When you walk

This book is dedicated to the memory of Shelagh Brown, writer, editor of *New Daylight*, and my friend, who died tragically in the year of its publication. Shelagh was an inspiration to myself and many others. She will be sadly missed.

When you walk

365 readings for ordinary followers of Jesus
who sometimes find the going a bit tough

ADRIAN PLASS

Text copyright © Adrian Plass 1997, 2007
The author asserts the moral right
to be identified as the author of this work

Published by
The Bible Reading Fellowship
15 The Chambers, Vineyard
Abingdon, OX14 3FE
United Kingdom
Tel: + 44 (0)1865 319700
Email: enquiries@brf.org.uk
Website: www.brf.org.uk
BRF is a Registered Charity

ISBN 978 1 84101 531 6

First edition 1997, reprinted twelve times
This edition 2007
Reprinted 2008, 2010, 2013
3 5 7 9 10 8 6 4
All rights reserved

Acknowledgments
The Revised Standard Version of the Bible, copyright © 1946, 1952, 1971 by the Division of
Christian Education of the National Council of the Churches of Christ in the United States of
America, used by permission. All rights reserved.

The New Revised Standard Version of the Bible, Anglicized Edition, copyright © 1989, 1995 by the
Division of Christian Education of the National Council of the Churches of Christ in the United States
of America, used by permission. All rights reserved.

The Holy Bible, New International Version, copyright © 1973, 1978, 1984 by International Bible
Society, used by permission of Hodder & Stoughton, a division of Hodder Headline Ltd. All rights
reserved. 'NIV' is a registered trademark of International Bible Society. UK trademark number 1448790.

The Good News Bible published by HarperCollins Publishers Ltd, UK © American Bible Society
1966, 1971, 1976, 1992, used with permission.

The New Jerusalem Bible, published and copyright © 1985 by Darton, Longman and Todd Ltd and les
Editions du Cerf, and by Doubleday, a division of Bantam Doubleday Dell Publishing Group, Inc. Used
by permission of Darton, Longman and Todd Ltd, and Doubleday, a division of Random House, Inc.

Extracts from the Authorized Version of the Bible (The King James Bible), the rights in which are vested
in the Crown, are reproduced by permission of the Crown's Patentee, Cambridge University Press.

Extracts from The Book of Common Prayer of 1662, the rights of which are vested in the Crown in
perpetuity within the United Kingdom, are reproduced by permission of Cambridge University Press,
Her Majesty's Printers.

A catalogue record for this book is available from the British Library

The paper used in the production of this publication was supplied by mills that source their raw
materials from sustainably managed forests. Soy-based inks were used in its printing and the laminate
film is biodegradable.

Printed in Singapore by Craft Print International Ltd

CONTENTS

Introduction 8

1   Narrow pathways 11
    John the Baptist

2   The shape of the real world..25
    The Sermon on the Mount

3   Trailblazing heroes..49
    Some Old Testament figures

4   Theory or practice—talk or walk..75
    A nervous look at the letter of James

5   Choosing the right direction...95
    Malachi

6   Travelling wisely 109
    Words of wisdom from Proverbs

7   Finding firm ground...133
    Reality in the Bible

8   Wise after the event? 153
    The character of Solomon

9   Getting lost..169
    Search and recovery in the 15th chapter of Luke

10   Long road to reunion 185
    Jacob

11   Clear signposts..199
    The promises of God

12   Fuelled by the Spirit 229
    Acts 9—11

13   Passionate parenting on the path to paradise 243
    Some reactions to Hosea

14 Unauthorized excursions 267
The story of David and Bathsheba

15 Clearing the way for us...287
Priesthood and sacrifice in Hebrews 8—10

16 New beginnings 301
Chances to get up and go—again

17 Travelling two by two 319
The sexy Song of Songs

18 Challenges on the road...339
Readings for Passiontide and Holy Week from Luke and John

19 Gathering as we go...353
Harvest in the Bible

20 Story power—tales to travel by...365
Parables

21 A wrong turning?...389
Readings from Job

22 Gaining fellow travellers 399
The woman at the well

23 Travelling with passion and a plan...413
Paul in Acts

24 Obedience—aiming for the planned destination...427
The sticky, sulky, salutary story of Jonah

25 Back to the eternal starting place? 445
Matthew 1 and 2

26 Heading for heaven—why did we leave in the first place?...455
1 Corinthians 15

27 Comfort for weary walkers 465
The Holy Spirit

28 Landscapes of beauty 487
Art and artists in the Bible

29 Power to persevere 501
     The miracle of resurrection

30 Pictures in the sky 517
     Revelation 19—22

When you walk through a storm,
hold your head up high...

OSCAR HAMMERSTEIN II

INTRODUCTION

Do I enjoy writing books? Yes, on the whole I do. Sometimes the battle to assemble a structure to contain words and ideas can drive me mad, but on those occasions when a piece of work really takes off it can be a wonderful, unparalleled experience. I am very bad at building aeroplanes, but I love flying them.

This book was born in a completely different way, one that brings its own very particular problems and elations. Each section of the book was originally a set of Bible reading notes for *New Daylight*, the Bible study booklet produced by BRF three times each year. Contributors are responsible for writing up to 14 notes on a theme, and I expect we all approach the task differently. No doubt there are highly disciplined individuals who set aside time to write one note each week over a long period, so that when the delivery date arrives the whole thing is neatly prepared and ready to go. I would like to be like that. I am not like that. This is how I do it.

Let us say the delivery date is on a Friday. Right. On the preceding Tuesday evening I lay out everything I will need for the following morning. There will be Bibles, commentaries, at least one concordance, the Concise Oxford Dictionary, Andrew Knowles' Bible guide and several sheets of paper on which to write notes as I proceed.

Wednesday morning arrives. My first, bleary-eyed, panic-stricken thought as I awake is that I *must* write seven notes today if I am to have any hope of reaching my Friday deadline. I don't hang about. Time is short. By eight o'clock I am sitting in front of my computer wishing that I was dead. As my wish is (to date) not granted I simply start to write my first note. By some miracle I always begin to take a deep interest in what I am reading and writing very soon after starting work. Soon I am steaming away, deeply buried and engrossed in the small world of my study, and the Bible verses in question and the lines of Times New

Roman print that are beginning to fill the screen of my computer. Every now and then I stop to agonize over some point, or to pray for relief from my foolishness, or to make an attempt to imagine and empathize with the reader who will eventually be sitting down with that slim BRF volume to share the things that are filling my heart at this moment.

Finally, when the seventh note is completed, I emerge, goggle-eyed and zombie-like from my hothouse of a study, filled with intense relief that once again the impossible has happened. I have filled my quota for the day.

Thursday is a repeat of Wednesday, but with slightly less pressure, and Friday—oh, Friday! I love you, Friday. Friday is the blessed day when I casually flick a button on my wife's computer and those 14 notes sail away into the ether to become someone else's concern.

There are advantages to my way of working, believe it or not, a major one being the unity of approach and style that results from working so intensively over such a short period. An uninterrupted flow of thinking and feeling achieves its own momentum and, I hope, imparts a common flavour to the entire set of notes.

The other advantage is that it suits me to grapple with my own responses to the Bible in the intense and concentrated way that is demanded by such a limited timescale. I have often said that we must deal with our very first response to a passage from the Bible, as opposed to editing our reaction until it falls in line with some worthy corporate view. Sometimes I twist and writhe physically in my seat as I go through the process of dragging the truth from myself before offering it to God and anyone else who cares to read it.

I have made so many friends through the publication of *When You Walk*. All over this country and in many other parts of the world I meet folk who, through the pages of this book, have joined me on a journey that really is for those of us who find the going a bit tough. I am delighted to be involved with the production of this new, expanded version containing more than 140 entries that were not included in the previous edition. There are now 365 readings in all, one for each day of the year, and they are not dated, so you can start on any day you wish, and take a break whenever you feel the need to turn to a proper theologian for more solid sustenance.

Because these notes were written over a period of years, there are references to events and people that are out of date in our lives and in the world context generally, but I am actually rather pleased that this should be the case. Journeys of the heart travel in all sorts of strange directions, forwards, backwards and, not infrequently, sideways. I hope you enjoy every single detour.

Above all, I pray that you will meet with God through the words on these pages. Jesus calls. Following him will be funny, tragic, puzzling, mysterious, frightening, intriguing and challenging. We don't have to go, of course. We can choose to stand still and watch him recede into the distance if we wish. But let's not do that. Come on. Walk with me.

NARROW PATHWAYS

JOHN THE BAPTIST

Disciplined, totally focused, unsure and vulnerable, strong but flexible. This list of attributes is not one that we would normally associate with the figure of John the Baptist. He is more often pictured as a hairy, wild-eyed headcase, snarling around the desert, stuffing his face with insects and honey and putting on a sort of loony sideshow for the locals.

The truth is that John was deadly serious about the job he had been born for and absolutely determined to play out his role as the one who would prepare the way for the Messiah. Educated, competent and much loved by his parents Zechariah and Elizabeth, who were more than a little surprised by his arrival, he might have done anything. In fact, he was obedient to the very specific call of God in his life and, because of that, his life was not a very long one.

There are many lessons to be learned from this extraordinary man's devotion to duty, his lack of possessiveness about men or ministry, his ability to remain solidly his own man while never deviating from the need to be God's man and his readiness to be as aggressive and uncompromising as it was necessary to be when faced with sin and hypocrisy.

For me, the most moving part of John's story is the moment in Herod's prison cell when, lost and alone, he loses his confidence and sends a message to Jesus seeking reassurance about the truth that he so confidently announced to the world only a short time before. In the end, John the Baptist was a man, with the weakness and vulnerability that all of us experience from time to time. He was also a hero of the Gospels. He took on the job that was specially his and he finished it.

HE WAS THE ANSWER TO A PRAYER

Luke 1:11–13, 18–20 (NIV)

Then an angel of the Lord appeared... When Zechariah saw him, he was... gripped with fear. But the angel said... 'Do not be afraid... your prayer has been heard. Your wife Elizabeth will bear you a son, and you are to give him the name John.' ... Zechariah asked the angel, 'How can I be sure of this? I am an old man and my wife is well on in years.' The angel answered, 'I am Gabriel. I stand in the presence of God, and I have been sent... to tell you this good news. And now you will be silent and not able to speak until the day this happens, because you did not believe my words.'

If you get the time, read the whole of this story, verses 5–20.

Can you blame Gabriel for taking such action? Angels do have a rough time occasionally. Imagine turning up full of enthusiasm to tell one of these awkward humans that, against the odds, he's going to have a son. Also, that this son will be great in the sight of God and filled with the Holy Spirit from birth and he'll bring lots of Israelites back to the Lord. Oh, and he'll be the one who prepares the way for the Messiah. All these good things and you get such a wet reaction from the said human.

You might think Zechariah would be just a bit pleased. Instead, the nervous old priest mumbles about feeling unsure about this because he and his wife are well on in years and so it's unlikely... No wonder Gabriel draws himself to his full height and lays down the law in no uncertain fashion. Perhaps he felt he'd been too soft all those years ago when Gideon came out with the same sort of rubbish. Is it possible that angels learn?

The really interesting aspect of the whole business is that, as Gabriel makes quite clear, Elizabeth's pregnancy and the birth of John would be a direct answer to Zechariah's own prayer. It is probably the thing that he and his wife wanted most in the world. Now that he is being offered his heart's desire, he doubts God has sufficient power to make it happen.

It's a lesson to all of us. Prayer is dangerous. We may talk to God about a particular need for years and simply get into the habit of believing it will never be answered. Not a good idea. Remember Zechariah!

Be careful with prayers—they might be answered.

HE WAS LOVED AND WANTED

Luke 1:14, 24–25 (NIV)

'He will be a joy and delight to you, and many will rejoice because of his birth.' After this his wife Elizabeth became pregnant and for five months remained in seclusion. 'The Lord has done this for me,' she said. 'In these days he has shown his favour and taken away my disgrace among the people.'

I was discussing with a friend recently whether or not he and I would have chosen to have children if we had seen our future with them in advance. We agreed that, probably, neither of us would have proceeded if we had. It's not, you understand, that our children have not been a joy and delight to us. They have been in their own particular ways, sometimes wonderfully so, but they've been other things as well. So many emotional cliffhangers, so many alarms and excursions, so much worry of various kinds. Of course you forget all that when things are good, but, yes, a clear and detailed vision of the future might have put me off altogether.

God was very good to this elderly couple. Once Zechariah had got over his negative response to the good news, he must have remembered and relished that promise from God that John was going to be a joy and delight to his parents. How wonderful for that fact to be furnished in advance from the most reputable source of all. As for Elizabeth, she was like a football manager whose team has just beaten Manchester United—over the moon. After years of barrenness, a son! A gift from God in the autumn of her life.

God gave John the best possible start for the tough times that were to come, didn't he? It is hard to imagine a son ever having been wanted more than this one. Being loved and wanted was the best possible launching pad for the rest of John's life. Indeed, being valued and appreciated is rocket fuel for the future of any child.

We must be very tender with those who have not had this kind of start. It's all very well to say how fellow believers should behave, but if you've never been loved it really is ever so hard to be good.

Father, may those whose hearts were broken before they even started learn what it means to be loved by you.

HE WAS FILLED WITH THE HOLY SPIRIT

Luke 1:41–45 (NIV)

When Elizabeth heard Mary's greeting, the baby leaped in her womb, and Elizabeth was filled with the Holy Spirit. In a loud voice she exclaimed: 'Blessed are you among women, and blessed is the child you will bear! But why am I so favoured, that the mother of my Lord should come to me? As soon as the sound of your greeting reached my ears, the baby in my womb leaped for joy. Blessed is she who has believed that what the Lord has said to her will be accomplished!'

Gabriel had promised that John would be filled with the Holy Spirit from birth, but it seems to have started even before that. In this, one of my favourite gospel moments, we learn that as the two pregnant women met, the unborn John seemed to recognize the unborn Jesus. The foetus inside Elizabeth jumped with a sudden spiritual awareness that the reason for his very existence was only inches away, in that younger, equally excited mother-to-be. I don't know if the presence of the Holy Spirit has an infectious quality, but it appears like that here, doesn't it? Suddenly Elizabeth is speaking inspired words, closely followed by Mary's famous hymn of praise. What a party! Both pregnant, both filled with the Spirit, both filled with babies filled with the Spirit, one bearing God himself within her body.

Much modern teaching about the Holy Spirit has attempted to set down processes or specific stages in connection with the moment when the Spirit enters a believer's life. Such teaching tends to draw heavily on events in the book of Acts and on sections of Paul's letters. Well, that's all right, as long as we don't end up tidying God and his way with us out of existence. I am afraid, brothers and sisters, that God does what he likes. You may have noticed that. It would be very helpful to the church as a whole if we abandoned the notion that theology can be kept in a paddock at the back of the house, and taken out for a bit of a gallop twice a week.

Anything can happen if we are open to being filled with the Spirit at any time.

We long to be filled with the Spirit and to speak out your words, Lord.

HE WAS HIS OWN MAN

Matthew 3:1–6 (NIV, abridged)

In those days John the Baptist came, preaching in the Desert of Judea and saying, 'Repent, for the kingdom of heaven is near.' ... John's clothes were made of camel's hair, and he had a leather belt round his waist. His food was locusts and wild honey. People went out to him from Jerusalem and all Judea and the whole region of the Jordan. Confessing their sins, they were baptized by him in the Jordan river.

What do Christians look like? How do they do their hair? How do they speak? How do they walk and eat and drink and sing and play Monopoly? Is there a distinctive Christian style to fit all these activities? There certainly has been, in this country at any rate, but it is less and less the case nowadays. Huddling together in conformity of dress and generally narrow lifestyles is not productive in terms of what the gospel demands. I am glad that religious cloning is gradually becoming a thing of the past. Of course, we are unified (one hopes) by a love for Jesus, each other and a desire to follow Jesus obediently, but those features can be expressed in a diversity of personal styles and approaches.

Having said this, a friend of mine is clearly not thrilled with this new acceptance. Having battled pleasurably through the 1960s and 1970s against elders who objected to his exceptionally long hair, he now finds himself not only accepted but invited to join the leadership team! Will he be able to overcome his disappointment?

As well as being God's man, John was his own man. Well-educated and competent, he chose to adopt an environment, diet and way of dressing that, although bizarre, related specifically to the task in hand and he wasn't interested in what others thought about it. We have to be careful, don't we? We may not like the way a person dresses, how he expresses himself, the details of his lifestyle or some of the places he frequents, but we are to estimate others (if at all) only on the basis of their love for God and their obedience to his call. How would John the Baptist get on at your next 'bring and share' lunch?

Lord, may we welcome the richness of variety in your family.

HE WAS AGGRESSIVE AND UNCOMPROMISING

Matthew 3:7–10 (NIV)

But when he saw many of the Pharisees and Sadducees coming to where he was baptizing, he said to them: 'You brood of vipers! Who warned you to flee from the coming wrath? Produce fruit in keeping with repentance. And do not think that you can say to yourselves, "We have Abraham as our father." I tell you that out of these stones God can raise up children for Abraham. The axe is already at the root of the trees, and every tree that does not produce good fruit will be cut down and thrown into the fire.'

John really laid into the Pharisees and Sadducees. Not only did he call them names, but he predicted what they'd probably claim about their spiritual heritage and why what they said would be wrong. His comment about the stones must have infuriated them. How I wish I'd been there. I wouldn't have been a Pharisee or a Sadducee, of course—I would have been a humble ordinary person, just as I'm sure you would.

One of my abiding fears is that, as a church, we let God down by refusing to take this kind of aggressive stance when the time is right. We are handicapped by the disease of politeness. We get cross about the machinations of those newly arrived upstarts on the flower rota or the movement of some dreary picture to a spot ten feet from where it has hung for the last 30 years. Meanwhile there are political, social and spiritual issues crying out for comment from those of us who claim or want to represent God's viewpoint.

Being a Christian is not about being nice to people, nor, obviously, is it about being nasty. It is about seeing what the Father is doing and then joining in. That's what John did imperfectly and Jesus perfectly. It is quite frightening and quite exciting.

Let's all pray that we will be more open to the prompting of the Holy Spirit. Beware, though. When that prayer is answered, some of us will have to turn away from that flower rota and instead get tough with the people and institutions that really need it.

Help us to be ready to speak out at the right time.

HE ACCEPTED TRUTH, HOWEVER STRANGE

John 1:32–34 (NIV)

Then John gave this testimony: 'I saw the Spirit come down from heaven as a dove and remain on him. I would not have known him, except that the one who sent me to baptize with water told me, "The man on whom you see the Spirit come down and remain is he who will baptize with the Holy Spirit." I have seen and I testify that this is the Son of God.'

Now, let's just think this through. Mary and Elizabeth were related, and we know that, in a sense, John and Jesus met before either of them was born. Surely it is inconceivable that the cousins failed to meet when they were growing up in separate but not inaccessibly distant parts of the country. They must have known each other. The manner and depth of their relationship is not something we can discover, but, from John's words, it seems that he was not fully or perhaps even partially aware that Jesus was the Messiah. Given the nature of both men, this seems strange. Nevertheless, it appears to be the case.

How remarkable, then, that, on seeing the Spirit alight on Jesus in the form of a dove, John immediately accepted that this familiar figure, this cousin of his, this son of Mary and Joseph, was the Son of God, the one whose way it had been his task to prepare. I wonder, might there have been just a single instant of jaw-dropping amazement as he registered the fact that God become man had been so close to him for so long? 'Oh! It's you...!'

An ongoing problem in the Church is the reluctance of many of us to allow that God may significantly use individuals who are of little worth in our eyes. I warn you and I warn myself that there is no class system in the kingdom of God. The person who sits three seats away from me every Sunday, the person whom I regard with indulgence or pity or slight scorn or I barely notice because his or her face is so very familiar, may be the very person God selects to speak his will or his discipline or his comfort to me. He who has ears...

Forgive our religious snobbery, Lord. Open our ears and eyes.

HE WAS STRONG ENOUGH TO BE FLEXIBLE

Matthew 3:13–15 (NIV)

Then Jesus came from Galilee to the Jordan to be baptized by John. But John tried to deter him, saying, 'I need to be baptized by you, and do you come to me?' Jesus replied, 'Let it be so now; it is proper for us to do this to fulfil all righteousness.' Then John consented.

A mighty hush must have descended over the hosts of heaven as this extraordinary rehearsal of death and resurrection was carried out. There can have been few more dramatic moments in the history of the world, and this one would not have been possible if John had not been ready and willing to be corrected in his assumption that it should have been the other way round. Fierce, focused and fanatical as he may have appeared to some, John was actually a man under authority who knew that orders from the highest source, however surprising, must be obeyed. It is so terribly easy for any of us to lock ourselves into an agenda or a process that was begun by God and refuse to come out even when the Holy Spirit himself issues orders for change.

When I began to write, I had a great deal to say about the emphasis placed by certain sections of the church on the avoidance of drinking, smoking and other such fundamentally neutral activities. The gospel is primarily about letting off spectacular fireworks; it is not about stamping on sparklers. I believe it was quite right for me to say these things, and I shall go on saying them as long as there are those who use the beating out of sin as an excuse for avoiding the awesome tasks that God has ready for them.

However, some time ago, an elderly lady wrote me a charmingly supportive letter, concluding with a plea that I should not joke quite so much about alcohol. Her son was an alcoholic and had made several suicide attempts. I receive a number of letters telling me what I should do or think or say. I ignore most of them, but this was a rebuke couched in love and God spoke to me through it. May he also grant me the strength and humility to be like John and to do what I'm told.

Lord, too often it is my agenda I pay attention to, not yours.

HE WASN'T POSSESSIVE OF MEN OR MINISTRY

John 1:35–39 (NIV)

The next day John was there again with two of his disciples. When he saw Jesus passing by, he said, 'Look, the Lamb of God!' When the two disciples heard him say this, they followed Jesus. Turning round, Jesus saw them following and asked, 'What do you want?' They said 'Rabbi' (which means Teacher), 'where are you staying?' 'Come,' he replied, 'and you will see.' So they went and saw where he was staying, and spent that day with him.

I know of a Christian leader who told his followers that if they transferred their allegiance to someone else, they would lose the blessing of God. Perhaps he should read this passage from John's Gospel. Hold on, what am I talking about? He probably uses it to support his position.

Superficially it appears a sad little story. John points out to his disciples that the man passing is the Son of God and, suddenly, they've gone! From that day onwards they seem to have become disciples of Jesus instead of John. They had been with the one who was preparing the way. Now they have gone to be with The Way.

Well, it would be a sad story if we thought that John was upset by their decision. I don't believe he was. I believe that, for John, this episode would have been a microcosm of the process that was inevitable, given the nature of his calling. Losing two disciples to Jesus was not a tragedy. It was a triumph for the plan that God had set in motion before John was born, and if John had had an ounce of pride in his locust and honey-nourished body, he might have considered it a personal triumph—the visible fulfilment of his ministry.

If it had been a contemporary fashion, I reckon John might have thrust his fist in the air at that point and cried 'Yes!!'

It's very hard to hand on the baton sometimes, but if our leg of the relay is run, we must rejoice in the eventual outcome of the race or face the fact that we never really wanted to belong to a team. Let's give up gracefully when our time comes.

For what we have been allowed to do, may the Lord make us truly thankful.

HE WAS HUMAN AND VULNERABLE

Matthew 11:2–5 (NIV)

When John heard in prison what Christ was doing, he sent his disciples to ask him, 'Are you the one who was to come, or should we expect someone else?' Jesus replied, 'Go back and report to John what you hear and see: the blind receive sight, the lame walk, those who have leprosy are cured, the deaf hear, the dead are raised, and the good news is preached to the poor.'

The devil tells lies in the darkness, doesn't he?

Sometimes, after a particularly successful evening in which I have made an impassioned plea for those present to respond to the love of God, I lie in the darkness of some obscure hotel room and ask myself if I have been talking complete nonsense.

How could John the Baptist possibly have plummeted to such a depth of doubt? After all, it hadn't been long since he had been proclaiming the need for repentance, aggressively taking on the Pharisees and Sadducees and baptizing hundreds in the waters of the Jordan. Not only that, but the Holy Spirit had enabled him to identify Jesus as the Messiah on the bank of that same river. He knew that Jesus was the one who was to come. Why on earth would he for one moment believe that he should expect someone else?

The sad and salutary truth is that John was human and, as such, he was subject to all the fear and uneasiness that any human being would suffer when shut away from their place and function and the light of the outside world.

The reply that Jesus sends is sometimes quoted as an example of the contradictions to be found in the Bible. Why, the cynics want to know, does Jesus give a different answer to John than he gave to the Pharisees when they asked him the same question? Well, it is just one example of the glorious, life-giving contradictions that offer evidence of the creative, ingenious God we try to serve. Jesus didn't want to comfort the Pharisees, but he did want to comfort John. Very soon he was to have similar experiences himself.

Call out to Jesus in the darkness and listen for his message of comfort.

Lord, I'll try to do my best. Catch me when I fall.

HE INSPIRED PASSION (1)

Matthew 11:7–11 (NIV, abridged)

Jesus began to speak to the crowd about John: 'What did you go out into the desert to see? A reed swayed by the wind? If not, what did you go out to see? A man dressed in fine clothes? No, those who wear fine clothes are in kings' palaces... A prophet? Yes, I tell you, and more than a prophet. This is the one about whom it is written: "I will send my messenger ahead of you, who will prepare your way before you." I tell you the truth: among those born of women there has not risen anyone greater than John the Baptist; yet he who is least in the kingdom of heaven is greater than he.'

This speech, delivered by Jesus as John's disciples hurried back towards Herod's prison with the Lord's answer to their master's question, has haunted me ever since I first read it more than 30 years ago. As with so many of the Gospel stories, and not least because of the literary style of the day, some of the most important truths seem to dwell between the lines.

Why do I sense unshed tears in the eyes of Jesus as he begins this impassioned speech about the man who was his cousin, his forerunner and his friend? Why can I almost hear the catch in his voice as he quotes the scripture that prophesies the coming of John? Do I sense his sadness at the thought of John, once so confident in his proclamations, now worried about whether or not Jesus really is the one for whom all his work was a preparation? Was he aware that this wild light would soon be extinguished? Was Jesus grieving for those who, over the centuries, would suffer pain and darkness and early death in order that the gospel should be preached?

I pray that you and I might inspire passion in the heart of our Saviour. Not by getting everything right, because we won't; not by understanding all that happens to us, because that will not be possible, but by doing the job we have been given as well as it can be done in the light of what we know and by calling out to him for the warm glow of his reassurance when darkness falls.

Give us the same passion for you as you have for us.

HE WAS DISCIPLINED IN HIS ROLE

Matthew 11:16–19 (NIV)

'To what can I compare this generation? They are like children sitting in the marketplaces and calling out to others: "We played the flute for you, and you did not dance; we sang a dirge, and you did not mourn." For John came neither eating nor drinking, and they say, "He has a demon." The Son of Man came eating and drinking, and they say, "Here is a glutton and a drunkard, a friend of tax collectors and 'sinners'." But wisdom is proved right by her actions.'

I am reluctant to write on this subject, being one of the least disciplined people I know. When I say this to people they laugh and ask how can I possibly get books written without discipline? The answer is that my motivation is a compound of fear that the job will never get done, a panic-stricken desire to be obedient and the deadline date printed so irrevocably in my contract. I do it, but my discipline is a small boat in a howling storm. I hope and believe that God can live with this arrangement.

John the Baptist was not like me at all, except in the sense that he was like all followers of Jesus. I mean that each of us has a role and a task or succession of tasks assigned by God and, by any means that do not contravene the laws of love, we must live out that role and fulfil those tasks. John was highly disciplined in his personal habits, as Jesus points out in this passage, and that particular way of living was appropriate to the job that God had given him. Jesus was able to eat and drink, go to parties and visit friends and have expensive ointment poured over his hair and feet because his fundamental task was to be himself—a free human being, fettered only to the continually revealed will of his father.

Take heart! You and I may sometimes feel we are only managing to do the job by the skin of our spiritual teeth, but, as always, God looks into our hearts and is pleased with an intention to do what we are told. He has learned to live with the scrambled means by which we attempt to be obedient.

Lord, help me to do my bit.

HE INSPIRED PASSION (2)

Matthew 14:6–11 (NIV)

On Herod's birthday the daughter of Herodias danced for them and pleased Herod so much that he promised with an oath to give her whatever she asked. Prompted by her mother, she said, 'Give me here on a platter the head of John the Baptist.' The king was distressed, but because of his oaths and his dinner guests, he ordered that her request be granted and had John beheaded in the prison. His head was brought in on a platter and given to the girl, who carried it to her mother.

John inspired passion in the heart of Herodias, but it was nothing to do with love. Rather, it was a wild hatred, the result of John's outspoken remarks about the unsuitability of her marriage to Herod. This passage tells us that Herod also wanted John dead, but was afraid to do the deed because popular opinion held him to be a prophet.

When hatred and weakness knot themselves together like a pair of snakes, disaster occurs before long. In our own age Nazi Germany is a grim reminder of what can happen. Here, because Herod was showing off in front of his guests and making extravagant promises to the daughter of Herodias, he destroyed John and also any chance of benefiting from contact with him. It may be pure conjecture, but perhaps Herod regretted the outcome of his thoughtless behaviour for reasons other than fear of the people. Perhaps he had developed a respect for John and was hoping that his prisoner would have something important to say to him. If so, he had blown it.

I don't have many opportunities for beheading people as a favour to others, nor do those I dislike tend to come to such a grisly end, but I cannot escape awareness in my own life of the way in which this deadly cocktail of weakness and passion can work. I have learned to be wary of opportunities to indulge any kind of inappropriate passion. It would be so easy—like poor old Esau with his soup—to give up the most important things in the world in exchange for a passing fancy. If that is what you are considering doing at the moment, please think again.

Protect us against our own weaknesses. Help us to be strong.

HE WAS MOURNED

Matthew 14:12–14 (NIV)

John's disciples came and took his body and buried it. Then they went and told Jesus. When Jesus heard what had happened, he withdrew by boat privately to a solitary place. Hearing of this, the crowds followed him on foot from the towns. When Jesus landed and saw a large crowd, he had compassion on them and healed their sick.

A few simple words don't convey very much, but we can guess and imagine. John's disciples took their master's body and buried it. Did they weep as they performed that sad task? Did they stand around the tomb or grave afterwards and ask themselves and each other what it had all been about? Who had this strange, dynamic, driven leader of theirs really been? Had he been right in the things he preached and said? Where was he now? What of the future? What should they do and where should they go? There was no one to give them the answers to those questions now that John had gone. First of all, they had to tell Jesus.

I wonder if he already knew? The idea that Jesus was aware of everything without having to be told is clearly not supported by scripture. He is said, for instance, to have been 'astonished' on a couple of occasions, and, of course, he could not be truly man as well as God if he was unable to experience or understand the shock of sudden realization or knowledge. It seems that special insights were doled out to him, as it were, when they became necessary.

Besides, one brief glimpse of John's wretchedly unhappy disciples as they approached must have given him a very big clue as to what they were about to say. Was there more weeping? Did Jesus place comforting hands on the arms and bowed shoulders of these men who had lost their master? I think so.

Then Jesus, deeply moved by his cousin's death, looked for just a few moments alone with his grief. Sitting in a little boat in a quiet place with his head in his hands, he mourned his loss.

He was not alone for long. The crowds found him. The crowds always found him. He must have let out a deep sigh, then business as usual.

Thank you for being as human as you are divine.

A good, honest and painful sermon.

SAMUEL PEPYS

THE SHAPE OF
THE REAL WORLD

THE SERMON ON THE MOUNT

How should I approach one of the greatest pieces of spiritual teaching that humankind has ever received? There is a strong temptation to cut and run. The Sermon on the Mount certainly doesn't need my flimsy footnotes to convey the depth and profundity that give it such central importance in the Christian faith. It feels like being asked to compose a limerick about Mount Everest. I can lose confidence very easily when faced with such a task. I was greatly helped on this occasion, however, by reading a comment by Red Smith, as quoted by Frederick Buechner. Smith said: 'Writing is really quite simple; all you have to do is sit down at your typewriter and open a vein.'

In other words, as Buechner points out, the aim is to effect—for better or worse—a transfusion from writer to reader. I can quite understand that this might sound affected and rather over the top, but it really does speak to me. I think that the idea of figuratively opening a vein makes a lot of sense, not just for writers, but for any of us who want to find within ourselves a true response to sections of scripture that are daunting or overfamiliar. Let me show you what I mean.

When I came to that part of this great discourse where Jesus talks about the broad way leading to destruction, and the narrow way leading to life that is only found by a few, I said to myself, 'Oh, yes, that's the bit that's always frightened me—now, what am I going to say about it?' I very nearly jettisoned my first, genuine, fearful response because it seemed too inward, inappropriate, personal and (ludicrously) trivial. But in fact the vein of fear was the vein that needed to be opened because that is where the life was flowing.

Forgive the violent change of metaphor, but, as we read the Bible, why should we not catch hold of those orphan responses, hanging about hopefully like ragged, starving children at a baker's window, and find out what they look like and what they're capable of when they're brought inside, fed, and warmed up a bit? God says that he will write his law on our hearts, and although others will certainly aid this process, it is essential that we do not simply think what we are told to think and believe what we are told to believe when it is not God who is doing the telling. We may be surprised at what we discover for ourselves.

This kind of approach is particularly important with the Sermon on the Mount because, broadly speaking, Jesus is challenging his listeners to make radical adjustments to the priorities instilled into them by a godless world, and to develop awareness of an eternal context for thoughts and actions and attitudes. It is not a game. It is a matter of life and death. If the way in which we react demands a little blood-letting—then, so be it. His example is before us.

Incidentally, the first of the following notes has become a particularly significant one for me because of a letter that I received in response to it.

I am very fortunate with my post, by the way. People write wonderful letters to me sometimes. Only this morning, for instance, a letter arrived with an Austrian postmark. It had been sent, as many letters are, via Harper Collins, who publish most of my books, but when I opened it I found the contents very puzzling. Inside the envelope was a piece of white paper folded twice. Nothing unusual about that, but when I unfolded this sheet it appeared to be completely blank. Why, I asked myself, has someone sent me a piece of unlined A4 sized white paper with nothing written on it? When I examined the paper more closely I discovered that it wasn't blank at all. There was just one word written in very small letters on the corner of one side of the page.

'*Danke.*'

That was the entire content of the letter, and it was quite enough, don't you think? However, I digress...

The response that I received to the first of these Sermon on the Mount notes was important to me because it further confirmed my belief that I had been right to offer God one of the weakest areas of my personality, that is, my disease of flippancy. I have suffered from this disease for as long as I can remember, and, as those readers who are fellow sufferers will know, the major symptoms of this disorder are not always easily tolerated by the sufferer's nearest and dearest. In fact, incredibly, they seem to think that *they* are the sufferers! What can they possibly mean?

The trouble is that these symptoms can flare up at any time and in any place. I was at a dinner a couple of years ago, for instance, seated on the same table as a retired bishop and his wife. (I had been pledged to non-flippancy by my wife, who wasn't able to be there, but knows what I'm like.) The bishop, a truly charming, pleasantly old-fashioned man, was talking about the pleasures of retirement, and, in particular, the fresh opportunities that he and his wife had found to take up activities that had tended to fall by the wayside during their busy working lives.

'For example,' said the bishop, 'we have very much enjoyed the renewal of our interest in art.'

'Oh, that's good,' I replied, 'that must be very enjoyable.'

'Yes, indeed, it is most enjoyable. In fact, we now attend a regular class in which a different topic is covered on each occasion.'

'Well, that sounds very good,' I said, conscious that my conversation was somewhat lacking in sparkle. 'I should imagine that's, er, very good.' At least I wasn't being flippant.

'Yes, it is good,' confirmed the bishop. 'This week, for instance, we were looking at hue, tone and intensity.'

Oh, dear. I did try. I promise you I did. I fought against temptation, but I lost. I fell.

'Oh, yes,' I cried merrily, 'I went down the pub with them last Friday. Hugh and Ton', nice couple of lads, and Intensity's that rather stressy girl they hang around with.'

The bishop was a little taken aback at first, but once he'd realized that it was a case of 'Christians having fun' everything was fine. Christians are allowed to have 'fun'.

On the face of it this kind of silliness has very little worth, doesn't it? But it really is quite amazing what God can do with the loaves and fishes of what we are, as long as we actually get round to offering them to him. When I wrote my first Bible note on the Sermon on the Mount I was a little worried that some readers might consider the opening comments too light-hearted for such a serious subject. That's why it was lovely to get a letter from a lady called Margaret who wanted to tell me the following story. I have her permission to retell it for the benefit of others.

Margaret's husband, David, who has MS, got very edgy and bad-tempered during a course of steroids. One despairing Sunday Margaret reached the end of her tether. She had a good weep in the garden shed, then wondered back into the house and happened to pick up a copy of *New Daylight*, the periodical in which most of these notes originally appeared. In the note for that day, as you will see when you read on, I had bemoaned Jesus' strange oversight in omitting 'Blessed are the irritable for they shall be given claret' from the beatitudes. Remembering that claret was her husband's favourite tipple (hallelujah—we are one with you, brother David) Margaret hurried to the mini-supermarket and queued for the only remaining bottle of claret on the shelf. When she gave it to David and explained why she'd bought it they had a good laugh together, and, as Margaret herself put it, 'All the tension was released.' And that was before they drank the claret. Wonderful!

Don't kid yourself. The Jesus who made his comeback by cooking breakfast for his friends instead of organizing a sky-filling Spielberg spectacular is still in touch with the real world, and here, in the most famous sermon in history, he tells us what the shape of the real world should be.

Prayer
Father, as we approach this most significant of sermons, open our hearts and minds in such a way that we are prepared to receive ideas and teaching that may displace responses from the past. We pray that we may feel genuine excitement as we listen to these words, heavy with eternal significance. Help us to freely offer ourselves, our weaknesses and our strengths to you, so that, through us, you can do unexpected and miraculous things in the lives of others.

THE POOR SHEEP

Matthew 5:1–6 (NIV)

Now when [Jesus] saw the crowds, he went up on a mountainside and sat down. His disciples came to him, and he began to teach them, saying: 'Blessed are the poor in spirit, for theirs is the kingdom of heaven. Blessed are those who mourn, for they will be comforted. Blessed are the meek, for they will inherit the earth. Blessed are those who hunger and thirst for righteousness, for they will be filled.'

I have searched this passage in vain for a statement tailored to my baser weaknesses and appetites:

'Blessed are the irritable, for they shall be given claret.'

'Blessed are the taller than average, for they shall develop a forehand that would send Bjorn Borg diving for cover.'

'Blessed are the fundamentally lazy, for their Bible notes will be done for them by divine intervention.'

Jesus doesn't make any of these rather superficially attractive promises, but the promises he does make are, ultimately, far more significant and encouraging than any individually oriented indulgences could ever be. As I read these famous words yet again I knew that they reminded me of something very familiar, but I couldn't quite put my finger on it. Where was I accustomed to encountering groups of people who were poor in spirit, sorely in need of comfort, meek by nature and yearning from the bottom of their hearts to be good?

The answer, of course, as even my feeble brain grasped in the end, was that Jesus was describing the Church—the people who make up his body on earth—almost exactly as I have experienced it and them in the course of my travels from town to town, and country to country. True, from time to time, I have encountered bold and vigorous spirits who don't appear to fit the pattern, but, in the main, they—or rather, we—are like sheep. And, whether we are High-Church mutton or house-church lamb, these extraordinary declarations invite us to rejoice in our weakness, because it is that very weakness, crying out for a shepherd, that brings Jesus to us.

A hunger and thirst for righteousness implies a serious lack of righteousness. We are allowed to fail, as long as we genuinely yearn to succeed.

Lord Jesus, you turned the world upside down with your teaching. Turn me now so that I am facing the truth.

A FRIGHTENING PROMISE

Matthew 5:7–12 (NIV)

'Blessed are the merciful, for they will be shown mercy. Blessed are the pure in heart, for they will see God. Blessed are the peacemakers, for they will be called sons of God. Blessed are those who are persecuted because of righteousness, for theirs is the kingdom of heaven. Blessed are you when people insult you, persecute you and falsely say all kind of evil against you because of me. Rejoice and be glad, because great is your reward in heaven, for in the same way they persecuted the prophets who were before you.'

Have you noticed how aggressively some people react to followers of Jesus nowadays? Adherents to other religions and philosophies are, quite rightly, accorded the respect that is due to any sincere group of believers, but there seems to be something about the Christian faith that provokes irritation, intolerance, scorn and even rage in folk who are otherwise perfectly reasonable. This used to puzzle me, because that kind of response is not just about the inadequate way in which we represent God—it seems to go much deeper than that. As I absorb passages like the one above, however, I think I begin to understand why people get so cross with Jesus.

You see, he wants to take their lives away.

In exchange he offers new lives that make sense only in the context of the kingdom of God. The divine madness says that it is good to be persecuted, insulted and lied about if such things are suffered for Jesus' sake. Will mercy, purity and a yearning for peace take us very far in this world? A lot of people think not. No wonder they become fearful and angry. Christianity is not a plan to improve the quality of life—it is God calling to the very depths of our being. He is calling to tell us that we must no longer huddle defensively into the three score years and ten that is our tiny corner of eternity. He is calling us to understand that many of the things we have valued most are trash. He is calling out that death is by no means the greatest disaster of all. He is calling with passionate urgency to say that the real madness lies in trying to put sticking plaster over the gaping wound of sin that is slowly killing the world.

He wants to take our lives away, and yes—we are frightened.

Open our eyes to eternity, Lord.

MY LIGHT, MY SALT

Matthew 5:13–16 (NIV)

'You are the salt of the earth. But if salt loses its saltiness, how can it be made salty again? It is no longer good for anything, except to be thrown out and trampled by men. You are the light of the world. A city on a hill cannot be hidden. Neither do people light a lamp and put it under a bowl. Instead they put it on its stand, and it gives light to everyone in the house. In the same way, let your light shine before men, that they may see your good deeds and praise your Father in heaven.'

I wonder if the disciples found it hard to accept that they were the light of the world. I find it extremely difficult until I stop thinking about myself, and realize that any light I may shed was switched on, and is maintained, by God himself. We Christians are scared stiff of advertising God, in case people think we are drawing attention to ourselves. This is a shame, because it is in the dark vessels of our lives that the light of God will be most apparent. I'm certainly not suggesting that we should go around crassly shoving the flashlight of our good deeds into people's faces, but there is a form of false modesty that results in missed opportunities.

When I first began to write and broadcast, a number of people who had known me at a much earlier age were frankly incredulous about my claim that I was now a follower of Jesus. One man in particular, a Christian who had been at the same secondary school as me, found it very difficult to believe that the person he had known in the 1960s was capable of change. I'm afraid that his scepticism was perfectly reasonable. As a teenager I had developed a habit of withering sarcasm to hide profound insecurity, and must have hurt and infuriated many people when I wielded the only defensive weapon I had. Now, God had transfigured, or turned his light towards, that sarcasm, turning it into satire and (hopefully) using it in a constructive way for the benefit of the Church. It must have taken people like that ex-schoolmate of mine a long time to accept that the change was a genuine one. But once he and others were convinced, they had to praise God really, because there was no other explanation.

We must be salt and light in the world, and that's all right, as long as everyone remembers who owns the saltmine and pays the electricity bill.

Father, you have given us the task of bringing flavour and illumination to this world. Teach us how to do it properly.

LUST AND REAL LIFE

Matthew 5:27–30 (NIV)

'You have heard that it was said, "Do not commit adultery." But I tell you that anyone who looks at a woman lustfully has already committed adultery with her in his heart. If your right eye causes you to sin, gouge it out and throw it away. It is better for you to lose one part of your body than for your whole body to be thrown into hell. And if your right hand causes you to sin, cut it off and throw it away. It is better for you to lose one part of your body than for your whole body to go to hell.'

My left earlobe might just about make it into heaven if I obey this command literally—but only if God stretches a point. Even my left earlobe has its seamier side. I'm afraid that the best of us is likely to enter heaven looking rather like Admiral Nelson.

When I was a very earnest young Christian we were taught that all sins and vices, including lust, can be overcome, and that failure to achieve such victories would constitute a denial of the efficacy of the resurrection power of Christ. This, as I am sure you will agree, is a very heavy thing to lay on a person of any age, let alone a teenager who has just awakened violently to the fact that the world is absolutely awash with desirable females. To make matters worse, my constant diet of testimony paperbacks included a book by some gleaming American Christian who actually claimed to have completely eradicated lust from his life. I can't remember the name of this paragon, or which part of himself he cut off to achieve such a spectacular result, but I do remember feeling utterly defeated by the contrast with my own puny efforts.

Honesty requires an acceptance of the fact that lust is a thorn in the flesh—or to use a more modern expression, a pain in the neck—for many, if not most of us. It really is a blinking nuisance, isn't it? But let's not all start gouging our flesh or cutting our heads off just yet. They tried that sort of thing in the distant past, and it never worked then.

I think Jesus is talking about the need to steer ourselves around publications, people, viewing matter and any other specific situations that we know are dangerous for us. Temptation is only the gateway to sin, but indulgence is a ski-slope.

Do you think it's possible that we approach this whole area too lightly and too seriously?

THE THIRSTY BEGGAR

Matthew 5:38–42 (NIV)

'You have heard that it was said, "Eye for eye, and tooth for tooth." But I tell you, Do not resist an evil person. If someone strikes you on the right cheek, turn to him the other also. And if someone wants to sue you and take your tunic, let him have your cloak as well. If someone forces you to go one mile, go with him two miles. Give to the one who asks you, and do not turn away from the one who wants to borrow from you.'

I was walking in Winchester late one cold evening with my friend, Ben. The street seemed deserted, until we were suddenly confronted by a shabby figure emerging from a shop doorway. With long matted hair, an overcoat tied with string, and terminally split shoes, he was what we used to call a 'tramp', although the loony political correctness of the present age would probably label him 'habitationally challenged'.

What was certain was that the poor chap was very cold and miserable. With considerable effort he cranked himself up to put the bite on these unexpected passers-by.

'Excuse me, Sir,' he embarked on a familiar script, 'could I speak to you as one man to another? I wondered if you might have some cash you could help me with.'

Now, I don't know about you, but I'm usually pathetic in these situations. I cringe and twist and dither about and perform theological triple somersaults in my head and go away wishing I'd done the thing I didn't do or that I'd not done the thing I did do. This occasion was different—thank God.

'Yes', I said briskly, 'I have.' I extended my hand towards him. 'I've got a five pound note here that I'm going to give you.'

My habitationally challenged friend was clearly taken aback. A new script! He managed to take the five pounds, though, and stood looking at it in a dazed fashion.

'I give you this money,' I continued, 'trusting that you will put it to the best possible use.'

'Well, actually,' he replied faintly, 'I was thinking of having a drink.'

'Precisely,' I said, 'that's exactly what we would have done with the money if I'd kept it. Goodnight to you.'

Father, I can be such a patronizing hypocrite sometimes. Help me not to judge or condemn others because they count for less in the eyes of the world. Let me see them through your eyes and deal with them as equals.

MUSIC IN A NEW PLACE

Matthew 5:43–48 (NIV)

'You have heard that it was said, "Love your neighbour and hate your enemy." But I tell you: Love your enemies and pray for those who persecute you, that you may be sons of your Father in heaven. He causes his sun to rise on the evil and the good, and sends rain on the righteous and the unrighteous. If you love those who love you, what reward will you get? Are not even the tax collectors doing that? And if you greet only your brothers, what are you doing more than others? Do not even pagans do that? Be perfect, therefore, as your heavenly Father is perfect.'

My experience of loving enemies is very similar to my experience of moving pianos from one room to another on my own. It's crashingly hard work, halfway through you begin to wish you'd never started, but in the end you hear music in a place where you've never heard it before.

What makes this whole area so difficult is that the line between enemies and friends is not as clear as one might think. Friendship can move so easily into enemy mode, and it's at such times that we fail most miserably to uphold this principle which, Jesus tells his disciples, should distinguish them from pagans. These shifts in the nature of relationships happen an awful lot in families, don't they?

A friend told me of a conflict between himself and his 14-year-old daughter, whom he loved very much. Having settled into mega-sulkdom over some minor incident, she refused to communicate with her father (other than with the occasional grunt) for more than two weeks. The levels of hurt and rage in my friend rose to such a height that just the thought of his 'little girl' made him grind his teeth and swear under his breath.

The crunch came one evening when she stormed up to her bedroom after being asked to perform the most undemanding of tasks. He thundered up in her wake with murder in his heart, and was about to crash into her room and pull her head off when something made him stop. My friend is a Christian and although he fails often he never gives up. Time for a little piano moving, he thought. My friend has become my enemy. With murder still crouching inside him he sat on the bed, spoke softly and lovingly, and held his arms out. She responded! Tears—music in a new place. Just as well, or he'd have chucked her out of the window.

Loving enemies—you don't have to feel it. You have to do it.

GIVE ME YOUR HEART

Matthew 6:19–21 (NIV)

'Do not store up for yourselves treasures on earth, where moth and rust destroy, and where thieves break in and steal. For where your treasure is, there your heart will be also.'

Three people arrived outside the gate of heaven. One, a well dressed man, carried a large sack.

'In this bag', he explained, 'is the wealth of a lifetime.' He patted it. 'If this little lot, plus a spot of the old wheeler-dealer chat, doesn't get me through those gates, I shall be very surprised. And, just to cover the religious angle, I've popped my heart in too, so they can have the lot if they want. There!'

The second person was a pious-looking woman in simple threadbare garments. She carried a much smaller bag.

'I have not collected great wealth,' she said, in a faint, burdened voice. 'Our Lord commanded us to store up treasure in heaven, and therefore my life has been spent in service to others.'

'What is in your bag?' questioned the rich man.

'Accounts,' she replied with modest pride. 'Notebooks, lists and ledgers recording every good deed and charitable act I have ever performed. I shall present them together with my heart, which, like you, I have placed inside in case it should be required.'

The third person, a weary looking fellow dressed only in a loincloth, and empty-handed, spoke nervously.

'I bring nothing,' he faltered. 'In life I neither accumulated wealth, nor did I pour myself out for others as selflessly as you, Madam. Most troubling of all, though, I have given away my heart—I fear I shall not enter heaven.'

The rich man and the pious woman walked ahead to the gates together, but returned very soon, faces dark with disappointment.

'No luggage allowed beyond the gates,' said the rich man sadly.

'And we are not allowed to leave our bags outside the gates,' sobbed the woman. 'We shall have them for ever!'

The man in the loincloth watched the pair walk slowly away, then approached heaven himself. True, he had no luggage, but his heart was lost. What hope for him?

The angel who opened the gates ushered him in with a sweeping bow, before placing into his hand something that shone and glittered like the most perfect diamond.

'Yours, I believe,' he said.

Look after our hearts, Lord, until we come to you.

WORRY OR LIFE?

Matthew 6:25-27 (NIV)

'Therefore I tell you, do not worry about your life, what you will eat or drink; or about your body, what you will wear. Is not life more important than food, and the body more important than clothes? Look at the birds of the air; they do not sow or reap or store away in barns, and yet your heavenly Father feeds them. Are you not much more valuable than they? Who of you by worrying can add a single hour to his life?'

A friend of mine who pastors a local fellowship told me once about a conversation with his five-year-old son.

'Dad,' said the little boy dolefully one morning, 'God's not answering my prayers any more.'

'I'm sorry to hear that, Tim,' said my friend. 'Anything in particular?'

'I asked him to close the window,' replied Tim in scandalized tones, 'but he didn't!'

Tim's slight misconception of the role of God in his life illustrates the kind of problem that can arise from key scriptures like this. I know people who have used these verses as a stepping stone towards the condition known as 'living by faith'. They stop worrying about where the next meal is coming from, while whole teams of other people start worrying on their behalf. God will not feed the canary while I am on holiday, and he will not (on the whole) supply the needs created by idleness. I'm sure God does call some people to live by faith, but it has to be his decision, and even then, as we learn from Paul's experiences and accounts, material needs are not necessarily going to come first on the Holy Spirit's agenda. The thing we can say in this connection is that if God does authorize and initiate a task, he will supply whatever is needed to get it done, although his idea of what is needed and ours may differ quite dramatically.

So what is this passage saying to the Church generally? It seems to be expressing yet again the divine frustration (can God get frustrated?) with the persistent, petty, potentially disastrous preoccupation of human beings with things of the body. Most of us are not just arranging the chairs on the Titanic, we're planning next week's menu and getting up teams for deck-tennis.

There are boats leaving for the kingdom. Can you see them?

Help us to trust you. Draw our eyes towards the cosmic vision.

IT'S NOT EASY, JESUS

Matthew 6:31–33 (NIV)

'So do not worry, saying, "What shall we eat?" or "What shall we drink?" or "What shall we wear?" For the pagans run after all these things, and your heavenly Father knows that you need them. But seek first his kingdom and his righteousness, and all these things will be given to you as well.'

Dear Jesus,

Over the last few days I've been writing very positively about all the things you said to your disciples in this famous sermon (yes, I know—big deal!) but this morning I feel jaded, and now, as I read your exhortation to avoid worrying about the precise things that this society trains us to worry about, I am confused. A Christian friend has just lost his one-man business through no fault of his own, and although his church has been warmly generous, he and his wife and four children are very bothered about what they're going to eat, drink and wear. What is your message to them and us? Is it up to the rest of your wider family to provide practical support? Does that sometimes constitute the miracle of faith? I don't undervalue that kind of miracle at all—I think it's wonderful. But is that 'it'? We've read books where miraculous provision happens constantly, but it's the exception rather than the rule in most churches I know.

You never had a problem in this area, did you? When you needed to pay tax you sent old Peter off to catch a fish, and there was the cash in the creature's mouth. When you had five thousand people to feed, you just kept breaking bits off one small meal until everyone had more than enough to eat. As for drink—well, gallons of water turned into top-grade wine at a snap of your fingers.

But then, you'd been through that gruelling 40-days sorting-out period in the wilderness, hadn't you? During that time you refused to use your spiritual cashpoint card, because (just as you say in this passage) the kingdom has to come first. After that battle was won the rest was a piece of cake, or a piece of fish, or a gallon of wine, or whatever. That became the easy part.

I guess the answer to my question is that most of us just haven't been through that sorting-out process—not really, and until we do, until we break through into the clean air of kingdom priority, we're bound to be stuck in a fog of worry and need.

It's not easy, Lord Jesus. It's not easy. Help us to understand the challenge, and then to face it. We pray for all those who, like my friend, are feeling worried and confused.

Thank you.

Love, Adrian

JUST LOOK AT HIM...

Matthew 7:1–5 (NIV)

'Do not judge, or you too will be judged. For in the same way as you judge others, you will be judged, and with the measure you use it will be measured to you. Why do you look at the speck of sawdust in your brother's eye and pay no attention to the plank in your own eye? How can you say to your brother, "Let me take the speck out of your eye," when all the time there is a plank in your own eye? You hypocrite, first take the plank out of your own eye, and then you will see clearly to remove the speck from your brother's eye.'

How true, and I should know, because we have someone in our house group who does just what Jesus is talking about. This person (whose name begins with 'Z' and who has a significant role in the second-tier leadership of our church—all the more surprising, really, wouldn't you agree?) is constantly judging others, and generally being negative. I've asked Stanley, our group leader, whether he intends to say anything to Z, but I'm afraid poor old Stanley is no more able to confront now than he ever was. When you consider he's allowed Eve thingy, who may or may not be a believer, to get away with something close to heresy for the whole year since she attached herself to us, it's clear not much can be expected in that quarter.

The pity of it is that Z's critical attitude and Stanley's weakness bring out the very worst in Jeanette, who, having paid her debt to society and been forgiven by God, is not going to benefit from having her anti-social proclivities stimulated, if you grasp my inference. That's leaving aside the fact that if Jeanette does give way to her subversive instincts we won't see Malcolm for dust, not that Malcolm (who's lived with his mother all his life and is a real Poirot of a—well, I was going to say 'man', but nobody's quite sure) would know dust if he saw it, him never having laid a finger on a Hoover in his life. I doubt if dear Malcolm's interested in any women, let alone Jeanette in full flow. The only one who's not affected by Z's nastiness is Violet Stratton, but then she's not been affected by anything for as long as I can remember, poor soul. She'd win prizes for nodding and smiling, but there's no edge to her since her 'holiday', if you get my drift.

So, that's the situation. Pray that Z will see the light—and become like me.

Let's build a cabin with all these planks—then set fire to it.

ASK ME...

Matthew 7:7–12 (NIV)

'Ask and it will be given to you; seek and you will find; knock and the door will be opened to you. For everyone who asks receives; he who seeks finds; and to him who knocks the door will be opened. Which of you, if his son asks for bread, will give him a stone? Or if he asks for a fish will give him a snake? If you, then, though you are evil, know how to give good gifts to your children, how much more will your Father in heaven give good gifts to those who ask him! So in everything do to others what you would have them do to you, for this sums up the Law and the prophets.'

I want to be touched by affectionate eyes,
I want to be welcomed when welcome is rare,
I want to be held when my confidence sighs,
I want to find comfort in genuine care.

I want to be given untakeable things,
I want to be trusted with hearts that might break,
I want to fly dreaming on effortless wings,
I want to be smiled on when I awake.

I want to see sunsets with people who know,
I want to hear secrets that no one should hear,
I want to be guarded wherever I go,
I want to be fought for when dangers appear.

I want to be chained to the lives of my friends,
I want to be wanted because and despite,
I want to link arms when the foolishness ends,
I want to be safe in the raging night.

I want to be sheltered although I am wrong,
I want to be laughed at although I am right,
I want to be sung in the heavenly song,
I want to be loved—I want to be light.

Father, I seem to find it awfully easy to assemble a list of things that I want from other people and from you. The problem comes when I turn the whole thing round and consider what it would cost me to give instead of to take. Please show me ways in which I can give pleasure to you and to the people I meet by doing for them the things I would want them to do for me. Thank you for your fatherly love. Teach me to see your hand in all the good things that happen to me.

IT FRIGHTENS ME...

Matthew 7:13–14 (NIV)

'Enter through the narrow gate. For wide is the gate and broad is the road that leads to destruction, and many enter through it. But small is the gate and narrow the road that leads to life, and only a few find it.'

These verses have always frightened me. The adult Adrian Plass, insubstantial, wraith-like creature though he is, does have a clean theological perspective on the question of faith and salvation. I am saved. I am going there. Oh, yes I am—hallelujah!

The other Adrian Plass, however, more formless but more authentic, the skinny 1960s kid with the long grey shorts that never did up properly, and the pudding-basin haircut, and the permanently worried expression, is in a bit of a panic, and needs to talk to Jesus. He finds him sitting alone beside the Sea of Galilee, gazing out over the water.

Adrian: Excuse me, could I ask you something?
Jesus: (*Smiles*) Anything.
Adrian: You know that bit about the little gate and the narrow road and only a few find it and all that?
Jesus: (*Solemnly*) Yes, I think I know that bit.
Adrian: (*Deep breath*) Well, it frightens me.
Jesus: (*Nods thoughtfully*) I can understand that. Did you want to ask something in particular?
Adrian: You don't mind?
Jesus: I never mind questions. Do you mind answers?
Adrian: I don't know yet—the thing is, what is the narrow gate, what is the narrow road, and—well, am I one of the few?
Jesus: (*After a long silence*) Answers can be very complicated or very simple. What sort of answer would you like?
Adrian: (*In a very quiet voice*) Simple, please, so that I understand.
Jesus: OK, then my answer to all three questions is a question.
Adrian: I sort of knew it would be.
Jesus: If I got up now and walked away without telling you where I was going, or whether I would ever come back, or what I would be doing, or how it would all end—would you take my hand and come with me?

Adrian: *(Throat suddenly dry)* Right now?
Jesus: Right now. Would you come?
Adrian: I... I think so...

Jesus, you said that you are the Way, the Truth and the Life. Help us to take your hand.

WHAT AM I, LORD?

Matthew 7:15–20 (NIV)

'Watch out for false prophets. They come to you in sheep's clothing, but inwardly they are ferocious wolves. By their fruit you will recognize them. Do people pick grapes from thornbushes, or figs from thistles? Likewise every good tree bears good fruit, but a bad tree bears bad fruit. A good tree cannot bear bad fruit, and a bad tree cannot bear good fruit. Every tree that does not bear good fruit is cut down and thrown into the fire. Thus, by their fruit you will recognize them.'

There is something deeply chilling about the idea of this unplanned, spiritual fancy-dress party, where in the midst of unsuspecting guests, ferocious wolves come as sheep, thistles dress up as figs, and thornbushes masquerade as vines. It's a horrible picture, isn't it, but let's be clear about something. Jesus is talking about deliberate, vicious deception by people who have an appetite for harming others. Dressing up as a sheep among other sheep, when you are actually a ravening wolf looking for food, is not a minor departure from moral rectitude, nor could it ever be done by accident. It is the devil's own work, and if that scares us, then so it should.

I emphasize this point because many anxious people ask themselves whether they are actually thistles pretending to be grapevines. After all, they say worriedly to themselves, the fruit I produce is a pretty varied crop. If, as Jesus says, a good tree can't produce bad fruit, and some of the fruit I produce is bad, then, logically, I must be a bad tree, or even a ravening wolf, without even realizing it. Help!

Enough of this neurosis—I've been through it myself. Good trees certainly produce fruit that's variable in quality, because (we might as well labour the metaphor while we've got it) sometimes the rich soil of fellowship is lacking, or the life-giving water of prayer has dried up, or the warm climate of scripture has—oh, never mind, you get the picture, don't you? It's difficult enough to keep my Jesus-planted tree in reasonable order, without worrying that I might be the antichrist in disguise as well.

We need to heed Jesus' warning. There are false prophets, and, like wolves, they do seek to destroy (the devil does all his best work inside the church), but if our hearts are yearning for God, even though we fail sometimes, that woolly stuff we find ourselves covered with is quite genuine.

Baaaa!

GOD WITH US

Matthew 7:21–23 (NIV)

'Not everyone who says to me, "Lord, Lord," will enter the kingdom of heaven, but only he who does the will of my Father... Many will say to me on that day, "Lord, Lord, did we not prophesy in your name, and... drive out demons and perform many miracles?" Then I will tell them... "I never knew you. Away from me, you evildoers!"'

A few years ago Bridget and I met a lady whose husband had recently died after contracting one of those appalling diseases that cause almost total physical helplessness. Mary and Chris (not their real names) had enjoyed a very happy marriage and were devastated. Quite apart from the dread of death, there was the fact that everyday living was now very hard work for Mary, and terribly frustrating for Chris. Two things happened towards the end of Chris's life that have some bearing on today's passage.

First, Chris was taken by a well-meaning friend, in his wheelchair, to a local healing meeting. When he was returned later that evening Mary was horrified to discover that both of his knees were grazed and bleeding. The distraught friend explained that the 'healers' had lifted Chris out of his wheelchair two or three times, and after praying loudly for his healing on each occasion, had dropped him on to his knees, telling him that he was now able to walk. It was an unimaginably awful experience on every level.

The second thing was the arrival on the doorstep one day of another Christian friend, whom I shall call Eileen, to announce quietly that the Holy Spirit had sent her to help look after Chris for as long as was necessary. Eileen was married and had a family herself, but from that day she was as good as her word. The burden of work was halved, and Chris could stop worrying about his wife wearing herself out. Mary was even able to take a brief holiday.

After Chris' death Eileen continued to support Mary, and was in fact with her when we met at a holiday house-party in Devon.

'Not long after Chris died,' Mary told us, 'my son, Martin, said to me one day, "Mummy, wasn't it good how Auntie Eileen came to be God for us that day?"'

It was indeed good that a true follower of Jesus had heard a command and obeyed it. It was the tougher, more committed way, but it was what God wanted, and that's the point. Of course God does heal in miraculous ways, but if a desire for spiritual gymnastics overcomes the rule of love and obedience—we'd better watch out.

Bind us to your will, Lord. Keep our eyes and ears on you.

*A hero is one who knows how to
hang on one minute longer.*

NORWEGIAN PROVERB

TRAILBLAZING HEROES

SOME OLD TESTAMENT FIGURES

One wonders why it never occurs to any of the characters in long-running television soap operas to ask themselves why such strange things tend to happen in their small worlds.

Why, for instance, do all soap 'marriages' seem doomed to end in premature death, inexplicable parting after recent declarations of undying love, and strange disappearances that are only ever solved if the actor concerned gets sick of doing talk-shows and (if they're Australian) pantomimes in England, and returns to the nice little earner that supported him or her in the past?

Why on earth, they might further ask themselves, do individual characters suddenly produce behaviour that is wildly, irrationally untypical of the personality that they have developed over the months or years?

Why, in pubs and other crowded places, do only two people at a time speak in voices loud enough to be heard, and why do third parties never come into a room until the first and second parties have reached the end of their significant conversation, and drifted into a brief snatch of small talk?

Most puzzling of all perhaps is the fact that entire geographical areas become totally repopulated over periods of just a few years. A truly extraordinary social phenomenon! Where do all those lost people go?

Could it be that, in some strange, shadowy world, long-abandoned soap stars meet to discuss and reminisce about the good old days when they actually existed, albeit at the mercy of writers and pen-twiddling, paperclip-twisting members of story-development conferences? Let us hope that such encounters are well-policed. Some of those legendary soap stars were pretty strong characters, weren't they? Imagine Ena Sharples from *Coronation Street*, Dirty Den from *EastEnders*, and Paul Robinson from *Neighbours* settling down in the corner of their local, a bizarre combination of The Rovers Return, The Queen Vic and The Watering Hole, to discuss the rival merits of their individual contributions to soap history. The fictional fur would certainly fly, and it's not easy to judge who would emerge the winner of the argument. If you press me, though, I must admit that most of my money would be on Ena Sharples.

I mention this unlikely scenario because it strikes me that a somewhat similar encounter must have occurred between the Old Testament figures that you are about to meet in the following section. Obviously there are major differences. They are not soap characters, of course, although the telling of their stories in so many different ways over so many generations has, for many people, tended to give them that same aura of pasteboard-like unreality. After watching four children grow up I have seen so many giants of the Old Testament coloured with crayons and cut out of cardboard with a little bit stuck on the back to make sure they stand up all right, that I have almost forgotten that they were real people.

Nor, I assume, will their meetings have taken place in a pub, although I suppose one can never be absolutely sure with God...

The other big difference is that Abraham and the rest of them must be retrospectively redeemed (unlike Ena, Den and Paul, who will have failed to qualify on the grounds that they don't actually exist) and will presumably get on pretty well.

Just imagine it, though—the whole crowd of them seated round a big circular table at lunchtime. There would be Jephthah, reunited with his daughter at last, and feeling more than a bit silly; Adam and Eve, politely refusing the fruit bowl every time it comes round, and effusively apologizing to everyone in sight; David, Uriah and Bathsheba having a bit of a laugh about the bad old days; Noah and Jonah, contrasting their very different experiences of being saved from drowning; Jacob and Esau sharing a bowl of soup; Samson showing off little strength tricks to Job, who is really only waiting for a chance to say some more about a really good treatment for boils that he's just come across; Joseph, closely attended by his brothers and wondering if there's any way he can claim royalties on the musical; Moses and Joshua selecting milk and honey as an ideal dessert experience; Daniel trying to talk the good-natured Zephaniah into adopting his highly successful and royally approved vegan diet, and, at the top of the table, Abraham himself, reunited for ever with his beloved son, Isaac, and beaming genially around at the assembled company.

Do you realize that we shall be with them one day?

On a more serious level, the stories that feature these great Old Testament figures are vital links in the chain of our understanding about how God deals and has dealt with those who claim him as their leader. The history of the Jewish people and their progress towards the time when it would be possible for God's law to be written on their hearts, offers countless parallels to the journey that we undertake today when we choose to follow Jesus, the new Adam, through a desert of earthly problems to the promised land of total unity with him. If we will accept them, there are lots of lessons to be learned.

And let us thank God that, as we take that journey, we are not like soap characters. Our authenticity will never be sacrificed to the needs of the plot, nor will we be 'dumped' out of existence because some more exciting idea has come along. We are real people who have been adopted into the real family of God, exactly the same family as that illustrious body whose members are seated around the heavenly table that I have just described.

Prayer

Father, help us to look more deeply into the lives of these people whose names have become so familiar that we are in danger of missing important aspects of their relationships with you and with each other. We understand that you have left a record of your dealings with them so that we can learn a little more of what it means to walk with Jesus in our own age. May the lessons go deep into our hearts, and enrich our spirits with their wisdom.

ABRAHAM AND ISAAC

Genesis 22:9–10 (NIV)

Abraham built an altar there and arranged the wood on it. He bound his son Isaac and laid him on the altar, on top of the wood. Then he reached out his hand and took the knife to slay his son.

When our first child was born, I remember gazing through the glass wall of the 'baby ward' at this little scrunched-up person. I'd never experienced the kind of love I felt at that moment. It was different from anything I felt for family, friends or even my wife—not more, just different. It filled me with a determination to care endlessly for his welfare, a determination that, as most parents know, doesn't lessen with the years.

At the same time, I had been spiritually 'raised' in a climate of self-sacrifice and denial. God had to come first, and the setting aside of strong feelings for friends or family was regarded as a positive virtue. The story of Abraham being asked to sacrifice Isaac just made me feel sick. A shadow fell over my perception of the relationship I had with God, because I knew that I would never sacrifice Matthew, neither actually nor symbolically. How could I, when I loved him much more than I loved the creator of the world? Inwardly, I flirted with atheism, preferring the prospect of human relationships followed by oblivion, to the shift in priorities that God seemed to be demanding.

The journey from that state of mind to my present one is too long and eventful to describe here, but some things I now know to be true. First, God stood beside me outside that baby ward, excited like me about the arrival of someone who was as much a new son for him as for me. His commitment to caring for Matthew was and is endless too, in the literal sense. Secondly, my love for my son has changed. It's more about him and less about me. I want him to enjoy eternal life. I want him to walk through the streets of heaven with a brand-new, indestructible body. I want him to be a child of God above anything else. Thirdly, perhaps most importantly, I have come to understand a little better what I would, with great respect, call the 'sanity' of God. He knows me and my weaknesses and strengths, and has done since the day when he chuckled fondly outside the baby ward where I was born.

He has been a good and very wise Father, and, as that fact becomes real to me, I come closer to loving him more than anyone in the world.

Father, I'm a long way from trusting you as Abraham did. Help me to learn that trust is the best way for me, and thank you for sacrificing your own Son so that mine can live.

DAVID

2 Samuel 12:19–20 (NIV)

David... realized that the child was dead. 'Is the child dead?' he asked. 'Yes,' they replied, 'he is dead.' Then David got up from the ground. After he had washed, put on lotions and changed his clothes, he went into the house of the Lord and worshipped. Then... he ate.

David's response to the death of the child conceived in his adulterous relationship with Bathsheba says something very profound about his understanding of God. He prayed and wept for seven days and nights, but when the child died, he accepted the judgment of the Lord. David loved God. His relationship was a real one. In crunch situations the reality of what we believe makes a demonstrable difference—or not, of course. A friend of mine, who was a traffic warden, recently died in hospital of cancer, amazing visitors with a new strength and authority as he approached his death. He really wanted to be healed, but he was ready to accept the will of the God he trusted. For his funeral service I wrote and read the following lines:

He stood at the crossroads of his own life
Directing the traffic of emotions, thoughts, events
Too watchful once, perhaps
For woe betide some maverick urge that tried to jump the queue
And overtake good common sense that ought to set the pace
He tried, he really tried to set his face against irregularity
Longed to see the day when all of life's unruly streams
Would be reorganized into an earthly paradise of dead straight lines
With no untidy tailbacks to upset him
Alas for all his dreams, his bosses wouldn't let him
He had three bosses
One in heaven, one in Hastings, one at home
The first and last of these instructed him in many things
They taught him that the waving through of tender thoughts
A blind eye turned when unashamed compassion
Does a sudden U-turn in the outside lane
Need not be crimes
That facts and feelings have to double-park sometimes

And in the end, in the main, love was flowing freely
Far too soon, far too soon for us, the traffic noises died
And on that soundless day
A chauffeur-driven certainty came softly in the morning
And carried him away.

A prayer: Father, may we develop the kind of trust in you that upheld these two
men who worshipped the same God. We want it to be real, Lord.

NOAH

Genesis 7:11–12 (NIV)

In the six hundredth year of Noah's life, on the seventeenth day of the second month—on that day all the springs of the great deep burst forth, and the floodgates of the heavens were opened.

A friend, whom I shall call Herbert, told me once about an encounter over coffee with someone whom I shall call Bertha. For some reason my name or one of my children's names came up in the conversation.

'Do you know the Plasses?' asked Bertha, settling into an I've-got-something-to-say sort of posture.

Herbert, who isn't a Christian but knows us very well, was quite unable to resist the temptation to find out what Bertha was going to say, and replied vaguely, 'Well—you know, I've come across them. Why do you ask?'

'You want to be very careful there,' replied Bertha darkly. 'Don't get more involved than you absolutely have to.'

Herbert was deeply intrigued to hear us talked about as though we were some sort of suspect political movement. 'Why do you say that?' he enquired innocently. 'Is there something wrong with them?'

'They're religious fanatics!' announced Bertha dramatically. 'They want to draw other people in, that's all they're interested in.'

'I didn't realize you knew them,' said Herbert.

'Oh, I've never spoken to them,' said Bertha, 'but it's common knowledge.'

Bertha wasn't very sure of her facts, but I found it interesting that 'common knowledge' held us to be fanatics—weirdos whose lives were centred on something not of this world. I would hate those who really know us to describe us in that way, but I guess it's inevitable that those who have heard and believed in the approach of a great disaster, and the possibility of great salvation, will seem slightly strange to the rest of the world. That's why nominal religion is such a crime. True Christianity might appear bizarre in some ways, but at least people notice it and wonder why it's there.

Few of us will be called upon to look quite as ridiculous as Noah must have appeared, but let's value our divine foolishness a little more than we have in the past. When the great rain of judgment comes, we won't look weird any more, and we might even have been able to hand out a few spiritual umbrellas in advance.

Father, it's so hard to get the balance right between openness about what we believe, and normal contact with the world. Give us courage and good judgment.

JOB

Job 29:21–24 (NIV)

'Men listened to me expectantly, waiting in silence for my counsel. After I had spoken, they spoke no more; my words fell gently on their ears. They waited for me as for showers and drank in my words as the spring rain. When I smiled at them, they scarcely believed it; the light of my face was precious to them.'

Job is one of my heroes, not just because his regard for God survived poverty, skin disease and extremely annoying friends, but because of the kind of man he was. The content of this passage, a description by Job himself of the way in which his counsel was received by others in pre-boil days, is the target at which I unsuccessfully aim in my writing and speaking. This servant of God clearly brought three things straight from the heart of God to all those who listened.

(I can't believe I'm about to make three points about something. Perhaps I should get out of the Anglican Church before it gets even worse.)

First, he says that his words fell 'gently' on their ears. Oh, for a few more gentle words in church. Many of the people I encounter have already been bruised by bawled accusation and crushed by echoing admonition. Jesus could be very tough, but he felt such compassion for the crowds. He still does, so let us all be gentle on his behalf, unless we're very specifically called to behave in some other way.

The second thing is about the showers and the spring rain. Job helped his listeners to feel refreshed and lightened in spirit. They would have felt more able to cope after hearing him, not less. Forgive me for repeating one of my constant bleats, but the blessing of God does not discourage and disable me, it makes me feel that I might be able to get somewhere after all.

The last bit is my favourite. When Job smiled at them they could hardly believe it. I cannot adequately express the sheer delight I have experienced on those few (too few) occasions when I have seen some frightened face suddenly illuminated by the awareness that God is actually smiling at his nervous, guilt-racked son or daughter. They can hardly believe it! God is nice! Why did no one ever tell them?

Father, help our gentle words to bring the refreshment of your smile to those of your children who need it.

URIAH THE HITTITE

2 Samuel 11:11 (NIV)

Uriah said to David, 'The ark and Israel and Judah are staying in tents, and my master Joab and my lord's men are camped in the open fields. How could I go to my house to eat and drink and lie with my wife? As surely as you live, I will not do such a thing!'

There are some memories that we fight to avoid, aren't there? In my own case, they are mainly recollections of those occasions when one of my children has been suddenly hurt or deeply upset about something, and especially when that hurt involved a significant erosion of their naturally optimistic view of the world. I hate it. When those memories surface, particularly late at night, my heart sinks and I pray that some bright distraction will soon lighten my darkness.

Other memories, however, are to do with my own misdoings. Even though God long ago forgave me for certain sins, I still experience a sickness in my spirit when I am forced for some reason to look at those dark things.

I am quite sure that the memory of Uriah's enthusiasm and loyalty haunted David for the rest of his life. He murdered that good man to cover up his own adultery. That's the trouble with sin committed by big-hearted people. Such folk throw themselves into wrongdoing with the same abandonment that is evident in their acts of generosity and goodness. Layer after layer of deceit is laid down until only an explosion of evil or an act of incredibly brave disclosure will change the situation. David managed (goodness knows how, when he knew God so well) to kid himself that he would get away with sin of the worst kind, simply because he had managed to hide his crimes from men. In the end, he had to face God, of course, through the prophet Nathan, and although he was forgiven, the consequences of his sin were appalling. I really do find it extremely difficult to read about David's agony of spirit over his son Absalom.

Please, if you are involved in wrongdoing that is bound to end up hurting people who are close to you, or the God who loves you more than you can imagine, do something about it now. Take the brave option rather than the evil one. Easy to say, I know, but we'll pray with you now.

Father, some of the people who are reading this note today are getting themselves into a lot of trouble. A world of remorse lies ahead. Please give them the courage to battle their way out of the darkness and into the light. It will be very tough, but you will be with them, and so, in spirit, will we. Thank you, Father.

JONAH

Jonah 3:10; 4:1–3 (NIV)

[God]... had compassion and did not bring upon them the destruction he had threatened... But Jonah was greatly displeased and became angry... 'O Lord, is this not what I said when I was still at home? That is why I was so quick to flee to Tarshish. I knew that you are a gracious and compassionate God, slow to anger and abounding in love, a God who relents from sending calamity.'

Of all the characters in the Old Testament the one I would most like to meet once a week in the pub is Jonah. I just know that our conversation about God, the universe and everything would be about as seamless as is possible in this fallen world. God was as much of a reality in this awkward prophet's life as a loaf of bread. Only the truest of believers would actually see the need to run away from the object of their belief purely because they knew all too well how he was likely to behave in a given situation. As for going into a sulk like a five-year-old because the nasty-wasty people in Nineveh didn't get deaded—well, what greater sign of faith could there be? Jonah knew God was there.

The reason I mention this is that I've recently become very aware of the different ways in which people talk about God, depending on where they happen to be, and who's listening at the time. I'm sure I'm the same. In public meetings or services most of us tend to speak of our faith in definite, formal words and tones, as if doubt is a disease that very few Christians suffer from. In private, however, there is often a quite distinctly different approach to such matters, one that, in many cases, suggests that public expressions of belief might have been more optimistic and expedient than truthful.

It can be quite a shock to settle down quietly for a drink with someone only to discover that the depth of their devotion to God is as evident in their private conversation as it was in a more formal situation. I love it when it happens, but it doesn't happen very often. Very few people are as closely engaged with the person of the Father as Jonah was, whether in a positive or a negative way.

Sadly, such awareness is not as popular as one might think. The kind of true faith that has explored the whole mountain is an enormous challenge to those who have half-decided to settle for a lifetime of pottering about on the lower slopes. But it is these people, the ones who talk about God in the same breath as they talk about the price of beans, who are needed in this generation.

Give us more prophets like Jonah, Lord, people who know you, and will argue with you, and speak for you.

HAGGAI

Haggai 1:3–8 (NIV)

Then the word of the Lord came through the prophet Haggai: 'Is it a time for you yourselves to be living in your panelled houses, while this house remains a ruin?... Give careful thought to your ways. You have planted much, but have harvested little. You eat, but never have enough. You drink, but never have your fill. You put on clothes, but are not warm. You earn wages, only to put them in a purse with holes in it... Go up into the mountains and bring down timber and build the house, so that I may take pleasure in it and be honoured.'

When I get to heaven I shall go searching round the various mansions until I find the one with Haggai's name printed over the front porch. Then I shall knock on the door, and when Haggai opens it I shall hold out my copy of the Bible and ask him to autograph his book for me. This summary of the problems faced by a society that does not put God first is absolutely masterful. However much we have or get, in the end it's worth nothing without the one who gives.

Nowadays, we work very hard at avoiding this fact, but God has an old and experienced assistant in this area of work, and the name of that assistant is Death. In the case of people like me, the process is as follows. A queue of worries, needs and concerns occupies most of our attention for most of the time. We work very hard at shortening this queue, not least because it really is possible to deal with some of the issues. Shortage of money, for instance, can be a real problem, but it is possible for hard work and a little luck to solve that problem, at least to the extent that we are comfortable. Next in the queue might be our failure to find a wife or a husband or perhaps just a good friend. Relationships can be tricky, but if we go to the right places and take a real interest in others—who knows?

Two down, 85 to go. Very few of us ever work our way through to the end of the queue, because so many difficulties are desperately hard, if not impossible, to deal with, and others tend to take their place as soon as they disappear. Sometimes, though—just sometimes—we reach a place where, by some miracle, we find ourselves staring at the very last item on the list. Death waits quietly and confidently, the problem that cannot be solved—unless we are inhabited by the living God.

Father, help us to make a priority of building a house for you in our hearts.

JEPHTHAH

Judges 11:30–32, 34–35 (NIV)

Jephthah made a vow to the Lord: 'If you give the Ammonites into my hands, whatever comes out of the door of my house to meet me when I return... will be the Lord's, and I will sacrifice it as a burnt offering.' Then Jephthah went over to fight the Ammonites, and the Lord gave them into his hands... When Jephthah returned to his home in Mizpah, who should come out to meet him but his daughter, dancing to the sound of tambourines!... When he saw her, he tore his clothes and cried, 'Oh, My daughter! You have made me miserable and wretched, because I have made a vow to the Lord that I cannot break.'

This little-mentioned tale contrasts bizarrely with the story of Abraham and Isaac, doesn't it? What an absolutely appalling situation! The more you think about it, the worse it gets. All I find myself able to do is ask a series of very obvious questions.

First—why did Jephthah open his big mouth and make rash promises when he didn't have to? What was the matter with him? It wasn't as if God had asked him to do it. Wild vows are dangerous, to say the least.

Secondly, what did he think was going to meet him when he returned in triumph, an earwig? Or did he perhaps expect some more dispensable member of the household to present him or her self. If he'd asked me (granted, I wasn't around at the time) I could have told him that it's always daughters who run to greet fathers when they come home from work. He just didn't think it through, did he?

Thirdly, why didn't he break his vow and take the consequences like a man? I don't suppose he knew what those consequences were likely to be, but if he was as fond of his daughter as he appeared to be he might have decided to find out. Instead, he killed her!

Last, but not least, why didn't God say to him, 'Look, Jephthah, old chap, let's forget that silly vow you made the other day, and just celebrate your victory over the Ammonites. I don't want your daughter to be sacrificed to me as a burnt offering—what kind of God do you think I am, for goodness sake?'

There are my questions, and I know the answers are located somewhere in the region of the ongoing revelation of the nature of God (have I got that right?), but what a story!

Father, help us to keep our mouths shut when we're overexcited, to think things through before we make a decision, and to go on searching for the truth about who and what you really are.

SAMSON

Judges 16:19–22 (NIV)

[Delilah] called a man to shave off the seven braids of his hair, and so began to subdue him. And his strength left him. Then she called, 'Samson, the Philistines are upon you!' He awoke from his sleep and thought, 'I'll go out as before and shake myself free.' But he did not know that the Lord had left him. Then the Philistines seized him, gouged out his eyes and took him down to Gaza. Binding him with bronze shackles, they set him to grinding in the prison. But the hair on his head began to grow again after it had been shaved.

Fortunately the Bible is full of good news for those who have failed. I've never been as powerful or as strong or as resourceful as Samson, but what I do have in common with him is the experience of giving in when the pressure becomes unbearable. This can apply at work or at home or in any situation where 'getting things right' requires consistent care and attention.

It can be so dispiriting. It's many years since I gave up smoking (I used to smoke 60 cigarettes a day and I enjoyed every single one), but I can still remember the attempts I made to stop when I was in my late 20s and early 30s. For some reason I got the idea into my head that God was going to 'get me' if I didn't stop smoking, so I was always worrying about it. Sometimes I'd manage to last for a week, a month, or even a couple of months, but then the pressure would become unbearable, especially if some other worry had become more dominant, and I'd fail again and feel a miserable failure. I didn't understand God at all in those days, so each time I was pretty sure I'd lose my salvation at the very least. Why would he want to be bothered with someone who had let the enemy batter him into submission?

But after each of these failures, and there were many, my hair began to grow again, as it were, just like Samson's. Some kind of divinely natural healing process restored both my belief that I was valued, and my intention to please God, and, in the end, I did give up smoking, although it was sheer agony for about six months.

Please don't think, by the way, that I'm getting at you if you're a smoker. God deals with each of us differently, and in my case, it was my experience that when people went on at me about giving up, there was only one thing I wanted to do—go and have a fag!

Father, sometimes we give in under pressure, and it feels as if we will never be quite as close to you ever again. Restore the strength of our trust in you, Lord, and keep us close to you in future.

DANIEL

Daniel 2:26, 29–30 (NIV, abridged)

The king asked Daniel... 'Are you able to tell me what I saw in my dream and interpret it?' Daniel replied, 'No wise man, enchanter, magician or diviner can explain to the king the mystery he has asked about, but there is a God in heaven who reveals mysteries. He has shown King Nebuchadnezzar what will happen in days to come. Your dream and the visions that passed through your mind... are these: As you were lying there, O king, your mind turned to things to come, and the revealer of mysteries showed you what is going to happen... This mystery has been revealed to me, not because I have greater wisdom than other living men, but so that you, O king, may know the interpretation and that you may understand what went through your mind.'

Do read the whole of Daniel as if it was a novel. It's a marvellous piece of storytelling (no, I'm not saying it didn't happen, just that it's a good read), and a very clear picture of the way in which God operates through a life that is genuinely dedicated to him. The impressive thing about Daniel, in all his dealings with the Babylonian kings, is his refusal to extract any personal glory from the situations in which God has given him special knowledge or protection. In this particular case he is at great pains to make it clear that it is God, not himself, who is the ultimate revealer of mysteries, and that his qualifications for passing on the wisdom of God do not include any extra or unusual wisdom of his own. The consistent purity of motivation shared by Daniel and his three famous friends makes them very strong. No one can truly damage the most important part of you if your first priority is to serve God.

We could do with a few Daniels in church leadership today. It's so easy, when involved in spiritual ministry, to put on a self-advertising show, instead of simply passing on whatever God has told you to. The great sadness is that, for both Christians and non-Christians, the glorious sanity of God can be obscured by unnecessarily dramatic and bizarre role-playing on the part of those who have power over others. I pray that the Church may be entering a new phase in this country, which will see God speaking and working more clearly and powerfully than ever before. I just hope that, when this happens, we'll be like Daniel, and get out of the way.

When the time comes to face the lions, relationship is going to be worth more than religion.

JOSHUA

Joshua 5:13–15 (NIV)

Now when Joshua was near Jericho, he looked up and saw a man standing in front of him with a drawn sword in his hand. Joshua went up to him and asked, 'Are you for us or for our enemies?' 'Neither,' he replied, 'but as commander of the army of the Lord I have now come.' Then Joshua fell face down to the ground in reverence, and asked him, 'What message does my Lord have for his servant?' The commander of the Lord's army replied, 'Take off your sandals, for the place where you are standing is holy.'

Thirty days after the death of Moses, Joshua, the new leader of the Israelites, was filled with the spirit of wisdom, which was just as well because he was going to need it. He must, in any case, have learned a great deal from his old master, described in Deuteronomy as the greatest prophet ever seen in Israel. Perhaps, in particular, he learned the folly of attempting to outguess God. And here's another good example.

Thank goodness he didn't rush bloodthirstily at this armed man and try to cut him to pieces. He might have done, mightn't he? Buoyed up by the reproach of Egypt having been lifted, and the experiences that year of eating from the produce of Canaan for the first time instead of being sustained by manna, Joshua must have been feeling pretty good. What an interesting answer the commander of the army of the Lord gave to his question. Why did he say 'neither'? Why didn't he say, 'Well, I'm for you of course'?

Perhaps Joshua needed a little reminder about who was actually in charge. Perhaps his question should have been: 'Are you for the Lord or for his enemies?' Perhaps it was essential that, like Moses, he should be humbled on holy ground, especially as the whole Jericho extravaganza was about to take place.

We can very easily find ourselves swept away by the excitement of doing things for God. But woe betide us if we lose touch with the roots of our excitement and begin to see the world in terms of those who are for us and those who are against us. We are not in charge of our own lives, and if we go around tackling our personal Jerichos without reference to the real commander, the walls are very unlikely to come down.

Meet us on holy ground, Lord, and remind us that you are in charge.

ZEPHANIAH

Zephaniah 3:18–20 (NIV)

'The sorrows for the appointed feasts I will remove from you; they are a burden and a reproach to you. At that time I will deal with all who oppressed you; I will rescue the lame and gather those who have been scattered. I will give them praise and honour in every land where they were put to shame. At that time I will gather you; at that time I will bring you home. I will give you honour and praise among all the peoples of the earth when I restore your fortunes before your very eyes.'

I used to think I was the only person in England who'd ever read Zephaniah, but there must be a few others, mustn't there?

This passage is very significant as far as I'm concerned, and I really hope it might be helpful to you as well. It became especially important to me when I was in the middle of a stress illness (yes, that's right— the same tedious old stress illness that I always seem to be bleating on about). I had arrived at just about the lowest point it was possible to reach, and I really could not see how I would ever achieve spiritual, emotional, or financial stability again. I had abdicated from work, church and proper family commitment to such an extent that I wasn't able to even look at the problems that I was facing.

God used a number of things to haul me out of that state, including friends, family and some specific experiences of his closeness, but this short passage from dear old Zeph, if I may call him that, was a small but key influence on my gradual return to normal lunacy. Don't ask me why some Bible verses stand out so vividly—I don't know how the Holy Spirit does it. What I do know is that the compassion and love expressed in these promises from God to his people became promises from him to me, like tickets for a Liverpool–Manchester match tucked away in my inside pocket. In particular, I loved the final line, as expressed in this translation. I sensed a delight in the heart of God about his plans magically to transform my fortunes.

I do hope that those of you who are in the same position as I was will also feel that delight, and tuck these promises away carefully so that you can take them out from time to time and draw a little strength from them.

Father, thank you for illuminating your words when it's necessary. Be with all those who have reached the end of their tether. Do some magic in their lives.

JACOB AND ESAU

Genesis 33:1–4 (NIV)

Jacob looked up and there was Esau, coming with his four hundred men; so he...
put the maidservants and their children in front... He himself went on ahead and
bowed down to the ground seven times as he approached his brother. But Esau
ran to meet Jacob and embraced him; he threw his arms around his neck and
kissed him. And they wept.

The power of these Old Testament stories is quite extraordinary, isn't it?
I've just read the section that leads up to this historic meeting, and
when the two brothers wept, so did I. Do the same and you'll see why
I ended up all gooey. Jacob was so worried that Esau's head would still
be full of the dastardly trick played on him by his brother all those years
ago when Jacob (famously 'a smooth man') got the blessing from Isaac
instead of Esau. Jacob was quite brave though, wasn't he? He was
determined to encounter his brother whatever the consequences, and I
suppose that shows how much he'd changed since the days when he
so easily outsmarted the slightly bovine Esau.

During the years that they'd been apart Jacob had met an even
sharper con-man than himself—Laban, his father-in-law—and he'd
wrestled with God and was still limping as a result. This was not the
same Jacob, and perhaps he should have realized that Esau would also
have moved on from the resentment of the past.

Reconciliation is often like this. Our fear of rejection or conflict can
separate us for years from people whom we once loved, would still love
if we felt sure that reconciliation was possible. When we do actually
take the plunge, it is often the case that both parties experience a
tremendous joy on rediscovering a relationship that was always greater
and more valuable than the reason for its fracturing.

Jacob's courage (despite his fear) didn't just result in peace between
the two brothers, important though that was. His return to the country
of his birth was an essential step in the history and destiny of what was
to be known as the Israelite nation.

My making-up with Auntie Ada over what she said about our Billy
35 years ago, when she'd had one sherry too many after Sunday dinner,
might not seem to be in quite the same league as Jacob and Esau, but
who knows? Shall we try?

Father, some of us have some peacemaking to do. It's frightening. Give us courage and determination, and an awareness that it's part of your plan for the future.

JOSEPH

Genesis 45:4–8 (NIV)

Joseph said, 'I am your brother Joseph, the one you sold into Egypt... Do not be angry with yourselves for selling me here, because it was to save lives that God sent me ahead of you. For two years now there has been famine in the land... But God sent me ahead of you to preserve for you a remnant on earth and to save your lives... So then, it was not you who sent me here, but God. He made me... ruler of all Egypt.'

This is one of the greatest Old Testament stories of all, but do you think Joseph got this bit right? I mean—obviously he was bowled over by seeing his brothers again, but was it really God who did it all?

Was it God who initiated the idea of slinging Joseph into a cistern, and then somehow silently persuaded the brothers to sell him to traders, just so that Jacob and his family wouldn't starve years later? And what about the fact that these incidents led eventually to the suppression and oppression of the Jewish people by an Egyptian nation that grew to hate them? Is that what God was planning all along?

If that was the case, then shouldn't we feel free to do whatever we feel like doing, however harmful it may be to others, confident in the knowledge that God is really behind our actions, and that therefore we can put the responsibility onto him? An attractive way to look at things, perhaps.

Forget it! Seductive though that approach to Christian living may be, we have been privileged to hear the words and sense the personality and presence of Jesus, who came to show us what God is actually like.

These Old Testament accounts are marvellously entertaining and profoundly instructive on many levels (Jesus himself quoted them often in support of his own teaching), but we would do well to temper both the unacceptable and the attractive aspects of this part of our Bible with the knowledge we have gained through the revelation of God in Christ.

Jesus made it clear that we are responsible for our own actions. He also showed us the depth of the love of God for us by going to the cross, and he did that for the very good reason that not a single one of us will be able to make our actions match the holiness of God.

The Bible—all of it—is full of God, but Jesus was God.

Father, we thank you for the passion and drama and humour and wisdom of the Old Testament. We wrestle with some of the nasty bits, but you've let them be there, so thank you for those as well (by faith!). Most of all we thank you for Jesus, who came to reveal you and save us.

*The supreme misfortune is when
theory outstrips performance.*

LEONARDO DA VINCI

THEORY OR PRACTICE— TALK OR WALK?

A NERVOUS LOOK AT THE LETTER OF JAMES

Some time ago I was speaking on the phone to a friend. The main part of what I wanted to say to him went something like this: 'The thing is, I've given Tony every chance in the past. No, I've done more than that —I've really worked hard at our relationship because I know how much it means to him. I've given him credit for things that he had hardly anything to do with, I've swallowed things he said and done my best to just put them to the back of my mind, I've spent hours talking through things he was worried about and I've forgiven him every time he messes something up and leaves me to sort the damage out afterwards. And now—after all that—I hear that he's run me down in a public meeting in front of people whose good will is important—no, crucial—to my future. So I've decided that enough is enough. I can't continue with our friendship on that basis, so I'm going to ring him and tell him that, as far as I'm concerned, I'd rather we didn't meet again.'

I waited for my friend to sigh and click his tongue and say that he would do exactly the same if he was me. Instead, there was silence for a few seconds.

'Right,' said the voice on the other end of the line at last, 'so I guess you'll be staying well away from the New Testament for a while, will you?'

'What?'

'I said, I guess you'll be staying away from—'

'Yes, I heard what you said, but what did you mean?'

'Oh, well, I suppose I was just thinking that Jesus said something or other about forgiving people 70 times seven times. Or have I got it wrong?'

'No, as you well know, you've got it right, but it doesn't matter because I've already forgiven Tony a lot more than 490 times, so he's had his allocation and now I'm going to stop.'

Another silence. Sometimes silences are not golden, they are very, very annoying indeed.

'All right,' I conceded, 'I was only joking. I know it means that there's not supposed to be any limit on forgiveness, but I've just had enough. I've run out of charity as far as he's concerned. I've tried so hard. Don't you think you reach a point where you have to just—part company?'

'Don't you want to be forgiven yourself, then?' asked my soon-to-be-ex-friend.

'I'm sorry?'

'Well, I was just thinking of the bit in the Lord's Prayer about how God forgives our sins as long as we forgive others, and then there's that parable, isn't there, where the steward gets let off his debts and then doesn't let someone else off and ends up going to prison. And there's the thing Jesus said about—'

'Yes, all right, you don't have to go through the entire Bible. I think I've just about got the point. You're not going to help me out by colluding with me, and you think I should forgive Tony and start all over again, don't you?'

'Sorry, it's just that I thought you were a Christian. I must have got it all wrong—have I?'

'Don't you think sarcasm might be a sin as well?'

'Yes, probably, but I know you'll forgive me…'

The book of James is mainly about the fact that Christianity is not just an abstract concept, but a relationship that will, if it is genuine, produce works reflecting the teaching and attitudes of Jesus. We Western Christians have a tendency to become so obsessed with theory and theology and a sort of academic spirituality, that we forget how practical the Holy Spirit is wanting to be in caring for others through us. In Jesus' parable of the two sons who are asked to perform a task for their father, it is the one with, if you like, the poor doctrine, who is obedient, while the one who produces all the right words does nothing.

Actually being what Jesus wants us to be, as opposed to talking about it, can be very tough indeed. Everything in me said that I had a right to reject Tony, but, as my friend pointed out (and as I shall point out to him on the very first occasion that he slips into sin and needs a little spiritual counselling from me), our personal rights have been subsumed into the will of God, and that will involve doing the right thing even when it hurts.

My wife learned this lesson painfully a few months ago. One morning she was about to set off for a warmly anticipated trip to visit her parents, when an elderly friend rang to ask if it was possible for Bridget to drive her to hospital in Brighton, as she was nervous at the prospect of going on her own. Bridget worked out that if she went straight to the hospital and straight back it would still just about be possible to arrive at her parents' house at the time she had planned. But, of course, it wasn't like that. It never is, is it? The elderly friend couldn't just be dumped at the hospital. She needed to be accompanied to the ward, and reassured, and calmed down, and all the other things that people need when they are frightened and in an unfamiliar place. By the time Bridget got back to the house she was in tears of frustration because it had got so late and and it would be dark by the time she arrived in Norwich.

I feel quite sure that Jesus would be sympathetic towards all three of the main characters in this little drama (I seem to remember that he kept his own mother waiting at one point) but I also think it was his idea that Bridget should go to Brighton.

The letter of James is enormously challenging, combining Python-esque humour with an almost Basil Fawlty-like rhetoric in places (try reading verses 13–15 of chapter 5 in Fawlty tones). The central message, that works are a natural byproduct of faith, is probably the one that the modern Church most needs to hear.

Prayer
Father, help us to face up to the challenge of 'doing' as well as believing.

PURE JOY

James 1:2–8 (NIV)

Consider it pure joy... whenever you face trials of many kinds, because you know that the testing of your faith develops perseverance. Perseverance must finish its work so that you may be mature and complete, not lacking anything. If any of you lacks wisdom, he should ask God, who gives generously to all without finding fault, and it will be given to him. But when he asks, he must believe and not doubt, because he who doubts is like a wave of the sea, blown and tossed by the wind. That man should not think he will receive anything from the Lord; he is a double-minded man, unstable in all he does.

A typical interchange in the Plass household:

Bridget: *(Entering euphorically)* You'll never guess what, Adrian!

Adrian: *(Filled with anticipatory pleasure)* What's that then, Bridget?

Bridget: Well, the car won't start and it looks as if the problem is a highly complex and expensive one.

Adrian: *(Clapping ecstatically)* That's really great, Bridget! Fancy that happening on the same morning that we get a huge electricity bill we can't possibly pay and the ceiling collapsing in the front room. I must say that I consider all these things pure joy, don't you?

Bridget: *(Almost dancing with delight)* Oh, yes! It's a wonderful opportunity for us to develop perseverance through the testing of our faith.

Adrian: *(With tears of sheer happiness in his eyes)* Yes, indeed! I should think we'll be as mature and complete as it's possible to be after this little lot, won't we?

Bridget: *(Excitedly)* Let's ask God for wisdom to deal with everything, shall we?

Adrian: *(Fascinated by such a novel idea)* Yes! After all, he does give generously without finding fault, doesn't he?

Bridget: *(Struck by yet another thought)* And let's not doubt!

Adrian: *(Amused at the very idea)* No, of course not, because then we would be like waves of the sea, blown and tossed by the wind. Then we shouldn't expect to receive anything, should we? *(They laugh heartily together)*

Bridget: *(Almost choking with merriment)* We don't want to be double-minded and unstable, do we? *(They collapse on the floor, laughing hysterically)*

Let's face it, Father, the concept of regarding trials with pure joy is an impossible dream for many of us. We accept, though, that you set this standard before us, and we humbly ask your help in moving towards it. Amen.

Is it possible for trials and troubles to be considered pure joy?

THE CROWN OF LIFE

James 1:9–12, 16–18 (NIV)

The brother in humble circumstances ought to take pride in his high position. But the one who is rich should take pride in his low position, because he will pass away like a wild flower. For the sun rises with scorching heat and withers the plant; its blossom falls and its beauty is destroyed. In the same way, the rich man will fade away even while he goes about his business. Blessed is the man who perseveres under trial, because when he has stood the test, he will receive the crown of life that God has promised to those who love him... Don't be deceived, my dear brothers. Every good and perfect gift is from above, coming down from the Father of the heavenly lights, who does not change like shifting shadows. He chose to give us birth through the word of truth, that we might be a kind of firstfruits of all he created.

I thought about the crown of life at a friend's funeral. Stan was elderly and had suffered terribly from emphysema, as well as recently diagnosed cancer. Now, thank God, the physical discomfort had ended, but the family was devastated. Betty, Stan's wife, a genuinely good person, couldn't contain the spasms of grief that continually rocked her body, while Stan's married daughter, Jane, cried so copiously that the very shape of her face seemed to melt and change.

Vicky, the youngest grandchild, was one big frightened question mark. She watched, wide-eyed, as the coffin was lowered. Grandad—in that box? Grandad gone? No more Nana and Grandad? Just Nana...? Suddenly it was too much. She buried her face in her auntie's jumper and burst into tears. Her older brother, Sam, was being tough. Only when the graveside ritual was over and everyone moved away, did he walk quietly back to the edge of the grave and release his tears.

Grief is infectious. But even as I wept with them all, I seemed to hear Jesus, saying in a voice fired with sympathy and excitement, 'Don't be afraid—I really have overcome death!'

Father, it's easy to forget that the crown of life—an eternity spent with you—is the reason that Jesus came and died and was raised to life again. Help us to get our priorities right.

Do I want this crown of life, and how am I dealing with the inevitability of death?

WHO'S WHO?

James 2:2–9 (NIV)

Suppose a man comes into your meeting wearing a gold ring and fine clothes, and a poor man in shabby clothes also comes in. If you show special attention to the man wearing fine clothes and say, 'Here's a good seat for you,' but say to the poor man, 'You stand there' or 'Sit on the floor by my feet,' have you not discriminated among yourselves and become judges with evil thoughts? Listen, my dear brothers: Has not God chosen those who are poor in the eyes of the world to be rich in faith and to inherit the kingdom he promised those who love him? … If you really keep the royal law found in Scripture, 'Love your neighbour as yourself,' you are doing right. But if you show favouritism, you sin and are convicted by the law as law-breakers.

One day, on tour in South Africa with the family, we were offered a lift from one town to another by a man who had been at one of our meetings. At his (very large) house next morning he told us his gardener had asked for a lift. Was that all right with us?

Gardeners in South Africa are black, and despite miraculously peaceful political change, master/servant roles are still evident. As we clambered into the car the gardener, Michael, hovered uncertainly. Katy (8) counted passengers and headed automatically for the back, assuming that, as usual, she'd be expected to fit into the luggage area. Our host soon nipped this in the bud, ushering Katy into the remaining seat-space while the gardener coiled his large frame into the place where dogs and suitcases usually fit. Later, we discovered that we'd all felt profound embarrassment at this treatment of a grown man.

I'm sure our host would have wanted to say that the gardener might have been just as embarrassed as us if he'd been given a seat in the car, and that things would probably change in future, etc, etc. But the fact is—I don't think it even occurred to him that Michael might have equal rights with us. Before we get too smug, let's ask ourselves who we regard as lesser simply because that's how we've always seen them.

Are there people in my church, my workplace, my road, my bus queue, who are 'obviously' less important than anyone else? If I take another look at them, might I see Jesus?

Am I a spiritual democrat?

BICKERING

James 2:10–13 (NIV)

For whoever keeps the whole law and yet stumbles at just one point is guilty of breaking all of it... If you do not commit adultery but do commit murder, you have become a law-breaker. Speak and act as those who are going to be judged by the law that gives freedom, because judgment without mercy will be shown to anyone who has not been merciful. Mercy triumphs over judgment!

Do your children argue? My four have argued in the past, still argue in the present and will undoubtedly continue to argue in the future. They don't all argue all of the time, but for as long as I can remember there has been a permutation of two who simply cannot encounter each other without finding some molehill of disagreement to turn into a mountain of raging, bickering, infuriating conflict. The maddening thing is that you know—you just know, that you never brought them up to behave in such a mindless, primitive way. Someone must surely have been creeping in during the night without you knowing and influencing their behaviour in this negative way.

One of the most sickening aspects of this sickening experience is the flood of accusations and counter-accusations upon which we poor suffering mums and dads are called upon to adjudicate. In our innocent pre-parent days, we vowed, didn't we, that we would always conduct negotiations and discussions with our hypothetical offspring in a calm, adult, constructive manner? Now, more often than not, we are reduced to screaming:

'If you two don't SHUT UP I shall—I shall kill you both! You're just as bad as each other! Why can't you be kind to each other?'

This is God's basic message (though expressed rather less frenetically, perhaps!) to those of us, his children, who constantly blame and judge and condemn other members of the kingdom we all inhabit, a kingdom that accommodates sinners only by the power of his mercy and grace.

We've said it before, we shall say it again, let's say it now: THE DEAREST WISH OF GOD IS THAT WE SHOULD LOVE ONE ANOTHER.

Father, we hurt and anger you with our negative treatment of each other. Forgive us for indulging attitudes of superiority or ill-feeling or resentment towards our brothers and sisters. We will try!

What kind of people make me cross?

DANCING VERSES

James 2:14–19 (NIV)

What good is it… if a man claims to have faith but has no deeds? Can such faith save him? Suppose a brother or sister is without clothes and daily food. If one of you says to him, 'Go, I wish you well; keep warm and well fed,' but does nothing about his physical needs, what good is it? In the same way, faith by itself, if it is not accompanied by action, is dead. But someone will say, 'You have faith; I have deeds.' Show me your faith without deeds, and I will show you my faith by what I do. You believe that there is one God. Good! Even the demons believe that—and shudder.

It has been suggested that the man called James who wrote this book might have been the natural brother of Jesus, and possibly one of the most important early leaders of the Church. This little section in particular seems to me to support that view. Its two distinctly Pythonesque comments are strongly redolent of the type of dry wit that we find Jesus using to such good effect in the Gospel stories and dialogues. The first of these, the comment about wishing your starving brothers well without offering practical help, has been making me chuckle since I first looked at it 30 years ago, and James' sardonic congratulation to those who believe in God just as the demons do could have come straight out of one of our modern situation comedies (one of the few funny ones, I mean).

I can't help wondering if James pinched these one-liners from his brother. Effective humour is memorable, isn't it? Verses like these dance an endless little jig in the mind, thereby constantly calling attention to themselves. This is good and useful for two reasons.

First, the message of the words themselves is such an important one. Again, James is driving home the self-evident but no less neglected truth that belief without action is useless. Second, and I suppose this appeals to me particularly because of the kind of work that I do, these verses remind me that God can be as Chestertonian as he can be solemn, and that I can look forward to a day when he and I will have a really good laugh together.

Thank you for the rich complexity of your personality, your creation and your dealings with us. Thank you that you laugh and cry, smile and frown. We look forward to knowing you better.

What makes God laugh? What makes him cry?

WORDS AND ACTIONS

James 2:20–26 (NIV)

You foolish man, do you want evidence that faith without deeds is useless? Was not our ancestor Abraham considered righteous for what he did when he offered his son Isaac on the altar? You see that his faith and his actions were working together... And the scripture was fulfilled that says, 'Abraham believed God, and it was credited to him as righteousness'... You see that a person is justified by what he does and not by faith alone. In the same way, was not even Rahab the prostitute considered righteous for what she did when she gave lodging to the spies...? As the body without the spirit is dead, so faith without deeds is dead.

Do you remember a television quiz called *Runaround*? A general knowledge question was asked, then 30 or so children raced across an open space to line up under one of three possible answers, including the correct one, displayed high up on the opposite wall. When a hooter sounded, the children had seconds in which to change lines. Quite a lot did.

Let's imagine that entrance into heaven is similar. Having covered the space between earth and heaven, people have formed lines outside the gates, all hoping they've got the right answer. Let's look at just two lines.

The first is straight and confident, men and women with well-thumbed fat black Bibles under their arms. They have perfected the art of worship and how to pray effectively. Some have been involved in healing and deliverance. The church was their lives. The second line is a bit of a mess, mainly because everyone is trying to not be at the front. Some of them have got Bibles, but they don't look very confident at all. To be honest, some of them seem downright inadequate. They've got just enough faith between them to stick around on the off-chance that they may be allowed in. These are the people who actually did things—the ones who got their hands dirty because, inadequate though they were in some ways, they sensed that the theory of love demands a practical response.

Now footsteps are heard on the other side of the gate. Those in the first line straighten up expectantly. The second line ceases to be a line altogether as its members hold on to each other nervously. A hooter sounds. Five seconds to change lines.

Show us how to be your hands, Lord.

What is the visible evidence of my faith?

MANIPULATION

James 3:1–6 (NIV)

We who teach will be judged more strictly... If anyone is never at fault in what he says, he is a perfect man, able to keep his whole body in check. When we put bits into the mouths of horses to make them obey us, we can turn the whole animal. Or take ships as an example. Although they are so large and are driven by strong winds, they are steered by a very small rudder wherever the pilot wants to go. Likewise the tongue is a small part of the body, but it makes great boasts. Consider what a great forest is set on fire by a small spark. The tongue also is a fire, a world of evil among the parts of the body. It corrupts the whole person, sets the whole course of his life on fire, and is itself set on fire by hell.

I don't think any of us would seriously argue with these comments about the potentially inflammatory nature of the tongue, but it's worth mentioning that, as well as the obvious problems, there are more subtle ones. Here's an example.

Working with children in care, as I did for many years, often involved case-conferences to discuss and decide on the next step in a child's life. Early in my career I would present my personal opinion passionately as soon after the beginning of the meeting as possible, only to find that it was lost or forgotten as the discussion continued and other attitudes were put forward. Eventually I learned that the most effective ploy was to let everybody talk themselves out, as it were, until mine was the only view unexpressed. One by one the other members of the conference would turn to me, vaguely assuming (quite erroneously) that as I'd said nothing so far, anything I did say must be worth hearing. Silence has an odd effect on people. Besides, as lunchtime approaches, any firm and apparently well-considered view is worth having.

My comment would begin with the words, 'Well, I've been listening carefully to everything that's been said, and I must say...' After that it was usually downhill, and I'm quite sure that on a number of occasions I was completely wrong.

Father, protect us from the temptation to manipulate others. Often we do it without even realizing that it's become a habit, especially in our own families, and with close friends. Amen.

Which kinds of talking are helpful, and which are not?

SALT AND FRESH WATER

James 3:7–12 (NIV)

All kinds of animals, birds, reptiles and creatures of the sea are being tamed and have been tamed by man, but no man can tame the tongue... With the tongue we praise our Lord and Father, and with it we curse men, who have been made in God's likeness. Out of the same mouth come praise and cursing. My brothers, this should not be. Can both fresh water and salt water flow from the same spring? My brothers, can a fig-tree bear olives, or a grapevine bear figs? Neither can a salt spring produce fresh water.

Why is there such a contrast between the things that we say? Same mouth, same brain—what goes wrong? How can salt and fresh water flow from the same spring? Yet they do in most of us. These early Church chaps tend to be very black and white, but many of us struggle to retain a reasonable shade of grey.

Let's be honest, the most dramatic contrasts occur between the way we are with our nearest and dearest, and the way we present ourselves to the rest of the world, and there's a sense in which that's exactly as it should be. We've got to relax somewhere. But it isn't just that. Much as I love my wife, I've never been as angry with anyone as I've been with her, and vice versa, only less so. There can be a gap between public and private morality. Bridget and I have been amazed by the depth of darkness we have seen in the private lives of some who spend their time calling others to the light.

What to do? Do we work hard at being as unpleasant in public as we are in private? An intriguing thought, but I don't think God would bless that one, do you? Should we doggedly roleplay polite warmth in private? Well, some of us could certainly offer a more natural courtesy to the people closest to us, but change has to be real or we shall quickly run out of steam and be back where we started.

No, there is little alternative to opening up the situation in four areas: honesty with ourselves, honesty with God, honesty with the people our behaviour affects most, and honesty with some trusted outsider in order to bridge the public/private gap. After that we shall have a job on our hands, but we shall have started, and we won't be alone.

Father, stand in the gap and heal us. Amen.

What difference would there be if I bridged the public/private gap?

PERSONAL FILTERS

James 3:13–18 (NIV)

Who is wise...? Let him show it by his good life... But if you harbour bitter envy and selfish ambition in your hearts, do not boast about it or deny the truth... For where you have envy and selfish ambition, there you find disorder and every evil practice. But the wisdom that comes from heaven is first of all pure; then peace-loving, considerate, submissive, full of mercy and good fruit, impartial and sincere. Peacemakers who sow in peace raise a harvest of righteousness.

Speaking as one who, in the course of listening quite frequently to other people's problems, has developed a habit of nodding solemnly as though I am nurturing profound insights into whatever the situation happens to be, but rarely if ever actually has the faintest idea what to say or suggest, I really would welcome a little of the wisdom that James is talking about here.

In this context I find it particularly interesting that he names purity as the first and most essential component of wisdom that comes from heaven, because it is often our less-than-pure personal agendas that impede useful communication on these occasions. Both hearing and responding have to make their laborious way through all the political, social, sexual, religious and idiosyncratic filters that make us what we are. Interestingly enough, it's usually the religious filter that gives me the most trouble. I still find it very hard to break away from a rather rigid worldview that was inserted into me like an extra skeleton when I was a young Christian. Sometimes I simply have to ignore a worriedly narrow little voice that tells me I'm committing some gross heresy merely by listening to, or not arguing with, something that doesn't 'fit'.

At the bottom of the list comes impartiality and sincerity, but I'm sure this is more of a summing-up than a relegation. These are the things that will set you and me free in our contacts with others, whatever the context may be. It might be useful to use this passage as an aid to prayer when we know that some tricky encounter is coming up. Wouldn't it be wonderful to feel that we had helped to raise a harvest of righteousness?

Give us wisdom, Father, the kind of wisdom that is yours rather than ours, a wisdom that sets us free from ourselves and thereby frees others. Thank you.

In which specific areas do I need wisdom today?

SURVIVING CHANGE

James 4:1–7 (NIV)

What causes fights and quarrels among you? Don't they come from your desires that battle within you? You want something but don't get it. You kill and covet, but you cannot have what you want. You quarrel and fight. You do not have, because you do not ask God. When you ask, you do not receive, because you ask with wrong motives, that you may spend what you get on your pleasures. You adulterous people, don't you know that friendship with the world is hatred towards God?... But he gives us more grace. That is why scripture says: 'God opposes the proud but gives grace to the humble.' Submit yourselves, then, to God. Resist the devil, and he will flee from you.

Meeting an old Christian friend called Tom in the pub, I found him very low. His problems concerned money, personal failure and God, all closely connected. Business collapse had left his family in a very difficult financial position, triggering feelings of inadequacy that have dogged Tom since childhood.

'It's not that I don't believe in God,' he said dolefully into his pint. 'That wouldn't be so bad in a way. What I can't understand is why he lets us carry on being miserable. If he's not interested in helping my family he must love them less than I do, and if that's the case—well, I'm not sure I like him very much.'

Basically, Tom's relationship with God had not survived the change in his material circumstances, but if you serve up raw truth like that you're likely to get it thrown back in your face. As I listened I wanted to say to Tom that 'friendship with the world', as James puts it, can be subtle. Tom's family has always had a siege mentality towards outsiders who are probably out to 'get them', and I suspect that God was only allowed a place at the table as long as he was paying his dues. Should I have said this to him, or just sympathized with his bad luck? What do you think?

What did I actually do, drawing on my vast reserves of wisdom, experience and skills of interpersonal communication? I bought him another pint.

Father, give us insight into our relationship with you, and courage when something needs to be said to somebody else.

How closely is my trust in God bound up with material security?

SPRING CLEANING

James 4:8–12 (NIV)

Come near to God and he will come near to you. Wash your hands, you sinners, and purify your hearts, you double-minded. Grieve, mourn and wail. Change your laughter to mourning and your joy to gloom. Humble yourselves before the Lord, and he will lift you up. Brothers, do not slander one another. Anyone who speaks against his brother or judges him speaks against the law and judges it. When you judge the law, you are not keeping it, but sitting in judgment on it. There is only one Lawgiver and Judge, the one who is able to save and destroy. But you—who are you to judge your neighbour?

There is no doubt that spiritual spring-cleaning needs to happen on a regular basis, particularly because of the way in which we continually slip back into being 'lifted up' by things and people other than God. In my own case it might be book sales or prospective speaking tours or food or alcohol or activities with the family or the pure joy of writing Bible notes or… well, all sorts of things. Not that any of those things are bad or un-Christian. On the contrary, most of them are the things for which I am mainly accountable to God. One of the major purposes of repentance, though, is to remind us that the most important part of us, the part that will live eternally, can only be lifted up and kept alive by the grace and mercy of God. It will always be humbling to realize how utterly dependent on him we actually are, but repentance, which is supposed to be a joyful thing (read the prodigal son), might also help us to express gratitude for the life and death of Jesus, the supreme gift which made repentance possible. My friend, Tom, whom you met in the previous note, had temporarily lost sight of that eternal dimension.

The two paragraphs in this passage, which at first glance appear to be about different things, actually fit together very well. If we really do humble ourselves before God in the wholehearted way described here, we're going to find it extremely difficult to sit in judgment on anyone else. Whatever the type or degree of our personal sins, we have all been equally lost, and we are all equally saved.

Father, we're back to the question of priorities again. Remind us that it is you who lifts us up. We have no reason to be proud.

What lifts me up?

NEO-NOMADS

James 4:13–17 (NIV)

Now listen, you who say, 'Today or tomorrow we will go to this or that city, spend a year there, carry on business and make money.' Why, you do not even know what will happen tomorrow. What is your life? You are a mist that appears for a little while and then vanishes. Instead, you ought to say, 'If it is the Lord's will, we will live and do this or that.' As it is, you boast and brag. All such boasting is evil. Anyone, then, who knows the good he ought to do and doesn't do it, sins.

The opening words of this passage have an extraordinarily modern ring to them, don't they? We live in a neo-nomadic age, where many people move frequently in pursuit of better jobs or to be close to the school they want for their children or for a variety of other reasons. I don't think James is criticizing that tendency, but he is saying what Jesus said so many times—that everything except our relationship with God must be held provisionally. In the end the practical concerns of this world will be meaningless, and that end can happen very abruptly.

Some years ago my mother suddenly became ill and was rushed to hospital at Pembury, which is more than 20 miles away from us. Late that night I rang the ward where she'd been taken, and was told that it was unlikely that she would still be alive in the morning. A friend drove me to the hospital, where I found my mother very ill and confused, but able to recognize me. When I kissed her goodbye an hour later I was sure that I would never see her again in this world.

Travelling home in the car was dream-like. I reflected on the fact that death is so big and so little—big in the sense that it removes one whole person and results in such loss and grief for the living; small in the sense that it can happen so quickly and be physically disposed of so totally. I felt frightened suddenly by the thought of how many of these neo-nomads are ambushed by death, and how shocked they must be by the realization that they were quite unprepared for this most important journey of their lives.

My mother survived for another four years, thank God, and the lesson continues.

Father, help us to turn our eyes upon Jesus, and to see all our decisions and plans in the context of his eternal gift to us.

Where does my plan begin?

KING RAT

James 5:1–6 (NIV)

Now listen, you rich people, weep and wail because of the misery that is coming upon you. Your wealth has rotted... Your gold and silver are corroded. Their corrosion will testify against you and eat your flesh like fire. You have hoarded wealth in the last days. Look! The wages you failed to pay the workmen who mowed your fields are crying out against you... You have lived on earth in luxury and self-indulgence. You have fattened yourselves in the day of slaughter. You have condemned and murdered innocent men, who were not opposing you.

Have you ever seen the film *King Rat*, in which the main character, a World War II soldier, is played by George Segal? Segal's anti-hero, a resourceful but amoral wheeler and dealer, is incarcerated in a Japanese POW camp, and becomes the wealthiest man in the camp through buying, selling, scrounging and stealing. Unburdened by scruples (officers buy rat meat from him, and cheerfully eat it believing it to be squirrel), he rapidly achieves a position of dominance, living in comparative luxury, dispensing or withholding favours according to the profit involved.

Particularly memorable is the scene where Segal fries eggs before someone who has something he wants. The staring, lip-licking agony of this man who hasn't seen an egg for two years is painful to behold. There is no doubt that, as far as the small world of that camp is concerned, and the small group of henchmen who defend and assist him in exchange for whatever scraps he throws at them, he is King Rat, the richest, most powerful man in the community.

The eventual liberation of the camp by allied troops corresponds to the picture drawn by James in this passage. Suddenly, the carefully hoarded supplies of food and bargaining items are worthless. Those who followed the 'King' in return for crusts are anxious not to be associated with him, especially as there is a strong indication that Segal's uniquely well-fed, healthy physical condition will result in investigation and punishment. The film ends with 'King Rat' isolated at the centre of the compound that, only yesterday, he ruled. If he had helped others in that little world he might have been a hero in the next. Instead, he is an outcast.

Father, whatever we are rich in, help us to share it.

What do I have in abundance? Do I share it?

PATIENCE

James 5:7–12 (NIV)

Be patient, then, brothers, until the Lord's coming. See how the farmer waits for the land to yield its valuable crop and how patient he is for the autumn and spring rains. You too, be patient and stand firm, because the Lord's coming is near. Don't grumble against each other, brothers, or you will be judged. The Judge is standing at the door!… You have heard of Job's perseverance and have seen what the Lord finally brought about. The Lord is full of compassion and mercy. Above all, my brothers, do not swear—not by heaven or by earth or by anything else. Let your 'Yes' be yes, and your 'No', no, or you will be condemned.

At a meeting that I attended in London, someone said, with a great tiredness in his voice, 'I'm so weary of being a Christian—I just want to be with Jesus.'

More recently, an acquaintance who is very active in the church had received some bad news, and phoned to ask if she could come round for a cup of tea and a chat. For a while we talked about what had happened, then, after a short silence, she suddenly burst into tears and cried out through her sobbing, 'All I want is to just know that God loves me—that's all I want!'

Another friend who has been used constantly for the comfort of others over a quarter of a century, reached a point where his faith simply drained away and the purpose of living seemed to have gone altogether. Unexpected weakness in pillars of strength is not popular, to say the least. I think my friend would have cheerfully opted for being swept off the face of the earth by the arms of God, and taken to a place where he didn't have to try any more. I know the feeling.

There are a lot of weary pilgrims around, folk who really have been patient for a long time as James says we should be, but are now at the point where they can't go on without a bit of help. If we need that kind of help, let's ask for it. If we find someone whose patience is all used up, let's not be Christians for them—let's be Jesus.

Father, we want to persevere and be patient as you command, but we break down every now and then. Help us to look after each other.

What breaks down patience? What builds it up?

INFORMAL ENCOUNTERS

James 5:13–20 (NIV)

Is any one of you in trouble? He should pray. Is anyone happy? Let him sing songs of praise. Is any one of you sick? He should call the elders of the church to pray over him and anoint him with oil in the name of the Lord. And the prayer offered in faith will make the sick person well; the Lord will raise him up. If he has sinned, he will be forgiven. Therefore confess your sins to each other and pray for each other so that you may be healed. The prayer of a righteous man is powerful and effective… My brothers, if one of you should wander from the truth and someone should bring him back, remember this: Whoever turns a sinner from the error of his way will save him from death and cover over a multitude of sins.

Have you noticed how 'The Pub' creeps into my writings on a fairly regular basis? Perhaps some of you are praying that my obsession with such establishments will be healed eventually. Well, don't hold your breath. It's not impossible that I may go teetotal one day, but that would be a silly reason to abandon The Ferret's Armpit, or whichever hostelry I'm frequenting at the time. After all, I'm supposed to be following Jesus, aren't I?

Why did this passage make me think about pubs? Well, it's full of things that happen there. My closest friends and I really do confess our sins to each other in such situations, and there really is an exchange of the things in our lives that are causing us to praise God or pray for rescue and release. In addition, and not infrequently, the business described in the last two verses of this book is very much on the agenda of such divinely secular occasions. We have to talk the nonsense out of each other sometimes, and that can be quite a tough prospect.

Of course, it doesn't have to be a pub. It may be morning coffee with a friend, or a walk on the hills, or half an hour in a launderette. I know that, but please don't relegate the meeting of close friends in informal situations to some lower-level, non-spiritual league. Jesus didn't, nor does the Holy Spirit.

Jesus will be wherever two or three are gathered together.

Where does my Christianity really happen?

He who has a choice has trouble.

DUTCH PROVERB

CHOOSING THE RIGHT DIRECTION

MALACHI

I gather that the Hebrew word *malachi* means 'messenger', but we have no way of definitely knowing if Malachi is the name of the prophet who delivered these messages. There is no record of anyone else using this name. Whatever the case, it doesn't really matter. The words of this prophet, whatever his name was, are very powerful ones and a weighty percentage of what he has to say is about uncommitted worship. At the time of writing, the temple had been rebuilt for quite a long time and it seems that the priests had become very half-hearted about their duties. In particular, they had stopped bringing the best of their animals for sacrifice, preferring instead to use sick or deformed creatures that would not be missed.

In addition, Jewish men were abandoning and divorcing the wives of their youth, taking up instead with women of exotic foreign faiths— something that had always enraged God. The whole nation at this time seems to have lost its faith and its nerve, moving away from God because it appeared, on the face of it, that the wicked were prospering more than the righteous.

Through his prophet, God calls the priests and the people to repentance, reminding them of what he has done for them in the past and warning them of the consequences if they fail to get their act together. He calls for a tenth of all that they produce to be brought to him and promises that, in return, the floodgates of his blessing will be thrown open. He will protect their crops and make sure that their harvests are greater than the capacity of storehouses that are supposed to contain them.

The book of Malachi is not exactly a barrel of laughs, but it does have some very relevant and important things to say to the Church of the 21st century. We are no longer obliged to sort through our flocks to select an appropriate goat for sacrifice, but we still have to decide the quality of our service to God—whether it is in terms of money, time, morality, care for others or general commitment. More than anything else, the book of Malachi is a cry from the heart of God for an adjustment of priorities. Who or what is the most important thing in our lives? If the honest answer to that question is not God, what, if anything, do we plan to do about it?

LOOKING BACK

Malachi 1:1–5 (NIV)

An oracle: The word of the Lord to Israel through Malachi. 'I have loved you,' says the Lord. 'But you ask, "How have you loved us?" Was not Esau Jacob's brother?' the Lord says. 'Yet I have loved Jacob, but Esau I have hated, and I have turned his mountains into a wasteland and left his inheritance to the desert jackals.' Edom may say, 'Though we have been crushed, we will rebuild the ruins.' But this is what the Lord Almighty says: 'They may build, but I will demolish. They will be called the Wicked Land, a people always under the wrath of the Lord. You will see it with your own eyes and say, "Great is the Lord—even beyond the borders of Israel!"'

My wife and I had a dip in spirits recently. Negative bombshells landed one after another. We felt battered and bruised and slightly resentful towards God, who, as the one with power, we thought might have done something about it. We human beings are so fickle. When we get into this frame of mind, everything tends to go out the window. Out goes the furniture of our faith, dumped unceremoniously so that we can more easily relish the misery of abandonment. For a while, a cold, Godless space is more attractive than any sense of his presence. Foolish thinking, of course. As far as I am concerned, sanity is only starting to return as I look at the things that God has already done in my life, things that vastly outshine this present moment of darkness.

That is what God is saying to his people here when they grumpily ask how he has loved them. 'Remember Edom,' he tells them through Malachi. 'That nation caused trouble when you made your desert journey from Egypt to Canaan and recently they joined in the looting when Jerusalem and Judah were overthrown. Now Edom has been finally defeated and destroyed and will never be rebuilt. Israel, on the other hand, has been amazingly restored, brought back from exile and encouraged to rebuild the temple. What other evidence do you need of my love?' Well, exactly.

Father, forgive us when we forget the love you have shown us in the past. Help us not to be childish. Thank you for watching over us.

SECOND BEST

Malachi 1:6–8 (NIV)

'A son honours his father, and a servant his master. If I am a father, where is the honour due me? If I am a master, where is the respect due me?' says the Lord Almighty. 'It is you, O priests, who show contempt for my name. But you ask, "How have we shown contempt for your name?" You place defiled food on my altar. But you ask, "How have we defiled you?" By saying that the Lord's table is contemptible. When you bring blind animals for sacrifice, is that not wrong? When you sacrifice crippled or diseased animals, is that not wrong? Try offering them to your governor! Would he be pleased with you? Would he accept you?' says the Lord Almighty.

This extract from Malachi has been on my mind for ages. There is a weight of hurt and outrage in these complaints from God that profoundly moves my spirit. These priests (we are all priests now, so it could be us) have stopped believing that God deserves the very best. When a beast is needed for sacrifice, they choose a goat that might have died anyway or a lamb so deformed that it has little worldly value.

Now, we human beings are rather simple creatures. When we stop valuing something, we no longer want to pay for it. On a level where it really matters, these priests had stopped believing that God had any real relevance to their lives. Why waste good, healthy, valuable animals on someone who offered them nothing in return?

Nowadays, I suppose the problem boils down to lack of belief. People might wish that they did believe wholeheartedly, but are wary of investing very much time, money, attention or involvement in a God or a community that may have no ultimate value for them.

Let us be quite clear. God is not interested in the jumble sale rubbish of our lives, the stuff that, because we have no use for it anyway, we don't mind giving away. It shows a lack of respect and love. It hurts and angers him. We don't want that, do we?

Father, some of us have tried to fob you off with cheap and tawdry offerings. Forgive us. We resolve to offer you the very best of our time, attention and material resources as a token of love and respect.

HEDGING THEIR BETS

Malachi 1:13—2:2 (NIV)

'When you bring injured, crippled or diseased animals and offer them as sacrifices, should I accept them from your hands?' says the Lord. 'Cursed is the cheat who has an acceptable male in his flock and vows to give it, but then sacrifices a blemished animal to the Lord. For I am a great king,' says the Lord Almighty, 'and my name is to be feared among the nations. And now this admonition is for you, O priests. If you do not listen, and if you do not set your heart to honour my name,' says the Lord Almighty, 'I will send a curse upon you, and I will curse your blessings. Yes, I have already cursed them, because you have not set your heart to honour me.'

A man wrote to me saying that he found it difficult to understand the story of Ananias and Sapphira. This unfortunate couple appear in Acts chapter 5. They donated half the proceeds from the sale of a field to a church's funds, claiming that they had given the full amount—a very silly move given that they were dealing with Peter. He instantly detected their lie. The husband and wife both dropped dead at his feet, causing the whole church (not surprisingly!) to be seized with fear. My correspondent thought that this was a startlingly harsh response to a 'fib'. The couple had, after all, given half their money to the church, so why was God so very tough on them?

I'm afraid I had no satisfactory answer to that question at the time, but thinking about it now, perhaps their offence was greater than it might appear at first sight. Ananias and Sapphira were under no pressure to give all, or indeed any, of their money to their church and the fact that they lied to the Holy Spirit indicates three things that also apply to the 'cheat' in this passage, who brought a manky old goat along to be sacrificed instead of the decent one that he had promised. First, they did not actually believe in the power of God to see into the hearts of men and women and, second, they were anxious to hedge their bets in case the whole thing turned out to be true. Third, they had no respect.

We cannot play these silly games with God. They make him extremely angry.

A cursed blessing is worse than no blessing at all.

A GRAPHIC THREAT

Malachi 2:3–6 (NIV)

'Because of you I will rebuke your descendants; I will spread on your faces the offal from your festival sacrifices, and you will be carried off with it. And you will know that I have sent you this admonition so that my covenant with Levi may continue,' says the Lord Almighty. 'My covenant was with him, a covenant of life and peace, and I gave them to him; this called for reverence and he revered me and stood in awe of my name. True instruction was in his mouth and nothing false was found on his lips. He walked with me in peace and uprightness, and turned many from sin.'

The descendants of Jacob's son Levi were set aside to be a tribe of priests and Levi himself was a shining example for those who were to follow. He was deeply reverent towards God and careful and faithful in his teaching of God's truth. His own way of life was the best example of all. Now God is calling for these pathetic priests of his to remember the relationship that existed between himself and Levi and mend their ways accordingly.

The threat that is issued against them if they fail to respond is graphic, to say the least. I can't help playing with the idea that, let us say, Anglican ordinands, might be warned in advance of taking up their posts that chronic disobedience and failure would be met with a divinely administered faceful of dung (so the NRSV has it). That should sort out the possibles from the probables, don't you think?

Bizarre though that specific concept might appear to us, it vividly illustrates the rage of God against those who were neglecting their sacred responsibility. As well as rejecting life and peace for themselves, they were failing those who might have turned away from sin and towards God if a good example and true instruction had been available to them.

In this age we say a lot about the love of God. We should—his love is behind every good thing that has ever happened to us. At the same time, though, let us not forget his anger. We are priests with a solemn responsibility for protecting his image. We are bound to let him down sometimes, but let's pray that it won't happen too often.

Lord, don't let it happen too often.

CAUSING OTHERS TO STUMBLE

Malachi 2:7–9 (NIV)

'For the lips of a priest ought to preserve knowledge and from his mouth men should seek instruction—because he is the messenger of the Lord Almighty. But you have turned from the way and by your teaching have caused many to stumble; you have violated the covenant with Levi,' says the Lord Almighty. 'So I have caused you to be despised and humiliated before all the people, because you have not followed my ways but have shown partiality in matters of the law.'

'By your teaching you have caused many to stumble,' says God. After reading these words, I sat and stared out of my study window, reflecting on the fact that I spend a lot of time telling people what I think about God and the Bible and the Christian faith. Has my incessant bleating caused anyone to stumble in the past? Would I be aware if it had? I honestly cannot answer these questions, but I know that sometimes I have continued with what one might loosely term 'ministry' at moments when my life was not in order and my ears were closed to the voice of the Spirit. Now that I think about it, I also recall the odd conversation where I have got out of my depth intellectually or emotionally and become a religious bully in order to protect myself from the possibility of sounding like an idiot. How might a performance of that kind have affected those who were listening from the side, as it were? Impossible to be sure, of course, but I think I might make an even greater effort in future to keep my mouth shut when I know that my three penn'orth is essentially self-serving.

I suppose one important aspect of this situation is that most of the Christian speakers and writers I know do really care about the consequences of their words and are not expecting to be despised and humiliated by God because of an occasional slip-up. The heart of that confidence is important. My experience is that, having known and received the love of God as a Father, the fear of hurting him is far more powerful than the threat of punishment. I shall ask him to protect me from the possibility of letting anyone else down and thereby grieving his heart.

Guard my lips, Lord.

FILTHY AND DETESTABLE

Malachi 2:10–12 (NIV)

Have we not all one Father? Did not one God create us? Why do we profane the covenant of our fathers by breaking faith with one another? Judah has broken faith. A detestable thing has been committed in Israel and in Jerusalem: Judah has desecrated the sanctuary the Lord loves by the daughter of a foreign god. As for the man who does this, whoever he may be, may the Lord cut him off from the tents of Jacob—even though he brings offerings to the Lord Almighty.

In one sense I take Genesis to Malachi with a pillar—sorry, I mean a pinch—of salt. We must use care and discrimination in applying parts of the Old Testament directly to this age. (The Anglican dung-smearing idea is one example, stoning your teenagers to death when they misbehave is another.) Everything should be viewed through the clearest revelation of God available to us—Jesus himself, who is described in Colossians chapter 1 as 'the image of the invisible God'. This is not the same as saying that the Old Testament is unimportant or irrelevant. On the contrary, it is crucial to our understanding of God's dealings with us, past, present and future. We must not neglect it. Now, having said all that, there are themes in the Old Testament that are so repeatedly and passionately expressed that they carry an immediate authenticity. This passage embodies one of them.

Our God is a jealous God. He has lavished love, guidance, discipline and redemption on the world he loves so much and is not about to share us with any other priority that has entered our lives, whether that is an actual foreign god or some more worldly pursuit or obsession that has stolen and occupied his rightful place in our hearts. For the one true God, our God, there is a disgusting filthiness, a detestable stench about the very notion that we, his children, might be drawn away to worship false gods or idols or windsurfing or sex or philosophies or alcohol or abstinence or religion or principles or anything else if it has become more important to us than him. He hates it and he will not put up with it in this or any other age.

Lord, you are Lord. We worship you.

REPENTING BOLDLY

Malachi 2:13–16 (NIV)

Another thing you do: You flood the Lord's altar with tears. You weep and wail because he no longer pays attention to your offerings or accepts them with pleasure from your hands. You ask, 'Why?' It is because the Lord is acting as the witness between you and the wife of your youth, because you have broken faith with her, though she is your partner, the wife of your marriage covenant. Has not the Lord made them one? In flesh and spirit they are his. And why one? Because he was seeking godly offspring. So guard yourself in your spirit, and do not break faith with the wife of your youth. 'I hate divorce,' says the Lord God of Israel, 'and I hate a man's covering himself with violence as well as with his garment,' says the Lord Almighty. So guard yourself in your spirit, and do not break faith.

I have heard quoted a letter from Martin Luther to a friend, urging him to sin boldly and repent boldly. Presumably Luther meant that, if you have sinned, you should be upfront about it and not make excuses.

'I'd had a bad day, you see...', 'You have to understand the context...', 'You have no idea what I'd been putting up with...'—I've used all those in the past, as well as a few others that I can't remember at the moment, and none of them transmute sin into anything other than what it is. If this passage challenges us to take our sin to God and repent of it boldly, then, for heaven's sake, let's stop moaning about what he has or hasn't done and get on with it.

Have you been involved in an adulterous affair or are you on the verge of being unfaithful? Stand up straight or kneel right down and tell God that you have done wrong and you are sorry. Do it for him and for the wife or husband of your youth. Do it boldly.

Have you turned away from Jesus and allowed other things to become the gods in your life? Have you been unfaithful in that way? You will know if you have. Spit it out. You'll feel much better afterwards.

Thinking about repentance is often much tougher than actually doing it. Won't it be good to feel clean again?

FIRE AND SOAP

Malachi 2:17—3:3 (NIV)

You have wearied the Lord with your words. 'How have we wearied him?' you ask. By saying, 'All who do evil are good in the eyes of the Lord, and he is pleased with them' or 'Where is the God of justice?' 'See, I will send my messenger, who will prepare the way before me. Then suddenly the Lord you are seeking will come to his temple; the messenger of the covenant, whom you desire, will come,' says the Lord Almighty. But who can endure the day of his coming? Who can stand when he appears? For he will be like a refiner's fire or a launderer's soap. He will sit as a refiner and purifier of silver; he will purify the Levites and refine them like gold and silver.

What an appalling notion it is that we might be wearying God with our words. Far worse than making him angry, don't you think? Just imagine it, God slumped on his heavenly throne, chin resting on one hand, bleary-eyed with the sheer tedium of listening to Adrian Plass moaning yet again about what's wrong with the world.

'It's not fair! All this following and trying to be good and pretending to like all the people at church and where does it get me? Can anyone tell me where it gets me? Don't bother. I'll tell you. Nowhere! That's where it gets me. In the meantime all the non-Christians get to lie in on Sunday morning while they plan their next batch of juicy weekend sins. I ask you—what is the point?'

I really don't want to weary God with my moaning, but I have to admit that I do descend into a sort of pit of miserable complaints from time to time. The threat of fire and soap is quite an effective one—imagine being scalded and scrubbed into the right frame of mind! The fact is, though, that I have become a son of God because of what Jesus did and, in my heart of hearts, his approval is what I really crave. Come on, my fellow moaners, let's allow that to be our motivation for coming to our senses. That should bring a smile to our Father's face.

Father, forgive us for moaning. You have done so much for us and we are grateful.

GOD'S AGENDA

Malachi 3:3–7 (NIV)

Then the Lord will have men who will bring offerings in righteousness, and the offerings of Judah and Jerusalem will be acceptable to the Lord, as in days gone by, as in former years. 'So I will come near to you for judgment. I will be quick to testify against sorcerers, adulterers and perjurers, against those who defraud labourers of their wages, who oppress the widows and the fatherless, and deprive aliens of justice, but do not fear me,' says the Lord Almighty. 'I the Lord do not change. So you, O descendants of Jacob, are not destroyed. Ever since the time of your forefathers you have turned away from my decrees and have not kept them. Return to me, and I will return to you,' says the Lord Almighty.

This list of sinful behaviour indicates the breadth and depth of God's social and spiritual agenda for the Church. It hasn't changed much. Concerns such as fair pay, proper treatment of foreigners and the oppression of vulnerable members of the community are as important to the heart of God today as they ever were, so they need to be just as important to us. In addition, within the Church itself, we urgently need to find the courage to weed out such issues as adultery and deliberate distortion of the truth so that we can turn to God with clean hearts and say, 'Here we are. We've returned. Please return to us.'

Don't misunderstand me. Not for one moment am I implying that there should be some sort of frenetic witch-hunt resulting in the detection and expulsion of wrongdoers. If all the sinners were to be removed from our church, for instance, Sunday mornings would be very quiet affairs. There would be no congregation and, let us be realistic, no vicar.

No, much more to the point is that we re-establish our corporate view of these matters and thus make it easier for all of us to see our behaviour in the context of responsible teaching and guidance. We don't want to lose our brothers and sisters—we want to keep them. Let the options be crystal clear and let us encourage each other to make the right choices. God will help us with that.

Father, help us to teach your standards and measure ourselves honestly against them.

TREASURE FROM HEAVEN

Malachi 3:7–12 (NIV)

'But you ask, "How are we to return?" Will a man rob God? Yet you rob me. But you ask, "How do we rob you?" In tithes and offerings. You are under a curse—the whole nation of you—because you are robbing me. Bring the whole tithe into the storehouse, that there may be food in my house. Test me in this,' says the Lord Almighty, 'and see if I will not throw open the floodgates of heaven and pour out so much blessing that you will not have room enough for it. I will prevent pests from devouring your crops, and the vines in your fields will not cast their fruit,' says the Lord Almighty. 'Then all the nations will call you blessed, for yours will be a delightful land,' says the Lord Almighty.

Predictably, this is a favourite passage for those who teach that God showers material benefits on Christians who respond appropriately. At its worst, the 'appropriate response' involves parting with a far greater percentage of income than is actually sensible. A friend in Sweden got caught up in this nonsense. He was paying out such huge sums of money every month that his wife had trouble feeding the family with what remained. After three tortured years, the expected shower of benefits had failed to materialize and the marriage collapsed in a storm of bitter acrimony. An extreme example, but hardly an isolated one. The path of greed disguised as virtue is ominously broad. Most of us fail to give enough financially, but do you believe that God will provide a sort of lump sum benefit when we do increase the cash payments? Don't hold your breath.

No, let us give generously from what we have, but we know the wealth that Jesus promises is treasure in heaven, while the deposit, the shower of blessings that we receive in this life, is the peace of being in his will and pleasure. I tell myself that I would give anything for that, but the requirement is greater than mere money. God wants to sit on the throne of our hearts and have the very best of us available for him. Am I willing to pay that price? Hmmm…

Open my heart, Lord. Fill me with you.

AFTER THE FURNACE

Malachi 4:1–3 (NIV)

'Surely the day is coming; it will burn like a furnace. All the arrogant and every evildoer will be stubble, and that day that is coming will set them on fire,' says the Lord Almighty. 'Not a root or a branch will be left to them. But for you who revere my name, the sun of righteousness will rise with healing in its wings. And you will go out and leap like calves released from the stall. Then you will trample down the wicked; they will be ashes under the soles of your feet on the day when I do these things,' says the Lord Almighty.

I have no desire to trample on the wicked—well, not many of them — but if this means that one day we will trample on the negative things that make our lives imperfect, then I am all for it. Having said this, in my more pessimistic moods I wonder how much of me will be left after the furnace phase. I don't know about you, but nowadays my concerns are less about more obvious sins in my life than about the fact that I so often arrive at the end of the day with a feeling that mine has been a very thin performance.

Two things help to combat these gloomy moods. One is the constantly self-refreshing fact that Jesus is on my side and represents me to his Father with more passionate eloquence than I can ever command. Thank goodness for that. The other is that I am learning to place myself, by an effort of will, within God's view of the world through my eyes. Do these words mean anything? Well, they do, actually. Here's an example. Shopping needs doing. As I walk into the supermarket, I give the whole experience to God. Every tiny contact with any other person—in fact, every aspect of the time I spend there—will be put into his charge. Sounds silly? Maybe it is, but, on the occasions when I stir myself up to do it, there are interesting consequences.

In the end, it won't be about what we have done for God, but what he has managed to do through us. The furnace won't be able to touch that.

Father, help us to concentrate on what you do instead of focusing on our own inadequacies.

HEALING IN RELATIONSHIPS

Malachi 4:4–6 (NIV)

'Remember the law of my servant Moses, the decrees and laws I gave him at Horeb for all Israel. See, I will send you the prophet Elijah before that great and dreadful day of the Lord comes. He will turn the hearts of the fathers to their children, and the hearts of the children to their fathers; or else I will come and strike the land with a curse.'

Turn to chapter 11 of Matthew's Gospel and you will be able to hear Jesus explaining that this promise of a returning Elijah was eventually fulfilled in the ministry of John the Baptist. John was the cousin of Jesus, sent by God to prepare a way for the Messiah. He was a tough, straight-talking sort of guy who, if he had shared a bag of honey and locust-flavoured crisps in the corner of a pub with Malachi, would have discovered that the two of them had much in common as far as their message to Israel was concerned. They both called the people of God back into the place that was fundamentally right for them, a place where God's laws were observed and respected and the atmosphere around creator and creation could approximate to a paradise that was long lost.

Interesting, isn't it, to see that Malachi signs out on a note of healing in relationships. Parents to children, children to parents, generation to generation, God to man, man to God. Both John and Malachi had a great deal to say about the specifics of conduct, but, for both of them, it was all a means to the same end—that end being the harmony of personalities relating to each other as they were supposed to from the beginning of time.

For many people, this is one of the most difficult things to understand about Christianity. Faith in Jesus is not about being seduced or drawn away to some ephemeral sphere that has no connection with what is real and central to human life. On the contrary, it is a means of returning to the granular, godly heart of existence. In other words—as Jesus himself explained so clearly—it is an invitation to come home.

Father, knowing you as we were meant to is a light in the far distance for most of us. Lead us forward.

*The most certain sign of wisdom is a continual
cheerfulness; her state is like that in the regions
above the moon, always clear and serene.*

MICHAEL DE MONTAIGNE

TRAVELLING WISELY

WORDS OF WISDOM FROM PROVERBS

Unfortunately, 'wisdom' is one of that increasingly long list of words
that have been devalued and, in fact, totally redefined by the commercial ploys of 20th-century advertising. Nowadays, if you were to tell
someone that the exercise of wisdom will be rewarded with a taste of
ambrosia, the received message will probably be that if you keep your
teeth nice and clean you'll be given a bowl of creamed rice. Sad, isn't
it? In an age when true wisdom is much more urgently needed than
toothbrushes we are not even quite sure what the word means any
more.

As far as the Church is concerned, the last 30 years have seen a
plethora (excuse me while I just press the thesaurus button and check
that) yes, a plethora of paperback books that offer a sort of bright easy-
stage wisdom on just about every problem that your average evangelical
Christian is likely to face.

My wife was given one of these books a few years ago, by someone
who must have felt that she was not coming up to scratch in certain
areas. This volume was all about how to become the ideal Christian
woman, and it helpfully included, on the front cover, a photograph of
just such an exemplary woman, so that readers would know exactly
what to aim for. This perfect looking creature was gifted with long
lustrous hair, beautiful, yet worn with dignified modesty. Her face was
blessed with a near-perfect complexion, and it shone with charity,
restraint, good will and potential (but strictly monogamous) passion.
One sensed that she had agreed to be photographed for the cover only
so that God might be glorified by her witness to the quality of his

handiwork when, as in her case, he really puts his mind to it.

Inside, the book was divided into handy sections, each dealing with a different aspect of being an ideal Christian woman. These included advice on how to say, think and do acceptable things in a church context, how to dress so that God is honoured but men are not tempted, how to support your husband in a submissive but godly and assertive way, how to balance the sacred requirements of hospitality with the sacred requirements of family, how to find time for prayer amid a busy schedule, and how to practise good stewardship with the Lord's domestic provision.

Bridget always tries to take it seriously when people present her with these heavily pointed gifts (my father, who used to worry about the fact that everyone gave him soap, spent most of his waking life taking baths), but she said that after reading about three-quarters of the book she noted in herself a growing desire to dress temptingly, boss me about, shut the door on visitors, ignore the family, give up praying altogether, splurge the Lord's domestic provision on cream cakes and an afternoon's shopping in London and find the woman depicted on the cover with a view to tying her up and pelting her with knobbly vegetables until she agreed to wipe that soppy grin off her face and do something coarse and unChristian.

This is the problem with so many of these easy-answer publications, isn't it? Each one seems to promise so much; whether it be the one that offers six simple steps to Prophetic Scuba-diving, or a beginner's guide to Knitting in the Spirit, or one of that plethora (I'm feeling quite confident about the use of this word now) of deeply depressing books that tell you exactly how to recover from depression. Just as the phrase 'Christian Counselling' has, in the past, sometimes tended to be a covering excuse for dangerously unskilled and untrained tinkering with people's lives, so these books of pop-wisdom can actually leave the reader feeling defeated and inferior because he or she stumbles over one of the six 'simple' steps and is unable to get up again without on-the-spot assistance.

Yes, I know that there are notable exceptions. I know because I have benefited from them myself, thank God, but I also know that a whole generation of believers has grown up with the notion that development as a Christian is rather like being in a junior-school classroom, where life is sliced up neatly into conveniently discreet subjects which can be learned quite easily as long as one pays proper attention to the teacher.

In fact, of course, for most human beings, Christian or otherwise, life never is as simple as that, and the wisdom that we need on the most basic level is of a rather different kind.

Where have I found wisdom? There have been books that have helped, and also particular individuals who were obedient enough to say the right word at the right time, but the following come to mind as being the most reliable sources of wisdom.

First, I believe that a resolve to follow Jesus is the purest form of wisdom that any of us can aspire to. We may be foolish followers, or intermittently sinful followers, or inadequate followers, but if, like the disciples, we have made the simple decision to go with him, then no one and nothing can harm the part of us that will join him in paradise. We would be very foolish indeed to follow anyone or anything else. We fail as we follow, but we mustn't give up.

Secondly, I find wisdom (about me) in my friends, if I care to listen. Few things are as valuable as the counsel of close friends who really do know me, and are willing to tell me the truth, even when I get stroppy about it. They are a practical, spiritual resource, and I thank God for them.

Thirdly, I rely heavily on my wife, who, as well as knowing me infuriatingly well, makes suggestions from time to time that seem to me quite definitely to come from the heart of God. Much as I complain about this process sometimes, I thank God for this blessing more than almost any other.

Last, but very far from least, I find wisdom from the Holy Spirit as he speaks to me from the pages of the Bible, a wisdom that is both accessible, and yet far greater in depth than I shall ever reach to or understand.

We need the wisdom of scripture. That is why I have written all the Bible notes in this book, including the ones in this section, which, as even the most dense among you might possibly have gathered by now, are on the subject of 'Wisdom'.

Prayer
Father, we meet so many people and get involved in so many things. We need the wisdom of your Holy Spirit. Help us to be humble enough to accept counsel from him, from those who know us well, and from the pages of scripture that we are about to read.

TRUE WISDOM

Proverbs 1:1–7 (NRSV)

The proverbs of Solomon son of David, king of Israel: For learning about wisdom and instruction, for understanding words of insight, for gaining instruction in wise dealing, righteousness, justice, and equity; to teach shrewdness to the simple, knowledge and prudence to the young—Let the wise also hear and gain in learning, and the discerning acquire skill, to understand a proverb and a figure, the words of the wise and their riddles. The fear of the Lord is the beginning of knowledge; fools despise wisdom and instruction.

I wonder how Solomon the Wise is dealing with the news that his words of wisdom are to be commented on in 1997 by Adrian Plass. 'They should have asked a theologian,' he's probably complaining, 'or a trained moral philosopher, or something. The man is a rank amateur!' Well, hard cheese, Solly, old mate. You've been dead a long time, now it's my turn.

And that response of mine sums up, in a way, the attitude to wisdom in the nineties, doesn't it? Like food and travel and many other areas of our lives, so-called wisdom is packaged and labelled and made available, particularly on television, for independent selection by those who may well not be wise enough to do the selecting. In America we discovered with horror the lengths to which those 'audience participation' programmes will go to attract viewers.

'Do you suspect that your husband or wife is having an affair? If so, would you like to confront them with the evidence on national television without them having any previous warning?'

That's no exaggeration, and the morality of such broadcasting is justified by the argument that, in this instance, it will be helpful to other married couples who are facing problems. Thus, the ancient Romans might have claimed that the spectacle of Christians being eaten by lions was actually a practical examination of feline dietary problems.

Far from giving prudence to the simple, or instilling discipline where there is personal chaos, these events offer nothing but emotional cream cakes to viewers, some of whom are desperately in need of a sensible diet.

Father, we know that the fear of the Lord does not sell many licences or much advertising but it remains the beginning of wisdom, and we pray that the young, the simple and the wise will find their counsel in you.

SPIRITUAL THOUGHTS

Proverbs 1:20–23 (NRSV)

Wisdom cries out in the street... 'How long, O simple ones, will you love being simple? How long will scoffers delight in their scoffing and fools hate knowledge? Give heed to my reproof; I will pour out my thoughts to you; I will make my words known to you.'

This passage reminds me of my friend Rabbi Hugo Gryn, who was well known and greatly appreciated as a broadcaster. Sadly, Hugo died recently. For four or five years Bridget and I met this master storyteller almost every week in the Maidstone studios of TVS to make a late-night 'God-slot' programme called *Company*. This regional programme catered mainly for insomniacs, taxi-drivers, publicans, nightwatchmen, and people who didn't manage to turn off the television quickly enough after the snooker finished, but it was fun to do, and we loved meeting people like Hugo.

In the course of many conversations we often discussed the differences, obvious and not so obvious, between Christianity and Judaism. One of the most interesting differences put forward by Hugo concerned knowledge and spirituality. In the Christian Church, he suggested, knowledge is generally supposed to be acquired through the development of spirituality, whereas in the Jewish faith the more knowledge and understanding you have, the closer you are likely to come to a relationship with God.

I'm sure that these general tendencies are sometimes taken to extreme lengths by adherents to both faiths. Over a decade ago I was struck by the anger with which a small minority of those who attended charismatic churches rejected any suggestion that an intellectual approach to Christianity could have real worth. There seemed to be a fear that thinking and spirituality were in some way mutually exclusive, ridiculous though such a notion obviously is. Happily, the balance has now largely been restored in these areas, but I still encounter the odd person who tells me that it is 'dangerous to think'.

As for Hugo—the interesting thing is that his first real experience of God was an emotional one. Seventeen years old, and hiding in a corner of a German concentration camp one day, he wept for himself and the Jewish race and the whole world, and felt, for the first time, the reality and 'otherness' of God.

I feel so sad that Hugo can't be here to argue the point out a little further, but the opportunity may well come.

Father, teach us to know you and to love you.

CRITICISM

Proverbs 1:29–31 (NRSV)

Because they hated knowledge and did not choose the fear of the Lord, would have none of my counsel, and despised all my reproof, therefore they shall eat the fruit of their way and be sated with their own devices.

After reading this passage I asked myself how willing I really am to accept criticism or rebuke from man or God. On one level I can answer the question easily. I have always hated all criticism, especially the constructive variety, because you can't dismiss it scornfully. You have to do something about it!

Having said that, I am painfully aware of my need for helpful criticism, but it has to come from someone who provenly values me already. When my wife, Bridget, makes negative comments about something I've said or done or written I'm quite likely to get cross, but I will then take my crossness and her comments away into a corner for closer examination in private. More often than not I have to admit that she is absolutely right, and I do genuinely value her insights. I just wish that I did not have to go through this process of childish resentment each time, though.

On another level I think some things have changed. I now truly believe that we are qualified for God's service by our weaknesses rather than by our strengths (although my use of the word 'we' instead of 'I' might be significant).

Bridget and I worked for a time at Burrswood, the healing centre founded by Dorothy Kerin, who died in 1961, seven years before we joined the staff. One evening we were taken out to dinner by an elderly, very wise lady of Russian origin named Marina, who had been one of Dorothy Kerin's closest friends. During the meal Marina said something that I found very hard to take.

'Adrian,' she said, 'you are capable of great good and great evil. You are weak, but Bridget is strong.' Turning to Bridget, she said, 'You will have to protect him, my dear.'

This image of me as a sort of schizophrenic wimp didn't go down at all well at the time. I struggled desperately to maintain my heroic self-image. In fact, although I don't think I showed it, I was furious. As the years have gone by, though, I have truly learned to value and appreciate that little nugget of wisdom. I carry it in a little side-pocket of my consciousness and take it out now and then when choices have to be made. I still hate criticism, but I do thank God for it.

Go on, say what you think—no, really, go on, say it. I don't mind...

HIDDEN TREASURE

Proverbs 2:1–9 (NRSV)

My child, if you accept my words and treasure up my commandments within you, making your ear attentive to wisdom and inclining your heart to understanding; if you indeed cry out for insight, and raise your voice for understanding; if you seek it like silver, and search for it as for hidden treasures—then you will understand the fear of the Lord and find the knowledge of God. For the Lord gives wisdom; from his mouth come knowledge and understanding; he stores up sound wisdom for the upright; he is a shield to those who walk blamelessly, guarding the paths of justice and preserving the way of his faithful ones. Then you will understand righteousness and justice and equity, every good path.

The idea of hunting for understanding in the same way that one might hunt for hidden treasure is a fascinating one. Ever since I was a child I have dreamed of discovering something old and precious in a place that has been undisturbed for generations. Even now (my children are tired of hearing me say this), I fantasize about being left a very old house whose cellars and attics have remained untouched and unexplored for years. I find myself positively drooling over the prospect of hunting through dusty boxes and cupboards in the search for long-forgotten books and objects and pictures. Marvellous!

As this is never likely to happen, I shall content myself with the Bible, which is itself a storehouse of treasure, albeit one that is not always immediately visible or recognizable. Over the generations the sparkling gems of truth that lie between the covers of this remarkable book have tended to be obscured by the dust of over-familiarity, poor teaching, even poorer reading-out-loud, denominational bias and sheer fear of the vivid, non-religious life that it offers.

There are times, not continually, but frequently enough to bring me back to the search again and again, when some old dry-as-dust verse cracks open quite unexpectedly and there before me is the pure, precious metal of God's truth, often in the last place I thought to find it. When that happens I want to rush around waving my arms in the air like one of those old-timers in the Westerns who've been panning for gold, and suddenly come across a shining reason to rejoice.

Thank you for this treasure chest. Guide us as we search through its contents.

THE PRIZE

Proverbs 2:12–22 (NRSV)

It will save you from the way of evil, from those who... delight in the perverseness of evil... You will be saved from the loose woman, from the adulteress with her smooth words, who forsakes the partner of her youth and forgets her sacred covenant; for her way leads down to death, and her paths to the shades; those who go to her never come back, nor do they regain the paths of life. Therefore walk in the way of the good... For the upright will abide in the land... and the treacherous will be rooted out of it.

I want to ask a question that will probably annoy some of my brothers and sisters in Christ because they think the answer is such an obvious one. And anyway, they will probably add, it's not the sort of question you should ask. Here it is. What's in it for us?

Vulgar, eh? But I have a feeling that a lot of Christians secretly want to ask that question, and I also believe that God wants us to be able to answer it, not just for ourselves, but also for people we meet who are outside the faith. Why should we want to be saved from the paths of wicked men? They seem to have quite a good time on the whole. And then there's the adulteress. Some of us might quite like to get involved with the adulteress or her male equivalent. It can't be less fun than Sung Eucharist at 8.00 a.m. on a wet Sunday morning, can it? Why should we be good? Why should we opt to be on the Lord's side? What is in it for us?

Well, forget the right and proper answers for a moment and think about the kind of reply Jesus might have offered (not a bad guide for answering most questions). In the previous note we were talking about the hidden treasure to be discovered in the Bible. Jesus spoke about treasure as well. He said that we should store up treasure in heaven rather than on earth, and I'm sure he meant exactly what he said. He used the image of treasure very deliberately, and was clearly saying that, in heaven, the currency is different, but just as valuable. We shall be rich in the best possible way—the eternal way. That richness is manufactured from the base metal of obedience and love, transmuted into the unfathomable joy of being with Jesus himself, a joy that is impossible to comprehend fully until we experience it in its fulness. That's what's in it for us.

Father, help us to keep our eyes on the true prize.

HEALTH AND WEALTH

Proverbs 3:1–8 (NRSV)

My child, do not forget my teaching, but let your heart keep my commandments; for length of days and years of life and abundant welfare they will give you. Do not let loyalty and faithfulness forsake you; bind them round your neck, write them on the tablet of your heart... Do not be wise in your own eyes; fear the Lord, and turn away from evil. It will be a healing for your flesh and a refreshment for your body.

Well, this is interesting, isn't it? Read verse 2 again and you might see what I mean. The writer appears to be saying quite clearly that conscientious application of his teaching and commandments will result in a long life and material gain.

When we were touring Australia in 1996 we found a growing interest in and adherence to what is commonly named the 'health and prosperity' movement. Those who embrace such teaching believe, as I'm sure you know, that if Christians make the kingdom of God a priority in their lives, God will be more or less obliged to bless them with material wealth and physical good health. I presume that verses like the one just quoted would be used by followers of this doctrine to support their claims.

So, perhaps they're right. The Old Testament's full of people getting rich when God's pleased with them. What do you think? After all, there it is in black and white—many years and prosperity. Let's go for it!

Actually, I'm not going for it, if you don't mind. There are very serious problems with using the Old Testament as a source of doctrine unless it is read and considered in the light of what Jesus teaches us in the Gospels. Without going into too much detail, I'd just like us to imagine how Jesus would react on being informed that his followers feel pretty confident that they are entitled to a reasonable income and substantial health benefits. This man who said that we would suffer just as he had, only more so; who sent out his followers without so much as a pair of sandals; who said that the poor are blessed; who sorrowed over the problems rich people would have in entering the kingdom of heaven; how would he have reacted?

I'll tell you how I think he would have reacted. I think he would have laughed until he cried. Or, come to think of it, he might have just cried.

Lord, how long will it be before your people know what being rich and healthy really means?

DISCIPLINE

Proverbs 3:11–14 (NRSV)

My child, do not despise the Lord's discipline or be weary of his reproof, for the Lord reproves the one he loves, as a father the son in whom he delights. Happy are those who find wisdom, and those who get understanding, for her income is better than silver, and her revenue better than gold.

A friend of mine was telling me about his divorce as we drove back from the north of England.

'We were married for a very long time,' he said, 'and hardly anyone knew there were problems in our relationship. When it reached the stage where divorce was looking like the only real option, my wife and I decided to send out a letter to quite a large number of people—close friends, of course, relatives, and some of the people at our church. It was easier than having to explain it a hundred times over.'

I nodded. 'And did they all write back?'

'Oh, yes, we had some wonderful replies—a lot of understanding and compassion. People were really warm in the way they responded.'

'Were there any replies you didn't like?'

'There was one,' he replied thoughtfully, 'I don't mean it was unpleasant. It wasn't. It was very friendly. The person who wrote it said that he was sure we were doing the right thing.'

'What's wrong with that?'

He tilted his head and sucked air through his teeth. 'I dunno, I suppose it was just that the person concerned didn't actually know me all that well, and he'd hardly ever met my wife, so it seemed a little bit— well, a bit unhelpful to sound so sure that divorce was the right way to go. By contrast,' he went on, 'the two replies I valued most were just as warm and supportive, but they included a firm but gentle question about whether there could be an alternative to divorce. In effect, they were asking if we'd properly thought and prayed through the issue before making such a serious decision. I really appreciated those two letters.'

Father, thank you for the times when our friends show real godly love by not letting us easily get away with things that could be bad for us, as well as supporting us with compassion and warmth. Help us not to reject your discipline, given directly or through someone else, when that's exactly what we need.

FEAR

Proverbs 3:19–21 (NRSV)

My child… keep sound wisdom and prudence, and they will be life for your soul and adornment for your neck… your foot will not stumble. If you sit down, you will not be afraid; when you lie down, your sleep will be sweet. Do not be afraid of sudden panic, or of the storm that strikes the wicked; for the Lord will be your confidence.

Here are some questions relating to this passage. Don't worry—I'm not putting these down to make you feel bad about yourself. I'm going to try to face up to my own answers. If your response is the same as I think mine is going to be, then we'll pray together. If it's not, you can pray for me and those like me.

When I sit down, am I afraid? The answer to that question is 'Yes, I am afraid.' There is a gloom that has shadowed my heart since I was a very young child. This shadow was cast by difficult events that I had no control over during that period, and also by some very injudicious reading of frightening books as I moved towards my teens. I would dearly like to be free of that shadow.

When I lie down, is my sleep sweet? Generally speaking, no, it is not sweet. I ought to say immediately that one substantial reason for this is my weight (too great), and my evening meal (too much and too late). Those aren't the only reasons, though. Sleep is still a fearful land for me, a place where you would be unwise to let yourself relax completely. I used to suffer from something called Sleep Paralysis, which didn't help. It comes back sometimes when I'm very tense. I would love to enjoy sweet sleep.

Do I have no fear of sudden disaster or of the ruin that overtakes the wicked? This question is not so easy to answer. That same shadow of gloom I have already mentioned is sometimes inhabited by phantoms of inevitable doom and destruction at the worst possible times, but I have much greater confidence nowadays that I cannot be overtaken by the consequences of my sin. God loves me, and because of Jesus I am saved. I don't think I've ever written it as bluntly before. Perhaps I believe it more bluntly.

That still leaves the problems with night-time and shadows and sleep. Let's pray about them.

Father, I know I'm not the only one who finds the nights difficult. Grant us judgment and discernment in dealing with the practical things that need changing, and give us your peace and wisdom to wear like ornaments around our necks at the moment when the shadows begin to fall.

GET WISDOM

Proverbs 4:7–8 (NRSV)

The beginning of wisdom is this: Get wisdom, and whatever else you get, get insight. Prize her highly, and she will exalt you; she will honour you if you embrace her.

Do you remember an item of news many years ago about a young couple who auctioned off everything they owned, including their house and furniture, in order to raise money for starving refugees in a distant country? I was quite young at the time, probably around 16, and I had only just become a Christian. I wasn't at all sure what to think about this extravagant gesture (we found out what we thought about things by asking the clergy usually), but I think I veered from admiration of such a generous, wholehearted act of giving, to concern that the young couple concerned were not exercising their stewardship properly (stewardship was a term I'd heard of for the first time only recently). Another part of me, pre-Christian and probably saner than the parts of me that had produced the first two responses, thought there was something very silly about ending up with nothing and having to rely on others to give you the things that you couldn't have because you'd just given them away to someone else. Or something like that.

Could this be the kind of wildly expansive act that the writer of the above passage is talking about when he says that we should acquire understanding, whatever the cost? Is there really a way in which we can exchange riches of some kind for the supreme gift of wisdom? I suspect that there is a way, but I am absolutely sure that the cost is much greater than the loss of material belongings or the contents of a bank account.

The clue lies in the readiness with which Jesus' disciples followed him when they were called. It was a readiness, not just to physically follow him, but to place him at the very top of their individual lists of what was most important to them. In dropping their own rights to decision and destiny those men gained the reality of his wisdom and power in their lives, despite the fact that there was no magical transformation of their personalities at that time. It can still happen today, but I don't think it happens much.

Father, show us individually what it means to put Jesus first in our lives. We can't follow him physically through Luton or Carlisle now. How should we do it?

KEEP YOUR HEART

Proverbs 4:20–24 (NRSV)

My child, be attentive to my words; incline your ear to my sayings. Do not let them escape from your sight; keep them within your heart. For they are life to those who find them, and healing to all their flesh. Keep your heart with all vigilance, for from it flow the springs of life. Put away from you crooked speech, and put devious talk far from you.

This injunction to 'keep your heart... for from it flow the springs of life' offers a deceptively simple challenge and a warning that is quite alarming. The challenge is to look clearly at what is in my heart, and the warning is that whatever my heart contains will be apparent in my life through actions or words.

Kinda makes you wanna sit tight an' say nuthin', don' it?

Those of us who have mapped the geography of our selves know what a dispiriting exercise this can be. We start off OK, marching boldly towards the edge of our talent or our goodwill or our patience or our generosity, and are suddenly brought up short by a precipice, usually at a point where it seemed as if the firm ground might go on for ever. Setting off in a different direction we discover that exactly the same thing happens. In fact, it happens again and again and again, until we start learning the shape and limits of what we are. For some this is a very welcome piece of learning—settle down and get on with it, they would say. For others, those with the blood of explorers in their veins, it is a kind of prison.

This is how many of us feel about the contents of our hearts. We look for enough compassion to care truly about the world and find a pathetically limited ability to place our arms around the suffering of others. We search for the strength of will and forgiveness to set ourselves and those we hate free from chains of resentment and bitterness, only to find weakness and a cherishing of hurts. We hunt within our hearts for the courage to fight when everything in us wants to lie down, and to wait quietly when we want to fight, but discover instead a self-indulgence that will have what it is greedy for.

We stand on the shore of our own lives, calling out to God that we can go no farther unless he provides a way.

Father, we know that we are weak and limited and that our hearts are not clean, but Jesus told us that he is the Way by which we shall find life and power. We ask that he should inhabit the throne of our hearts and live his righteousness through us.

SEX

Proverbs 5:15–20 (NRSV)

Drink water from your own cistern, flowing water from your own well... Let your fountain be blessed, and rejoice in the wife of your youth, a lovely deer, a graceful doe. May her breasts satisfy you at all times; may you be intoxicated always by her love. Why should you be intoxicated, my son, by another woman and embrace the bosom of an adulteress?

A young man called Steve said to me, 'Is it normal to fancy other women after you're married?' He was one of those clear-eyed individuals who spend the first part of their lives expecting, and generally speaking discovering, that life is a good, wholesome, rewarding sort of affair.

He and his wife, Samantha, had fallen head-over-heels in love when they were 20, and enjoyed a fairytale wedding. Now she was pregnant, and Steve was dismayed to find his young wife's hugely inflated body not attracting him as it had done. Indeed, his eyes were straying lustfully in the direction of other, slimmer females who were—well, not Samantha.

For Steve, this was a shadow over his life, a profound failure in his relationship with Sam and with God. He felt somehow mucky and diminished by the experiences he was having.

'I keep thinking,' said Steve, 'about Jesus saying that if you just look at another woman with desire you're already committing adultery. That means I've already committed adultery 15 times since I got up today.'

I think my friend might have been a little taken aback by the matter-of-fact way I responded to his problem.

'Consider these points, Steve,' I said. 'One, there may be some men who haven't fancied other women after getting married, but if you got them all together they'd fit quite easily into a large wardrobe.

'Two, Jesus wasn't silly or unrealistic. He knew what human beings are like. He was one. He never compromised the truth, but he knew all about temptation, and he's more interested in helping you deal with that, than organizing thunderbolts because you're fantasizing about Bessie next door.

'Third, sex is a crucial part of being married, but real love is a complex, maturing thing. It takes a lot of time and work, but you can end up with something rich and right and priceless. The sex'll get sorted out, you'll see. Don't give up before you've started, mate. The best is yet to come.'

Father, marriages are falling apart all around us. Help us to be strong and wise in our relationships, and to depend on you like children.

BETTER THAN GOLD

Proverbs 8:1–5, 10–11 (NRSV)

Does not wisdom call, and does not understanding raise her voice? On the heights, beside the way, at the crossroads she takes her stand; beside the gates in front of the town, at the entrance of the portals she cries out: 'To you, O people, I call, and my cry is to all that live. O simple ones, learn prudence; acquire intelligence, you who lack it… Take my instruction instead of silver, and knowledge rather than choice gold; for wisdom is better than jewels, and all that you may desire cannot compare with her.

Why don't people choose wisdom instead of silver or gold? Why are the very things that attract us to other people, whether they be kindness, gentleness or quiet wisdom, the last things we want for ourselves? Strange, isn't it?

I have seen this phenomenon very clearly in the lives of my own children as they've grown up. They have always loved and instinctively wanted to be close to people who had the qualities I've just described, but, certainly through their teenage years, for themselves they wanted something tougher and more brassily impressive to show off than these unselfish talents. I suppose most children pass through this phase, but some of us never come out the other side.

Take me, for instance. Even now, when I'm well into my 40s, and ought to know better, I occasionally find myself carefully setting out to impress another person with some pathetic achievement or other. Almost invariably this other person will be one of these truly nice people who really, really do seem to want to hear me mouthing off vainly about myself. Even as I speak, I find myself looking at the person opposite and wishing that he or she could see in me the qualities of receptivity and kindness that I see in them.

When this happens I get quite disturbed, and I pray sincerely to God that I will eventually lose my obsession with myself and the way in which the rest of the world sees me. In the end, I would like to be so genuinely interested in other people that their image of me doesn't concern me any more.

An interesting thought occurs to me. If this miraculous change ever occurs—I won't know it's happened, will I? So, perhaps it's happened! No, I don't think so either…

Father, lots of us want the applause without the rehearsal. Help us to value the qualities that are truly attractive and to keep our mouths shut until we gain some of them.

WISE NOTES

Proverbs 8:22–26 (NRSV)

The Lord created me at the beginning of his work, the first of his acts of long ago. Ages ago I was set up, at the first, before the beginning of the earth. When there were no depths I was brought forth, when there were no springs abounding with water. Before the mountains had been shaped, before the hills, I was brought forth— when he had not yet made earth and fields, or the world's first bits of soil.

Wisdom is a recurring tune in the symphony of creation, running on for ever, whatever else fails.

Have you ever written any music? Until about ten years ago I had never even thought about writing serious songs. Working in a succession of residential establishments, we did have a go at putting together lyrics for songs to be performed in pantomimes and revues, but we always relied on the nearest keyboard wizard to supply the actual music.

Then, during a period of enforced idleness, as I was just beginning to find out how invigorating it could be to tell the truth, I suddenly wanted to write songs more than anything else. I felt terribly frustrated because I didn't know how to do it. I had an old guitar that I swear tried to hide in corners when it saw me coming, but I was limited by the fact that I could only play three chords with confidence. The dull, throbbing, strumming noise that I produced was equally uninspiring, and I was beginning to feel a bit discouraged when a friend suggested that I should just write the words and the tune of each song and then he'd 'turn them into music'.

The joy of it! I shall never forget the first occasion that he turned up with a tape and put it on my cassette player. MY TUNE came out of those speakers sounding so splendid that I hardly recognized it. It was sung by someone who could really sing, and it was accompanied by drums and guitars and a keyboard and goodness knows what else. My little tune had been turned into music!

It was a small parable, applying not just to my miserably unproductive life at that time, but to the lives of many people who feel it's hardly worth offering God the unsophisticated melody of time, effort or talent that they possess. My advice is—offer it! You'll be amazed what an expert can do with a simple tune.

Father, make beautiful music with our lives.

BEING THERE

Proverbs 8:27–31 (NRSV)

When he established the heavens, I was there, when he drew a circle on the face of the deep, when he made firm the skies above... when he assigned to the sea its limit... when he marked out the foundations of the earth, then I was beside him, like a master worker; and I was daily his delight, rejoicing before him always, rejoicing in his inhabited world and delighting in the human race.

I feel rather jealous of Wisdom in this passage, don't you? Fancy having been there! Just imagine being present when God was drawing up the blueprints for creation at the beginning of time, and watching as those plans were carried out on such an awe-inspiring scale. Nothing that Hollywood has ever produced comes close to the reality of what happened then. I love the thought of Wisdom being filled with delight as each day brought yet another amazing spectacle. In fact, I feel very sad that I won't ever see it, and this brings me to a little private fantasy that I'd like to share with you.

I've arrived in heaven, right? Some kind of conference-centre-managing-type angel has shown me to my mansion, no doubt situated right next door to someone I was sure would never make it, and I'm just flicking through the Heaven brochures before taking a stroll around. I learn to my surprise that there's a video shop just up the golden street, and I decide to pay it an immediate visit. When I get there I discover to my unutterable joy that the videos on offer cover every period of history from the beginning of time to the moment when I shuffled off my own particular mortal coil.

Incredible prospect, eh? Just think—on my heavenly Friday nights I can take out *The Battle of Waterloo* and *The Invention of the Wheel*, or I might decide to settle down and watch *Henry the Eighth*. Or perhaps I'd decide to get out a tape called *The Jurassic Era*, and enjoy footage of dinosaurs that would make Spielberg's efforts look pale by comparison. I might get a few friends together and spend the whole of one week watching *Genesis*, followed on Sunday by *Exodus*, starring the real Moses, who will almost certainly look nothing like Charlton Heston. Come to think of it, I could get Moses to come over and watch it with me—fill me in on all the details. Yes, that's what I'll do...

Father, forgive my silliness, but I would love us all to warm up to the idea of heaven, and particularly to the idea of experiencing the joy described in this passage, simply because we are in your presence.

We are but shadows till the heart be touched.
That touch creates us—then we begin to
be—thereby we are beings of reality and
inheritors of eternity.

NATHANIEL HAWTHORNE

FINDING FIRM GROUND

REALITY IN THE BIBLE

There's a lot of talk about reality in the Church nowadays, and I'm sure most of us would reckon that's a very good thing. Certainly, I could hardly say otherwise, as I've made a fair bit of noise about it myself. And yet, how hard it is to pin down what is real and unchangeable with total confidence, not just in spiritual things, but in all sorts of areas. Let me give you one or two examples. The first one concerns our oldest son, Matthew. It may seem a minor and unimportant thing to you, but it amazed me.

Matthew was always a tea fanatic. Ignoring the trivial fact that Bridget and I had been making what we thought to be perfectly adequate pots of tea for 40 years or so, he would, from time to time, lecture us sternly on the correct procedure for producing the perfect cup of tea. We had, he pointed out kindly but firmly, totally misunderstood the proportions, sequence and timing with which the essential components of this wonderful beverage should be brought into contact with each other. He generously donated substantial periods of his time, free of charge, to the task of ensuring that our education in this area should be completed. This removed our confidence altogether, of course. We became jitteringly nervous about preparing tea for him in case it should fail to meet with his approval and high standards—he being a sort of high priest of the tea-worshipping fraternity.

The rest of the fraternity, Matthew's friends that is, were similarly addicted to the hot brown stuff. The very mention of the word 'coffee' (a drink which we loved, but almost felt obliged to drink in dark corners where our shameful apostasy could not be witnessed) seemed to be regarded as a shocking heresy. They gathered like some loony sect in our kitchen, fussing and fiddling and muttering over their boiling and brewing and sugaring and adding of milk before bearing the sacred vessels on the sacred tray aloft to the high priest's chaotic Holy of Holies at the top of the house. Unfortunately, the ensuing ceremony rarely seemed automatically to conclude with a ritual return and cleansing of the sacred vessels. We humble, coffee-drinking acolytes were clearly more suited to that particular role.

This obsession with tea persisted throughout the whole of Matthew's school career, and was unabated as he began his degree course at Exeter University. This and his equally violent loathing for just about every vegetable under the sun were two of the most fixed and reliable facts in our universe. They were reality.

Then, one day, not long before finishing his course, Matthew arrived home for a weekend and offered to cook the dinner for that evening. Bridget, always open to new experiences, accepted the offer with alacrity, and watched with interest to see what was going to be on the menu. It was when Matthew started to throw all manner of vegetables into a large saucepan that the world began to rock on its axis, but it was when he lightly declared, 'Think I'll make myself a nice cup of coffee while I'm waiting for that lot to boil up,' that she had to sit down quite abruptly on the nearest kitchen chair.

'B-b-b-but, Matthew,' she stammered, 'you don't drink coffee. You've never drunk coffee! And what are you doing with those vegetables? You hate vegetables!'

At first, Matthew stared at Bridget as if she had gone mad, then a reflective look appeared on his face. Brows furrowed, he stared down the long tunnel of his past seeking some basis for what his mother had said. His face cleared at last.

'Ah, well, yes, that's right, I was a bit off vegetables, wasn't I? I like 'em now.' He looked at the cup in his hand. 'I always drink coffee now—can't stand tea. It's so insipid, don't you think?'

I know it sounds absurd, but Matthew's defection from the tea-drinking, non-vegetable-consuming community was as surprising as anything else that's ever happened to me. And it gives hope for all sorts of people and situations where what we have believed to be reality really might be able to alter. How well God can use such a propensity for change.

Some adjustments of reality are just as surprising but very much more worrying. I think in particular of those occasions when a person recreates his or her own past in a form that coheres more easily with present needs, biases and circumstances. This can often happen on a level that is not even quite conscious. I'm terrified that I've done it myself, especially as I probably wouldn't know it had happened unless someone else told me, and then I might not accept what they said. It occurs to me that you might not know what I'm talking about, so I'll give you an example.

I once found myself being driven from one meeting to another (for the benefit of those who don't know—I am a proud non-driver) by a lady named Vera who obviously had something on her mind. I knew that I'd met her before, actually, but for a long time I couldn't for the life of me remember where this meeting had taken place. Then, quite suddenly, it came back to me.

'Weren't you at that church down on the west coast where I came to speak a couple of years ago?' I asked.

She nodded vigorously. Bingo! I was right, and this recollection was obviously what she'd been waiting for.

'I've left there now,' she said, pressing her lips firmly together and shaking her head as if trying to rid herself of some dark and terrible memory.

I took my cue obediently.

'Something go wrong, did it? I seem to remember that your pastor down there was a good sort of guy. Phil, wasn't it?'

'I'd rather not talk about him if you don't mind.'

'Fine.' I nodded understandingly, settled back and waited patiently for her to talk about him.

Seconds passed.

'Only, you see, he's the reason I left the church and then moved up here.'

'I see—look,' I said, rather unkindly, 'you don't have to talk about it if you'd rather not, you know.'

'No, no,' she reassured me hurriedly, 'it's all right, I don't mind telling you. You see, I had to leave because Phil accused me of being a child of the devil.' Turning her head and glancing momentarily at me to gauge my reaction, she paused to allow the enormity of the offence to register, then fixed her eyes on the road again. 'I mean, I don't object to being told off if I do something wrong, but that's right over the top, don't you think? I couldn't stay after that, could I?'

I made a vague noise that might have indicated agreement or otherwise, but as we continued our drive I pondered on what Vera had said. I remembered Phil quite well. He'd struck me as being a very good man, committed to the people in his church and certainly not the sort of person who was likely to make the kind of statement that I'd just heard. We arrived soon after that, but every now and then, in the course of the evening meeting, and during the period when we all had coffee and biscuits afterwards, I went over those words in my head:

'He accused me of being a child of the devil.'

No! I shook my head as I got into the same car to make the return journey. I couldn't imagine Phil saying that unless he had some truly exceptional reason. As we travelled towards home I decided to bring up the subject once more. I didn't want to very much. After all, it was none of my business, was it? On the other hand, I really had thought Phil was a nice bloke.

'Vera,' I said, 'just going back to what Phil said to you for a moment—'

'Yes,' said Vera, more than willing to return to the subject, 'he said I was a child of the devil. That's why I had to—'

'Let's just get this straight. He actually said that, did he? He said those words—"Vera, you are a child of the devil"—just like that?'

'Well...'

I could see Vera's eyes in the driving mirror. A funny little jump happened in them, as though an inner adjustment had been made. She looked almost surprised.

'Well,' she continued slowly and much less confidently, 'he didn't actually use those exact words, but, I mean, that's what he meant—that's what he implied.' Her eyes had a worried, hunted look in them now.

I moved in for the kill.

'So what were his exact words?'

Vera swallowed hard. 'Well, err, what he actually said was that the way I was behaving wasn't what he'd expect from a child of God. But, surely, that means...'

Her voice trailed away as she realized that the implied step from one statement to the other was an impossibly large one. The rest of the journey was not very comfortable for either of us.

The interesting thing about this incident is that I am quite sure Vera had repeated her 'child of the devil' story so often that she had temporarily forgotten the words that Phil had actually used, and that little jump of the eyes had signalled the moment when she was forced back to a truth that had been too threatening for her to face in its genuine, original form.

I wondered how many people had been told what Phil 'said' in the year or two since he didn't say it?

Before we get too critical of old Vera, it's worth asking ourselves whether we have 'reconstructed' the truth in one or two areas of our lives. We might be surprised!

So, what is real? Let's explore.

Prayer
Father, as we begin to look at the issue of reality, help us to be honest about ourselves, our past, present and future.

REALITY

John 8:32 (RSV)

And you will know the truth, and the truth will make you free.

A few years ago I travelled up to London for an evening discussion. It was a very hot summer night, and the upstairs meeting room was packed solid.

Sitting on the floor with my knees jammed under my chin, hot and uncomfortable, I was thanking God that the meeting was drawing to a close, when I suddenly realized that the man sitting three feet away from me on a chair was a very well known Christian speaker and Bible scholar. He was the sort of man whose reputation for spiritual insight sometimes causes people to gabble hysterically about how well their walk with the Lord is going, or emit shrill cries of 'Hallelujah!' and 'Praise the Lord!' to indicate soundness. How awful it would be, I thought, if he 'saw' something I did in 1972, just by looking into my face. Just then he took a piece of paper from his pocket and began to write something on it. He then folded the paper and, to my abject horror, leaned over and handed it to me. I unfolded it with trembling fingers and was about to read it when—the lights went out!

Sitting in the darkness, holding my piece of paper with 1972 scrawled over it for all I knew, I just wanted to die. When power was restored I saw that the man had written: 'Can you give me a few moments afterwards?' A few minutes later I followed him down the stairs like a little doggy to a small room, where he further alarmed me by announcing that he was in the habit of having visions, and that one of his recent visions involved me. It had nothing (I was thankful to hear) to do with 1972—not that I did anything in 1972, I hasten to add. Oh, the relief!

As we stood up to leave I couldn't help wondering if he'd read my books. He must have known what I was thinking. 'I've read your books,' he said, 'and I'd like you to know that the verse that's usually translated "The truth will make you free" can also be translated "Reality will make you free".'

It was a confirmation and an assurance, and it has been at the centre of everything I've thought, written and spoken about since that day.

Can I handle reality?

THE FUNNY BIKE

John 3:1–3 (RSV)

Now there was a man of the Pharisees, named Nicodemus, a ruler of the Jews. This man came to Jesus by night and said to him, 'Rabbi, we know that you are a teacher come from God; for no one can do these signs that you do, unless God is with him.' Jesus answered him, 'Truly, truly, I say to you, unless one is born anew, he cannot see the kingdom of God.'

The reality of what we refer to casually as 'the Christian life' is quite different from the reality of life outside the kingdom of God. I hope that doesn't sound too airy-fairy or abstract, because the spiritual life is, in fact, more practical and gritty than any other. Read again about the carpenter who got involved in mass catering and ended up nailed to a piece of wood, if you don't believe me. Jesus was telling Nicodemus that the whole axis of his life needed to change if he wanted to enter the kingdom. Being born again means a new context, a new perspective, new priorities and new behaviours.

My wife and I once went to a summer fair at the junior school where Katy is a pupil. One of the outdoor attractions was a bicycle that steers the wrong way. You've probably seen them—most annoying contraptions. When you turn the handlebars to the left the front wheel turns to the right, and vice-versa. The owners of this awkward vehicle were offering a prize of one pound to anyone who could ride the bicycle for six yards without putting a foot on the ground. It cost 20 pence for each attempt, and they were making lots of money because not a single person was able to adjust mentally and physically to this change in cause and effect. It was very funny to watch them trying.

Following Jesus involves a rather similar revolution in our steering habits, and many people fall by the wayside because of poor teaching in this area. 'Love your enemies.' How about that one? The world steers to the right, but we are called to do the opposite. My heart fails me sometimes when I look at the commitment that's required, but I want to live in the kingdom of God, so I shall go on practising, however many times I fall off.

Teach me to steer, Lord.

STRAIGHT TALKING

Matthew 16:21–24 (RSV)

From that time Jesus began to show his disciples that he must go to Jerusalem and suffer many things from the elders and chief priests and scribes, and be killed, and on the third day be raised. And Peter took him and began to rebuke him saying, 'God forbid, Lord! This shall never happen to you.' But he turned and said to Peter, 'Get behind me, Satan! You are a hindrance to me; for you not on the side of God, but of men.' Then Jesus told his disciples, 'If any man would come after me, let him deny himself and take up his cross and follow me...'

There is a dearth of healthy confrontation in the Church nowadays. Here we see Jesus reacting with explosive anger to Peter's inappropriate and obstructive heroics. Immense, eternal issues were under discussion, and there was Peter trying to lob a very worldly spanner into the cosmic machinery. The cross was a price that Jesus was willing to pay so that men and women could inherit eternal life, and he had no intention of being distracted by sentimental assertions.

I used to feel that Peter was rather unfairly battered by Jesus on this occasion, but when I think about my own dealings with people I'm not so sure. I was infected, very early in my Christian life, with the politeness disease. Everything I said had to be expressed 'nicely', and if I did have anything negative to say it had to be done 'in love', which meant that I had approached the point in such a circumlocutory way that the recipient of my wonderful wisdom found it very difficult to know what I was talking about. I'm all for courtesy and love, but I think I have often used them as excuses for not being direct when it's necessary.

It's a matter of reality again. For a long time I saw one particular man every week for two or three hours. After months of nervously skirting around the issue I finally told him what I thought about his situation. 'Why didn't you say that before?' he asked. Exactly.

How can we develop a proper assertiveness?

STANDING FIRM

Daniel 1:11–16 (RSV)

Then Daniel said to the steward whom the chief of the eunuchs had appointed over Daniel, Hananiah, Mishael and Azariah; 'Test your servants for ten days; let us be given vegetables to eat and water to drink. Then let our appearance and the appearance of the youths who eat the king's rich food be observed by you, and according to what you see deal with your servants.' So he harkened to them in this matter, and tested them for ten days. At the end of ten days it was seen that they were better in appearance and fatter in flesh than all the youths who ate the king's rich food. So the steward took away their rich food and the wine they were to drink, and gave them vegetables.

Here's a chap who understood the 'funny bike' principle. As far as we know, Daniel never once compromised his religious principles, no matter which Babylonian king he happened to be dealing with at the time. This was his first challenge, and he came through it with flying colours. After ten days he and his companions were fitter and stronger than those who had eaten the rich court food. What a fortune he would have made nowadays. Daniel the Israelite's low-fat, vegetable only, hip 'n' thigh diet would have hit the bestseller list within a fortnight. Daniel's only interest was in doing the will of his God, his reward—the discovery that he would receive divine support if he stood up for what he believed in.

This unwavering attitude of Daniel's makes us feel quite threatened. I'd like to be him after his brave stance was endorsed by God, but I suspect that when faced with the original dilemma I would have said in sensible, no-nonsense tones: 'Look, I honestly think that fanaticism is a poor witness. I reckon it takes more courage to eat the king's food— I honestly do…' For Daniel, though, it was the thin end of the wedge. From now on it could only get easier to do the right thing and make the right decisions. By the time he arrived (as an old man) at the famous lion sketch he must have had a profound understanding of the principle that our most crucial needs are met and satisfied by doing what we are told.

Lord, I am not brave, but I want to be.

THE EYES OF A CHILD

Matthew 18:2–3 (RSV)

And calling to him a child, he put him in the midst of them, and said, 'Truly, I say to you, unless you turn and become like children you will never enter the kingdom of heaven.'

Jesus seems to be saying here that the reality of heavenly things is more apparent to childlike eyes than to the eyes of sophistication and 'grown-upness'.

Some time ago we took our bicycles down to Newhaven, crossed on the ferry to northern France, and spent a few very enjoyable days pedalling from town to town along the river valleys. Our last day was set aside to explore the port of Dieppe before recrossing the Channel that evening.

Just after lunch we entered the cool interior of a big church near the centre of town. I lost touch with the others for a while, but after a few minutes I discovered Katy, aged four at the time, staring silently at a life-size sculpture of Mary, the mother of Jesus, holding her son's dead body in her arms, and looking into his face with an expression of real pain and loss. Katy turned and saw me.

'Daddy,' she asked, 'why has Jesus got a hole in his side?' Stumblingly, I explained that a Roman spear had been responsible. Katy was horrified. She studied the sculpture again. 'Daddy, he's got holes in his feet. Why's he got holes in his feet?'

'Look.' I pointed to a small crucifix on the wall above us. 'They nailed his feet to that piece of wood called a cross, and those are the holes where the nails were.' 'Nailed his feet?!' She turned to look at the stone figures again. Her voice broke a little as she spoke. 'Daddy, he's got holes in his hands as well. They didn't nail his hands as well, did they?' Sadly, I explained. Katy moved closer to the sculpture, put her arm around Jesus and rested her face down on his knee.

Suddenly I longed to go back to the time when I first understood that Jesus died for me and it really hurt, before I covered my faith in words and worries. I wanted to be like a child again.

Father, give me the eyes of a child.

WHAT IS YOUR NAME?

John 3:16 (RSV)

For God so loved the world that he gave his only Son, that whoever believes in him should not perish but have eternal life.

I've had a love/hate relationship with this verse since I was converted (whatever that means) at the age of 16. It expresses, of course, the greatest reality of all, but back in the 1960s it seemed to be used almost as a talisman by the young evangelicals who thought that the Bible might be the fourth person of the Trinity. I swallowed my hate for John 3:16 years ago. Now I love it, because it encapsulates the great truth that God is crackers about us. It ought to make us feel glad and proud (in the best sense) but an awful lot of Christians feel neither of those things. Many of us have a very poor self-image, a phenomenon that has little or nothing to do with pride and humility.

I remember a woman I met when I was signing books after a meeting one evening at some church in the north of England. She held a book out for me to sign and I asked, as I always do, for her name, so that I could write a dedication to her on the title page.

'Oh,' she said, shaking her head uncertainly, 'I'm not anybody really. Just sign it...'

'Go on, tell me your name,' I coaxed. 'You must be somebody.'

She blushed slightly.

'Oh, well, I'm just Sarah...'

God so loved just Sarah that he gave his only beloved son, that if just Sarah believes in him, she will not perish but have everlasting life. Why doesn't she believe that? There could be all sorts of reasons, but perhaps one might be that the Church puts far less value on Sarah than God does. The last couple of decades have seen an increased emphasis on individual spiritual achievement in certain areas. Getting and gaining from God in all sorts of quick-fix ways has tended to obscure and replace the kind of long-term care and valuing of individuals that should characterize the body of Christ. God loved the person who sits beside me in church enough to send Jesus. There aren't any nonentities.

Father, teach us to value each other and ourselves. Thank you for sending Jesus just for me.

BLESSINGS AND TROUBLES

Luke 1:26–30 (GNB)

In the sixth month of Elizabeth's pregnancy God sent the angel Gabriel to a town in Galilee named Nazareth. He had a message for a young woman promised in marriage to a man named Joseph, who was a descendant of King David. Her name was Mary. The angel came to her and said, 'Peace be with you! The Lord is with you and has greatly blessed you!' Mary was deeply troubled by the angel's message, and she wondered what his words meant. The angel said to her, 'Don't be afraid, Mary; God has been gracious to you...'

Mary is one of my all-time heroes, or heroines, or heroic persons, and this particular passage contains a clue to the reason why I hold her in such high regard. She was a realist, a good servant, and a very puzzled lady. Mary is told by the angel that she is 'greatly blessed'. She is immediately 'deeply troubled'. For the rest of her life Mary continues to be greatly blessed and deeply troubled as she observes the development of her extraordinary son's ministry, his appalling death and subsequent resurrection.

Mary's example should have a freeing effect on folk like myself who have somehow got the idea that the 'greatly blessed' mode is the only legitimate one. Nearly all of the Christians that I know well have passed through, are passing through, and certainly will pass through periods of being deeply troubled. How could it be otherwise? This is a wild, fallen world, and we are weak, vulnerable people with widely differing backgrounds and personalities, but sharing the same hope as Mary, that we have life and ultimate healing in Jesus.

How important it is that we accept this reality in each other without offering inappropriate ministry or implicit condemnation. Share blessings, share troubles, and, above all, share Jesus. We'll get by.

Father, help us to look after each other without unreal expectations or unhelpful responses. Thank you for Mary who was obedient and genuine.

BACK TO BASICS

Luke 24:13–17 (RSV)

That very day two of them were going to a village named Emmaus, about seven miles from Jerusalem, and talking with each other about all these things that had happened. While they were talking and discussing together, Jesus himself drew near and went with them. But their eyes were kept from recognizing him. And he said to them, 'What is this conversation which you are holding with each other as you walk?' And they stood still, looking sad.

A rich mix of troubles and blessings is one thing, but a long desert-like experience of spiritual loneliness is quite another. As I travel around the country I am quite often faced with the fact that some folk have felt neglected by God for a very long time. I know a free-church minister in the north-east, for example, who simply cannot understand why there has been little or no spiritual development in the church that he leads. He's a talented, caring man who seems to have done all the right things, but, like the two fellows in this passage, he has ended up 'standing still, looking sad' because Jesus seems to have disappeared and the future is pointless. This man (and many others like him) are yearning to feel their hearts burn within them again, so that they too can tell others, with the deep wild excitement they once knew, that 'The Lord is risen indeed!'

There are no universal solutions to the problem of spiritual depression (I once bought a 'universal' roof-rack that fitted every model of car in the cosmos except the one that we had) but the experience of these two travellers is interesting. First, they received a metaphorical clip round the ear for being silly, but it didn't put them off—Jesus gets that sort of thing right. Then they were taken back to first principles via the scriptures. Finally they received blessed bread from the stranger who turned out to be Jesus. Then their hearts burned!

It's worth a try. No-holds-barred repentance, followed by a quiet return to Bible-basics, leading to warm and intimate communion with the person who was with us all the time, even when we were standing still and looking sad.

We want to burn with life, Lord. Meet us, teach us and eat with us, please.

BURGLARS

Luke 21:34–36 (RSV)

'But take heed to yourselves lest your hearts be weighed down with dissipation and drunkenness and cares of this life, and that day come upon you suddenly like a snare; for it will come upon all who dwell upon the face of the whole earth. But watch at all times, praying that you may have strength to escape all these things that will take place, and to stand before the Son of man.'

The Bible is a strange book. There's always a bit you never noticed, usually right in the middle of a very familiar passage. Take this extract from Luke, for instance. When I tell people that Jesus mentioned three areas of worldly distraction that weigh the heart down, and that these include drunkenness, they usually look very surprised and demand to know exactly where the quote appears. The situation is not helped by the fact that I almost invariably forget the chapter and verse and have to leaf feverishly through the New Testament searching for evidence.

Dissipation, drunkenness and cares of this life. In my time I've had a paddle in the first, got out of my depth in the second, but jolly nearly drowned in the third. Some of us who are in the 'standing still, looking sad' bracket may have to face the reality that we are hanging on to concerns and preoccupations so ponderous that they cast a perpetual shadow of gloom over all other aspects of life. The habit of worry can be a crippling one.

No burglars came again last night
Just as they failed to come the night before
And for as many nights as I remember
No burglars yet again
Although I listened, as I always do, for them.
They did not come
They were not here again last night
And what if they should never come?
A waste of nights—I might have slept
But if I had, I feel quite sure
They would have come—those burglars,
Yes, they would have come.

A prayer: *Lord, our worries cling to us like poultices. Sometimes we pray about them and they seem to go away for a while. Then they come back and we are close to despair. Help us, Lord, we don't want to be distracted from you.*

THE FAILED FATHER?

Luke 15:11 (RSV)

And he said, 'There was a man who had two sons...'

If the story of the prodigal son had been told for the first time in this age, it would undoubtedly have been called 'The parable of the failed father'. After all, neither of his sons turned out very well, did they? One left home and spent all his money on riotous living and harlots, while the other grew up to be a sulky, po-faced individual who had no idea how to enjoy life. Something wrong with the parenting there, wouldn't you say?

Of course, Jesus was making a different point altogether and views on individual responsibility were very different at that time, and in that society. However, if we are trying to deal with reality, let's face the fact that very many people outside the Church, and not a few inside, have a big problem with this 'other view' of God's dealings with men and women. It's an old question, but here it comes again: If the creator really is omniscient and omnipotent, why did he produce creatures who were going to fail and rebel and experience suffering and pain as a result? Why doesn't he take responsibility for his own poor handiwork and planning? Doesn't he owe us a slice of heaven?

My evangelical training pops up answers to these questions with Pavlovian ease: God didn't want robots so he gave us free will. He is the potter and we are the clay, so we have no right to object. Our finite minds are incapable of comprehending his infinite and eternal purposes.

These arguments may or may not have virtue, but I can only say that they've never satisfactorily solved the problem for me. I wouldn't be a Christian now if my faith depended on an acceptance of the logic of creation and the fall. It doesn't depend on that—it depends on Jesus. Right at the centre of my chaotic, shifting, strangely shaped religious belief lies the person of Jesus and the relationship that exists between us. He is the still point from which all references are taken and I have gradually learned that he is reliable.

I can't solve the problem of the 'failed' father, but Jesus knows the truth and I trust him. In the end—that is my answer.

Father, there are lots of things I don't understand. Help me not to pretend I do when I don't. Thank you again for Jesus.

TIME OUT

Matthew 14:6–14 (RSV)

But when Herod's birthday came, the daughter of Herodias danced before the company, and pleased Herod, so that he promised with an oath to give her whatever she might ask. Prompted by her mother, she said, 'Give me the head of John the Baptist here on a platter.' And the king was sorry; but because of his oaths and his guests he commanded it to be given; he sent and had John beheaded in the prison and his head was brought on a platter and given to the girl, and she brought it to her mother. And his disciples came and took the body and buried it; and they went and told Jesus. Now when Jesus heard this, he withdrew from there in a boat to a lonely place apart. But when the crowds heard it, they followed him on foot from the towns. As he went ashore he saw a great throng; and he had compassion on them, and healed their sick.

There was a time when even Jesus became still and sad. He was a real man, so it isn't surprising. Jesus and his cousin must have been very close. Their parents knew each other, they were the same age, and they lived within a day's journey of each other. Even before they were born John had leaped in his mother's womb when the excited Mary hurried to Elizabeth's hill-country home to describe her encounter with an angel. I may be wrong, but I've always felt that Jesus' impassioned outburst about John in the seventh chapter of Luke's Gospel contains a very personal note as well as a logical argument.

Now, on hearing that John is dead, he tries to find a place to be alone, a place to grieve, but the crowds are like baby birds, knowing only their own hunger, and as he sets foot on the shore they all are waiting for him. Business as usual. No more time for grief.

Thank you, Father, for this special view of one of your son's very personal moments. I'm sorry he was made so sad by his cousin's death, and I want to thank you that he got on with the job so determinedly after drawing apart for a while. It gives me permission to do the same.

GOD OF THE GAPS

Zephaniah 3:15–20 (RSV)

Do not fear, O Zion; let not your hands grow weak. The Lord, your God, is in your midst, a warrior who gives victory; he will rejoice over you with gladness, he will renew you in his love; he will exult over you with loud singing as on a day of festival. 'I will remove disaster from you, so that you will not bear reproach for it. Behold, at that time I will deal with all your oppressors. And I will save the lame and gather the outcast, and I will change their shame into praise and renown in all the earth. At that time I will bring you home, at that time when I gather you together; yea, I will make you renowned and praised among all the peoples of the earth, when I restore your fortunes before your eyes,' says the Lord.

This passage, and the last sentence in particular, became very important to me twelve years ago when I retreated from my normal activities because of a stress-related illness. One thing that assisted my recovery was the daily discipline of writing, a completely new occupation for me. There was something very therapeutic about taking feelings and memories from inside and placing them outside, on a sheet of paper. Gradually, the notion of becoming a full-time writer began to form in my mind. My family were very supportive, but most other people displayed a thinly veiled scepticism when I described what I intended. I can hardly blame them. I had a mortgage, three children and a dog to support. How was I going to pro-vide for them? Then, one morning, I read the final part of Zephaniah, and those last few words stood out like divine Braille, relieving the spiritual blindness that I was suffering at the time. God was going to restore my fortunes before my eyes, and although it was difficult to picture how it would happen, I felt sure that writing would be involved. Soon after that I sent a selection of written pieces to the American writer Elizabeth Sherrill, who, with her husband John, had been responsible for a string of bestselling books, including *The Cross and the Switchblade*. Elizabeth replied with the kind of letter raw beginners dream of. Armed with her generous encouragement I continued to wear out biros and tear up rejection slips from publishers informing me that 'our readers would not approve of our Lord Jesus Christ being written about in that fashion…'

But God kept his promise.

Are we too quick to plug 'gaps'?

LONG LIVE LOVE

1 Corinthians 13:8–10 (RSV)

Love never ends; as for prophecies, they will pass away; as for tongues, they will cease; as for knowledge, it will pass away. For our knowledge is imperfect and our prophecy is imperfect; but when the perfect comes, the imperfect will pass away.

Most people are fond of this passage, but there is nothing sentimental about what Paul is saying. All of the spiritual gifts will pass away, but love will remain. We are not saved by tongues, prophecy, words of knowledge, or any of the other useful pots and pans that equip the Christian kitchen. God is love and we are saved by the power of love. The other things are good but imperfect.

I have a friend who is a Jewish rabbi in the reformed movement. We have often looked for common ground. He is a very spiritual man and I am an Anglican. When David came to tea with his wife one day I put the following scenario to him.

'I arrive in heaven, right?' David nodded. 'And God says to me, "I'm awfully sorry, Adrian, but Jesus wasn't the Son of God. The Jews got it right and you didn't. But will you trust me anyway?"'

'Yes,' smiled David, 'I can imagine that quite easily.'

'Hold on,' I said, 'I haven't finished yet. While I'm chewing over what God's said to me—you roll up.'

'Oh,' said the rabbi, his smile fading a little.

'"Hello, David," says God, "I'm awfully sorry, but Jesus was the Son of God. You missed out on the Messiah. But will you trust me anyway?"'

'And what happens then?' asked David.

'Well, I guess you and I talk it over just outside heaven's gate, then we go to God arm in arm and say that as long as the three of us can be together nothing else matters.'

'Hmmm,' said David thoughtfully.

Don't throw scriptural thunderbolts at me. I do believe that Jesus is exactly who and what he said he was, but I also believe that the love between David and me is as real and as lasting as anything else.

John Lennon was right. 'Love is real...'

COMING LAST

Micah 4:6–7 (RSV)

In that day, says the Lord, I will assemble the lame and gather those who have been driven away and those whom I have afflicted; and the lame I will make the remnant; and those who were cast off, a strong nation; and the Lord will reign over them in Mount Zion from this time forth and for evermore.

A friend and I took some members of the local youth club to Wales. I was a little nervous because I knew that the weekend itinerary included the climbing of a very high mountain, and I seriously doubted that I was fit enough to manage it. No rock-climbing was involved, just walking and clambering forever. I was sure my lungs and legs would rebel long before I reached the top.

Because of this apprehension I set off like an express train when we started, anxious to put failure or success behind me as quickly as possible. Some of the kids kept pace with my frenetic attack on the hillside, while others—the plump, the wrongly shod, the frail and the disinclined—dribbled slowly along at the rear. It wasn't until I was about three-quarters of the way to the top and I stopped to admire the view (I claimed) that I took any notice of what was happening to the stragglers. Far, far below me, I could see a little line of bent figures toiling laboriously up the slope, and, right at the back, my friend and co-leader, Michael, who was much fitter than me and could easily have been further on than I was by now. As I watched, he stopped to encourage the smaller figure in front of him who seemed to have given up temporarily. I reached the top long before Michael. It took him hours to shepherd his reluctant lambs to the summit.

Sometimes it can look as if the elevated, front-running, high-profile Christians are the significant, successful ones, but it is not so. Those who are carrying out the commission implied by these verses in Micah are the winners in God's eyes, for their example and their inspiration is Jesus himself.

Father, give us patience and pleasure in helping those who are having trouble making it.

Wisdom is ofttimes nearer
when we stoop than when we soar.

WILLIAM WORDSWORTH, 'THE EXCURSION'

WISE AFTER THE EVENT?

THE CHARACTER OF SOLOMON

Solomon was the son of David and Bathsheba—clearly a man of talent and insight even before God specifically gifted him with yet greater wisdom. As he started to emerge as the most glorious of Israel's kings, David died, having passed on the plans for the temple to his son. Most of Solomon's reign (probably about 40 years) was a peaceful and prosperous period for Israel. Politically astute and very adept in his handling of people, the king amassed huge wealth and used much of it to construct the temple that his father had never been allowed to build. This magnificent construction was sited on Mount Moriah, the hill that had been Araunah's threshing floor, the place where God halted the plague that was about to devastate Jerusalem, as recorded in the first book of Chronicles. David offered a sacrifice here and bought the site for the temple. Mount Moriah was also the place where Abraham once prepared to sacrifice Isaac and, in the future, it was to be the hill to the north of the city where Jesus was crucified. Nowadays, the site is covered by the Dome of the Rock, one of Islam's holiest shrines.

In addition to building the temple, Solomon erected a palace for himself that took 13 years to build. There is reason to believe that this may have been even more sumptuous than the dwelling-place he designed and completed for God.

For many years, Solomon was a devoted follower of the one true God, continually praying and offering sacrifices on behalf of himself and his people. He was actually visited by God on at least two occasions and it would have seemed inconceivable in the early years that he could ever stray from the path of virtue. Perhaps because of the cumulative effects of such massive wealth and power, however, a time came when, as an old man, Solomon was seduced by his foreign wives into following gods such as Ashtoreth and Molech. Such foolishness is almost inexplicable in a man gifted with such wisdom, but it happened and it made God extremely angry. He punished Solomon by allowing only one tribe of Israel to be ruled by his son after Solomon's death.

What kind of man was Solomon? Well, as usual in the Bible, this kind of information lies both in the lines and between them, so that's where we'll look.

HE WAS JUST AND COMPASSIONATE

1 Kings 1:49–53 (NIV)

At this, all Adonijah's guests rose in alarm and dispersed. But Adonijah, in fear of Solomon, went and took hold of the horns of the altar. Then Solomon was told, 'Adonijah is afraid of King Solomon and is clinging to the horns of the altar. He says, "Let King Solomon swear to me today that he will not put his servant to death with the sword."' Solomon replied, 'If he shows himself to be a worthy man, not a hair of his head will fall to the ground; but if evil is found in him, he will die.' Then King Solomon sent men, and they brought him down from the altar. And Adonijah came and bowed down to King Solomon, and Solomon said, 'Go to your home.'

Read from the beginning of this chapter to see how this little drama has unfolded. David's son Adonijah has set himself up as the one who will succeed David as king without any reference to David himself or to Nathan, the prophet who, years ago, had confronted David with his sin over Bathsheba and Uriah. Adonijah and his supporters are in the middle of a celebratory feast when they hear that Solomon has been made king. The feast breaks up in confusion. Adonijah is terrified, believing that his younger brother will certainly have him killed.

Why did Solomon not do exactly that? Adonijah, poorly disciplined by a father who was as weak with his sons as he had been strong in most other situations (see v. 6), was a genuine threat to the peace and stability of the new king's reign. Perhaps Solomon loved his brother. Perhaps he didn't. Perhaps he wanted this first decision of his reign to be characterized by the best and finest qualities. Mercy and justice were the attributes of God himself. It was a time for new beginnings. If Adonijah behaved himself, there would be no reason for conflict or punishment in the future.

OK in theory, but, as we shall see presently in the case of Shimei son of Gera, theory and practice do not always coincide.

Lord, let our actions reflect your heart when we deal with others. Let us be ready, whenever it is possible and right, to show compassion and forgiveness, even with those who may seek to do us harm.

HE KEPT HIS PROMISES

1 Kings 2:8–9, 36–38 (NIV, abridged)

'And remember, you have with you Shimei son of Gera... who called down bitter curses on me the day I went to Mahanaim. When he came down to meet me at the Jordan, I swore to him by the Lord: "I will not put you to death by the sword." But now, do not consider him innocent. You are a man of wisdom; you will know what to do to him. Bring his grey head down to the grave in blood.' ... Then the king sent for Shimei and said to him, 'Build yourself a house in Jerusalem and live there, but do not go anywhere else. The day you leave and cross the Kidron Valley, you can be sure you will die; your blood will be on your own head.'

One of Solomon's first tasks as king was to decide about his father's old enemies, like Joab and Shimei, both of whom had been allowed to live in David's lifetime. The first passage here details David's words to his son in the matter of Shimei. Perhaps his attitude was a compound of vengeful feelings and genuine fear for Solomon's welfare, but there was no doubt about the content of his advice. Shimei should be put to death.

Once more, why did Solomon not do this immediately? His kingdom could never be totally secure and at peace as long as these potentially subversive elements survived. However, intelligence and compassion tend to walk parallel paths. Perhaps he believed that it must be possible to arrive at an understanding with Shimei, although events had already driven him to command the execution of Adonijah, his older brother, and Joab, who had once commanded the king's army.

Whatever the reason for this forbearance, he does his best for Shimei, just as we have seen him attempting a new beginning with Adonijah. He offers him a place to live and a promise that he will remain unharmed as long as he stays in Jerusalem.

The king certainly kept his promise. For three years Shimei stayed put, and not a hair of his head was harmed. He must have realized that the king's word could be trusted, but he made the mistake of forgetting the other, far more ominous promise that had been made.

Lord, make us strong in our promises, accountable to you.

HE CARRIED OUT HIS THREATS

1 Kings 2:41–46a (NIV)

When Solomon was told that Shimei had gone from Jerusalem to Gath and had returned, the king summoned Shimei and said to him, 'Did I not make you swear by the Lord and warn you, "On the day you leave to go anywhere else, you can be sure you will die"? At that time you said to me, "What you say is good. I will obey." Why then did you not keep your oath to the Lord and obey the command I gave you?' The king also said to Shemei, 'You know in your heart all the wrong you did to my father David. Now the Lord will repay you for your wrongdoing. But King Solomon will be blessed, and David's throne will remain secure before the Lord for ever.' Then the king gave the order to Benaiah son of Jehoiada, and he went out and struck Shimei down and killed him....

An intriguing story. I wish it were more detailed. What did Shimei say when he was tackled about his excursion to Gath? Did he try to justify himself? Did he claim that he'd forgotten the promise made three years ago?

'After all,' he might have argued, 'all I did was go and get a couple of runaway slaves back. Hardly a threat to your kingdom, is it?'

Of course, in itself, it wasn't. The fact was, though, that Shimei had disobeyed a direct order from the king and deliberately broken the terms of his suspended sentence. Did he think Solomon had not really meant what he said? Did he suspect that the king was soft, and would never actually carry out his threat? Had he convinced himself after three uneventful years in Jerusalem that a tiny infraction of the rule would barely be noticed? Was the man mad?

Infuriatingly, we shall have to wait until we meet Solomon before we know the answers to these questions. We know, though, that Solomon, faced with a potentially dangerous instability in the attitude and behaviour of this old enemy of his father's, now took the step David had advised in the first place. Shimei was executed.

The final threat to the stability of Solomon's kingdom had been removed.

Is it easier to keep a promise than to carry out a threat?

HE WAS WISE (PART 1)

2 Chronicles 1:7–12 (NIV)

That night God appeared to Solomon and said to him, 'Ask for whatever you want me to give you.' Solomon answered God, 'You have shown great kindness to David my father and have made me king in his place. Now, Lord God, let your promise to my father David be confirmed, for you have made me king over a people who are as numerous as the dust of the earth. Give me wisdom and knowledge, that I may lead this people, for who is able to govern this great people of yours?' God said to Solomon, 'Since this is your heart's desire and you have not asked for wealth, riches or honour, nor for the death of your enemies, and since you have not asked for a long life but for wisdom and knowledge to govern my people over whom I have made you king, therefore wisdom and knowledge will be given you.'

This is like a fairy story, isn't it? You know, the one where the hero gets three wishes and he makes disastrous mistakes with the first two before sorting it out at the third go.

Solomon made no mistakes. God gave him the wisdom he asked for, but this king's head must have been screwed on the right way before that, mustn't it? Instead of going for what most human beings want, he requested something that would enable him to perform adequately the huge task lying before him. As I mentioned last time I wrote about Solomon, he must have been sincere, because God would have known if he was only trying to impress. He got his wisdom and, if you read on, you'll see he was promised wealth, riches and honour as well. Jackpot! He'd won the lottery.

So, what would you choose? What would I choose? Well, actually, I know exactly what I'd choose, in fact have chosen already. It hasn't changed for years and I think I'm being given it in instalments. Peace— that's what I want most and, of course, there are many different things that come under that heading. There are things connected with faith and family and friends and the future. Total peace this side of heaven? I suspect not, but one day…

Do you dare to pray the prayer at the bottom of this page?

Lord, the thing I want most in the world is…

HE WAS WISE (PART 2)

1 Kings 3:24–27 (NIV)

Then the king said, 'Bring me a sword.' So they brought a sword for the king. He then gave an order: 'Cut the living child in two and give half to one and half to the other.' The woman whose son was alive was filled with compassion for her son and said to the king, 'Please, my lord, give her the living baby! Don't kill him!' But the other said, 'Neither I nor you shall have him. Cut him in two!' Then the king gave his ruling: 'Give the living baby to the first woman. Do not kill him; she is his mother.'

Yes, Solomon was extremely wise, and here, in the story of two suppliant women and a baby, is the best-known illustration of that wisdom. A sparkling piece of decision making, but certain things occur to me.

First, it can only have been a one-off solution, can't it? I mean, we learn in the next verse that the whole nation heard what had happened, so if the king had tried the same trick again, the women involved would have said to themselves, 'Ah, it's the old let's-cut-the-baby-in-half ploy.' Both would beg Solomon to give the child to the other rather than killing it. What then?

What if, on this first occasion, both women had given up their claim rather than see the baby harmed? Would he have tossed a shekel and awarded the prize to the winner?

What if neither woman had really cared about the welfare of the child and both had agreed with the decision to cut the poor little thing in half? Not so tricky, that one. Presumably Solomon would have given the baby to someone else altogether.

What if—I've started so I'll finish—the real mother had agreed to the gory division and the other had abandoned her false claim out of compassion for the child? Again, not so difficult. You give the baby to the non-mother on the grounds that the real one has forfeited her rights.

What if... Enough!

Real life presents us with a succession of 'What if...?'s. One thing is for sure, dealing with it requires the wisdom of Solomon. He, of course, got his from God and so, amazingly, can we.

Father, the simplest decisions can be challenging. Clear our minds, give us wisdom.

HE WAS AN ARTIST AND A SCHOLAR

1 Kings 4:29–34 (NIV)

God gave Solomon wisdom and very great insight, and a breadth of understanding as measureless as the sand on the seashore. Solomon's wisdom was greater than the wisdom of all the men of the East, and greater than all the wisdom of Egypt. He was wiser than any other man, including Ethan the Ezrahite—wiser than Heman, Calcol and Darda, the sons of Mahol. And his fame spread to all the surrounding nations. He spoke 3000 proverbs and his songs numbered 1005. He described plant life, from the cedar of Lebanon to the hyssop that grows out of walls. He also taught about animals and birds, reptiles and fish. Men of all nations came to listen to Solomon's wisdom, sent by all the kings of the world, who had heard of his wisdom.

Pretty impressive, eh? Philosopher, poet, musician, botanist, zoologist and teacher. Ladies and gentlemen, the next competitor on *Mastermind* is King Solomon, specialist subject—everything!

Given this vast range of interests and absorptions I suppose the king might have selected almost any area in which to direct most of his energies. In fact, predictably perhaps, he decided to concentrate on the temple that his father had never been able to build in his lifetime. Conditions for such a project were excellent. The nation was rich and well-organized. Potential troublemakers had all been removed. There was peace and stability in the land. It was time to honour God by creating an earthly dwelling-place that would surpass anything seen before.

There is no doubt—as we shall see if we take the trouble to read through the detail of the following three chapters—that all the arts and abilities and interests of the king fed into the planning and construction of what must have been a truly magnificent piece of work. I imagine he was a very hands-on project coordinator!

There are those who argue that we have nothing to offer God and, of course, they are right in the sense that God is the true author of all things. Having humbly acknowledged that fact, though, we must not be afraid to pour all that we are into the work we do for him. Solomon did.

I offer you everything that I am, Lord. Take it and use it.

HE COULD GET OTHER PEOPLE ON HIS SIDE

1 Kings 5:3–6 (NIV)

'You know that because of the wars waged against my father David from all sides, he could not build a temple for the Name of the Lord his God until the Lord put his enemies under his feet. But now the Lord my God has given me rest on every side, and there is no adversary or disaster. I intend, therefore, to build a temple for the Name of the Lord my God, as the Lord told my father David, when he said, "Your son whom I will put on the throne in your place will build the temple for my Name." So give orders that cedars of Lebanon will be cut for me. My men will work with yours, and I will pay you for your men whatever wages you set. You know that we have no one as skilled in felling timber as the Sidonians.'

This is Solomon's message to Hiram King of Tyre and if you read on you will see that Hiram produced a very pleased response. You can see why.

First, Solomon does Hiram the courtesy of explaining the context of his request. David was unable to build the temple, but now there is peace and stability enough to begin this huge project. The principle of inclusion holds good in all situations (including DIY stores, I have discovered). Let people into your plans and they might travel with you.

Second, he did not attempt to prescribe or set a wage limit for the workers that would join Hiram's men. Open-endedness in matters of finance has a genuinely liberating effect on relationships, whereas meanness and that awful narrow-eyed wariness that we see so often in our society has exactly the opposite effect. I'm not talking about being silly or irresponsible with money. We are called to be good stewards, but good stewardship sometimes demands an extravagant vulnerability that reflects the very heart of God.

Third, Solomon includes a simply expressed acknowledgment of the special timber-felling skills that the Sidonians are able to offer. Finding that our particular strengths or skills are genuinely appreciated always lifts us and makes us even more able.

Respect, generosity and appreciation. He was no fool, this Solomon, was he?

Help us to win the goodwill of others with the tools of grace.

HIS PRIORITIES MAY HAVE BEEN CONFUSED

1 Kings 7:1–4; 10:4–6 (NIV)

It took Solomon 13 years, however, to complete the construction of his palace. He built the Palace of the Forest of Lebanon 100 cubits long, 50 wide and 30 high, with 4 rows of cedar columns supporting trimmed cedar beams. It was roofed with cedar above the beams that rested on the columns—45 beams, 15 to a row. Its windows were placed high in sets of three, facing each other... When the queen of Sheba saw all the wisdom of Solomon and the palace he had built, the food on his table, the seating of his officials, the attending servants in their robes, his cupbearers, and the burnt offerings he made at the temple of the Lord, she was overwhelmed. She said to the king, 'The report I heard in my own country about your achievements and your wisdom is true.'

A very simple piece of mathematics for you here. How long did it take for the temple to be built? Seven years is the answer. How long did it take for the king's palace to be built? This time, the answer is thirteen years. Take seven away from thirteen and you are left with six. Six more years were given to the construction of the king's residence than to God's house. That's a long time. Did Solomon get a bit carried away? Is it possible that all the power and the wealth and the admiration went to his head without him even being properly aware of it? What was the effect of being visited by such celebrities as the Queen of Sheba and finding himself and his possessions so openly and fulsomely admired? Note that, quite soon after this visit is recorded, there is a description of the great throne that Solomon had constructed for himself, inlaid with ivory and overlaid with fine gold. Nothing like it, we read (10:18–20), had ever been made for any other kingdom. He soaked himself in splendour.

We know that Solomon was a man of prayer and a follower of the true God, but he was neither the first nor the last to be seduced from the path of pure virtue by things that are tempting but ultimately worthless.

Lord, preserve those with leading roles in the Church from the folly of believing their own publicity and being drawn aside by glittering trifles.

HE APPRECIATED THE MYSTERY OF GOD

2 Chronicles 5:13—6:1 (NIV)

The trumpeters and singers joined in unison as with one voice, to give praise and thanks to the Lord. Accompanied by trumpets, cymbals and other instruments, they raised their voices in praise to the Lord and sang: 'He is good; his love endures for ever.' Then the temple of the Lord was filled with a cloud, and the priests could not perform their service because of the cloud, for the glory of the Lord filled the temple of God. Then Solomon said, 'The Lord has said that he would dwell in a dark cloud.'

This is one of my favourite moments in the Old Testament and there are fascinating ideas to be drawn from it. Today, though, I was reflecting on something said by a bishop on television. I only caught the tail-end of his comments, but it was something about the way in which a desire for immediacy and informality can rob us of an appreciation of the mystery and grandeur of God. It is a difficult tension to maintain, isn't it? We all need the close, uncomplicated love of our heavenly father, the father we are allowed to call 'daddy'. There was a divine ordinariness about the ways of Jesus with vulnerable human beings that, thank God, warms and reassures my heart. The bishop is right, though. In this life we are only able to touch the outermost rim of the farthest edge of the garments of the glory of God. The mystery and splendour of the creator of the universe is as real and as rich as those aspects of him that we do seem to understand.

Here is Solomon, fully in control because he knows that God is as likely to dwell in a dark and mysterious cloud as he is to inhabit the most beautiful dwelling-place constructed by the hands of man.

A small, trusting child confidently clutches his daddy's hand, despite understanding nothing of the big, mysterious world where his father operates. That little world within a much greater universe is all he needs for now. It is a perfectly safe place and how exciting, inspirational and informative it can be to peep out at the mystery and the splendour from a place where no one can hurt the most important part of you.

We trust you, Father.

HE HAD A SENSE OF HISTORY AND DESTINY

1 Kings 8:17–21 (NIV)

'My father David had it in his heart to build a temple for the Name of the Lord, the God of Israel. But the Lord said to my father David, "Because it was in your heart to build a temple for my Name, you did well to have this in your heart. Nevertheless, you are not the one to build the temple, but your son, who is your own flesh and blood—he is the one who will build the temple for my Name." The Lord has kept the promise he made: I have succeeded David my father and now I sit on the throne of Israel, just as the Lord promised, and I have built the temple for the Name of the Lord, the God of Israel. I have provided a place there for the ark, in which is the covenant of the Lord that he made with our fathers when he brought them out of Egypt.'

Given half a chance, I start raving on about metaphorical pendulums and that's what I'm going to do now. There is a serious danger of moving too far in the direction of immediacy and total clarity (don't make me laugh!) in spiritual matters. In some groups and congregations there is a fear that acknowledgment of history and tradition in some way impedes the work of the Holy Spirit. We only need to stop and think clearly for a moment to see that this is nonsense. Jesus himself was at great pains to place himself and his ministry in the context of God's dealings with men and women over the centuries. Also, it would be foolish and ungrateful of us to forget the heroes of faith who have toiled through the years to build the spiritual platforms that we caper about on nowadays.

Let's be aware of our past. Let's understand how the love of God has landed us in this place at this time. Let's enjoy our various traditions and allow them to enrich experiences of the living God who has been present and working in every phase of our history.

Here is Solomon doing exactly that and what a satisfaction one senses in his awareness of the way in which his very special 'today' completes the jigsaw puzzle of the past.

Thank you, Lord, for past, present and future.

HE RECOGNIZED PHYSICAL AND HUMAN LIMITS

1 Kings 8:27–29, 46, 50 (NIV, abridged)

'But will God really dwell on earth? The heavens, even the highest heaven, cannot contain you. How much less this temple I have built! Yet give attention to your servant's prayer and his plea for mercy, O Lord my God. Hear the cry and the prayer that your servant is praying in your presence this day. May your eyes be open towards this temple night and day, this place of which you have said, "My Name shall be there," so that you will hear the prayer your servant prays towards this place... When they sin against you—for there is no one who does not sin—and you become angry with them and give them over to the enemy, who takes them captive to his own land, far away or near... And forgive your people.'

Do read the whole prayer (8:23–53). It is fascinating to see how this realistic king seeks to cover all possible contingencies in his nation's life. He has few blind spots about things or people.

It took Solomon seven years to build that temple, every tiny detail crucially important to him. It was to be an ideal dwelling-place for the creator, the greatest architectural feat in history. Nevertheless, the king acknowledges that God is too vast to be contained within the finest building. He pleads with God, though, to let his eyes be open towards the temple, so that the king's prayers will be heard.

Similarly, he is clear-eyed about human beings. Solomon is not addressing some hypothetical situation in which the people of Israel might sin. He knows that no one can avoid sin and he is pleading in advance for forgiveness and return from exile if that is to be the nation's punishment. Good lessons.

You may spend millions on church buildings. Some are doing exactly that. Those places will not contain God, nor persuade him to be any more present than when he is invited into the single room of a praying pensioner who can no longer leave home.

As for the problem of sin, well, like the poor, it is always with us and that realization should encourage us to be very, very gentle with each other. The temple of the Holy Spirit is being built and rebuilt daily within each one of us.

Dwell in me, a sinner.

HE WAS NOT INSULAR IN HIS THINKING

2 Chronicles 6:32–35 (NIV)

'As for the foreigner who does not belong to your people Israel but has come from a distant land because of your great name and your mighty hand and your outstretched arm—when he comes and prays towards this temple, then hear from heaven, your dwelling-place, and do whatever the foreigner asks of you, so that all the peoples of the earth may know your name and fear you, as do your own people Israel, and may know that this house that I have built bears your Name. When your people go to war against their enemies, wherever you send them, and when they pray to you towards this city you have chosen and the temple I have built for your Name, then hear from heaven their prayer and their plea, and uphold their cause.'

Here is another extract from Solomon's great prayer of dedication, offered before the whole assembly of the people. Perhaps it constitutes a message to them as much as a request to God. The second part of the passage—a prayer that God will uphold the king's army when it is away at war—would have been familiar to those who were listening. Of course it was to be hoped that the righteous pleas of their troops would be heard and granted. The first part, however, is a declaration to all who are present that the God of Israel is likely to listen to the prayers of outsiders, to those who have seen and appreciated the goodness of the Lord and wish to throw themselves on his mercy. The welcoming of strangers was already traditional in Israel, but this was a plea from Solomon that the whole world should come to know and worship the one true God.

How sad to contrast the wide-armed spiritual optimism of this prayer and attitude with the scrunched-up little prejudices that we continue to suffer from in some sections of the modern Church. Even within the Christian faith itself, there are denominations that refuse to have contact with other denominations, let alone with strangers to the faith. How have we allowed this to happen? May the Lord send us leaders who will throw their arms wide like Solomon and pray strangers into the kingdom of God.

Send them, Lord!

HE WAS ASSURED OF GOD'S PRESENCE IN THE TEMPLE

2 Chronicles 7:11–16 (NIV, abridged)

When Solomon had finished the temple... the Lord appeared to him at night and said: 'I have heard your prayer and have chosen this place for myself as a temple for sacrifices. When I shut up the heavens so that there is no rain, or command locusts to devour the land or send a plague among my people, if my people, who are called by my name, will humble themselves and pray and seek my face and turn from their wicked ways, then will I hear from heaven and will forgive their sin and will heal their land. Now my eyes will be open and my ears attentive to the prayers offered in this place. I have chosen and consecrated this temple so that my Name may be there for ever. My eyes and my heart will always be there.'

We don't build temples out of wood and brick and stone any more, do we? Instead, the Bible tells us, we are temples (1 Corinthians 6:19). Each one of us can be a place where God lives. Bearing this in mind, you may find it interesting to read this passage again, as I've just done, and see how it applies as an assurance from God to us as individual Christians.

Bridget and I once hosted an evening on behalf of the Kenward Trust, a Christian organization that offers light at the end of the long dark tunnel of drug and alcohol misuse. It was a highly inspiring evening for us, quite apart from anyone in the audience. Two of the men who have been helped by a residential placement at one of the Kenward houses were up on the stage answering questions about the past, the present and, thank God, the future. Certainly a plague had passed across the lives of these two people, but now they were following Jesus and the healing process was well under way. I am quite sure that God's eyes and ears are open and attentive to the prayers that they offer. Our prayer for them is that his name will be on their lips for the rest of their days.

Father, you are building temples all over the world. May they remain strong and beautiful and may your eyes and heart be always with them.

HE COULD NOT RESIST THE WRONG WOMEN

1 Kings 11:1–4, 9 (NIV)

King Solomon, however, loved many foreign women besides Pharaoh's daughter—Moabites, Ammonites, Edomites, Sidonians and Hittites. They were from nations about which the Lord had told the Israelites, 'You must not intermarry with them, because they will surely turn your hearts after their gods.' Nevertheless, Solomon held fast to them in love. He had 700 wives of royal birth and 300 concubines, and his wives led him astray. As Solomon grew old, his wives turned his heart after other gods, and his heart was not fully devoted to the Lord his God, as the heart of David his father had been... The Lord became angry with Solomon because his heart had turned away from the Lord, the God of Israel, who had appeared to him twice.

(If you can, read the whole of chapter 11.) Oh dear, he was his father's son. As well as inheriting many fine characteristics, Solomon seems to have ended up with one of David's major weaknesses.

Years earlier, on a spring night in the battle season, another king had paced the palace walls, wondering how the battle was going and wishing he was there (2 Samuel 11). He had spied the beautiful figure of Bathsheba, Solomon's mother, and seduced her. In this, and in concealing his adultery with the murder of Uriah, her husband, he had greatly angered God. God forgave David, but his punishment was the dire calamity that came upon him from his own household. David had never worshipped false gods, but sheer lust started trouble in his life.

Solomon fell for the same reason. There's no fool like an old fool, they say and, as Solomon grew elderly, he allowed his foreign wives to seduce him into following the Sidonian Ashtoreth and Molech, the god of the Ammonites. As a result of this treachery, God raised up enemies against him and allowed his son only one tribe of Israel after the king's death.

How could he have done it? How? After all God had given and done for him, how could Solomon, with his riches and his concubines and his hundreds of wives, have been so foolishly wicked as to chase after foreign gods? It beggars belief, but I'm afraid the same sort of thing still happens.

Lord, we are weak and easily tempted. Help us to be strong and obedient in your service.

Cut your losses and let your profits run.

AMERICAN PROVERB

GETTING LOST

SEARCH AND RECOVERY IN THE 15TH CHAPTER OF LUKE

For as long as I can remember I have identified and empathized with people and things that are lost and damaged. In this connection I would like to tell you about two paintings that mean a great deal to me.

In our sitting-room at home hangs a picture that used to be in the centre of the longer wall that faces you as you walk in through the door. It has now been relegated to a corner position on the opposite side, somewhat obscured by the opened door, where it waits, like one of those plain daughters in Victorian fiction, to be noticed by somebody. This relegation is not, I can assure you, a sign of any diminished appreciation on my part, but rather a mildly defensive reaction to the responses of some of our visitors. I have seen so many of them regarding it with bemused stares, rocking back on their heels and pursing their lips as they try to think of something to say. As a matter of fact, I can feel myself delaying an explanation of the actual content of this picture in case you also frown and shake your head in a puzzled, pitying sort of way, and secretly ask yourself if that man who was so good and patient with your sadly afflicted second cousin might be able to offer me a similarly helpful course of treatment.

Oh, all right, I'll tell you—it's a picture of a car.

'Well, what's wrong with that?' I hear many of you say. 'Lots of people develop an interest in transport of various kinds, and whilst we may not actually share that particular interest we fully understand why, in your own home, you would want to hang a—'

No—hold on, you don't understand. This isn't one of those meticulously executed, full-colour representations of an XP47 Cougar Vincenzo with streamlined triple-vaning and double overhead camshaft

—I can't imagine anything more boring—no, this is something quite different. This is a broken-down, abandoned small vehicle of the Mini Traveller type, the sort with wooden frames around the windows, and it appears to have been dumped at the edge of a field. In fact, it must have been there for some time, because the undergrowth has crept up around the wheels and lower chassis, and the back doors are open and hanging crazily from twisted hinges. In the background an ominously dark wood seems to be waiting to swallow up the remains of what might once have been someone's pride and joy. It is a very sad little car indeed.

The unspoken, and occasionally spoken, question from a number of our guests has been: 'Why? Why on earth do you want a picture of a dead car on your wall, a car that will certainly remain unmended, a useless heap of metal and wood that will never again fulfil its original function?'

Ah, but that's exactly the point, you see. Having been in a broken down state myself, and having worked for many years with children who had been abandoned and despaired of, and having encountered a God who specializes in taking lost, broken things and miraculously restoring them to working order, I find my picture immensely inspiring. It's a bit like having a picture of Jesus on the cross, only less oppressive. That old car (and it is a brilliantly executed piece of work, by the way) is a constant reminder to me that nothing and nobody is beyond rescue and redemption in the kingdom of God.

I feel a bit guilty about bowing to the pressure of opinion as far as the position of my picture is concerned, but you should see what I've hung on that long wall in its place! As visitors enter now they are confronted by a large charcoal drawing of Jacqueline Du Pré, a shining talent who, as a result of illness and depression, became as lost and broken as the Mini Traveller that humbly awaits a little attention on the wall behind my sitting-room door.

The second picture—well, just thinking about the second picture brings back feelings of great excitement and anticipation. It isn't hanging anywhere in our house as I write, because we're going to take it into town to be valued as soon as we get a bit of spare time, but I'd love to see it on our bedroom wall, for instance, once that's been done. This is the story that lies behind it.

After my mother died at the end of 1996 my brothers and I set about the dismal task of disposing of all her belongings, including various items that must have been lying around in the loft for years. This collection included three or four dusty old religious pictures of the bleeding-heart variety, a genre which I have personally always found vaguely repellent. One or two of them were encased in quite impressive frames, but the general feeling was that they should be dumped, and because Bridget and I offered to do the dumping, they all ended up at our house, victims, as the days went by, of the chronic Plass inability to get things done with any urgency.

One evening, sitting in the kitchen on my own, I found myself idly wondering whether it might be worth removing the pictures and hanging on to the frames. Picking up one of the largest, I tore off the backing paper and found, to my intense interest, that a second, smaller picture had been used as a support for the picture that actually appeared behind the glass. Examining my discovery, I found that it was a photograph of rocks and sea, probably cut from a magazine many years ago and stuck onto a piece of card. Valueless, no doubt, but you can imagine the eagerness with which I picked up the next example of religious excess and ripped away the backing to see if anything inter-esting might be concealed underneath. Nor was I disappointed. This time I pulled out a print, dated just after the turn of the century, mass-produced and, again, probably worthless, but you can imagine how excited I was by now. I felt as though I had walked unexpectedly into an Aladdin's cave. Who could tell what I might come across next?

The third picture was smaller than the other two, but it looked older, and was, if anything, even more representative of that depressingly grim style of religious art that abounded in the Victorian age. This time I savoured each step in the process, slitting the crackling, fragile old brown paper carefully around the edge of the frame before bending back each of the nails that had held the picture in place for so many years. Holding my breath, I lifted out the sheet of card that formed the next layer and turned it over. There in front of me, in its own card frame, was an enchanting little original painting of a seaside scene, done in what my uneducated eye took to be watercolours. Looking more closely at the corner of the painting I saw that the artist had written the date 1879, and that the setting was Bournemouth. There was no signature. More than a century ago someone, feeling that this small picture was dispensable, had sealed it up inside the larger one, and mine were the first eyes to see it since then.

Whether or not this jewel of a find turns out to have any monetary value, I shall always love the fact that something so precious and attractive was hidden for so long behind such a garishly distorted portrayal of the Christian faith. Do forgive the obvious parallel, but it seems such a clear picture of how the sweet, strong reality of Jesus continues to be itself, however many mistakes the Church as an institution might make. And it is also a reminder to all of us that Jesus hides the most important part of what we are within himself, ready to be revealed to his Father when the right moment comes.

Our God is the God of the damaged and the lost.

Prayer

Father, as we walk with you, we pray for all those people who have become lost and hurt along the way. We all know some people like that, Lord. Some of us are those people. Thankfully, you know where the lost ones have got to and what's happening to them, so we ask that, if there are ways in which we can be helpful in bringing them back to the right path or healing their hurts, we won't chicken out of making uninviting detours, nor make religious excuses for avoiding heavenly tasks.

Thank you so much, Lord Jesus, that you have hidden each one of us, your valuable works of art, safely within yourself. Sometimes we wonder how the public face of your Church can possibly represent the person that you are, but we know that you are always working from inside to change things for the better. Help us to be courageous and faithful in helping you to accomplish this.

BUT WE'RE CHRISTIANS!

Luke 15:1–3 (NJB)

The tax collectors and sinners, however, were all crowding round to listen to him, and the Pharisees and Scribes complained saying, 'This man welcomes sinners and eats with them.'

When I do an evening of 'funny stuff' for a church or group of churches, the event is usually well attended, I'm pleased to say. People love to laugh, and if there's a serious thought or two thrown in as well, they seem to accept that quite happily. When, however, I have been involved in concerns to raise money or consciousness for AIDS sufferers, or Prison Fellowship, or Third World poverty, the attendance has been considerably lower.

The material I use is exactly the same, but there seems to be a reluctance to come close to these sorts of issues, even in such an in-direct way. Some folk have quite openly expressed their distaste for any Christian activity connected with AIDS, and Prison Fellowship is consistently underfunded and poorly supported, despite the fact that they do some marvellous work.

Not many Christians want to get their hands dirty, but those who do see miracles sometimes. Jesus didn't stay at the Jewish Hilton and make evangelistic visits to sinners. He was with them—eating with them, making real friends with them, telling stories, answering questions, untainted but fully involved. The scribes and Pharisees couldn't stand it, just as some people still can't stand it nowadays.

Recently, a friend of mind came out of prison and was looking for lodgings in a nearby town. We found an establishment listed in the local directory as a 'Christian hotel'. When I phoned the number and explained what was needed the lady on the other end of the line said, 'Well, I'm not sure. We do have to be very careful who we take, because we are a Christian hotel, you see...'

God help us as a church, if we're saying, 'We do have to be very careful who we take, because we are a Christian church, you see...'

Do we make real friends with those we don't approve of? Are we ready to get our hands dirty in God's service? Read Matthew 25:31–46.

SHEPHERDS OR POLICEMEN?

Luke 15:4 (NJB)

'Which one of you with a hundred sheep, if he lost one, would fail to leave the ninety-nine in the desert and go after the missing one till he found it?'

Here, Jesus is asking the scribes and Pharisees to take a 180 degree turn in their attitude to sinners. From scolding to caring; from abandoning to searching out; from indifference to love.

Some years ago one of our major universities undertook studies into the nature and components of successful counselling. After much research, observation and discussion, three major factors were identified as essential characteristics of an effective counsellor. They were as follows:

1. The effective counsellor must be willing to enter the world of his client.
2. He must not be condemnatory of the person he is counselling.
3. He must value that person demonstrably.

A little reflection might have saved that university an awful lot of time and trouble. Two thousand years ago Jesus (who is sometimes called the Mighty Counsellor) entered our world, not to condemn us, but to show how much he valued us by dying on that horrible cross.

I wonder how the scribes and Pharisees coped with a suggestion that they should be shepherds rather than policemen; that it was worth an enormous expenditure of time and effort to seek out just one of those grubby little sinners and save him from the consequences of his separation from God.

Some years ago I was a lost sheep myself, despite the fact that I had been a Christian for more than 20 years. Emotionally distraught, out of work, and no longer attending a church, I said to my wife one day that if there was a God who loved me he could come and help, and if there wasn't, it didn't matter anyway. The good shepherd heard my bleat and came, particularly through certain friends who worked for the shepherd, rather than the religious police force.

Thank you for coming into our world, Jesus. I'd like to help you in your search. Show me something specific that I can do.

SEARCHING WITH TEARS

Luke 15:5–7 (NJB)

'And when he found it, would he not joyfully take it on his shoulders and then, when he got home, call together his friends and neighbours saying to them, "Rejoice with me, I have found my sheep that was lost." In the same way, I tell you, there will be more rejoicing in heaven over one sinner repenting than over ninety-nine upright people who have no need of repentance.'

When my youngest son, David, was a little boy, we went to Cornwall for a family holiday. One afternoon we decided to spend some time on the beach at Newquay. After an hour or so of sandcastle building, paddling and ice-cream consumption, we realized that David was missing. An hour later, after searching every square yard of the beach, we could still find no trace of him. Bridget, my wife, was pacing aimlessly up and down the beach, tears in her eyes, desperately hoping that the small figure would appear.

Meanwhile, I made my way to the lifeguard point and asked the young man on duty to call David over the public address system. That didn't work either. A great darkness began to settle over my heart. My mouth had dried up and I was unable to keep my eyes from the thin white line where the sea met the shore. I was terrified. It must have been half an hour later when the friend who was with us on the beach found David playing quietly on the sand two hundred yards or so from where we had last seen him. The relief and joy in our little party was palpable. I hoisted David up on to my shoulders and carried him back to the car.

Jesus wanted his listeners to understand that his search for the lost —the shepherd's search for his sheep—is conducted with even more passion and urgency than our desperate hunt for David on that summer day. No wonder they rejoice in heaven when one sinner repents. God is crackers about us.

Jesus searches for us with tears in his eyes. When he finds us, the whole of heaven goes bonkers with happiness.

SHARING SORROW AND JOY

Luke 15:8–10 (NJB)

'Or again, what woman with ten drachmas would not, if she lost one, light a lamp and sweep out the house and search thoroughly till she found it? And then, when she had found it, call together her friends and neighbours, saying to them, "Rejoice with me, I have found the drachma I lost." In the same way, I tell you, there is rejoicing among the angels of God over one repentant sinner.'

This story (presumably told so that contemporary ladies could get the point of the sheep story) reminds me of the occasion when Bridget lost all our holiday money when she was pushing one of the children round the shops at Hailsham. She rang me at work to pass on the bad news and was clearly astonished by the calm and muted manner with which I responded.

'OK, Bridget,' I purred soothingly, 'not to worry—I'll sort it out somehow. It's only money…' Little did Bridget know that this warm act of forgiveness and understanding was solely attributable to the fact that I was surrounded by a little circle of childcare trainees who had been enduring my views on the need for warmth and forgiveness in dealing with kids in care. When I arrived home later I discovered that the money had been found and returned to Bridget, so I was able to perpetuate the myth of my tolerance and generosity of spirit.

We certainly rejoiced together over the return of that cash, but we didn't invite any neighbours in to share our joy. Perhaps that is one of the lessons of this little parable. We are not very good at inviting others into the centre of our joys and our tragedies. Births, weddings, house-warmings and deaths tend to be the only occasions when this happens in grey old England. But we are the body of Christ, and we belong to each other. Some of the warmest and most memorable moments in the history of the little house-group that Bridget and I lead have been the times when individuals have made a gift to the rest of us of quite small joys and sorrows. This kind of sharing often requires an act of the will.

Father, I'm not really very good at giving my life to other people. Please help me to be more generous and courageous.

A STORY OF GOD

Luke 15:11–13 (NJB)

Then he said, 'There was a man who had two sons. The younger one said to his Father, "Father, let me have the share of the estate that will come to me." So the father divided the property between them. A few days later, the younger son got together everything he had and left for a distant country where he squandered his money on a life of debauchery.'

The Bible tells us that Jesus used stories all the time in his contacts with the crowds who flocked to hear him. Now, I happen to know, as a feeble but committed storyteller myself, that the best stories are the ones that are based on fact—things that have really happened to me or to people I know. This famous story has the same ring of truth about it. During that invaluable period of 16 years or so, when he was (presumably) a working carpenter, Jesus must have put together a sizeable mental portfolio of memories and anecdotes. This is probably one of them. I wish there was more storytelling and less preaching in the Church these days.

I have often wondered why the prodigal left home so deliberately. Unlike sheep and drachmas, he didn't get lost—he went. Perhaps he looked at his elder brother, po-faced, aridly virtuous and miserable, and decided anything was better than ending up like that. It seems more likely, though, that he made the common mistake of separating the gifts from the giver. It can take a long time to realize that we have lost touch with the springs of our own joy and pleasure, and the process can be a subtle one. Some Christians, convinced that they are working for God, arrange religious activities that seem quite laudable, but if those activities don't have their roots in the will of God they are going to bloom once, then die.

The prodigal is incapable, at this stage, of realizing that as the good things flow away from him, nothing else will flow in to replace them—not as long as he is away from home, that is. The principle holds good for all of us.

Jesus took his life, rolled it up in a ball and gave it to us. He lost the life he loved, so that we would never be hungry. Maybe it's best to work from home...

STUCK IN A PIGSTY

Luke 15:14–16a (NJB)

'When he had spent it all, that country experienced a severe famine, and now he began to feel the pinch; so he hired himself out to one of the local inhabitants who put him on his farm to feed the pigs. And he would willingly have filled himself with the husks the pigs were eating but no one would let him have them.'

Much of my early working life was spent caring for children in trouble. Some of them came from appalling backgrounds, and, inevitably, I came into contact with many of the parents of these confused teenagers. I met wives who had endured continual battering from their husbands, and men who had served frequent sentences in prison as a result of their consistently inexpert criminal activities. The children themselves were often locked into patterns of behaviour that had never brought them anything but negative responses.

Again and again I was struck by the apparent inability of unhappy people to explore alternatives in lifestyle or behaviour that would immediately make a difference. Why stay with a man who beats you up every other day? Why persist in acts of petty crime when the police catch you every time? It was only when I reached a point of intolerable pain and had to make an involuntary withdrawal from work and church that I realized I was exactly the same. I had completely ignored the need to tackle some very obvious problems in my own life.

The prodigal son in this story is just the same. His descent from riches and riotous living to the ignominy of the pigs must have been a relatively gradual one. He could have made the decision to go home at any stage, but he seems to have been unaware of this option until he reached a point where his need was so great that he had to consider any alternative.

Lots of us are blinkered to obvious needs in our lives, and others usually see where we are heading long before we come to our senses. Prayer, sensitivity and practical help could prevent a few of us from hitting rock-bottom.

Father, take the blinkers away so that we can see the changes that need to be made in our lives. If there are people known to us who are heading for disaster, give us the sensitivity and wisdom to help them.

AT LEAST I'LL EAT...

Luke 15:16b–19 (NJB)

'Then he came to his senses and said, "How many of my father's hired men have all the food they want and more, and here am I dying of hunger! I will leave this place and go to my father and say: 'Father, I have sinned against heaven and against you; I no longer deserve to be called your son; treat me as one of your hired men.'" So he left the place and went back to his father.'

Let's not get too sentimental about this lad. No doubt he has some very warm and nostalgic memories of home. But his primary motivation for returning is an eminently sane and practical one. He wants some food. He is hungry. He is lacking the fuel that sustains life at its most basic level. Sin isn't much fun when you're dying of starvation.

Coming to our senses in a spiritual sense is a very similar experience. When worldly distractions lose their potency and props are snapped or fatally weakened, men and women know suddenly that their spirits are thin and emaciated. Only the bread of life can make any difference to this sort of terminal malnutrition.

It is worth mentioning, though, to those who are dithering about whether to leave the pigs or not, that this God who is offering sustenance is the one who created kites, and sex, and good wine, and spring flowers, and children's eyes. Coming home to him will not just be survival—it could turn out to be an awful lot of fun.

I can easily picture this 'oik' of a prodigal—a sort of New Testament Baldrick—crawling up the road towards home, rehearsing his little set speech over and over again, boldly perhaps, and then with cringing humility, hoping to strike a note that will be effective with a potentially furious parent. Most of us expect very little from God, especially if, like myself, we have been encouraged at an early stage to look at ourselves as miserable, crawling, verminous little creatures, tolerated by God, but only when he holds his nose and averts his eyes. The prodigal wasn't expecting much, but he was in for a shock.

For those who are thinking of starting the journey back to the Father, we pray for courage. If there's anything we can do to help, please show us clearly, so that we don't mess things up.

A HURRICANE OF LOVE

Luke 15:20–21 (NJB)

'While he was still a long way off, his father saw him and was moved with pity. He ran to the boy, clasped him in his arms and kissed him. Then his son said, "Father, I have sinned against heaven and against you. I no longer deserve to be called your son."'

I have annoyed some of my evangelical friends occasionally by telling them of an acquaintance who came to his Christian faith as a result of attending classes in Buddhism. After obediently emptying his mind of almost everything that normally occupied it, he found that Jesus filled the mental vacuum that remained. Eventually he cancelled the Buddhist classes, joined a local church and made a commitment to Christ.

The same thing happens to the prodigal son in this story. He is a 'long way off' when his father spots him (probably from an upstairs window) and can hardly have expected such an early response. Too often the attitude of Christians to their non-believing acquaintances reminds me of the old joke about a country yokel who is asked for directions by a traveller.

'Well,' says the yokel, 'Oi wouldn't start from 'ere if I was you...'

God knows where people are and when he should meet them. Sometimes they come along very strange roads indeed.

Here we see the dear old prodigal hit by a hurricane as he lopes along, learning his little speech by heart as he goes. The hurricane is his father, of course, overjoyed to see the son he has always loved so much, and not ashamed to sprint down the road, holding his robes up with one hand. What an extraordinarily vulnerable picture of God that is.

With his father's arms wrapped round his head, the surprised prodigal manages to bleat out a muffled version of the set speech he's been rehearsing. His repentance is embraced with joy. Repentance and forgiveness are not opposite ends of the spectrum. They are parts of the same joyful experience.

We know nothing about how and when God will call and meet people. Our job is to be obedient and carry out orders, however strange they may seem sometimes.

SO HAPPY YOU'RE HOME!

Luke 15:22–24 (NJB)

'But the father said to his servants, "Quick! Bring out the best robe and put it on him; put a ring on his finger and sandals on his feet. Bring the calf we have been fattening, and kill it; we will celebrate by having a feast, because this son of mine was dead and has come back to life; he was lost and is found." And they began to celebrate.'

Having children of my own has taught me more about the fatherhood of God than anything else. When one of my children is naughty I feel an intensity of love towards him or her that yearns for a resolution of the problem. I don't mean that I never lose my temper or act irrationally (such a claim would qualify me for a degree in hypocrisy). But I do greet them, when they stumble through the apology barrier, as if they had never done anything wrong. It's so nice to have them back!

What a surprise for the prodigal. He would have settled for three meals a day and a bed in the barn. Instead he's covered with gifts and told that there's going to be a party to celebrate his return. The fragile little pose that he'd prepared for this first big encounter would hardly have been proof against such extravagant, limitless generosity. The face would have crumpled, a tear or two would have appeared—Daddy really wanted him back.

I met a modern prodigal in Australia once, a man who ran away from home when he was 14, and didn't return until he was nearly 20. He planned to drive home in style to surprise his Dad. But on the way his car broke down. He had to ring his parents for help. The stylish return lost some of its dignity as the young man was towed home in a lifeless vehicle by his beaming father. Lots of people break down on their way back to God. Don't worry if it happens to you—he'll come and get you.

Thank you for loving us so much when we are naughty. I wish I really knew how much you like to be with me. I still break down from time to time. Please rescue me when it happens.

FURIOUS!

Luke 15:25–28a (NJB)

'Now the elder son was out in the fields, and on his way back, as he drew near the house, he could hear music and dancing. Calling one of the servants he asked what it was all about. The servant told him, "Your brother has come, and your father has killed the calf we had been fattening because he has got him back safe and sound." He was angry then and refused to go in…'

People often ask me if the characters in my books are based on real individuals. They are particularly interested in a couple called Stenneth and Victoria Flushpool, self-appointed moral watchdogs in the imaginary church community that we encounter in *The Sacred Diary of Adrian Plass*. Do they really exist? I refuse to answer that question on the grounds that it may incriminate me, but I can tell you that people from different places all over the country claim that I must have visited their church before writing the book, because the Flushpools (under another name) are definitely members of their congregation.

One thing is sure; no one has ever openly identified himself or herself with any negative character of the Flushpool variety. Perhaps some defensive mechanism prevents such recognition. I wonder if the Pharisees and scribes recognized themselves in the elder brother of the prodigal story? These ancient Jewish Flushpools hated to see sinners relaxing with Jesus. Like the prodigal's miserable sibling, they had never taken the trouble to discover the true nature of the God whom they claimed to serve. They could have had a party if they'd wanted—they never asked.

Watch out for Flushpools in the church. They coax people into conversion, then tell them off afterwards because they're not perfect immediately; they elevate man-made activities onto a sacred level; they mistrust laughter and relaxation; they are stern and unhappy.

We must pray for them—especially if we are them…

We pray for relaxation and joy throughout your Church, Father. Forgive us for allowing religious activities to atrophy and become meaningless. Help us to be shepherds rather than policemen.

COME TO THE PARTY!

Luke 28b–30 (NJB)

'And his father came out and began to urge him to come in; but he retorted to his father, "All these years I have slaved for you and never once disobeyed any orders of yours, yet you never offered me so much as a kid for me to celebrate with my friends. But, for this son of yours, when he comes back after swallowing up your property—he and his loose women—you kill the calf we had been fattening."'

Do you sulk? I do. It is recorded elsewhere that I am a master of the shuddering sigh, the kind that indicates profound suffering, bravely borne. The whole point of a sulk is that you advertise your misery, and then refuse comfort or help when it's offered. My wife ruins my best sulks by tickling me.

Here we see the elder brother locked into a monster sulk. Hanging about outside the life and light of his brother's party he is clearly hoping that his father will come and plead with him to come in. That will give him the opportunity to refuse. Sure enough, out comes Dad, anxious that his other son should share the fun, the joy, and the fatted calf. The resentful lad pours out his anger and hurt at this point, unable to contain himself any longer.

Many Christians would be able to identify with this deep, stress-filled anger towards God. I met a bank manager once who, years ago, prayed for his younger brother to be healed from a terminal illness. The brother died, and the resulting disappointment and fury remained unexpressed for decades.

Strange as it may sound, many of us need to forgive God for what he has done to us, or failed to do for us. Of course, we know that he can't really have got it wrong, but that doesn't take the hurt away. Let's climb up on his lap and cry out our frustration and pain. Let's beat our fists against his chest like small children and let him see our confused passion.

He can handle it. He will put his arms round us until our anger dissolves in tears, and we realize that he loves us after all, and always did.

Father, if there are unresolved issues between us, I'd like to face them and sort them out. It's very hard to argue with someone who's perfect, but I do feel angry with you sometimes. Help me to express my feelings to you and trust your response.

GETTING IT RIGHT

Luke 15:31–32 (NJB)

'The father said, "My son, you are with me always and all I have is yours. But it was only right we should celebrate and rejoice, because your brother here was dead and has come to life; he was lost and is found."'

The elder brother has the same problem as many Christians in this age. He simply cannot understand that families at their best operate on the same principle as the Three Musketeers—'all for one and one for all'. When one is happy everyone rejoices, and when one mourns, the rest mourn with him or her.

The apostle Paul (who never read Dumas, but must have met him by now) put it rather differently. He said that each of us is part of Christ's body on earth, and that all parts, including the unusual ones, are vital to the function of the whole.

I used to belong to a Bible-study group which included a lady who made superb cakes, and a man who had a deep understanding and appreciation of God's forgiveness. We shared the cake and the forgiveness with equal enthusiasm, and we did not insist that the cake maker should have hands laid on her to increase her sense of forgiveness. Nor did we send the man off for an intensive course in cake making. Over the past couple of decades there has been a lot of emphasis on individual spiritual success. Articles entitled 'Washing up the Christian Way' and 'Carpet-laying in the Spirit' have implied that every aspect of life must be victoriously and overtly claimed for God. Perhaps there is some truth in that, but how much more important it is that we share, value and appropriate each other's talents and blessings, and that we add our strength to the carrying of each other's burdens.

The elder brother got it wrong. The scribes and Pharisees got it wrong. Perhaps we could have a shot at getting it right.

Perhaps we have undervalued some people because their gifts or perceptions do not come high on our list of priorities. Perhaps we hug what we have and are to ourselves, instead of letting it belong to the body. Let's take a fresh look at the people around us.

*The first and fundamental law of nature is
to seek peace and follow it.*

THOMAS HOBBES, *LEVIATHAN*, 1

LONG ROAD TO REUNION
JACOB

The story of Jacob is one of those Old Testament epics of which most people have 'edited' or muddled memories. 'Something to do with some soup and being hairy or not hairy or something? Doesn't he climb a ladder and wrestle with a bloke who turns out to be God? I seem to remember a bit about speckled goats or am I going completely mad?'

If these are the sorts of things that spring to your mind, don't worry because you are absolutely right, except that there are other things as well. There are two sisters—one beautiful and shapely, the other rather plain with some sort of eye condition. They both want Jacob and they both get him. Mind you, he gets both of them as well, which is perhaps not quite as wonderful as it might seem. There is the story of a callous rape and a truly excruciating, eye-watering revenge wreaked on the guilty party by the enraged brothers of the victim. There is an account of a strange, tumultuous night and a tale of deep, deep fear in the heart of a changed man—fear that the darkness of the past will blot out the light of possible reconciliation—and a burst of joy when that fear is not realized. Most important of all, this is the story of God working hard to turn Jacob into Israel, a father of his people and the man after whom the chosen people of God were to be named.

So, where do we start? After being cheated out of his father's blessing by Jacob, Esau is planning to kill his brother in revenge. These readings begin at the point where Jacob has decided to leave home while he is still in one piece. His mother Rebekah has advised him to travel to Haran to seek refuge and a new home with Laban, her brother, and so Jacob leaves Beersheba. (Do also read the section indicated in brackets before reading the printed extract and the note. Get the full scope of the story and, above all, enjoy it.)

STAIRWAY TO HEAVEN

Genesis 28:10–15 (NIV, abridged)

Jacob left Beersheba and set out for Haran. When he reached a certain place, he stopped for the night because the sun had set. Taking one of the stones there, he put it under his head and lay down to sleep. He had a dream in which he saw a stairway resting on the earth, with its top reaching to heaven, and the angels of God were ascending and descending on it. There above it stood the Lord, and he said: 'I am the Lord, the God of your father Abraham and the God of Isaac. I will give you and your descendants the land on which you are lying. Your descendants will be like the dust of the earth, and you will spread out to the west and to the east, to the north and to the south... I am with you and will watch over you wherever you go, and I will bring you back to this land. I will not leave you until I have done what I have promised you.'

Do you think Jacob really laid his head on a stone? Bearing in mind that they ate a lot of cheese in those days as well, it's not surprising that he had such extraordinary dreams!

I wish I could stop feeling so envious of these biblical characters who had such vivid and inspiring messages from God. I mean, this is real Warner Brothers stuff, isn't it? A stairway to heaven with angels processing grandly up and down as they conducted their business between earth and heaven. At the top, God himself waiting to offer the sleeping Jacob some mind-boggling promises. It certainly beats the kind of thing we tend to hear nowadays, doesn't it? 'I sort of have a feeling that the Lord might sort of be saying that maybe I ought to sort of do something or other, but I could easily be wrong.'

I suppose we must conclude that, in this or any other age, God will communicate whatever needs to be communicated in the best way possible. Having said that, it may well be that the low level of our expectations militates against the kinds of encounters with God that we read about here. I have a feeling in my gut (a theological expression) that my expectations are low in just about every area of the faith that means so much to me. I would love to be open to more.

Remove the veil, Lord.

BETHEL

Genesis 28:16–22

When Jacob awoke from his sleep, he thought, 'Surely the Lord is in this place, and I was not aware of it.' He was afraid and said, 'How awesome is this place! This is none other than the house of God; this is the gate of heaven.' Early the next morning Jacob took the stone he had placed under his head and set it up as a pillar and poured oil on top of it. He called that place Bethel, though the city used to be called Luz. Then Jacob made a vow, saying, 'If God will be with me and will watch over me on this journey I am taking and will give me food to eat and clothes to wear so that I return safely to my father's house, then the Lord will be my God and this stone that I have set up as a pillar will be God's house, and of all that you give me I will give you a tenth.'

Some years ago, in a book called *The Final Boundary* (HarperCollins, 1990, 2000), I wrote a story about a snail called Bethel. At the time I had no idea what the word actually meant. I am intrigued to learn, on studying this passage, that it actually means 'House of God'—a fitting definition in the context of my story. I'm pleased. It's like something clicking into place.

Something certainly clicked into place for Jacob. God had promised him and his descendants a spectacular future and absolute security for as long as it took for those promises to be kept. I find Jacob's response interesting and a little amusing. He was impressed and awed by what had happened, but that didn't stop him from setting out the terms of the contract in a manner that can only be described as 'businesslike'. God's side of the bargain was to provide protection, food, clothing and an eventual safe return. If all these things were forthcoming, Jacob would accept the Lord as his God, undertake that the stone he had set up would be God's house and, practical to the last, would give back to God a tenth of everything that he was given.

This is not the evangelical way, is it? Or is it?

It wouldn't do some of us any harm to set out clearly what we can do for God in return for what he has done for us.

THICKER THAN WATER

Genesis 29:9–14 (NIV) (Read also vv. 1–8)

While he was still talking with them, Rachel came with her father's sheep, for she was a shepherdess. When Jacob saw Rachel daughter of Laban, his mother's brother, and Laban's sheep, he went over and rolled the stone away from the mouth of the well and watered his uncle's sheep. Then Jacob kissed Rachel and began to weep aloud. He had told Rachel that he was a relative of her father and a son of Rebekah. So she ran and told her father. As soon as Laban heard the news about Jacob, his sister's son, he hurried to meet him. He embraced him and kissed him and brought him to his home, and there Jacob told him all these things. Then Laban said to him, 'You are my own flesh and blood.'

There used to be a television series called *Surprise, Surprise!* The programme drew huge audiences, largely because it specialized in bringing together relatives who had not met for years and feared that they might never meet again. Mothers were suddenly confronted with long-lost sons. Brothers were reunited after a lifetime of separation. Grandmothers were able to cuddle the grandchildren who, until then, had been voices on the telephone or photographs in the post. I was always annoyed with myself for crying when I watched this programme because that is exactly what the programme makers intended me to do. I'm just a softy.

When I read this passage, I find, again, that there are tears in my eyes about something that happened thousands of years ago to a man called Jacob. It isn't even as if Jacob has met cousin Rachel or Uncle Laban before. It must have been wonderful, though, mustn't it, after travelling so far, to discover people who were a part of him, linked by blood and by all the ties of family.

I have travelled quite a lot over the last couple of decades and I cannot begin to tell you what a difference it has made to meet up with members of my family in strange and perhaps slightly threatening places. I thank God for them, just as Jacob must have thanked God for Rachel and Laban at a time when his future looked uncertain, to say the least.

Thank you so much that we belong to someone. Our hearts go out to those who don't.

THE OTHER WOMAN

Genesis 29:18–25 (NIV, abridged) (Read also vv. 14–17, 26–30)

Jacob was in love with Rachel and said, 'I'll work for you seven years in return for your youngest daughter Rachel.' … So Jacob served seven years to get Rachel, but they seemed like only a few days to him because of his love for her. Then Jacob said to Laban, 'Give me my wife. My time is completed, and I want to lie with her.' So Laban brought together all the people of the place and gave a feast. But when evening came, he took his daughter Leah and gave her to Jacob, and Jacob lay with her. And Laban gave his servant girl Zilpah to his daughter as her maidservant. When morning came, there was Leah! So Jacob said to Laban, 'What is this you have done to me?'

If I could transport myself through time to this exact point in the history of Israel, I would take two presents for Jacob. The first would be a portable CD player (with plenty of batteries, for obvious reasons) and the other would be a Rolling Stones album that includes a track with enormous relevance to his situation. For several days, wives, workers, sheep and goats would hear nothing from the inside of Jacob's tent but the rasping petulance of Mick Jagger's voice singing, 'You can't always get what you wa-ant!'

A tinge of malice in my motivation? Yes. After all, he had it coming, didn't he? The con-man had been soundly conned, so it is difficult to feel great sympathy for him. Apart from anything else, Jacob seems to have slept with Leah without any inkling at all that she was the wrong woman. This means, if we are to believe the contrast in the descriptions of the two girls, either that Jacob was so drunk after the feast that he was incapable of telling the difference or that he invested an absolute minimum of verbal and emotional communication in the consummation of his marriage. I suppose the seven-year wait might explain that.

What goes around comes around. Jacob would have understood that very modern saying. Perhaps he would have hung it above his bed to meditate on as he listened to Mick telling him what he already knew.

You can't always get what you want, even if God is on your side.

MARRYING SISTERS!

Genesis 30:1–6 (NIV) (Read also 29:31–35; 30:7–24)

When Rachel saw that she was not bearing Jacob any children, she became jealous of her sister. So she said to Jacob, 'Give me children, or I'll die!' Jacob became angry with her and said, 'Am I in the place of God, who has kept you from having children?' Then she said, 'Here is Bilhah, my maidservant. Sleep with her so that she can bear children for me and that through her I too can build a family.' So she gave him her servant Bilhah as a wife. Jacob slept with her, and she became pregnant and bore him a son. Then Rachel said, 'God has vindicated me; he has listened to my plea and given me a son.'

Friends of mine had two girls. The older girl was physically attractive, with a natural grace in her movements and the most beautiful dark eyes. The younger was plainer, but brighter and more tomboyish—a lively presence. I liked them both and I was amazed when their father said he couldn't wait to have at least one taken off his hands.

'But they're lovely girls,' I said. 'Why would you want rid of them?'

'It's all right for you,' he said darkly. 'You don't live with them. They've shared a bedroom all their lives and they'll have to go on doing that right up to when the first one leaves home, if that ever happens, which I doubt! Their arguing and bickering and fights and borrowing each other's stuff and—and all the other things that happen are just about driving me round the bend.'

'Well, they're very nice when they're out,' I said, trying to cheer him up a little.

'I'm afraid,' he said, 'that has ceased to be a comfort.'

My suffering friend should have written this bit about Rachel and Leah. He would have understood. What an extraordinary catalogue of conflicts and collisions is recorded here. Babies, servants, mandrakes, jealousy, anger. Being the father of two daughters can obviously be problematic, but marrying two forceful sisters—one beautiful and one plain—it doesn't bear thinking about.

There never was some shining, biblical, ideal world. People are people, and ever more shall be so.

DIRTY WORK

Genesis 30:31–35 (NIV, abridged) (Read also vv. 25–30)

'What shall I give you?' he [Laban] asked. 'Don't give me anything,' Jacob replied. 'But if you will do this one thing for me, I will go on tending your flocks and watching over them: Let me go through all your flocks today and remove from them every speckled or spotted sheep, every dark-coloured lamb and every spotted or speckled goat. They will be my wages. And my honesty will testify for me in the future, whenever you check on the wages you have paid me. Any goat in my possession that is not speckled or spotted, or any lamb that is not dark-coloured, will be considered stolen.' 'Agreed,' said Laban, 'Let it be as you have said.' That same day he removed all the male goats that were streaked or spotted, and all the speckled or spotted female goats (all that had white on them) and all the dark-coloured lambs, and he placed them in the care of his sons.

This Laban character makes Robert Maxwell look like an angel of light. What a twister!

You might remember a television series called *Minder*. The central character was called Arthur Daley. Arthur lived by buying items that were cheap and useless and selling them for as much as he could possibly get. His idea of satisfaction was to end each day with a pocket full of other people's money and the knowledge that he had given nothing to anyone. His promises were worthless. Occasionally, a victim of this chronic double-dealing would seek revenge. Usually Arthur avoided retribution by the skin of his teeth.

Jacob must have been tempted to seek revenge on his devious relative as soon as he realized that he had been cheated. In 14 years of hard work he had hugely increased the wealth of his uncle, but in terms of his own personal wealth, he had nothing. Fortunately, instead of letting his anger overwhelm him, he seems to have hung on to God's promises and, as we shall see tomorrow, albeit in a rather bizarre way, God did not let him down.

Father, sometimes we rage at unfairness. Why should we put up with the bad things others do to us without seeking revenge? Help us to follow your agenda when these things happen and to leave the pursuit of justice to you.

TIME TO GO HOME

Genesis 31:3–7, 17–18 (NIV) (Read also vv. 1–2, 8–16, 19–21)

Then the Lord said to Jacob, 'Go back to the land of your fathers and to your relatives, and I will be with you.' So Jacob sent word to Rachel and Leah to come out to the fields where his flocks were. He said to them, 'I see that your father's attitude towards me is not what it was before, but the God of my father has been with me. You know that I've worked for your father with all my strength, yet your father has cheated me by changing my wages ten times. however, God has not allowed him to harm me.' ... Then Jacob put his children and his wives on camels, and he drove all his livestock ahead of him, along with all the goods he had accumulated in Paddan Aram, to go to his father Isaac in the land of Canaan.

During a recent visit to America, someone spoke about the concept of 'terminating friendships'. Apparently it is fashionable in certain quarters to review one's relationships in order to establish whether or not they continue to be positive and productive. If you decide a particular friendship is going nowhere, you may wish to consider the option of informing your 'friend' (face-to-face with courage, by letter or e-mail without) that the relationship must end because it has ceased to be functional. This seems to me one of the worst and most potentially destructive ideas in the entire history of bad ideas, but, as is often the case with over-the-top notions, it does spring from a grain of truth. There are times, hopefully few and far between, when contact with another person may have become so negative, counterproductive or damaging to either or both that it is more helpful to break the connection than to attempt to mend it yet again.

That is what happened with Jacob and Laban. For different reasons, they had had enough of each other. Now was the right time to make the break. Add to this the fact that God had instructed Jacob in a dream to return home and there could be little doubt about what the right course of action was.

Father, the last thing we want is to make silly, hurtful decisions about ending relationships. If a friendship is not good for us, however, and we know you disapprove, give us the courage to act.

LABAN'S LOST LABOURS

Genesis 31:33–37 (NIV) (Read also vv. 22–31, 38–42)

So Laban went into Jacob's tent and into Leah's tent and into the tent of the two maidservants, but he found nothing. After he came out of Leah's tent, he entered Rachel's tent. Now Rachel had taken the household gods and put them inside her camel's saddle and was sitting on them. Laban searched through everything in the tent but found nothing. Rachel said to her father, 'Don't be angry, my Lord, that I cannot stand up in your presence; I'm having my period.' So he searched but could not find the household gods. Jacob was angry and took Laban to task. 'What is my crime?' he asked Laban. 'What sin have I committed that you hunt me down? Now that you have searched through all my goods, what have you found that belongs to your household?'

Some passages of scripture are so rich in life and detail, that our belief in the Bible as, among other things, a record of fact, is revived and refreshed.

Here is a graphic picture of Laban, certain he will find what he wants, but in a state of high tension because Jacob's God has warned him to watch his mouth (v. 24). Into his nephew's tent he goes, flinging stuff around as he hunts these personal 'gods' that he is convinced are hidden somewhere. Nothing! He turns the maidservants' dwelling upside-down, then Leah's and finally he rushes into Rachel's tent, only to find his youngest daughter sitting on her camel's saddle, complaining of period pains. The gods are nowhere to be found in this tent either. Baffled, Laban gives up. Time for Jacob to get something off his chest at last.

'Come on!' he says, passionately righteous because he knows nothing of Rachel's theft and cunning. 'This stuff I've stolen—stick it out here and let's see what everyone thinks about it! Nothing? Right, well I've got one or two things to say to you, Uncle Laban. I've been with you for 20 years now. Your sheep...' and so on and so on. My questions are these: did Rachel tell Jacob the truth after Laban had gone and, if she did, what did he say?

Thank you, Father, that, apart from everything else the Bible is and does, it can be very entertaining.

OUT OF BOUNDS

Genesis 31:51–55 (NIV) (Read also vv. 43–50)

Laban also said to Jacob, 'Here is this heap, and here is this pillar I have set up between you and me. This heap is a witness, and this pillar is a witness, that I will not go past this heap to your side to harm you and that you will not go past this heap and pillar to my side to harm me. May the God of Abraham and the God of Nahor, the God of their father, judge between us.' So Jacob took an oath in the name of the Fear of his father Isaac. He offered a sacrifice there in the hill country and invited his relatives to a meal. After they had eaten they spent the night there. Early the next morning Laban kissed his grandchildren and his daughters and blessed them. Then he left and returned home.

This arrangement between Jacob and Laban transports me to childhood days when my two brothers and I argued over how much of the sitting-room floor each of us could reasonably claim for playing with toys. After 30 minutes or so of loud complaints and counter-complaints, my long-suffering mother would use anything handy to mark off three areas, threatening that anyone who strayed out of bounds would not play any more and—worst of punishments—his area would be divided between the others. This ensured peace for a while, but I recall my mother's regret that we couldn't settle our differences without barriers imposed by outside authority.

The compromise reached by Jacob and Laban was not ideal. Jacob had worked hard for crafty old Laban for years and had every right to all he had brought from Haran. There was no obligation to compromise. Laban, on the other hand, must have finally realized that he had squeezed all he was going to get out of Jacob. Perhaps he feared that with this powerful God on his nephew's side it would be safer to have Jacob safely and permanently on the other side of a witness heap. Still, they did part on good terms after a meal and Laban did get to kiss his daughters and grandchildren goodbye. A far better ending than might have been predicted.

Father, may our differences be resolved in love rather than witness heaps.

NIGHT WRESTLING

Genesis 32:24–29 (NIV) (Read also vv. 1–23, 30–32)

So Jacob was left alone, and a man wrestled with him until daybreak. When the man saw that he could not overpower him, he touched the socket of Jacob's hip so that his hip was wrenched as he wrestled with the man. Then the man said, 'Let me go, for it is daybreak.' But Jacob replied, 'I will not let you go unless you bless me.' The man asked him, 'What is your name?' 'Jacob', he answered. Then the man said, 'Your name will no longer be Jacob, but Israel, because you have struggled with God and with men and have overcome.' Jacob said, 'Please tell me your name.' But he replied, 'Why do you ask my name?' Then he blessed him there.

I feel I can identify with Jacob as I write this. I am suffering pain in my right hip—not because I have wrestled with God, but because I have sciatica. I expect the pain is about the same, though.

This bizarre experience of Jacob's happened at a crossroads in his life, the point where his dealings with Laban were over and he was full of dread about encountering his brother Esau the following day. It is not surprising that such a night should be filled with wrestling and conflict. I have known nights like that and so have many of you I'm sure, but what was going on here? It's all so strange. What can possibly be meant by the suggestion that Jacob was actually wrestling with God? Why was the man who turned out to be God unable to overpower a mere mortal? Why did God 'cheat' in the end by throwing out Jacob's hip?

Clearly it has something to do with the establishment of Jacob's new and more substantial identity as Israel, the father of a people—a man who has struggled with God and himself and survived. Perhaps the vigour with which Jacob fought and held on to the man/God was a significant measure of his determination to make the Lord's blessing his number one priority for the first time in his life. The touch on the hip was simply a reminder that, in the final analysis, the boss is the boss.

Some of the best people bear the scars of God.

BROTHERLY LOVE

Genesis 33:1–5 (NIV) (Read also vv. 6–20)

Jacob looked up and there was Esau, coming with his 400 men; so he divided the children among Leah, Rachel and the two maidservants. He put the maidservants and their children in front, Leah and her children next, and Rachel and Joseph in the rear. He himself went on ahead and bowed down to the ground seven times as he approached his brother. But Esau ran to meet Jacob and embraced him; he threw his arms around his neck and kissed him. And they wept. Then Esau looked up and saw the women and children. 'Who are these with you?' he asked. Jacob answered, 'They are the children God has graciously given your servant.'

'There are times when you get what you wa-ant!' This might have been Jacob's personal adaptation of Mick Jagger's song following the joy and relief of his restored relationship with Esau. After his endless, dream-filled, tumultuous night, his feverish, strategic dispersal of personnel and flocks and his general gut-wrenching dread of what the morning would bring, suddenly, amazingly, everything is all right, and the two brothers are almost competing over who can be the most generous.

Some years ago I 'brokered' a reconciliation between two Christians. One lady (let's call her Sally) had done something truly unspeakable to another (whom we'll call Vera). Sally wanted to sort this out, but lacked courage. She asked me if I would tell Vera what she had done and then be present at a meeting between the two of them. I shall never forget the encounter. It happened in the late evening in an old caravan at the end of our garden. Sally, terrified, and I, apprehensive, sat and waited in a silence that was broken only by the hissing of the old-fashioned gas lamps that lit the interior of the caravan. Then, the door opened, and in came Vera. The two women looked at each other for what seemed like several minutes but can't have been, then Vera took a step forward, opened her arms wide and embraced the person who had treated her so badly. It wasn't just a gesture—she meant it.

Father, thank you that, when it is working as it should, the body of Christ is able to heal its own deepest wounds.

THE UNKINDEST CUT OF ALL

Genesis 34:24–29 (NIV) (Read also vv. 1–23, 30–31)

All the men who went out of the city gate agreed with Hamor and his son Shechem, and every male in the city was circumcised. Three days later, while all of them were still in pain, two of Jacob's sons, Simeon and Levi, Dinah's brothers, took their swords and attacked the unsuspecting city, killing every male. They put Hamor and his son Shechem to the sword and took Dinah from Shechem's house and left. The sons of Jacob came upon the dead bodies and looted the city where their sister had been defiled. They seized their flocks and herds and donkeys and everything else of theirs in the city and out in the fields. They carried off all their wealth and all their women and children, taking as plunder everything in the houses.

This passage makes my eyes water. I'm not talking about crying. I'm talking about imagination working far too well in identifying with someone else's pain. What a comprehensive revenge these brothers wreaked on Shechem and the other male Shechemites. I have no idea what would have been used to circumcise adult males at this point in history. I'm not sure I want to know. I have a nasty feeling that Simeon and Levi would have found a way of insisting that the implement in question must be blunt. Perhaps they claimed that horrible, unspiritual old sharpness would render the ceremony ineffectual. However, it was done. Three days later, the newly snipped Shechemites were still in so much pain that the attack by Dinah's brothers must have seemed nothing more than a whirling blur out of which swords and spears emerged to end their pain and their lives.

Jacob seems to suffer something of a dip in his faith on learning what his sons have done. Despite God's earlier promises, he expresses a fear that, because of what has happened, he and his household will be attacked and destroyed by surrounding forces.

'You shouldn't have done that to Shechem,' he complains. 'Well,' reply the sons, in the manner of all sons since time began who have gone their own way regardless of what anyone else thinks, 'he shouldn't have treated our sister like a prostitute.'

Why is it that, at times, close family can seem so unspiritual and so right?

PURE PROTECTION

Genesis 35:1–5 (NIV) (Read also vv. 6–15)

Then God said to Jacob, 'Go up to Bethel and settle there, and build an altar there to God, who appeared to you when you were fleeing from your brother Esau.' So Jacob said to his household and to all who were with him, 'Get rid of the foreign gods you have with you, and purify yourselves and change your clothes. Then come, let us go up to Bethel, where I will build an altar to God, who answered me in the days of my distress and who has been with me wherever I have gone.' So they gave Jacob all the foreign gods they had and the rings in their ears, and Jacob buried them under the oak at Shechem. Then they set out, and the terror of God fell upon the towns all around them so that no one pursued them.

One of the interesting things about writing these notes is that often the message of the passage is specifically for me. If it happens to be for you also, well, that's wonderful. Here's a good example. Jacob has been told by God to go back to Bethel (where he used his stone pillow to build an altar, remember) and settle there. Jacob's response is a sort of frenzy of purification. False gods and anything else that God might not approve of are collected, bundled up together and buried under an oak tree at Shechem. Having done that he and his people are ready to march—a purified body acting in obedience to God's will. No wonder they seemed invincible to all those they passed.

I have something to do in obedience to God and I believe God is telling me through this part of Jacob's story that some purification is needed in my life before I take the next step in my personal odyssey. I'm not sure that I am completely happy about the obedience or the purification, but I do want to get things right. You may be facing the same kind of crucial challenges in your life. If so, let us pray together.

Father, we are weak and flawed, but we want to be obedient. Show us the parts of our lives that are not clean and help us prepare to do what we are told.

A promise is a kind of debt.

MOROCCAN PROVERB

CLEAR SIGNPOSTS

THE PROMISES OF GOD

I have been asking myself the following question.

In which circumstances do I feel most confident that the general promise of God will be kept? I mean, I suppose, the promise that he is what he says he is, that we will become what he says we will become, and that the whole happy-ever-after potential of the Gospel narratives will one day be fully realized in our lives.

I know some people feel that such questioning indicates a lack of respect, but it is important to grasp the fact that those of us who do question in such a way are actually dealing with our own weakness and doubt, not with the trustworthiness or otherwise of God. One of the greatest and most helpful revelations in my largely revelationless life has been the knowledge that God is God and I am me. I am sure you will be gasping in wonder at the banality of this statement, but, however silly it sounds, that simple separation does mean a great deal to me. God will continue to be who and what he is despite me, while I, relieved beyond measure that he continues to love me even when I am in the most frightful messes, will continue to be me, and pray for change as farmers pray for rain in a drought.

So, where do I feel confident in the promise of God? There are a number of answers to this question, but, for the moment, I want to talk about just one.

I see the promise of God being fulfilled in the lives and spirits of my friends.

One night I was having a quiet drink and a bowl of chips with my friend Ben Ecclestone. Ben and I worked together on *Learning to Fly*, a book of poems and pictures charting the journey of our friendship over the last decade or so. Fortunately we no longer need to pretend anything to each other concerning what we feel and believe about our common faith. Last night we were discussing the problems we have both encountered with doubt and assurance.

'Sometimes,' said Ben, 'I've found myself feeling that deep down I know it's all a load of nonsense, and it's just lack of courage that stops me from admitting it to myself.'

'I know what you mean,' I replied, dipping a chip in his tomato sauce because I'd finished mine, 'I sometimes think it would take a lot more courage for us to give up our faith than to hang on to it. Imagine all the fuss and palaver if we told everyone that we'd decided we weren't Christians after all. I couldn't be a Christian writer any more, unless I joined A.N. Wilson firing on the retreat, and you'd have to give up being an elder, wouldn't you? Hassle all the way, eh? Besides, I reckon there's an even deeper level where you know that it is all true. Uncovering that would be a problem—you wouldn't have anything left to worry about then, would you?'

'Maybe it's a matter of temperament,' suggested Ben. 'There's a chap I know in a church near ours who wouldn't even know what we were talking about if he was sitting here now. Everything's black and white in his world. No problems about doctrine or faith or doubt or anything like that—all completely straightforward. But I reckon he's always been like that. It's just the way he's made. He's not like us. He doesn't have to keep taking his entrails out and studying them miserably to see if they're all right, he just lives his life. Sometimes I really wish I was like him. I'd be a lot more use if I was.'

'No you wouldn't,' I said, 'I know the bloke you're talking about. He's got about four things to say, and if someone comes along with a problem that doesn't fit one of them he's lost without even knowing that he's lost. You've helped loads of people because you don't pretend to know all the answers. Besides,' I dipped another chip deep into Ben's ketchup and studied the bright red sauce for a moment before popping it into my mouth, 'I rather like entrails.'

I have sat over so many bowls of chips and bottles of wine with Ben, 'finally' sorting out our own difficulties and the problems faced by the Church, formulating radical solutions that we alone are able to understand and offer. I'm sure we talk an awful load of rubbish at times, but as I looked at Ben last night, I sensed, as I have sensed so many times in the past, the profound love that God feels for this son of his who has done so much for so many people in the name of Jesus, but has never quite been able to make the final step into a real assurance that he is truly valued and loved by his heavenly Father.

I know for a fact that Ben's worst nightmare involves an encounter with an angel holding a clipboard at the gates of heaven. The angel runs his finger down a list and shakes his head unemotionally. 'No Ecclestone here, I'm afraid,' he says, and the gates clang shut behind Ben as he trudges off towards Hades to consume soggy chips and vinegary wine with me for ever.

My faith for Ben is unshakeable—I just know that the person he is, the person who is complex, artistic, stubborn, loyal, fretful, self-effacing and fearful of rejection is as safely held in the palm of the hand of God as any man or woman ever was or ever will be. As a matter of interest I think he probably feels as confident about my eternal future as I do about his. And that, in a nutshell, is why Christians need Christians. For it is in each other that we see the promise of God coming to fruition.

You see, as I've just said, I have no doubt about Ben's salvation, but if you ask me about mine—well, I'm really not quite as sure…

Prayer
Father, thank you so much for our friends, and the assurance of salvation that we see so clearly in them. Help us to love them and pray for them.

FISHERS OF MEN (PART ONE)

Matthew 4:18–20 (NIV)

As Jesus was walking beside the sea of Galilee, he saw two brothers, Simon called Peter and his brother Andrew. They were casting a net into the lake, for they were fishermen. 'Come, follow me,' Jesus said, 'I will make you fishers of men.' At once they left their nets and followed him.

The fishing record of my immediate family is far from distinguished. My youngest son did once catch a moderately sized fish off a pier in Australia, but I ruined the moment when, in a sudden fit of compassion, I threw it back before he had a chance to take a photo.

My middle son has never caught a fish, but he did once catch me. With a metal imitation minnow on the end of his line he drove one of the three large hooks into my right ear. Walking into a nearby health centre with this bizarre decoration dangling from my earlobe was not one of the high spots in my life.

This same son never did quite perfect the art of casting. On one occasion, bravely putting behind him a series of miserably unsuccessful attempts and applying every available ounce of concentration to one last try, he hurled himself bodily into the water, leaving his rod and line lying neatly on the bank.

My own attempts at angling have been equally useless.

Jesus promises that we will become fishers of men, but I have to confess that most of my attempts at one-to-one evangelism are sadly reminiscent of the Plass family's angling exploits. I think that, through my books, I can sometimes be the simplest sort of signpost, pointing people towards Jesus, but when it comes to the people next door I'm absolutely useless at talking about what I believe. This doesn't trouble me as it used to.

As a young Christian I got the idea that everyone ought to be evangelizing in just about every situation all the time, and an automatic pang of guilt hit me every time I bought a piece of cod in the fish shop and didn't offer salvation along with my £1.50. I think I was being very silly. Jesus promised the disciples that he would make them fishers of men, and, of course, they went on to do very specific jobs. Let's trust that he will give us the job that is right for us, whether it's up-front evangelism or something less overt but no less essential.

Lord Jesus, we all want to be part of your promise that we can be fishers of men, but we also want to make sure that we're doing the job that is right for us. Give us either the courage or the humility that we need to accept the role that you've planned for us.

FISHERS OF MEN (PART TWO)

Matthew 4:18–20 (NIV) (again)

A fishing disaster I failed to mention in my previous note was the dramatic occasion when one of us hooked a seagull. It wasn't funny at the time. We were horrified. These birds had been wheeling around us since our arrival at the estuary. They wanted our bait, which consisted of little frozen fish from a local shop. At every cast, one or two birds would swoop down hoping to capture the tasty snack on a hook. We thought they'd never be quick enough—but one was. He flapped triumphantly up with his prize in his beak, only to catapult back to the water as he reached the full extent of the line. We were distraught.

Hurriedly I cut the whole thing free next to the reel, and we watched the puzzled bird fly up again with endless nylon cord trailing from its beak. Finally, to our enormous relief, bait, hook and all got dislodged and dropped into the water. I began to wonder if someone was trying to say something...

Later that year I took my youngest son to a trout farm. Here they provided set-up tackle, buckets to put your catch in, and, most importantly, a lake full of fish whose one apparent aim in life was to be caught by the general public. Those fish were almost jumping out of the water in their eagerness to take our bait. At first it was wonderful. We caught seven good-sized fish in an hour! Unheard of!

Was it the lorry arriving to dump vast quantities of replacement stock into the lake that put us off a bit after that? These fish had obviously been raised on the sweetcorn provided to us for use as bait. As far as the trusting incoming fish were concerned it was simply lunchtime in a different place. We took our seven fish home and grilled and ate them, but we couldn't think of ourselves as proper anglers. Those fish were not wild fish—those fish were in captivity before we caught them...

The trout farm reminds me of an awful lot of evangelism that I've encountered. All over this country converted Christians have the gospel preached to them every Sunday whether or not they need it or like it— placid fish volunteering to be caught yet again by those who want to feel like real fishermen.

Perhaps genuine evangelism is going to be rather more like the Plass family's experiences of angling. You might have a few disasters as you learn patience and technique, you might have to stand faithfully by strange waters that are 'known' to be a waste of time—you might even catch the odd seagull by mistake, but at least you'll know that you are fishing where the wild fish are, and that when you catch something it'll be worth it.

Give us the courage to fish in strange waters.

WHEN?

Jeremiah 29:13 (NIV)

'You will seek me and find me when you seek me with all your heart.'

This verse has dogged me for years. Why? Well, I suppose because it asks a question of me that I have never satisfactorily answered. I am always, like Goethe on his deathbed, crying, 'More light—more light!', but when opportunities come, am I prepared to seek God and the knowledge of God with my whole heart? Do I even really know what that means? The merest glance at my performance so far is not too encouraging.

Take me when it's late at night, for instance. Quite often I'll be the last one to bed, because I've sat up in my favourite armchair watching some obscure sporting contest. God is probably sitting in the other armchair getting very bored and sleepy. Round about midnight it suddenly occurs to me that there's a burning issue in my life, and I really need to discuss it with God. So vital is the issue that I almost turn the television off, but not quite. When the next commercial break comes, however, I finally get round to doing something dynamic—I turn the sound down. Hurriedly, I outline my problem or concern to God, still keeping one eye on the screen because I don't want to miss any of the Ukrainian formation chisel-balancing championship quarter-final if I can help it.

As the programme comes back on I say something along the lines of, 'Well, I'll leave it with you,' and then it's up with the volume and back to the chisels.

A bit of a caricature, perhaps, but not so far from the truth, I'm afraid. When I am disciplined and committed to prayer—and I mean disciplined, not chained—the burdens that constitute my particular cross become no less heavy, but are more neatly packed. It's rather like using one properly organized rucksack instead of 15 over-full plastic carrier bags that are about to break.

So, why am I still wrestling with the carrier bags? Oh, I don't know!

Father, I'm well aware that you aren't going to stop loving me because I don't spend enough time and concentration on my communication with you. I hope we're all beginning to understand that the place we occupy in your heart doesn't require any kind of religious rent from us. On the other hand, we miss out on so much when we don't get close to you. Forgive us for those times when we fail actively to seek you. Help us to be wholehearted in all our dealings with you—even when there's something good on the telly.

DINING WITH THE KING

Revelation 3:19–20 (NIV)

'Those whom I love I rebuke and discipline. So be earnest, and repent. Here I am! I stand at the door and knock. If anyone hears my voice and opens the door, I will come in and eat with him, and he with me.'

Regular readers of my vapid outpourings will be well aware that certain ideas occur in everything I write, and that eating—or rather, the enjoying of meals—is definitely one of those.

Allow me a little indulgence as I describe one or two of my favourite scenarios.

There's a country pub about three miles from where I live that, on a weekday evening in particular, is a real joy to visit. Settling down at one of the bar tables with a good friend, two wine glasses, a bottle of house red and a large bowl of chips comes as close to heaven on earth as most things I've experienced.

It was in exactly this situation that a close friend of mine and I decided that if we saved, scraped, borrowed and schemed it might actually be feasible jointly to buy some kind of small property in France. A big decision for us, but now we've done it. We have a dumpy little cottage in Normandy, and it's wonderful.

Here's another scenario.

I have a friend who regularly takes me to speaking engagements and the like. I can't eat much before speaking, but afterwards we quite often find a restaurant (usually Indian) on the way home, and enjoy a late meal. It may not be good for the digestion, but I can tell you that it's pretty good for the soul. I would say that we talk at more depth and with more mutual benefit at those times than on any other occasion. Unforced fellowship—that's what I'd call it.

I could continue the list.

Bridget and I, for instance, love to eat out in some quiet place where we can be 'us', instead of us defined by our responsibilities. We need that so much. It isn't just the food, or the place, or the company that makes these times so enjoyable and meaningful—it's a rich mix of everything, and it goes very deep, way down into the heart of habit and history and tradition and the real meaning of things.

And look—Jesus, the same Jesus who cooked fish and ate breakfast with his friends on that wonderful Galilee morning two thousand years ago, says to us today that, if we will open the door, he will come in, not to pray with us, not to worship with us, not to read the scriptures with us, not to supervise our quiet times, but to eat with us. How clearly we recognize the authentic voice of Jesus, and what a pleasure to eat with him.

Come in, Lord. Please sit down. Let's eat and talk together.

WHOSE APPROVAL?

Matthew 6:3–4 (NIV)

'But when you give to the needy, do not let your left hand know what your right hand is doing, so that your giving may be in secret. Then your Father, who sees what is done in secret, will reward you.'

Giving secretly is not easy for mere mortals like me. I always like someone to know, don't you?

This very challenging (and annoying) passage roots around at the base of our faith like a very determined dog after a bone. Will that dog's snuffling activities uncover some foundations down there, or will it become clear that the structure of what we believe is far less stable than we thought? Because, dear reader, a very simple question is being asked here, and the answer to that question, whatever it happens to be for you and me as individuals, needs to be faced if we are to claim any reality for our faith. The question boils down to this: is my belief in the presence of God real enough, close enough and personal enough to motivate giving or prayer or acts of kindness without the need to receive 'applause' from anyone else?

This is really a question about relationship, isn't it? Do I need to tell someone else if I send some flowers to my wife when I'm away from home? No, I don't, because I can imagine her pleasure on receiving them, and I look forward to the moment when we are reunited because then I shall actually see, hear and touch her response. That will be my reward and it will be enough. Whilst I'm away and going about my work I hug to myself the secret knowledge of what I've done, and—the crucial point, this—I enjoy it as much as she does. (At this point my wife looks over my shoulder and comments that she could do with it happening a bit more often.)

The points that Jesus makes here are fearsomely clear and uncompromising. Whatever I do to attract the applause and approval of the world has no validity in the Father's eyes. Those things mean nothing. The things that I do in secret and that spring from a genuine desire to please him will be rewarded. But don't lose heart if your answer to that essential question left you feeling a bit depressed. I didn't come out of it too well either. Let's talk to God about it—he really is very nice...

Father, some of us fall very short of the mark when it comes to the reality of our relationship with you. We want to value you and love you so much that our only concern is your approval, but we're not there yet. Teach us and hold us for as long as it takes.

MY FRIEND

Luke 23:34 (NIV)

Jesus said, 'Father, forgive them, for they do not know what they are doing.' And they divided up his clothes by casting lots.

Some people reckon that when Jesus said these words he was asking God to forgive all of us for our corporate sin in putting him on the cross as we did then, and as we have continued to do again and again and again ever since. Well, that makes sense, of course, but it's wrong. God told me it was wrong last night. He didn't really, but I wish he had, because it would support what I think.

You see, I think Jesus was a very immediate sort of character, and when you're having nails driven into your hands and you're an immediate sort of character, you tend not to produce carefully formulated prayers concerning the corporate sin of humankind. The interesting thing is that if the response is localized, it actually has a more powerful implication for all of us.

It almost sounds as though Jesus had a sudden, awe-inspiring awareness of the vengeful fury his Father was feeling towards the men who were wielding those murderous hammers on his beloved Son's hands and feet. Hurriedly he throws up a preventative prayer to make sure that they don't get thunderbolted before they have a chance to be saved by the very event that they were preparing Jesus for.

Those men must have approached the gates of heaven with a certain trepidation, to say the least. Perhaps the duty angel recognized them and frowned as he mentally replayed the scene in which they had played such a brutal part. Perhaps he whistled up a few of his mates and they all stood with folded arms, ranging themselves in a solid, accusing phalanx in front of the gates, silently conveying the message that if these killers of the Son of God thought they were coming in they could think again. And perhaps, just as those men turned away guiltily, Jesus himself broke through the ranks of angels and cried out, 'What are you doing? These are my friends—let them in. I've been so looking forward to seeing them...'

I'm sure this is a foul slur on angels, but they'll be able to get me later. The point is that I have to approach the gates of heaven one day as well, and I don't think I'll be waving an insurance policy called The

Salvation Plan. I think—I know—that I'll be craning my neck to catch a sight of Jesus, my friend, who has promised to forgive the particular sins that are mine, and who will, without doubt, keep his promise.

Father, forgive us, we don't know how much we hurt you…

GETTING CLEAN

Luke 7:47–48 (NIV)

'Therefore, I tell you, her many sins have been forgiven—for she loved much. But he who has been forgiven little loves little.' Then Jesus said to her, 'Your sins are forgiven.'

Do read the whole of this story. It begins at verse 36, and it embodies one of the greatest promises of all, a promise so familiar, and yet so difficult to believe for oneself, that it is easily overlooked or avoided.

Jesus will forgive our sins.

I've always been vaguely grateful to the woman in this story for showing me so clearly that real repentance will involve two important things. First, having recognized the authoritative personality of Jesus and his claims on our lives, we are likely to feel deeply sad and sorry that we are not as he would like us to be. Second, though, and this is so important, we will want to express this to him. And please don't be put off by those who say that feelings are to be avoided at all cost. People who say that may have a bit of a point—sometimes—but just look at the state of this poor woman, for goodness' sake! She is absolutely devastated by the knowledge that God knows and is affected by what she does and what she is.

Mustn't it have been unutterably wonderful when, after supporting her in front of this stuffy old bigwig, Jesus turned to her and very simply told her that everything was going to be all right because her sins were forgiven? The only one in the world who had the power and the authority to make her clean had, with four life-changing words, done exactly that. No emotion? Who's kidding who?

Would you like to feel that clean?

Lord Jesus, there are things in our lives, past and present, that make us feel wretched and sad. You know what they are. You're the only one who knows about some of them.

(Tell him about the particular things in your life—go on, there's no one else listening. If you get all upset it's not the end of the world. Tell him now...)

Jesus, that woman in today's reading heard your voice clearly saying that she was forgiven and made clean. Some of us are not very good at hearing your voice, and some of us don't believe it's really possible, but would you please help us to achieve anything from a tiny gleam to a blinding flash of awareness that you do indeed forgive us in exactly the same way? Thank you, Lord Jesus.

THE SECOND DEATH

Revelation 2:10–11 (NIV)

Do not be afraid of what you are about to suffer. I tell you, the devil will put some of you in prison to test you, and you will suffer persecution for ten days. Be faithful, even to the point of death, and I will give you the crown of life. He who has an ear, let him hear what the Spirit says to the churches. He who overcomes will not be hurt at all by the second death.

A friend of mine came round fairly late one night for a coffee and a chat. He leads quite a large church in the next town, and he was a bit low on this occasion. A member of his church, a 40-year-old married man with three children, had collapsed and died earlier in the week.

'The thing is,' said my friend, 'there was no warning of any kind, no preparation possible. One minute he seemed to be as fit as a fiddle, and the next minute—gone.' He shook his head. 'I just seemed to run out of things to say this time.' He sat back and stared at the ceiling for a moment. 'I wonder if any research has ever been done on whether Christians have lower incidence of accidental or sudden death than other groups. I must say, despite all the stuff about counting the hairs on our heads, it looks exactly the same to me.'

I felt a lot of sympathy for my friend, and for the family who are hurting so much, but I also felt that much of the teaching about suffering that we receive is blinkered and blinkering, if I can put it like that. Suffering has always been a part of Christian living, beginning with Jesus and continuing to the present day in the lives of ordinary people like this young widow and her children. It's horrible, but let's not pretend that it doesn't happen. Christians appear to be afflicted by exactly the same things as everyone else. The difference is that Jesus inhabits our suffering and pain as well as our joys. He is in it with us.

Sometimes, certainly, God will intervene to remove suffering, but perhaps we should focus on the fact that he also intervenes to not remove suffering, and if he doesn't know what he's doing we've had it! He holds the most valuable part of us in the palm of his hand, and no one can harm or steal that part.

He asked the Christians in Smyrna to be faithful even to the point of death. Like them, the man who died this week will not be hurt at all by the second death. At the moment that won't be much help to those who loved him, but by the time he is reunited with his family they will realize that this was always the most important thing of all.

Father, Jesus never said it would be easy, but he promised to be with us always. Help us to trust you whatever happens.

UNCONDITIONAL LOVE

Romans 8:38–39 (NIV)

For I am convinced that neither death nor life, neither angels nor demons, neither the present nor the future, nor any powers, neither height nor depth, nor anything else in all creation, will be able to separate us from the love of God that is in Christ Jesus our Lord.

These are very grand, stirring words, aren't they? The promise they contain is exactly what most of us (me included) want to hear, but there was a time when I felt sick every time I heard them because they sounded so hollow and meaningless to my ears. Why was that? Well, I was going through a difficult time, and confidence in God was part of those difficulties. Someone would read out a verse like the one quoted above, speak about the unchanging, never-ending love of God, then, a little later quote some other verse that apparently indicated the ease and finality with which any one of us could separate ourselves from God. It used to drive me mad. Since then, I've met other Christians, especially those whose confidence is never very high anyway, who are puzzled by the way in which this paradox is trotted out so readily by people who haven't really thought it through. For all those people (and for myself) here are a few humble(ish) observations.

God loves us without any condition whatsoever. Whatever we are or aren't—whatever we do or don't do, he will go on loving us just the same. Consider the story of the prodigal son. Could anything be more transparently clear than the passion with which this father regards the son who has left home. Let me spell it out.

Even as the prodigal was in the act of sleeping with prostitutes and pursuing whatever other vile activities he was engaged in, his father, knowing full well the sort of thing he was doing, was loving him and watching out for his return and planning the kind of celebration that would accompany that return. Do we honestly think that this consistency and depth of love and affection is going to be changed or reduced by lapses and mistakes made by the prodigal after he has returned home? Don't misunderstand me, I don't mean that we have a licence to sin. What I'm trying to convey is that this whole thing—this whole salvation/Jesus/crucifixion/resurrection/repentance/heaven thing is God's idea and initiative. He so loved the world…

Father, thank you for the passionate, eternal love you offer us. Perhaps some of us have drifted away from home again. Call us back—help us to remember what Jesus told us about you.

A BURST OF COLOUR

Genesis 9:13–15 (NIV)

I have set my rainbow in the clouds, and it will be the sign of the covenant between me and the earth. Whenever I bring clouds over the earth and the rainbow appears in the clouds, I will remember my covenant between me and you and all living creatures of every kind. Never again will the waters become a flood to destroy all life.

The rainbow guarantees that our world will never again be covered in water. This is good news, of course (although it can't be much comfort to those whose small corner of the world is destroyed by local flooding), but I think the rainbow promises much more than that.

It might be seen as a declaration that God has permanently abandoned the idea of wiping out humanity—a commitment, if you like, to working with the problem rather than against it. This promise has been kept. The life and death of Jesus is powerful evidence of the depth of that commitment. Nothing could be more important.

A less obvious interpretation of the rainbow promise was suggested to me by the work my wife was doing with a junior class on the subject of 'Light'. It was rather fun looking through all the stuff about prisms and mirrors and experiments involving pieces of black card with holes cut in them. I remembered all sorts of things that I'd almost completely forgotten. Prominent among these was the fact, astonishing and frankly unconvincing to me when I was a small child at school, that light is not really white at all, but is actually a mixture of colours known as the spectrum.

Richard Of York Gave Battle In Vain. Of course he did! Red, orange, yellow, green, blue, indigo and violet—the colours that, when spun rapidly together on a cardboard spinning top, became white, proving that our teacher's ridiculous claim was entirely justified.

The spectrum that we call the rainbow is a clue, a hint, a promise, a guarantee, that the love of God is not a single, unvaried beam of light shining impersonally on us all, but a veritable explosion of colours, one of which will be the exact wavelength of light needed to reach and illuminate the dark places in my heart and yours.

Next time rain and sunshine happen together, and you feel as if you're living in a washing-machine, look up, and see how God is offering you, individually, what we Anglicans would call the sign of peace—in glorious Technicolor.

Richard of York may have given battle in vain, but he did make a very solid contribution to junior science.

SOMETHING TO LOOK FORWARD TO

1 Corinthians 2:9 (NIV)

However, as it is written: 'No eye has seen, no ear has heard, no mind has conceived what God has prepared for those who love him.'

A group of us were talking about heaven. I was putting forward the view that the quality of eternal life will be much more closely linked to our lives on earth than we imagine. 'Surely,' I said, 'the essence of all those beautiful things in the world must be there because they're part of him and part of us. I reckon anything good and innocent and beautiful down here has a chance of surviving in some form up there. For instance, I fully expect to play cricket in heaven.'

'Well, I'm not going, then,' said one of the ladies spiritedly. 'If you think I'm going to watch cricket in heaven you've got another think coming. It already lasts for ever down here.'

'No, no,' I protested, 'you won't have to. Each of us has got our own list of things that mean a lot to us. We won't have to get involved in anything we don't like.'

Most of us had contributed something to this enjoyable if highly speculative discussion, but there was one chap, called Jim, who had said nothing. Jim was a man who really loved Jesus, but his language and general conversation in this context tended to be abstract and rather unimaginatively Bible-based. He listened to our discussion with a little smile of gentle scepticism on his face.

'It's quite a thought, isn't it,' said someone else, 'that we might be allowed to do or have the very thing we've always wanted most and never been able to have?' I was just about to answer when I noticed the smile had gone from Jim's face. In its place was an expression of what appeared to be deep spiritual longing. Rarely have I seen anyone with as much of his heart in his eyes as I saw in Jim's at that very moment. Probably some Bible verse, I thought, that will neatly dismiss everything we've been saying. 'Penny for 'em, Jim,' I said.

'Oh!' He seemed to come to with a start. 'I was just thinking how much I've always wanted—' The faraway look came back into his eyes—'I was just thinking how absolutely wonderful it would be if he would let me have, well—a lathe of my own...' Somewhere in heaven a note was made.

Father, we don't really know any of the details about heaven, but we do know that you love us and that you care for us as individuals. The verse we've read today seems to be full of your excitement about planning good things for us, and we would like to feel a little of that excitement ourselves. Help us to remember that you made heaven and earth.

EVER PRESENT

Matthew 28:19–20 (NIV)

'Therefore go and make disciples of all nations, baptizing them in the name of the Father and of the Son and of the Holy Spirit, and teaching them to obey everything I have commanded you. And surely I am with you always, to the very end of the age.'

How do we react to the idea—the fact—that Jesus is with us always? Is it embarrassing, encouraging, alarming, or doesn't it mean very much at all because he's not actually visible?

I remember an occasion, recorded in fictional form elsewhere, but a very real part of my experience, when a member of our church who'd been asked to do the talk on this particular Sunday set an empty chair before the congregation and invited everybody to consider it carefully.

'Just suppose,' he said dramatically, 'that Jesus were to suddenly appear sitting in this chair. How would you feel? Wouldn't you be deeply worried? Wouldn't you want to run away and hide because you were ashamed of your sins? Wouldn't you decide to stay well out of the way until he'd gone?'

Well, how would that have made you feel? On this occasion I felt almost the exact opposite of what the speaker said I should. I don't mean that I would have welcomed the chance to see Jesus because I hadn't committed any sins—don't make me laugh! No, I just wanted to be with him. The thought almost made me weep. I wanted him to take charge and tell me what to do and make everything all right. And that's what I want now, even if I can't see him. I want him with me— always.

What if he had not been with us always? Have a look at Psalm 123.

I'LL BE BACK

John 14:1–3 (NIV)

'Do not let your hearts be troubled. Trust in God; trust also in me. In my Father's house are many rooms; if it were not so, I would have told you. I am going there to prepare a place for you. And if I go and prepare a place for you, I will come back and take you to be with me that you also may be where I am.'

Have you noticed how some rock stars like to dwell on their humble origins and the fact that underneath the glitz and glamour they're just ordinary folk like you and me? You sometimes see TV programmes in which they visit their old haunts and pose with picturesque locals as if they'd never left. You almost get the feeling (you're meant to, of course) that for two pins they'd move back into a little semi-detached house as near as possible to the one they grew up in. That might be true for one or two, but generally speaking—I don't think so! Most 'stars' also become very inaccessible, admittedly for the best of reasons. If your face is known by everyone, you guard your privacy at any cost—if you've got any sense.

But there never was a greater star than Jesus. He voluntarily left his seat beside his Father to begin a human life in the most humble fashion imaginable. When his ministry began, he chose ordinary people to accompany him and carry the message on after his death. He refused all offers to take personal advantage of the power which was his to command, and in the end suffered an agonizing criminal's death, no doubt leaving those who even bothered to think about it with a clear conviction that whatever he'd intended to start was now well and truly finished.

The resurrection restored Jesus to the highest possible place, beside his Father. Now was the time, if he had wanted to use his glory as most humans do, to forget his short life, his miserable death and the little people who for three years had followed him round that tiny corner of time and space that was Israel two thousand years ago. But he didn't. Jesus is the megastar who doesn't stay separate, the top man who will never forget his friends, the multimillionaire who wants to share. He busies himself preparing nice rooms for us. And one day, when everything's ready, he'll come and get us, and we shall live in his Father's house, and I suspect we shall have a bit of a party. You, who read this now—you'll be there.

He is coming back, you know…

A BIT BLAND?

Revelation 21:3–4 (NIV)

And I heard a loud voice from the throne saying, 'Now the dwelling of God is with men... God himself will be with them and be their God. He will wipe every tear from their eyes. There will be no more death or mourning or crying or pain, for the old order of things has passed away.'

For those of us who suffer, it's a wonderful thought that God will take out his divine hanky, dry our eyes and tell us to have a jolly good blow. A lovely concept, but it leaves me uneasy. I can't imagine life with no tears at all, can you? I'm not sure that existence without negative content is very appealing. I don't mean that I have a loony wish to be constantly miserable, and, let's face it, I live in a country with little lacking in physical comfort so I'm very spoilt anyway. I like being fed, clothed and generally happy.

No, my problem is that most of my inspiration for writing in general and poetry in particular has its roots in personal difficulty and pain. I enjoy the business of mining these seams of conflict, digging out the raw material of experience and extracting the truth that it invariably contains. What kind of life will it be where the spices of mood-change and confrontation and anger and forgiveness and debate and clash and Frank Bruno's attempts to regain the world championship are all missing? Won't it be rather bland?

Panic in heaven. God clutches his head, crying, 'Goodness me, yes, of course! It'll all be rather bland. Of course it will. Fancy Adrian Plass spotting a glaring error like that and me missing it completely. I've been so stupid! I'll have to start all over again...'

I reach out through the mist of my own foolishness for an answer, and it comes, as always, in the form of a question.

'On the rare occasions that you've enjoyed real *shalom* peace, the gift you've always wanted most, would you happily have exchanged it for a little more conflict and confrontation?'

'No, but—'

'Was there anything lacking in those moments?'

'No, but—'

'If I offered you that peace now and for ever would you take it?'

'Yes, but—'

'Well, I'm not going to.'

'Oh, but—'

'That's why you feel the need to transmute experience into poetry. It's unlikely that you'll achieve total peace this side of heaven.'

'What about the other side of heaven?'

'Precisely.'

Perhaps conflict is raw peace—much tastier when it's cooked and allowed to cool.

INSPIRATION

Matthew 25:34–40 (NIV)

'Then the King will say to those on his right, "Come... take your inheritance... For I was hungry and you gave me something to eat, I was thirsty and you gave me something to drink, I was a stranger and you invited me in, I needed clothes and you clothed me, I was sick and you looked after me, I was in prison and you came to visit me." Then the righteous will answer him, "Lord, when did we see you...?" The King will reply, "I tell you the truth, whatever you did for one of the least of these brothers of mine, you did for me."'

C.S. Lewis and G.K. Chesterton are my literary heroes. Both make words dance. Clarity, profundity and entertainment are hallmarks of their work. Recently, though, I found my old copy of *The Unutterable Beauty* by Studdert Kennedy, the Anglican clergyman nicknamed 'Woodbine Willie' because of his habit of handing out cigarettes in the trenches during the First World War. I bought this anthology of poems soon after conversion at the age of 16. The vulnerability and reality of some pieces impressed me no end. Here's an extract from 'It Is Not Finished':

I cannot read this writing of the years
My eyes are full of tears
It gets all blurred, and won't make sense
It's full of contradictions
Like the scribblings of a child,
Such wild, wild
Hopes, and longings as intense
As pain, which trivial deeds
Make folly of—or worse.
I can but hand it in, and hope
That Thy great mind, which reads
The writings of so many lives,
Will understand this scrawl
And what it strives to say—but leaves unsaid...

I met an elderly lady once who recalled how her father became too sick to earn money to feed his family for some weeks. 'Studdert Kennedy came round every day,' she said, 'with a pint of milk and a loaf of bread, and I sat on his knee while he chatted to mother and father. Mind you, I don't know how he managed it, because he gave away everything he'd got. My mother would see him going out in the morning in jacket and waistcoat, and come back later with just a shirt.'

Kennedy thought nothing of his own good deeds, and, for the sake of others, he was vulnerable to the point of rawness in his art—a good and faithful servant who long ago entered his Master's peace. I thank God for his example and inspiration.

Loving humility really is a beautiful rose.

And the disciples were filled with joy and
with the Holy Spirit.

FUELLED BY THE SPIRIT

ACTS 9—11

These notes cover the Pentecost period and look at the impact of the Holy Spirit on the life of the Church in the period including and following the conversion of the apostle Paul.

You're not going to believe this, but I got quite excited writing these notes. I was quite excited in the wrong sort of way at first because I was behind in my writing and I knew I was going to have to bury myself like a mole in my study for two days to get them done. Once I got started, though, I found that I was recovering some old excitements about the work of the Holy Spirit in the early Church—Saul's conversion, Peter's rooftop vision and his encounter with Cornelius and his household, developments in the church at Antioch… All these happenings and events, so brilliantly recorded by Luke, have been part of my Christian life for well over 30 years, but I had forgotten just how attractive a world full of the power of God can be. I want it now. I want it in the year 2006. I want to live in the drama and fear and amazement and novelty and unexpectedness that makes the book of Acts such a cracking read.

I think we may have given up a little bit, and that is a terrible shame. Pray with me as we read these passages together that we shall be as open to the work of the Spirit today as were those ancient pioneers who had no Bible to refer to, but were forced to depend on the living presence and guidance of God.

WHO?!

Acts 9:1–2 (NIV)

Meanwhile, Saul was still breathing out murderous threats against the Lord's disciples. He went to the high priest and asked him for letters to the synagogues in Damascus, so that if he found any there who belonged to the Way, whether men or women, he might take them as prisoners to Jerusalem.

The scene is heaven and the angel canteen is flapping with activity. It's 11 o'clock in the morning two thousand years ago (in a timeless, eternal sort of way) and those who worked on Michael's early shift are filling in Gabriel's late bunch on last night's events. Suddenly, their chatter is interrupted by someone clapping his hands together by the door. Only one person (or three, depending on your theology) could produce such thunderous sounds. The angels listen respectfully.

'Good news, everyone!' announces God cheerfully. Excitement buzzes through the assembled host. When God says 'good news', he means good news. The precedents have been truly extraordinary. 'Yes,' continues God, boundlessly enthusiastic, 'my good news is that I've found someone to preach to the Gentiles. How about that?!' A burst of spontaneous applause erupts, filling the canteen with gusts of air and loud noise from the beating of angels' wings and the clapping of angels' hands.

'That's wonderful!' exclaims Gabriel. 'What's he like?' 'Well,' says God, 'for a start, he's extremely well educated. A very clever man indeed. Very bright!' Murmurs of approval. It was not always thus with God's chosen servants.

'Excellent!' nods Gabriel happily. 'What else?' 'Well, he's deeply passionate, in fact, an incredibly determined type. Once he gets his teeth into something he never gives up!' 'Better and better! So, what's he doing now?' God's enthusiasm seems to wilt slightly. Twisting his fingers together, he hesitates. The angels lean forward on their seats.

'Ah, yes, well, umm, just now he's planning the best way to murder Christians, but, but, look, I have every confidence that we can overcome that little hurdle…' Stunned silence. At the back of the room a cockney angel mutters incredulously under his breath, 'E's bin an' gorn an' dun it agen…'

God sees the best in me.

A WILD LONGING

Acts 9:3–9 (NIV)

As he neared Damascus on his journey, suddenly a light from heaven flashed around him. He fell to the ground and heard a voice say to him, 'Saul, Saul, why do you persecute me?' 'Who are you, Lord?' Saul asked. 'I am Jesus, whom you are persecuting,' he replied. 'Now get up and go into the city, and you will be told what you must do.' The men travelling with Saul stood there speechless; they heard the sound but did not see anyone. Saul got up from the ground, but when he opened his eyes he could see nothing. So they led him by the hand into Damascus. For three days he was blind, and did not eat or drink anything.

'Why do you persecute me?' Why indeed? People often talk about Saul's road to Damascus experience as though it was the epitome of a particular kind of encounter with God that has no roots in or connection with past experience; a flash in the pan that leaves the pan illuminated, as it were. In fact, as John Stott points out in his commentary on the book of Acts, there is a good chance that Saul actually encountered Jesus during the three years of his ministry. Also, there is absolutely no doubt that he was present at the stoning of Stephen, when he was a sort of cloakroom attendant for some of the people who were doing the damage.

Something had to have fuelled the 'murderous' feelings that characterized Saul's attitude towards Christians up to this point. What was it, I wonder? Later in Acts, a little more information is added to the story when the apostle reveals how, in the course of that same experience, Jesus illuminated his difficulty in resisting the 'pricks' or 'goads', but what was he being pricked or goaded towards?

Like an indoor flower pressing its face against the window in an instinctive search for the source of light, perhaps a part of Paul had been leaning, yearning and growing in the direction of Jesus for a long time. Perhaps he thought he would never really be allowed to belong. Perhaps that aching desire to be part of the Way was close to unbearable. Could it have been this wild longing in himself that he hoped to extinguish in the act of destroying those who possessed what he wanted so much? I think so.

Father, there are those in this age who rage against you, but long for your love. Help them to give in.

WORRIED BUT WILLING

Acts 9:10–15 (NIV)

In Damascus there was a disciple named Ananias. The Lord called to him in a vision, 'Ananias!' 'Yes, Lord,' he answered. The Lord told him, 'Go to the house of Judas on Straight Street and ask for a man from Tarsus named Saul, for he is praying. In a vision he has seen a man named Ananias come and place his hands on him to restore his sight.' 'Lord,' Ananias answered, 'I have heard many reports about this man and all the harm he has done to your saints in Jerusalem. And he has come here with authority from the chief priests to arrest all who call on your name.' But the Lord said to Ananias, 'Go! This man is my chosen instrument to carry my name before the Gentiles and their kings and before the people of Israel.'

And lo, after a pause Ananias again addressed God in a strangled, high-pitched voice. 'Mmmm… truly, Lord, naturally I can barely restrain myself from sprinting away to perform this worthy act that you have kindly selected me to undertake, but it just occurs to me that my name features with great abundance in the Damascus telephone book, and I would hate—for your own sake and for the sake of the gospel, you understand—if you should end up sending the wrong Ananias. Are you with me?

'Also, Lord, and truly I could kick myself all the way to Jericho and back for failing to mention this at the very commencement of the vision you have so generously made known to me, but, by a curious coincidence, this very day is that on which an elderly and sick aunt of mine has implored me to deliver to her a particular elephant, one that is, indeed, crucial to… to her spiritual well-being. Moreover, Lord, now I think about it, correct me if I am in error, but has not Straight Street been cleared away to make room for the new one-way system? Maybe Saul now resides in some other street, I know not which, that sounds a bit like "Straight". Tell you what, Lord, my flatmate Thribbiel is a bit of a road system freak. What old Thribbiel does not know concerning Damascus might fit on the back of a first-class stamp. What it boils down to, Lord, is this. Here am I—send Thribbiel.'

Father, I want to be like the real Ananias, worried but willing. Help me not to make pathetic excuses for walking away from your clear demands.

DELUSION

Acts 9:13–16 (NIV)

'Lord,' Ananias answered, 'I have heard many reports about this man and all the harm he has done to your saints in Jerusalem. And he has come here with authority from the chief priests to arrest all who call on your name.' But the Lord said to Ananias, 'Go! This man is my chosen instrument to carry my name before the Gentiles and their kings and before the people of Israel. I will show him how much he must suffer for my name.'

We live in Sussex, near where eight-year-old Sarah Payne lived a short, happy life, brutally cut short when she was abducted and murdered. That happened some years ago, but people still talk about it.

Only a few weeks later, a friend's daughter ended years of misery by deliberately overdosing on drugs. Jane was in her early 20s, a Christian suffering chronic depression just as others suffer acute physical pain. In the end, she literally did not know where to put herself, so she threw herself away. Another friend is wrestling with a terminal illness. Valery enhances the lives of every person she comes into contact with. She is a follower of Jesus and a wonderful friend.

Paul was specially chosen by God to take the life-saving gospel of Jesus to Gentiles and Jews. During his ministry he was imprisoned, flogged, starved, in despair, shipwrecked and finally beheaded.

Jesus Christ was and is the Son of God, burdened with the awesome combination of unlimited power and human capacity for sin. He was made deeply unhappy by the general lack of response to his message, and was finally betrayed by a close friend, imprisoned, beaten, jeered at and nailed to a wooden cross. Three hours later he died.

Thousands prayed for Sarah's safety before her body was found. Jane grew up in a Christian family, surrounded by prayers all through her life. Valery belongs to God. Prayers are offered constantly for her healing. Paul also prayed constantly, and accepted all negative experiences for the sake of the gospel. Jesus spent nights in prayer and would only do what he saw the Father doing. He resisted all temptation and only for one desolate moment on the cross did he gasp out the agony of his temporary separation from his Father. Prayer is essential and effective, but let's stop kidding ourselves that prayer or belief in God is an insurance policy against suffering. To do so only produces more suffering.

OH, BROTHER!

Acts 9:17–19 (NIV)

Then Ananias went to the house and entered it. Placing his hands on Saul, he said, 'Brother Saul, the Lord—Jesus, who appeared to you on the road as you were coming here—has sent me so that you may see again and be filled with the Holy Spirit.' Immediately, something like scales fell from Saul's eyes, and he could see again. He got up and was baptized, and after taking some food, he regained his strength.

Good old Ananias! He did what he was told in the end, didn't he? His obedient, fearful heart probably melted at the sight of Saul. For three days, the latest convert to the Way had taken neither food nor water as he dwelt in the darkness behind useless eyes, speaking and listening to his new master. A fresh light was to burn in the heart of this man who had so recently been a murderous hunter of Christians, but, at this moment, it was a physical and emotional wreck that confronted Ananias when he tentatively entered the house of Judas in Straight Street.

Do you think Saul wept on hearing himself addressed as 'Brother Saul'? What a moment. I hope they have it on video in heaven! At the touch of his new brother's hands and the sound of his voice, a wave of belonging, understanding and unconditional acceptance must have flowed through that weakened body, healing and lifting Saul's bruised spirit to a place he had previously known only in dreams.

We can discuss technical aspects of conversion until the cows come home, but if we only manage to understand the truths embodied in this famous story, we are doing pretty well. When Jesus enters the life of another human being we have immediately gained a new brother or sister, and we may then be required to be a crucial part of that conversion, offering love and practical support in any way the Holy Spirit directs. How exciting, beautiful and disturbing that is.

Presumably it was Ananias who prepared the food that broke Saul's fast. A feast of relief—for Saul because he belonged at last and could see again; for Ananias because he had been used by God and all his fears had turned out to be groundless. A wonderful meal. How the three of them must have enjoyed it.

Father, thank you for those who obediently bring your love to us.

SWEETNESS

Acts 9:32–35 (NIV)

As Peter travelled about the country, he went to visit the saints in Lydda. There he found a man named Aeneas, a paralytic who had been bedridden for eight years. 'Aeneas,' Peter said to him, 'Jesus Christ heals you. Get up and tidy up your mat.' Immediately Aeneas got up. All those who lived in Lydda and Sharon saw him and turned to the Lord.

What kind of inner confidence enables a man to pronounce healing loudly and publicly enough to be ridiculed if nothing happens? Perhaps in Peter's case it sprang from memories of that great Pentecost event in Jerusalem, quickly followed by the healing of a paralysed man (Acts 3:1–10). But when we read of the Holy Spirit inspiring someone in this way, what is the nature of that inspiration? Is it an interior voice, a very strong feeling, a profusion of trust or just a strong hunch coming, apparently, out of nowhere? These questions seem important for one or two reasons.

First, many prayers for healing and 'words' for sufferers seem to be homemade cocktails of compassion and optimism with just a dash of hope. I have known great damage from ministry that is loud, enthusiastic but spiritually uninformed. Illness is enough without the burden of guilt about not feeling better after someone has taken the trouble to pray for you and perhaps even announced that 'in a very real sense' you are no longer ill.

Second, I do believe in healing. I don't see it happening much, but I know that God still touches people's lives and bodies dramatically in this age. Because I believe in God's willingness to heal, I determinedly do not accept the comfortably vague concepts that accompany many so-called healing ministries nowadays. Jesus didn't mess about when it came to healing—people got better. Bodies and minds worked properly again, just as here Aeneas' body worked properly after eight years of paralysis.

Third, I've been rereading John Wimber's account of the beginning of his healing ministry. He was shown a honeycomb in the sky, dripping sweet healing in abundance on to the world beneath, and he heard the voice of God telling him never to beg for healing again. Don't you hate the thought of wasting so much goodness?

Peter did not heal Aeneas. He said, 'Jesus Christ heals you...'

HEARTFELT

Acts 9:36–40 (NIV, abridged)

In Joppa there was a disciple named Tabitha (which, when translated, is Dorcas), who was always doing good and helping the poor. About that time she became sick and died, and her body was washed and placed in an upstairs room. Lydda was near Joppa; so when the disciples heard that Peter was in Lydda, they sent two men to him and urged him, 'Please come at once!' … Peter sent them all out of the room; then he got down on his knees and prayed. Turning towards the dead woman he said, 'Tabitha, get up.' She opened her eyes, and seeing Peter she sat up.

I have commented on this passage many times. I don't mind—good Bible stories are like everlasting lemons: always a few more drops to be squeezed out.

This time I am asking a new question. Why did the Joppa disciples fetch Peter? I mean, why did they not do it themselves? They were Christians in a vibrant spiritual climate and they must have believed the dead could be raised or they wouldn't have bothered to send for him at all. Given the affection in which Tabitha was held and the strength of the Christian community in that town, was nobody at Joppa capable of doing what Peter was likely to do?

The answer must be that they had tried. They must have faithfully prayed for their talented, beloved sister during her illness, and probably after her death as well. It hadn't worked. Put it any other way you want, the fact was it hadn't worked. Hearing Peter was nearby, they must then have decided to pull in someone with more clout. Peter came—just as Jesus always came when people brought their frantic concerns for loved ones to him—and Tabitha was raised from the dead.

Were they right to call on Peter? Recently an extremely level-headed Christian man who is the father of a very sick little girl asked if I thought he should take his daughter to healing meetings. Might it indicate a lack of faith on the part of himself and his wife, bearing in mind that family, friends and church prayed continually for healing?

I said he should go with his heart, but I felt a little uneasy. Now, after this visit to the story of Tabitha, I am strangely reassured.

Hear our hearts, Lord.

THE GOOD LIFE

Acts 10:1–6 (NIV)

At Caesarea there was a man named Cornelius, a centurion… He and all his family were devout and God-fearing; he gave generously to those in need and prayed to God regularly. One day at about three in the afternoon he had a vision. He distinctly saw an angel of God, who came to him and said, 'Cornelius!' Cornelius stared at him in fear. 'What is it, Lord?' he asked. The angel answered, 'Your prayers and gifts to the poor have come up as a memorial offering before God. Now send men to Joppa to bring back a man named Simon who is called Peter. He is staying with Simon the tanner, whose house is by the sea.'

A rather malicious little pseudo-evangelical imp took up residence on my shoulder soon after I became an 'expert' Christian at the age of 16. Nowadays, weary of being swatted away, he rarely appears, but in the bad old days he was a terribly negative fixture. Any dialogue about a man like Cornelius would have proceeded as follows.

Me: This looks like a very good man indeed.

Imp: Christian?

Me: No, but…

Imp: Well, it doesn't matter how good he seems. None of that counts with God. Does this good man realize what a sinner he actually is?

Me: Err, probably not.

Imp: Well, until he does know, these moral baubles of his are valueless. All God sees is an unrepentant sinner.

Me: Mmm, yes, well, I suppose you must be right…

What nonsense! Of course God sees and appreciates the good lives and clean hearts of any human being, Christian or otherwise. It was precisely because of the qualities evident in Cornelius and his family that God sent his angel to organize the link-up with Peter.

In these nervously indulgent days, the concept of holiness can seem a bit of a nuisance in the context of church life. Our anxiety to avoid being judgmental towards others must never be allowed to erode the ideal standards of behaviour that Jesus taught. We all have problems measuring up to those high standards and we always will, this side of heaven. The fact is that God likes good people such as Cornelius and we'd better believe it!

Lord, you love me as I am. Move me nearer to what I shall become.

I DID IT HIS WAY

Acts 10:9–15 (NIV)

Peter went up on the roof to pray. He became hungry and wanted something to eat, and while the meal was being prepared, he fell into a trance. He saw heaven opened and something like a large sheet being let down to earth by its four corners. It contained all kinds of four-footed animals, as well as reptiles of the earth and birds of the air. Then a voice told him, 'Get up, Peter. Kill and eat.' 'Surely not, Lord!' Peter replied. 'I have never eaten anything impure or unclean.' The voice spoke to him a second time, 'Do not call anything impure that God has made clean.'

Was Frank Sinatra a Christian? Did God make him an offer he couldn't refuse? I hope so. I hope everyone was or is or will be whatever they need to be to spend an eternity with Jesus. The thing is, I've been reading this passage and wondering how Simon Peter and Sinatra are getting along in Paradise. One thing they might have in common is the last line of the famous song that Sinatra probably had to promise never to sing again before being allowed into a place where things have a tendency to go on for ever and ever—'I did it my way...'

It hardly seems credible that Peter was still arguing the toss with his Master after those famous happenings in the garden and then in the courtyard and then after a hard night's fishing by the edge of the softly lapping water at breakfast time. Reassuring in a way, though, isn't it? The Spirit came at Pentecost, but Peter was far from being a clone of Jesus. Still stubborn, still thinking he knew what was what, still having to be reminded that the agenda is set by God, not by man, but still ready to carry out the commission with all his heart once he finally understood what it was.

The message of God's words is the same for us as it was for Peter: 'You are hungry to do great things for me. That is very good because there are great things to be done, but please do them my way or not at all. Lay down your right to say "I never will" or "I always do" or "Of this I'm certain", then follow me.'

Everything is provisional except Jesus.

CATCHING THE VISION

Acts 11:1–18 (NIV, abridged)

The apostles and the brothers throughout Judea heard that the Gentiles also had received the word of God. So when Peter went up to Jerusalem, the circumcized believers criticized him and said, 'You went into the house of uncircumcised men and ate with them.' Peter began and explained everything to them precisely as it had happened... 'So if God gave them the same gift as he gave us, who believed in the Lord Jesus Christ, who was I to think that I could oppose God?' When they heard this, they had no further objections and praised God, saying, 'So then, God has even granted the Gentiles repentance unto life.'

This passage depressed me slightly, but why? The story is positive enough. The circumcised believers criticized what Peter had done, Peter explained why he'd done it and then everything was OK. On reflection, it's the very simplicity of the process that causes my sadness. In today's Church, such a situation would result in Peter's words passing through the critics' filters of their own prejudices, then the critics splitting into at least four factions, each convinced that theirs was the ultimate revelation of truth. It is hard for us to grasp how massive the gap between Jews and Gentiles was at the time of Acts, yet Peter had the kind of authority that resulted in circumcised believers saying, 'Oh, fine, great, that's all right then...'

Where did that authority come from? Well, first, he had been one of the twelve who had been close to Jesus. We Christians have no higher calling than to spend time with Jesus. In particular, those in authority are wasting time if their ministry does not have its roots in a close, childlike relationship with God. Christianity is the only boardgame where you lose if you do not go back to square one after each move.

Second, it was a time of spiritual adventure and derring-do. Healings and miracles were happening, angels broke people out of prison, God spoke directly and urgently to his followers in dreams and visions. When Peter described the vision in today's passage his listeners heard and believed what he said. Is there a book of Acts waiting to be written in our own age? Let's hope so.

Lord Jesus, assert your authority through those who stay close to you and are willing to be part of an adventure.

DISASTER REDEFINED

Acts 11:19–21 (NIV)

Now those who had been scattered by the persecution in connection with Stephen travelled as far as Phoenicia, Cyprus and Antioch, telling the message only to Jews. Some of them, however, men from Cyprus and Cyrene, went to Antioch and began to speak to Greeks also, telling them the good news about the Lord Jesus. The Lord's hand was with them, and a great number of people believed and turned to the Lord.

You would have to be a particular kind of loony to pray for persecution to come to the Church in this country. I am a completely different kind of loony, so I pray for other things, but isn't it interesting that this flurry of evangelism was made possible by the persecution and eventual killing of Stephen. Even more remarkable perhaps is the fact that these men, who had probably watched their brother being stoned to death, were anxious to pass on something that they still referred to as the 'good' news. It would have been more than understandable if, by now, it had become the 'not really that good at all' news.

Earlier I was talking about the fact that Paul was happy to accept personal hardship if it meant that Jesus' words would be preached. He was able to do that because he knew that, in the world of the Spirit, the real real world, the concept of disaster is completely redefined. A shipwreck, for instance, becomes an opportunity for witness and healing. A stoning provides the impetus for evangelistic outreach. A crucifixion becomes a resurrection. The Holy Spirit can be in any event or situation, giving shape to chaos and bringing light into dark places. The real disasters occur when men and women turn their backs on the call of God on their lives or are deliberately disobedient to the commands of the Spirit.

Of course, we must not pray for persecution, but what we might pray for is an openness to the work of God in every situation, however difficult and negative it might seem at the time. We may see some remarkable things happening.

Father, our logic is the logic of the world. Free our spirits so that we expect to see you working in all situations.

A BIT OF A PROD

Acts 11:27–30 (NIV)

During this time some prophets came down from Jerusalem to Antioch. One of them, named Agabus, stood up and through the Spirit predicted that a severe famine would spread over the entire Roman world. (This happened during the reign of Claudius.) The disciples, each according to his ability, decided to provide help for the brothers living in Judea. This they did, sending their gift to the elders by Barnabas and Saul.

Do you get the sense, as I do, of the Holy Spirit being a voluntarily restrained member of the Christian community, as opposed to a dominant presence, enforcing attitudes and behaviour against the will of ordinary men and women? Certainly it was the Spirit, through Agabus, who provided the information about a forthcoming major famine, but the disciples themselves decided to provide help for their Judean brethren. Anyone who has ever worked with young people will concede the benefits of allowing them to initiate their own good works. All it needs sometimes is a bit of a prod.

It is also worth noting that the disciples gave variable amounts according to what they could afford. There are two interesting conclusions to be drawn from this. The first is that they must have earned or possessed different amounts of money. A tedious Christian movement emerges from time to time which tries to suggest that the early Church was universally organized on some kind of communist system. Parts of it may have been, but clearly 'having all things in common' meant something quite different for these generous Christians at Antioch. If we are not allowed to take charge of our own generosity or meanness, the whole point is lost.

The second conclusion concerns the far more tedious Christian movement whose adherents claim that all true followers of Jesus should be wealthy or at least comfortably off. How and where did such a ludicrous notion ever gain credence? Surely not in Antioch, certainly not from Paul and definitely not via the Holy Spirit.

Father, thank you for the sane atmosphere in this part of your early Church. Open our ears to your voice speaking wisely and challengingly into our overly comfortable lives. Thank you that in your earthly kingdom we are neither drilled nor indulged.

A man in a passion rides a wild horse.

BENJAMIN FRANKLIN

PASSIONATE PARENTING ON THE PATH TO PARADISE

SOME REACTIONS TO HOSEA

Dear Father,

I am addressing this letter to you at the beginning of my notes on Hosea, because writing them was such a strange, emotional experience, and because there is one thing about the content of this book that I simply cannot understand, however hard I try. Of course, the fact that there is something I can't understand is hardly an earth-shattering surprise—why on earth should I expect to grasp more than anyone else? But, you see, it's not that I'm craving theological insight, or spiritual vision, or exegetical illumination (that's what they have in Blackpool during Bible weeks, isn't it?—sorry), or anything like that. It's just that everything I've thought and felt as I've read about Hosea's unending struggle to make people comprehend the depth of your love, and the intensity of your hurt and anger, leads me towards one genuine and serious question:

HOW CAN YOU, THE CREATOR OF THE UNIVERSE, BE A PARENT AND A PERFECT BEING?

I hope you don't think this is an impertinent question, by the way. Some people find the way I speak to you quite unacceptable. They say I should be in awe of you, and that, if I was, I would never address you in such familiar tones. Well, I've got news for them. I am in awe of you. The last thing in the world that I would ever want to do is get on the wrong side of you, partly because it would frighten me, but also because I know that you love me, and I hate the idea that I might be responsible for hurting you. I treasure our relationship. The knowledge that it is this relationship between father and child that you have chosen to describe the way things should be between you and me, is something that I hold carefully in my hands like the most precious of jewels. And, to an extent, it helps me to understand you, because I have four children of my own (not quite as many as you've got, of course), and I've learned so much about you through having them. We have much more in common than I thought.

For instance, I have learned that when one of my children is really naughty the love I feel for them burns, if anything, more brightly than ever. Everything in me wants the rift to be healed as soon as peace with honour becomes possible. In the past I tended to think that you probably 'went off me' when I misbehaved, and that a good long period of perfect behaviour would be required before you unbent sufficiently to smile in my direction again. I'm sorry that I misjudged you so badly. I should have known, shouldn't I, just by reading the Bible, that you always were more than ready to forgive anyone who is truly sorry.

I've learned also about that razor-sharp knife that cuts into the very centre of a parent's heart when a child is hurt or unhappy or abandoned or disappointed, and there is no immediate means of solving their problems. I know now that you feel all those things, but far more intensely than I do, and the knowledge of that point of identification makes me want to put my arms around you to comfort and be comforted. Is that wrong? It doesn't feel wrong.

I've learned that all sorts of different things happen between a child and a parent. Sometimes I simply play with my daughter. We do ridiculous things together and laugh a lot and play silly tricks on one another. Sometimes I help her (or try to help her) with work she brings home from school. We sit at the kitchen table together, puzzling jointly over maths problems that seem to bear no relation at all to anything I ever tackled when I was being educated. From time to time I get cross with her, especially when she deliberately annoys her older brother and ignites one of those dreadful squealing, squabbling, bickering arguments that are based on nothing, but drive everyone else mad. Sometimes I go and look at her when she is fast asleep and think about how much I love her. And you do all these things with us, don't you, Father? You laugh with us, and teach us, and discipline us, and look on us with great love when we are at peace.

All these things I have learned about you through having my own children, and the knowledge that you and I feel the same things (albeit on such a different scale) is a source of warmth and reassurance.

But what about the differences between you and me, Father? In one of the poems that I've written for this section there's a line that says you are 'burdened with perfection and with passion'. How do you do it, Father? How do you do it? How do you deal with those storms of feeling, when you are not allowed (not able?) to sulk for a while, or to blow your top when it would have been better to go out of the room and come back in again, or to blame somebody else when it was your fault in the first place, or to seek solace in three fingers of whisky, or to blame your own parents and their parents before them for the problems that have actually been caused by your own poor parenting, or to make threats that you can't carry out and have to climb down from later on?

How can you, the creator of the universe, be a parent and a perfect being? In this book, the story of the prophet Hosea, I can feel great waves of love and anger pouring from you towards those infuriating Israelites who meant so much to you, and, as a parent myself, I, in my own feeble way, feel so sorry for you. And it's still going on with us, isn't it?

Do you sometimes wish that you were not perfect?

Love,

Adrian

VICIOUS CIRCLE

Hosea 1:1 (NIV)

The word of the Lord that came to Hosea son of Beeri during the reigns of Uzziah, Jotham, Ahaz and Hezekiah, kings of Judah, and during the reign of Jeroboam son of Joash king of Israel.

Commentaries on Hosea speak of the difficulty involved in finding coherent meaning in the book as a whole, but it looks as if the prophet gave an ear-blasting to at least six different kings of Israel, so we're actually talking about a long and complex period in the nation's history. The repeated pattern of anger and forgiveness needs to be seen as happening over a period of many years.

What a pain in the neck this chap Hosea must have been. Every time those in authority—kings or priests—cobbled together some morally threadbare system designed to accommodate the sinful excesses of the people, a system that would necessarily exclude the one true God, along would come Hosea to 'spoil' everything by telling the truth.

Some marriages (not mine, of course) can be a bit like this. Paul Tournier speaks about some wives becoming 'policemen' in their husband's lives, continually wagging a metaphorical finger when their spouses stray from the straight and narrow. A relationship once full of tenderness and mutual idealism becomes cold and strained as love is transformed to disapproval on one side, and annoyed resentment on the other. The wife takes on a parental role in order to cope with her husband's regression to teenage-style awkwardness.

This is more or less what's happening here with God and Israel, at least, as far as Israel is concerned. The God who provided for their every need, passionately caring for them when they needed him most, has become an irritating interference, a nagging marital partner who is no longer wanted, or a preaching parent who wants to stop everybody from 'having a good time'. The vicious circle of disapproval and resentment, one that is very difficult to break out of, is expressed here in very human terms. Much of Hosea's message from God is filled with the desperate pain-filled fury that characterizes those who have been betrayed and neglected.

Frankly, I can't believe that Hosea was on many people's Passover-card list, and he'd be no more popular now than he was then, but, oh, how we could do with him in this age.

You loved us then, you love us now. Through Jesus you revealed that you are not a policeman, but a father. Forgive our neglect and draw us back to you, Father, so that we don't have to face your anger.

FAMILY MATTERS

Hosea 1:4–9 (NIV)

Then the Lord said to Hosea, 'Call him Jezreel, because I will soon punish the house of Jehu for the massacre at Jezreel, and I will put an end to the kingdom of Israel...' Gomer conceived again and gave birth to a daughter. Then the Lord said to Hosea, 'Call her Lo-Ruhamah, for I will no longer show love to the house of Israel...' Gomer had another son. Then the Lord said, 'Call him Lo-Ammi, for you are not my people, and I am not your God.'

Dear Miss Osborne,

Early contact with the family provides the following information:

Father is unemployed, but states, usually very loudly from the upstairs window of his house, that he is a mouthpiece for God. Hosea the Prophet claims that God instructed him to marry an adulterous woman and use their relationship as a sort of visual aid to illustrate people's religious shortcomings. This did not produce queues of eager applicants, but Hosea did—incredibly—find a willing candidate with the somewhat muppet-like name of Gomer, a member of the Diblaim family, who have been known to this office for a number of years.

Hosea then moved to the fathering of three offspring by Gomer, and it is their welfare that causes concern. Hosea's choice of names alone indicates that all three are at risk.

Jezreel, the oldest boy, is named after a bloody and brutally inhuman massacre, because he is the symbol of God's decision to destroy the whole community. This has not exactly endeared the boy to local residents.

The second child, a girl, is called Lo-Ruhamah, which means 'Not Loved', a further sign of God's refusal to forgive the world in general. Such a name is unlikely to enhance a developing child's self-confidence.

Lo-Ammi, the second son, completes the set, as it were. His title conveys a message from God to all and sundry that they are not his people and he is not their God. Lo-Ammi doesn't get many party invites.

I recommend a social worker be appointed immediately, as 'Hosea the Prophet' and Gomer seem incapable of understanding that the God Hosea claims to represent would never allow children to be subjected to the hardship that these three have endured.

Yours, Vic Stapley

Father, the Old Testament continually throws up things about you that I just won't—can't—don't want to accept, but lead us into all truth, whatever the truth turns out to be.

PRACTICAL FORGIVENESS

Hosea 3:1–4 (NIV)

The Lord said to me, 'Go, show your love to your wife again, though she is… an adulteress. Love her as the Lord loves the Israelites, though they turn to other gods…' So I bought her for fifteen shekels of silver and about a homer and a lethek of barley. Then I told her, 'You are to live with me for many days; you must not be a prostitute or be intimate with any man…' For the Israelites will live for many days without king or prince…

Defining forgiveness and working out how you actually do it is an ongoing preoccupation of many Christians. Those of us who try to follow Jesus are all too aware that we are directly commanded to forgive those who hurt us. When Peter asked his master how many times he was supposed to forgive his brother he probably assumed the answer would be something like, 'Well, two or three's more than enough—four at the most…' In fact, of course, as we all know, Jesus said that Peter should forgive ' up to seventy times seven', and he didn't mean that, having put up with your brother annoying you 490 times, you were then free to smack him in the mouth. Forgiveness is meant to be for ever.

But isn't it difficult? The experience many of us have is that we try hard to change the way we feel about someone who's wronged us, and perhaps feel that we've succeeded, only to discover that all the old bitterness and anger comes flowing back when we least expect it. I suspect the reason is that 'being a Christian' tends to be a rather cerebral business nowadays. God is very practical, and, contrary to the belief of many, practicality and spirituality are not mutually exclusive. Read the book of James.

Hosea was commanded not just to forgive Gomer, but to buy her back and physically reinstate her as his wife, even though she had committed adultery. Forgiveness would occur within the framework of this practical act of reinstatement, an act that depended not on Hosea's feelings about his wife, but on his obedience to God's will. Perhaps, if we can, by an act of obedience, allow or actively draw those who have injured us into areas of our lives where we would really rather not have them, forgiveness will have a chance to become real. I'm not for one moment claiming that it will be easy, but then, whoever started the ridiculous rumour that it would?

Who have I not forgiven? What can I do?

HURTING THE LAND

Hosea 4:1–3 (NIV)

The Lord has a charge to bring against you who live in the land: 'There is no faithfulness, no love, no acknowledgment of God in the land. There is only cursing, lying and murder, stealing and adultery; they break all bounds, and bloodshed follows bloodshed. Because of this the land mourns, and all who live in it waste away; the beasts of the field and the birds of the air and the fish of the sea are dying.'

Nothing changes much, does it? The first two verses could easily be describing the moral decline that seems to be common to all so-called civilized nations at present, and the third reflects the concerns and warnings constantly expressed by those who feel that the natural environment is in real danger of being damaged and misused by us.

Sometimes, you know, a deep, dark pool of fear is stirred in me. It happens when I face the fact that our society does not, by and large, give any credence to the idea that an all-powerful God will eventually react to this general decline. 'There is no acknowledgment of God in the land', says Hosea in this passage, and if anyone is looking for a strong theme on which to pray, this may well be it. Pray that more and more people will discover the missing piece of the jigsaw that makes sense of the whole picture. Pray that the terrible distortion of God's image that we as Christians are responsible for will not obscure the truth. Pray for healing in this increasingly immoral society and in the natural world. Pray that, at last, God will be acknowledged in the land.

Don't you find it interesting that God links death and decay in nature with moral and spiritual decline? What can he possibly mean by saying that 'the land mourns'? The New Testament view is that the whole of creation groans as it waits for redemption. Apparently everything that exists is from God, is linked with God, and is indivisibly part of his total creation. Somehow—and I certainly don't understand this—the pain and sin or elation and virtue that enter into our lives are registered in the very rocks themselves, and in the seas that surround us. We don't begin to comprehend the nature and complexity of this masterpiece of God's, but perhaps that ignorance is quite a good place to start.

Jesus tells us that there is great rejoicing in heaven over one sinner who repents, and that rejoicing permeates the physical world as well. Likewise, when we perform some small selfish act, the vibrations, however small, will be felt everywhere. Let's work towards a wider acknowledgment of God, and give the land a break.

PROPHETS AND PRIESTS

Hosea 4:7–9 (NIV)

The more the priests increased, the more they sinned against me; they exchanged their Glory for something disgraceful. They feed on the sins of my people and relish their wickedness. And it will be: Like people, like priests. I will punish both of them for their ways and repay them for their deeds.

One morning I received an extraordinary letter from a Christian hotel in an exotic part of the world. After reading the first couple of paragraphs I laughed loudly, and Bridget looked enquiringly at me over the top of her coffee mug.

'I've been invited to be "Prophet in Residence" at a holiday hotel,' I said.

Bridget laughed at the title, but when I told her where the hotel was located her eyes reflected the greedy gleam in mine. Miraculously, we both felt strongly guided to accept the offer of a free holiday on this tropical island, one that we'd always wanted to visit. Alas, as I read on, I discovered that (rather surprisingly) I was expected to pay all my own travel expenses, a condition which abruptly ended my dreams of enjoying sun-soaked relaxation in exchange for the occasional, gently benevolent prophecy to my fellow residents.

'Oh, well', said Bridget, looking disappointed, 'you're not a prophet, so you couldn't have done it anyway.'

I nodded resignedly and reached for the marmalade.

I forgot all about it until fairly recently when a friend asked me quite seriously if I thought I was a prophet or not. My immediate reaction was to snort sardonically, but he persisted, so I said that apart from one or two isolated occasions, I had never been aware of God literally speaking through me. Later I reviewed what I'd said, and was a little horrified when I thought about how much (considering my non-prophet status) I've talked and written about God. What a cheek! In any case, I reflected, all Christians are priests nowadays, according to scripture, so the responsibility for what we say to others, and the way we represent our faith, is enormous, whoever we are.

I went all hot and cold as I remembered some of my verbal excesses —and this passage from Hosea hasn't helped much. God seems to be saying that the priests of Israel had completely misused the power that they held—instead of representing the ways and the will of God, they were, for their own benefit, fitting in with what sinful people wanted.

It can happen in such a way…

Prayer

Father, whether we're prophets or priests, help us to make sure when we talk to others about you, that we are speaking for you, and not for us.

TURNING ROUND

Hosea 4:12 (NIV)

They consult a wooden idol and are answered by a stick of wood. A spirit of prostitution leads them astray; they are unfaithful to their God.

Here is an extract from a conversation I had with an old friend whom I shall call 'Rita'. Rita is one of those people in whose world everyone appears to make one physical revolution before speaking. Rita made us a pot of tea, then she sat down and said (after turning round, of course), 'I was out with Plank an' Emma last night, an' she was saying—'

Me: Plank?
Rita: Plank an' Emma, yea, an' she was saying—
Me: Plank? How can anyone be called Plank?
Rita: He just is. That's his name. What?
Me: It just seems a bit of an odd name. He can't have been christened Plank, surely? (*We both turn round before continuing our conversation*)
Rita: Oh, no, his actual name's Ricky, but we all call him Plank.
Me: Yes, but why?
Rita: 'Cos he's thick.
Me: Ah! As in two short... yes, I see. And he doesn't mind?
Rita: No, you call him Ricky and he won't even turn round, but if you call him Plank he says, 'Yea, what?' He knows he's thick, see?
Me: I see.
Rita: Anyway, Emma turned round an' she said to me...

Whatever these Israelites were called, God must have been tempted to call each one 'Plank'. People made in the image God—indeed, a particular people rescued, nurtured and protected by him—had put its faith in wooden idols. Planks seeking revelation from planks. How could they have been so thick?

Where there is sin and self-absorption and no genuine will for change, it is virtually impossible to meet the eye of one who will never dilute his response to evil. Later, God complains that people do not cry out to him from their hearts, but 'wail upon their beds'. This reminds me of when I have persisted in deliberate sin, and paused only for long enough to moan that God isn't interested in me any more—you know the sort of thing I mean. No hint of repentance, just the complaint that I'm not allowed to have my self-indulgent cake topped with the icing of spiritual comfort. It's a small step from there to 'Plank Allegiance', and then nothing will go right until, like Rita's friends, we turn round and say something (from the heart) to God.

We take the risk of turning to you, Father, because we know that not doing so is a much greater risk.

RELIGION AND RELAXATION

Hosea 6:6 (NIV)

For I desire mercy, not sacrifice, and acknowledgment of God rather than burnt offerings.

Some years ago I wrote a book called *Broken Windows, Broken Lives*, a fictional account of my experiences as a residential worker in a boarding school for maladjusted boys. That horrible word 'maladjusted' simply meant that these children were unable to cope with the situations they had found themselves in. My job as Housefather was to look after the daily physical and emotional needs of about 25 of these kids, half the school in fact. I was 21, and the fact that I thought I could do the job shows how naïve I must have been.

At first it all looked terribly easy. I accompanied an experienced member of staff called Bob as he woke the children, supervised showers and dressing, joined them for breakfast, and checked the small domestic tasks that each one performed before school-time. It all looked so relaxed and effortless. The boys were fully cooperative at every stage, and Bob never needed to raise his voice, let alone get cross. They just—did it. I remember, on that first morning, hearing screamed orders and swearing coming from the other side of the house, and congratulating myself on being on the side where the pleasant children were. I did just wonder why they'd put all the nice children on one side and all the difficult ones on the other...

The next morning, the first one on my own, I thought they must have switched the groups of boys around. But they hadn't. It was the altered staffing that made the difference. Where there had been cooperation and friendliness there was resentment and argument, where there had been calm there was loud noise and chaos, and where there had been willingness and industry there was laziness and grumbling. I hated it. To make matters worse, those on the other side, now looked after by Bob, had been transfigured, and were behaving like little angels.

I went through a long, painful period of instituting procedures, rules, fixed penalties and other aids to gaining control. The reaction of my charges was negative and grudging, and it was a very long time before I came anywhere near acquiring Bob's deceptively relaxed style of supervision, but I was so relieved when, eventually, temporary structures could be replaced by genuine relationship. Why, oh, why, did it take them so long to understand that I cared for them?

Why, oh, why does it take us so long to understand that you care for us? Roll on the day when religion rolls away.

POOH-STICKS

Hosea 10:7 (NIV)

Samaria and its king will float away like a twig on the surface of the waters.

Have you ever played Pooh-sticks? A.A. Milne invented it, and it's very simple. You stand with someone else on a bridge over a river or a stream, and you each throw a stick into the water. Then you hurry to the other side of the bridge, and the person whose stick comes floating through first is the winner. It doesn't call for any great skill, but our family has always enjoyed it. The bridge we especially like is on the outskirts of Alfriston, a beautiful old village set among the Downs, a few miles from where we live. You must go and see it if you haven't already.

In this passage God is saying through Hosea that he is capable of causing the most powerful nations, people and institutions to simply float away and disappear like one of those Pooh-stick twigs. You and I might find this fact very depressing or extremely encouraging, depending on what our 'twig' happens to be.

We might think it depressing, for instance, that money, or looks, or power, or human achievement, or life itself, or any of the other things that the world offers can be removed and discounted with such casual despatch. Many of us have invested everything we have and are and hope for in such trifles. The image of God leaning over a parapet and dropping our precious bundle of things into a slow-moving inexorable current that will take them away for ever is not an attractive one.

On the other hand, if our priorities have been rightly adjusted, we might be mightily heartened by the fact that he is just as capable of taking our blackest sins and sorrows—nasty charred old bits of wood, if you like—and dropping them with equal abandonment into the moving stream. If we then hurry across the bridge we shall be in time to see them come out on the other side, and we can watch as they become smaller and smaller before disappearing altogether in the far distance.

Play Pooh-sticks with God. Stand beside him on the bridge and, with due consideration, hand him the things that you want to get rid of, one by one. When they've all gone, rush across with him and watch them float away. Then, I suggest that you walk off the bridge, across the green, and into Alfriston to celebrate, possibly with one of their very good cream teas...

LOOKING BACK

Hosea 11:1–4 (NIV)

'When Israel was a child, I loved him, and out of Egypt I called my son. But the more I called Israel, the further they went from me. They sacrificed to the Baals… It was I who taught Ephraim to walk… but they did not realise it was I who healed them. I led them with cords of human kindness, with ties of love; I lifted the yoke from their neck and bent down to feed them.

The person who wrote this passage must have been chosen by God because he knew what it was like to have difficult or rebellious teenage children (sorry—that's a tautology, isn't it?).

It may be foolish fancy, but I picture God sitting at home in an armchair flicking through old photograph albums in which his rescue of the children of Israel from Egypt is recorded. I've done the same sort of thing myself, sighed and wiped away the beginnings of a tear as those carefully preserved snapshots remind me of when my children were so dependent on Bridget and me for their most basic physical needs that there was no question of division or serious conflict between us. We looked after them and they cuddled us—that was more or less the deal. As they get older, the loss (temporary though it usually is) of that simple arrangement can come close to breaking a parent's heart. This change in relationship is actually the door to a different but equally profound closeness, as long as we mothers and fathers will walk willingly through the door and close it firmly behind us, but the pain of the process can be unbearable sometimes.

Here is God the Father, then, cooing over the first tottering steps of his little ones, recalling the pleasure with which he healed them, fed them and removed obstacles from their path, but, at the same time, shaking his head in anguished disbelief over the fact that those same cherished children have now put their trust in other, man-made gods, and forgotten the one who loves them with genuine power and passion.

I don't want to appear disrespectful, but, as far as the pain is concerned, he sounds just like me, and I find that rather helpful. If God really does regard me with anything like the same torrential love as I regard my own children (and, of course, that's an understatement) then I probably hurt him far more than I have realized when I ignore him and turn to the alien gods who inhabit this little corner of the 21st century.

We are used to the idea of God being angry, but how will we react to the knowledge that he is hurt?

Father, we have hurt you. Forgive us, and let us be close again.

JUST FOR NOW

Hosea 11:8–11 (NIV)

'How can I give you up, Ephraim? How can I hand you over, Israel? How can I treat you like Admah? How can I make you like Zeboiim? My heart is changed within me; all my compassion is aroused. I will not carry out my fierce anger, nor will I turn and devastate Ephraim. For I am God, and not man—the Holy One among you. I will not come in wrath. They will follow the Lord; he will roar like a lion. When he roars, his children will come trembling from the west. They will come trembling like birds from Egypt, like doves from Assyria. I will settle them in their homes,' declares the Lord.

Forgive us if we say
We want to take you in our arms
Sad Father, weeping God
Breathless with the storms
Of anger—of compassion
Fists clenched hard around your grief
Around the marks
The cost
The proof
How can you give us up?
How can you hand us over?
Of course you never can
Never could
Never will
Burdened with perfection and with passion
Lay your head down
Let us hold you for a while
We will try to be to you
What you have been to us so many times
Peace, Lord, be a child once again
Do you remember Mary's arms?
So warm
So different
Rest quietly and soon you will be strong enough
To be a lion thundering from way beyond the east
We will come trembling from the west

We promise you
Like birds
Like doves
Like children who have suddenly remembered
Who taught them how to laugh
But just for now
Forgive us if we say
We want to take you in our arms
Sad Father, weeping God.

FREE LOVE

Hosea 13:4–7 (NIV)

But I am the Lord your God, who brought you out of Egypt. You shall acknowledge
no God but me, no Saviour except me. I cared for you in the desert, in the land of
burning heat. When I fed them, they were satisfied; when they were satisfied, they
became proud; then they forgot me. So I will come upon them like a lion, like a
leopard I will lurk by the path.

If I wanted I could take the light
One shining sheet of paper
Crush it in my fist
And so, it would be night
If I was so inclined
I could destroy the day with fire
Warm my hands at all your charred tomorrows
With the smallest movement of my arm
One flicker of my will
Sweep you and all your darkness from the land
But I cannot make you love me
I cannot make you love me
I cannot make you, will not make you, cannot make you love me
If I wanted I could lift the sea
As if it was a turquoise tablecloth
Uncover lost forgotten things
Unwritten history
It would be easy to revive the bones
Of men who never thought to see their homes again
I have revived one shipwrecked man in such a way
The tale of that rescuing
That coming home
Might prove I care for you
But though I can inscribe I LOVE YOU
on the sea and in the sky
I cannot make you love me
I cannot make you love me
I cannot make you, will not make you, cannot make you love me.

HOSEA-FIED?

Hosea 13:16; 14:4–6 (NIV)

'The people of Samaria must bear their guilt, because they have rebelled against their God. They will fall by the sword; their little ones will be dashed to the ground, their pregnant women ripped open... I will heal their waywardness and love them freely, for my anger has turned away from them. I will be like the dew to Israel; he will blossom like a lily.'

The vivid contrast between these two passages is a recurring feature of much of the Old Testament. God appears to swing wildly from crashing, vengeful fury to warm, compassionate forgiveness with bewildering swiftness. I asked someone else to tell me honestly what they thought about the personality that seems to be revealed here. I needed to because I couldn't quite focus on what I thought myself. It's difficult to face one's own response to some of these passages because each response passes through the sieve of religious conditioning. I have to give myself permission to look at what I really think.

'Well,' said my friend, wrestling inwardly, but, unlike me, determinedly pinning half-truth to the floor, 'he comes over as rather immature, doesn't he? I mean, he's doing all the things that teachers and parents are told they should never do—making huge threats and then not carrying them out, getting murderously angry and then going all sort of sentimental. That's how I see it. Bound to be wrong, of course.'

'Mmm...' I felt the same. This God didn't seem much like Jesus.

Well, here's a thought. It's only a thought. Don't unofficially excommunicate me. Discuss it—consider it.

Hosea marries a woman who turns out unfaithful and unstable. Hosea is a maritally loyal but emotionally immature fellow of extreme passions, who loves this wife of his, and her waywardness drives him into bouts of irrational fury, followed by tearful expressions of love and forgiveness. God, who is casting around for someone to convey to Israel his anger, his pain and his willingness to start again, decides to use this inadequate but (crucially) available vehicle, even if the message gets grossly Hosea-fied on the way through. Hosea decides that a little licence is allowable in the area of his reasons for marrying Gomer in the first place, and there we are. God filtered through man. Not the first time—and, I can assure you, certainly not the last.

Forgive me if I'm up the creek here, Lord, but this is a real problem for a lot of us. What we do know is that Jesus is the living expression of you, and for that we are deeply thankful.

All sin is a kind of lying.

ST AUGUSTINE

UNAUTHORIZED EXCURSIONS

THE STORY OF DAVID AND BATHSHEBA

Yes, that's right, we're talking about David; the same David who killed Goliath, the Philistine giant; the same David who slew lions and bears when he was just a shepherd boy looking after his father's sheep; the same David who played soothing harp music to the manic-depressive King Saul, and was later driven into exile by that insanely jealous king when he could no longer stand the chant of the Israeli people: 'Saul has killed his thousands and David his ten thousands!'

We are talking about David, who mourned for his closest friend, Jonathan, the son of Saul, when he died next to his father on the field of battle, and then came back to Jerusalem and was made king, years after the great prophet Samuel had anointed the young shepherd boy with oil and declared that, against all the odds, it would be so.

This is David, who brought the ark of God back to the holy city at last and danced with joy in front of it, and, when his first wife, Michal, mocked him, said: 'I was dancing before the Lord who chose me and appointed me as leader of Israel, the people of God. So I don't mind acting like a fool in order to show my joy in the Lord. Yes, and I don't mind looking even more stupid than this.'

This is David, who was promised by God through the prophet Nathan that he would become one of the most famous people in the world.

David.

You know, David really loved God. He really loved him. He loved his generosity, couldn't understand why he showered blessings on someone who had started out as nothing, with nothing. He said: 'You know what I'm like. Why do you do it? Because you want to. Because you said you would. Well, go ahead, and—thank you.'

David was so well set up! Wives, concubines, children, property—he had everything. Fair to everyone, justice to all, that was David's style. A good king. God's man. Every battle, every campaign began with the same questions to God: 'Should I go? Is it right? What do you want?' And always, the questions were answered, and the battles, the campaigns—hugely successful.

All was well. Life was rich and fulfilling. Israel was in good hands. How could a man like David possibly go wrong?

WHERE IS THE BATTLE?

2 Samuel 11:1–3 (NRSV)

In the spring of the year, the time when kings go out to battle, David sent Joab with his officers and all Israel with him; they ravaged the Ammonites, and besieged Rabbah. But David remained at Jerusalem. It happened, late one afternoon, when David rose from his couch and was walking about on the roof of the king's house, that he saw from the roof a woman bathing; the woman was very beautiful. David sent someone to inquire about the woman. It was reported, 'This is Bathsheba... the wife of Uriah the Hittite.'

It is so easy to go wrong.

One night David took a walk on the palace roof. It was springtime, the battle season, the season when kings usually went to war. It was a beautiful night. The air was vibrant, electric. He had tried to sleep, but he was just unable to relax. Not surprising. The army was away under the leadership of the great Israeli general, Joab. Joab's brief was a simple one—destroy the Ammonites, and he had already begun by laying siege to the city of Rabbah.

Of course the king couldn't sleep! David, the soldier, the ex-guerilla leader, the commander, the man of action, must have been regretting his decision to stay home. He must have been itching to abandon the luxury of his palace, to be where he knew he belonged, out in the field with his fighting men. It would take something very powerful, very stimulating, to push these thoughts of blood and battle from his mind.

He strolled slowly along the edge of the palace roof, gazing out over the city lying quietly in the moonlight before him. Suddenly he stopped, his gaze fixed on the courtyard of a dwelling house not far from the royal residence. A woman was bathing. She was naked—beautiful, more beautiful than any woman he had ever seen. He wanted her. He sent a servant to find out who she was.

He wanted her.

Never mind that he had wives and concubines of his own. Never mind that this woman turned out to be the wife of Uriah, a loyal warrior, who, at this very moment was fighting under David's banner in the struggle to capture Rabbah.

He wanted her. Her name was Bathsheba.

He burned for her, and he wanted her—now.

Father, sometimes when we should be at the battle we stay home. Forgive us and protect us.

SELF-DELUSION

2 Samuel 11:4 (NRSV)

So David sent messengers to fetch her, and she came to him, and he lay with her. (Now she was purifying herself after her period.) Then she returned to her house.

David didn't burn for long. He sent for Bathsheba that night. He slept with her that night. And in the morning he sent her home.

Now, this is where we part company with all those who have never done anything wrong, because they just won't understand. You see, David knew he had done wrong. Oh, yes! No doubt about that. He knew God's law as well as anyone else: Thou shalt not commit adultery.

For commoners and kings alike the law was just the same, and he knew it. Probably for the first time in his life, David had deliberately left God out of the reckoning. Now that the deed had been done it occurred to him that it might be better to avoid Nathan the prophet for a time. The old man could have heard something on his hotline from God, and David had never been told off by God before.

Anyway, perhaps the whole thing would blow over soon. Was it such a terrible sin? He had wanted her so much. The very power of his feelings had somehow seemed to make it right at the time. And Uriah, the husband, need never know. Bathsheba and her servants were silenced by royal command. No problem there. Yes, perhaps it would just blow over, and later on he'd make his peace with God too—when the dust had settled, as it were. And when Uriah came back from the war, he'd give him a fine present—in appreciation of his soldierly feats, of course. Uriah would feel very honoured. Well, anybody would, wouldn't they? Bathsheba would like that too.

David could continue to be the great and good king, loved and respected by all. It had just been a silly slip, quite out of character. Surely he was allowed to make one mistake. He'd got so many things right, for goodness' sake! Granted, Nathan might not see it that way, but he needn't see him for a while. Yes, surely the whole thing would blow over soon.

Thus, David talked himself into an uneasy peace, but deep in his heart he knew with dark and lonely certainty that, for the time being at least, he had lost God and was on his own.

Father, protect us from the dangerous self-delusion that sin doesn't really matter.

WEBS

2 Samuel 11:5 (and read 6–11) (NRSV)

The woman conceived; and she sent and told David, 'I am pregnant.'

It didn't blow over. It got worse—much worse. One of Bathsheba's servants arrived at the palace. She had a message. She would speak only to the king. No, she would not speak to David's servant. Yes, she must speak to the king himself, with no others present. When she was finally ushered into his presence she could hardly bring herself to speak. David was kind to her—coaxed her. At last, she told him. Her mistress, Bathsheba, was pregnant. What did the king suggest?

What indeed?

White-lipped and tense with shock, David dismissed the girl and considered alternatives.

Tell all? Confess to Uriah when he returned? Call Nathan? Confess to God? Confess that good king David had stolen a fighting soldier's wife and used her casually for a night?

No! He was David! He could never bear to be less than the sum of rich qualities that his name had come to mean throughout the land of Judah and far beyond. Self-preservation, that was all that mattered right now. There was another way, and it could work. If Uriah were to sleep with his wife in the very near future, then everyone would assume that the baby, when it came, was his. But Uriah was at the war. Uriah was at Rabbah.

David summoned him, and, when he arrived a few days later, greeted him personally, asked how the battle was going, talked as one old soldier to another, shook him by the hand, sent him home for the night, sent a present to his house.

That night David slept. The nightmare was over—or so he thought.

Uriah, an honest captain of fighting men, and a stickler for the rules, had refused to stay in the comfort of his own home while his troops suffered hardship at the front. He slept by the palace door.

How his eyes must have shone as he explained to the king why he hadn't gone home. David would understand. He knew what it was like. He too was a leader of men. Of course he would understand.

Oh, what tangled webs we weave...

INTO THE DARKNESS

2 Samuel 11:12–13 (NRSV)

Then David said to Uriah, 'Remain here today also, and tomorrow I will send you back.' So Uriah remained in Jerusalem that day. On the next day, David invited him to eat and drink in his presence and made him drunk; and in the evening he went out to lie on his couch with the servants of his lord, but he did not go down to his house.

How did you feel when you learned that your clever ploy with Uriah had failed to work, David? Did you feel ashamed, or did you just feel wild panic driving your mind to work, to plan, to find a way—any way—to remove the problem?

Did Uriah guess that all was not well? That night, when you entertained him again at the palace, feasted him well, made sure that he drank far too much, talked about war and wives, did he suspect that something else was going on—something that he couldn't quite understand? Because he didn't go home that night either, did he? He slept in the servants' room again.

I wonder, David, do you think Uriah slept easy that night, or did he suffer strange nightmares of pointless, bloody fighting and dying, of a woman running naked through a storm, of another battle fought with something other than swords—a battle that he had already lost without ever being given the chance to fight?

And what about you, David? Did you sleep on that second night of Uriah's stay? I bet you didn't. I bet you lay awake thinking and thinking and thinking—what do I do if he doesn't go home again? And in the morning, when you knew that Uriah was still there, still in the palace, when you knew that plan A was not going to work, was that when you finally faced the fact that, other than the confession you would not contemplate, there was only plan B left?

Uriah had to die, didn't he? You had reached the point where you couldn't care less what you had to do as long as your crime was concealed, even if it meant committing another, even worse crime to do it.

Father, give those who are about to step into utter darkness the courage to turn back.

DANGEROUS SAFETY

2 Samuel 11:14–16 (NRSV)

In the morning David wrote a letter to Joab, and sent it by the hand of Uriah. In the letter he wrote, 'Set Uriah in the forefront of the hardest fighting, and then draw back from him, so that he may be struck down and die.' As Joab was besieging the city, he assigned Uriah to the place where he knew there were valiant warriors.

The morning after Uriah's second night at the palace, you wrote a letter to Joab, field commander of the armed forces. Joab would do whatever he was told. He knew which side his bread was buttered on. Was any part of you sickened by the words you wrote in that letter, David? You remember the words, don't you? It was quite a short message really.

'Joab, place Uriah in the front line where the fighting is at its hottest, then draw back and leave him. I want him dead.'

And who delivered this instruction to Joab? No prizes for guessing. Good old trusting Uriah, wasn't it? Reported smartly back at camp to deliver his own death sentence. Went out to face the fiercest of the Rabbah defenders without question, and died at the foot of the city walls, puzzled by the sudden, unaccountable lack of support, but proud to give his life in the service of the king who had so generously wined and dined and talked intimately with him only a few short days ago.

Plan B worked like a dream, didn't it, David? And all you felt was relief. In the space of a few short weeks you had trained yourself to stay deaf to the once-familiar voice that said:

'Thou shalt not lie.

'Thou shalt not covet.

'Thou shalt not commit adultery.

'Thou shalt not murder.'

Like so many people before and since, David discovered that after only a few steps into the swamp of deceit and cruelty, he almost forgot what it meant to be clean. He was safe—safe from the judgment of men, that is. Uriah was well and truly fixed. Time to relax? Maybe.

Being safe according to the world's terms can be very dangerous indeed.

NAILS

2 Samuel 11:25 (NRSV)

David said to the messenger, 'Thus you shall say to Joab, "Do not let this matter trouble you, for the sword devours now one and now another; press your attack on the city, and overthrow it." And encourage him.'

Surely, in some remote corner of David's heart, as he pronounced these hollow words, the shepherd boy, the honourable soldier, the servant of the Lord, was in anguish—furious with himself and everyone else.

Was David looking for someone to blame? If so, I wonder if God was his first choice.

Didn't you mean what you said when you called me?
Didn't you mean it at all?
When I was young and you knew you enthralled me,
Did you know then I would fall?
I was so sure, I was sure I would never,
Never be parted from you,
I'm just a king who has taken his pleasure,
What did you think I would do?

Was it a lie? Did you deceive?
Do you not love me at all?
Better to die if I believe,
That you don't love me at all.
I get the picture, you're talking of murder,
Let's put a name to the crime!
But I never wanted to go any further,
And you weren't around at the time.

Let's not pretend I'm the only offender,
I'm only joining the queue,
No, don't try to tell me your love is so tender,
I am just spoiling your view.
Will you forgive? I need to know,
Can it all be like before?
How can I live if you say no,
If it can't be like before?

You won't forgive, You will say no,
No, it can't be like before,
Somehow I'll live when you say no,
No, it can't be like before.

Didn't you mean what you said when you called me?
Didn't you mean it at all?
When I was young and you knew you enthralled me,
Did you know then I would fall?
I wish I could know and be sure in the morning,
That you will be there when I call.

A thought: *Before and after Calvary, the nails are constantly hammered in.*

A SOCK IN THE JAW

2 Samuel 11:26–27 (and read 12:1–7) (NRSV)

When the wife of Uriah heard that her husband was dead, she made lamentation for him. When the mourning was over, David sent and brought her to his house, and she became his wife, and bore him a son. But the thing that David had done displeased the Lord.

Bathsheba mourned.

Yes, that's right. Bathsheba mourned for her dead husband. When the king of Israel sends for you to sleep with him, you don't send a note back saying, 'I'm not that sort of girl.' You have no choice. Bathsheba didn't give away anything. Her husband was dead. She mourned for him.

As for God being displeased—yes, you could put it like that. God must have been, at the very least, displeased. But, however angry he might have been, it was more than nine months since David's stroll on the palace roof, and so far, not a word from God—no sign of Nathan. Everything had settled down. Perhaps it had blown over.

As David warmed himself by the fire in a corner of the royal palace one night his mood matched the winter season—cold but settled. The fear had almost gone, but so had the joy. The baby was a great pleasure, but real happiness was rare, to say the least. Still, the panic had passed. It was possible to relax nowadays. Sometimes he almost managed to forget the nightmare events of last year. It really began to look as if there was to be no comeback—no punishment.

He hardly heard the servant announce a visitor, and when he did turn towards the door he was not particularly interested—until he saw who it was. Then, his stomach seemed to turn to ice, and the old fear gripped him tight, so that, for a moment, he could only stare dumbly at the figure standing in the doorway. It was Nathan.

How relieved David must have felt on discovering that Nathan had only come round to tell a little story, but what a sock in the jaw that punchline must have been!

Sock it to us, if necessary, Lord.

FACING UP

Psalm 51:1–12 (and read 13–19) (NRSV)

Have mercy on me, O God, according to your steadfast love; according to your abundant mercy blot out my transgressions. Wash me thoroughly from my iniquity, and cleanse me from my sin. For I know my transgressions, and my sin is ever before me. Against you, you alone, have I sinned, and done what is evil in your sight, so that you are justified in your sentence and blameless when you pass judgment. Indeed, I was born guilty, a sinner when my mother conceived me. You desire truth in the inward being; therefore teach me wisdom in my secret heart. Purge me with hyssop, and I shall be clean; wash me, and I shall be whiter than snow. Let me hear joy and gladness; let the bones that you have crushed rejoice. Hide your face from my sins, and blot out all my iniquities. Create in me a clean heart, O God, and put a new and right spirit within me. Do not cast me away from your presence, and do not take your holy spirit from me. Restore to me the joy of your salvation, and sustain in me a willing spirit.

Oh, David, what a shock that little story was! What a heart-stopping, dumbfounding shock! Nathan played you like a fish, and now you were well and truly caught. He knew everything, and that meant that God knew everything as well. The whole thing was out in the open, and for the first time in your life you were face to face with a very upset God. The prophet went on to spell out every detail of your crimes, didn't he? And he left you in no doubt about the way God felt about what you'd done. Sadness, disappointment, anger.

Now, I have to tell you, David, I was very impressed with the way you handled the situation at this point. Nathan's accusation must have broken through all that brittle hardness that had built up over the last nine months, and reached the heart of the old David, the man who feared and loved his God. No excuses, no bluster, no attempt to blame anyone but yourself. You really spoke to God. And the amazing thing is that, all these thousands of years later, we know exactly what you said, because here are your very words in the 51st psalm, in God's book, the Bible.

Thank you for the example of David's wholehearted repentance.

ANOTHER?

John 3:16 (NRSV)

For God so loved the world that he gave his only Son, so that everyone who believes in him may not perish but may have eternal life.

Nothing changes much, does it, David? Burnt offerings, church services, prayer meetings, Bible reading; all useless as long as they're being used as smart gear to cover up the grubby underwear. You really came clean when you talked to God about what you'd done, and I admire you for that. It took some courage.

But it didn't change the facts.

Charges: Adultery and murder.

Verdict: Guilty.

Statutory sentence on both counts: Death.

Jewish law, you see. Absolutely clear, and you can read it for yourself if you want. Leviticus, chapter 20, verse 10:

If a man commits adultery with another man's wife, both the man and the woman shall be put to death.

Leviticus, chapter 24, verse 17:

All murderers must be executed.

You should have died, David. You knew that, Nathan knew that, God knew that. You should have died, but you didn't. God listened to that prayer of yours, and it must have touched him in the same way that Nathan's words touched you. He forgave you—he let you live. He preferred to have you back as a loving friend rather than let the law take its course and lose you altogether, and it says in one translation of the story that God 'laid your sin upon another'.

Laid your sin upon another? Who?

Might it have been someone who was born thousands of years later in a small Judean town called Bethlehem (you knew Bethlehem well, didn't you, David?), someone who came specially to take the blame for people like you, and to make it possible for all of us to get back into friendship with God? He's even more famous than you, David. You didn't know him then, but you must have met him by now. His name is—well, you know his name, don't you?

I would imagine you and he have a lot in common. You were a man after God's own heart, despite your sins, and he is God's beloved Son

279

who never put a foot wrong. I would love to be a fly on the wall when you two get together.

God so loved you...

DOMINOES

2 Samuel 12:14–17 (NRSV)

'Nevertheless, because by this deed you have utterly scorned the Lord, the child that is born to you shall die.' Then Nathan went to his house. The Lord struck the child that Uriah's wife bore to David, and it became very ill. David therefore pleaded with God for the child; David fasted, and went in and lay all night on the ground. The elders of his house stood beside him, urging him to rise from the ground; but he would not, nor did he eat food with them.

David didn't die, but there was an immediate and chilling penalty to pay. The child, Bathsheba's child, David's child, a living testimony to the king's crime, was going to die.

Only a little baby, but he too had David's sin laid upon him. He became deathly sick. David lay on the bare earth day and night for seven days without eating, weeping, and begging God to let the child live. Meanwhile, Bathsheba watched daily as the little body lost strength, and the eyes that should have sparkled with interest and curiosity became dulled and lifeless, as though the baby knew somehow that this world was not for him.

Perhaps she sang softly as she sat and rocked him.

Peace now, baby,
Your daddy's praying outside
And your mummy's already cried,
For you,
Now your eyes are asking me why
She needed to cry,
Oh, baby, if only you knew.

Special baby,
You won't be staying for long,
But can you tell from the love in my song,
For you,
And the tears in your daddy's prayers,
That somebody cares?
Oh, baby, if only you knew.

Sorry, baby,
You won't see much of the sky,
But you have to learn how to fly,
Yes, you do.
Remember you after you die,
We won't have to try.
Oh, baby, if only you knew.

Listen, baby,
I'm all wrapped up in my pain,
And my tears are falling like rain,
For you,
But I know that we'll meet again,
And I will explain,
Oh, baby, if only you knew.

A thought: *People get hurt like toppling dominoes after certain kinds of deliberate sin.*

WHAT MATTERS?

2 Samuel 12:18–20 (and read 21–23) (NRSV)

On the seventh day the child died. And the servants of David were afraid to tell him that the child was dead; for they said, 'While the child was still alive, we spoke to him, and he did not listen to us; how then can we tell him the child is dead? He may do himself some harm.' But when David saw that his servants were whispering together, he perceived that the child was dead; and David said to his servants, 'Is the child dead?' They said, 'He is dead.' Then David rose from the ground, washed, anointed himself, and changed his clothes. He went into the house of the Lord, and worshipped; he then went to his own house; and when he asked, they set food before him and he ate.

On the seventh day the baby died. The king's aides were afraid to tell him the bad news. All that week he had been broken up by his son's worsening condition. Exhausted by lack of sleep and food, emotionally drained by hour after hour of tearful prayer, how on earth would David react to the news that the child was dead? Breakdown? Total collapse? Nobody could summon up the courage to tell him. In the end he couldn't help but see for himself that something was being kept from him.

Now, here are some things that David did not do at this point when he realized that, despite his pleadings, the baby had died.

He didn't collapse.

He didn't rave at God because his prayers hadn't been answered.

He didn't lose himself in wild living in order to forget.

He didn't descend into the sludge of self-pity.

This is what he actually did, to the amazement of his aides, and every detail of it is recorded in this passage. He got up, brushed his hair, changed his clothes, went into the tabernacle to worship God, then returned to the palace and ate an extremely good meal.

Heartless? No. You really cared about that baby, David. Mind you, I can see why the people around you were puzzled. I suppose the fact was that they hadn't really understood how close you were to God before all this business started, and how intensely relieved you were to be back on speaking terms, as it were. He had become your first priority again, and that was what really mattered to you.

What really matters to me?

WHY?

Matthew 7:8 (NRSV)

For everyone who asks receives, and everyone who searches finds, and for everyone who knocks, the door will be opened.

David, I genuinely did want to understand how your relationship with God made it possible for you to cope with the death of your baby, but it took me a long time. You see, it was different for you. You were more or less brought up by God. You were never that important to your own father, and Saul swung from rage to affection and back again with bewildering speed and frequency. You loved them both, but it was God who really looked after you. It was God who gave you the love and guidance that you needed so much. You seemed to have known something about him that most of us don't, something that made it possible for you to accept the death of your baby without bitterness or anger. For your sake I am glad of that, but when I read that part of the story for the first time, I was left with one overwhelming question that I had to ask, because I'm me, and not you.

Why did God kill the baby? I mean—why did he?

I don't mean that I hadn't followed the logic of what happened. I understood the mechanics—cause and effect and all that. I could see that, but—why did God kill the baby?

The idea of him doing that hurt me, opened up a dark place inside me. It frightened me. Why did he do it? How could he do it?

Of course, there were answers. I'd heard them—used them even, when people had asked me the same sort of question.

It was a different age and culture. Life was cheaper. The baby might have died anyway. God has his own reasons that we don't understand. It's wrong to question God, in any case.

Take your pick. They all make a bit of sense, and they may be absolutely right. I nearly gave up, but, fortunately, God cares about the things that trouble us deeply.

Father, thank you for listening to us when we are lost or confused. Help us to trust that you will not condemn us for genuinely needing to be at peace about issues like this one. We know that there are no final answers in this life, but we are grateful for the temporary ones.

AN ANSWER

Isaiah 53:5–6 (NRSV)

But he was wounded for our transgressions, crushed for our iniquities; upon him was the punishment that made us whole, and by his bruises we are healed. All we like sheep have gone astray; we have all turned to our own way, and the Lord has laid on him the iniquity of us all.

Why did God kill the baby?

I hadn't stopped hoping for an answer to that question, but in the meantime I had started to leave things like that out when I was talking to people about what I believed. It was a bit like when a friend asks you to write a reference for her and you don't exactly tell lies, but you avoid much mention of the weaknesses that might lose her the job. Well, that's just plain silly, isn't it? God doesn't need that kind of nonsense, surely. I know that the apostle Paul said the clay has no right to question the potter, but I couldn't help it. I really wanted to know—about the baby, I mean, David—your baby.

Why?

If there were prophets like Nathan around today (and if there are any, I haven't met them—not like Nathan, anyway) I would have asked one of them, but I couldn't, so I went on asking God directly, and, in the end, he gave me, not the answer, but an answer. His answer was about his own Son. It was about how he allowed Jesus to be put on trial and beaten and jeered at and kicked. He let his own dearly loved child be hurt and abused by the very people he came to save. He allowed us to crush him under the weight of the cross as he dragged it towards the site of his own death, refusing to release him from his burden for our sakes.

He let his 'baby' be nailed to a piece of wood without lifting a hand to save him, because if he had done, we would have been abandoned to judgment.

He endured the unspeakable pain of hearing his Son cry out that he felt forsaken, and let the situation be, because he loves us.

I began to understand, David, that, though there are many questions still to be asked, when it comes to the death of babies, he does know exactly what he is doing.

Thank you for placing your child into our arms.

FULL CIRCLE?

2 Samuel 12:24–25 (NRSV)

Then David consoled his wife Bathsheba, and went to her, and lay with her; and she bore a son, and he named him Solomon. The Lord loved him, and sent a message by the prophet Nathan; so he named him Jedidiah, because of the Lord.

It all sounds pretty good, doesn't it? David is not only back with God, he also gets to keep Bathsheba as well. The first baby's death was a great sorrow, but there are plenty more sons—Solomon, Absalom, Amnon, Adonijah—and David is back on track with God.

It looks like a full circle.

It looks like the end of a nightmare.

It looks as if the only way to end the story is to say that they all lived happily ever after. Unfortunately that is not the case. It is true that David stayed on good terms with God for the rest of his life, except for the foolish affair of the census, years later, and there is little doubt that this relationship continued to be a priority for the king, but the rest of it, well, the rest of it was a bit of a mess.

Nathan had warned David that another penalty of his crimes would be trouble in his family, and the prophet was absolutely right. Terrible trouble. Terrible times. Terrible hurts from Absalom, the son he probably loved most. Absalom was—well, you can read about Absalom and David in the second book of Samuel, one of the most heart-wrenching stories in the Bible. You can read about the death of Amnon, the treachery of Adonijah, and the end of David's life.

David never quite recovered the purity of intention and motivation that had so distinguished him before the Bathsheba incident, but then, in David's life, as in the lives of believers before and since, there can only be one hero, and that is God, the God of whom David himself said: 'He has rescued me from my troubles.'

Thank you, Father, for allowing us access to this detailed and exciting account of David's life. It helps us to understand that everyone, no matter how close to you, is liable to fall. We pray that followers of David's type will be raised up to work for you in this age of respectable moderation in the Church—people capable of great virtues and great sins, who, in the end, choose to follow you. May you be the only hero in the lives of us all.

My faith looks up to Thee,
Thou Lamb of Calvary,
Saviour divine!

RAY PALMER, 'THE LAMB OF GOD'

CLEARING THE WAY FOR US

PRIESTHOOD AND SACRIFICE
IN HEBREWS 8—10

I have it on good authority that there is no particularly good basis for saying who actually wrote the epistle to the Hebrews. If you want to believe it was Paul, I don't suppose he or the actual writer of the letter will mind in the slightest any more. What we do know for sure is that the person who produced this original and creative piece of writing was passionately excited about the sheer greatness of Jesus Christ and the new life he has made possible for those who follow him. Using the Old Testament themes of priesthood and sacrifice, he sets out to explain how man-made means of achieving access to God have been replaced by the real thing. Jesus himself, because of his obedience in going to the cross, dying and rising again, has become our great high priest, defending and representing us to his Father. The writer invites us to grasp a new and deeper understanding of Jesus and the completeness of his triumph over death.

Chapters 8 to 10 are specifically concerned with Jesus' role as the only high priest necessary to our encounters with God, the fulfilment of Jeremiah's prophecy about God's Law being written on our hearts, the need to take hold of the absolute forgiveness offered by Jesus and the need to persevere and be courageous because the eventual rewards will be richer than we can possibly imagine.

This all sounds nice and neat and tidy, but the truth is that my own response to these chapters has been fairly ragged and emotional. The idea that there is a place where everything comes right and the real thing turns out to be infinitely better than its shadow or counterfeit, well, that is my yearning and my dream. There are times when I get so chronically weary of what we have come to perceive as Christianity and all its trappings. Human beings can't help it, I suppose. They just have to make up pictures and shapes and rhymes and patterns and mantras and all manner of religious bits and pieces. All this will fall away in the end, like those bits that drop off space rockets as they go higher and higher. I look forward to that. My little excursion into Hebrews has encouraged me to believe that the place we are heading for on that final journey might be exciting beyond belief. See what you think.

INEFFABLY PARENTAL

Hebrews 8:7–9 (NIV)

For if there had been nothing wrong with that first covenant, no place would have been sought for another. But God found fault with the people and said: 'The time is coming,' declares the Lord, 'when I will make a new covenant with the house of Israel and with the house of Judah. It will not be like the covenant I made with their forefathers when I took them by the hand to lead them out of Egypt, because they did not remain faithful to my covenant, and I turned away from them,' declares the Lord.

There is something ineffably parental about God, isn't there? Leaving aside the slight differences between the creator of the universe and myself, his ways of dealing with Israel, and indeed with all of his children, remind me so much of the relationship Bridget and I have had with our children over the years. This passage brings to mind those many occasions when we have had to abandon our carefully thought-out plan A because the child it was designed for has failed to agree to his or her part in the arrangement.

Perhaps this makes us angry. Perhaps it makes us turn away, but, as all our fellow parents know, we can only turn away for a season. Why is that? You know why it is. We love them. We love them beyond their disobedience and their refusal to cooperate. Even as the cross expression on our faces is still visible, we are mentally devising a plan B, something that will allow everything to be all right again. A different approach, a new angle, a fresh attempt to produce the right response.

I would suggest that God is doing exactly that here. Being God, he is unable to go against his own nature by turning a blind eye to sin, but neither is the great lover of the world able to turn his back on those he loves with such a passion. In my opinion, our chronic failure to comprehend the ocean of love with which God yearns to flood the Church is responsible for much of the individual spiritual breakdown that is all too common nowadays. God can be very fierce, but watch his eyes...

Father, thank you for being so fatherly, so loving. Open our eyes so that we can see you properly.

THE GOLDEN GRACE OF GOD

Hebrews 8:10–13 (NIV)

'This is the covenant I will make with the house of Israel after that time, declares the Lord. I will put my laws in their minds and write them on their hearts. I will be their God and they will be my people. No longer will a man teach his neighbour, or a man his brother, saying, "Know the Lord", because they will all know me, from the least of them to the greatest. For I will forgive their wickedness and will remember their sins no more.' By calling this covenant 'new', he has made the first one obsolete; and what is obsolete and ageing will soon disappear.

Well, here is plan B—God's intention of establishing a new (or perhaps very ancient) intimacy between himself and his people, as prophesied by Jeremiah. This plan involved the death and resurrection of Jesus, events that were essential if the Holy Spirit was to come and live in the hearts of men and women as God promises here.

So far, so good—indeed, so far, so exceedingly good. There is one problem, though, and it is one that has made life difficult for many Christians during the last two thousand years. It centres on one of the words in this passage—'obsolete'. How, my dear brothers and sisters, are we to persuade the sad and striving ones among us that the old covenant really is obsolete and that we are only saved by the golden grace of God?

Yesterday I listened to a troubled young man called Alan who is anxious to follow Jesus, but deeply worried about his acceptability to God. Is he showing the right fruits? Are there enough fruits? Is he being sufficiently sacrificial in his giving of time and money and effort? When he arrives at the gates of heaven, will God look down his nose and refuse to admit this quivering would-be Christian? Alan was and is very tense and concerned.

I told him what I thought. These things are important. Of course we should consider them, but only because, having discovered the freedom that comes from knowing we are loved by God, we now want to please him as much as we can. We are adopted, not employed.

Are you motivated by God's love or are you stranded in plan A?

SMALL WORLD

Hebrews 9:1–5 (NIV)

Now the first covenant had regulations for worship and also an earthly sanctuary. A tabernacle was set up. In its first room were the lampstand, the table and the consecrated bread; this was called the Holy Place. Behind the second curtain was a room called the Most Holy Place, which had the golden altar of incense and the gold-covered ark of the covenant. This ark contained the gold jar of manna, Aaron'.s staff that had budded, and the stone tablets of the covenant. Above the ark were the cherubim of the Glory, overshadowing the atonement cover. But we cannot discuss these things in detail now.

'We cannot discuss these things in detail,' says the writer of Hebrews, having discussed them in considerable detail. I like the detail. I like hearing about the set-up in the tabernacle. I have always been a lover of small worlds. Perhaps that explains why, in the course of my work with children in care, I worked in two different secure units—one in Birmingham and one in Sussex. It was nothing to do with finding enjoyment in locking children up—indeed, whenever possible, the secure unit in Sussex had its doors wide open. No, it was something to do with reducing the big, complicated world to a small, precisely defined area that could be managed with comparative ease and simplicity.

I would love to have gone into the tabernacle, to have moved slowly through the Holy Place and the Most Holy Place, gazing at all those amazing relics and decorations as I went. Imagine poring over the very tablets that Moses had brought down from the mountain or handling the staff that Aaron had once held in his hand.

It is remarkable when we reflect on the fact that the theoretically boundless cosmos of God's communication with man had, for eminently practical reasons, including our inability to handle any but small worlds, been reduced to this tiny area filled with symbols of the greatest escape of all. Even more remarkable is that, in this age, the Holy Spirit is willing to inhabit the small world of your spirit or my spirit, a world where we are allowed to enter the Most Holy Place and meet with the God of the Israelites whenever we wish.

I will meet you in the tabernacle of my heart, Lord.

DAD'S HOME!

Hebrews 9:6–10 (NIV)

When everything had been arranged like this, the priests entered regularly into the outer room to carry on their ministry. But only the high priest entered the inner room, and that only once a year, and never without blood, which he offered for himself and for the sins the people had committed in ignorance. The Holy Spirit was showing by this that the way into the Most Holy Place had not yet been disclosed as long as the first tabernacle was still standing. This is an illustration for the present time, indicating that the gifts and sacrifices being offered were not able to clear the conscience of the worshipper. They are only a matter of food and drink and various ceremonial washings—external regulations applying until the time of the new order.

When children are small, they can only manage for a limited time without drawing on the special blend of assurance, affection and natural authority that the best mums and dads are so good at giving them. You can hear children on a thousand street corners, and in ten thousand back gardens, loudly shouting at each other about what they will allow each other to do or not do in the course of a game: 'You have to wait there and I have to come along and you have to not see me until I'm just behind your back and then I have to shoot you...' One of the others replies, 'Yeah, and then I have to come alive again and you have to give me the gun and I have to shoot you...'

The embattled, stentorian tones in which these commands are uttered is some indication of the lack of real confidence that children feel in their self-imposed rules. When mum or dad come back, though, well, it's different. Different ethos. Different sense of safety. Different awareness of love lying at the heart of authority.

God's new order is the same. We are not left on our own any more. He is no longer issuing orders from a distance or sending messages through someone else. Now, we can know for sure that the things we do, good or bad, will be dealt with properly, on the spot, by the only one who really does see right to the heart of what we are. Dad's home.

Father, sit on the doorstep and watch us as we play.

A STEP FORWARD?

Hebrews 9:11–14 (NIV)

When Christ came as high priest of the good things that are already here, he went through the greater and more perfect tabernacle that is not man-made, that is to say, not a part of this creation. He did not enter by means of the blood of goats and calves; but he entered the Most Holy Place once for all by his own blood, having obtained eternal redemption. The blood of goats and bulls and the ashes of a heifer sprinkled on those who are ceremonially unclean sanctify them so that they are outwardly clean. How much more, then, will the blood of Christ, who through the eternal Spirit offered himself unblemished to God, cleanse our consciences from acts that lead to death, so that we may serve the living God!

The exclamation mark at the end of this passage was not my idea. I don't like exclamation marks (other than when they follow exclamations) and I especially loathe them when they are added to the end of a sentence by some self-deluded writer who thinks he has said something clever!

Seriously, though, why is it there? Perhaps it is telling us that something important has just been said. If that is its purpose, I agree with it. I have previously mentioned talking to a young man who was very worried about not being good enough for God. One of his main concerns was that he had never truly been forgiven. He knew the Bible inside out and he quoted it constantly, but it didn't seem to be helping him with his problem. I think if I had produced half a mug of bull's blood, a basin of goat's blood and a pinch of heifer ashes and thrown it over him he might have felt better, but only for a while. Like many others, he is trapped in a little virtual biblical prison. He needs to get out and meet Jesus, who will forgive his past sins once and for all through his own shed blood and be happy to do it again tomorrow when Alan rolls up with a fresh crop of interesting sins to talk about. Perhaps then he will stop worrying about forgiveness and start worrying about how he might serve the living God. That would at least be a step forward!!

We really can be clean!!!!

A TRUE PICTURE

Hebrews 9:24–28 (NIV)

For Christ did not enter a man-made sanctuary that was only a copy of the true one; he entered heaven itself, now to appear for us in God's presence. Nor did he enter heaven to offer himself again and again, the way the high priest enters the Most Holy Place every year with blood that is not his own. Then Christ would have had to suffer many times since the creation of the world. But now he has appeared once for all at the end of the ages to do away with sin by the sacrifice of himself. Just as man is destined to die once, and after that to face judgment, so Christ was sacrificed once to take away the sins of many people; and he will appear a second time, not to bear sin, but to bring salvation to those who are waiting for him.

This is a magnificent picture, isn't it? Spielberg would have a job coming up with anything to equal this. I have never been to heaven, but I can dream. After the long history of God's protracted and painful strivings with mankind, Jesus steps into heaven, applauded by the ranks of angels and saints, to claim forgiveness and salvation for Adrian Plass, for you, dear reader, and for one or two others who need not concern us at the moment.

'I've done it!' he exclaims. 'No more tabernacles, no more high priests, no more blood sloshing around. In future, if anyone has any-thing against Adrian Plass or the person who is reading his Bible notes at this very moment, you can refer them to me. The pain is for ever, but so too is the joy. All debts are paid and death has been overcome. I shall be going back for Adrian and his reader later on.'

A million angels and ten million saints cheer themselves hoarse—in a spiritual sort of way. The devil gnashes his teeth and asks himself where it first went wrong for him.

In case my tone deceives you into thinking I'm joking, I'm not. My life, my future, everything that I am or will ever be depends on the truth of the picture that I have so inadequately painted here. It is reality. You and I will be waiting for him and he will come.

Thank you.

READY TO FLY?

Hebrews 10:1–4 (NIV)

The law is only a shadow of the good things that are coming—not the realities themselves. For this reason it can never, by the same sacrifices repeated endlessly year after year, make perfect those who draw near to worship. If it could, would they not have stopped being offered? For the worshippers would have been cleansed once for all, and would no longer have felt guilty for their sins. But those sacrifices are an annual reminder of sins, because it is impossible for the blood of bulls and goats to take away sins.

Bridget and I will never forget our first trip to Australia. We had been invited to speak at the first national convention of the Uniting Church, a denomination made up of Methodists, Presbyterians and Congregationalists. We were so excited. Hitherto, our travels had been limited. Imagine flying all that way across the world to a place we had only read about in books and seen on television. It was like a dream.

As the weeks went by, a flood of practical concerns swamped our dream. Katy, our youngest, was coming with us, but that left the three boys, who were 16, 12 and 11. We arranged for friends to move in and look after them while we were away. There were visas to be obtained, one passport to be renewed, clothes to be bought, money to be saved, a week of speaking material to be prepared and a whole host of fears and uncertainties to be faced. In the fortnight before flying, it got so complicated that we lost sight of the reason for our trip. It was difficult to see the object of our efforts amid such a swirling haze of essential but uninspiring considerations.

We left and the dream not only returned, but became a reality that far outstripped our hopes. That first experience of Australia remains in our memories as a truly golden time. We were so warmly welcomed, so well looked after, so much appreciated that, from then onwards and during each of the three trips that we have subsequently made, the country shines like a beacon and will always call us back. All the work and the worry were worth it.

I won't labour the point, but the Law is only a shadow of the golden times that are coming.

Ready to fly?

A SIMPLE SOUL

Hebrews 10:5–10 (NIV)

Therefore, when Christ came into the world, he said: 'Sacrifice and offering you did not desire, but a body you prepared for me; with burnt offerings and sin offerings you were not pleased. Then I said, "Here I am—it is written about me in the scroll—I have come to do your will, O God."' First he said, 'Sacrifices and offerings, burnt offerings and sin offerings you did not desire, nor were you pleased with them' (although the law required them to be made). Then he said, 'Here I am, I have come to do your will.' He sets aside the first to establish the second. And by that will, we have been made holy through the sacrifice of the body of Jesus Christ once for all.

He never has been that interested in the familiar metaphors of sacrifice and worship. Burnt animals, symbolic gifts, ceremonial bun fights and extravaganzas never really touched the spot. They had their place, of course. Filled a gap, as it were. In the purest sense, God has always been a very simple soul. Hope he doesn't mind me saying that. I don't think he will.

No, but it is true. Since the world began, throughout the ages of the Bible, down through the last two thousand years, God has been trying to make his voice heard. 'Look,' says God, 'I don't actually want any of that stuff. It does nothing for me. What I want is for you to be just and kind and to look after the poor. I would like you to be obedient. My son was obedient to the point of death and that's why I'm able to welcome you home. I wouldn't give you tuppence for religion—not even some of the wild, sizzling stuff that's taken the place of burning animals nowadays. Be loving to me and to each other. That's the scent I love— have always loved.'

This is a voice that many people, many Christians, do not want to hear. Too natural, too godly, too liable to insinuate itself into the cracks between our humanity and our faith, supergluing the two together, making us whole, but robbing us of all the old securities. Scary and sweet, isn't it?

Walk quietly with us in the cool of the afternoon, Lord. We need to talk.

THE HOLINESS VACUUM

Hebrews 10:11–18 (NIV)

Day after day every priest stands and performs his religious duties; again and again he offers the same sacrifices, which can never take away sins. But when this priest had offered for all time one sacrifice for sins, he sat down at the right hand of God. Since that time he waits for his enemies to be made his footstool, because by one sacrifice he has made perfect for ever those who are being made holy. The Holy Spirit also testifies to us about this. First he says: 'This is the covenant I will make with them after that time, says the Lord. I will put my laws in their hearts, and I will write them on their minds.' Then he adds: 'Their sins and lawless acts I will remember no more.' And where these have been forgiven, there is no longer any sacrifice for sin.

There is an intriguing phrase in this passage, one that you have to repeat again and again before it starts making sense: '…by one sacrifice he has made perfect for ever those who are being made holy.' What does this mean? No, it's no good clicking your tongue irritably and saying that you worked it out eons ago. My brain is the sort that has to take its time.

The people who have been affected by Jesus' sacrifice—people like you and I—have been made perfect by his death on the cross. In other words, we have been turned into qualifiers for heaven, heaven being unable, by its very nature, to admit anything but perfection. Good news. We're in!

In that case, what's this other bit about these same people still being in the process of being made holy, even though they have already been perfected? What does that mean? Well, having considered the question carefully for many minutes, I feel quite encouraged. I know that I am far from holy. I know also that the Holy Spirit has been working slowly on the holiness vacuum in my life for nearly four decades. By the time I reach the grave, I shall still fall far short of perfection, but that, I assume, is when the divine life insurance kicks in—thank God. It may be rubbish theology, but it'll do me.

It's all in hand, and the hand it's in is pierced.

THE ELBOW AND THE KNEECAP

Hebrews 10:19–25 (NIV)

Therefore, brothers, since we have confidence to enter the Most Holy Place by the blood of Jesus, by a new and living way opened for us through the curtain, that is, his body, and since we have a great priest over the house of God, let us draw near to God with a sincere heart in full assurance of faith, having our hearts sprinkled to cleanse us from a guilty conscience and having our bodies washed with pure water. Let us hold unswervingly to the hope we profess, for he who promised is faithful. And let us consider how we may spur one another on towards love and good deeds. Let us not give up meeting together, as some are in the habit of doing, but let us encourage one another—and all the more as you see the Day approaching.

Not many people actually draw near to God in full assurance of faith. Lots of Christians, myself included, find that their spiritual confidence dips dramatically at times. Here, in this passage, are four points that might help.

First, are the words 'draw near to God with a sincere heart'. Take the truth of what you are to God, lack of assurance and all. Be straight with him. As we have seen, Jesus died to make up the shortfall. Trust him.

Second, we should spur one another on to good deeds. We take turns at this, being generous with our assurance when we have it and getting plumbed into someone else's when we haven't. We are supposed to be a body.

Meeting together provides the opportunity for such things to happen. I value being alone very highly, but it goes flat in the end—like champagne without a cork. In any case, how long can the body manage without its elbow or its kneecap? Assurance is in the linking of hands, metaphorical or actual.

Encouragement of one another is like the caress of God for a church community. Taking the trouble to recognize value and achievement in our brothers and sisters can have what appears to be a disproportionately positive effect on the recipient. Do you enjoy watching flowers open?

The general message is clear. We're in this together, Jesus and us. Be assured of that and you won't go too far wrong.

Jesus had a dark moment on the cross. He understands.

THE PRIMAL URGE

Hebrews 10:32–34 (NIV)

Remember those earlier days after you had received the light, when you stood your ground in a great contest in the face of suffering. Sometimes you were publicly exposed to insult and persecution; at other times you stood side by side with those who were so treated. You sympathized with those in prison and joyfully accepted the confiscation of your property, because you knew that you yourselves had better and lasting possessions.

The picture of anyone joyfully accepting the confiscation of their property is, to my modern Western eyes, almost irresistibly Python-esque: 'Whee! They've taken my stuff! Fantastic! It's all gone! Whee! (Breaks into song) Come on, let's celebrate…!'

It only goes on being funny for a while, though. When my schoolboyish sense of humour has chortled itself to a standstill, I begin to see my own past. Pictures float into my mind of how I used to be, the things I once did, when the staggering awareness of what Jesus had done was still a flashing white light in my consciousness. Oh, I know I was a pain in the neck. I would have avoided myself like the plague. I had a Bible with me constantly and I would talk endlessly to anyone who would listen—and quite a few who wouldn't—about salvation and damnation and the need for them to make a personal commitment immediately because the world might well end before four o'clock that day. It was a passion and a preoccupation. I must have got on so many people's nerves on the streets and in the cafés of Tunbridge Wells.

I was doing it all the same. You know what I mean? I was doing it. I wasn't cuddling my passion for Jesus to myself as I sometimes do nowadays. I was treating the message of salvation as though it was vitally important that others should hear it, letting it flow from me in its raw, shapeless, unrefined state. I probably made a fool of myself from time to time, but that didn't seem to be so much of a problem then.

A lot of what I did was probably bad, but I also suspect that a lot of it was good. The same feeling—that spiritually primal urge—is just beginning to resurface. I'm glad.

Catch me, Lord, I'm coming back.

THE LITTLE ONES AT THE BACK

Hebrews 10:35–39 (NIV)

So do not throw away your confidence; it will be richly rewarded. You need to persevere so that when you have done the will of God, you will receive what he has promised. For in just a very little while: 'He who is coming will come and will not delay. But my righteous one will live by faith. And if he shrinks back, I will not be pleased with him.' But we are not of those who shrink back and are destroyed, but of those who believe and are saved.

Oh, dear. Am I a back shrinker? Are you?

One of the first stories I told was about my son Matthew, aged 4, arriving miserably home from school one day. After three tear-dampened jam sandwiches, he explained that, at assembly, the headmistress had frightened him by threatening terrible punishment for any child who brought money to school. Mrs Shaw was frightening—she frightened me. Matthew, shaking in his small shoes, had resolved never to bring a penny to school. Later, in the yard, he put a hand in his pocket and found, to his horror, a coin! Panicking, he tugged it out and dropped it. A passing girl said with relish, 'When I tell Mrs Shaw you brought money to school you'll be in big trouble tomorrow.'

Matthew was terrified. What to do? Simple. I wrote to Mrs Shaw, challenging her to a duel with swords or pistols. If she won she could punish Matthew, if I won she couldn't. A reply arrived the next afternoon.

Mrs Shaw thanked me for making the teachers laugh. It had also made her think carefully about saying loud, forceful things at assembly that were never meant to terrify the little ones at the back. She sounded nice in her letter.

Maybe it was like that with Jesus. After one of his stern pronounce-ments, a nervous disciple tugs his sleeve and says, 'Look, I don't think I'm up to this!'

'Don't worry,' Jesus replies from the corner of his mouth, 'you're OK. It's that lot over there I'm getting at...'

Don't worry. We'll be as courageous as necessary. We may be the little ones at the back, but we also know that God is almost as nice as Mrs Shaw—perhaps even nicer.

Thank goodness she didn't accept my challenge.

There is nothing new save that
which has been forgotten.

MME BERTIN

NEW BEGINNINGS

CHANCES TO GET UP AND GO—AGAIN

The fact that Bridget and I have made three trips to Australia during the last few years is, in itself, evidence of a fairly dramatic new beginning. There was a time when financial pressures and the demands of seemingly eternal shiftwork in childcare establishments were such that we felt very little hope of ever going much further than the corner shop. Once you've done it, of course, you know that you can do it, and therefore it's more likely that you'll do it again. We really are grateful to God for allowing us the opportunity to do things and to go to places that we would never have thought possible, and, of course, for inspiring people to believe that it's actually worth paying for us to come and speak to them. I still find that idea extremely difficult to accept, as do my close friends, who have stubbornly refused to pay me a heavily discounted sum per sentence for speaking to them when we meet at the pub.

Bridget has found the whole business of travelling and speaking just as exciting as I have, but, as she has recorded elsewhere, there has always been a gnawing worry in her mind that people are only tolerating her contribution to our presentations because she happens to be married to me, the one who writes the books. This deep insecurity tends to persist in the face of overwhelming evidence to the contrary. She won't thank me for saying this, but wherever we have appeared together she has received fulsome praise and expressions of appreciation. But then, that's the way it is with deep insecurities, isn't it? As a young teenager I was quite convinced that no normal girl would ever want to go out with me, and this conviction persisted even though I found myself going out with an extremely attractive one. Any girls who did like me, I reasoned, must have faulty powers of perception, and therefore, in this area at least, their views didn't count. Bridget's just the same. If an entire audience of 500 people were to pin her to the ground and scream loudly and in unison in her ear that they appreciated her in her own right, there would be a short pause, and then you would hear a small voice from the bottom of the human pile saying, 'You don't really mean that.'

During our third trip to Australia this problem came to a head because of one particular comment during a radio interview, and seemed to be getting worse until a story told by a friend, and inspired by God, I'm sure, produced a new beginning in Bridget's ability to keep things in perspective.

The radio interview, live and conducted over the telephone, was set up as a promotional aid to our forthcoming appearance in Sydney, and included the following question, delivered in a flat, Australian drawl:

'What exactly does Bridget do? Does she hold up cue-cards, or come on stage wearing a leotard, or what?'

Bridget later said that, on hearing those words, she felt as if she had received a vicious punch in the solar plexus, a sense of reeling back, doubled up and breathless with pain and humiliation. Only pride enabled her to laugh and smile as though nothing had happened instead of bursting into childlike tears of hurt and anger.

All evening and all of that night Bridget fought to subdue the sense of rage and upset that was determinedly welling up in her. She said that it felt like emotional bruising. The same questions and fears ran through her mind over and over again as she lay awake.

'How could that man say such a thing? What a sexist, chauvinistic idiot! But supposing he was right! Am I being ridiculous? Even if I'm not, what's wrong with me that I've taken it so much to heart? Why am I still so vulnerable to the idea that I'm worth nothing in my own right?'

By morning the waves of pain had receded, but, just as is the case with acute homesickness for many people, when reason appeared to have achieved some level of healing, the memory of how threatened she had felt sent her reeling again. Bridget's peace had been stolen, and it was difficult for her to see how it was going to be recovered or replaced.

The day after that interviewer had unknowingly caused such a problem found Bridget and me, together with other people involved in our concerts, scrunched together in a van on our way to the next venue. It was during this trip that Karen Beckett, a marvellous singer and ideal travelling companion who accompanied us throughout the tour, suddenly announced, 'It was just around here that my husband and I nearly ruined a small turtle's life.'

It sounded too good a story to miss.

'What happened,' said Karen, 'was that we were travelling along the main road, when I spotted this little turtle right over on the other side of the dual-carriageway. He was just climbing up from the road to get on to the grass verge, so he must have spent ages crawling from one side to the other. I don't know how he'd avoided getting flattened by cars and trucks, but he'd done it somehow. Anyway, my kids had never seen a turtle before, so we stopped, and my husband, Trev, dodged the traffic to get across the road, and brought the turtle back across to where we were waiting in the car. The kids were knocked out by the little fellow, and they wanted to take him home, but then he did an amazing amount of wee all over us—frightened I suppose—and that sort of brought out the conservationist in all of us. It encouraged us to think it would be better to leave him in his natural habitat. So I put him down on the grass verge beside the car and we drove on.

'Well, we hadn't got much further down the road when I suddenly realized what we'd done. We'd left him on our side! The poor little creature was going to have to dice with death all over again, and the odds against him getting across unsquashed a second time were pretty heavy, to say the least.'

Bridget told me later that, on hearing the story up to this point, she said to herself, 'That's just how I feel. After years of trying to get to the other side of this dreadful self-image of mine, and just about managing to dodge the stuff life throws at me, one stupid remark has taken me all the way back to the place where I started.'

I wondered at the time why Bridget asked her next question with such a degree of intensity.

'What did you do?'

'Well,' said Karen, 'we turned around as soon as we got to a junction and went back. We felt pretty stupid, actually, but we couldn't face the idea of that little thing having to take such an awful risk all over again. He'd just started the repeat trip when we got back, so Trev picked him up, wee and all, and carried him over to the place where we'd found him. He must have had a great story to tell his mum! Eh?'

We all enjoyed the story, but Bridget not only laughed, she also felt the lingering remains of that recent bruising fade quietly away. She thought of all the times when family and friends had helped her to pick herself up in the past, leading her across roads that seemed too difficult to navigate on her own—phone calls she couldn't bring herself to begin; encounters she dreaded; apologies that were difficult to make; reconciliation that depended on her being more forgiving than she felt able to be. She thought also about the times when she and God had been on their own in situations where she felt totally inadequate, and she had been able to lean on him.

And it isn't only Bridget, of course. It's all of us. We all depend on each other and on God. Jesus promised that we would be left with a peace that can't be taken away, whatever the world throws at us. He will not leave us stranded on a roadside verge, so paralysed by our overwhelming sense of failure that we are incapable of moving forward.

No matter how deep the old wounds may go, and I know that they threaten to cut some of us in two, by God's grace it will always be possible to have a new beginning.

Prayer
Father, some of us are in desperate need of a new beginning. As we read your words and think about what they mean, give us fresh hope that we can move safely to the other side of difficulty and disaster. Be with us as we watch closely for opportunities to help others who need to make a fresh start, and clear our heads so that we may hear your voice offering wisdom and guidance. We trust that you will never forsake us, Lord—help our lack of trust.

A NEW SONG

Psalm 40:1–3 (NRSV)

I waited patiently for the Lord; he inclined to me and heard my cry. He drew me up from the desolate pit, out of the miry bog, and set my feet upon a rock, making my steps secure. He put a new song in my mouth, a song of praise to our God. Many will see and fear, and put their trust in the Lord.

I identify with all of this section except for the first six words. I never have been a very patient person, with God or anyone else. As someone who is constantly required to put words on paper, however, I have special reasons for willingly testifying to the truth contained in the other 59 words.

This process of crawling out of the bog (don't laugh, please) and having a new song put into my mouth is one that I experience every single time I begin a new piece of writing. It doesn't matter how successful the last project might have been, because I still end up slumped gloomily in front of my computer, filled with the certainty that I will never write anything else ever again. As I sit there, I might pick up my last book and glance through it. 'How on earth,' I ask myself, 'did I manage to write all this? How could someone with a mind as empty and unproductive as mine feels now produce an entire book that other people might want to read?'

I really do get very depressed. Convinced that my professional life is over, I dejectedly push a key or two, just for old times' sake, before putting my coat on and setting out for the Job Centre. A couple of words appear on the screen; they grow into a bad sentence; I put the sentence right; I have to write a second sentence in order to explain the first one; suddenly my interest is caught by some aspect of what I have written; I sit up in my chair and wriggle into a comfortable position; my fingers do a sort of piano-playing mime as they hover over the keyboard; I plunge headlong into composition; I am writing again.

I am not talking about God giving me the words to write. What I am talking about is this eternally present divine principle of movement from despair to a new beginning. Don't give up. Whether your inspiration is lost in the area of looking after a dependent relative or composing a concerto, put yourself in the place where the work is to be done and listen hard. The music may begin with a few faint notes in the far distance, but there is always a new song to be sung.

Father, may others hear you in the music of our lives.

A NEW START

Isaiah 62:2–4 (NRSV)

The nations shall see your vindication... and you shall be called by a new name... You shall be a crown of beauty in the hand of the Lord, and a royal diadem in the hand of your God. You shall no more be termed Forsaken, and your land shall no more be termed Desolate; but you shall be called My Delight Is in Her, and your land Married; for the Lord delights in you, and your land shall be married.

Since my mother died, I cannot tell you how sad Bridget and I feel that we can no longer jump in the car and drive up to Tunbridge Wells to see her. She was such a very significant part of our lives, and the pain of loss has not diminished much. She was a tough, generous, sometimes cantankerous enjoyer of life, who allowed people to be exactly what they were. Bridget described her as 'my best friend'.

For the four years prior to her death, Mum was confined to a wheel-chair as the result of a stroke, and though she remained very much the person that we loved, there was an inevitable deterioration in the optimism and outgoingness that had characterized her before she became ill. Sometimes she was downright crabby.

Interestingly, most of our memories of Mum go back automatically to the days before her stroke, when she was vigorously active in the village where she lived, and a warm, involved grandma in the lives of her grandchildren. That person was the real Marjorie Plass, but we had almost lost sight of that fact in the period before her death.

In our kitchen stands a framed photograph of Mum when she was ten years old. The picture, taken in 1928, shows a tall, skinny little girl holding her skirts up as she paddles in the sea. She is gazing up inquiringly towards the shore, as if trying to hear what someone is calling to her. Young Marjorie's face, captured for ever in this long-ago moment, is strong and confident, full of an optimism that needs no expression because it is a part of her. That child lived on in the adult that Mum became, sustaining her through some very difficult years. Strangely, in that 62-year-old portrayal, I see more of the person I knew than in any other memory or photograph, which is just as well, because it will be the clear-eyed face of a child that Bridget and I shall recognize when we join her in heaven.

In heaven the child in us will be able to start again.

A NEW WORLD

Isaiah 65:17–19, 25 (NRSV)

For I am about to create new heavens and a new earth; the former things shall not be remembered or come to mind. But be glad and rejoice for ever in what I am creating... I will rejoice in Jerusalem, and delight in my people; no more shall the sound of weeping be heard in it, or the cry of distress... The wolf and the lamb shall feed together, the lion shall eat straw like the ox; but the serpent—its food shall be dust! They shall not hurt or destroy on all my holy mountain, says the Lord.

Are you engaged in an eternal struggle to develop a life that you wouldn't cope with if you ever succeeded in creating it? Let me explain.

Take our family—please do. In my pathetic vision of the future there is total cooperation between all the members of the household. My second son would spend a long time cleaning and preparing the bathroom for its next occupant after using it himself, my daughter would insist on doing her violin practice at least twice every day (without being reminded) at times convenient to the rest of the family, my third son would regularly wrest the carpet cleaner from my wife's hand, refusing to allow her to wear herself out when he could just as easily do it, and my oldest son would pop over every weekend to take his brothers and sister out for the whole of Saturday, leaving Bridget and me to potter about in the sort of happily pointless way we used to before we foolishly started begatting.

There are a couple of problems with this scenario. First, I contribute to the general air of chaos as much as anyone else. I am either fanatically, cataclysmically, intolerantly tidy in very short explosive bursts, or utterly slob-like for much longer periods. I'd have a job changing that very much now. Secondly, despite the fact that we always seem to be fighting our way towards this domestic utopia, I'm not sure that I'd actually enjoy it if it came. Our family life has always been as rich as a Christmas cake, and I think I'd miss it if it became that civilized.

No, I think I'll leave the new earth to God. Something tells me that he will be able to pick out the very best of what was, and reproduce it in a new and excitingly shining form that will lose nothing of the granular richness of family life, and gain a great deal in addition because he'll be in charge instead of me!

I've said it before and I'll say it again—heaven will be wonderful.

A NEW KIND OF LAW

Jeremiah 31:31–34 (NRSV)

The days are surely coming, says the Lord, when I will make a new covenant with the house of Israel and the house of Judah. It will not be like the covenant that I made with their ancestors when I took them by the hand to bring them out of the land of Egypt... But this is the covenant that I will make... I will put my law within them, and I will write it on their hearts; and I will be their God, and they shall be my people. No longer shall they teach one another, or say to each other, 'Know the Lord', for they shall all know me, from the least of them to the greatest, says the Lord; for I will forgive their iniquity, and remember their sin no more.

For some people this particular new beginning may be the only real hope left in their lives.

I remember watching news of the roadside murder of Bill Cosby's only son, a socially concerned young man, often referred to by his famous father as 'my hero'. As I watched pictures of the griefstricken comic leaving home with his wife to collect the body of his son, I reflected on the fact, hackneyed but true, that wealth and position become meaningless in the face of such loss. I am sure that Bill Cosby would give his last dollar and every shred of his international fame for the chance to be with his son once more. I have no idea what the religious beliefs of these two men were or are. I hope that God's law has been written on their hearts, because if so, there will be new and wonderful beginnings for both of them in the future, despite the agony that Mr Cosby was sure to be feeling at that moment.

I really cannot imagine how anyone survives such a loss without the hope of reunion that Jesus promises. It's bad enough to lose someone close when you do believe, isn't it? What must it be like to face the solid wall of blackness that confronts those who see death as a complete full-stop?

People sometimes suggest that the readers of these notes are bound to be believing Christians, and most of them are, but I know that a minority are not. Please, if you have never known God, speak to him, and speak to those who do know him. Perhaps, if you do that, you, and eventually those you love, will experience your own new beginnings and be ready for anything that life throws at you.

Father, hear the voices of those who need you. Write your law on their hearts and forgive their sins.

A NEW MORNING

Lamentations 3:15–23 (NRSV)

He has filled me with bitterness… my soul is bereft of peace; I have forgotten what happiness is; so I say, 'Gone is my glory, and all that I had hoped for from the Lord.' The thought of my affliction and my homelessness is wormwood and gall!… But this I call to mind, and therefore I have hope: The steadfast love of the Lord never ceases, his mercies never come to an end; they are new every morning; great is your faithfulness.

This sort of testimony infuriates some Christian groups. They dislike it so much because it's ragged and untidy and failing and just about impossible to contain within a neat religious package. For those who like their Christianity to proceed along man-made straight lines, these wild and hopeless cries from the heart are disturbing and threatening. And yet, for two very good reasons, it is absolutely essential that we hear and appreciate the meaning of such loud and painful shouts to God.

First, they reflect the way things actually are for many people, and you can argue until your face is bright purple with pink spots about how life ought to be for Christians, because all I shall say to you is that 'oughts' rarely work with clockwork precision. People get bashed and bewildered by events, and if we are honest we must admit that troubles fall with equal weight on believers and unbelievers alike. Being Jesus to our neighbour, the highest calling known to men and women, involves hearing and embracing pain in each other without feeling obliged to trot out religious platitudes that make us feel better but bring the sufferer nearer to despair than ever. Jesus pleaded that we should love one another. Isn't it difficult?

Second, this kind of cry is immensely encouraging, because it concludes with a sudden surfacing of the knowledge, presumably based on past events, that the love of God will never end and is new every single morning. When a man as unhappy and bowed down as this is rescued by that awareness, then his testimony is valuable indeed. This is no airy-fairy, pseudo-religious thing. In my life, and in the lives of many who are reading these words at this moment, it has sometimes only been possible to go on because, when you dwell in the kingdom of God, nightmares may come, but there is always the miraculous possibility of a new morning.

Help us to be honest and faithful, Lord.

A NEW HEART

Ezekiel 36:25–28 (NRSV)

I will sprinkle clean water upon you, and you shall be clean… and from all your idols I will cleanse you. A new heart I will give you, and a new spirit I will put within you; and I will remove from your body the heart of stone and give you a heart of flesh. I will put my spirit within you, and make you follow my statutes and be careful to observe my ordinances. Then you shall live in the land that I gave to your ancestors; and you shall be my people, and I will be your God.

I have experienced no more powerful drive than the desire to make everything 'all right' for my children. Sometimes this leads to mistakes. Children should not always be protected from the consequences of their actions, and certainly there have been times when Bridget or I have jumped in far too quickly to rescue one of them from disaster. It's just that we love them so much, and we can't bear the thought of them being less than content. No doubt, in my case, this has more to do with my past than their present, but—well, you know what I mean.

Occasionally I've been really glad that we have this knee-jerk reaction to their problems. Once, the phone rang at five o'clock in the morning. When the phone goes at that time of day it can only be bad news or an Australian. It was actually my oldest son, living in Kent at the time, and all he said was, 'Can you come down straightaway? I'm all right, but something bad has happened and I need you to come as soon as you can.'

I think Bridget and I were dressed and in the car within five minutes. Arriving 35 minutes later, we found a police car outside the building, and learned that someone in the next-door flat had been attacked in the early hours of the morning. Hearing a banging noise, my son opened the door to find this unfortunate individual bound, gagged and covered in blood on the landing outside the door. He was still in a very shocked state by the time we got him home. We weren't able to make everything all right, but, thank God, we were able to be there for him when he needed us.

Read this passage, and you will hear the passionate cry of a Father's heart for his children simply to be all right. This is a list of the things that he will do to make sure it happens. Until that work is completed, God is there for us whenever we need him, and we don't have to use a telephone.

Put your Spirit within us, Lord.

A NEW COMMANDMENT

John 13:34–35 (NRSV)

'I give you a new commandment, that you love one another. Just as I have loved you, you also should love one another. By this everyone will know that you are my disciples, if you have love for one another.'

How would the Church change if this commandment were to be generally obeyed? Would such a new beginning be welcomed? I have my doubts. The problem, you see, is that Jesus doesn't say, 'Love one another as you have always loved one another in the past.' He says, 'Love one another just as I have loved you.' This is a very tall order indeed, not least because the love that Jesus showed to his disciples was a (to them) bewilderingly mixed bag of uncompromisingly tough straight-talking, overwhelming compassion, and a quite extraordinary willingness to trust them with powers and tasks that they can't possibly have understood. In other words, the principle of only doing what he saw his Father doing was applied as rigorously by Jesus to individual relationships as to his broader ministry.

How many of us would be ready to abandon items of our personal agenda because the love of God for the person before us demanded it? Would I? Would you? My heart sinks whenever another major issue arises in the life of the Church, not because I don't think we should confront issues, but because there will always be a little bunch of single-issue fanatics at both ends of the argument whose voices are louder and more strident than the saner arguments of those who have put Jesus first in their lives, and are prepared to be wrong if necessary.

The acid test will never change. Jesus himself appears in the flesh, right in front of me, and says, 'Look, I see what you're getting at, Adrian, but, as it happens, you're wrong.' My two possible responses are: 'Nevertheless, I think I have to pursue this point—I've thought it through very carefully' or: 'OK, Lord, you know best, I'll follow you.'

If I find that the first answer is the one I would give, then I have no business commenting on matters of faith and life at all. The business of loving as Jesus loved demands identification with the spirit of personal sacrifice that, in the end, sent him to the cross. Tough, isn't it?

Lord, teach us how to love you and each other. Heal your Church.

COMMUNION

Luke 21:19–20 (NRSV)

Then he took a loaf of bread, and when he had given thanks, he broke it and gave it to them, saying, 'This is my body, which is given for you. Do this in remembrance of me.' And he did the same with the cup after supper, saying, 'This cup that is poured out for you is the new covenant in my blood.'

The church that we attend in Hailsham is small, and, being a sort of hall, has none of the grandeur or dignity of your average parish church. And yet, on those Sundays when we celebrate Communion, I experience a sense of mystery and fathomless significance that could not be more profound if I was worshipping in the most extravagantly impressive cathedral in the country.

There is a danger in pulling to pieces the things that you love, but I have been trying to work out why this simple ritual has such an effect on me. One Sunday I sat at the back, watching the congregation make their way, row by row, to the front of the church, where they waited in a rough semicircle to receive bread and wine from the priest and his helper. I know quite a lot of the people in our church, some very well indeed. As I looked at my brothers and sisters waiting like children to be given their share of the body and blood of Jesus, I felt like crying. I know the struggles that some of them have been through, as they know of mine. I know that quite a lot of people in our church feel far from worthy to be receiving such precious, jewel-like gifts from God. And yet, there we are, each time Communion happens, going out like junior-school kids from their desks, tentatively putting out our hands in the eternally renewed hope that Jesus will place a share of himself into our humble safekeeping just as God placed his baby son into the world all those years ago.

We are a communion of uncertainty and hope, human beings of all shapes and sizes, but with exactly equal rights as children adopted into the family of God. In taking those few short steps from our seats to the front of the church we are, however nervously, expressing our faith in that proposition. Once we get there—he does the rest. It's beautiful.

Thank you for your smiling presence at Communion.

A NEW CREATION

2 Corinthians 5:17–21 (NRSV)

So if anyone is in Christ, there is a new creation... All this is from God, who reconciled us to himself through Christ, and has given us the ministry of reconciliation; that is, in Christ God was reconciling the world to himself, not counting their trespasses against them, and entrusting the message of reconciliation to us. So we are ambassadors for Christ, since God is making his appeal through us; we entreat you on behalf of Christ, be reconciled to God.

I was terrified when we first went to America. My books hadn't done very well there, except in a few individual churches and small pockets of the Christian community. I had been told some grisly tales about widespread puritan attitudes that would find the sort of material I use offensive and unfunny. I suppose I'd been a bit spoilt really. Most audiences come to my meetings because they've already read something I've written and are therefore unlikely to be hostile. Many of those who bought tickets for our first meetings in the USA had no idea what they were coming to.

In the end it was a nerve-racking experience, but only for as long as it took to discover that Americans reacted in very much the same way as people in other parts of the world. One of the three venues Bridget and I spoke at was a huge church on the outskirts of Los Angeles. That evening there must have been more than a thousand people attending, and we had a wonderful time, the highlight of which was meeting and spending some time with the leader of the church. This man, an Australian as it happened, was precisely the kind of ambassador for Christ that American Christianity seems to need. Relaxed and vulnerable in public about his faults and shortcomings, Barry was totally committed to the task of presenting Jesus to those who are desperately in need of him, without allowing personal biases and attitudes to stand in the way. In the words of this passage, God was making his appeal through the minister, and, as far as we could tell, that appeal was emerging in a relatively pure form. The result was a very lively and unusually relaxed congregation in which individuals were free to pursue the business of conforming to Christ rather than to the man or woman at the front.

America is not the only place that could do with more leaders like this.

Father, may people meet you in us, instead of us in us.

A NEW HUMANITY

Ephesians 2:13–16 (NRSV)

But now in Christ Jesus you who once were far off have been brought near by the blood of Christ. For he is our peace; in his flesh he has made both groups into one and has broken down the dividing wall, that is, the hostility between us. He has abolished the law... that he might create in himself one new humanity in place of the two, thus making peace, and might reconcile both groups to God in one body through the cross, thus putting to death that hostility through it.

The bitterness with which some Christians talk about their brothers and sisters takes my breath away.

I spoke at a weekend somewhere in England once for a church more or less divided down the middle over one issue. The issue was the vicar. One faction seemed sure their minister was, at best, useless, and at worst, some kind of devil's agent. The other faction felt—surprise, surprise—that he was the most saintly figure in the history of the Christian Church.

The leader of the anti-brigade picked me up from the station. All the way to the conference centre he filled me in on the vicar's failure as a preacher, his insensitivity to parishioners, his lack of hospitality in a home which had been supplied to him 'for that very purpose!', his inept chairmanship of the PCC, and his stubborn tendency towards sacramentalism. I asked him to tell me something good about the vicar. He grudgingly admitted that the vicarage garden was looking better nowadays. If only, he added, spoiling it, the vicar spent as much time with his parishioners as his flowers they would all be a lot better off. Later, at the Centre, I was cornered by members of the pro-vicar faction, anxious to put forward their point of view in case I had already been nobbled.

The vicar turned out to be a charming man close to cracking under the strain of a conflict that he clearly found quite inexplicable. It was a terrible weekend. When I openly challenged people there was temporary agreement that things were not as they should be, but nothing changed. I very rarely talk about such things, but it was as if something maliciously evil had crept into the very centre of that community.

Let's pray that the power of the cross will bring a new beginning for Christians locked in conflict.

Lord Jesus, you are our peace. God forbid that your death should be in vain. Where there is bitterness and anger speak into the minds of those who need to change, and cast out evil from communities that have been deceived into losing sight of you.

A NEW SELF

Ephesians 4:17–24 (NRSV)

You must no longer live as the Gentiles live, in the futility of their minds. They are darkened in their understanding, alienated from the life of God because of their ignorance and hardness of heart. They have lost all sensitivity and have abandoned themselves to licentiousness, greedy to practise every kind of impurity. That is not the way you learned Christ! For surely you have heard about him and were taught in him, as truth is in Jesus. You were taught to put away your former way of life, your old self, corrupt and deluded by its lusts, and to be renewed in the spirit of your minds, and to clothe yourselves with the new self, created according to the likeness of God in true righteousness and holiness.

I sometimes think that I've been a Christian for too long. Let me explain.

I began toddling after Jesus at 16, so it's 32 years since I had any kind of perspective on life from the non-believer's point of view. Because of this I tend, like many Christians, to give myself a hard time over passages like this one. The guilt trap opens before me and I step meekly in, assuming that when I measure myself against such expectations I shall be revealed as a total failure. Now, there is some truth in that assumption, but it is not the whole story. Let's be positive for once. I'll tell you what I'm thinking, and you see if you agree with me.

First, I read this passage with the eyes of one who really does want to follow Jesus. Thank God for that! Good start, eh? Next, I may not measure up to what is demanded of me here, but I am at least conscious of that deficiency, and the gap between what I am and what I should be matters to me very much. I want to put away my former way of life. I want to be renewed in the spirit of my mind. I want to clothe myself with the new self. Thirdly, I have made some steps in the direction that God wants me to go. They might have been small ones, and they might have been interspersed with the odd backward one from time to time, but I know that they have happened and I thank God for that as well.

It would be very sad if the effects of that guilt trap were to obscure the good work of God in our lives. We may not be much, but what we are and what we shall be is made possible by him, so let's thank him for it.

Thank you, Father, for helping us to grow, however slowly, into the likeness of yourself.

A NEW NAME

Revelation 2:17; 3:12 (NRSV)

'To everyone who conquers I will give... a white stone, and on the white stone is written a new name that no one knows except the one who receives it'... 'If you conquer, I will make you a pillar in the temple of my God; you will never go out of it. I will write on you the name of my God, and the name of the city of my God, the new Jerusalem that comes down from my God out of heaven, and my own new name.'

One of the most interesting pieces of graffiti I ever saw was on a bridge that crossed a stream in a very upmarket area to the east of Harpenden. The first interesting thing was that these three words were the only defacement of the stonework. The houses on either side of the little stream and in the whole of that part of the world were very, very large and expensive, not at all the sort of places that are generally supposed to produce wall-scribblers. One young rebel, however, had obviously decided to break the mould by leaving his mark in bright yellow chalk. In large capital letters he had written: NIGEL IS OBDURATE

Somewhat obscure and tentative perhaps, in comparison with the daubs that one sees on the walls of public toilets nowadays, but no doubt the writer felt better for it, and I expect Nigel was mortified, don't you?

Psychiatrists tell us that the act of writing on walls and doors has a lot to do with identity. Once you have written your name or made your mark on a surface that is bound to be seen by others, you make that place your own and feel a greater confidence in being who you are. Or something like that.

Now, before the Thought Police saddle up and ride out to get me, I am not about to say that God goes around scribbling nasty things in public places, but I am interested to note from this passage that Jesus declares his intention of writing the name of God, the name of the city of God and (intriguingly) his own new name, not on a wall or a door, but on us. Don't you find it encouraging that Jesus might believe in us enough to write his name on you and me so that we are publicly and eternally connected to him? The deal is that if we are obedient to him he will demonstrate his total confidence in us by intertwining his identity with ours.

Should we go for that? I think the writing's on the wall, don't you?

We would be proud to bear your name, Lord Jesus. Be patient with us.

A NEW HEAVEN

Revelation 21:1–5 (NRSV)

Then I saw a new heaven and a new earth... And I heard a loud voice from the throne saying, 'See, the home of God is among mortals. He will dwell with them; they will be his peoples, and God himself will be with them; he will wipe every tear from their eyes. Death will be no more; mourning and crying and pain will be no more, for the first things have passed away.' And the one who was seated on the throne said, 'See, I am making all things new.'

I enjoy most of my life, but sometimes I feel weary and sad. As a child I knew some unhappy nights, but the morning had miraculous powers of regeneration. I particularly liked going out in the summer just after the sun came up so that I could watch the light streaming like a river of gold over the red brick footpath that ran along the front of our house. That wonderful daily display of brand-newness suggested that any change for the better might be possible.

Years went by and the magic of the morning became diluted. Waking up no longer had the automatic effect of dispelling inner darkness, and the dull ache of lost innocence was perpetually present. I still loved the early morning sun, but the feeling that it heralded change was a memory instead of a reality.

Becoming a Christian helped a lot once I understood that instant and total joy was not handed out with each copy of *Journey Into Life*. The concept of a fallen world explained a lot about the way in which life seemed to offer so very much, but to deliver in such a variable way. The world may be imperfect, but all around us, and particularly in the natural world, are clues to the way God originally intended that things should be.

Things have gone well for me in so many ways. I know that. I have a family that loves me and a job that brings an enormous amount of satisfaction. I have travelled to places that I never thought I would see and met people who have become very important to me, and yet there is a part of me that is sick of this fallen planet. I look forward to nothing more than the wonderful, brand new morning that is promised in this passage. All things will be made new and we shall no longer feel weary or sad, because heaven and earth will be exactly as they were always supposed to be.

Can't wait to see it, Father.

Can it be true, what is so constantly
affirmed, that there is no sex in souls?
I doubt it, I doubt it exceedingly.

S.T. COLERIDGE

TRAVELLING TWO BY TWO

THE SEXY SONG OF SONGS

Reactions to this particular set of notes have been most interesting and varied. A few Christians clearly identify and agree with Mr Cholmondley-Warner, one of Harry Enfield's comic creations, who describes sex as 'conjugal unpleasantness'. I received a distinct impression from some of the people who talked to me that they felt God must have had some kind of brainstorm on the day when he allowed this particular book to be included in the Bible.

I remember, on a different occasion, one of those same people expressing the view that, although Jesus was a normal man in every other way, it was highly unlikely that he ever experienced sexual temptation. I can understand this person's reluctance to attribute such a basic and intrusively unruly human experience to someone who, for her, epitomizes purity, but, as I have said elsewhere, if he was not tempted in that way, then he was definitely not 'tempted as we are'.

Those who do react to the content of the poem with extreme distaste might like gently to ask themselves why they have such a personal aversion to this aspect of God's creation. They might also reflect on the fact that, as far as Orientals are concerned, the Song of Solomon is considered to be eminently chaste, honouring marriage and the joys of married life. Far from being an unfortunate and inexplicably accidental addition to God's otherwise admirable book, it is actually a vigorously positive endorsement of the kind of committed marital relationship that is under such constant attack in these days.

If anyone suggests to you that God is coldly legalistic and negative about this side of life—show 'em the Song of Songs!

By contrast, others, and especially women, have reported a sense of liberation as they enjoyed the celebration of simply being a woman that lights up these stanzas. One quite elderly lady talked with bright innocence about being 'thrilled' by the extravagantly appreciative way in which parts of the female body are described. For two pins I would pass her exact comments on to you, but unfortunately the Bible Reading Fellowship has only supplied me with one.

A second and more general objection has been that, while one might choose to read and interpret the book as an allegory of Christ's love for the Church, there is little substance in the text itself to support the view that it is intended to be understood in this way. As a non-theologian I have little to say in reply to this comment, except that, in a sense, I don't really think it matters either way. I consider it perfectly legitimate to enjoy the whole thing as poetry and nothing else (I hope all who use these notes will read right through it from that perspective in any case before looking at the different sections I've commented on). The trouble is that getting on to the old allegory trail is a bit like those times when, as kids, we used to ride down steep, bumpy hills on our rickety go-karts that never had any brakes. Once you've started it really is very difficult to stop—so I didn't.

Whatever the legitimacy or otherwise of this approach, I feel quite safe in assuming that the passion of God for his Church is at least as extreme and all-embracing as the love that is declared in these verses. It is, after all, Jesus who casts himself in (among many others) the figurative role of bridegroom to the Church that makes up his body on earth, that Church being composed, as you know, of you and me. Perhaps it is a measure of how far humanity has fallen, that some of us trip so heavily over the physical aspects of this relationship when it is used as a metaphor, that we forget to look up and see the value and significance of parallels with the fierce love, the passionate loyalty, the deep commitment and the rich fulfilment of married life at its best.

In any case, physical passion is not fornication, any more than a sunset-soaked poppy is a life-destroying drug. Both were created to be beautiful, and God has not changed his mind about either.

Prayer

Father, help us to read and enjoy this beautiful poem on any and every level that will provide nourishment for our spirits. We thank you for the gift of love between those men and women who dedicate their relationships to you, and we ask your forgiveness for those times when we have tended, in our minds, to turn something beautiful into something smutty. Thank you particularly for the relationship of Jesus to his Church. Help us to understand the depth and richness of that relationship, and to receive the passion of your love for us.

THE POWER AND THE PERFUME

Song of Solomon 1:1–4 (NIV)

Solomon's Song of Songs. Let him kiss me with the kisses of his mouth—for your love is more delightful than wine. Pleasing is the fragrance of your perfumes; your name is like perfume poured out. No wonder the maidens love you! Take me away with you—let us hurry! Let the king bring me into his chambers. We rejoice and delight in you; we will praise your love more than wine. How right they are to adore you!

It's refreshing to plunge into an atmosphere as rich with the ecstasy of lovers as the Song of Solomon. I pray you will feel closer to the heart of God, and more safely held by the divine intelligence than ever, as you read this passionate allegory of spiritual desire and union. There is something reassuring about God electing to use such a human scenario in which to reveal his feelings for us.

One line in this early passage, though, the one about the lover's name being like perfume poured out, makes me rather sad. Don't misunderstand me, I love the idea. It reminds me of visits to our home by special friends and family members. When one of my children calls out that one of these favourite people is at the door, the very mention of the name seems to add a new and sweeter scent to the day. I felt the same thing even more pungently as a child. One of my brothers would yell, 'Mum's back!', and suddenly everything was—well—all right again. The house was warm and normal and scented with safety.

My sadness is about the name of Jesus. Since becoming a Christian in the mid-1960s that name has had the power to strengthen me, warm me, support me, make me cry, remind me who I belong to and what I should be doing, or a combination of those things. For some, however, the word 'Jesus' triggers feelings of something very close to disgust and repulsion, largely because the man who bore that name has been relentlessly presented by far too many of those who claim to follow him, as a passionless and really rather pathetic personality, who bleats thinly and unattractively about the need for people to stop doing bad things. How sad.

The Song of Solomon tips the balance way over in the other direction, without one jot of moral or spiritual compromise, and the sweet scent of the name of Jesus is on every page.

Restore the power and perfume of your name, Lord.

THE PLACE WHERE WE ARE

Song of Solomon 1:5–6 (NIV)

Dark am I, yet lovely, O daughters of Jerusalem, dark like the tents of Kedar, like the tent curtains of Solomon. Do not stare at me because I am dark, because I am darkened by the sun. My mother's sons were angry with me and made me take care of the vineyards; my own vineyard I have neglected.

Some aspects of this poem are very difficult to understand, but it appears that the girl in this passage has been sent by her brothers to work in their vineyard under the hot sun. As a result she is bronzed and beautiful, and in this state she is later encountered by Solomon (disguised as a shepherd?), who falls in love with her and eventually makes her his bride.

The theme isn't an uncommon one—I suppose Cinderella is more or less the same story in a different form—but, as a picture of Christian experience it has a particular significance, namely, that the Holy Spirit will find us and demonstrate the power of love to us in the place where we are, rather than in the place where we perhaps thought we ought to be. Often, in addition, the face of God appears to us at first in the guise of a person or set of events that are without specifically Christian labels of any kind.

Today, as I look back to the days before I became a Christian, I can see, as I was unable to see then (or for some years after my conversion, to be honest), the ways in which God fathered me in times of desolation. I recall, for instance, a café in Tunbridge Wells where, as a lost, bored, broke and singularly unattractive teenager I spent much of my time. The manageress, an Italian lady named Inez, was one of the very few rays of light in an otherwise bleak world. She fed me occasionally, smiled at me, talked to me, made me feel I was not entirely a waste of time. I hope she reads this. I'd love her to know how grateful I was and am. Today, I also thank God for being there for me, in her, at a time when I didn't even know he existed.

If you want to meet Jesus you are not in the wrong place, because that is the place where he will find you, and then you will go to the ball.

Father, some of us feel that we have been badly treated and have ended up in the wrong place. Visit us with your love, Lord, in the place where we are.

FOR EVER IN LOVE

Song of Solomon 1:12–17 (NIV)

While the king was at his table, my perfume spread its fragrance. My lover is to me a sachet of myrrh resting between my breasts. My lover is to me a cluster of henna blossoms from the vineyards of En Gedi. How beautiful you are, my darling! Oh, how beautiful! Your eyes are doves. How handsome you are, my lover! Oh, how charming! And our bed is verdant. The beams of our house are cedars; our rafters are firs.

Being in love is such a total thing, isn't it? This passage has that dreamy, all-absorbed, repetitive quality that one associates with the whole business of falling head over heels in love.

Two friends of ours fell in love when we were living in the Midlands. We knew them both very well, but separately, if you know what I mean. In fact, they probably first met at our house. Philip and Jane were both halfway through their 50s, and we were surprised and a little alarmed on first hearing that a relationship had not only begun, but was rocketing down the road towards marriage! How would these two very distinct and independent personalities cope with sharing personal space at this stage in their lives? I went out for a drink with Philip and asked him how things were going. He was in a state of terminal gooiness. Apparently he and Jane felt exactly the same about absolutely everything.

'Isn't that a remarkable coincidence?' said Philip.

'Yes, Philip,' I confirmed superfluously, 'that's a remarkable co-incidence.'

'Do you know,' went on Philip dreamily, 'I was sitting in this very same pub with Jane the other evening, and she accidentally spilt some of her drink on my trousers.'

'Oh, dear,' I said, 'how annoying that must have—'

'I said to her, "Jane, don't worry, I count it a privilege to have your drink spilt on me—I really do…"'

I didn't listen to any more after that. Philip and Jane are happily not counting it a privilege to spill drinks all over each other nowadays, and I hope they'll have a very pleasant life together.

Why have I been rambling on about my friends? Well, it interests me to reflect on the fact that the idyllic 'in love-ness' expressed in these verses from Solomon's poem will never actually fade when it comes to our relationship with God. Read it again and reflect on the fact that this dream is for ever.

Help us to never fall out of love with you, Lord.

A LILY AMONG THORNS

Song of Solomon 2:1–3 (NIV)

I am a rose of Sharon, a lily of the valleys. Like a lily among thorns is my darling among the maidens. Like an apple tree among the trees of the forest is my lover among the young men. I delight to sit in his shade, and his fruit is sweet to my taste.

This is a beautiful piece of writing, isn't it? No comment of mine can add very much. There is one little thing that strikes me, though. (Yes, yes, you're right—there's always some little thing that strikes me.) It's the line where the man compares his love among maidens to a lily among brambles. What does this mean? Here are two possible interpretations, both of which have interesting implications.

First, there's a suggestion of vulnerability. Brambles are notoriously apt to choke or impede the growth of more tender plants. Perhaps there's a hint here of the risk taken by God in allowing Jesus to be exposed as a real man to the tangles and thorns of unsaved humanity. Certainly, the sight of that baby, fragile and dependent, in the stable in Bethlehem, is one which God and all his angels must have gazed on with great pride and great fear. How would we look after him? What would happen to him in the end? The answer, of course, is that Mary and Joseph seem to have done very well, but, between us all, we crucified him. The lily was crushed but not destroyed.

This principle of the vulnerability of Jesus is, I believe, an important part of our understanding of how the body of Christ on earth should function today. A later note mentioning Mother Teresa might explain more of what I mean by that.

The second interpretation is simply that something very beautiful and special is growing in the midst of us, however wild and cheap life on *News at Ten* (and in our living-rooms) may seem sometimes. In each one of us, in the centre of every situation, at the heart of every storm, plague and tragedy, the flowering, or the first shoots, or, at the very least, the seeds of the growth of love can never be destroyed. And, just in case anyone thinks that's soppy talk, let me say, on behalf of myself and many others, that it is the lily among the brambles that has made it possible to survive on many, many occasions.

Jesus, so vulnerable, so beautiful, so strong, help us to stand.

ORDINARY HEROES

Song of Solomon 2:4–7 (NIV)

He has taken me to the banquet hall, and his banner over me is love. Strengthen me with raisins, refresh me with apples, for I am faint with love. His left arm is under my head, and his right arm embraces me. Daughters of Jerusalem, I charge you by the gazelles and by the does of the field: Do not arouse or awaken love until it so desires.

'Mum! I'm home, Mum, guess what—Robert Wilson's asked me to go round his tonight, an' I'm faint with love. Get the raisins out an' bung us an apple—I need a bit of sustaining...'

Initially it seems difficult to relate the stylized romance of such a distant culture and time to contemporary experience, but, in fact, human beings have been more or less the same throughout history, and especially when it comes to affairs of the heart. Only the context and the details change (although even raisins and apples reappear nowadays as muesli, don't they? Presumably Solomon's lover's mum made sure she had a good nourishing breakfast before going out romancing every morning).

Understanding the 'ordinariness' of biblical characters can help to develop a constructive relationship with scripture. For years, presumably influenced by grimly dramatic lithographs in our family Bible, and feature films in which Charlton Heston or Victor Mature gazed at the horizon accompanied by a full orchestra, my notion was that people like Moses and Samuel were (a) American (b) 15 feet tall, and (c) incapable of speaking any sentence that didn't drip with cosmic significance. What rubbish!

God has always dealt with frail human beings because there isn't any other sort about. Some of the great characters of the Old Testament had particular talents, but, on reading accounts of their lives we discover that they also had pronounced faults. A barrier to personal involvement in passages like today's, and in much of the rest of the Bible, is this illusory feeling that our emotions, experiences, relationships and spiritual battles are puny and unimportant by comparison with the 'heroes' of scripture.

Rest assured; if you've ever been in love, you will understand the Song of Solomon, and if you're serving God in the 21st century, you are already starring in an epic all of your own.

If the Bible had been written today, in our society, would we have the Book of George, and the Book of Irene, and the Book of Stan, and the Book of...?

A SEASON FOR ALL MEN

Song of Solomon 2:10–13, 16–17 (NIV)

My lover spoke and said to me, 'Arise, my darling, my beautiful one, and come with me. See! The winter is past; the rains are over and gone. Flowers appear on the earth; the season of singing has come, the cooing of doves is heard in our land. The fig-tree forms its early fruit; the blossoming vines spread their fragrance. Arise, come, my darling; my beautiful one, come with me.'... My lover is mine and I am his; he browses among the lilies. Until the day breaks and the shadows flee, turn, my lover, and be like a gazelle or like a young stag on the rugged hills.

This must be one of the most famous springtime rhapsodies of all time, sung by one, not only enraptured by the new season, but also in love, a pretty unbeatable combination.

One of the clichés of Christianity is the spiritual symbolism of the seasons, isn't it? We're born, we live, we pass through the evening of our lives, we die, we are born again. These parallels have only become clichés, of course, because they really do resonate not just with specifically Christian cycles, but with the very rhythm of living itself. As the years go by my gratitude for seasonal change intensifies. Living through a year in this country is like travelling in majestic slow motion on the most magnificent theme park ride that could ever be devised.

The symbols? Well, for me there are symbols within symbols. Here's an example. In front of our house stands a large Japanese flowering cherry. The tree has obviously been there for years. For 49 weeks of the year, this sturdy growth is undistinguished, but when the spring comes it explodes into a triumph of pink blossom. For three weeks a huge orb of colour shines over the street like the most precious of precious jewels, glowing with particular magnificence under blue skies. After this brief but spectacularly successful run the performance ends, and our neighbours start getting annoyed about soggy blossom all over their front gardens.

When I was ill over a decade ago, the blooming of that tree was like a sign from heaven, suggesting to me that God employs a special magic to bring beauty out of dullness. Every year I look forward to a repeat of that little exercise in optimism, a sort of arboreal rainbow, a symbol within a symbol. I love springtime.

Thank you for the seasons and the possibility of change.

LOST LOVERS

Song of Solomon 3:1–4 (NIV)

'All night long on my bed I looked for the one my heart loves; I looked for him but did not find him. I will get up now and go about the city, through its streets and squares; I will search for the one my heart loves. So I looked for him but did not find him. The watchmen found me as they made their rounds in the city. "Have you seen the one my heart loves?" Scarcely had I passed them when I found the one my heart loves. I held him and would not let him go till I had brought him to my mother's house, to the room of the one who conceived me.'

Of all the heart-rending letters that people send me from time to time, the ones that upset me most (perhaps because I can identify with them) are those in which a desperate but unfulfilled desire for God is expressed. Like the speaker in this passage these unhappy souls cry out in the dark night of their desolation for some sign or indication that they are not alone—that God really does hear them and love them, that they will eventually be united with him and that—well, you know— that everything will be warm and fuzzy and wonderful.

Often, these folk have already sought and received most of the statutory varieties of advice, and are hoping I might offer some new, super-effective idea that will transform their lives. Oh, dear!

I suppose if God was a system, or a mechanism, or even a sheet of MFI instructions, I might be able to help in that way, but he isn't—he is a creative, dynamic personality who cannot be adjusted or programmed to produce a particular effect.

When you set against that the complexity of each of the human beings who has dealings with him, the problem appears to become even more insoluble. What I can say, from personal experience, is that if you are one of these lost lovers, a right time will come to rise from your bed and go about the city, in the streets and in the squares, looking for your God, and then you will meet him. But it must be the right time, the moment that he has chosen for you.

When you do find him—and you will—don't take him for granted. Don't let him go.

Father, hear the cries from the dark and stretch out your arms towards us. We want to be with you so much.

TOO GOOD TO BE TRUE

Song of Solomon 4:1, 5–7 (NIV)

How beautiful you are, my darling! Oh, how beautiful! Your eyes behind your veil are doves. Your hair is like a flock of goats descending from Mount Gilead... Your two breasts are like two fawns, like twin fawns of a gazelle that browse among the lilies. Until the day breaks and the shadows flee, I will go to the mountain of myrrh and to the hill of incense. All beautiful you are, my darling; there is no flaw in you.

When I was a teenager an advert appeared in *The Times*. The small panel on the back page simply offered a free car—a mini—to the first person who replied. There were no strings attached, nothing to be paid, in fact, no catch at all. Someone could have had a car for nothing, but not a single person responded. Presumably readers thought they'd be 'done' in some way. Of course, that was exactly the reaction the advertisers had expected; nevertheless, the car really was there for the taking.

Do you think people were silly to be wary? Well, look at this passage, which offers something rather more valuable than a mini, and ask yourself whether you think it's for real. Let me explain.

The Song of Solomon is many things, including, as I mentioned in the introduction, a picture of God's love for his bride, the Church. That, in case you didn't realize it, means you—and me. Now, I'd like us to ask ourselves the following question. Leaving aside items such as having breasts like two fawns, do we honestly believe that this is what God sees when he looks at us?

Are we—not just beautiful—but very beautiful to him? Does he really think us lovely? Could we possibly be without flaw in his sight? Is it conceivable that we stir such excited pleasure in his breast?

He says this is all true. Perhaps there's a catch. I don't think so. Even less than when the Plass family go fishing. We are so much in the groove of self-criticism that we forget we are caught up with Christ. We are as beautiful as he is, not because of what we are or do, but because he is in us and we are in him. Can we accept that? Come on—we missed out on the mini—let's have a go.

Some of us don't feel very beautiful, Lord. Help us to get lost in your love.

SWEET NOTHINGS

Song of Solomon 4:9–11 (NIV)

You have stolen my heart, my sister, my bride; you have stolen my heart with one glance of your eyes, with one jewel of your necklace. How delightful is your love, my sister, my bride! How much more pleasing is your love than wine, and the fragrance of your perfume than any spice! Your lips drop sweetness as the honeycomb, my bride; milk and honey are under your tongue. The fragrance of your garments is like that of Lebanon.

I wish I was a little better at the old sweet nothings. Mind you, my wife would be deeply suspicious if I suddenly nestled up and told her that honey and milk are under her tongue, and the scent of her garments is like the scent of Lebanon. As for claiming that I regard her love as much better than wine—I'm not at all sure she'd believe me.

Seriously, it does seem a pity that many marriages deteriorate, not just into lack of romance, but actual conflict. A dismally common view of marriage is exemplified by a scene I once witnessed in a laundrette. As I entered, a loud argument was going on between a man and woman in their early 60s.

'You don't understand listenin', do you?' shouted the lady. 'All you can do is make a noise!'

'Go on, get out of it!' returned the man furiously. 'You're nothin' but a stupid, mouthy old ratbag!'

'Don't worry!' she snapped. 'I don't want to be anywhere you might be!'

And with that, she swept through the door and disappeared.

A pear-shaped lady who'd observed hostilities from beside the drying machines shifted slightly on her seat and addressed the man in dispassionate tones. 'She your wife, then?'

The man stopped muttering and stared at her.

'Married to 'er!' he said incredulously, 'I wouldn't marry 'er if she was the last woman on earth!'

'Oh,' said the pear-shaped lady, dispassionate as ever. 'I thought she must be your wife the way you was talkin' to 'er.'

An extreme example of how marriage is seen, perhaps, but it does seem such a shame that so many marriages begin as romances, only to decline to the point where your marriage partner is the only person you're ever really nasty to.

Lord, we can't reach Solomon's standard, but we'd like to bring some romance back into our marriages. Help those of us who are married to see our partners with fresh eyes, and begin to appreciate them all over again.

UNLOCKING

Song of Solomon 4:12–16 (NIV)

You are a garden locked up, my sister, my bride; you are a spring enclosed, a sealed fountain. Your plants are an orchard of pomegranates with choice fruits, with henna and nard, nard and saffron, calamus and cinnamon, with every kind of incense tree, with myrrh and aloes and all the finest spices. You are a garden fountain, a well of flowing water streaming down from Lebanon. Awake, north wind, and come, south wind! Blow on my garden, that its fragrance may spread abroad. Let my lover come into his garden and taste its choice fruits.

I mentioned earlier that I occasionally look back with horror to the time when, as a teenage truant, I wandered aimlessly around Tunbridge Wells with no money and no prospects. It isn't the idea of the aimless wandering that causes my horror—that has remained one of my favourite hobbies—it's the memory of how I dealt with feelings of gross inadequacy about most of my relationships. I developed a habit of scathing sarcasm that probably alienated more people than I imagined at the time. Lowest form of wit it may have been, but for a pain-filled loser like me, it was the most effective way of making some impact on someone, sometimes.

I'm sure people were infuriated by my sardonic attitude. I don't blame them. But I think if they'd known what a yearning there was within me to give and receive warmth and emotion at exactly the same time as I was attempting to cut every other ego in sight down to size, they would have been amazed. With a few friends, predictably those who demonstrated unequivocally that they valued me, I dropped my act, but those people were few and far between.

A significant effect of encounters with God over the last few years has been a release of the natural, childlike desire in me to love and be loved for what I am, however unimpressive that might be. I believe and hope that my sarcasm has been transfigured into satire nowadays. As I read today's passage, I sense in the heart of it God's promise that all the locked, beautiful gardens within us will be thrown open one day, and all the sealed fountains allowed to overflow with feelings and thoughts and words that have hardly seen the light of day before. I know that some of you who are reading these words today need that more than anything else in the world.

Unlock us and release us, Lord. Walk in this garden. Drink from this fountain.

WHAT DO YOU THINK ABOUT GOD?

Song of Solomon 5:8–11, 16 (NIV)

O daughters of Jerusalem, I charge you—if you find my lover, what will you tell him? Tell him I am faint with love. How is your beloved better than others, most beautiful of women? How is your beloved better than others, that you charge us so? My lover is radiant and ruddy, outstanding among ten thousand. His head is purest gold; his hair is wavy and black as a raven... His mouth is sweetness itself; he is altogether lovely. This is my lover, this my friend, O daughters of Jerusalem.

Because I travel so much as a speaker, I see an enormous number of churches in the course of a year, and I meet hundreds of Christians doing work of various kinds, from full-time ministry to the making of coffee on a Sunday morning. I never tire of hearing what's happening, especially from people who are really caught up in their activities. James Herriot wrote that enthusiasts are attractive, but fanatics are irresistible. I agree. Quite often, though, when I have been listening for some time to a description of recent youth-group activities or progress with the new church extension, I throw in a question that I've asked more times than I've had cold dinners that were supposed to be hot at missionary fundraising meetings: 'What do you think about God?'

The usual reply, after a moment's puzzled silence, is, 'What do you mean?'

'Well, what do you personally think and feel about God—about Jesus?'

Some people wouldn't be able to answer this question if I stood and waited all day, because, at this stage in their lives, they have not met him in any conscious sense. Others speak with varying degrees of eagerness or devotion, but the ones I really enjoy are those whose eyes and manner soften, as they attempt, incoherently or lucidly, to tell me how much they love him, and, perhaps, how proud they are to be working for him.

That's more or less what is happening in this passage.

'What's so special about this man of yours?' the women ask.

The reply is lyrical and overwhelming, containing words that, for two thousand years, have summed up the feelings of true believers about Jesus.

'This is my beloved and this is my friend.'

Help us to put you at the centre of our work for you, Lord, and to give a good, warm account of you when we are asked.

OPEN OUR EYES

Song of Solomon 6:1–5 (NIV)

Where has your lover gone, most beautiful of women? Which way did your lover turn, that we may look for him with you? My lover has gone down to his garden, to the beds of spices, to browse in the gardens and to gather lilies. I am my lover's and my lover is mine; he browses among the lilies. You are beautiful, my darling, as Tirzah, lovely as Jerusalem, majestic as troops with banners. Turn your eyes from me; they overwhelm me. Your hair is like a flock of goats descending from Gilead.

Have you ever wondered why God allowed Mother Teresa to become known to such a wide public? Wouldn't it have made more sense to leave her to quietly get on with her work among the poor in India, while the blow-wave evangelists do all the up-front stuff? Clearly, God wanted to make some sort of point, and this passage may offer a clue as to what it was.

'Where has your beloved gone?' When that question is asked of Christians you can expect a wide variety of responses. Some are quite sure he is contained within a specific liturgical framework, others just know that the only venue at which he can be reliably expected to put in an appearance is their very own church between 10.30 and 12 o'clock on a Sunday morning. Yet others have him stuck down solidly to the pages of the Bible, a number are certain he lives at Butlin's, and there are even a few who would locate him somewhere inside a television set, firmly under the control of a steely-eyed American evangelist.

What would Mother Teresa say? I suspect that she might reply in a rather similar way to the maiden in these verses, that he has gone to pasture his flocks in the gardens. But for Mother Teresa the flocks are sick, filth-ingrained, homeless people, and the gardens are the teeming streets of India. I believe that God raised this remarkable woman to prominence to remind us that our beloved is still to be found among those who need him, and to help us understand that if our spiritual sight is corrected we might be able, like Mother Teresa, to see Jesus in the eyes of beggars, and lilies on the streets of Calcutta.

Open the eyes of our understanding, Lord, to see where you are to be found. May we see hope where there was only despair, and beauty where there was only ugliness.

ON THE CONTRARY

Song of Solomon 7:1-2, 6-9 (NIV)

How beautiful your sandalled feet, O prince's daughter! Your graceful legs are like jewels, the work of a craftsman's hands. Your navel is a rounded goblet that never lacks blended wine. Your waist is a mound of wheat encircled by lilies... How beautiful you are and how pleasing, O love, with your delights! Your stature is like that of the palm, and your breasts like clusters of fruit. I said, 'I will climb the palm tree; I will take hold of its fruit.' May your breasts be like the clusters of the vine, the fragrance of your breath like apples, and your mouth like the best wine. May the wine go straight to my lover, flowing gently over lips and teeth.

Solomon must have been a wow at parties, mustn't he? What a chat-up line! I wonder how he would have got on nowadays. I'm not sure how the average modern girl would react to being told that her navel is a rounded bowl that never lacks mixed wine. I'm a bit confused about the rounded thighs like jewels as well. Jewels? I expect those references had cultural significance. The rest of this passage, though—my goodness!

If those who condemn the Bible (without reading it) for being bland and passionless were to study passages like this, they might have to shift their attack to a different front altogether. Perhaps they would end up complaining that such blatantly sensual expressions of sexual desire are inappropriate to a book claiming to be the living word of God. After all, they might point out, he is uncompromisingly critical of sexual immorality in many other parts of the very same book. But, of course, that is precisely the point. Sadly, the Church has tended to emphasize the negative aspects of sex, so that for many it has become an area of dark repression and guilt. God is often perceived as being concerned only with preventing people from enjoying themselves.

Read the passage again. Allegorically or literally, its message is clear. This climber of palm trees, this holder of branches, this connoisseur of wines and kisses, is as far removed from being anti-sex as it is possible to be. God is not just mildly, benignly tolerant of physical love, he is extravagantly in favour of it when it is enjoyed within the context of a spiritually committed relationship. He designed it, and saw that it was good. And it is.

Lord, help us not to be frightened about things that you have given us. We'll try to be positive when talking about these things to people who don't know you.

NOWHERE IN PARTICULAR

Song of Solomon 7:10–13 (NIV)

I belong to my lover, and his desire is for me. Come, my lover, let us go to the countryside, let us spend the night in the villages. Let us go early to the vineyards to see if the vines have budded, if their blossoms have opened, and if the pomegranates are in bloom—there I will give you my love. The mandrakes send out their fragrance, and at our door is every delicacy, both new and old, that I have stored up for you, my lover.

A few weeks before this note was written, Bridget and I took David and Katy over to France to spend a few days at the small cottage in Normandy that we own jointly with some local friends. This dumpy little dwelling, blessedly lacking in everything beginning with the prefix 'tele', stands next to a tiny junior school in a sleepy village, and has only three rooms, one dining-sitting-doing-things sort of room, and two bedrooms. The optimistically named 'bathroom' is designed for people at the lower end of the not-very-tall range, but it allows you to do whatever you need to do, albeit in rather contorted postures. Ours is not a smart cottage. It probably qualifies for a quarter-star rating, but it and the fascinatingly lit valley it overlooks are full of strong magic. Those who stay there invariably seem to relax, and that's exactly what we did on this occasion.

I'm potty about France anyway, but there was something extra special about this visit. Something inside me sat down and took it easy for the first time in a very long time. We went for little walks to nowhere in particular, we cycled through farms to a place where the river runs beneath an old crumbling bridge and talked to a little brown goat who seemed anxious to get to know us, we went up to the nearby forest and collected kindling for the open fire, we ate long lingering breakfasts at the table by the window that overlooks the valley and we played French cricket on the lawn (an area of rough grass at the side of the house).

Something about this passage is almost tearfully reminiscent of those all too few peaceful days when we laughed together and looked at things together and simply rejoiced in being people who loved each other in a place that was lovely. It doesn't happen very often, does it? When the Lord and his bride are truly united it will happen for ever and ever.

Come soon, Lord Jesus.

At Easter let your clothes be new,
Or else be sure you will it rue.

OLD ENGLISH RHYME

CHALLENGES ON THE ROAD

READINGS FOR PASSIONTIDE AND HOLY WEEK FROM LUKE AND JOHN

I must tell you honestly that there was no clear plan or theme in my mind as I selected passages, mainly from Luke, to take us towards Easter. As so often happens, though, a theme does emerge when this number of notes is written intensively over a relatively short period, and in this case it appears to be the theme of 'challenge'.

It seems important to me that we do not confuse 'being challenged' with 'being told off'. Jesus was not attempting to weigh his beloved disciples down with guilt, but to supply them with very necessary spiritual weapons and equipment, and to teach them, in the days that he had left, how these things should be employed in the tough times that lay ahead. Do you think that tough times lie ahead of us? I do. And I think that the church—that is, you and me and the others—has become a trifle flabby and uncertain about some of the most fundamental aspects of our faith. However, Jesus is risen, and the Holy Spirit is alive in us. There are a million 'nows' in which to start again. Let's choose one and do exactly that.

Be challenged.

THE BREATHLESS PAUSE

Luke 17:1–6 (NIV)

Jesus said to his disciples, 'Things that cause people to sin are bound to come, but woe to that person through whom they come. It would be better for him to be thrown into the sea with a millstone tied round his neck than for him to cause one of these little ones to sin. So watch yourselves. If your brother sins, rebuke him, and if he repents, forgive him. If he sins against you seven times in a day, and seven times comes back to you and says, "I repent," forgive him.' The apostles said to the Lord, 'Increase our faith!' He replied, 'If you have faith as small as a mustard seed, you can say to this mulberry tree, "Be uprooted and planted in the sea," and it will obey you.'

Do you sense the breathless pause between Jesus' incredibly tough line on forgiveness, and the disciples' strangled request for more faith? The staggering challenge to them two thousand years ago was exactly the same as it is for us today, and there is no escaping that challenge if we want honestly to follow our Master day by day through this fortnight to the place of his death and the moment of his resurrection. Yet again, the message is about the giving up of rights, a command to those of us who call ourselves Christians to echo, in our dealings with each other, the ultimate sacrifice that he is about to make.

We do well to ask ourselves if we are prepared to love those who hurt or offend us, relinquishing our rights to the shoddy tools of resentment, sulking or revenge. Let's not kid ourselves or make idle promises. It is so very difficult truly to walk in the way that he sets before us, but the Holy Spirit will help and comfort us in our task. Let's pray that our heavenly Father will grant us at least a tenth of a tenth of a tenth of a mustard seed of faith, so that we can be obedient to him. A church that is at war with itself is of no use to God or man.

Father, we do not want to be followers of Jesus in name only. In this breathless pause before we follow him towards Jerusalem, we pray for the faith and courage to love one another as you have commanded.

MAKING CONNECTIONS

Luke 17:11–19 (NIV) (Also read Psalm 124)

Now on his way to Jerusalem, Jesus travelled along the border between Samaria and Galilee. As he was going into a village, ten men who had leprosy met him. They stood at a distance and called out in a loud voice, 'Jesus, Master, have pity on us!' When he saw them, he said, 'Go, show yourselves to the priests.' And as they went, they were cleansed. One of them, when he saw he was healed, came back, praising God in a loud voice. He threw himself at Jesus' feet and thanked him—and he was a Samaritan. Jesus asked, 'Were not all ten cleansed? Where are the other nine? Was no one found to return and give praise to God except this foreigner?' Then he said to him, 'Rise and go; your faith has made you well.'

Perhaps Jesus was occasionally tempted to save the Samaritan nation and leave the rest to get on with it. Certainly, they emerge from the Gospels in a very positive light—rather nicely brought up, judging from the behaviour of this ex-leper, one of a group of ten who seem to have tithed their gratitude.

The trouble with problems is that, once solved, they are no longer problems. They disappear, don't they? It's so easy to forget who cleared the path when we are celebrating our arrival in the clearing.

A friend of mine, for instance, told me when we first met of a major concern about which he prayed with fervent regularity. His grown-up son, after a couple of painful relationships, seemed unlikely ever to risk the closeness that might lead to marriage. My friend found it hard to accept that God had not yet answered his prayer. Two years later his son did, in fact, marry a girl from the church, but it was not until my friend was talking one day about yet another major prayer concern that I realized he had never expressed any awareness of the connection between his son's marriage and all those heartfelt prayers. My friend was flabbergasted when I recalled our previous conversations. The problem had disappeared, and so had its connection with the problem-solver.

Here is a practical suggestion. Let us read Psalm 124, look back on what God has done for us, and ask ourselves the same question as the psalmist: 'What if the Lord had *not* been on our side…?'

Thank you.

A QUESTION OF ATTITUDE

Luke 18:9–14 (NIV)

To some who were confident of their own righteousness and looked down on everybody else, Jesus told this parable: 'Two men went up to the temple to pray, one a Pharisee and the other a tax collector. The Pharisee stood up and prayed about himself: "God, I thank you that I am not like other men—robbers, evildoers, adulterers—or even like this tax collector. I fast twice a week and give a tenth of all I get." But the tax collector stood at a distance. He would not even look up to heaven, but beat his breast and said, "God, have mercy on me, a sinner." I tell you that this man, rather than the other, went home justified before God. For everyone who exalts himself will be humbled, and he who humbles himself will be exalted.'

And behold, the following week, the same two men went up to the same temple, but this time the tax collector stood really quite close and said, 'God, I thank you that I am not like this Pharisee, who, despite fasting twice a week and giving a tenth of all he gets, thinks himself better than me, not realizing that after my endearingly humble request of last week for you to have mercy on me, a sinner, I am, in fact, in a somewhat better spiritual state than he is.'

You can tie yourself in hopelessly tangled, unproductive knots over this. I know—I've done it. As a young Christian, I gulped this wonderful parable down like a glass of water in the desert, overjoyed that openness with God about my continual failure was all that seemed to be required. Sadly, all too soon the sensation of spiritual refreshment was translated into fierce pride in the 'rugged simplicity' of my faith, especially compared with the pathetic attempts of those who were—huh!—trying to be good enough for God.

It's actually about attitude, of course. Jesus is saying that there is no position from which one Christian may look down on or judge another, however deliciously tempting it may sometimes be. The denial or deep-down acceptance of this inescapable truth is—always has been—an absolutely crucial factor in deciding whether the Church is to be the Body of Christ or just another social club.

Thank you for your mercy.

FLESHING IT OUT

Luke 18:31–34 (NIV)

Jesus took the Twelve aside and told them, 'We are going up to Jerusalem, and everything that is written by the prophets about the Son of Man will be fulfilled. He will be turned over to the Gentiles. They will mock him, insult him, spit on him, flog him and kill him. On the third day he will rise again.' The disciples did not understand any of this. Its meaning was hidden from them, and they did not know what he was talking about.

Nailing down my actual reaction to this Bible passage before it turns into something more spiritually respectable, I am forced to ask this question: Why did Jesus tell his disciples things that they completely failed to understand? It wasn't as if they were likely to *ask* him to explain. Elsewhere in the Gospels we find the disciples unwilling to ask their Master what he means because he might get cross!

The common answer to my question is that Jesus knew his words would be understood and recorded at some later day; and that does, of course, make sense. But, for a moment, consider something else.

A while ago, I was present at a gathering of Christian booksellers when a highly respected biblical scholar stated publicly that anyone who believed that Jesus never doubted his own divinity had failed to understand the Gospels. Predictably, an uneasy *frisson* passed through the company at this point, but I found the comment a very helpful and stimulating one.

As Jesus came closer and closer to the cross that would cut his life so hideously short, there must have been, in that truly human heart of his, fleeting moments when he did ask himself if he had indeed got the whole thing wrong. What if, despite everything, he was actually in the grip of a complex delusion? What if he was about to throw away his sweet, sweet human life for the sake of a dream from which he would never awake? At moments like that, however swiftly passing, was it necessary for Jesus to insert the skeleton of divine prophecy into the flesh of his intention, and actually to say the words out loud, partly perhaps for other people's benefit, but mainly for his own?

Father, when tough obedience is called for, the doubts creep in. Thank you that Jesus leads the way in this as in everything else.

WHAT DO YOU WANT ME TO DO?

Luke 18:35–43 (NIV)

As Jesus approached Jericho, a blind man was sitting by the roadside begging. When he heard the crowd going by, he asked what was happening. They told him, 'Jesus of Nazareth is passing by.' He called out, 'Jesus, Son of David, have mercy on me!' Those who led the way rebuked him and told him to be quiet, but he shouted all the more, 'Son of David, have mercy on me!' Jesus stopped and ordered the man to be brought to him. When he came near, Jesus asked him, 'What do you want me to do for you?' 'Lord, I want to see, ' he replied. Jesus said to him, 'Receive your sight; your faith has healed you.' Immediately he received his sight and followed Jesus, praising God. When all the people saw it, they also praised God.

A friend of mine suffers from a disease that threatens her sight and will eventually kill her.

Our church believes that God can heal, but there is a nervous, tentative, not-wanting-to-blow-our-only-chance feel about the way in which many of us actually present petitions to God in such a situation. This kind of thing always feels strange and difficult to understand, doesn't it? If we ask God to heal our friend on Friday, is it all right to ask him again on Sunday? And what about Tuesday? I mean—presumably he heard the Friday and Sunday prayers perfectly clearly, so there can't be much point in repeating it for a third time—can there? So, should we just wait? Or could there be something wrong with our technique, something we could adjust if we knew what the problem was?

As I read this account of the blind man who was determined to be heard, I suspect that what is actually missing from our petitions is the full and genuine expression of our desires. It is like showing someone the picture of a flower instead of the flower itself. Perhaps if our calling out were to pass the bounds of 'how it is usually done' and to be truly inhabited by the passion and pain with which we fear the death of our friend, Jesus would hear our shouts and call us to him, and ask, 'What do you want me to do for you?' And then we would tell him with tears, and our friend would be healed.

Release us, Lord…

SMALL CHANGE

Luke 19:2–7 (NIV)

A man was there by the name of Zacchaeus; he was a chief tax collector and was wealthy. He wanted to see who Jesus was, but being a short man he could not, because of the crowd. So he ran ahead and climbed a sycamore-fig tree to see him, since Jesus was coming that way. When Jesus reached the spot, he looked up and said to him, 'Zacchaeus, come down immediately. I must stay at your house today.' So he came down at once and welcomed him gladly. All the people saw this and began to mutter, 'He has gone to be the guest of a "sinner".'

For a time I worked in a secure unit for very difficult teenagers. One day a big, tough-looking lad of 18 was brought in by two policemen and left with me. My new guest's demeanour suggested that he was aggressively intent on becoming as dominant in this environment as he probably had been elsewhere. And yet—I thought I saw something else behind that darkly challenging glare.

'What am I s'posed to do in 'ere, then?' was his first, heavily scorn-laden question as we confronted each other in the unit office.

I pointed. 'Well, we've got some Airfix kits over there—planes and tanks and things. You could do some of those if you like.'

'Airfix!' Incredulous disgust and derision mingled in his reaction to this suggestion.

'Anyway,' I continued, with the quiet politeness that I found so helpful in dealing with new admissions, 'first things first. Would you be so good as to slip those boots of yours off and I'll give you some slippers to wear around the unit. It's a rule.'

This was the crunch. He eyed me speculatively, unsure about this unusual combination of physical size and polite confidence. Slowly he bent to undo the laces in his 'fourteen holers'. I placed the boots carefully in a cupboard and handed him a pair of slippers to wear. The lad was looking slightly dazed and oddly relieved. Life as he knew it had suddenly stopped, and in this place his customary weapons seemed useless.

'What do you want to do now?' I asked.

'Wouldn't mind 'avin' a look at them Airfix kits,' said the mild twelve-year-old I had spotted earlier.

Father, Jesus saw possibility for change in people like Zacchaeus when nobody else did. Teach us to keep our eyes open so that lost things might be found.

THIS IS GETTING US NOWHERE

John 12:12–19 (NIV)

The next day the great crowd that had come for the Feast heard that Jesus was on his way to Jerusalem. They took palm branches and went out to meet him, shouting, 'Hosanna!' 'Blessed is he who comes in the name of the Lord!' 'Blessed is the King of Israel!' Jesus found a young donkey and sat upon it, as it is written, 'Do not be afraid, O Daughter of Zion; see, your king is coming, seated on a donkey's colt.' At first his disciples did not understand all this. Only after Jesus was glorified did they realize that these things had been written about him and that they had done these things to him. Now the crowd that was with him when he called Lazarus from the tomb and raised him from the dead continued to spread the word. Many people, because they had heard that he had given this miraculous sign, went out to meet him. So the Pharisees said to one another, 'See, this is getting us nowhere. Look how the whole world has gone after him!'

Jesus was one of the few human beings to understand that although B undoubtedly follows A, it is a completely different letter. You hear Christians say, in desperate tones, 'It was all going so well! Why has everything gone so wrong all of a sudden? How can God be in the things that are happening to me now?'

Well, the broad answer is in front of us as we read this passage and think ahead to the darkness of betrayal and crucifixion. If the latter constitutes B, then this wonderful little excursion into praise and joy is the A that preceded it. Both necessary, both right and ordained before time began, their only visible connection is that one follows the other.

Neither disciples nor Pharisees understood this principle until later, but it is one that will help a great deal in our daily lives if we truly accept it. God brings or allows both joy and pain into our lives. He just does, and that's that. We resist either at our peril, because both are servants to the wise purposes of the Father.

Besides, if we do not willingly accept jolly old A and rotten old B, we may miss out on strange and amazing old C, which in the case of Jesus turned out to be different again, but really rather crucial...

Teach us to enjoy, to trust, to accept.

A SLIP OF THE TONGUE

Matthew 26:27 (NIV)

Then he took the cup, gave thanks and offered it to them, saying, 'Drink from it, all of you...'

Recently, in the course of a Communion service, I heard a nervous curate say, 'In the same way, after supper he took the cup and gave you thanks; he broke it and gave it to them, saying, "Drink this, all of you..."'

Thank goodness Jesus was word-perfect on these crucial occasions. No Penultimate Supper for rehearsal purposes. It had to be right first time. Imagine if Jesus had made the same mistake. Every Sunday, ministers would break little pieces from a chalice fashioned out of thin biscuit (or chocolate?), drop them into liquid of some sort, then offer them solemnly to the congregation, to be drunk in their dissolved state as the scriptures so mysteriously commanded.

'Excuse me,' Jesus might tentatively enquire during a surprise visit, 'I was wondering why you use those chocolate cups at Communion.'

'Ah, well, they dissolve better.'

'They dissolve better?'

'Yes, you said we should break the cup and drink it. This is the easiest way of doing it.'

'I said... oh dear! I'm so sorry. I meant *take* the cup. And you've been... for two thousand years?'

Son of God laughs helplessly.

A ridiculous scenario, but the Church has had great difficulty in preserving essential truths that Jesus expressed with complete accuracy, so it is just as well he was not guilty of any verbal errors.

'What?' he might say, surveying the Church worldwide. 'I said you were to love one another. What's this new religion you've started that allows and encourages bitter division and unloving conflict? Why have you done that? Why?'

'And what on earth are these?' he might further ask, encountering a succession of dumbly unwelcoming church buildings catering for the sterile religious habits of a few. 'I called you to be fishers of men, not inward-looking ignorers of the real world. I was *passionate* about the harvest. Why are you not out in the fields? People are dying out there!

And why are Pharisees and hypocrites still putting impossible burdens on my brothers and sisters when they should be free and rejoicing instead of shackled and guilty?'

Never mind chocolate chalices and slips of the tongue. The truth is hard enough to handle.

Most of us probably know quite enough theology to be going on with.

HARDLY GETHSEMANE

Luke 22:39–43 (NIV)

Jesus went out as usual to the Mount of Olives, and his disciples followed him. On reaching the place, he said to them, 'Pray that you will not fall into temptation.' He withdrew about a stone's throw beyond them, knelt down and prayed, 'Father, if you are willing, take this cup from me; yet not my will, but yours be done.' An angel from heaven appeared to him and strengthened him.

It was hardly Gethsemane, but that made it worse in a way. It was Thursday evening and I was booked to speak to a public school sixth form in the Midlands the next day. I didn't want to do it. Why are occasions like this always scheduled on those long, yawn-filled Friday afternoons when healthy sixth-formers feel reluctant to do anything at all, let alone listen to some strange man bleating on about his naff religion?

A great idea in the posing stage, of course. It feels good to see oneself as part of the great army of evangelists bravely taking Christ to an unbelieving world. No posing on that Thursday night, though. I really didn't want to face an array of young faces registering hostility or bored resignation. My audiences usually come because they know me. Often, they're smiling before I even start to speak. On occasions like the one I had been sentenced to on the following day, the mountain of gaining their interest would be very steep indeed. I slept badly.

I woke on Friday hoping for symptoms of some non-fatal, incapacitating illness. No such luck. I was horribly well. During the three-hour train journey, I fantasized every conceivable scenario in which the event might be cancelled. I came perilously close to phoning home and asking my wife to contact the school to say I was too ill to come. In the end I dragged myself heavily into the school and did it, because, in my heart of hearts, I knew this was a very important matter of obedience. I wasn't being asked to like it—I was being asked to do it.

And yes—yes, of course, you guessed it—it went really well and I was glad I'd done it. But there was a little death involved. You see, it was not my will that did it, but his. I was happy, but not proud.

Father, our small challenges are hardly Gethsemane, but we need your strength in order to be obedient. Thank you.

I DON'T KNOW THE MAN

Matthew 26:69–75 (NIV)

Now Peter was sitting out in the courtyard, and a servant girl came to him. 'You also were with Jesus of Galilee,' she said. But he denied it before them all. 'I don't know what you're talking about,' he said. Then he went out to the gateway, where another girl saw him and said to the people there, 'This fellow was with Jesus of Nazareth.' He denied it again, with an oath: 'I don't know the man!' After a little while, those standing there went up to Peter and said, 'Surely you are one of them, for your accent gives you away.' Then he began to call down curses on himself and he swore to them, 'I don't know the man!' Immediately a cock crowed. Then Peter remembered the word Jesus had spoken: 'Before the cock crows, you will disown me three times.' And he went outside and wept bitterly.

I have written about this passage more times than I can remember, but it still draws my attention like a magnet. Originally, like thousands of others, I found it immensely comforting to rest my failed head back on a cushion of identification with the flawed personality and swirling passions of the big fisherman. I think I still do. As I am reading through the story again today, though, something else occurs to me.

This is a man in whom, at this point in his life, intense love and total denial are operating at exactly the same time. I don't suppose anyone loved Jesus more than Peter did, and it must have been from that deep well of love that the fire of his denial was fuelled. How could those who challenged him on that dreadful night have suspected that such violent denial concealed such raging love? Is it foolish to suspect that this principle operates more frequently and encouragingly than we realize? It certainly has been my own experience that, in some people, a growing regard for and acceptance of Jesus are, as it were, dammed up until the moment when the wall of denial breaks and a flood of faith is released.

We should be very sensitive and tender with those who are vociferously opposed to the Christian faith. In some cases the love of Jesus has entered their hearts, and they can only restrain its expression by forcefully denying that it exists. How exciting!

Father, may we be open and sensitive to the work you have done in those who deny you. We look forward to the day when they openly declare allegiance to Jesus.

MISSED OPPORTUNITIES

Luke 22:63–65; 23:33 (NIV) (Also read Luke 18:18–30)

The men who were guarding Jesus began mocking and beating him. They blindfolded him and demanded, 'Prophesy! Who hit you?' And they said many other insulting things to him… When they came to the place called the Skull, there they crucified him, along with the criminals—one on his right, the other on his left.

'Jesus was a fool. He could have done much—been much. Why, once— I witnessed it myself as a young man—he was offered the crown of a king, and refused. I tell you, he was a fool.'

The old man rubbed his bearded chin with one hand, waving the other towards his guests, all listening respectfully to their host's words.

'Few of you are old enough even to remember what he looked like, but I remember. Oh, yes, I hear his voice in my inner ear and see his face in my mind's eye. Once, you see, I did think he had something to offer, but—well, I ask you with modesty to observe my age, and to look around my house. See how the Lord blesses me.'

A murmur of approval passed through the assembly. The revered provider of their feast was surrounded by evidence of enormous wealth.

'Whereas he,' continued the old man, 'barely lived beyond the age of 30. He owned nothing. He was beaten and jeered at by Roman soldiers before suffering a criminal's death among common thieves and vagabonds. He had opportunities, but he missed them. Jesus was such a fool.'

Later, when his guests had departed, the old man remained seated, staring into the dying embers of the fire lit earlier against a chill night. His wife sat beside him.

'Why do you never tell them the truth, husband?' she asked quietly.

He turned to her, his eyes red-rimmed, full of unspeakable sadness.

'Because I know that I would weep, wife,' he replied, his voice breaking a little. 'I would weep, and in my weeping reveal to those blinded by my possessions that I am but a poverty-stricken old man who wasted his best, his greatest opportunity. That blessed fool, who looked at me with such love, told me to sell all I had, give it to the poor, and follow him. I did not do it, and—oh, how I wish from the bottom of my heart that I had.'

'Perhaps,' she said softly, 'it is not too late?'

Give us the courage and wisdom to follow you when the opportunity comes.

STANDING STILL, LOOKING SAD

Luke 23:48–49 (NIV)

When all the people who had gathered to witness this sight saw what took place, they beat their breasts and went away. But all those who knew him, including the women who had followed him from Galilee, stood at a distance, watching these things.

I have shamelessly pinched the title for today's note from later in Luke, where two disciples on the road to Emmaus are 'standing still and looking sad'. These people who had known Jesus were the same. The one they loved was crucified and gone. There was nothing to be done about it.

Last year, Bridget and I did a short speaking tour in Germany. Three out of four evenings were enjoyable but uneventful. The Friday night event, however, was strange and challenging. One of the young men from the church hosting our visit died suddenly on that same day. He was 22. Because people from all around the area had bought advance tickets, it was decided that cancellation of our talk would be impractical.

We found a church filled to overflowing with grief. Little knots of people clung to each other, weeping openly. Eventually, unwilling to intrude, we drifted outside, but it was the same there. All around us, people were standing still and looking sad. It was heartbreaking.

We assumed that none of these intensely unhappy people would be coming to hear us speak, but we were wrong. The younger ones seemed reluctant to face the pain of solitary grief at home. Twenty or thirty of them filed into the hall to fill three rows at the back, many still weeping, while, disconcertingly, the rest of the hall was filled with people who knew nothing of the tragedy, and had come for an evening out and 'a bit of a laugh'.

We are so glad that God is in charge. Somehow we adapted our programme as we went along, so that the laughter was gentle and the love and closeness of God were emphasized. At the end we said a simple prayer asking not that we should avoid pain, but that we should know Jesus in the centre of it. We were privileged to be there, and to be part of what had happened. We Christians may not know much, but we are privileged to have been taught the most important secret principle of all. Wherever there is death and loss, there is potential for resurrection and reunion.

Thank you for being with us in our pain.

The great storm comes at harvest time.

FRENCH PROVERB

GATHERING AS WE GO

HARVEST IN THE BIBLE

It's so easy to forget important things, isn't it?

I was in a group that was being asked to talk about the experience that had excited each of us more than any other. It was a Christian group, and therefore, for better or worse, most of the answers tended to be about conversion or baptism or healing or something similar. One or two people did mention things like hang-gliding and the birth of their children, but, in the main, specifically spiritual adventures dominated.

I didn't say anything for a long time, because I was trying as hard as I could to answer the question with strict accuracy. In the back of my mind I felt that I knew what that answer was, but, although a long list of candidates jostled for front position in my mind, it was very hard to pin down the truth.

What about the time in Africa in 1995, for instance, when we hired a small plane and flew out from Johannesburg to spend three days at a game lodge on the edge of the Kruger National Park? Now, that was exciting! Very early each morning we were taken out in an open-topped jeep to spot animals in the wild. We would then return for a huge breakfast at the lodge. In the evening, we would set out once more, equipped with powerful torches on the front of the vehicle, to explore the vast acres of African bush as darkness fell. Both of these daily trips lasted for at least two hours. I cannot begin to convey the thrill of seeing, in their natural habitat, creatures that I had only ever seen in zoos or circuses before. We tracked the path of a lion right into the undergrowth, and saw where her recent kill had been hidden. As we gazed at the remains we suddenly realized that the lioness herself was regarding us with ominous suspicion from the top of a very adjacent hillock. We caught a leopard in the beam of our torch and followed it through the long grass as it sought cover. We came across giraffes, elephants, wild dogs, and one very satisfying rhinoceros. This experience could easily have been the one that I was thinking of, but—no, that wasn't it.

Something to do with writing? Well, that could easily be what I was trying to remember—that amazing day when I signed copies of *The Sacred Diary* for two and a half hours at Spring Harvest, at a time in my life when everything else seemed to be going wrong. Surely that must have been the most exciting moment in my life? No—still not it.

Seeing my children born? Mindblowing, but—no.

First kiss? Definitely not (I was trying to eat fried chicken at the time).

Getting married? No, too frightening.

What about the day when we moved into the first house that we'd ever owned. That was tremendously exciting. But it still wasn't the thing tickling the back of my mind.

So what on earth was it? I strained to remember. It was frustrating. The finger-tips of my memory were just managing to touch the extreme edge of whatever this thing was. It was something much further back than those other experiences—something so vibrantly, electrifyingly exciting that the very aura of this unidentified recollection set my nerves tingling and jingling in anticipation of—what, for goodness' sake?

'Radishes!'

My sudden triumphant cry was received by the rest of the group as though I had uttered some sort of vegan swear word.

'Radishes,' I repeated, 'my most exciting experience of all time was seeing my radishes come up when I was about three.'

Of course it was. Nothing had come close to it since. I remembered it all now. I could see the small square of garden at the edge of my father's allotment, the one that was specially mine. I could see myself carefully making a groove in the earth with a stick, then sowing seeds from the packet that I'd bought at the shop in the village where they seemed to sell everything under the sun. On the back of that packet was a picture illustrating the Platonic ideal of radishness, a bunch of huge radishes, their luxuriant, emerald growth sprouting from crimson red tops that merged into creamy white at the base. That was how my radishes were going to look. After covering up the seeds with earth I impaled the empty packet in two places on a stick as I had seen my father do, and stuck the stick into the ground at the end of the row, just in case, by some miracle much greater than the miracle of plant reproduction, I should forget what I was growing there. I think, also, I had a vague and strictly private notion that the plants might appreciate some kind of reminder of what they were supposed to be as they emerged from the earth.

Kneeling by my newly planted row, I would study the length of raised earth intently, wondering if the mysterious underground process of turning into radishes had actually begun yet, and hoping that if I hung around for a few minutes more I might actually spot the very first tiny spot of green to appear as the pioneers of my crop struggled towards the light.

For part of every single day I squatted by that bed, checking my radishes, becoming very slightly agnostic about the promised metamorphosis as time went by. Then—oh, the indescribable joy of discovering one morning that minuscule green shoots had begun to appear in exactly the right places—the places where little me had ordained that they should appear by sowing the seeds in that very nearly straight line the other day. The promise had come true—things did grow!

As all ex-radish enthusiasts will clearly remember, in the early stages of growth a radish plant consists of two tiny oval leaves pushing out in opposite directions, for all the world, I used to think, like two little hands extended in such a manner that each plant seemed to be saying, 'Well, here I am!' I believe I only just stopped short of naming each radish individually.

All I dreamed of from that first day of visible growth was harvest. I was terribly impatient. Days went by. At the first sign of embryonic red globes emerging from the earth I wanted to pull my radishes up. I so wanted to pull my radishes up! I was restrained by higher authority, but only just.

'What if they grow too much?' I inquired worriedly. 'What if they grow right up out of the ground and fall over and get eaten by—by cats?'

'Cats don't eat radishes.'

'Oh.'

At last the shining day arrived. Higher authority decreed that some of my radishes might be ready for pulling up. There can be few more profound and innocently sensual experiences than harvesting your own crop from the rich earth. And, at three, or any other age really, can there be a greater thrill than to walk into your own kitchen, as casually as you can in view of the fact that you are positively shivering with delight, to present your own mother with the firstfruits of your own labour? Real, proper teatime on that first day of harvest always featured my radishes. I was so proud.

This section is all about harvest, the first and last notes concerning prayer, without which there can be no harvest. As we work our way through it, let's bear in mind that the planting, preparation, daily attention and eventual reaping of our personal harvest for God needs to be conducted in exactly the same spirit of wonder and innocent excitement that I experienced as a child with my garden. Our limited contribution to the needs of the kingdom of God may appear small to us, but I can assure you that, if we offer them in the right spirit, they will be taken from our hands with the same seriousness and gratitude that my mother showed when she took those radishes from me when I was three, and which Jesus himself must have shown when he took two loaves and five small fishes (and a couple of radishes?) from a little boy on a hillside two thousand years ago.

Prayer

Father, our harvest for you will be small, but we offer it to you with the confidence that you love all gifts from your children. Thank you for the miracles you do with radishes and the like.

HONESTLY!

Isaiah 29:13 (NIV)

The Lord says: 'These people come near to me with their mouth and honour me with their lips, but their hearts are far from me. Their worship of me is made up only of rules taught by men.'

Prayer can be so many things, but I think I find a sort of respectful friendship at the centre of all my honest dealings with God. The honesty is a relatively recent addition to my prayer life. Until I reached my mid-30s I was very similar to the people who God is addressing through Isaiah in this passage. My mouth produced some well-rounded, well-organized sounds in the theoretical direction of God, but my heart was occupied elsewhere. Things changed after my wife and I said a very honest prayer for once. 'God,' we said, 'we know that we haven't done very well with anything up to now, but we really want to go all the way with you. We realize that we don't understand what that means, but whatever it costs, and however much it hurts, please let it happen. Amen.'

For once our prayer didn't bounce off the ceiling and fall on our heads, and it was in that same year that, through illness and recovery, I discovered the reality of God's fatherly love in a completely new way. Part of that new way was a relaxation in prayer, an understanding that, as the friends of Jesus, we are warmly welcomed to the presence of God. There seemed to be only two requirements—be there, and be honest. God could handle anger, tears, boredom, badly phrased prayers and just about anything else as long as they were offered to him as a child offers its moods to a parent.

I am not a disciplined sort of person at all, but I found myself settling into a flexible routine which included some sort of apology, prayers for friends and enemies, and, most important of all, a period spent just being with God, enjoying his joy in being with me. I wish I could pretend that this idyllic-sounding scenario has continued without pause since then, but I am a perverse human being. I abandon regular prayer times for weeks on end and wonder why my life feels shapeless and un-supported. Then I begin again and wonder why I ever stopped.

But it's always OK—as long as I'm honest, we just start again.

Let us pray.

GIVE AS GOOD AS YOU GET

Exodus 23:15–16 (NIV)

No-one is to appear before me empty-handed. Celebrate the Feast of Harvest with the firstfruits of the crops you sow in your field.

God must be so tired of receiving our leftovers.

I remember sitting with friends in a local restaurant, discussing the need for new elders in their church, a quite large Brethren assembly along the coast from us. 'The problem is,' said Jean, 'that everyone's so busy. There are three or four people who'd be really good, but they just can't spare the time. It's not fair to ask.'

I nodded and sighed automatically as I usually do. There's probably far too much sympathetic nodding and sighing in the Church nowadays. Afterwards I realized what my response ought to have been. Why should God be offered leaders on the basis that they have time? Why shouldn't he be offered leaders on the basis that they are right for the job, or (forgive me for suggesting such a thing) that he is calling specific individuals to become whatever he wants them to become? Why shouldn't priorities be altered so that we create time for the most important purpose of all?

I don't think God wants the fag-ends of our time, or our effort, or our money, or our concentration, or our love. Whatever the harvest of our lives might be, he wants the firstfruits, not the scraps. If you want to encounter God at his most scathingly angry on this subject, read the book of Malachi. I tend to avoid it.

I am reminded of an ancient aunt of mine who lived in Wales. After breaking several bones in one leg she was confined to a wheelchair and unable to take part in the village activities that had meant so much to her. One of the local ladies organized a collection among Auntie Susan's contemporaries, and used the proceeds to purchase a rather straggly plant in a pot, which was duly presented to the invalid.

'The thing is,' the collector confided to my wife, 'I only asked them for ten pence each, so they hardly noticed they'd parted with anything.'

Sums it up, really, doesn't it?

Father, help us to offer our best to you. We want to seek the kingdom of God above all things, but we get distracted. Show us what we should be giving from our harvest.

URGENT MESSAGE

John 4:35 (NIV)

Do you not say, 'Four months more and then the harvest'? I tell you, open your eyes and look at the fields! They are ripe for harvest.

I entirely agree with C.S. Lewis when he says that there are going to be a lot of surprises in heaven. I believe that God is just, and I suspect that a lot of people are going to receive rewards that they never knew they had earned. If that's not true, then the 25th chapter of Matthew doesn't mean anything. Conversely, there will be others, Jesus tells us, who will be unacknowledged by God despite their loud claims that they wrought miracles in the name of his Son. I would like to believe that everyone will be saved (no, I can't claim to know exactly what that means) but if I also want to follow the Jesus of the New Testament, I can't help but be infected with the passionate urgency revealed in passages such as this. Jesus came to save sinners from some kind of eternal separation. He was perfectly clear about that, whatever anyone else wants to think. We leave the surprises to him, and get on with the harvest, that seems to be the plan.

I joined a church for a street mission in London once. Before we left the church building we prayed, and one lady gave a very dramatic prophecy about the 'scythe descending, and a mighty harvest to be reaped'. When we reached the spot, on this very cold day, there were only two 'ears of corn' to listen to us, and neither of them seemed very interested. Our speaker, a man who has a real ear for God, said that the Lord was calling someone with a marriage problem, someone with a hearing disorder and someone with respiratory difficulties. None of these materialized and we all trudged dismally home. A year later, the speaker was stopped by a man who said, 'I was walking past when you did that street thing. I had trouble with my ears, bronchitis, and my marriage was falling apart. I was too embarrassed to stop, but I found a church and I became a Christian.'

God had mobilized that whole event to save one man. The harvest goes on.

Father, show us what you're doing, and we'll join in.

MEAN?! ME?!

Leviticus 19:9–10 (NIV)

When you reap the harvest of your land, do not reap to the very edges of your field or gather the gleanings of your harvest. Do not go over your vineyard a second time or pick up the grapes that have fallen. Leave them for the poor and the alien. I am the Lord your God.

One of the vices I hate most is meanness and penny-pinching. There's nothing worse than being on holiday, for instance, with the kind of person who waits outside the café for you because 'there's no point in paying for coffee when we can have it for nothing back at the cottage'. I don't mean that I approve of spending indiscriminately (although I'm pretty good at doing that on the rare occasions when I've got any money to do it with). It's just that I get depressed when any streams of availability dry up. I guess that goes back to my own childhood when we never knew for sure whether my father would part with the housekeeping money on a Friday, or take offence over some imagined misdeed of my mother, leaving us all to wonder how we would eat for the rest of the week. I've hated all wilful withholding of resources ever since.

Imagine, then, my horror at discovering that I have exactly the same vice developed to the point of miserliness in my own make-up. It only erupts occasionally, like some underground molten river, and it isn't only to do with money, but it's very real. A sort of panicking insecurity drives me to greedily clutch to myself every scrap of time, or ready money, or attention from others, or whatever is around at the time. I reap to the very edge of my field, and I gather the gleanings of my harvest. It is a far from attractive characteristic, and I'm always very relieved when the tension relaxes in me and I'm able to, as it were, release my grip.

I realize that it's a rather alarming prospect, and it's probably very cheap psychology as well, but try having a look at the thing you dislike most in others, then honestly assess the extent to which it's replicated in your own character. Maybe I'm the only one!

Father, let the weakness we see in ourselves encourage generosity towards others in their weakness.

WHAT'S THE CATCH?

Luke 5:4–11 (NIV)

When he had finished speaking, he said to Simon, 'Put out into deep water, and let down the nets for a catch.' Simon answered, 'Master, we've worked hard all night and haven't caught anything. But because you say so, I will let down the nets.' When they had done so, they caught such a large number of fish that their nets began to break. So they signalled to their partners in the other boat to come and help them, and they came and filled both boats so full that they began to sink. When Simon Peter saw this, he fell at Jesus' knees and said, 'Go away from me, Lord; I am a sinful man!' For he and all his companions were astonished at the catch of fish they had taken, and so were James and John, the sons of Zebedee, Simon's partners. Then Jesus said to Simon, 'Don't be afraid; from now on you will catch men.' So they pulled their boats up on shore, left everything and followed him.

Saatchi and Saatchi would have found Jesus a very frustrating client to have. He refused just about every opportunity to exploit his natural advantages. Here's a good example. After a night remarkable only for its barren fish harvest, Peter and his mates, having heard some great stuff from the benevolent hijacker of their boat, go along with Jesus' suggestion that they should let their nets down one more time. Peter's reactions of fear and astonishment when the huge catch comes in are very understandable, but I wonder if the Saatchi and Saatchi side of him peeped through for just an instant, speculating perhaps on the possibility of this strange man joining the piscatorial team on a full-time basis. There would be two good reasons for not suggesting such a thing.

First, Peter must have sensed that this was far from being a commercial gesture. Jesus was saying—or rather showing—that material success was easily and abundantly available to him. It was a one-off, almost casual demonstration of power. And that leads directly into the second reason.

Peter must have been puzzled, fascinated and strangely thrilled by the fact that this Jesus, who seemed to have total control over the environment, was calling him, a simple fisherman, to join in some inexplicable task called 'fishing for men'. Thrilling for us as well to realize that he needs us to help bring in the only harvest that really counts.

Have we seen the power? Would we follow?

HOW MUCH?

Haggai 1:5–10 (NIV)

Now this is what the Lord Almighty says: 'Give careful thought to your ways. You have planted much, but have harvested little. You eat, but never have enough. You drink, but never have your fill. You put on clothes, but are not warm. You earn wages, only to put them in a purse with holes in it.' This is what the Lord Almighty says: 'Give careful thought to your ways. Go up into the mountains and bring down timber and build the house, so that I may take pleasure in it and be honoured,' says the Lord. 'You expected much, but see, it turned out to be little. What you brought home, I blew away. Why?' declares the Lord Almighty. 'Because of my house, which remains a ruin, while each of you is busy with his own house. Therefore, because of you the heavens have withheld their dew and the earth its crops.'

'There's a hole in my bucket...'

As I intimated in the section on Old Testament figures, the message of Haggai is timeless. The recipients of the prophet's message were lurching from disappointment to disappointment; from dismal failure to dismal failure. They were working hard, eating and drinking well, dressing in good clothes and earning plenty of money, but somehow they were never quite full or refreshed, never warm, and never in funds. Nothing satisfied them because the most important dimension of their lives was lacking. They had failed to build a house for God. The old temple lay in ruins while they lived in their smart panelled houses.

No wonder the so-called 'health and wealth' movement is dying a death. The notion is fundamentally ludicrous. Any Christian movement that fails to accommodate Jesus at the very heart of itself will go through that same cycle of trying and failing endlessly, until the ruins of humility and dependence are swept away and rebuilt at the centre.

The present-day Church is paying heavily for the Debenham's sale style of evangelism that says you can have the whole salvation package in return for one small down-payment of an assenting prayer. Jesus' teaching on repentance and cost is not popular. How could it be when its clear implication is that you give your harvest freely to him, and happily accept whatever he gives back to you?

We cannot have our divine cake—and eat it.

Come and live in me, Jesus. Just give me a minute while I clear out all this stuff...

HEAVY ROCK

Matthew 13:5–6 (NIV)

Some fell on rocky places, where it did not have much soil. It sprang up quickly, because the soil was shallow. But when the sun came up, the plants were scorched, and they withered because they had no root.

For a while my wife worked in what used to be called an approved school. The teenage girls who were resident in this grim establishment were mainly delinquent or out of control. Many of them were very disturbed and all were grossly inadequate. The lives of these kids were characterized by disruption, conflict, divorce and general emotional chaos. Some had been abused sexually, and others had been beaten regularly. The atmosphere of this boarding school was far from jolly.

Very occasionally the school would be visited by Christian outreach groups, who spent an evening describing the faith and calling girls to repentance. Hearing that everything would change once they invited Jesus into their lives, many of the girls would repent in floods of tears, desperate to embrace something that offered so much. The hit-and-run evangelists would depart rejoicing over their success, leaving the new 'converts' to wonder why nothing seemed to have changed when they woke up the next morning. Quite apart from the fact that evangelism without follow-up is irresponsible, these poor girls had no root in themselves. The good earth that is formed by consistent experiences of trust and love and security was simply not present in their lives. They were rocky places, the hearts of those children.

But there will be a harvest there as well. God loves each of those desperate kids, and he is quite capable of breaking up rock to form new soil. It can be a long process, though, and it will probably require Christians who are not infected with quick-fix disease to commit themselves to long-term support and contact and caring for individuals whose lives were shattered before they even had a chance to get started.

If you really want to help someone like that, ask God to show you who needs a friend. But, be warned, he'll probably answer your prayer.

We are all responsible for our own actions, but some of us don't know how to take responsibility. We need to share the burden of learning with someone who won't give up too easily.

ENVELOPED BY LOVE

Luke 11:5–7 (NIV)

Then he said to them, 'Suppose one of you has a friend, and he goes to him at midnight and says, "Friend, lend me three loaves of bread, because a friend of mine on a journey has come to me, and I have nothing to set before him." Then the one inside answers, "Don't bother me. The door is already locked, and my children are with me in bed. I can't get up and give you anything." I tell you, though he will not get up and give him the bread because he is his friend, yet because of the man's boldness he will get up and give him as much as he needs.'

My children were fascinated to know why I started to spend a part of each morning sifting through a pile of brown envelopes that lay on my desk in the upstairs sitting-room a few years ago.

'Well,' I explained, 'each of these envelopes has got a letter inside it. All of the letters are written to God, and each one is about someone I know or someone I want to pray for.'

'Are you going to send them, then?' asked David.

'Well, I don't think there's much point in posting them,' I replied seriously, 'but every day I hold each one up to God and ask him to look after the person I've written about.'

The boys looked through the pile of sealed envelopes with great interest, noting the name written on the front of each. Joe became very animated when he discovered one marked 'ENEMIES'.

'Those are the difficult ones,' I said, 'but I'm supposed to pray specially for them, so I just grit my teeth and do it.'

'Tell us who your enemies are, Dad,' said David.

'No, that wouldn't be fair.'

'Does it work?'

'I'll tell you in a few months.'

And in a few months I was able to tell them that it really did seem to work! Persistent prayer seems to gradually massage events and circumstances and people and attitudes into a position nearer to God, or nearer to what he wants.

I hope I'm in someone else's envelope—even as an enemy...

*People who are anxious to shine can never
tell a plain story.*

GEORGE BORROW

STORY POWER—
TALES TO TRAVEL BY

PARABLES

A good story is such a wonderful thing, isn't it? Ever since I was a small boy, books, mainly fiction, have been an essential item on the list of things-that-comfort-me. We tend to take such basic skills as reading for granted, but even when I didn't quite know who to thank, I was always immensely grateful for this simple path to distraction. I may have been uncertain and nervous as an infant, but I developed reading skills very early, and learned that, whatever storms might be brewing in the outside world, it was nearly always possible to slip quietly and quickly away into the warm safety of a book.

By the time I was ten or eleven I had become a sort of print monster, seeking out and indiscriminately devouring every scrap of reading matter that presented itself to me. Bizarre combinations of books would be scattered around the end of my bed—Pope's translation of Homer nestling up to *Little Grey Rabbit*, a couple of *Famous Five* books piled on top of Conrad's *Nigger of the Narcissus*—they were all grist to my fiction-consuming mill, whether or not I understood them (certainly, the deeper meanings of some passages in *Little Grey Rabbit* elude me to this day).

I once made the mistake of telling one of my own children how I went about persuading my parents to buy me a particular book that I wanted.

I explained that I had read all of a certain series of books by Enid Blyton (that terrible writer whose books are mysteriously enjoyed by generation after generation of children who stubbornly refuse not to like them), and that I now desperately wanted the latest in the series, a book entitled *The River of Adventure*. Neither Christmas nor my birthday were in sight, and as my parents were not very well off, I was well aware that seven and sixpence was far more money than they would care to part with, especially as the book was bound to appear in the library eventually anyway. But I was merciless. I embarked on a callous, long-term campaign which simply involved saying the words 'River of Adventure' over and over again, the theory being that eventually my parents would crack under the pressure and I would get my book.

'River of Adventure—River of Adventure—River of Adventure—River of Adventure—River of Adventure…'

Those were the words that began to drive my mother and father mad over the weeks that followed. I was as stubborn at the age of ten as I sometimes can be now, and I WANTED THAT BOOK. I was determined to go on repeating the phrase until my mission was accomplished, and nothing was going to stop me. Looking back, I find it interesting to reflect on the stages that my poor parents went through in their response to this ploy. They were mildly amused at first, perhaps thinking my insistence rather touching, but that phase soon passed. Their amusement turned swiftly to irritation as they discovered that their every waking hour in my presence was filled with the same phrase, accompanying all else that happened, like the bass-line of a track being played on someone else's hi-fi in the next room.

Irritation was followed by downright anger and threats, all of which failed to stem or even briefly interrupt my flow, the content of which had, by now, resolved itself into a sort of condensed version of the original.

'Riverererventure—Riverererventure—Riverererventure—Riverererventure—Riverererventure…'

They never really stood a chance, did they? But they did try everything. They ignored me.

I went on saying it.

They talked reasonably to me.

I went on saying it.

They made promises for the distant future.

I went on saying it.

They told me in serious, end-of-our-tether tones that enough was enough.

I went on saying it.

'Riverererventure—Riverererventure—Riverererventure—Riverererventure—Riverererventure….'

Finally, wild-eyed, haggard and defeated, they bought me the book.

It was one of the few victories in a not very victorious childhood.

When, some years ago, I told one of my sons this story, he listened with enormous interest, then gazed speculatively at me for a moment.

'Nintendo,' he said, 'Nintendo—Nintendo—Nintendo— Nintendo...'

My love affair with books, and particularly my use of them as a distraction from the tricky business of living, grew so intense at one stage that it was almost life-threatening. I am somewhat embarrassed even to recall this fact, but I got into the habit of cycling to school with a book resting on my handlebars so that I could have a little read as I went along. Yes, yes, you are absolutely right—the results were utterly catastrophic. I can still recall the sensation of shock and horror when my world exploded because I had smashed into the back of a parked car or delivery van. And the unbelievable fact is that it happened several times. Nothing put me off!

As a pedestrian I was in no less danger. I gave up smoking many years ago now, but at the time it was just about the only other thing I did apart from reading. A packet of cigarettes and a novel—that was my distraction kit. The trouble was that, when I grew older and was out of work, I took to walking the streets with a cigarette in one hand and a book in the other, with as little regard for what was in front of me as I'd had in the days when I rode my mobile reading desk to school. I even continued to read—oh, blush!—as I crossed the road. What a trail of disgruntled drivers and fellow-pedestrians I must have left behind me.

I can only imagine that God had a whole legion of angels on my case, working overtime to prevent me from being prematurely dispatched to a place where I would be judged on the absence of my name from the most important book of all.

By the time I got married my reading habits had become a little more sane, but I can still recall Bridget's puzzlement on witnessing the lengthy procedure that I usually went through before going to bed. I might spend as much as half an hour selecting three or four books to take to bed with me, and then, exhausted by the lengthy selection process, read one of them for two minutes before turning off the light and settling down to sleep. She was no less puzzled by the complex explanation that I offered for this strange behaviour.

'You see,' I explained, 'I have to have one very worthy, serious sort of book that I can tell myself I might read—although I know I almost certainly won't, and then I have to have one of my old thumb-sucking books in case I need to feel safe, and I do like to have at least one book that I haven't read yet but really want to some time but probably won't start tonight, and last of all I have to have the book I'm actually in the middle of reading at the moment—to actually read, you see....'

All right, I may be slightly crackers, but I think it is this lifelong love of stories that enables me to go on finding so much satisfaction in being a writer myself. People sometimes ask me where ideas come from when you have to write all the time, but a very large part of the answer is that I am probably more interested in finding out what happens at the end of my stories than anybody else. When I was in the middle of writing *An Alien at St Wilfred's* I had no idea what the outcome of the story would be, but I so relished the fact that I was there with those five characters in the dimly lit interior of the church on those four Thursday evenings, waiting to find out how the arrival of 'Nunc', the alien, would change the lives of those who encountered him. In *Stress Family Robinson* I wasn't sure until near the end of the book whether Dip, family friend of the Robinsons, would move in to live with the family or not. I didn't want to know until then. I was enjoying the story too much.

I have also very much enjoyed narrating stories to live audiences over the last ten years. It is in this situation that one learns how stories grow and change and improve with the telling.

Here, in this section, which describes the beginning of Jesus' ministry and the way in which he taught through parables, we focus on the work of one of the greatest natural storytellers of all time. It is such a joy for me to know that Jesus used the medium of fiction to communicate cosmic facts, and I do not think I am imagining the sense of satisfaction with which one feels these stories were developed and honed over the course of his ministry. Here is a performer who knew his audience intimately through years of gritty, day-to-day contact with them, and who worked hard at recycling events and experiences from real life until they became the multi-layered, verbally economical masterpieces that we know, and perhaps undervalue, today.

As those who have been bored by countless sermons will be aware, a good point cannot be made by a bad story. The parables of Jesus are not just arid, minimum requirements for passing on dry old chunks of teaching. They are in the very best tradition of 'Once upon a time' and I love them.

You are a God of stories. Thank you for teaching your Son all the best ones.

BUTTERFLIES

Matthew 4:12–17 (NIV)

When Jesus heard that John had been put in prison, he returned to Galilee... to fulfil that which was said through the prophet Isaiah: '...Galilee of the Gentiles—the people living in darkness have seen a great light; on those living in the land of the shadow of death a light has dawned.' From that time on Jesus began to preach, 'Repent, for the kingdom of heaven is near.'

The butterflies must have fluttered in Jesus' stomach when he heard the news about John's imprisonment. Clearly, this was, to use an appropriately theatrical term, the 'cue' he'd been waiting for. Three years of ministry lay before him, to end, not with applause but with a very unpleasant death. It was a long way from the wings to the stage—from Nazareth down to Capernaum; long enough, no doubt, to wonder whether his recent victory over temptation in the desert was really going to carry him through the teeth-grindingly difficult events and encounters that were about to begin. So very lonely.

Did he carefully control the panic in his breathing as he approached the place and time when the words he said and the things he did would be remembered, recorded and subsequently studied by millions of people for thousands of years? If the thought of that didn't make him nervous he wasn't human—and he was, so it must have done.

My own experience is that it's much better when you've actually got started. The waiting is awful. I don't feel the gut-wrenching fear that used to accompany all my speaking engagements, but my sweat glands still get a bit of violent exercise at times. In 1993 the most difficult situations I faced were a prison service where disruptive inmates had already been removed before I started to speak, and a spot at the London Palladium in a Christmas show attended mainly by Christians. These vastly disparate settings caused equal terror in my frail psyche. The disgruntled prisoners had certainly never heard of me, and it was clear I'd have to earn every second of their attention. The Palladium audience probably knew who I was, but this was the Palladium, for goodness' sake! What on earth was I doing here?

These events turned out all right in the end, but on both occasions, when my cue came, I was terrified. The bad news is that we don't escape the fear, the challenge, or the need to use an act of will to step onto the centre-stage of God's plan for us. Jesus went through it, and so, in our own small way, shall we. The good news is that God is in charge of the epilogue.

No resurrection without crucifixion.

FOND FATHERS

Matthew 4:18–22 (NIV)

Jesus... saw two brothers, Simon called Peter and his brother Andrew. They were casting a net into the lake... 'Come, follow me,' Jesus said, 'and I will make you fishers of men.' At once they left their nets and followed him. Going on from there, he saw... James son of Zebedee and his brother John. They were in a boat with their father... Jesus called them, and immediately they left the boat and their father and followed him.

Do you remember *The Magic Roundabout*? It was a TV programme that always ended when a funny little character called Zebedee bounced in on a spring, and told everyone it was time for sleep. The biblical Zebedee came to my notice much later, so that, even now, I picture the father of James and John ricocheting around the boat, trying to persuade his piscatorial sons to go to bed. I need to dispel this image, because I suspect that, like the father of Simon and Andrew, he was actually quite an impressive fellow. What kind of parenting produced, in each case, two sons who were fit and ready to join the Son of God as he stepped out to save the world? We have no details, but it seems likely that years of care, teaching and prayer had been invested in those four boys.

We once met an elderly man named George who had spent over 30 years praying each day that his son, Frank, would one day love Jesus. George was a quiet, devout Christian, more concerned with deeds than words, and his devotion was rewarded when, aged 36, Frank was well and truly converted.

We met Frank. Not only was he converted, but he had become an air-punching, Spirit-intoxicated, promise-claiming, chorus-singing servant of the living God. When we bowed our heads for grace, Frank spoke in tongues, interpreted his own tongue, sang a solo chorus and praised God for the fellowship and the food. We felt quite exhausted by the time he'd finished.

Frank chided his father for not entering more vigorously into things of the Spirit. I watched George's face as he listened. In the quiet, loving smile with which he regarded his son, I read a deep and serene trust that the same God who had answered his prayers after so many years would temper and focus the zeal of this exuberant new disciple.

George was proud of his son, and so, I suspect, were Zebedee and the father of Simon and Andrew. They might not have quite understood what was going on, but perhaps, in their spirits, they sensed that losing a son is not really a loss if he has gone to be with Jesus.

Help us not to grow weary in prayer.

ROOTS

Matthew 13:3–9 (NIV)

He told them many things in parables, saying: 'A farmer went out to sow his seed. As he was scattering the seed, some fell along the path, and the birds came and ate it up. Some fell on rocky places, where it did not have much soil. It sprang up quickly, because the soil was shallow. But when the sun came up, the plants were scorched, and they withered because they had no root. Other seed fell among thorns, which grew up and choked the plants. Still other seed fell on good soil, where it produced a crop—a hundred, sixty or thirty times what was sown. He who has ears to hear, let him hear.'

In the section on Harvest, I mentioned the girls my wife used to work with in connection with this passage, but it also reminds me of some of the children I encountered in residential establishments. I remember Steve, for instance, who despite being the most inefficient thief in the universe, seemed quite incapable of curtailing the activities that con-stantly got him into trouble. Steve always got caught.

'I don't understand it,' said his mother to me one day. 'I've always been a good mother—given him stuff for his birthdays and all that. Last year I gave him this big construction set. Twenty-five quid that cost—at least, it would have done if I'd paid for it...'

Then there was Tony, who lived on a notorious local estate, and had been placed in the secure unit after being arrested and charged with arson. Tony's explanation of the motivation behind his crime went as follows: 'What happened was, my mate asked me to burn his flat down for the insurance, so I said, "Look, I'll burn your flat down for you, but I don't want to get involved."' As I pondered this elus-ive piece of logic, Tony, who was actually a very warm-hearted lad, offered graphic descriptions of everyday life in his large, tumultuous family.

'When people come to the door,' he said cheerfully, 'we might beat 'em up, or we might not. It depends on how we're feeling at the time.'

The seeds of these children's lives had been planted in such rocky ground. The soil of consistent love, good example and self-control was very shallow. I've described elsewhere how readily such children will reach for the gospel, only to despair when it seems to take no root. But it is worth repeating that rocky places can be broken up. Soil can be deepened and enriched. Thorns can be cleared. It's hard, long-term, sweaty work that sometimes lasts a lifetime, but it can be done.

Father, increase our willingness to support people who had a rotten start. Help us not to give up.

IT'S NOT WHAT YOU KNOW

Matthew 13:10–13 (NIV)

The disciples… asked, 'Why do you speak to the people in parables?' He replied, 'The knowledge of the secrets of the kingdom of heaven has been given to you, but not to them. Whoever has will be given more, and he will have an abundance. Whoever does not have, even what he has will be taken from him. This is why I speak to them in parables: "Though seeing, they do not see, though hearing, they do not hear or understand."'

When I come up against passages like this I wish I was a theologian or a Greek scholar or an intellectual. Being none of these things, my normal inclination is to rush to the little row of William Barclay commentaries on my shelf. 'Oh, William,' I cry in panic, 'please tell me what this means, so that I can rearrange your explanation and pass it on to the readers as if it were my own.'

But I'm not going to do that this time. You can look up Barclay for yourself if you want to. I'm going to tell you what I think it means.

The odd thing about Jesus' reply to his disciples is that, in fact, they didn't understand the secrets of the kingdom of heaven any more than the people did, except in one very important sense. The disciples had, as we saw in chapter 4, responded immediately and spontaneously to the person or the personality of Jesus.

They followed him.

They were still vulnerable, flawed human beings, but their special knowledge—the thing that they had, and which would be added to, was a commitment to, and a relationship with, Jesus. The crowds who listened to Jesus did not yet have this, so that the truths expressed in the parables (and in this one particularly, perhaps) took away even the spiritual security that had been theirs. Whether or not they understood in detail is irrelevant if we define a parable as a story that keeps the listener occupied at the front door while the truth slips in through a side window. Now they had to deal with that truth.

What all this means, if you're getting as confused as I am, is that we shall never have a more precious possession than our relationship with the Son of God. The knowledge of our need for him is the core of all wisdom, and though we may well meet people who can argue our faith to pieces, no one can destroy our love for Jesus.

Wisdom is very much to be desired, but, when it comes to the crunch, knowledge of Jesus is all the knowledge we shall need.

FLYING BLIND

Matthew 13:14-17 (NIV)

'In them is fulfilled the prophecy of Isaiah: "You will be ever hearing but never understanding; you will be ever seeing but never perceiving. For this people's heart has become calloused; they hardly hear with their ears, and they have closed their eyes. Otherwise they might see with their eyes, hear with their ears, understand with their hearts and turn, and I would heal them." But blessed are your eyes because they see, and your ears because they hear. For I tell you the truth, many prophets and righteous men longed to see what you see but did not see it, and to hear what you hear but did not hear it.'

When I first became a Christian I was terribly shocked by everyone else's short-sightedness. I read about the slave trade and knew without a doubt that if I'd been alive at the time I would have seen how evil it was. What idiots those bygone Christians must have been! I was also quite sure that I could never have been taken in by Hitler's ravings—it would have taken more than a bunch of crazed Nazis to fool someone as spiritually aware as me. In the present day, I found it difficult to believe that most people were blinded to the truth about Jesus as I clearly saw it. In fact, by and large, I was probably the most clear-eyed and perceptive person in the universe.

Curiously, the realization that my spiritual vision was actually very limited coincided with an abrupt deterioration in my physical sight. For the first time in my life I had to wear glasses, and, apart from the fact that I could now sing 'We will magnify' with real gusto, I didn't like it very much. The first time I put spectacles on I felt as if an insect was gripping my head from the front. The good thing was that I could see the words I was reading without having to screw my eyes up and develop a headache.

Spiritual vision works in a very similar way. Clear sight can only be achieved with outside (inside?) help from the Holy Spirit. Without this help, Christianity is about as exciting as eating a recipe, and it gives you a terrible headache. The thrilling thing about what Jesus is saying here is that it is possible to see clearly who he is, and what his message means, otherwise he wouldn't have bothered to come. Calloused hearts can be softened, and dimmed eyes can be filled with light.

I thought I saw everything, but now I know that I see very little. I want to see, Lord. Please open my eyes.

GRAPPLING WITH GREED

Matthew 13:18–23 (NIV)

'Listen then to what the parable of the sower means: When anyone hears the message... and does not understand it, the evil one comes and snatches away what was sown... This is the seed sown along the path. The one who received the seed that fell on rocky places is the man who hears the word and at once receives it with joy. But since he has no root... when trouble or persecution comes... he quickly falls away. The one who received the seed that fell among the thorns is the man who hears the word, but the worries of this life and the deceitfulness of wealth choke it, making it unfruitful: But the one who received the seed that fell on good soil is the man who hears the word and understands it. He produces... a hundred, sixty or thirty times what was sown.

Is the sower in this parable wasteful, generous, or just very enthusiastic?

That was the question that first came to my mind as I read this story, but it was very quickly eclipsed by another question provoked by the phrase 'deceitfulness of wealth'.

I recently travelled to the north-east of England to do an evening at a local theatre on behalf of a Christian retreat centre that was about to open. The basis on which I had agreed to go was that, after expenses had been deducted, profits from the evening would be split 60/40 in my favour, an arrangement that usually works very well. As far as I was concerned, it was one of those really enjoyable evenings. The theatre was packed to capacity with more than 500 people, and the response was as positive as I could have wished.

Afterwards, as I ate an Indian meal with the organizers, I knew inwardly that I should ask only for my expenses and donate the rest of my 60 per cent to the project. Imagine my horror on discovering that, although I'm usually fairly generous on a personal level, a small but dominant part of me was too greedy to give up the cash. I wanted to scoop it in and make it mine. I didn't want to give it away. I felt very miserable about being me, so, as I sat there, filling my face with Tandoori chicken, I gave the whole problem to God. 'You sort it out,' I said, 'I can't.' I was very relieved a little later to find myself giving away the money with hardly a thought. I was very grateful to God—I really was.

So, my question on reading this passage was about this newly discovered tendency to grasp at money. Am I deceived by wealth? The answer is, I think I could be, but the generous sower has cleared a few thorns that were choking me, so I think I'll be all right.

Does he come first?

LARGE FIELD—SMALL CROP

Matthew 13:24–30 (NIV)

Jesus [said]: 'The kingdom of God is like a man who sowed good seed in his field. But... his enemy came and sowed weeds among the wheat... When the wheat sprouted... the weeds also appeared. The owner's servants... said, "Sir, didn't you sow good seed in your field? Where then did the weeds come from?" "An enemy did this," he replied. The servants asked him, "Do you want us to go and pull them up?" "No," he answered, "because... you may root up the wheat with them. Let both grow together until the harvest. At that time I will tell the harvesters: First, collect the weeds and tie them in bundles to be burned, then gather the wheat and bring it into my barn."'

This parable is an aerial photograph of the entire history of the Christian Church. For centuries critics have tended to see the weeds rather than the wheat, and have judged Jesus accordingly. The Inquisition, the endless sectarian conflict, the cruelty that has been inflicted in the name of Christ by those who don't know him, the agonizing boredom of many church services—these are just some of the ugly growths that have done the devil's work for him over the years. God has allowed the mess that men and women make of the Church for the sake of saving those who truly follow him, and it happens on all sorts of levels.

At one time Bridget and I were heavily involved in the running of a church youth club which, at its busiest, attracted anything from 40 to 60 young people to the rather small house we shared with the curate. From those large numbers a much smaller group of five or six was, as it were, distilled. Out of this little band which met on a different evening for discussion and Bible study (because they wanted to), three have become ministers of the Church. Not for one moment am I suggesting that all the other club members were disposable weeds, but it does seem that in many situations you need a large field to produce a small crop.

The principle operates on an individual level as well. Your life may be producing a 100 per cent crop, but mine certainly isn't. God is allowing a lot of weeds to flourish beside the worthwhile things that are growing in me. Fortunately, like the owner in the parable, he knows where they came from, and he will know how to get rid of them when the right time comes.

Father, protect the part of us and the Church that is yours.

GROWN BY GOD

Matthew 13:31–32 (NIV)

He told them another parable: 'The kingdom of heaven is like a mustard seed, which a man took and planted in his field. Though it is the smallest of all your seeds, yet when it grows, it is the largest of garden plants and becomes a tree, so that the birds of the air come and perch in its branches.'

The idea that wonderful things grow out of something very small and simple is not an easy one to grasp, but it has always been God's way. I can't imagine any earthly committee, however wise, agreeing that the birth of Jesus in a stable in Bethlehem would make the ideal start for a salvation plan. God sees mustard seeds where others see none. Take my own case.

Imagine the scene: a decision-making meeting in heaven about twelve years ago. Around the table an angelic committee is studying files, each of which has the words ADRIAN PLASS embossed on its front cover.

'No,' says one angel, shaking his head as he leafs through the file, 'not much here. He's cracked up and useless. Doesn't go to church any more, he's left his job. How he can do that with three kids depending on him...'

'Look at this.' Another heavenly being takes up the dismal story. 'Getting drunk most nights and disappearing for hours on end. I don't know how his poor wife has put up with it. He seems to enjoy letting himself sink into a moral swamp.'

'Have you read what he's saying to people about the Church?' A third angel holds up his opened file and taps the page with his finger. 'So scathing and destructive. It's hard enough keeping that outfit going as it is, without this kind of negative talk.'

'So,' says yet another committee member, shutting his file with a bang, 'what we have here is a drunken, critical, irresponsible, spiritually bankrupt, morally deficient no-hoper. An ideal case for dumping. Am I right?'

A murmur of agreement passes round the table as, one by one, the angels close their files and sit back in their chairs. Only one member of the committee has not yet expressed an opinion. God, who has been listening silently at the head of the table, gazes thoughtfully into the distance, and speaks for the first time. 'I think,' he says quietly, 'we'll give him an international writing and speaking ministry...'

Father, some of us have reached the bottom. You once planted a mustard seed of faith in us. May it begin to grow now. Thank you.

REAL LIFE

Matthew 13:33–35 (NIV)

He told them still another parable: 'The kingdom of heaven is like yeast that a woman took and mixed into a large amount of flour until it worked all through the dough.' Jesus spoke all these things to the crowd in parables; he did not say anything to them without using a parable. So was fulfilled what was spoken through the prophet: 'I will open my mouth in parables, I will utter things hidden since the creation of the world.'

Whether you regard the life, death and resurrection of Jesus as a mustard seed or as yeast, it is easy to forget how remarkably that small beginning has grown into a situation where, in this country alone, almost every city, town, village and hamlet contains at least one building that celebrates the coming of the Son of God. This is certainly evidence of the power of the gospel, but, sadly, it is also evidence of the way in which the devil has been able to prevent the yeast of God's presence from working itself right into the dough of everyday living. When a friend of mine took over a big city mission, he raised more than a few religious eyebrows by immediately closing down the three mission churches that were operating at the time.

His explanation was simple. 'They aren't doing any mission,' he said. 'Each church has got its own little congregation that turns up on Sundays, and that's all right as far as it goes. They don't do anyone any harm. But they're not there to be harmless. The mission churches are supposed to be bringing God to the community, and they're not, so we'll close them down until we've decided how to do what we're here for.'

Christianity cannot be stored in barns called churches.

Why should things hidden since the creation of the world be uttered in parables? Why? Because, when the world was created, man was able to walk with his God through a garden in the cool of the afternoon. He didn't have to wait until the verger had unlocked the church and the vicar had arrived. Parables are about real life. The yeast was part of the dough when Adam walked with God.

We need our churches. But let's not forget that the end of all our work for God will be the removal of buildings, rituals and religion, because he will be in all things. We will have him, he will have us, and all will be one.

Those of us in ministry are working enthusiastically towards doing ourselves out of a job.

UNAUTHORIZED

Matthew 13:36–43 (NIV)

Then he left the crowd and went into the house. His disciples came to him and said, 'Explain to us the parable of the weeds in the field.' He answered, 'The one who sowed the good seed is the Son of Man. The field is the world, and the good seed stands for the sons of the kingdom. The weeds are the sons of the evil one, and the enemy who sows them is the devil. The harvest is the end of the age, and the harvesters are angels. As the weeds are pulled up and burned in the fire, so it will be at the end of the age. The Son of Man will send out his angels, and they will weed out of his kingdom everything that causes sin and all who do evil. They will throw them into the fiery furnace, where there will be weeping and gnashing of teeth. Then the righteous will shine like the sun in the kingdom of their Father. He who has ears, let him hear.

Now, you're in luck here, because I can throw an entirely new light on these verses. Recently, a distant relative called Bill Rae died leaving me everything. In his will Bill insisted I should investigate an ancient Eastern pot in his attic, because 'the contents would help communicate parts of the Bible more accurately than hitherto'. I found the pot and, inside, an ancient scroll, which I submitted to experts.

Their report estimates the scroll's age at two thousand years (well, they say two years, but I'm sure that's a typing error) and describes the content as 'a copy of Matthew's Gospel, with significant differences from the familiar version'. It certainly looks authentic, right down to the chapter divisions and verse numbers. I'll quote you a little of what I believe to be the original version of the above scripture. We've been so naïve!

'The Son of Man will send out his angels, and they will gently remove from his kingdom everything that causes what we rather archaically refer to as sin, and all who, for reasons beyond their control, do evil. They will install them in a rather comfortable private hotel where there will be counselling and laughing and cleaning of teeth, and a general sense of relief that all the fiery furnace stuff was just for effect. And the righteous need not have bothered really, nor the Son of Man if it comes to that. Still, never mind, he said some good things...'

He who has ears, let him hear.

What is the one-word anagram of Bill Rae?

THE INSPIRATION OF JOY

Matthew 13:44 (NIV)

The kingdom of heaven is like treasure hidden in a field. When a man found it, he hid it again, and then in his joy went and sold all he had and bought that field.

For all too many people this parable ends rather differently: 'The kingdom of heaven is like treasure hidden in a field. When a man found it he hid it again, and set off with great joy to sell all he had, but he dithered about so much that he missed that day's market, and by the time he'd asked a few close friends for advice and slept on it for a night his joy had faded, and it didn't seem such a good idea after all. He was able to think of a thousand good reasons why it would be better to leave buying the field for a while, and anyway, the treasure would probably still be there when he went back in a few years' time. By then he'd be able to afford the field without having to sell absolutely everything. Much more sensible…'

Opportunities to act on the inspiration of joy don't happen very often in most people's lives, and they can result in great blessing or great sadness depending on whether they're taken or not. Sadly, much treasure is lost, for the 'best possible' reasons.

It can happen to writers sometimes, when consciousness is suddenly illuminated by an idea burning with such brilliance that you know it will work. After a night's sleep, these inspirations can look very drab indeed, especially if you then share them with somebody else, and that person's unenthusiasm dulls whatever shine might have remained. I'm beginning to learn to trust the memory of these shining moments, to believe that the excitement will return when I actually put them into practice, and not to spill them to anyone else before pursuing the original vision.

We live in a society where nostalgia has become an industry, and for many people the future functions as distraction from an unacceptable present. Jesus is suggesting here that when we do discover the secret treasure of joy—the eternal now of union with him, it is worth giving, losing, selling everything so that it becomes truly ours. The world is very deceptive, and we shall be a long time dead. Grasp the chance.

Lord, we discovered you—our treasure—in a moment of joy, but some of us never came back to make sure of owning that joy. Give us new resolve now to give all that we are and have for you.

SELLING UP

Matthew 13:45–46

The kingdom of heaven is like a merchant looking for fine pearls. When he found one of great value, he went away and sold everything he had and bought it.

I have a friend who is continually finding the only thing he ever really wanted. The problem is that it's something different each time. Neglected and abused in his childhood, Sam has a bottomless pit of emotional need, made worse by disastrous relationships in the past. He has more or less given up the idea of marriage, fearing that he will never be able to sustain that kind of lifelong closeness. Nowadays, Sam's 'pearls' tend to be things rather than people. I can't count the number of times Sam has rung me, full of excitement because, at last, he really does know what he needs to make him happy. There was the art studio in the back garden: Sam was going to devote himself to developing a neglected talent for sketching, and he simply had to have a special place and special equipment with which to do it. He nearly bankrupted himself in the process of finding enough money for this project, but today the 'studio' has become a garden shed and Sam sketches nothing.

He arrived outside our house once, driving an almost brand new Land Rover. 'It's been my dream for years,' he said. 'I'll probably be in debt for the rest of my life, but everything's going to be different now. I shall probably sell up and drive round the world.' He didn't do anything of the sort, of course, and it wasn't long before the new vehicle was replaced by a heap of rust, thus releasing credit potential for the incredibly versatile electronic keyboard that was going to give Sam what he really wanted.

Now and then Sam gives up for a while. During these periods he phones us a lot and comes close to despair. He is a Christian—has been for years—but, perhaps because he is such a damaged personality, his faith doesn't bring him much peace. He does encounter Jesus, though, in the caring and concern of many Christian friends, and I think he is aware of the reality of that encounter. We pray that one day he will stop sorting through the worldly pearls of buildings and cars and the countless other things he's tried, and settle for Jesus, who will certainly cost everything, but will at last give him what he always needed.

Sometimes our task is to be temporary guardians of someone else's fine pearl.

BAD FISH

Matthew 13:47–50 (NIV)

'The kingdom of heaven is like a net that was let down into the lake and caught all kinds of fish. When it was full, the fishermen pulled it up on the shore. Then they sat down and collected the good fish in baskets, but threw the bad away. This is how it will be at the end of the age. The angels will come and separate the wicked from the righteous and throw them into the fiery furnace, where there will be weeping and gnashing of teeth.'

The people who first heard this parable can have had no idea that, in 2000 years' time, fried fish, cooked in furnaces of a more compact and worldly nature, would be available on the streets of every town and village in this country. Jesus' account is about something very different. Can you imagine the smell when bad fish get slung into the eternal ovens of hell? Ugh!

Do you sometimes worry that you're a bad fish? I do. I'm in the net, but am I fresh? It's not easy to feel the kind of assurance that we would like to feel, and it's no use holding Bible verses under my nose to show that we should be absolutely sure, because lots of us aren't—so there!

Elsewhere Jesus points out, for instance, that people will say to him that they healed the sick and drove out devils in his name but he'll say that he never knew them. He'll call them doers of evil. I know churches where people do those sorts of things all the time. Do you honestly think that any of those engaged in such—apparently—crucial spiritual tasks believes that he or she is a bad fish? I don't think so.

In another place he says that calling out 'Lord, Lord!' is meaningless if you don't really do what you're told. Well, I hear lots of marvellous prayers—really impressive ones. Would some of the performers of these offerings recognize the scent of bad fish in the air around them, or is it so familiar that they can't even smell it any more?

Then there's the 25th chapter of this Gospel. Read it. Worrying, isn't it? Do I feed the hungry or give water to the thirsty? Do I invite strangers in? Do I clothe the naked? Do I care for the sick or visit prisoners? If I don't give these things proper priority, I need to take a long deep breath. There'll be a smell of bad fish around, and I'd better do something about it.

I will read the Gospels as though I had never read them before, and find out what being a good fish really means.

UNDERSTANDABLE

Matthew 13:51–52 (NIV)

'Have you understood all these things?' Jesus asked. 'Yes,' they replied. He said to them, 'Therefore every teacher of the law who has been instructed about the kingdom of heaven is like the owner of a house who brings out of his storeroom new treasures as well as old.'

I love this bit, don't you? Can't you just picture the disciples sitting and listening with great enjoyment to the stories Jesus was telling, and then suddenly, to their horror, being confronted with an inquiry as to whether they had understood everything? I should imagine there was a brief, jaw-dropping pause, followed by general, quite spuriously confident nods of agreement.

'Understood all these things? Oh yes. Eh, lads?'

'No trouble at all…'

'Got it, yes—quite clear, thanks.'

'Yep! Yep! Bad fish—yep!'

'Seeds, yeast, weeds, treasure—'

'Don't forget the pearls.'

'Ah, yeah, that's right, yeah, pearls as well, yeah.'

'Nets.'

'Nets, yeah…'

'It's all about the kingdom of er—'

'God.'

'That's it, God, yeah.'

'Yeah…'

A little smile of amusement must have played around Jesus' lips as he listened to the 'yes' of his disciples. I think it's extremely unlikely that they had anything but the haziest idea of what their master was talking about at this stage. Later, of course, after Jesus had died and risen, and the Spirit had come, they would have pored over every recollected word, catching for the first time a vision of the great reality that is contained in these deceptively simple little stories.

We have the Spirit with us now, so don't worry if you feel you don't understand all that you read in the Bible. He will reveal anything that you need to know.

Father, thank you for the new treasures—the teachings of Jesus. We want to understand what he is saying, and particularly what he is saying to us as individuals. Holy Spirit, be with us as we read—let us adventure together.

A WRONG TURNING?

READINGS FROM JOB

Well, here I am, standing nervously at the end of an enormously long line of eminent people who have all written significant things about the book of Job. However, what I lack in theology and learning I hope I might just make up for in enthusiasm. The story of Job is one of the most illuminating, amusing and intriguing books in the entire Bible, and it feels a great privilege to be able to join you as we look at chapters 29, 30 and part of 31. In these verses Job is looking back over the years and trying to work out why God has brought him so low, when his life was so carefully and conscientiously attuned to the commands of his creator.

Because Job was such a virtuous man, we learn a great deal in these chapters about the way in which a godly life should be led. I feel as sure that you will benefit from this information as I am certain you will forgive me for my hopelessly anecdotal approach to these notes.

Let me just say, for the benefit of those who believe this book to be an entirely factual account of the events that befell Job, that I absolutely agree with you. There is no doubt whatsoever that this is the literal history of a real person.

As for those who believe it to be a wonderful example of Jewish humour and poetry containing layer upon layer of meaning, but not a literal account at all, well, I absolutely agree with you as well. How right you are. It's that kind of a story.

Let us proceed…

WHAT AM I?

Job 29:7–13 (NRSV)

'When I went out to the gate of the city, when I took my seat in the square, the young men saw me and withdrew, and the aged rose up and stood; the nobles refrained from talking, and laid their hands on their mouths; the voices of princes were hushed, and their tongues stuck to the roof of their mouths. When the ear heard, it commended me, and when the eye saw, it approved; because I delivered the poor who cried, and the orphan who had no helper. The blessing of the wretched came upon me, and I caused the widow's heart to sing for joy.'

Goodness! The young men, the old men, the chief men—all deferring to Job, obviously a celebrity cubed. The combination of power and compassion is usually an attractive and popular one, is it not? And an ability to hush the voice of the noble *and* cause the widow's heart to sing is impressive, to say the least. But it had all gone. Poverty-stricken, pizza-faced, pathetic, Job must have asked himself the question that most of us do eventually.

What, in truth, am I?

How much was Job's identity bound up with how he was perceived by the general public and the kowtowing bigwigs? Who or what was he without those regular doses of affirmation?

I once had a complete year of abstinence from any form of public speaking, a sort of sabbatical, although that term overdignifies it somewhat. One real purpose of the exercise was to create space to ask myself the question I've already mentioned.

What am I?

No rude, anonymous answers on postcards, thank you very much. It was a serious enquiry. How much was my identity bound up with public response to what I do? If I were to take speaking and performing (or perhaps even writing—please, God, no!) out of the equation suggested by that question, what would be left of me? That's what I talked to God about all through that year, and I was a little bit frightened, if I'm honest. The future was a blank page, and I was doing my very best to give away the pen. Poor old Job had no choice!

May what we are be what we are for you,
Not flimsy shadows of applause for what we do.

ONE BODY

Job 29:14–20 (NRSV)

'I put on righteousness, and it clothed me; my justice was like a robe and a turban. I was eyes to the blind, and feet to the lame. I was a father to the needy, and I championed the cause of the stranger. I broke the fangs of the unrighteous, and made them drop their prey from their teeth. Then I thought, "I shall die in my nest, and I shall multiply my days like the phoenix; my roots spread out to the waters, with the dew all night on my branches; my glory was fresh with me, and my bow ever new in my hand."'

A highly successful generic social worker with an amazingly good pension scheme, that's how Job seems to have seen himself before all his troubles began. I sympathize, though. Job genuinely helped those who were handicapped or in trouble, and now he was in trouble himself. I wonder if, after losing everything, he ran into folk he'd assisted in the good old days. And if he did, do you think he felt a sudden stab of humiliation about actually *being* one of them?

More than 20 years ago, after working with children in care for a number of years, I was retired through ill health and found myself in at least two dignity-shredding situations. One happened when I was arrested for punching a pane of glass out of a telephone box in a fit of temper. At the police station I was placed in the very cell from which I had collected a variety of offending teenagers in the past. I've written before about properly understanding their frustration for the first time as a result, but I have never truly confessed to the depth of sheer humiliation I experienced that day. I was supposed to be the social worker, not the client!

The other occasion was signing on at the dole office, and finding a couple of the kids I'd worked with standing in the same queue. I hated it! For the first time I realized the extent to which I had operated from a position of superiority, and I felt ashamed.

These experiences were helpful. I finally began to understand that God truly sees us all as equals. Job probably knew that already, but it must have been a shock all the same.

Do I really believe that every part of Christ's body on earth is equally valuable?

FOUNDATIONS

Job 30:9–15 (NRSV)

'And now they mock me in song; I am a byword to them. They abhor me, they keep aloof from me; they do not hesitate to spit at the sight of me. Because God has loosed my bowstring and humbled me, they have cast off restraint in my presence. On my right hand the rabble rise up; they send me sprawling, and build roads for my ruin. They break up my path, they promote my calamity; no one restrains them. As through a wide breach they come; amid the crash they roll on. Terrors are turned upon me; my honour is pursued as by the wind, and my prosperity has passed away like a cloud.'

We moved house a few years ago. Bridget and I were always nomadic by nature and, as ex-actors, somewhat theatrical in our perception of life. We regarded moving as actors regard the transition from one play that's ended its run to the opening of another one in a different theatre. This time, though, we had been in the same house, hauling our children towards adulthood, for 16 years. A *very* long run in *very* tricky roles, as all parents will testify, particularly as there's no script. Nevertheless, I doubted that there would be much of an emotional factor to the move. I was wrong.

One night, just before the move, I was suddenly overwhelmed by crashing waves of panic. Just about every doubt and fear I had ever known threatened to destroy any sense of safety in me. The impending loss of my habitual, warmly familiar environment did indeed seem to have created a gaping breach in my defences and, amid the ruins, dark despairing questions flowed in.

What kind of flawed father had I really been to my children?

What if I were to contract some terrible illness and die?

Was all this business about God and heaven just a load of optimistic nonsense?

What were love and relationships worth if, in the end, there was to be blind oblivion?

What if there were burglars downstairs…?

The panic passed with the morning, thank goodness, and we are now happily ensconced in our new house, but, a little like Job, I had learnt that true dignity and safety are ultimately found only in relationship with God. It's not such a bad thing to have the road broken up from time to time.

Father, be our firm ground.

BEATEN UP

Job 30:16–23 (NRSV)

'And now my soul is poured out within me; days of affliction have taken hold of me. The night racks my bones, and the pain that gnaws me takes no rest. With violence he seizes my garment; he grasps me by the collar of my tunic. He has cast me into the mire, and I have become like dust and ashes. I cry to you and you do not answer me; I stand, and you merely look at me. You have turned cruel to me; with the might of your hand you persecute me. You lift me up on the wind, you make me ride on it, and you toss me about in the roar of the storm. I know that you will bring me to death, and to the house appointed for all living.'

Do you hear the voice of a child suffering inexplicably hard treatment from its father? There is an unbearable poignancy in the image of Job standing to gain God's warm attention, but instead being subjected to cold stares and ruthless attack. It all suggests some crazily uneven wrestling match—Giant Haystacks against Little Red Riding Hood.

My friend Mark Jessop was inexplicably attacked by his father once.

Mark describes his family as solidly, militantly working-class people of a particular kind, impatient of any airy-fairy nonsense. Mark committed two serious crimes. First, he showed a bent towards art and music, both alien to the Jessop culture. Then, his major offence, he became an evangelical Christian at the age of 15. Not long after this, Mark's father quite simply beat his son up, an explosion of his own inexpressible fears. When Mark described this, the hurt and bewilderment of that experience, many years in the past now, still filled his eyes. Mark adored and still does adore his father, and they get on nowadays, but he is still waiting for signs of real approval. Sadly, Mark's perception of God is seriously distorted by dealings with his earthly father.

I know many of you who read this now will, like Job and my friend Mark, be asking why God, your heavenly Father, seems to be throwing you around the room at present. There are no easy answers to that question, but please leave a little space in the back of your mind to store this message from me, that he knows what he's doing, and he loves you—he really does.

Why?

TUNING UP

Job 30:24–31 (NRSV)

'Surely one does not turn against the needy, when in disaster they cry for help. Did I not weep for those whose day was hard? Was not my soul grieved for the poor? But when I looked for good, evil came; and when I waited for light, darkness came. My inward parts are in turmoil, and are never still; days of affliction come to meet me. I go about in sunless gloom; I stand up in the assembly and cry for help. I am a brother of jackals, and a companion of ostriches. My skin turns black and falls from me, and my bones burn with heat. My lyre is turned to mourning, and my pipe to the voice of those who weep.'

Things are not looking up for Job, and he *was* innocent, wasn't he? I've done plenty of complaining, but in my case it's been heavily tinged with awareness of my own guilt. That's what makes the last two verses of this chapter so interesting.

A local elder told me about somone who for years had been a peripatetic problem peddler, going from person to person with the same sonorous set of problems, never finding a solution to any of them. From church member to church member he went, clutching his invisible emotional begging-bowl, seeking scraps of attention from folk who never found him anything but tedious.

'One evening,' said the elder, 'he arrived as we were about to eat, saying he needed someone to talk to. As usual I had to scratch my blessed got-to-help-anyone-in-need itch, so there I was, picturing my cold pork chops and waiting for Lamentations to begin. He said, "I'm so worried. I feel everyone's fed up with me." I nodded, like you do, waiting for the usual therapeutic babble to emerge, but I couldn't get it out. "Well, they *are* fed up with you," I said, "because you never do anything but complain and talk about your problems. People are sick of it."'

He smiled and shook his head in wonder. 'Believe it or not, Adrian, but that's really done the trick. He's a different man.'

My friend's inadvertent method of dealing with such a problem certainly can't be recommended in general terms, but it's true that some of us have had our harps tuned to mourning and our flutes to the sound of wailing for so long that we've forgotten what music is for.

Write new tunes for us, Lord.

STRANGE TRUTH

Job 31:1–8 (NRSV)

'I have made a covenant with my eyes; how then could I look upon a virgin? What would be my portion from God above, and my heritage from the Almighty on high? Does not calamity befall the unrighteous…? Does he not see my ways, and number all my steps? If I have walked with falsehood, and my foot has hurried to deceit— let me be weighed in a just balance, and let God know my integrity!—if my step has turned aside from the way, and my heart has followed my eyes, and if any spot has clung to my hands; then let me sow, and another eat; and let what grows for me be rooted out.'

You can see why Job's friends got fed up with him, can't you? What a paragon! No lust, no deceit and no defilement. They must have found it very difficult to believe that anyone could be quite so virtuous. But it really is a mistake to let worldly-wise instincts blind us to the truth.

I was amused once when my oldest son's ex-landlord phoned.

'Could I speak to Matthew Plass,' said the voice. 'I'm his ex-landlord and I've rung about a damaged saucepan that needs paying for.'

'I'm awfully sorry,' I said, 'but he's in Azerbaijan.'

'Azerbaijan?' The tone was rich with scepticism.

'Yes, Azerbaijan, that's right.'

'Well, can you tell me where I can get hold of his flatmate, Dave?'

Short pause. 'I'm afraid Dave's in Uzbekistan.'

'Look,'—the voice was openly cynical now—'can you just tell them that I need one of them to do something about paying for this saucepan.'

'I'll pay for it,' I said. 'Matthew really is in Azerbaijan and Dave really is in Uzbekistan.' And they were. Both had done a TEFL course, and both were teaching conversational English in those two crumbling ex-Soviet republics. It's not at all uncommon for the truth to sound rather strange.

Job's 'comforters' made the mistake of judging him according to their own standards, so they were useless to him and to God and to everyone except people like me who love reading the nonsense they talked. Jesus said that we should be as cunning as serpents, but also as harmless as doves. Being realistic about life doesn't mean we blind ourselves to truth and goodness when they do appear.

Open our eyes to what is good, Father.

SNIFFY BUT TRUE

Job 31:9–15 (NRSV)

'If my heart has been enticed by a woman, and I have lain in wait at my neighbour's door; then let my wife grind for another, and let other men kneel over her. For that would be a heinous crime; that would be a criminal offence; for that would be a fire consuming down to Abaddon, and it would burn to the root all my harvest. If I have rejected the cause of my male or female slaves, when they brought a complaint against me; what then shall I do when God rises up? When he makes inquiry, what shall I answer him? Did not he who made me in the womb make them? And did not one fashion us in the womb?'

The church seems seriously infected with the disease of adultery, particularly among leaders. Perhaps it always was but we never heard about it because in the past it happened in a much more secretive way—I don't know. There are some odd things happening nowadays, though, and they seem very much related to the age we live in.

Recently, for instance, I learned that a married worship leader in a church some miles from where we live had confessed to a long-term affair with a single woman of the same congregation. As a result of this revelation the married couple had parted and were planning divorce. This, in itself, is highly regrettable, of course, but not unusual. The thing that staggered me was that the church elders had asked the wife to leave and the husband to stay, because—wait for it—he was so valuable as a worship leader!

I'm all for compassion and a new start. In most cases sincere repentance should be followed by acceptance, but this seemed an extraordinary decision. This man had been leading worship throughout his long affair. Job makes the point that if *he* had strayed, his harvest would have been uprooted, and in the case I've just mentioned, might not this be true in terms of spiritual harvest?

I would advise that church to think carefully about priorities. God hates immorality as passionately as he forgives those who repent of it. We cannot afford to reflect the shift in moral boundaries that has occurred in the rest of the world just to keep the music nice, and I don't care how sniffy that sounds, because it's true.

Father, we're all tempted—keep us clean.

THE BLATANT CHALLENGE

Job 31: 16–23 (NRSV)

'If I have withheld anything that the poor desired, or have caused the eyes of the widow to fail, or have eaten my morsel alone, and the orphan has not eaten from it—for from my youth I reared the orphan like a father, and from my mother's womb I guided the widow—if I have seen anyone perish for lack of clothing, or a poor person without covering, whose loins have not blessed me, and who was not warmed with the fleece of my sheep; if I have raised my hand against the orphan, because I saw I had supporters at the gate; then let my shoulder blade fall from my shoulder, and let my arm be broken from its socket. For I was in terror of calamity from God, and I could not have faced his majesty.'

What a wonderfully full-blooded hymn of commitment to godly living this is. Read it through again out loud. It's always nice to snuggle into the rather cosy proposition that salvation doesn't come through works. But just look at the kind of caring behaviour inspired by Job's total belief in the living God. In the same way that the book of James identifies true religion as something that will, by its nature, involve practical charity, so Job is saying that the very splendour of God demands, as Mother Teresa often said, that our hands must be Christ's hands ministering to those in need.

As we read these words today, let's, for once, blatantly challenge ourselves with the principal question that they raise.

If I was afflicted as Job was, could I claim that the poor and the widows and the fatherless and the unclothed had got the kind of deal from me that might rightly be expected from someone who claims to follow Christ? And if my answer is that I am not actually making significant efforts in that directin, let me not get bogged down with guilt, which never fed anybody, but let me *do* something about it. Goodness knows, there are enough agencies around to make that extremely easy.

And if I really mean business, let me risk asking the Holy Spirit to show me who needs help in my immediate neighbourhood as well. And let me do it now.

I want to be like Job, Lord. Give me courage, and show me where to start.

RESERVES

Job 31:24–28 (NRSV)

'If I have made gold my trust, or called fine gold my confidence; if I have rejoiced because my wealth was great, or because my hand had gotten much; if I have looked at the sun when it shone, or the moon moving in splendour, and my heart has been secretly enticed, and my mouth has kissed my hand; this also would be an iniquity to be punished by the judges, for I should have been false to God above.'

I gather gold is losing its value. So? Well, when I was little, I heard that Great Britain measured its wealth in gold reserves. I pictured a vast cavern under the Houses of Parliament, stuffed with mountains of glittering gold bricks, presided over by dwarf-like creatures rubbing their hands and licking their lips as they counted the bricks. I wanted to do it. It made me feel greedy. And just for a moment, the little boy in me felt worried about gold dropping in value. Silly, isn't it?

This passage is about how you measure true wealth and security. Job says that, despite being an extremely rich man in worldly terms, he never allowed possessions or money to usurp God as the source of true safety in his life or as the object of his worship. Nor was he seduced by the grandeur of the natural world, the sun and the moon.

Interesting, isn't it, how these two elements in life can take central place in the lives of spiritually inclined people? Money and the natural world offer seductively distracting options for those who are weary in following Jesus. Take me, for instance. One morning I realized that I had got into the habit of flicking through the post for cheques, and feeling nothing of interest had arrived if I didn't find any. Mind you, this is a familiar disease with self-employed people, but it alarmed me at the time.

Distraction by beauty in the natural world is more subtle, not least beause I'm sure God loves my appreciation of his world. Sometimes, though, a dreamy voluptuousness enfolds my enjoyment of such things and—you're going to think I'm mad—I want to drown in it...

Job placed God at the very centre of his life, a good man with a truly horrendous problem. Why had God dropped him in it? Do read the whole book from beginning to end. It's worth it.

Be our security, Lord.

GAINING FELLOW TRAVELLERS

THE WOMAN AT THE WELL

Personal evangelism, or rather my failure to do it, was one of the things that caused me quite a lot of guilt when I was a young Christian. Mind you, I started off with enormous vigour. For a time, as I have already recorded in *The Unlocking*, I spread the word indiscriminately, and, I have no doubt, extremely annoyingly, all over Tunbridge Wells. On reflection, I was probably fortunate to escape public execution by a mob composed of all those who had, quite reasonably, decided they would rather spend an eternity in the hell I was trying to save them from, than ten minutes trapped in the corner of a café by me and my large Bible.

As time went by, a conspicuous lack of results caused my zeal to be abated (my tongue was writing cheques that my experience and scholarship couldn't cash, to borrow an expression I heard in a film), but the feeling that I should be telling everyone I met about Jesus never really went away, and has remained with me, although its outworking has been highly modified since those early days.

Interestingly, in one sense my attitude to evangelism has come full circle. The stark message of judgment and salvation with which I harangued people when I was sixteen is exactly the message that now seems to me the most crucial thing for people to hear. The difference is, quite simply, my awareness that the gospel is driven by the love of God, and not by the neurotic need of any organized branch of Christianity to fit each potential convert into its own unvarying pattern of behaviours and attitudes. The need for people to be saved is paramount, but, as Saint Paul would undoubtedly have said if he had been alive in this age,

'Verily, there existeth more than one way to skinneth an cat.' I certainly had not appreciated this when I was converting the world at 16.

The fact is that almost any form of evangelism can be effective, including the traditional ones.

Bridget and I were very struck, for instance, during a large Christian festival that we attended in Australia, by the work of one South American evangelist, unknown in this country, as far as I am aware, who spoke for a fairly short time in a not particularly impressive way, but was immediately besieged by hundreds of people wishing to make some kind of movement towards Jesus. It seemed to me, especially after we had met and spoken to this chap over one or two meals, that this was a man who was as near to being fully committed to his master as it is possible to be, and, much more importantly, that he was a man who had actually received the specific gift of evangelism that Paul mentions in the fourth chapter of Ephesians. There were other speakers at the same conference who produced talks that were longer, wittier and far more obviously seductive than those of the South American, but they simply did not achieve anything like the same results. God had tapped this fellow on the shoulder.

The provision of such useful services as mother and toddler groups to the secular community by individual churches can be a valuable means of evangelism, as long as the service is offered in a genuine spirit of charity, and God is allowed to direct the means and the pace of evangelism.

Keeping one's mouth shut can be an excellent form of evangelism.

Making real friends with someone can result in highly effective evangelism—the most effective as far as I can tell from what I hear as I travel around the world.

I'm sure this is only the beginning of a much longer list of ways in which the message of salvation can be given to those who need to hear it, but is there one thing that they all have in common? Well, I would venture to suggest that wherever people are drawn to Christ, you will find someone who really has tackled the business of sorting out priorities. This is what Jesus himself had to do before beginning his three-year ministry, and we learn about it in the following verses, which come from chapter four of Luke's Gospel:

Jesus, full of the Holy Spirit, returned from the Jordan, and was led by the Spirit in the desert, where for forty days he was tempted by the devil. He ate nothing during those days, and at the end of them he was hungry.

The devil said to him, 'If you are the Son of God, tell this stone to become bread.'

Jesus answered, 'It is written: "Man does not live on bread alone."'

The devil led him up to a high place and showed him in an instant all the kingdoms of the world. And he said to him, 'I will give you all their authority and splendour, for it has been given to me, and I can give it to anyone I want to. So if you worship me, it will all be yours.'

Jesus answered, 'It is written: "Worship the Lord your God and serve him only."'

The devil led him to Jerusalem, and had him stand on the highest point of the temple. 'If you are the Son of God,' he said, 'throw yourself down from here. For it is written: "He will command his angels concerning you to guard you carefully; they will lift you up in their hands, so that you will not strike your foot against a stone."'

Jesus answered, 'It says, "Do not put the Lord your God to the test."'

When the devil had finished all this tempting, he left him until an opportune time.

LUKE 4:1–13 (NIV)

In Matthew's version of the same story angels appear at this point and minister to Jesus.

The trouble with passages like this is that, over the years, they become almost impossible to see clearly, just as a painting on the sitting-room wall can become such a familiar part of the domestic scenery that the content and meaning of the picture, which meant so much once, no longer makes any impact on those who see it every day. An additional problem with this crucially important event in the life of Jesus, is that the common perception of those forty days in the wilderness, the one that is, as it were, fixed on the walls of our minds, is a religious picture, a tidy, formalized, cleaned-up, harmless version of one of the greatest and most gritty acts of heroism in the history of this world. Behind those silly images of a tall, blue-eyed, freshly showered and shampooed Son of God, dismissing Satan with a casual waft of the wrist, is something much deeper, much more ragged, much more meaningful and challenging to us, and, ultimately, much more beautiful because it is full of love.

During the sheer hell of 40 hungry days and 40 freezing nights in the desert Jesus had to learn, through facing these three temptations of the devil, to steer away from material prosperity, indulgent use and enjoyment of power and an illusory sense of personal safety, the very items that topped the priority list of most human beings then, and still do today. Only by doing this could he bring about the greatest miracle of all, the reunion of his Father with millions—billions of people who were and are profoundly loved, but profoundly lost. Grasping the logic of this divine principle is so difficult for limited human beings like us. It doesn't appear to make any sense.

We are not helped by the way in which that side of the Church which is vulnerable to temptation has, in recent years, tried to rationalize—forcibly to steer—these low spiritual priorities back on to the top of the list. Some churches have almost redefined material prosperity as a sort of spiritual gift; some misguided aspects of what is called Holy Spirit ministry offer power without loving responsibility to people who shouldn't be in charge of a sausage sizzle, and, perhaps most subtly of all, there is a form of 'Kingdom Now' teaching that manages to avoid, for the 'best possible theological reasons', the realities of death and heaven and especially hell. These movements are all the more dangerous because their mutant growths emerge from seeds of truth.

Prosperity, power and personal safety—these are the things that Jesus deprioritized, as the Americans put it, and the message is pretty clear for us as well. While we are, in the very heart of ourselves, depending more on these worldly assets than on the God who sent his Son to die for us, we are not free to offer him the best possible job of evangelism, or anything else for that matter.

I know it's not easy—even I'm not stupid enough to think that—but it wasn't easy for Jesus either. He didn't go through the desert experience on a bye, like some fortunate Wimbledon competitor. He could have failed. He could have decided that he wanted money and women and power more than he wanted to be obedient to his Father, in which case we wouldn't be sitting in our churches every Sunday morning because there wouldn't be any churches to sit in. Jesus had no idea whether he would overcome temptation or not. If that was not the case, then he wasn't really tempted and he wasn't really a man.

He came through in the end as we know, and he did it for us. He did it because he knew he was our only chance. He knew that disaster on a vast scale was just waiting to happen if he didn't overcome those temptations. I must say that I think the Church seems to have lost sight of this dramatically urgent reason for the coming of Jesus.

Earlier in the week that has just ended as I write, I was talking to someone in the street, and he was saying what a shame it is that Christianity doesn't have as many interesting activities and events attached to it as other religions. I was just embarking on the old familiar nodding and agreeing that we Christians are so good at, when I suddenly thought—what are we talking about? The central issue is not (or shouldn't be) reminiscent of some *Blue Peter* versus *Magpie* competition (remember *Magpie* on ITV?). It's not about who can offer the best way to make working models of combine harvesters out of milk-bottle tops. If Christianity is true, and I think it is, we are talking about a looming cosmic disaster, and, as well as presenting things in the best possible way—of course we want to do that—we should primarily be saying to people, 'Look, you do what you like—believe what you like, but I tell you this, if you're going to reject Jesus, you'd better be pretty blinking sure you've got it right!'

Two thousand years ago the Son of God gritted his teeth, locked his priorities firmly in place, and set out, steering in a very straight line towards certain death. He did it for us.

Prosperity, power and personal safety—where do they come on my list, and what am I going to do about it? Once they have descended to their proper place, and commitment to God has become my priority, I shall be prepared to pass on the message of salvation as well as it can be done, in the way and the place that is appointed and right, just as Jesus did with this woman from Samaria 2,000 years ago.

Prayer
Father, we really would like to be involved in passing on the message of salvation, but some of us are unsure and nervous about what might be involved. Please help us make a serious attempt to place you at the top of our list of priorities, and to be so filled with the excitement of your love and the urgency of your desire to save, that, impossible though it may seem at the moment, our very lives are alight with the gospel.

ALL THE THIRSTY PEOPLE

John 4:6–10 (NJB)

Jesus, tired by the journey, sat down by the well. It was about the sixth hour. When a Samaritan woman came to draw water, Jesus said to her, 'Give me something to drink.' His disciples had gone into the town to buy food. The Samaritan woman said to him, 'You are a Jew. How is it that you ask me, a Samaritan, for something to drink?'—Jews, of course, do not associate with Samaritans. Jesus replied to her: 'If you only knew what God is offering and who it is that is saying to you, "Give me something to drink," you would have been the one to ask, and he would have given you living water.'

Nowadays we hear quite a lot about groups of Christians marching around the edge of a town or part of a city 'claiming it for the Lord'. One hopes that they get involved with the centre of such areas as well. A friend of mine was asked to run a house for homeless men in the East End of London when he was still very young. Each night he set off in the dark to seek out places where these men (many of them alcoholics) settled for the night. Sometimes he was so frightened that he turned round and ran home again. He was only a part-time coward, though. He persisted, and the project thrived. He took Jesus to people who might not have met him otherwise.

Here we see Jesus taking himself into an area that Jews normally avoided like the plague. He did not walk round it; he walked into it.

Having despatched the disciples (why did it take twelve men to collect the groceries?), he then defied convention even further by not only speaking to a Samaritan woman, but actually asking her for a drink. Like the homeless men that my friend visited on their own ground, she was curious about the motivation for this unusual behaviour. The answer in both cases was the same—Jesus had come, bringing the water of life.

It is not easy to go into places that are unfamiliar or threatening in some way, but if we want to follow Jesus, that is what will happen. It may be the people next door, it may be the pub down the road, it may be deepest Borneo, but if he calls us, we either go—or disobey.

Lord, am I avoiding anyone or anywhere that you want me to visit? I need courage. Please give it to me when I need it, so that I can take you to those who need living water.

UNPOISONED WATER

John 4:11–18 (NJB)

'You have no bucket, sir,' she answered, 'and the well is deep: how do you get this living water? Are you a greater man than our father Jacob, who gave us this well and drank from it himself with his sons and his cattle?' Jesus replied, 'Whoever drinks this water will be thirsty again; but no one who drinks the water that I shall give him will ever be thirsty again: the water that I shall give him will become in him a spring of water, welling up for eternal life.' 'Sir,' said the woman, 'give me some of that water, so that I may never be thirsty or come here again to draw water.' 'Go and call your husband,' said Jesus to her, 'and come back here.' The woman answered, 'I have no husband.' Jesus said to her, 'You are right to say, "I have no husband"; for although you have had five, the one you now have is not your husband. You spoke the truth there.'

Sometimes self-indulgence and sin appear very much more attractive than the path of virtue, especially when it is the path of arid, bloodless duty. When a stress-related illness forced me out of work and my world was collapsing around me, I wrote these words:

Who made these poison pools in desert lands
So sweet and cool?
A welcome lie,
The chance to die with water on my lips.
I've seen how others try to die
Unpoisoned in the sun,
I do not think that I can do as they have done.

In this passage, Jesus is offering clean, healthy, running water to replace both the poisoned water of negative behaviour and the aridity of loveless virtue.

In the case of the Samaritan woman, it is her predilection for a broad choice of close gentlemen friends that constitutes the poisoned water that will kill her in the end. What a mind-numbing shock it must have been when this rather impressive stranger's innocent-sounding suggestion was followed by such an accurate stab of insight.

God understands our failings. He knows the weaknesses that are responsible for bad decisions and developments in our lives. But the living water is still on offer, water that will purify our minds and bodies and make virtue a byproduct of joy.

Lord, I know you will not be soft with me when straight speaking is needed. Let us meet and talk. You will tell me what is not clean in my life, and I shall ask you for living water to wash it away.

HE LIVES IN OUR HEARTS

John 4:19–26 (NJB)

'I see you are a prophet, sir,' said the woman. 'Our fathers worshipped on this mountain, though you say that Jerusalem is the place where one ought to worship.' Jesus said: 'Believe me, woman, the hour is coming when you will worship the Father neither on this mountain nor in Jerusalem. You worship what you do not know, we worship what we do know, for salvation comes from the Jews. But the hour is coming—indeed is already here—when true worshippers will worship the Father in spirit and truth: that is the kind of worshipper the Father seeks. God is spirit, and those who worship must worship in spirit and truth.' The woman said to him, 'I know that Messiah—that is, Christ—is coming; and when he comes he will explain everything.' Jesus said, 'That is who I am, I who speak to you.'

The Samaritan woman's religious understanding was sketchy and intuitive, but on one point she was quite clear. 'The Christ is coming and he will explain everything.'

One summer holiday we entertained 17 Russians to a barbecue in our garden on a Saturday evening. Our guests were in a party mood. They had come to England as tourists, but, because of a breakdown in communications at an early stage, the local man who had organized the trip mistakenly believed them to be 17 youth leaders on a fact-finding tour. Frequent, inexplicable trips to scout troops, schools and youth clubs had left the Russians completely bewildered and just a little resentful.

Now, with their host's eccentricities explained, they danced and sang under our apple trees, determined to enjoy themselves.

'What do you think about God?' I asked one of them through an interpreter, thinking that I could predict his answer.

'We have no education in God,' he replied, 'but'—and he thumped his barrel chest—'he lives in our hearts.'

Can you understand what I mean when I say that I envied that man slightly? In this part of the world it may be that we have too much education in God, and not enough simple awareness of his presence with us. Like my Russian, the Samaritan woman was in possession of one simple, certain truth: 'The Christ is coming...'

Imagine the heart-stopping amazement that this woman must have felt when the man who had already proved his power to her said, 'You're right, and I'm him—I've come.'

Is there such a thing as a more sophisticated faith? How does the tension between intelligence and simplicity help or hinder us? Are we too ready to assume that some groups, races or religions know nothing of Jesus?

COME AND SEE JESUS

John 4:27–32 (NJB)

At this point his disciples returned and were surprised to find him speaking to a woman, though none of them asked, 'What do you want from her?' or, 'What are you talking to her about?' The woman put down her water jar and hurried back to the town to tell the people, 'Come and see a man who has told me everything I have done; could this be the Christ?' This brought people out of the town and they made their way towards him. Meanwhile, the disciples were urging him, 'Rabbi, do have something to eat'; but he said, 'I have food to eat that you do not know about.'

We are told that when the food-buying committee came back from the Samaritan equivalent of Tesco's, they were surprised to find their master talking to the Samaritan woman, but that they declined to comment. Some people suggest that this indicates sensitivity and tactfulness on the part of the disciples, but I doubt it. We hear in another part of the Gospels that they were afraid to tell Jesus what they were discussing because it might make him angry. It seems much more likely that they were simply beginning to learn that if he was doing something, however strange, it must be worth doing, and the best thing they could do was to cooperate.

The principle holds good today. Find out what God is doing and join in, as a friend of mine once put it, and don't ask unnecessary questions.

The Samaritan woman, in defiance of many modern three-point sermons on outreach, now rushes off full of excitement to evangelize before she gets round to repenting. Whenever and wherever the power of Jesus is genuinely manifested we are bound to see this kind of natural, spontaneous spreading of the good news that Jesus has come. She simply could not contain herself, and soon the sheer infectiousness of her enthusiasm brought a congregation out to the well.

We talk a great deal about evangelism (a fact which must excite God greatly!) but if what we are doing is devising and organizing events, then asking God if he would care to help with the chairs or the refreshments, or some other little task not yet allocated, we shall get nowhere. Jesus himself, his power and his love, must be at the very centre and forefront of our efforts, exciting people so much that they rush off to tell others.

Help us to follow you unquestioningly, Lord, and to keep you at the front of all we do.

PASSION AND PRIVILEGE

John 4:33–38 (NJB)

So the disciples said to one another, 'Has someone brought him food?' But Jesus said: 'My food is to do the will of the one who sent me, and to complete his work. Do you not have a saying: Four months and then the harvest? Well, I tell you, look around you, look at the fields, already they are white for harvest! Already the reaper is being paid his wages, already he is bringing in the grain for eternal life, so that sower and reaper can rejoice together. For here the proverb holds true: one sows, another reaps. I sent you to reap a harvest you have not laboured for. Others have laboured for it; and you have come into the rewards of their labour.'

I have never been good at talks based on three points beginning with the same letter, but this passage is about priorities, passion and privilege.

Fired by this productive encounter with the Gentile world, Jesus refuses the food that the disciples have brought, and reasserts his chief priority, which is obedience. Notice that his 'food' is not seeing thousands of people converted, or sick people healed, but simply to do the will of the one who sent him. It is about relationship. What is our priority?

The passion in this section is unmistakable. The time has come for the harvest to be brought in, and Jesus is filled to the brim with Holy Spirit excitement at the urgency and the wonder and the power and the splendour of God's salvation plan nearing its climax. What is our passion?

The privilege is for the disciples and for us. We are fellow labourers with Jesus himself in the fields that have been planted and tended by the prophets, and died for by our friend, brother and king. An immense amount of work has been done by others. Now it is our turn. Into our hands is placed a shining sickle of love and truth and judgment. The harvest is waiting for us. Does it feel like a privilege?

The challenge of this passage is immense. If we are only playing at Christianity, it will have no appeal for us at all. There is a powerful symbolic message in Jesus' refusal of earthly food in favour of spiritual sustenance. It suggests and invites a commitment that will remove our fundamental dependence on the things of this world. I find that quite frightening, don't you?

Lord, we want to share your passion and your priorities. We are weak and blind. Open our eyes to your power and our great privilege.

SHE TOLD THEM ABOUT JESUS

John 4:39–42 (NJB)

Many Samaritans of that town believed in him on the strength of the woman's words of testimony, 'He told me everything I have done.' So, when the Samaritans came up to him, they begged him to stay with them. He stayed for two days, and they said to the woman, 'Now we believe no longer because of what you told us; we have heard him ourselves and we know that he is indeed the Saviour of the world.'

This Samaritan woman must have been quite something! She obviously set up a very dynamic little one-woman mission team, probably standing on a Samaritan soapbox in the marketplace and describing her vivid encounter in graphic detail. If present-day Christian publishers had been around at the time, she would undoubtedly have been snapped up to write one of those testimony paperbacks that begin with the old life (five husbands) and end with the new life (one-woman mission team… and so on). Clearly her audiences did not condemn her on hearing about her lurid past, so presumably the new life in her was powerful indeed.

Nor did she make the mistake that many evangelists and church leaders do, of drawing her listeners to herself instead of to Jesus. They insisted on seeing for themselves, and having seen him, they wanted to keep him, as I am sure we all would. They were then able to say, as one hopes and prays that all converts will be able to say eventually, 'You told us about him, but now we've met him for ourselves, and we know who he is.'

The most any of us can hope for, whatever our dreams of spiritual progress may be, is to become an effective signpost pointing to Jesus. Generally speaking, signposts are not required to pontificate about means of transport or the way in which passengers should position themselves. They simply point the way.

I cannot help feeling that this little period of time spent in a Samaritan town must have been a pleasant respite for Jesus. He had left Judea to avoid the Pharisees, and here, in the middle of a country that the Jews despised, he found acceptance and a warm response. Perhaps it is not surprising that, in a certain parable, the hero was a Samaritan.

Is our new life more dynamic than the old one? Do we draw people to us or to Jesus? Do we mind our own business after that? Could Jesus relax with us for a while?

A man in a passion rides a wild horse.

BENJAMIN FRANKLIN, *POOR RICHARD'S ALMANAC*

TRAVELLING WITH PASSION AND A PLAN

PAUL IN ACTS

The old 'Who likes Paul?' debate has been going on in the church for as long as I can remember, and probably for centuries before that. His is undoubtedly a massive, volatile presence in the New Testament, and it is hardly surprising that he attracts such a widely varying set of responses from readers of every imaginable shape and shade. The most common, of course, is the wild and totally inexplicable claim that he was in some sense a woman hater. The following readings do not explore that particular and, in my view, groundless accusation, but they do give us an opportunity to see Paul at his muscularly intellectual, highly ingenious, totally committed best. This man positively fizzed with faith in a God whose grip on the life and future of his servant was absolutely sure. Tradition suggests to us that Paul was eventually executed in Rome, but these episodes of his life make it quite clear that until the very special work given to him by God had been completed, there was no force on earth or in hell that could divert him from his spiritual destiny.

When the ship in which Paul was being transported to Rome was wrecked, he was the only man present who knew without any shadow of a doubt that his life (as well as all the others on board) would be saved from a watery grave. God had said it would be so, and that was that.

Are we encouraged or intimidated by Paul's approach to Christian living? Both, in my own case. I love the idea that God is wholly in charge of my future as long as I truly give myself to him, but do I actually want to hand over control in the same manner as this extraordinary man? I want to want to, but there is a dimension of fear in me. We must pray for courage as we read and digest these passages.

FITTING IN FOR THE GOSPEL

Acts 21:22–26 (NIV, abridged)

'What shall we do? ... Take these men, join in their purification rites and pay their expenses, so that they can have their heads shaved. Then everybody will know there is no truth in these reports about you, but that you yourself are living in obedience to the law. As for the Gentile believers, we have written to them... that they should abstain from food sacrificed to idols, from blood, from the meat of strangled animals and from sexual immorality.' The next day Paul took the men and purified himself along with them. Then he went to the temple to give notice of the date when the days of purification would end and the offering would be made for each of them.

I was talking to my wife (a bit of a Paul groupie) about this passage. She repeated her view that the apostle was willing to do just about anything within faith and reason to ensure that the gospel continued to be preached. Here, the Christians in Jerusalem are asking Paul to scotch rumours about his intolerance of Jewish customs by identifying himself with four men in the middle of their purification rites. He appears happy to do so.

It seems to be a mark of those who are truly zealous for the gospel that they are ready to fit in with the customs of others, as long as their consciences can remain clear in doing so. I have written elsewhere about a moment when, in the company of David Watson, we encountered a man who had a present for the famous preacher. It was a little plastic envelope containing a scrap of cloth. 'Relic of Padre Pio,' said the man. 'Oh, thank you so much!' replied David. 'Very active in Kent and Sussex since his death, you know.' 'Is he? Is he really?' That infernal evangelical imp that lives on my shoulder started jumping up and down and getting quite cross, but David was right. The things that this man was saying were very important to him. The continuing conversation depended on David's willingness to step into the arena of another man's concerns, and that is exactly what he did.

Lord, give us insight, courage, ingenuity and determination in spreading the gospel.

Note: This section of Acts should be read from beginning to end as a 'ripping good yarn'. These extracts are snapshots along the way.

A CITIZEN OF HEAVEN—AND ROME

Acts 22:25–29 (NIV)

As they stretched him out to flog him, Paul said to the centurion standing there, 'Is it legal for you to flog a Roman citizen who hasn't even been found guilty?' When the centurion heard this, he went to the commander and reported it. 'What are you going to do?' he asked. 'This man is a Roman citizen.' ... The commander went to Paul and asked, 'Tell me, are you a Roman citizen?' 'Yes, I am,' he answered. Then the commander said, 'I had to pay a big price for my citizenship.' 'But I was born a citizen,' Paul replied. Those who were about to question him withdrew immediately. The commander himself was alarmed when he realized he had put Paul, a Roman citizen, in chains.

Why do I continue to find this little story so richly rewarding as the years pass? It does, of course, involve all the elements and emotions that keep thousands glued to soap operas several days a week. There is the threat of violence, significant knowledge withheld, revelation on the brink of disaster, surprise, envy and alarm—all in less than 150 words. Luke tells a story well. We feel that we are right in the centre of events.

Paul's casual question to the centurion carries echoes of that moment in the Gospels when Jesus suggests that the first stone to strike the woman taken in adultery should be thrown by someone who has never sinned. Jesus was saying, 'Yes, you're absolutely right about the law, but here is a simple question that will make your heartless legal processes grind to a halt.'

Paul is saying, and I suspect he is enjoying saying every word of it, 'Yes, yes, of course you must flog me. Perfectly reasonable, logical thing to do. Off you go! Oh, by the way, just as a small matter of interest. Have you given any thought to the fact that it's illegal to flog a Roman citizen who hasn't even been found guilty? Small point. Still, mustn't keep you. I expect you'll want to be getting on with the flogging...'

Poor old commander. Saved for years for his citizenship. This bloke was born a Roman. Lucky beggar! Who was he, and what was going on?

Albert Square could do with some input from Doctor Luke.

A SMACK IN THE MOUTH FOR PAUL

Acts 23:1–5 (NIV)

Paul looked straight at the Sanhedrin and said, 'My brothers, I have fulfilled my duty to God in all good conscience to this day.' At this the high priest Ananias ordered those standing near Paul to strike him on the mouth. Then Paul said to him, 'God will strike you, you whitewashed wall! You sit there to judge me according to the law, yet you yourself violate the law by commanding that I be struck!' Those who were standing near Paul said, 'You dare to insult God's high priest?' Paul replied, 'Brothers, I did not realize that he was the high priest; for it is written: "Do not speak evil about the ruler of your people."'

What an extraordinary man Paul was—a tumultuous mixture of courage, anger and regard for duty. All three qualities are displayed here.

First he makes his opening statement, one certain to provoke angry reaction from the Sanhedrin. I know about being deliberately provocative and how difficult it is to choose the right moment to do it, a moment that will result in something constructive rather than simply giving me a feeling of personal satisfaction. Sometimes, though, things just have to be said, and this is one of those times. Paul looks straight at them, takes a deep breath and courageously says it.

The response is immediate. He gets a smack in the mouth for his pains and lashes out angrily in response, offering the same 'whitewashed wall' insult to the high priest that Jesus offered to the Pharisees, but with rather less control.

Was his sight still less than 100 per cent after the blinding that had accompanied his conversion? Was that why he had failed to realize that the one who had issued the order to hit him was Ananias the high priest? Throughout his ministry, Paul trod the line of correctness, both for his conscience's sake and, occasionally, as we saw with the issue of Roman citizenship, to extricate himself from difficulties. On this occasion, he seems genuinely sorry that he has violated the law. He apologizes humbly, but the situation is still extremely volatile. What should his next move be? Being Paul, he has another trick up his sleeve!

Lord, may we be brave and dutiful—and watch our mouths.

CAT AMONG THE PIGEONS

Acts 23:6–10 (NIV)

Then Paul, knowing that some of them were Sadducees and the other Pharisees, called out in the Sanhedrin, 'My brothers, I am a Pharisee, the son of a Pharisee. I stand on trial because of my hope in the resurrection of the dead.' When he said this, a dispute broke out between the Pharisees and the Sadducees, and the assembly was divided. (The Sadducees say that there is no resurrection, and that there are neither angels nor spirits, but the Pharisees acknowledge them all.) There was a great uproar, and some of the teachers of the law who were Pharisees stood up and argued vigorously. 'We find nothing wrong with this man,' they said. 'What if a spirit or an angel has spoken to him?' The dispute became so violent that the commander was afraid Paul would be torn to pieces by them.

This Paul was a rascal sometimes, wasn't he? The trick up his sleeve is usually summed up nowadays in the phrase 'divide and rule'.

His second statement—the one about being made to stand trial because of his hope in the resurrection of the dead—really put the Christian cat among the Jewish pigeons. He didn't need to add his actual belief that resurrection was only possible through Jesus (are we really allowed to tell half-truths?) because the Pharisees were immediately up in arms, claiming him as one of their own. In any case, as he said, he was a Pharisee and he was the son of a Pharisee. The Sadducees were furious. Suddenly, these two groups who claimed a monopoly on righteousness were at each other's throats and Paul, though not ruling, was rescued and returned to the barracks.

I guess this tendency to weigh in on the side of the person you identify with is what Paul elsewhere called 'party spirit' and it can be a subtly negative force in church communities. I believe we all need at least one friend who is in tune with us and a real pleasure to be with (Jesus enjoyed that kind of relationship). However, we are also called to love and serve brothers and sisters who are not our natural soulmates in the worldly sense. They are members of the body of Christ, though, so they are Jesus' too, and he is our priority.

Help me to love the family.

CAN IT BE TRUE?

Acts 23:11–15 (NIV)

The following night the Lord stood near Paul and said, 'Take courage! As you have testified about me in Jerusalem, so you must also testify in Rome.' The next morning the Jews formed a conspiracy and bound themselves with an oath not to eat or drink until they had killed Paul. More than 40 men were involved in this plot. They went to the chief priests and elders and said, 'We have taken a solemn oath not to eat anything until we have killed Paul. Now then, you and the Sanhedrin petition the commander to bring him before you on the pretext of wanting more accurate information about his case. We are ready to kill him before he gets here.'

Were these words of encouragement delivered in a dream or was Jesus actually present in the cell with Paul on the night before the Jews formed their conspiracy? These were tense, dramatic days in the setting up of the early Church, weren't they? It is very easy to see the need for visions and dreams that offered advice or encouragement for this man who had been precipitated into something that was to take over his whole life.

When I read about moments such as these, I am sometimes hit—stunned—by the fact that the whole thing is absolutely true. It's true! The whole strange business has happened—is happening. There really is a God who made a world, saw it overcome with evil and had to devise a plan involving his Son to pluck as many as possible from disaster. It's true!

If the British government realized how practically, crucially true it was, it would divert massive resources into a Ministry of Salvation and ensure that far more energy was put into evangelism than into such areas as the defeat of terrorism. The spiritual disaster that looms is much more important, the numbers involved unimaginably more massive, the consequences more unspeakably serious than anything that has ever been reported in the newspapers or on the television.

Let the sheer drama of Paul's adventures enter into your soul and make it shiver, because the drama continues today and we are part of it.

Father, we've lost our sense of urgency. Wake us up to the drama!

FELIX THE FEARFUL

Acts 24:22–26 (NIV)

Then Felix, who was well acquainted with the Way, adjourned the proceedings. 'When Lysias the commander comes,' he said, 'I will decide your case.' He ordered the centurion to keep Paul under guard but to give him some freedom and permit his friends to take care of his needs. Several days later Felix came with his wife Drusilla, who was a Jewess. He sent for Paul and listened to him as he spoke about faith in Christ Jesus. As Paul discoursed on righteousness, self-control and the judgment to come, Felix was afraid and said, 'That's enough for now! You may leave. When I find it convenient I will send for you.' At the same time he was hoping that Paul would offer him a bribe, so he sent for him frequently and talked with him.

This Felix was, by all accounts, a very nasty piece of work—cruel, self-centred and oppressive. Despite being such a cad, however, this passage suggests that he had something in common with the rich young ruler who begged Jesus for the key to eternal life. Jesus clearly thought very highly of that young man, and must have been very distressed when the prospect of separation from his wealth prevented him from actually following the Master. In a way, the same thing is happening with Felix here. There is obviously something fascinating about Paul and his message, but a call for self-control combined with the threat of judgment is too much for the governor of Judea. He hurriedly rids himself of the source of these disturbing ideas, unable to look into the mirror that the apostle is holding up to his blackened soul.

We cannot exclude ourselves from the challenge that is implied here, a challenge that has been facing men and women ever since Jesus began his ministry two thousand years ago. Will we—you, I—willingly give up the thing that defines us and makes us safe if the Master demands it from us? This is a very serious matter, because we cannot follow Jesus if we are not so willing. It will be a different issue for each of us, but the question is always the same.

What is keeping me from you, Lord? Show me and help me.

ALL ROADS LEAD TO ROME

Acts 25:9–12 (NIV)

Festus, wishing to do the Jews a favour, said to Paul, 'Are you willing to go up to Jerusalem and stand trial before me there on these charges?' Paul answered, 'I am now standing before Caesar's court, where I ought to be tried. I have not done any wrong to the Jews, as you yourself know very well. If, however, I am guilty of doing anything deserving death, I do not refuse to die. But if the charges brought against me by these Jews are not true, no one has the right to hand me over to them. I appeal to Caesar!' After Festus had conferred with his council, he declared: 'You have appealed to Caesar. To Caesar you will go!'

Paul knew perfectly well that he would end up in Rome. God had told him so on the night before the Jews formed their conspiracy. He may not have known how it would happen, but his experience of God was that once the word was spoken, it would be fulfilled.

I know the whole experience was a bit nerve-wracking, but it must have been rather fun as well, don't you think? Might it have been a little like being a character in a book that you had opened and read how it all turned out on the last page before going back and starting at the beginning? What a strange thing to see the spiritual outworking and destiny of your life running parallel with the worldly machinations and devices of those who believed that their power over you was absolute.

'To Caesar you will go!' cries Festus, imperiously. Paul must have smiled.

If that makes you a little envious, reflect on the fact that exactly the same is true of you and me. The only difference (for most of us) is that we haven't been allowed to have a peek at the final page of the book of our lives. Perhaps that's just as well: there may be storms ahead. Rest assured, though, that God knows to the final millimetre where you and I are going, and nothing will be allowed to stop us from getting there. We may hit painful times, but we are perfectly safe in our adventure.

Father, thank you for making sure that we arrive where you want us to be.

DEAD OR ALIVE?

Acts 25:18–22 (NIV)

[Festus said] 'When his accusers got up to speak, they did not charge him with any of the crimes I had expected. Instead, they had some points of dispute with him about their own religion and about a dead man named Jesus whom Paul claimed was alive. I was at a loss how to investigate such matters; so I asked if he would be willing to go to Jerusalem and stand trial there on these charges. When Paul made his appeal to be held over for the Emperor's decision, I ordered him to be held until I could send him to Caesar.' Then Agrippa said to Festus, 'I would like to hear this man myself.' He replied, 'Tomorrow you will hear him.'

I wonder if King Agrippa (latest in the bloodstained line of Herods) ever realized how lucky he had been to hear Paul preaching. He lived for another 30 years, but the chance almost certainly never came again. Well, when we get to heaven, we shall know if that one meeting made any real impact, shan't we?

No wonder Festus admitted to being at a loss. Why all this fuss about a dead man called Jesus? He was either dead or alive and, as the records showed that he was dead, there didn't seem much to discuss. In a way, though, that is precisely how the power of God has manifested itself to non-Christians since Jesus came. How can it be, in the present age, for instance, that people profess a passionate, personal love for someone who has been dead and buried for two thousand years? Why do they talk about him as if he was still involved in the everyday affairs of men and women in the 21st century?

Paul knew that Jesus had been raised from the dead. So do I. So, I hope, do you. Without this very personal awareness of the presence of the living Jesus, it is difficult to see how others can respond to him in us. That is why respectable, lifeless churches are not just meaningless, but are actually deeply harmful to the work of the Holy Spirit. They proclaim that Jesus is dead, but he is not—he is very much alive.

Help us to fall in love once more with the living Jesus.

TAKING A CHANCE

Acts 26:24–29 (NIV)

At this point Festus interrupted Paul's defence. 'You are out of your mind, Paul!' he shouted. 'Your great learning is driving you insane.' 'I am not insane, most excellent Festus,' Paul replied. 'What I am saying is true and reasonable. The king is familiar with these things, and I can speak freely to him. I am convinced that none of this has escaped his notice. King Agrippa, do you believe in the prophets? I know you do.' Then Agrippa said to Paul, 'Do you think that in such a short itme you can persuade me to become a Christian?' Paul replied, 'Short time or long—I pray that not only you but all who are listening to me today may become what I am, except for these chains.'

Festus might explode into accusations of madness, but King Agrippa was a Jewish convert and would have been familiar with the aspects of Jewish law and history that Paul so eloquently expounded. Whatever else he thought of the words he was hearing, he must have clearly perceived the logic of Paul's argument.

He had his chance.

His great-uncle Herod had had his chance as well when John the Baptist was imprisoned at his palace. Instead of taking that chance to save his soul, he had ordered John to be beheaded because of a foolish promise to a scheming woman.

Perhaps one of the things that prevented Agrippa (who arrived to meet Festus with Bernice, his sister and mistress) from responding to the gospel was Paul's declaration (v. 22) that he was testifying to small and great alike. Agrippa clearly had a strong sense of his own importance and might have found it difficult to conceive of espousing a religion that allowed no difference in spiritual importance between a slave and a king. Perhaps, also, he felt it due to his dignity to ponder the matter for a much longer period than might be the case with a person of humbler status. Who knows?

There is one thing that we do know, though. He had his chance.

Lord Jesus, may we not regard the worldly rank of those we meet, but fearlessly preach the gospel to all men and women, so that they may have a chance to be with you.

THE SHIP AND THE PLANET

Acts 27:21–25 (NIV)

After the men had gone a long time without food, Paul stood up before them and said: 'Men, you should have taken my advice not to sail from Crete; then you would have spared yourselves this damage and loss. But now I urge you to keep up your courage, because not one of you will be lost; only the ship will be destroyed. Last night an angel of the God whose I am and whom I serve stood beside me and said, "Do not be afraid, Paul. You must stand trial before Caesar; and God has graciously given you the lives of all who sail with you." So keep up your courage, men, for I have faith in God that it will happen just as he told me.'

If you would like to be able to address men and women using the same assurance and authority that Paul used with these tired, hungry, desperate fellows, there is good news and bad news for you.

The good news is that the situation Paul and his shipmates are in is an almost exact parallel to the situation of this planet and all the men and women who sail—or spin—on her. The world is doomed to be wrecked because of separation from the one who created it and it is our privilege to be able to announce that it is not the will of God that a single person should be lost. We know, because of the teaching of Jesus (and, of course, such people as Paul), that a rescue plan is in place, and that individuals can activate it by turning their lives around and placing their trust in Jesus. We need no angel to impart this information to us: it is written in the Bible. However, one very important section of it was not available to Paul, for the very good reason that it did not yet exist and he was in the middle of writing most of it. He needed angels.

The bad news is, of course, that very few people realize that they are in the middle of a potentially fatal storm. We must find the words to explain, and the courage and opportunity to say them.

Father, help us to announce salvation from the wreckage.

PROMISES AND PRIORITIES

Acts 27:31–37 (NIV)

Then Paul said to the centurion and the soldiers, 'Unless these men stay with the ship, you cannot be saved.' So the soldiers cut the ropes that held the lifeboat and let it fall away. Just before dawn Paul urged them all to eat. 'For the last 14 days,' he said, 'you have been in constant suspense and have gone without food—you haven't eaten anything. Now I urge you to take some food. You need it to survive. Not one of you will lose a single hair from his head.' After he said this, he took some bread and gave thanks to God in front of them all. Then he broke it and began to eat. They were all encouraged and ate some food themselves. Altogether there were 276 of us on board.

By now Paul was effectively in command of the ship, wasn't he? How had he impressed these soldiers and sailors to such an extent that they obeyed his commands with no apparent question? I suspect there were two things that gave him the air of authority I mentioned yesterday.

First, he believed God's promise that nobody would be killed and only the ship would be lost. What a truly remarkable position to find yourself in. All around you people are praying and screaming and struggling to stay alive, whereas you, strong in the absolute knowledge that all will be well—knowledge conveyed to you personally by God—are able to remain completely calm. After a time, all eyes and hopes are bound to turn towards a calm point in the centre of confusion.

Second, Paul's priorities were not the same as those of his shipmates. Paul lived for the gospel and for Jesus. I don't suppose for one moment that he relished the prospect of a watery grave, but he knew that the most important part of himself was safe and that if he did perish, it would be within the will of God.

Promises and priorities can change the lives of others through us as well, if we will practise the habit of embracing them.

Father, teach us to trust you and put you first.

MIRACLE AND MISCONCEPTION

Acts 28:2–6 (NIV)

The islanders showed us unusual kindness. They built a fire and welcomed us all because it was raining and cold. Paul gathered a pile of brushwood and, as he put it on the fire, a viper, driven out by the heat, fastened itself on his hand. When the islanders saw the snake hanging from his hand, they said to each other, 'This man must be a murderer; for though he escaped from the sea, Justice has not allowed him to live.' But Paul shook the snake off into the fire and suffered no ill effects. The people expected him to swell up or suddenly fall dead, but after waiting a long time and seeing nothing unusual happen to him, they changed their minds and said he was a god.

For me, there is a pleasant shock about moving from the Gospels to Acts. I love reading the Gospels because there is a great fascination in corkscrewing my way down through the collected memories of those who heard and saw Jesus in search of the man himself. In Acts, I feel I am in the presence of a man with whom I could sit in the corner of a pub and talk about writing. Here is a good example of the detail with which Luke observed events.

It thrills me to know that, all those years ago, Paul, now very much in charge of events, thrashed about in the falling rain, gathering a pile of brushwood for the fire. I can see him doing it, can't you? The man's energy would have worn me out!

The reaction of the islanders to the business of the snake is typical of mobs and congregations. Both their estimates were completely wrong. Paul was not a murderer (not any more) and neither was he a god.

There is a tendency for people to detect extremes of virtue and uselessness in their leaders and to swing from one perception to the other on the basis of relative trivialities. Those who take on the un-enviable task of leading us are human and vulnerable. Respect and support are what they need from us, not snakebites, and especially not in the back.

Gossip and criticism are such fun, Lord. Help us to not do it.

PAUL'S PASSION

Acts 28:24–28 (NIV)

Some were convinced by what he said, but others would not believe. They disagreed among themselves and began to leave after Paul had made this final statement: 'The Holy Spirit spoke the truth to your forefathers when he said through Isaiah the prophet: "Go to this people and say, 'You will be ever hearing but never understanding; you will be ever seeing but never perceiving.' For this people's heart has become calloused; they hardly hear with their ears, and they have closed their eyes. Otherwise they might see with their eyes, hear with their ears, understand with their hearts and turn, and I would heal them." Therefore I want you to know that God's salvation has been sent to the Gentiles, and they will listen!'

How would Paul fit with the modern generation of evanglists? In some ways, well, I think. Most evangelists I have known are single-minded, stubborn, lovable, occasionally bad-tempered, alternately proud and humble, sure that they are right, worried that they are wrong and partial to late-night curries. Leaving aside the curries (maybe he'd have loved them), I think Paul had something of all those qualities.

Would he, though, have been troubled by modern tendencies to elasticate the walls of acceptance in order to admit anyone with the slightest inclination towards faith? I'm reminded of the swimming certificates my children used to earn. I seem to recall a 'Getting up in the morning, thinking I might go for a swim, then changing my mind and going back to sleep' badge.

Paul's passion was winning souls for Christ but, as this passage shows, he was not going to dilute the medicine for anyone, not even if it resulted in them turning away.

The modern Church has drifted from the teachings of Jesus on cost. This is an age of credit and deposits and value for money. We are, quite laudably, at pains to present an attractive Church, but Christianity is really about the claim of God on our hearts and the path he has created through Jesus to allow us to return to him. It costs everything that we have and are. We could do with another Paul.

Father, may we offer the gospel, simple and unsullied, to those who need it.

Woe to him that claims obedience when it is not due; woe to him that refuses it when it is!

THOMAS CARLYLE

OBEDIENCE—AIMING FOR THE PLANNED DESTINATION

THE STICKY, SULKY, SALUTARY STORY OF JONAH

Just about every discussion I've ever had about the authority of scripture (and we've had some crackers around our kitchen table, I can tell you!) has, at some point, concerned itself with either Job or Jonah, or both. Why? Well, I'm no biblical historian, but I gather that these two wonderful accounts of the dealings of God with man are, to the objective and knowledgeable eye, clear examples of a particular type of contemporary storytelling.

I shall never forget the outrage I felt at the age of 18 or 19 when a close Christian friend of mine went away to study theology, and, returning after his first term, announced, with the calm insouciance that so often accompanies newly acquired knowledge, that Jonah was a 'typical Jewish folk tale'. Time to bring in the Spanish Inquisition! How could he have been so corrupted in such a short time? After all, he knew as well as I did, because we'd been taught it at the church youth group, that every last semicolon in the Bible had been installed carefully into scripture by God himself, and that the whole edifice of our belief in that fact would have to be condemned and demolished if one small brick was found to be faulty. The curate had said so, for goodness' sake! So necessary was it for us to feel sure in those early days, that we preferred to wear such 'certainties' like ill-fitting uniforms, rather than face the chill of a difficult world with the scanty, individual rags of honest enquiry and constructive doubt. At the time, my friend's statement sounded like the worst kind of heresy.

Nowadays, of course, I know that God may admit into heaven even those who, when asked about doctrine, suggest that it might be 'what they do up at the health centre'. He is mainly concerned with heart and relationship. In any case, we grow into some of those badly fitting clothes as the years go by, don't we?

What is my view of scripture today? Forgive me if I repeat myself, but it does seem very important to make this plain. I regard the Bible as a letter from God to me. He has personally supervised every aspect of its contents, and there is nothing in it that should not be there. It includes every kind of writing that you can imagine, including poetry, history, storytelling, prophecy and teaching. This long letter begins with 'Dear Adrian' and ends 'Love, God', and I am very grateful for it.

As for the book of Jonah in particular, it is without doubt one of the most entertaining narratives in the Bible, and, frankly, it doesn't matter a jot to me whether it describes a historical event or not, because, like the parables of Jesus (are they true?), it contains so much information and truth about God and man that I am quite sure the Holy Spirit inspired its inclusion in the Old Testament.

So what does this authoritative piece of scripture have to say to us? Perhaps the major theme of the book is obedience, a feature of Christian living that Jesus returned to again and again. I find obedience extremely difficult, not least because it is in the (apparently) small things that God challenges us most directly and intrusively. OK, I know people often say that sort of thing about small things, but I really mean it. Let us suppose that the phone were to go right now, even as I was typing these words, and someone from America or Africa or Australia asked if it was possible for me to drop everything and fly out immediately to speak to five thousand people. I would find it much easier, in the most important sense, to be obedient to that sort of call, assuming it was from God as well as from some frantic organizer, than to adapt my normal responses in a purely domestic situation.

Only last night (you're going to think this sounds so daft) I was in the kitchen doing something or other, and I said to myself, 'I think I'll have a cup of tea.' The only other person in the house was one of my teenage sons, who was watching television in the sitting room. He and I usually get on very well, but that day we'd had a pretty stormy row and I wasn't feeling very charitably disposed towards him. We hadn't spoken for a couple of hours. As I filled the kettle and put a teabag into my cup it occurred to me that the most generous—and helpful—thing I could do, would be to offer him a cup of tea as well. But I didn't want to. Why should I? He hadn't been very reasonable with me earlier on. Why should I make him a cup of tea? Let him make his own cup of tea. After all, it wasn't as if he'd even know I'd made myself a cup of tea without offering him one, because I'd drink it in the kitchen. So, there!

It's at times like this that being a Christian is so very annoying and so very rewarding. My son wouldn't know, but God's Son would. It was an opportunity to begin the peace-making process, and I could either take advantage of it or waste it. I made a second cup of tea, and suddenly we were talking again.

I know that sounds like a trivial little incident, but the fact is that genuine change in behaviour and attitudes, as opposed to the theoretical total transformation that we are sometimes promised by certain sections of the Church, usually grows in the good soil of moral self-confidence resulting from these tiny experiences of victory in obedience. God is very clever, you know.

It was rather similar for Evie, a lady I met in South Africa, who worked as a housemaid for a Christian doctor friend of mine called Jane. Jane often talked to Evie about Jesus, and eventually Evie herself became a believer. Asked what difference being a Christian had made to her life, she replied that she now dusted the space behind the furniture as well as the bits you could see, because, whereas Jane didn't often check those hidden places, the Lord always did, and he demanded her obedience in such things.

I would like briefly to mention two other important things about the Jonah story.

First, Jesus used it as a picture or parallel of his own death and resurrection, hence the connections with the Easter story that I have made in some of the notes.

Secondly, the story offers us a quite fascinating and challenging insight into what is possible in terms of a relationship between God and one of his people.

I promise you, there is much to learn from dear old Jonah.

Prayer
Father, may we have a whale of a time with Jonah.

WHERE NOW?

Jonah 1:1–2 (RSV)

Now the word of the Lord came to Jonah the son of Amittai, saying, 'Arise, go to Nineveh, that great city, and cry against it; for their wickedness has come up before me.'

When I became a Christian, in the 1960s, guidance was one of the items included in a sort of invisible evangelical kit-bag that was issued to all new recruits. From in front or from behind (depending on which scripture was quoted) God would direct every step that we took. We would always know where to go and what to do because he would tell us.

I can't speak for others, but this subtle misteaching left me frequently paralysed (when God seemed to be saying nothing) and sometimes neurotic and twitchy (when a random thought invaded my mind). Did the Lord really want me to get a train to Walsall and give a blue cardigan to the first person that I met?

It was during this period that a friend told me he was being led to work in the Holy Land because every time he opened his Bible he found a reference to Israel.

It is precisely because the Holy Spirit does guide people clearly and specifically when necessary that we need to avoid the rather superstitious view of God's leading that prevails in many parts of the Church.

God's communication system is not based on some mouldy old hand-operated printer that produces documents too fuzzy to read. If he speaks to you—you'll know it!

Paul the apostle is a good model. He prayed constantly, made common-sense decisions, and was always ready to change his plans when a dream or a vision or a direct word from God told him he'd got it wrong.

Of course God is concerned with every step we take, but we're not involved in some ghastly spiritual version of *Come Dancing*. Jonah knew exactly what God wanted him to do. That's why he cleared off. On Palm Sunday Jesus knew exactly what God wanted as well. He didn't clear off, though. He entered Jerusalem knowing that death was inevitable.

Lord, help me to stay close to you in prayer and study, so that our relationship affects all the decisions that I make. I trust that I will hear you clearly and specifically when necessary.

NOT MY WILL...

Jonah 1:3 (RSV)

But Jonah rose to flee to Tarshish from the presence of the Lord. He went down to Joppa and found a ship going to Tarshish; so he paid the fare, and went on board, to go with them to Tarshish, away from the presence of the Lord.

I wonder what Jonah did when he was not out being a prophet? Perhaps there was a sign over his door saying: AMITTAI AND SON— STICK WHITTLERS. Every now and then, as Jonah sat happily at home, whistling through his teeth and doing a spot of bespoke whittling, the Spirit of God would whisper in his ear and his heart would sink as he realized that it was time to move into prophet mode once again. Why had he got so fed up with it? What was the reason for his deliberate act of disobedience when he was told to go to Nineveh? We can't be sure—but we can guess.

My guess is that his lack of enthusiasm dated from the time when he began to realize that he would never be anything more than a messenger. It would have been quite exciting at first—rather exhilarating. How powerful it must have felt to threaten the enemies of Israel with the hammer of God as a consequence of their evil ways. Perhaps the first one or two failed to repent and suffered destruction as a result.

Then (as far as Jonah was concerned, anyway) the rot began to set in. Following the prophet's impressive forecast of doom and gloom, people repented, and Jonah began to sense that the God whose message he had delivered much preferred to forgive sinners. I guess Jonah felt a bit of a twit when this happened. All that ranting he'd done, and now God had changed his mind. Very hard to walk away keeping your back view dignified in those circumstances.

Unlike Clark Kent and Bruce Wayne, Jonah was not at all keen to don his super-prophet costume, not if he was going to end up feeling an idiot yet again.

God reserves the right to follow up our obedience in any way that seems fit. If we don't like it we can try to run away, but, as Jonah was about to discover, that doesn't always work.

Am I willing to have my cake but give up the right to eat it?

TROUBLE FOR OTHERS

Jonah 1:4–6 (RSV)

But the Lord hurled a great wind upon the sea, and there was a mighty tempest on the sea, so that the ship threatened to break up. Then the mariners were afraid, and each cried to his god; and they threw the wares that were in the ship into the sea, to lighten it for them. But Jonah had gone down into the inner part of the ship and had lain down, and was fast asleep. So the captain came and said to him, 'What do you mean, you sleeper? Arise, call upon your god! Perhaps the god will give a thought to us, that we do not perish.'

I find these verses a little disturbing. If I weren't doing these notes for you I'd skip this bit and go on to something more comfortable. Can it really be true that my disobedience could cause a whole lot of trouble for folk who've done nothing wrong? Honesty compels me to admit that I know it to be true in my own life. I haven't gone down to New-haven and taken ship to Dieppe to flee the will of God recently, but I have quite deliberately failed to tackle problems, heal relationships or perform tasks that should be top priorities in my life. The innocent fellow-travellers who suffer as a result are usually members of my family. Guilt makes me grumpy. Failure makes me fret. I become a little cloud, inflicting bad weather on my small part of the world.

In this account the little cloud called Jonah is lying, like a baby in its womb, down in the depths of the ship, hoping perhaps to hide in unconsciousness as so many of us do when we feel like fugitives.

What an awakening! The sensation of being dragged violently back into reality must have been dreadful—it always is. The fear and panic in the captain's voice, the sounds and movements of the storm, and the inescapable knowledge that God had taken the situation by the scruff of the neck and was shaking it until his disobedient servant fell out— all these things must have combined to become a waking nightmare for the prophet. The crew had dumped the cargo, a multi-faith prayer meeting had been held, everyone was quite terrified, and it was all Jonah's fault!

Will I do what I'm told at last?

OWNING UP

Jonah 1:8–9 (RSV)

Then they said to him, 'Tell us, on whose account this evil has come upon us. What is your occupation? And whence do you come? What is your country? And of what people are you?' And he said to them, 'I am a Hebrew; and I fear the Lord, the God of heaven, who made the sea and the dry land.'

Isn't it difficult to own up sometimes? When I was about nine years old my father made a bow and arrow for myself and my brother, Ian, who was two years younger than me. He spent hours hunting in the woods for the right—absolutely straight—lengths of hazel, and then sat outside the shed on our allotment, trimming, cutting, tying, sharpening, and fashioning flights out of cardboard. Ian and I tried the weapon out. It worked marvellously. Later that day, when no one else was around, I did what I'd been wanting to do ever since I saw the completed implements. I fired the arrow as far as I possibly could. It was inexpressibly wonderful to draw back the string and feel the potential power in that strong, flexible length of hazel. When I released the arrow, it flew in a majestically huge and regular arc, curving up towards the sun, and curving down into a thick and impenetrable mass of undergrowth. That beautiful arrow was lost. I didn't tell anyone.

For some reason my father got it into his head that it was Ian who had lost the arrow. When I got to the allotment next morning Ian was in tears, and my father was angrily trying to make him confess. A block of ice gripped my heart as the crying and shouting escalated. Words crouched miserably just inside my mouth, too frightened to come out. Then my brother was clipped round the ear and I couldn't stand it any more. The smallest voice you ever heard in your life said, 'Dad, it wasn't Ian who lost the arrow, it was me.'

My father had used up all his anger on Ian, so I didn't get shouted at, but the ice took a long time to melt.

Poor old Jonah. Poor old Ian.

Lord, if there are things lodged in our hearts that chill us when we remember them, give us the courage to confess to the right person at the right time.

OVERBOARD

Jonah 1:12–15 (RSV)

He said to them, 'Take me up and throw me into the sea; then the sea will quiet down for you; for I know it is because of me that this great tempest has come upon you.' Nevertheless the men rowed hard to bring the ship back to land, but they could not, for the sea grew more and more tempestuous against them... So they took up Jonah and threw him into the sea; and the sea ceased from its raging.

This is a very heart-warming story, don't you think? I like the sound of the fellows on this ship. The whole of their profits had gone overboard with the cargo, they'd been buffeted and terrified by an appalling storm, but they still tried as hard as they could to avoid throwing the author of their misfortunes into the sea. Of course, they must have been a little puzzled. Did this powerful, weather controlling God really want them to throw his prophet into the ocean? Wouldn't he be angry with them? They failed to understand, just as Peter failed to understand when he provoked the famous 'Get thee behind me, Satan' speech from his master, that, in the context of God's planning and special knowledge, negative events and circumstances are sometimes essential. As we think about Jesus' horrendous death on the cross, this central truth becomes very evident, but enlightenment usually comes only by hindsight.

I got thrown overboard when illness left me with no job, no church, and no prospects. If you had suggested to me then that this was all part of God's plan for me I would have gone for your throat. I guess that as Jonah travelled the short distance from the ship's rail to the boiling sea, he must have reflected that he had known better days. But he knew God better than I did when my crisis happened. I don't doubt that he was very frightened, but there is a sort of wry awareness in his brave assertion that the tempest would abate if the sailors threw him over the side.

'Maybe I'm going to drown,' he might have said to himself as he hit the water, 'but I have an awful feeling that I'm going to Nineveh...'

We are not really capable of assessing the divine perspective on any situation or circumstance. Perhaps its more useful to develop trust and obedience than insight.

THE SCREAMING MOMENT

Jonah 1:17—2:3 (RSV)

And the Lord appointed a great fish to swallow up Jonah; and Jonah was in the belly of the fish three days and three nights. Then Jonah prayed to the Lord his God from the belly of the fish, saying, 'I called to the Lord, out of my distress, and he answered me; out of the belly of Sheol I cried, and thou didst hear my voice. For thou didst cast me into the deep, into the heart of the seas, and the flood was round about me; all thy waves and thy billows passed over me.'

When the scribes and Pharisees asked Jesus for a sign, he told them that the only sign they'd be given was the sign of the prophet Jonah.

On the day that we call Good Friday, Jesus allowed us to 'throw him overboard' so that the storm of God's displeasure would not destroy us. He spent three days in a place that was far darker and more dismal than the belly of a whale. From the cross he cried out his desolation and anguish to his Father, whose back was turned on his son for that one screaming moment in eternity. Unlike Jonah, Jesus was innocent. He went where he was told, said what he was told, and died when he was told.

I have to say that I don't understand the crucifixion. I accept that this is more a measure of my understanding than a comment on the crucifixion, but I suspect that many others will identify with my lack of comprehension. I don't mean that I can't see the basic logic of somebody taking the blame and being punished for what I have done and not done; nor am I saying that I don't accept or appreciate the power of what Jesus did. How could I? The wordless truth and significance of the cross is in my bones, and in the bones of every suffering body or situation that ever was. I think I mean that there is a great mystery enshrouding that strange, cosmic event, and that I prefer the mystery to half-baked, glib explanations of what was going on.

What about Jonah? I wonder if he knew what this dark, wet, heaving environment was. We shall never know for certain, but one thing's clear enough from the prophet's impassioned prayer—there's nothing like being swallowed by a whale to stimulate revival!

Thank you so much, Jesus, for being obedient.

RAGING AT GOD

Jonah 2:5–6 (RSV)

'The waters closed in over me, the deep was round about me; weeds were wrapped about my head at the roots of the mountains. I went down to the land whose bars closed upon me for ever; yet thou didst bring up my life from the Pit, O Lord my God.'

I sometimes find myself thinking rather dark thoughts, especially on the day before Easter Sunday. When I read these words of Jonah, spoken from the belly of the whale, I suddenly remembered that horrible incident (widely covered by the media at the time) when a young Italian boy was trapped at the bottom of a disused well. Attempts to rescue the poor lad went on for days with the whole world watching via newspapers and television. Everywhere people prayed that he would be brought up alive from the pit. But he wasn't. He died at the bottom of the well while his mother wept at the top.

I raged at God. I hated God. I told God what I thought of his weakness or his cruelty or whatever it was that prevented him from doing something so obvious, especially in the face of such a barrage of prayer from every corner of the globe.

'You must have seen him!' I raved. 'How could you watch him go through that and not do anything about it? How? Tell me!'

I won't bother trotting out the statutory answers to these questions. I know them. I've used them when others have asked me about such things, and they're not really satisfactory. Two things help me.

First, the God I meet through Jesus weeps and hurts and cares and loves. I've grown to trust him despite getting so angry with him. That isn't an answer—it's a relationship.

Secondly, I take heart from the experience of the disciples on the night following Jesus' death. I believe that they too must have raged at God, unable to believe that he could have allowed such a cruel, pointless, waste of a life that had so much to offer. How could a loving Father stand by and watch as his Son was nailed to a piece of wood between two criminal scum? What a mess! What a waste! What a dark night of tears. Nothing would ever mean anything again.

Then came the dawn.

Hold my hand, Lord, it's dark.

SOLID GROUND

Jonah 2:10 (RSV)

And the Lord spoke to the fish, and it vomited out Jonah upon the dry land.

As soon as God had had a chat with this very cooperative whale the creature obligingly deposited Jonah on dry land, and, for the first time since leaving Joppa harbour, the prophet felt solid ground beneath his feet.

This is what Easter is all about. Until Jesus rose quietly but triumphantly from the dead, the world was an island in creation that sank beneath the feet of every man and woman as soon as their mortal bodies became too old to function. The resurrection redefined solid ground. Now, death is no longer relevant, because we can be admitted into the true reality of eternal life with Jesus in the place where he lives with his Father. As soon as death had been overcome, a return to Eden—spiritual and physical—became possible.

All that and chocolate eggs as well!

I've rarely been able to celebrate Easter on Easter Day, but I do celebrate it on all those occasions when, like Jonah, I am rescued yet again from some whale of a problem that is about to digest me into nothingness. I know I am saved once and for all, but every now and then the resurrection principle acts as a structure within my confusion and I know I'm saved all over again.

One of the few occasions when my mood matched the day was an Easter Sunday when I attended the morning service in Norwich Cathedral, one of my all-time favourite buildings. It was one of those incomparable spring mornings full of rippling light and hope. The place was packed, the singing was wonderful, and the prayers seemed to buzz and resonate with the will of God. The deep bass note of tradition and the high and beautiful living presence of the Holy Spirit made my heart soar. Tears filled my eyes and I, who have almost never raised my arms in worship in the most informal situations, suddenly wanted to thrust my open hands as high into the air as they would go in the middle of a formal Anglican cathedral service. I didn't. I wish I had done. I was an Easter chicken. I bet, if the truth were told, there was a whole flock of us there that day.

Thank you for setting our feet on the mainland. May Easter be always in us.

COMPLETING THE LOOP

Jonah 3:1–2 (RSV)

Then the word of the Lord came to Jonah the second time, saying, 'Arise, go to Nineveh, that great city, and proclaim to it the message that I tell you.'

Poor old Jonah! If he had gone to Nineveh when he was first told to, he wouldn't have ended up in the mess he found himself in and having to hear God give him exactly the same order as before. The prophet's personal rebellion had been nipped in the bud before it had the chance to get going. No doubt he was relieved and grateful to be saved from a blubbery death, but as he squelched off in the direction of this strong-hold of the national enemy, all the old misgivings must have fallen over him like a shadow.

But how thankful we should be that God does organize and allow these 'loops' in our lives. Have you done a loop? I have. On at least one occasion in my life I have deliberately taken a direction that is opposed to the will of God. One day I shall write a book with the title *Life in the Loops*. These little drifts and diversions are almost always interesting (ask Jonah!) but they become progressively more hollow, unsatisfying, or just plain dangerous—more dangerous, indeed, than those things that the world fears most. I don't know if Jonah really believed that he could escape God by changing his geographical position, but a greater and more horribly permanent fate would have resulted from real separation from the creator.

Yes, the good news is that God will sort our mistakes and wrong turnings out. He would never have taken us on in the first place if he wasn't prepared to cope with the inevitable dips in our behaviour and response. (Most of the prophets were temperamental, awkward, passionate people who wouldn't last two minutes in most of our modern churches.)

The bad news is that the job we've been given doesn't change. As far as God is concerned, completing the loop means 'business as usual'.

Off to Nineveh!

Thank you, Lord, that you rebuke us when we get in a mess, but that you don't give up on us.

INTO ACTION

Jonah 3:3–4

So Jonah arose and went to Nineveh, according to the word of the Lord. Now Nineveh was an exceedingly great city, three days' journey in breadth. Jonah began to go into the city, going a day's journey. And he cried, 'Yet forty days, and Nineveh shall be overthrown.'

Do you get the impression, as I do, that Jonah slipped straight into top prophesying gear as soon as he actually reached Nineveh? Prophets and evangelists are like that in my experience. They may moan or complain or even become sullenly uncommunicative at times (modern ones as well as Old Testament ones) but as soon as they start to do what they are called and born to do there's no stopping them. A sort of spiritual professionalism takes over. Vanity and vulnerability take a back seat as God drives his message into the listeners. I'm quite sure that Jonah's warning to the citizens of Nineveh was not even slightly diluted by his reluctance to be there. His 'ministry' was part of him, which is more than can be said for many of us.

I know at least two people who have spent most of their lives denying (or trying to deny) a part of themselves that God has almost certainly been wanting to use for years. One of them is a very talented artist who, when he became a Christian more than 30 years ago allowed the climate of Christian disapproval that befogged art at the time to dissuade him from continuing with his career as a painter. He has recovered from this foolishness now, but many years were wasted as he tried to pretend that this essential part of him had been painlessly amputated, and that he didn't care. God cared. If Jonah had been ordered to paint pictures he would have been wasting his time at Nineveh.

My other friend is a musician—a cellist. This chap has wanted to 'do something for the Lord' for ages. He gets quite depressed when things don't seem to work out. He's just beginning to realize—with some amazement—that what the Lord wants is some really good cello-playing, and not just 'Christian stuff'.

Painting, prophesying or playing the cello—whatever is right is all right.

Are we doing what we are?

AND THE POWER OF FEAR

Jonah 3:5–9 (RSV)

And the people of Nineveh believed God; they proclaimed a fast, and put on sackcloth, from the greatest of them to the least of them. Then tidings reached the king of Nineveh, and he arose from his throne, removed his robe, and covered himself with sackcloth, and sat in ashes. And he made proclamation and published through Nineveh, 'By the decree of the king and his nobles: Let neither man nor beast, herd nor flock, taste anything; let them not feed, or drink water, but let man and beast be covered with sackcloth, and let them cry mightily to God; yea, let every one turn from his evil way and from the violence which is in his hands. Who knows, God may yet repent and turn from his fierce anger, so that we perish not?'

How could one disobedient little prophet have such a dynamic effect on such a huge community? In scale and depth of response this mission of Jonah's makes a Billy Graham rally look like a Quaker meeting in a telephone box. How did he do it? Well, first of all, of course, he didn't do it. His threat of destruction after 40 days carried the authority and authenticity of the Holy Spirit, yet another lesson for all of us that it is both pointless and perilous to claim that we speak for God when we are only guessing.

Secondly, and precisely because the prophecy was so convincing, the citizens of Nineveh were clearly terrified. Modern evangelism tends to major on the attractiveness of God's love for us, and the logical desirability of being reunited with our creator, and we need those emphases to counteract the influence of the Pharisees who surround us, but fear has a long and respectable pedigree in the history of God's dealings with men and women. Why? Quite simply because God knows that for those who do not belong to him there is a lot to be frightened of. If someone whom you love is in danger you warn them, and you hope against hope that they will save themselves.

The people of this city threw themselves into repentance wholeheartedly, inspired and commanded by their king, who ordered a suspension of all normal activities while everybody turned to God.

This kind of head–heart–body repentance is rare today. Why?

UNLESS YOU BECOME...

Jonah 3:10 (RSV)

When God saw what they did, how they turned from their evil way, God repented of the evil which he had said he would do to them, and he did not do it.

In a magazine article, my wife described an occasion when, after working in Germany for a few days, I flew into Heathrow, arriving at about 7 o'clock in the evening. Bridget drove up to meet me, bringing our two younger sons with her. Joseph, aged twelve, and David, aged eleven, knew how much I would be looking forward to seeing them. They pushed to the front of the waiting crowds so that their shining faces would be the first thing I saw as I came out of the green channel with my luggage. It was such a pleasure for me to see them there.

The God who so freely forgave these Assyrian penitents, and who describes himself through Jesus as a Father, takes a similar pleasure in our confident awareness that he wants to see us. Not because we have earned his affection, nor for any other motives of personal pride, but because, like Joe and David at the airport, we know that he loves us with a passion that is graphically illustrated in the story of the prodigal son. Let's not get smug about the rotten old sinners in Nineveh. We all need to go through the repentance door if we want to be hugged by God.

What sort of door is the repentance door? I found a clue once. A few miles along the coast from us there's a place called Jungle Tumble. It's a highly coloured maze of tunnels, ladders, netting and plastic balls— a little paradise for children who want to enjoy the ecstasy of physical abandonment. When Katy was four and David was eleven we visited this place that we'd heard so much about. On arriving we discovered that only children under a certain fixed height were allowed. Katy was little enough. David was too big. What to do? Fortunately the lady in charge invited David to duck his head under the bar. 'Look,' she said, 'now you're small enough!'

We bow our heads and become a bit smaller before we enter joy.

Chesterton said, 'A man is never so tall as when he bows.'

GETTING CROSS WITH GOD

Jonah 4:1–3 (RSV)

But it displeased Jonah exceedingly, and he was angry. And he prayed to the Lord and said, 'I pray thee, Lord, is not this what I said when I was yet in my country? That is why I made haste to flee to Tarshish; for I knew that thou art a gracious God and merciful, slow to anger, and abounding in steadfast love, and repentest of evil. Therefore now, O Lord, take my life from me, I beseech thee, for it is better for me to die than to live.'

Well, who's an angry little prophet, then? Jonah is very bold with God, isn't he? Mind you, he must have known him very well. It reminds me of the way one of my sons used to respond to being told off when he was very small. After a minute or two of my parental raging he would look me in the eye and say triumphantly, 'Anyway, you love me, so you'll be nice to me in a minute...' I wouldn't recommend that as a way of responding to the wrath of God, but I'm glad David knew I loved him, and I find the interchange between Jonah and God a refreshingly real and familiar one. The prophet is doing a real Basil Fawlty here, furious that God has done exactly what he feared he would do. He's forgiven them! Huh!

It's interesting to note that God did not insist on Jonah sharing his intention or motivation as far as Nineveh was concerned. He simply wanted him to do as he was told. Jesus made exactly the same point in his parable of the two sons. One said he would do what was asked of him, but didn't. The other got stroppy and refused to obey, but then went and did what he'd been told. Similarly, when Jesus called Zacchaeus down from his tree, the little man wasn't required to sort his attitudes and behaviour out before nipping home to sort a meal out. Again and again throughout scripture the same point is made. Those who love God are those who obey him.

Now it was time for Jonah's little attitude problem to be sorted out.

Do I trust God enough to get cross with him? Do I love him enough to obey him?

THE INCREDIBLE SULK

Jonah 4:4–5 (RSV)

And the Lord said, 'Do you do well to be angry?' Then Jonah went out of the city and sat to the east of the city, and made a booth for himself there. He sat under it in the shade, till he should see what would become of the city.

I really like God in this story. I don't like him in all the Old Testament accounts, particularly the bits where mass killings are ordered, but I shall understand what that was all about one day. The thing I like in this story is that, having shown such compassion and taken such trouble with the enormous community at Nineveh, God now concentrates on one confused individual—Jonah.

If the prodigal son's elder brother is the heavyweight sulking champion of the New Testament, Jonah must be a front-line candidate in the Old. There he sits on the hillside, probably muttering about Joppa and ships and storms and whales and people not doing what they say they're going to do...

God tries to talk to him about it, but it seems that Jonah is one of those people who just can't understand anything without concrete examples or visible object lessons. The whale was the first and most dramatic one, but now it was time for something a little more agricultural. It has been most refreshing over the last few years to find that God does not have a set of unvarying procedures that he applies to anyone who comes within his orbit. In my own case, for instance, there have been times when my rather negative expectations led me to predict a divine clip round the ear as a response to less than wonderful behaviour. In fact, because he knows and loves me, God has used encouragement and humour to lift me out of my lower self. Mind you, when the aforesaid clip round the ear is necessary he doesn't seem to have any qualms about applying it, and that's as it should be, even if I don't like it much at the time.

Jonah and you and I may be very different in outlook and personality, but don't worry—although we shall all finish up in the same place, a very individual and carefully designed route has been prepared for each of us.

Thank you, Father, for loving me as an individual and planning things specially for me.

THE FINAL LESSON

Jonah 4:6–11 (RSV)

And the Lord God appointed a plant, and made it come up over Jonah that it might be a shade over his head, to save him from his discomfort. So Jonah was exceedingly glad because of the plant. But when dawn came up the next day, God appointed a worm which attacked the plant, so that it withered. When the sun rose, God appointed a sultry east wind, and the sun beat upon the head of Jonah so that he was faint; and he asked that he might die, and said, 'It is better for me to die than to live.' But God said to Jonah, 'Do you do well to be angry for the plant?' And he said, 'I do well to be angry, angry enough to die.' And the Lord said, 'You pity the plant, for which you did not labour, nor did you make it grow, which came into being in a night, and perished in a night. And should not I pity Nineveh, that great city, in which there are more than a hundred and twenty thousand persons who do not know their right hand from their left, and also much cattle?'

My sulks are fairly fragile. If someone tickles me or says something absurd, my glum expression is likely to crack, and once I've smiled my sulk is usually ruined. Jonah, on the other hand, is so determined not to give an inch to God that he walks straight into the logical trap that is set for him. The writer of this book fails to record the prophet's response to the final, telling argument that 120 thousand people must be as important as a plant, but I have no doubt that Jonah got the point. Perhaps the mention of cattle swung it in the end. A real waste!

A sad footnote to this story, recorded a few pages further on in the Old Testament in the book of Nahum, is that the people of Nineveh learned very little from their great deliverance. As far as we can tell they returned to their sins and were destroyed.

Jonah teaches us that obedience is essential; that God would rather forgive than punish; that he takes as much trouble with individuals as whole communities; and that he can be very humorous and nice.

Do I share these attributes of God?

BACK TO THE ETERNAL STARTING PLACE?

MATTHEW 1 AND 2

Christmas laughs at you when you try to write about it.

'Oh no, not you as well!' it cackles. 'Surely you can't fail to be aware that everyone, from the best to the worst, has been scratching their heads and snapping their pencils over me for the last two thousand years. I've been uglified, prettified, used up, pulled to pieces and scraped out. So why don't you do yourself a favour and write about something easy, like—well, how about predestination and free will?'

'Ah, but,' I protest feebly, 'I'm not planning to write about Christmas as such, but the first two chapters of Matthew.'

'Oh, I see. The first two chapters of Matthew being almost exclusively concerned with what, may I ask?'

'Well, events around Christmas, but the thing is—the thing is…'

I run out of dialogue. I can't think what the thing is. What is the thing? Is there a thing—a less-than-tediously-familiar thing buried somewhere underneath the rockfall of history and tradition? After all, when you think about it, the Christmas story doesn't really have much to do with Christmas, does it? It was cold and difficult and dangerous and—well, as ordinary as it was strange.

Ordinary and strange. Mmm. Maybe that's the thing. Let's have a look.

SPONTANEOUS, YET PLANNED

Matthew 1:12–17 (NIV)

After the exile to Babylon: Jeconiah was the father of Shealtiel, Shealtiel the father of Zerubbabel, Zerubbabel the father of Abiud, Abiud the father of Eliakim, Eliakim the father of Azor, Azor the father of Zadok, Zadok the father of Akim, Akim the father of Eliud, Eliud the father of Eleazar, Eleazar the father of Matthan, Matthan the father of Jacob, and Jacob the father of Joseph, the husband of Mary, of whom was born Jesus, who is called Christ. Thus there were fourteen generations in all from Abraham to David, fourteen from David to the exile to Babylon, and fourteen from the exile to the Christ.

I left out the first eleven verses of the genealogy to avoid anyone getting too hysterically excited this close to Christmas. Thirty-five theologians will now write to tell me just how electrifyingly interesting these things actually are when you know something about them. I should have learnt my lesson about making flippant remarks by now, shouldn't I?

I haven't. I was down at a church in Devon last year to preach on the feeding of the five thousand. Just before my slot, the vicar got up to do a little piece from the front. He had brought along several different types of bread and was holding them up one by one for the congregation to look at. 'Now,' he enquired brightly, picking up a long French loaf, 'can anyone tell me what we call this kind of bread?'

Misguided inspiration struck. 'Yes,' I said, from my place on the front row, 'isn't it the same as the word they use in genealogies in French Bibles?'

An expectant silence fell. The vicar raised his eyebrows. 'The word they use in…?'

'Yes, you know—Boaz baguette Obed, and Obed baguette Jesse, and Jesse baguette David, and David baguette Solomon, and so on…'

Thin laughter. I die a little.

There is one serious point that might be made by an ignoramus like me. It is simply that this genealogy points up a fascinating tension between detailed plans and prophecies devised and given by God and the dynamically vibrant, patently spontaneous events of the Gospels and the book of Acts. I'm afraid we are unlikely to solve that paradox this side of heaven.

Father, thank you for letting Jesus join the list at exactly the right time.

A REMARKABLE MAN

Matthew 1:18-21 (NIV)

This is how the birth of Jesus Christ came about: His mother Mary was pledged to be married to Joseph, but before they came together, she was found to be with child through the Holy Spirit. Because Joseph her husband was a righteous man and did not want to expose her to public disgrace, he had in mind to divorce her quietly. But after he had considered this, an angel of the Lord appeared to him in a dream and said, 'Joseph son of David, do not be afraid to take Mary home as your wife, because what is conceived in her is from the Holy Spirit. She will give birth to a son, and you are to give him the name Jesus, because he will save his people from their sins.'

Fascinated by the silently powerful presence of Mary in the Gospels, I have tended to neglect Joseph.

No one would have taken on Joseph's task if its pain-filled future prospects had been revealed in advance. God scanned eons of human history to find one woman suitable to bear his Son, but what about the crucial issue of fathering him? The right man needed exceptional personal qualities as well as being contemporary with Mary and a descendant of David. God was very fortunate—all right, very clever: Joseph was the perfect choice. He was heartbroken at first, of course, that the girl promised to him had somehow got herself pregnant. Disappointment and anger vanquish compassion in many, but not in Joseph. He decided to protect her from public disgrace. He was a good man.

Joseph's situation reflects the generosity of God's dealings with us. He was wholeheartedly to accept a child with whom he had no bio-logical connection—more, to accept that Jesus' lineage was claimed through his adoptive father's line as if they were blood relatives. Similarly, we are invited to become adopted children of God, despite the chasm of sin between Creator and creation. By accepting, we join the bloodline of God's family as if we had always been his natural children, and are therefore heirs with Jesus to all that heaven offers.

The angel told Joseph that this embryonic acquisition, this Jesus, was the Saviour of the world. A huge responsibility to take on. Joseph must have been a remarkable man.

I'm so glad Mary and Joseph had each other.

THE PEARL AND THE PARCEL

Matthew 1:22–25 (NIV)

All this took place to fulfil what the Lord had said through the prophet: 'The virgin will be with child and will give birth to a son, and they will call him Immanuel'—which means, 'God with us.' When Joseph woke up, he did what the angel of the Lord had commanded him and took Mary home as his wife. But he had no union with her until she gave birth to a son. And he gave him the name Jesus.

If you had been a Christian at the time of the slave trade, would you have recognized that evil practice for what it was? If I had been a follower of Jesus in Nazi Germany, how would I have reacted to the persecution of the Jews, and the general vileness of Hitler's regime? These are two of the more dramatic questions that Christians quite often ask each other, but, as we all know, being so closely related to social and historical context, they are almost impossible to answer. They do illustrate, however, the need for all who genuinely want to follow Jesus at least to attempt to step out of the context of the age we happen to live in and the social and religious conditioning that has made each of us what we are.

What happens when we do that? When we remove the religious accretion of two thousand years; when we strip away the legalism, denominationalism, pomp, corruption, pettiness, selfish striving, spiritual oppression, stuffiness, modern self-righteousness, timidity and respectability; when we dispense with the glitter, coloured paper, greed and garishness; when we have finally hacked our way through this forest of irrelevancy to find ourselves at last in a clearing where the baby Jesus really is being born, what might we learn about Christmas?

I would not presume to try to answer that question for you. You will make your own journey and draw your own conclusions. Me?

I see a man and a woman doing what they were told in very difficult circumstances because their obedience was going to help God in ways they cannot possibly have understood. I see the humblest, most ordinary setting one can possibly imagine for the most extraordinary event in history. A pearl hidden in the least likely field. A diamond in a ditch.

Nothing has changed?

A RULER AND A SHEPHERD

Matthew 2:1–6 (NIV)

After Jesus was born in Bethlehem in Judea, during the time of King Herod, Magi from the east came to Jerusalem and asked, 'Where is the one who has been born King of the Jews? We saw his star in the east and have come to worship him.' When King Herod heard this he was disturbed, and all Jerusalem with him. When he had called together all the people's chief priests and teachers of the Law, he asked them where the Christ was to be born. 'In Bethlehem of Judea,' they replied, 'for this is what the prophet has written: "But you, Bethlehem, in the land of Judah, are by no means least among the rulers of Judah; for out of you will come a ruler who will be the shepherd of my people Israel."'

Those who are worshipped for the wrong reasons are never truly safe.

My wife gave me a complete collection of the letters of Oscar Wilde, whose tragically short life and bewilderingly variable works have always fascinated me. I was particularly interested in letters from America, where Wilde was engaged in a long speaking tour. The tour was, generally speaking, a great success. Wilde's first address to the American public was far too long and theoretical, but he adapted his approach immediately and from then on became something of a prophet in the areas of art, style and beauty. Some audiences reached numbers in excess of a thousand, and it is clear from Wilde's reports that the feeling extended to him (other than in some very scathing newspaper articles) was akin to worship. Was the development of Wilde's spirit ambushed by this huge dose of adulation? Self-image inflated by approval has little connection with reality. The dangers are immense.

Herod, who, like all despots, coerced his people into worship and then told himself that they meant it, must have been profoundly threatened by the complex nature of this prospective 'King of the Jews'. The Magi wanted to find the newborn king in order to worship him. But the priests and teachers were telling him that Christ would be a 'shepherd to his people'. A king, but a king who would also be a shepherd. Being and doing. Worship and love. No, Herod could never handle that.

Lord, protect us from assessing ourselves in any light but yours.

POTENTIAL FOR DISASTER

Matthew 2:7–9 (NIV)

Then Herod called the Magi secretly and found out from them the exact time the star had appeared. He sent them to Bethlehem and said, 'Go and make a careful search for the child. As soon as you find him, report to me, so that I too may go and worship him.' After they had heard the king, they went on their way, and the star they had seen in the east went ahead of them until it stopped over the place where the child was.

Could it have gone wrong? Was there potential for failure? If Herod had ordered his secret police to follow the Magi on unmarked camels and kill the baby at the first opportunity, would God have stepped in to protect his Son at the last moment, whatever the means or the cost?

The trouble is, in the course of my 57 years, I've been to too many carol services where Jesus is trying to get out of the manger, Mary is way below childbearing age, Joseph is picking his nose, the shepherds are dressed in tablecloths and tea towels and the Magi are three feet tall with impossible beards on their faces. And then there are pantomimes. My mental picture of Herod as I read this passage is a sort of Abanazar-like figure, twirling long mustachios and speaking in a guttural Terry Thomas voice.

These things inoculate us against the truth. It was a deadly serious business and, yes, of course it could have gone wrong.

If he had wanted, God could have destroyed the enemies of his Son with a mere flicker of his will. Much later in his life, Jesus makes exactly that point at Gethsemane when one of his disciples draws a sword with the intention of defending his Master: 'Put your sword back in its place,' Jesus said to him, 'for all who draw the sword will die by the sword. Do you think I cannot call on my Father, and he will at once put at my disposal more than twelve legions of angels?' (Matthew 26:52–53).

It is as a real man in the real world that Jesus must fulfil his destiny. Only thus can he call real men and women to follow him. More exciting and fraught with danger than any fiction, the story might have ended in complete disaster.

It was not sweet.

WARNED IN A DREAM

Matthew 2:10–12 (NIV)

When they saw the star, they were overjoyed. On coming to the house, they saw the child with his mother Mary, and they bowed down and worshipped him. Then they opened their treasures and presented him with gifts of gold and of incense and of myrrh. And having been warned in a dream not to go back to Herod, they returned to their country by another route.

These three very bright cookies were clever enough to work out the significance of the star; successfully complete the complicated journey to Israel; bring exactly the right kinds of gifts with them. So, given all that, how come they weren't bright enough to latch on to the fact that Herod was a devious villain who had lied through his teeth about wanting to come and worship Jesus?

Actually, as I ponder this question, I find myself recalling a number of Christians I know, and have known in the past, whose sheer intellectual power is equalled only by the simplicity and innocence of their faith and their dealings with other people. The Magi were 'overjoyed' to see the star, and it is this capacity for bright delight that is such a charming feature of these clever men and women who are childlike in their faith.

I think of my friend Norman in particular—an anthropologist whose knowledge and expertise have made him a leader in his own field. Meeting this man has never failed to be a positive experience as far as I am concerned. He listens to my pathetic bleatings, however rubbishy they might be, with little gasps of awe, as though he were enjoying sparkling revelations from an exceptionally brilliant mind. When I'm with Norman—and only when I'm with Norman—I'm a genius! He believes in people, and it is a belief that survives way past the point where they let him down. Despite being terribly used and taken advantage of at times, nothing seems to dim his optimistic attitude towards God and man.

If it had been this friend of mine who rode his camel all that way to see the baby Jesus all those years ago, God would certainly have needed to whisper in his ear, 'Err, Norman, you've done very well, but best go back the other way…'

Father, thank you for clever, simple people who go on believing in you and us.

A PLACE OF SAFETY AND PEACE

Matthew 2:13–15 (NIV)

When they had gone, an angel of the Lord appeared to Joseph in a dream. 'Get up,' he said, 'take the child and his mother and escape to Egypt. Stay there until I tell you, for Herod is going to search for the child to kill him.' So he got up, took the child and his mother during the night and left for Egypt, where he stayed until the death of Herod. And so was fulfilled what the Lord had said through the prophet: 'Out of Egypt I called my Son.'

It's not always wrong to escape.

Soldiering away against the odds or exposing oneself to imminent danger may feel heroic and vaguely Christian, but if the end result is not a continuation and development of the plan that God has made, it is meaningless. Sometimes it is necessary and right to draw back into a safe place where we can wait for the call of God to take us on to the next stage of our lives. (Incidentally, if you happen to be a person God has called to dangerous work somewhere, don't you go using this as an excuse for getting out of it. God would never forgive me. Well, he would, but—oh, you know what I mean...)

Perhaps drawing apart to a place of safety and peace is necessary for the person closest to us. So many of us who feel we have a job to do for the Lord are failing to see the God-given ministry right under our noses or beside us in our beds.

There are times when sheer tiredness demands that we find refreshment. There is no guilt in gathering our strength.

Some hardworking disciples have lost touch with the roots of their faith. They work harder and harder to hide from themselves and everyone else the fact that dryness and disappointment have taken the place of hope and fulfilment. Go and spend time with Jesus.

God did not command Joseph to go and be anxious in Egypt. He just told him to move—quickly—away from the danger. They probably had a wonderful time in Egypt, who knows? Certainly there would be danger and to spare for that little baby in the future. In the meantime, it was not wrong to escape.

Egypt: a place to escape from and to?

LOVE IS AT THE CENTRE

Matthew 2:16–18 (NIV)

When Herod realized that he had been outwitted by the Magi, he was furious, and he gave orders to kill all the boys in Bethlehem and its vicinity who were two years old and under, in accordance with the time he had learned from the Magi. Then what was said through the prophet Jeremiah was fulfilled: 'A voice is heard in Ramah, weeping and great mourning, Rachel weeping for her children and refusing to be comforted, because they are no more.'

Hideous, isn't it? Is there such a thing as the opposite of a shepherd? If there is, Herod was it.

How does this pointless massacre make you feel? When I first became a Christian, I got so angry with God about these poor little children being cut to pieces by Herod's brutal henchmen, and what about their mothers and fathers? Whole streets running with blood, ringing with grief, echoing with hollow desolation. Why didn't God do something to prevent all that? He could have. He was full of tricks in just about every other department, wasn't he? Surely he didn't let it happen just so that another prophecy could be fulfilled and enable him to fit one more piece into the cosmic jigsaw that seemed to mean so much to him.

I'm glad I felt that raging, raving anger then. I'm even more glad I don't feel it now. I certainly don't find the event any less horrific, but my Christianity has turned inside out, if I may put it like that. In the early days of my faith, I would begin at a problem, dragging it to the feet of the God I hardly knew, demanding to know how he would reconcile the contradictions I had discovered. If you like, the problems were at the centre of my thinking and God was on the periphery. Nowadays I apprehend the love and good intentions of God in a way that I would not have thought possible then. He is at the centre of the circle now and the problems are at the edge. These problems and contradictions and, indeed, agonies are no more soluble and no less frustrating than they ever were, but I trust him now, and that has made all the difference.

Those little children and their parents understand completely now, and they are at peace.

THE ADVENTURE OF OBEDIENCE

Matthew 2:19–23 (NIV)

After Herod died, an angel of the Lord appeared in a dream to Joseph in Egypt and said, 'Get up, take the child and his mother and go to the land of Israel, for those who were trying to take the child's life are dead.' So he got up, took the child and his mother and went to the land of Israel. But when he heard that Archelaus was reigning in Judea in place of his father Herod, he was afraid to go there. Having been warned in a dream, he withdrew to the district of Galilee, and he went and lived in a town called Nazareth. So was fulfilled what was said through the prophets: 'He will be called a Nazarene.'

Good heavens! Joseph must have found dropping off to sleep quite an exciting business during this phase of his life! If he had been unsure about the immediate presence of God before meeting Mary, there can't have been much doubt in his mind by now. The whole exercise was like some giant boardgame. Throw a four and land on 'Herod's death means you can return to Israel—move forward ten squares.' Throw a six—'Archelaus is in charge: you must divert to Galilee—go back three squares.'

It was far from being a trivial pursuit, though. Every move was crucial. Jesus must survive and grow, become a man and exercise his ministry, be crucified and come back to life again so that I would be able to write these words about what happened and you would be able to read them. Joseph's role was to be alert and obedient, to go or stay or change direction according to commands from the ultimate master of the game.

If anyone is seriously looking for a good New Year's resolution, I can do no better than suggest that you join me in the following prayer. I warn you, though, if you don't mean it, don't pray it.

Father, I would like to be more aware of the immediacy of your presence in my everyday life. Give me the strength and obedience to hold my own agenda with such a light hand that I am ready to abandon it at a moment's notice. Lord, I want an adventure with you.

The way to heaven out of all places is of like length and distance.

THOMAS MORE

HEADING FOR HEAVEN— WHY DID WE LEAVE IN THE FIRST PLACE?

1 CORINTHIANS 15

After my mother died and her body had been cremated we were left with a smart, polished wooden urn that, according to the undertaker, contained her ashes. Someone told me once that these urns often do not contain the actual remains of one's relative, but a mixture of the ashes of all those cremated on that particular day. I have no idea if this is true, but it didn't really matter to me. That sealed box was more of a symbol than anything else, a mini-coffin that we could lodge in a place that might help us to focus our memories of Mum in the future.

There was even a hint of humour in our response as a family to this sombre object. Ian, my younger brother, was the one who collected it from the undertaker's office in Tunbridge Wells, and when Bridget and I visited his home a few days later he said, 'Mum's in the back room.' For some reason this made us both slightly hysterical, not least because Mum herself would have been highly amused by the idea that she was stored in a small container on the sideboard. My mother was too large a character to be contained in a small anything.

What were we to do with the urn?

After some discussion it was agreed that Mum's preference (we may have been wrong, but she could hardly argue with us now) would have been burial in the same grave as her parents in the graveyard of a little non-conformist chapel near Rushlake Green in East Sussex. None of us had been to this place since we were children, and although church records indicated that a stone had been placed at the head of the grave, we found no trace of it on the plot where Mum's parents had been buried many years ago.

Digging at one end of the grave to make a hole for the urn on the day before the burial, Ian's spade suddenly came up against something hard and unyielding. Careful excavation revealed the missing gravestone which must have sunk gradually into the soft earth over the years, until it had disappeared altogether beneath the grass that covered the grave. After a sluice-down, the names of John and Kitty Baker, my grandparents, were visible once more. I never knew my grandfather, but I loved Nanna with that special variety of openly excited passion that I find so endearing in small children nowadays. Travelling on the bus to visit her house in Heathfield had always been a trip to heaven. I liked the idea that my mother would, in a symbolic sense, at least, be reunited with her mum and dad, here on this quiet Sussex slope, overlooking a view which happened to be her favourite one in all the world.

Next day, the day that we had chosen for the burial of the urn was the windiest, wettest day of the year so far. It seemed as if the whole world was weeping in sympathy with us as we huddled around that oblong of turf with the little patch of newly turned earth at one end, trying to turn a wild, ragged experience into something that had a shape. Turning away at the end seemed like a form of treachery. Silly though it was, both Bridget and I, and probably the others as well, found it hard to leave Mum alone on that hillside in the wind and weather. We wanted to take her home with us.

On St Patrick's day, Mum's birthday, we returned to put some daffodils and greenery on the grave. This time the feeling was quite different. Spring sunshine bathed the hillside in bright hope, and in the field next to the graveyard two horses rolled and galloped and sported out of sheer high spirits. Mum loved horses. In the clear March air the view across the valley was spectacular, and I remained for a while after the others had gone back to the car, just gazing out towards the far horizon. I felt no less sad about Mum's absence from our lives—I'm still trying to deal with it on the most basic level—but I knew in my heart, as I stood there, that we who follow Jesus must not betray him and his death and resurrection by accepting death as a finality. We come to terms with our temporary loss because normal living demands that we must, but, as David Watson said repeatedly as he approached his death, the best is yet to come. As I walked away from the place where I am sure we shall often come to remember my mother, I knew, with rare conviction, that, as surely as that stone in my grandparents' grave re-emerged when it seemed no longer to exist, I shall meet her and my grandmother again, and we shall have new bodies and new understandings, but those two people who loved me will undoubtedly be themselves, and I shall certainly be me.

If that is not so, we are wasting our time, and that is primarily the subject of this great chapter from the New Testament.

Prayer

Father, it is agony to lose people whom we love, but we know that Jesus died in order that we can be reunited one day. Help us to be properly balanced in the way that we deal with death. We can't help mourning, because we miss those we've lost so much, but let us keep in mind the hope that we have in you, not just as an airy-fairy, abstract thing, but as an excited anticipation of genuine contact with people who will be equipped with new bodies that cannot ache as my mother's did, because they are eternal bodies. Thank you for lending us those who have loved us. Help us to hand them back to you with as good a grace as we can. May the sense of heaven-waiting be strong and evident in us so that others can take heart from our example, and truly believe that the rising of Jesus from the tomb guarantees that all those who follow him will rise in exactly the same way.

THE RIGHT DIRECTION

1 Corinthians 15:1–8 (NIV)

Now, brothers, I want to remind you of the gospel I preached to you, which you received and on which you have taken your stand. By this gospel you are saved, if you hold firmly to the word I preached to you. Otherwise, you have believed in vain. For what I received I passed on to you as of first importance: that Christ died for our sins according to the Scriptures, that he was buried, that he was raised on the third day according to the Scriptures, and that he appeared to Peter, and then to the Twelve. After that, he appeared to more than five hundred of the brothers at the same time, most of whom are still living, though some have fallen asleep. Then he appeared to James, then to all the apostles, and last of all he appeared to me also, as to one abnormally born.

Paul is determined to put the erring Corinthians firmly back on track. There is only one right way to go and here he reminds them what it is.

I remember making one of those interminable tube journeys from central London to some nameless suburb in the middle of nowhere. Two businessmen of the thrusting executive type got on at Baker Street and began talking in fruity, overloud voices. They spoke of 'oil' and 'productivity' and 'corporate industry' and 'international awareness'. As I listened to their confident tones, and admired their advanced strap-hanging techniques, I felt slightly inferior. Here were these hugely competent captains of industry on their way to clinch some multi-million pound deal, while I trundled off to my latest speaking engagement with a suitcase full of books for sale. My reverie was interrupted when the train arrived at about the third stop since Baker Street, and one of the two men peered out at the platform in sudden alarm.

'We're going the wrong way!' he bleated.

The two high-flyers ducked out of the train, leaving me to reflect on the fact that while I might be a bit of a twit, at least I was going the right way.

Paul is reminding his readers of the basic truths of Christian faith. Jesus is the way, and everything else depends on following his lead. This requires obedience rather than talent.

Am I still on board?

BOASTING

1 Corinthians 15:9–11 (NIV)

For I am the least of the apostles and do not even deserve to be called an apostle, because I persecuted the Church of God. But by the grace of God I am what I am, and his grace to me was not without effect. No, I worked harder than all of them— yet not I, but the grace of God that was with me. Whether, then, it was I or they, this is what we preach, and this is what you believed.

I have heard Paul described by some critics as a conceited evangelist. Quite apart from the fact that this is an obvious tautology, I believe that it shows a complete misunderstanding of the man. Paul's real problem is that he believes in the power of God and he isn't afraid of telling the truth. The result is that he can say 'I worked harder than all of them' without any self-consciousness at all because he honestly believes that any success he achieves is attributable to the grace of God working in him. There is a right kind of bold assertiveness, and we see too little of it in this age. Very few people are broken and humble enough to boast about God as naturally and loudly as Paul.

I once spoke at a meeting in the north-west of England, under the title 'Wounded in action'. I talked about my own experience of suffering, the way in which genuine friendship had helped, the perils of looking for quick-fix solutions to long-term problems, and the dreadful (and inaccurate) feelings of spiritual failure when depression or breakdown occurs. As soon as I stood up to speak I could sense the pain in many of those present and by the time I had finished the air was heavy with need.

Then the organizer of the meeting stood up. 'I'm sure we've all enjoyed listening to Adrian,' he said, 'and of course we know that all these questions and problems are answered when the Lord Jesus Christ comes into our hearts…' Saying that probably made the organizer feel a lot better, but down in the body of the hall a lot of very miserable people (who had asked Jesus into their lives a long time ago) were feeling much worse. I know that I should have offered to pray with the people then, or at least invited them to pray with each other. I didn't because I felt inadequate and not 'spiritual enough'. I was refusing to believe that God could use me until I was good enough. Now that's conceit!

Sorry, Lord. Use me.

SILLY SHEEP

1 Corinthians 15:12–15 (NIV)

But if it is preached that Christ has been raised from the dead, how can some of you say that there is no resurrection of the dead? If there is no resurrection of the dead, then not even Christ has been raised. And if Christ has not been raised, our preaching is useless and so is your faith. More than that, we are then found to be false witnesses about God, for we have testified about God that he raised Christ from the dead. But he did not raise him if in fact the dead are not raised.

Christians are like sheep. I suppose that's a good thing really, isn't it? The metaphor was selected at a rather high level, after all. But problems arise when false or misguided shepherds appear and lead the bleaters into poisoned pasture. It seems almost beyond belief that these Corinthians allowed themselves to be persuaded that a lifetime of faith and discipline would be followed by oblivion. What sort of pressures resulted in their acceptance of such a foolish distortion?

I have a young friend who attends a very lively and ultra-charismatic fellowship in the West Country—the sort of church where you can't own a canary unless it's been hatched-again. David described how a north European evangelist had visited the church for a fortnight, bringing with him a conviction that God wanted to miraculously change his followers' dental fillings from dull grey to solid gold. Wide-eyed, the congregation listened to this message, and then submitted themselves as a body to the evangelist's prayer that God would touch their gums like a sort of divine Midas. This was followed by much celebration as the speaker announced that God had indeed worked in the mouths of many. So intensely positive was the feeling in the church that on the following day David was persuaded to publicly testify to the metamorphosis in his own fillings—this despite the fact that his bathroom mirror showed clear evidence to the contrary.

Much ashamed, he subsequently got a (very close) friend to check his fillings, and confessed to the church that his previous testimony had been false. Strangely, he discovered that he was not alone…!

Beware! God is quite capable of doing whatever he likes with teeth, but technique and cultivated atmosphere are no substitute for spiritual reality.

Sheep need to be serpents and doves. What a menagerie!

WHAT IF...?

1 Corinthians 15:19, 29–34 (NIV)

If only for this life we have hope in Christ, we are to be pitied more than all men... Now if there is no resurrection, what will those do who are baptised for the dead? If the dead are not raised at all, why are people baptised for them? And as for us, why do we endanger ourselves every hour? I die every day—I mean that, brothers—just as surely as I glory over you in Christ Jesus our Lord. If I fought wild beasts in Ephesus for merely human reasons, what have I gained? If the dead are not raised, 'Let us eat and drink, for tomorrow we die.' Do not be misled: 'Bad company corrupts good character.' Come back to your senses as you ought, and stop sinning; for there are some who are ignorant of God—I say this to your shame.

This part of Paul's letter challenges me in a dark and dangerous part of myself, and I would like to share that challenge openly because I believe that many others will identify with my experience. It is about the final barrier between partial and total commitment to the demands of Jesus on the very centre of my will. Paul no longer cares about preserving his life in the worldly sense. Why should he, when he has encountered a dynamic, joy-inspiring God who beckons him on to an eternity of unspeakable rightness? He experiences terrible physical hardship and will eventually be executed because he pursues the path of obedience. It doesn't matter—he's not troubled. He's going to live with Jesus. It is this certainty that causes his incredulity over the Corinthians' acceptance of Christianity without resurrection. Why bother?

Sometimes a chill fear creeps over me. 'What', I ask myself, 'if I've got it all wrong? What if I'm giving my energy and time and concentration to something I've dreamed up—something that will collapse in darkness when the end comes? What if there is no resurrection?'

These fears (or lies, if you like) don't inhabit me constantly, and I do have great faith in Jesus, but I know that a little part of my will stands back from the precipice of total trust, afraid that if I step out, I may not be caught.

Father, help us to give up the world, and thereby gain everything. Forgive us for not trusting you.

NEW BODIES FOR OLD

1 Corinthians 15:35–38, 42–44, 49 (NIV)

But someone may ask, 'How are the dead raised? With what kind of body will they come?' How foolish! What you sow does not come to life unless it dies. When you sow, you do not plant the body that will be, but just a seed, perhaps of wheat or of something else. But God gives it a body as he has determined, and to each kind of seed he gives its own body... So will it be with the resurrection of the dead. The body that is sown is perishable, it is raised imperishable; it is sown in dishonour, it is raised in glory; it is sown in weakness, it is raised in power; it is sown a natural body, it is raised a spiritual body. If there is a natural body, there is also a spiritual body... And just as we have borne the likeness of the earthly man, so shall we bear the likeness of the man from heaven.

I'm afraid I would have made a rather good Corinthian—I mean in the sense that I can easily identify with their problems. Paul is dealing with their worries about life in the hereafter in this passage. What kind of bodies will we have? The same? Different? Will we know each other? Will we be able to talk to each other? The apostle suggests that our heavenly bodies will be like blooms that have grown from seed that has died (our earthly bodies) and that the contrast between the one and the other will be as dramatic as a sunflower emerging like magic from a scrap of parrot food. Now, we are like Adam. Then, we shall be like Jesus.

I must confess that when I look at my own body (an experience to be avoided whenever possible) I am very glad that the responsibility is God's and not mine.

I shall never forget hearing about a girl called Jayne, who had cerebral palsy. Jayne was a devout Christian who brought joy into many lives. She died at the age of 16 after a totally wheelchair-bound life. Shortly before her death she had a vision of herself entering heaven.

'Oh, Mummy,' she said, 'I'm walking through the gates of heaven! Mummy, I'm dancing with Jesus!'

Let's get excited—I think it's probably going to be wonderful.

Father, show us more of Jesus so that we will want to be like him.

IS IT WORTH IT?

1 Corinthians 15:56–58 (NIV)

The sting of death is sin, and the power of sin is the law. But thanks be to God! He gives us the victory through our Lord Jesus Christ. Therefore, my dear brothers, stand firm. Let nothing move you. Always give yourselves fully to the work of the Lord, because you know that your labour in the Lord is not in vain.

How we need our dulled eyes to be opened and brightened by Paul's enthusiasm and certainty. He carries through his earthly life a cosmic view of existence that seems to be denied to most Christians. In my travels around the country and the world I meet so many believers who are weary, or disappointed, or disenchanted, and sometimes I am one of them. There are times when I yearn with all my heart for some clear sign that my labour in the Lord is not in vain. Every now and then, God graciously gives me such a sign.

A few weeks ago a friend visited from London. He quite often drives over for a morning—there's nothing unusual about that. But, on this particular morning, as we walked the dog in a nearby field, something different happened. A ripple of pure excitement passed through me, and the colours around us seemed to acquire a new intensity and brightness, rather like the effect of sunlight suddenly shining through a crack in a leaden sky. I knew that God was crowning the moment with significance, but I didn't know any details. Not many years previously I would have crinkled my eyes into the classical smile of evangelical concern and insight and said, 'I think the Lord wants to speak to you, brother.' Instead, I said, 'Something's going on, Steve. God's involved in our meeting today, but I don't know what it's about. Is there anything you ought to say to me?'

There was something Steve had to say to me, and it was significant.

The point I want to make, though, is that in that short period when the Holy Spirit was so evidently in command, all problematic issues became totally irrelevant, and it was impossible to doubt the benefits of walking in the Lord. I would like to live in that experience for ever—and I will. Jesus has risen.

Remind us of reality, Lord.

The letter killeth, but the spirit giveth life.

2 CORINTHIANS 3:6 (AV)

COMFORT FOR WEARY WALKERS

THE HOLY SPIRIT

As I sit down to write the introduction to this section, it is just after 7 o'clock in the morning. I was the first one to get up, because I'd booked an alarm call for 6.50, and I had to leap out of bed and sprint to the phone before it woke everybody else up. The phone in our bedroom was over on the piano by the door. It could have been placed nearer to the bed had it not been for the fact that I am quite capable of reaching a hand out, lifting the receiver, saying 'Thank you very much', replacing it and going back to sleep. Nowadays, Bridget and I are usually recalled to consciousness by our new automatic tea-making device (bought last Christmas as a brave declaration that we are beginning to accept middle-age), but Bridget's parents are staying for a few days so we've lent it to them.

After having a shower (our shower has only two settings—'boiling' and 'arctic'), I went back to the bedroom to dress, observing when I arrived that Bridget was also up now. 'Last one up makes the the bed' is the rule in our bedroom. This tradition has occasionally resulted in an unseemly scramble to be the first one to actually get a foot on the floor, but this morning I had won by a mile, and the bed was already made. On the sofa at the other end of the room a small form was still enjoying the relaxed sleep of the innocent. Katy, aged ten, has relinquished her room for a few days so that her brother, David, can sleep in her room, in order that their nanna and grandpa can sleep in his room. It sounds complicated but it works, not least because Katy would much rather sleep on the sofa in our room than in her own bed. As I finished dressing I leaned down and kissed my daughter gently on the cheek. She stirred and peered balefully at me through one half-opened eye before settling down to go back to sleep. Downstairs my wife had ensured that the kettle was performing its accustomed task, and soon the first cup of tea of the morning, the one that truly resurrects, was in my hand.

Now, I am sitting at the computer typing these words. Katy is up, and commencing the crucial daily battle to make her hair look exactly as she wants it to; Joe, who has got an agency job for the Easter holidays, has crawled out of his bed on the third floor and is making low but resonantly penetrating groans of despair as he contemplates another eight hours spent in the incessant noise and tedium of the plastics factory; Bridget is trying to make sandwiches for Joe and lay the table for breakfast and find a hairband for Katy all at the same time; Bridget's mother has just called down the stairs to ask if it's all right for them to use the bathroom now, and David is still dead to the world in Katy's bedroom upstairs. Through the window beside me I can see that one of those super-fresh early spring days is gathering itself delicately together, and I find myself wishing that I wasn't disciplined enough to stay in this chair until I've produced my daily quota of one thousand words.

Katy has just come in and leaned on my shoulder to ask what I'm writing about, then gone away disgusted because I said I was going to write about what she'd just said.

An average day in the Plass household is under way.

Where does the Holy Spirit fit into all this? Well, more to the point is that if he doesn't fit into this everyday ordinariness, then he doesn't really fit into any situation. Interpersonal relationships in a family like ours are filled with complexities, tensions and subtleties that have been shaped, controlled or altered by the practical ministry of the Holy Spirit. In case that sounds too vague, I mean that, over the years, Bridget and I have prayed for our children and each other a million times, sometimes in tears; we have implored his help to fight against impulses in ourselves that would assuredly have had very negative effects; we have tried to allow the direct and immediate influence of the Spirit to change very specific situations, occasionally with dramatic results; it would not be an exaggeration to say that we have survived as a family because the Holy Spirit is here with us as Jesus was with his disciples.

Much of the confusion and disappointment that one encounters among Christians seems to spring from a reluctance to allow that it is in the ordinary circumstances of life that we are most likely to see God working out his purposes. As a young Christian I went through agonies because it seemed so very difficult to transfer all the life and vibrancy of formal situations to the place where I actually was, to the dark space of solitude, the 'at home' part of myself where religion meant nothing and I needed a God who was willing to become a small friendly person who would tolerate my weakness and just be with me. Today, I have moved very much closer to understanding that he was there—and he was there, all the time—but the clearing of my sight and perceptive faculties has taken—is taking—all my life. What I can say for sure, though, is that the Holy Spirit, in his most influential role, is a house guest.

Prayer
Father, we want the Holy Spirit to be involved in the very centre of our lives. We invite him to join us when we are at our most ordinary and defenceless, and we thank you that you have provided us with a comforter to be with us in the same way that Jesus was with his followers two thousand years ago. May we not be afraid to seek his help at the most dismal, despairing times, those times when religion means nothing, and we just need a friend.

DIVINE TRIVIALITY

Acts 1:14–18 (NIV)

They all joined together constantly in prayer... In those days Peter stood up among the believers... and said, 'Brothers, the Scripture had to be fulfilled... concerning Judas...' (... Judas bought a field; there he fell headlong, his body burst open and all his intestines spilled out.)

I have written elsewhere about the ease with which the apparent ordinariness of life can seduce us into doubting the reality of a spiritual dimension. When you come back from an uplifting Christian meeting to find that the dog has messed in the middle of the living-room carpet, or the children have done something so unspeakably awful that you lose your temper and respond in equally unspeakable ways—or both—it is easy to believe that the uplift was caused by religious falsies of some kind.

In fact, God is more ordinary than the most ordinary thing that we can imagine. He made this world, and he inhabits it in a much broader and more secular way than the churches do. One of the most effective deceptions of the devil is the idea, fixed firmly in the minds of many Christians, that certain arenas are spiritual ones, while others are not. Couple this with subtly false teaching about the Holy Spirit working in us without any cooperation on our part, and you have the dismally frequent phenomenon of the paralysed Christian. When the Spirit works in us it will never be without our assent. That assent will require the virtue that Jesus rated so highly—obedience. Doing what you're told can be very tough indeed.

Peter stands up, filled with the Spirit, at this early and highly dramatic stage in the history of the Church, to perform obediently the job that is required at that particular moment, but let's not kid ourselves. The Holy Spirit does not confine himself (unlike some speakers) to large meetings. We might not have experienced tongues of flame, and we may never be called upon to act as the hinge upon which the history of the Church turns, but the Holy Spirit is just as keen to find arenas in our personal lives where, given our obedient cooperation, he can change a life or a situation for the better, however trivial ·or ordinary that situation may seem to us.

'And Adrian, filled with the Spirit, stood up in the kitchen, and did not get irritable and sulk as he would normally have done, and those who saw this were amazed, and said, "Surely this man has been drinking." But he hadn't (not this time). He was just doing what he was told for once…'

Holy Spirit, inspire me in the ordinary things.

LEAST OF THE GIFTS

1 Corinthians 14:39–40 (NIV)

Therefore, my brothers, be eager to prophesy, and do not forbid speaking in tongues. But everything should be done in a fitting and orderly way.

I've written little about speaking in tongues, despite the fact that this gift has become a very important part of my life. There are two reasons for this reticence, one quite unworthy, another that springs from genuine concern.

The unworthy reason is connected with the look one sometimes gets when this subject arises. 'Here's another one for the funny-farm' just about sums it up. This negative response has been intensified by the unfortunate way this gift has been elevated to a status that it was never supposed to have. How foolish to suppose that Christians must have this gift. I confess that there were times in the past when I kept my mouth shut during discussions about 'The Gifts', just to avoid being thought a loony. I should have spoken up, and didn't.

The more sensible reason for restraint (even now, when being thought a loony is the least of my problems) is an awareness that love is the gift of gifts and I would rather talk about that great sea of generosity than one little drop of benefit, however shiny it may be. An unhealthy appetite for 'magic' has caused a lot of trouble in the past.

Having said all that, I am glad that, on a Thursday night more than 25 years ago, a Christian friend called Marian nervously demonstrated the new gift she had received, so I could begin to understand what she was talking about when she said that the Holy Spirit was doing new and unexpected things in her life. Since that time I have spoken to God in a language that I don't understand on countless occasions, always (apart from one notable and alarming occasion which is recorded elsewhere) in private.

How can I describe this experience? Well, all I can say is that there are times when I run out of prayer and understanding and intelligence and just about everything else. When that happens a child—a baby perhaps—cries out to his daddy from inside me, and the language, or baby-talk, is what we call tongues. Sometimes—not often in my case because I'm a miserable beggar—it is an overflowing of sheer joy.

I remain sceptical about many tongues that I hear in churches, and about my own occasionally, and I know it's only another tool in the spiritual kit-bag, but it really has been such a helpful gift and I thank God for it.

Lord, if you want to add this gift to the ones I've already got, help me to take it. If not, help me to be happy for those who have received it.

WHOSE AGENDA?

Revelation 1:19–20 (NIV)

'Write, therefore, what you have seen, what is now and what will take place later...
The seven stars are the angels of the seven churches, and the seven lampstands
are the seven churches.'

At a big Christian festival over in Europe recently, a friend told me, the
number of people requesting counselling from the onsite team (of
which he's a member) was considerably less than in recent years. My
friend couldn't explain the change, but as I listened to a variety of
festival speakers I felt that I'd found a clue. The fact was, that if you
picked the right seminar or discussion, and carefully avoided others,
you would be able to hear justification for just about any point of view
you wished to take.

Gay Christianity is a good example. A large proportion of those who
used the counselling team in the past were seeking help with problems
relating to that issue. Many of them felt that scripture, and the Church,
had established a norm of disapproval towards homosexual practice,
sometimes seasoned with non-judgmental love and compassion, but,
sadly, very often not. Those gay Christians who accepted this view as
an expression of the mind of God experienced agonies of guilt and
resentment, often expressed to members of the counselling team. Now,
however, with the climate of opinion in the Church changing so quickly,
it was possible to hear one speaker stating categorically that homosexual
practice is perfectly compatible with Christian belief, while in the next
tent but one the opposite view was being put, less dogmatically (politics
creep in everywhere, don't they?), but with an equal underlying conviction. Why should you need counselling about something that is
openly and unequivocally given the public seal of approval?

The same dichotomy of view was evident in the general area of sex
outside marriage. I'm not concerned here to express my view on these
matters. I just want to say two things. First, how much we need to hear
what the Spirit says to the churches in this age, as opposed to what we
concoct to support our own inclinations. I would like God to lay it on
the line. Where are the mad, brave, genuine, unpopular, effective
prophets of this age? Secondly, are those who stand and claim to speak
for God—on whichever side of whichever argument, myself included—

prepared to change, adapt or totally dump their ideas when the Spirit tells them they're wrong? If not—what's the point of it all?

Holy Spirit, speak truth into the Church. Give us the grace to listen and respond.

USING THE GIFTS

John 15:12; 16:7 (NIV)

My command is this: Love each other as I have loved you... But I tell you the truth: It is for your good that I am going away. Unless I go away, the Counsellor will not come to you; but if I go, I will send him to you.

A man called Bill had two grown-up daughters, whose names were Imogen and Sally. Imogen, a handsome, impractical girl, gifted with a powerful imagination, was perhaps just a little too intense for her own or other people's good. Sally, the younger sister, was a relaxed, intelligent creature with a homely smile and a lot of common sense. She annoyed Imogen from time to time by being, not only right, but nice as well.

One day Bill had to go away. He got up early, got ready, then woke his daughters and spoke kindly to them.

'Girls, I have to go away for a while, and I have two things to say before I leave. Most important, I want you to be nice to each other. Nothing matters much compared with that. OK?'

Both girls nodded, but only Sally was able to be upset and take in what her father was saying.

'The other thing,' continued Bill, 'is that, in the kitchen, you'll find a present, or rather some presents, that should make it easier for you to remember me and do what I've asked. Now I must go.'

A little later the girls crept excitedly into the kitchen to discover a brand-new set of pots and pans on the table.

'Oh, Sally,' cried Imogen, 'what a wonderful way to remember Father! Every day we'll put the pots and pans on the table and look at them and think about how much we love him, and then, after giving them a good polish, we'll put them away until the next day.'

'You're joking,' laughed Sally. 'We're not going to just look at them—that's not what they're for.'

'Well, what are they for, then, clever-clogs?' grumped Imogen.

'They're for cooking with, of course. That's what Father meant. He wants us to prepare lovely meals for each other every day. We're supposed to use them, not sit and look at them! You are funny.'

Imogen was horrified. 'Mess up these beautiful things Father has given us with horrible, dirty old food, and then have to wash them up? Never!'

'Come on,' coaxed Sally, 'let me make you something tonight.'

But Imogen cradled the set of utensils and glared at her sister. 'Get out of the kitchen!' she shouted, 'You don't belong here—you'll cook with these over my dead body!'

What happens when Bill gets back? When a church has gifts but lacks love, it may be a dead body.

THREESOME

2 Corinthians 13:14 (NIV)

May the grace of the Lord Jesus Christ, and the love of God, and the fellowship of the Holy Spirit be with you all.

How do you imagine the members of the Trinity? Do you think it matters if we picture them in a human setting? I don't see how it can. After all, two thousand years ago it actually happened. God became man. Those are the three words that changed the world. If you do think it matters— well, you'd better not read any more of this note. Bye!

It's late at night. Three figures are sitting around a campfire on the banks of the sea of Galilee, enjoying the way the sparks fly, and the smell of freshly caught fish sizzling over the flames. It's not a bottle party. Instead, the trio have contributed large measures of the grace, love and fellowship that are specialities of this particular house. The Father is an older man (well, be fair—he's got to be, hasn't he?), a bearded, deep-eyed, still personality, rich with potential for earth-shattering anger, or extravagant, all-embracing love. He gazes into the flickering tongues of orange and red, his head filled with an eternity of thoughts.

Poking the embers with a long stick on the other side of the fire, in charge of the fish because he has previous, hands-on experience, sits Jesus, the Son, the only one who has ever known or ever will know how it feels to be God with a human skin. The marks of death are still on that skin, and will stay there until the victory that is already won has been claimed by the least, lost soul. He has a wonderful smile, laced with pain.

The third member of the party is more difficult to describe, except that he is like one of the flames in the fire—vital and restless, beautiful, moving, constantly changing shape, alternately reflecting light and seeming to disappear into the shadows. The Holy Spirit is the one who is out and about and doing—but he does enjoy fish as well.

So, when the meal has been cooked and eaten, and the family gets down to business, what is the subject of their intense, concerned conversation? The answer, believe it or not, dear reader, is that they are talking about—you.

May the grace of our Lord Jesus Christ, the love of God, and the fellowship of the Holy Spirit be with us all, evermore. Amen.

TRANSPORTED

Acts 8:39–40 (NIV)

When they came up out of the water, the Spirit of the Lord suddenly took Philip away, and the eunuch did not see him again, but went on his way rejoicing. Philip, however, appeared at Azotus and travelled about, preaching the gospel in all the towns until he reached Caesarea.

What an amazing period of church history this was. And for someone like me who spends hours on trains and in cars, the speed and simplicity of Philip's transport after finishing his task is highly enviable. But as I read this story I find myself asking one of those questions to which you never really expect to find a totally satisfactory answer.

Why, if the Holy Spirit is capable of such dramatic activity (activity that appears easily to bypass the limitations of nature), doesn't he sort out all the problems of creation with a series of divine conjuring tricks? The usual answer is, of course, that human beings have free will, and God would never use his power to change people who don't want to be changed. I don't dismiss this argument—it's the best one I've heard—but it still doesn't really explain why God doesn't intervene dramatically and miraculously in order to provide all the information people need to make the changes in their thinking and behaviour that the Bible tells us they so urgently need. Why not organize thousands of Damascus Road experiences for people who are unsure, or, like Saul, desperately resisting the awareness that faith is developing inside them. What about huge messages inscribed across the sky by a giant hand, like Daniel's writing on the wall? Why not chuck a thunderbolt at well-known evildoers? Some significant public healings? I've got lots of ideas. For instance, what about—

'Enough!' says the small, definite voice that heads off some of my less productive mental indulgences. 'My ways are not your ways. My solutions are not your solutions. You're not even asking the right questions—I don't know how you expect to understand the answers. Tell people something you do know for sure, like the fact that I forgive you every time you're not available to do the things that might bring someone a bit nearer.'

'Sorry.'

'It's all right.'

Thank you for the things that we do know. We'll go on asking questions, but help us to accept that sometimes the answers will be beyond us.

EACH TO HIS OWN

Galatians 2:11 (NIV)

When Peter came to Antioch, I opposed him to his face, because he was in the wrong.

'You wouldn't mind if I made a comment, would you?'

After hearing me speak, folks had lingered for a chat. Now there were two left, a man, and the woman who'd asked the question.

'No.' I adopted my always-willing-to-accept-constructive-criticism expression. 'Of course I wouldn't mind. Go ahead.'

'Well,' she said, 'I just want to say I think it's not a good idea to trivialize sin like you do. Adultery's nothing to joke about. A lot of people get very hurt when something like that happens.'

I knew what she was referring to. I'd talked about the adulterous relationship between David and Bathsheba, and David's subsequent confrontation with Nathan the prophet. Nothing trivial about that, but then I said something like this: 'Right, anyone who's committing adultery at the moment, raise a hand—no, don't! I didn't mean it!'

I could see how she might have thought I regarded this sin as trivial, but experience has shown that, as far as my own work is concerned, this kind of approach is far more effective than simply telling people off. Still, perhaps this lady was right—perhaps I had got it all wrong.

'Thank you,' I said (humble, eh?), 'I'll certainly think about that.'

I could sense that the man who was waiting to speak to me was getting rather agitated. The woman left and I turned to him. 'Hello,' I said.

'Hello,' he said, 'I've been committing adultery with my neighbour's wife,' and he burst into tears.

We prayed together and he went off with Jesus to wrestle with the world, the flesh and the devil. I tell this story because it further confirms my growing conviction that God takes a Peter, a Paul, a Felicity, an Agnes, a Bert or an Adrian, and says, 'The Holy Spirit shall work through the personalities of these people, and though the style of that work may vary from person to person, the fruits will not. Lay off each other.'

Father, I don't like criticism, but I need it. Help me to listen and learn from what other people say to me. But help me also to be true to the task you have given me, and to do it in a way that honours you. I will try to respect the way in which my brothers and sisters work for you, however strange or different it may appear.

LIES AND DAMNED LIES

Acts 5:3–5; 7–10 (NIV)

Then Peter said, 'Ananias, how is it that Satan has so filled your heart that you have lied to the Holy Spirit and have kept for yourself some of the money you received for the land?… What made you think of doing such a thing? You have not lied to men but to God.'… Later his wife came in, not knowing what had happened. Peter asked her, 'Tell me, is this the price you and Ananias got for the land?' 'Yes,' she said… Peter said to her, 'How could you agree to test the Spirit of the Lord?…' At that moment she fell down at his feet and died.

Good bit this, isn't it?

'No,' you reply, 'it's not a "good bit", it's a horrible bit. These two people get bumped off for telling a fib. Horrible!'

Nobody likes this story much. I've sat in many Bible studies watching people wrestle with the idea that the God whose name is love could be capable of causing someone's death because of a lie. That aspect doesn't actually trouble me too much—I do moan about God occasionally, but, deep down, I trust he knows what he's doing. What interests me is an idea I have that most of us tell many more lies than we care to face. Maybe that's what makes this story so unpopular.

Take me, for instance. I've practically made a living out of telling the truth, and I do try to be as honest as possible whenever I write or speak, but, as with many others, there are some shadowy areas that just don't get talked about. And the way in which wives and husbands cover for each other is a good example. It's become a habit over the years for my wife and I to shade or bend the truth, if necessary, when one of us is particularly vulnerable or under attack from the 'outside world'. Do all couples do this? I've no idea. Is it wrong? Well, I've always told myself that it's a sort of special case—dishonesty made honourable by the fact that we are protecting each other. But is this what happened with Ananias and Sapphira? We're told that she knew exactly what was going on and quite readily, almost automatically perhaps, supported his attempt to cheat the Holy Spirit. Maybe she was just being loyal, but it came to the same thing in the end.

I suspect that there may be an area of subtle danger here. We are certainly taught that husband and wife become one flesh, but the neglect of individual development and responsibility can result in corporate acts of dishonesty that may seem comparatively small and reassuringly domestic at the time, but—well, read the story again.

Father, help us to remember that we are accountable to you before anyone else.

THE BOTTOM LINE

Romans 8:12–17 (NIV)

We have an obligation—but it is not to the sinful nature, to live according to it... For you did not receive a spirit that makes you a slave again to fear, but you received the Spirit of sonship. And by him we cry, 'Abba, Father.' The Spirit himself testifies with our spirit that we are God's children. Now if we are children, then we are heirs—heirs of God and co-heirs with Christ, if indeed we share in his sufferings in order that we may also share in his glory.

One criticism levelled against the church in Victorian England is that it dulled the edge of resistance among the poor. Preachers exhorted worshippers to look forward to an eternity of joy that would totally eclipse the misery and hardship of this life, one minister whose sermon I read even claiming that the death of a young boy through starvation was actually a form of healing. Of course, the pendulum has swung violently since then, partly for the very good reason that many Christians are now aware that social issues are not just secular concerns, and partly for the very bad reason that people are frightened stiff (an apt expression) of dying, and are looking for a faith that focuses on this life rather than the life to come. This pendulumic swing has sometimes resulted in an odd form of Christianity. It might be best expressed by slightly rewriting a famous portion of scripture.

'For God so loved the world that he gave his only Son, that whosoever believes in him, keeps his nose clean and makes a significant but sensibly balanced contribution to church life in terms of time and cash, shall have a reasonable expectation of material comfort, physical good health and ongoing prosperity in the fields of business and emotional relationships, with guidance provided as and when necessary so that opportunities in all these areas shall not be missed or wasted. Oh, yes—and eternal life gets thrown in as well.'

Have you noticed how ratty some Christians can get when their lives stop running smoothly? I know, because I've done it myself. How could God let this happen to me? I've had to sell the car. I'm eating into my capital...

I don't want to minimize these problems, but perhaps the pendulum has swung too far. Jesus died so we could 'share in his glory'. That's what he bought for us—not a semi-detached in Bromley. The bottom line for those of us who, by the Spirit, cry 'Abba, Father', is that we shall be with him for ever in paradise, and then we shall find out what that 'glory' really means.

Thank you for eternal life. I prioritize it—help my unprioritization.

THE MOST IMPORTANT THING

Matthew 7:21–23 (NIV)

'Not everyone who says to me, "Lord, Lord", will enter the kingdom of heaven, but only he who does the will of my Father who is in heaven. Many will say to me on that day, "Lord, Lord, did we not prophesy in your name, and in your name drive out demons and perform many miracles?" Then I will tell them plainly, "I never knew you. Away from me, you evildoers!"'

Here is perhaps the most ominous warning of all, from Jesus himself, that what is generally called 'Holy Spirit' activity is utterly useless if it is not accompanied or motivated by love. Not only is it useless—it can be very dangerous.

An elderly friend of mine, a devout Christian who has most unusual spiritual vision at times, told me of a visit she paid many years ago to a spiritualist meeting led by a famous 'healer' who was a close acquaintance of hers. My friend had no illusions about the spiritualist church, and would never have allowed this man to pray for her, but she occasionally went to his meetings to pray silently for him and for all those present. On this occasion she was sitting in a row of people feeling very conscious of a back pain that she suffered from periodically. Without warning (and without previous knowledge of her affliction) the man sitting next to her placed his hand on her back and prayed for the pain to be removed. The pain did go immediately, but my friend was very angry. She hadn't asked for prayer, and certainly wouldn't have wanted it from a member of the spiritualist church in any case. Later, her concern was fully justified. She collapsed at the sink in her kitchen, unprepared by the pain that usually warned her that it was necessary to lie down for an hour or two. How did the removal of that pain come about? I don't pretend to know, but I do know that I would not want any counterfeit benefits from the same source.

The alarming thing is that similar things are happening in those churches that evangelical Christians would describe as 'sound'. Let us never tire of reminding ourselves and each other that an appetite for spiritual fireworks needs to be curbed until we have learned how to care. Heaven is not the headquarters of the Magic Circle, it's the home of love.

May Jesus be or become the most important thing.

CUDDLING FEAR

Romans 8:15–16 (NIV)

For you did not receive a spirit that makes you a slave again to fear, but you received the Spirit of sonship. And by him we cry, 'Abba, Father.' The Spirit himself testifies with our spirit that we are God's children.

For as long as I can remember, darkness and light have both been only a step away from the place where I am. Sometimes it feels easier and safer to stand absolutely still.

When I was little, this was not just a metaphor, it was a fact as well. There were many nights when I woke to find the darkness pressing upon me like a weight. So frightened was I that I would heave the weight aside, scramble from my bed and creep out onto the landing intending to seek refuge in my parents' room. Our landing received very little light from the frosted-glass window at the top of the stairs, and there were many occasions when I simply froze, midway through my journey. When I close my eyes I can still feel the cold emulsioned wall against which I placed the palm of my left hand, and the metal radiator on which my right hand rested, as I stood, paralysed, too scared to move forwards or backwards. This, despite the fact that I knew the door of my parents' room was very close, and that as soon as I opened it the light from their big front window would illuminate the path to safety. There was an intensity of fear in those locked, motionless minutes that has not been surpassed by any experience since, but there was something else as well. How can I describe that extra sensation without sounding completely mad? There was a cosiness about the pocket of velvet black in which I stood like a human statue, that was compounded of independence and excitement because no one knew that I was there, and, ludicrous though it sounds in view of all that I've already said, a kind of safety. I wasn't anywhere, and in the sort of childhood I had, that wasn't a bad place to be.

I have always, for as long as I can remember, been just a step away from darkness and light, and I am still tempted to stay exactly where I am.

Father, there are real dangers in cuddling our fears to ourselves. We are supposed to be free children of God, but a lack of trust prevents us from taking the step that might make all the difference. Lead us gently from the landing to the light, Lord. Lead us to the kind of security that doesn't need to play games.

BROODING SPIRIT

Genesis 1:1–2 (NIV)

In the beginning God created the heavens and the earth. Now the earth was formless and empty, darkness was over the surface of the deep, and the Spirit of God was hovering over the waters.

Autumn is a fierce reply
To those who still deny your brooding heart
Flaming death in fading sun
The yearly mulching of elation, sadness, pain
A branch unclothed
The tatters flying, tentatively lying
Far more beautiful for dying
Rainbowed floating rain
The final breath
Softly whispering 'enough'
But memories come down like leaves
On old uneven pathways
Such a sweetness
See my breathing stands upon the air
And you, my oldest friend, are there
As evening falls
We pass between the tall park gates
A short cut to the town
A shiver moves the children's swings
The earth is soft and dark and rich
A Christmas cake
We know the grass
Will not be cut again this year
So down the tiled streets
The peopled rivulets
Perhaps towards some tea
In places that were ours but now have changed
Though early Autumn darkness
Stares as hungrily through plate-glass windows
Velveted by bright electric embers
We are glad to be there pouring tea

And pleased that we are laughing once again
Relieved that we are us once more
I have been troubled by a fear
That everything is gone
The fingertips of friendship cold and numb
But Autumn is a season that returns
With intimations of the death of pain
And so, my friend, shall we
Spirit, you have brooded well
Melancholy Autumn beauty
And the Spring to come

Prayer: *The creation is still beautiful, Father, even in its fallen state. Help us to hear the message that the Spirit offers us through the seasons. How wonderful it must have been when it was new. How wonderful it will be when it is new again.*

In every art it is good to have a master.

GEORGE HERBERT, 'OUTLANDISH PROVERBS'

LANDSCAPES OF BEAUTY

ART AND ARTISTS IN THE BIBLE

When this section came to mind, I felt quite excited. Some topics are so bursting with potential that it feels necessary only to plunge one's hands into the great treasure chest of scripture, scoop out armfuls of material, and then do just a little judicious editing. Occasionally it does happen a bit like that, but this time, for a long time, it did not. I simply was not able to think of a way into the theme, until, as is so often the case, I stopped thinking and did the most obvious and simple thing. I made a list. I listed all the different art forms that entered my head, from dance to dressmaking. Then I ran down the list once more, noting next to each item a place in the Bible where that particular skill or art is featured. I confess to drawing a blank on one or two, but I was amazed to discover the extent to which the arts are explicitly or implicitly mentioned in the Old and New Testaments.

I found this very invigorating. As we all know, there is a long and rich tradition of art and drama in the life of Christian communities. However, sections of the modern Church have passed through a phase of extreme wariness, especially towards artists who are unable to squeeze their productivity into the tight confines of a fear-shrunken religion. As a result, we have had to endure some Christian art that is reminiscent of those dreadful pictures from Communist Russia in which tractors seem to take centre stage. Thank God for those who have continued to follow their star as the wise men did, in order to arrive at the place where they were supposed to be, however odd the direction may have seemed. My prayer is that Christian artists will increase in numbers and confidence and be encouraged by the Bible. It rings with echoes of the wonderfully original work done by the greatest artist of all.

DRESSMAKING

Acts 9:36–40 (NIV)

In Joppa there was a disciple named Tabitha (which, when translated, is Dorcas), who was always doing good and helping the poor. About that time she became sick and died, and her body was washed and placed in an upstairs room. Lydda was near Joppa; so when the disciples heard that Peter was in Lydda, they sent two men to him and urged him, 'Please come at once!' Peter went with them, and when he arrived he was taken upstairs to the room. All the widows stood around him, crying and showing him the robes and other clothing that Dorcas had made while she was still with them. Peter sent them all out of the room; then he got down on his knees and prayed. Turning towards the dead woman, he said, 'Tabitha, get up.' She opened her eyes, and seeing Peter she sat up.

Every now and then, the writer of the book of Acts opens a little window to let us witness the exquisite ordinariness of life and death in the early Church.

Dorcas is described as someone who was always doing good and helping the poor, but when Peter arrives he is not—praise the Lord!—presented with a hastily published paperback testimony of her life. Nor is he assailed with a list of sonorously posthumous virtues. Instead, the women who had known Dorcas flock tearfully around the apostle to show him the garments that their friend and sister had so lovingly made for others. No doubt one or two of them were actually wearing the work of her hands. A wonderful legacy, this glowing evidence of the love of God physically and visibly clothing those in need.

In this age when hierarchies of spiritual activity are still dominated by abstract religious practices, it is good to remember that the beauty of God is, more often than not, expressed through practical service offered by one person to another. And, at its best and most truly reflective of the heart of God, that service will never be merely functional. Do you honestly think those heartbroken women would have been drawing Peter's attention to plain old bits of cloth thrown together with just enough care to do their basic job? Of course not. Dorcas had the heart of an artist, but Jesus was the Lord of her art.

Thank you for the way things really are.

DANCE

2 Samuel 6:12–16 (NIV)

Now King David was told, 'The Lord has blessed the household of Obed-Edom and everything he has, because of the ark of God.' So David went down and brought up the ark of God from the house of Obed-Edom to the City of David with rejoicing. When those who were carrying the ark of the Lord had taken six steps, he sacrificed a bull and a fattened calf. David, wearing a linen ephod, danced before the Lord with all his might, while he and the entire house of Israel brought up the ark of the Lord with shouts and the sound of trumpets. As the ark of the Lord was entering the City of David, Michal daughter of Saul watched from a window. And when she saw King David leaping and dancing before the Lord, she despised him in her heart.

Leaving aside the fascinating question of how Obed-Edom felt about having the source of blessing on his household so abruptly removed, my immediate response to this famous passage is uneasiness. You see, I would like to feel my sympathy was solidly with David. Why shouldn't he dance and leap about (somewhat lewdly according to linen ephod experts) because the ark was returning to his own city? Fancy nasty old Michal despising him just because he was expressing joy so un-inhibitedly.

The trouble is that I really am not yet as released in my appreciation of God as David was, and I might just have found myself up at the window with Michal, talking earnestly about meaningful, silent worship being just as valid as 'all this happy-clappy stuff'.

I wish I was more like David. I wish I had that deep-down knowledge of divine parenting that allowed him to break religious rules and flip his lid in the sure and certain knowledge that everything but the state of his heart in relation to God was provisional. I know he went on to do some terrible things, but even then, the manner of his repentance and the way he picked himself up again were a direct function of the uncluttered relationship he had enjoyed with God as a young shepherd on the hills.

Yes, I would like to be more like David. One day I'd like to dance as he danced, but with trousers on…

Free us, Lord!

POETRY

Job 38:4–12 (NIV)

'Where were you when I laid the earth's foundation? Tell me, if you understand. Who marked off its dimensions? Surely you know! Who stretched a measuring line across it? On what were its footings set, or who laid its cornerstone—while the morning stars sang together and all the angels shouted for joy? Who shut up the sea behind doors when it burst forth from the womb, when I made the clouds its garment and wrapped it in thick darkness, when I fixed limits for it and set its doors and bars in place, when I said, "This far you may come and no farther; here is where your proud waves halt"? Have you ever given orders to the morning, or shown the dawn its place…?'

The other day, when everyone was out, I spent an indulgent hour in the kitchen reading aloud from one of those treasuries of verse that you can pick up in second-hand bookshops. And what forgotten treasures there were in that little book. After reading the whole of 'Hohenlinden' in stirring tones, I regaled my invisible but appreciative audience with sonnets from Keats and Shakespeare, mournful Victorian accounts of the deaths of famous men, large chunks of the poetic soul of William Wordsworth, numerous stanzas from 'The Ancient Mariner', and a wide and delightful selection of other gems rediscovered and delivered with the sort of passion that is only possible in an empty house. My invisible audience was ecstatic. The applause went on and on.

Do it with the Bible. Go on—get a Bible, open it at Job and read it aloud to God and all his angels, especially the section that begins with the above passage. It will roll like thunder out of your mouth. Turn to the Song of Songs, a warmly sensuous hymn of love that has so much to say on so many levels, and says it with such lilting, haunting beauty. Treat your empty kitchen to the severely practical, divinely expressed 13th chapter of the first epistle to the Corinthians, one of the most famous and most misunderstood treatises on love ever written. Lamentations, Isaiah, Ecclesiastes, Hosea and, of course, the wonderful Psalms—the list is long. All on its own, the Bible is a treasury of verse, and it's there for you.

Thank you.

WRITING

Jeremiah 31:33–34 (NIV)

'This is the covenant that I will make with the house of Israel after that time,' declares the Lord. 'I will put my law in their minds and write it on their hearts. I will be their God and they will be my people. No longer will a man teach his neighbour, or a man his brother, saying, "Know the Lord," because they will all know me, from the least of them to the greatest,' declares the Lord. 'For I will forgive their wickedness and will remember their sins so more.'

It may be trivializing this great gift of God to equate it with a computer program, but for one as ill-equipped to use modern technology as I am, it is actually quite a helpful comparison. The program I am using right now in order to write these words consists of a huge body of knowledge assembled by someone else, and installed into my computer in its entirety. Like a small boy on a beach for the first time, I paddle timidly on the extreme edge of a sea of word-processing, wondering if I shall ever have the nerve or knowledge to travel to the strange, distant oceans of spreadsheet and database. I suspect not. Recording on a floppy disk is enough to make me seasick.

In this passage we learn the astounding news that God has installed a much more significant body of knowledge into the minds and hearts of those who have returned to him through the saving power of Jesus. Everything that we ever need to know about the will and the ways of God has been writtten indelibly by the Holy Spirit into our own attitudes and approaches. This is the case even if we have not yet understood or appropriated the wisdom that is available in the secret places of our own hearts.

Have we really understood that this action—this promise of God— is intended to make it possible for us to think with his thoughts, to feel with his responses and to act with his intentions? The power and scope of this 'program' is awesome!

Father, you are the great author of mankind, and you have written your heart on our hearts. Teach us how to become so good at reading your will and ways that, in the end, they become the things we spontaneously think and feel and do.

HORTICULTURE

Genesis 2:8–9, 15–17 (NIV)

Now the Lord God had planted a garden in the east, in Eden; and there he put the man he had formed. And the Lord God made all kinds of trees grow out of the ground—trees that were pleasing to the eye and good for food. In the middle of the garden were the tree of life and the tree of the knowledge of good and evil... The Lord God took the man and put him in the Garden of Eden to work it and take care of it. And the Lord God commanded the man, 'You are free to eat from any tree in the garden; but you must not eat from the tree of the knowledge of good and evil, for when you eat of it you will surely die.'

There is one line in this passage which might serve as a guide for all sorts of church activities. I mean the one telling us that the trees God planted in the garden were not only good for food, but pleasing to the eye as well.

One year, because of mix-ups in that fearsomely vulnerable area of church life that we loosely term 'The Arrangements', our harvest festival service was sadly lacking in design or decoration. Because offerings from members of the congregation were mainly in tins or jars, the building ended up looking more like a poorly stocked and stacked supermarket than a church desiring to celebrate the bountiful harvest of God. A number of people were very disappointed by the minimalist response to the most voluptuous season of the year, but one person suggested to me that it didn't really matter how the church looked because the only important thing was getting stuff out to needy people. I fear I disagreed to the point of needing to repent.

That comment aroused exactly the same feelings in me as when another person said she knew a place where she could get really cheap sausages for the church barbeque.

'They're not very nice,' she added, 'but that doesn't matter, does it? They'll fill people up.'

'Doesn't matter! Fill people up!' More repentance.

Our God is not a functionalist. He is creative and caring, an artist and a provider. He makes good things that are pleasing to the eye and good for food.

May our gardens grow flowers and vegetables.

TRANSFIGURATION—HIS FINEST WORK

Mark 9:2–8 (NIV)

After six days Jesus took Peter, James and John with him and led them up a high mountain, where they were all alone. There he was transfigured before them. His clothes became dazzling white, whiter than anyone in the world could bleach them. And there appeared before them Elijah and Moses, who were talking with Jesus. Peter said to Jesus, 'Rabbi, it is good for us to be here. Let us put up three shelters—one for you, one for Moses and one for Elijah.' (He did not know what to say, they were so frightened.) Then a cloud appeared and enveloped them, and a voice came from the cloud: 'This is my Son, whom I love. Listen to him!' Suddenly, when they looked round, they no longer saw anyone with them except Jesus.

The question I have frequently asked myself and other people about this passage (without getting a satisfactory answer) is this. How did Peter, James and John identify Elijah and Moses? Well—how? Was it like the Parkinson show? Did Jesus introduce his special guests one by one as they stepped down through designer clouds? Surely not. Or could it be that the two great prophets were wearing helpful little identity badges like the ones people pin on to themselves at Christian conferences in order to play those excruciatingly awful getting-to-know-you games? I don't think so, do you? Whatever the truth of the matter, the three disciples definitely knew exactly who they were looking at, and they were terrified. Hence Peter's high-pitched, bleating attempt to turn the whole thing into a sort of early version of Spring Harvest. Perhaps he thought the two visiting VIPs might use their tents to do seminars on Nation Transference and Prophet-Slaying for Beginners.

I suspect the truth is that for a short period those nervous disciples were privileged to witness a private preview of God's greatest work of art—the perfection that is planned. A window to heaven was opened on the mountain that day, and when you're on earth gazing into heaven I doubt if labels are necessary.

Won't it be wonderful to see Eden replanted, to know the truth without being told, and actually to be a transfigured part of a design more beautiful than any earthly eye has ever seen?

Give us a vision of heaven, Lord.

STORYTELLING

Matthew 13:35–36 (NIV)

Jesus spoke all these things to the crowd in parables; he did not say anything to them without using a parable. So was fulfilled what was spoken through the prophet: 'I will open my mouth in parables, I will utter things hidden since the creation of the world.' Then he left the crowd and went into the house. His disciples came to him and said, 'Explain to us the parable of the weeds in the field.'

Jesus told some jolly good stories. That must surely be one of the few statements concerning the Christian faith that is pretty well beyond debate. People flocked to hear him because they so loved to hear the parables that, according to this passage, were the Master's sole means of verbal communication when addressing the crowds.

Let us now engage in a little simple logic. Why did Jesus select the art of storytelling for use in his ministry? The answer, unless we are all completely mad, is that they worked. The combination of entertainment, relevance and message was clearly irresistible. Apart from anything else, any attempt to hold the attention of thousands of people on a Judean hillside without the benefit of a microphone would have been doomed from the start if the content of the talk was heavily and exclusively theological or glumly punitive. Storytelling worked.

That being the case, why do we hear so little of this useful craft in the Church nowadays? Certainly not because people don't like stories any more. They love them as much as ever. They always did and they always will. The true answer may well be that storytelling is much more difficult than is generally realized. Putting a good story together, trying it out on an audience, adapting it according to response, trying it again with a different group of people, adding, subtracting and chipping away until a final version emerges, all takes time and application. And I am quite sure Jesus himself went through that process. His parables were conceived and crafted out of day-to-day experience, not handed to him ready written by the divine quartermaster, to be learned in time for the start of his ministy. Let us pray that God will bless the Church by energizing people who are able and willing to apply themselves to continuing the storytelling tradition established by its most famous exponent.

Thank you for the storytellers that we have. Please give us more.

SONG

Song of Songs 2:9–13 (NIV)

Look! There he stands behind our wall, gazing through the windows, peering through the lattice. My lover spoke and said to me, 'Arise, my darling, my beautiful one, and come with me. See! The winter is past; the rains are over and gone. Flowers appear on the earth; the season of singing has come, the cooing of doves is heard in our land. The fig-tree forms its early fruit; the blossoming vines spread their fragrance. Arise, come, my darling; my beautiful one, come with me.'

Let us have a moment of quiet honesty here. For all the triumphalist statements that one hears nowadays, there is, at the heart of many believers' experience, a bittersweet sadness, and a yearning for the coming true of all that our walk with Jesus once seemed to promise. We are cluttered with so many things, are we not? And most of those 'things' don't really take us much further forward as far as Jesus is concerned. We want the season of singing to come. We want to believe that our beloved will see us as truly beautiful, and will one day call us to come with him through the wonderful after-rain fragrance of the blossoming vines. Does that prospect seem distant to you? It does to me much of the time.

And yet, there are moments when just a few clear notes in the back of my mind suggest that this season of singing will come, perhaps has already begun on the other side of the thicket of nonsenses that surround me. Such moments, significantly, are usually connected with an experience of—well, of giving up.

When my daughter was a little younger, she would sometimes have days when she became overtired and, as a result, was snappy and aggressive or argumentative. Towards the end of these difficult days she would suddenly run out of steam altogether. Tears would fill her eyes and she would extend both arms in my direction, entreating me to take over and just love her.

So it is with me and God. In those moments when I give up my strivings and my religion and my certainties and my fragile little strengths and cry out desperately for the love of Jesus, I hear the sound of singing, and I sense in my heart that everything will be all right.

Help me to give up.

MUSIC

Ezekiel 33:30–32 (NIV)

As for you, son of man, your countrymen are talking together about you by the walls and at the doors of the houses, saying to each other, 'Come and hear the message that has come from the Lord.' My people come to you, as they usually do, and sit before you to listen to your words, but they do not put them into practice. With their mouths they express devotion, but their hearts are greedy for unjust gain. Indeed, to them you are nothing more than one who sings love songs with a beautiful voice and plays an instrument well, for they hear your words but do not put them into practice.

A disconcerting thing about writing Bible reading notes is that the passages often speak with as much clarity to the writer as to those who read his notes. And here's a good example. It speaks to me particularly because the talks I do tread a line between entertainment and ministry —not, I hasten to add, that I dismiss either. The problem comes when people enjoy the humour and even shed a tear at the 'moving bits', but are actually no more shifted in their attitudes or intentions than if they had been watching a movie tearjerker on a Friday night, cuddled up to a curry and a pint.

'Wonderful to hear about the love and the sense of humour of God,' a man says as he files out and sets off homeward, but if absolutely nothing changes as a result, then something is wrong with him or me or both of us. I have always stubbornly refused to consider such a thing as a call to the front at the end of meetings, but I had a bit of a shock recently. A friend's non-Christian husband had come to one of our meetings. Afterwards he said to his wife, 'If that bloke had asked me to come up and do whatever, I would've gone, you know.' Perhaps I should try to be as flexible in this area as I claim to be in others.

The message of the love and power of God makes beautiful music, but it is not just entertainment, to be taken or left, or played like a favourite track on a CD or tape. The music of heaven should move folk right off the spot where they had always felt safe to stand.

If music really is the food of love…

DRAMA

Ezekiel 12:3–6 (NIV)

Therefore, son of man, pack your belongings for exile and in the daytime, as they watch, set out and go from where you are to another place. Perhaps they will understand, though they are a rebellious house. During the daytime, while they watch, bring out your belongings packed for exile. Then in the evening, while they are watching, go out like those who go into exile. While they watch, dig through the wall and take your belongings out through it. Put them on your shoulder as they are watching and carry them out at dusk. Cover your face so that you cannot see the land, for I have made you a sign to the house of Israel.

The position of drama in the church in this country seems to have changed somewhat over the last 20 years. In the 1960s and '70s, there were a number of full-time drama groups more or less making a living out of appearances at conferences, church weekends and other events. They seemed to function most successfully when providing illustration or adding emphasis to a central theme or talk. Nowadays many of those groups have either shrunk drastically or disappeared altogether, but as I read about this vivid piece of acting demanded from Ezekiel by God, I find myself wondering if there might possibly be a brave new role for Christian thespians in the future. They will certainly need to be brave if they are to follow in Ezekiel's footsteps.

This particular piece of roleplay, for instance, is a clear message from God to Israel, stating that the whole nation will shortly go into exile because of the rebelliousness of their hearts. Anything could happen to a prophet after a performance like that. I wonder how a drama group which presented that kind of sharp edge to a modern church audience would be received.

It is something of a generalization, but in the past drama tended to be thought of as an evangelistic tool. Perhaps the time has come for those with skills in this area to ask God how they might be used to speak fearlessly to a church which tends to be terribly nice.

Father, we really are not very good at plain speaking nowadays. We pray for the emergence of Christians who will genuinely seek your will, and be prepared to use their dramatic skills as obediently as Ezekiel.

ARCHITECTURE

2 Chronicles 3:1–2 (NIV)

Then Solomon began to build the temple of the Lord in Jerusalem on Mount Moriah, where the Lord had appeared to his father David. It was on the threshing-floor of Araunah the Jebusite, the place provided by David. He began building on the second day of the second month in the fourth year of his reign.

We all have a temple to build or, at any rate, to maintain. And that temple is, of course, our physical body. 'Do you not know that your body is a temple of the Holy Spirit, who is in you, whom you have received from God?' (1 Corinthians 6:19).

Your body may not look like the temple of the Holy Spirit—mine doesn't—but in a practical and spiritual sense it is the place where the Holy Spirit resides, so we must take Paul's words seriously. The degree of repair and adaptation required to turn our temple into something worth inhabiting might seem intimidating, but that's why this passage from Chronicles inspires me. Solomon started with empty space and a deep conviction that the thing must be built. And it took a long time, just as it might take us a long time, whatever would-be workers of spiritual magic may say.

Take me, for instance. Twenty-four years ago I smoked 60 cigarettes a day. No, don't stop reading if you're a smoker. I'm talking about me, not getting at you. I knew I should stop, and I hoped that God would lift the problem painlessly out of my life. He'd done it for others I knew. He didn't do it for me—thank God! That experience of gritting my teeth through nine months of absolute misery before the pressure eased was one of the most useful things that ever happened to me. And, of course, God knew it would be.

More recently I have launched a major attack on my vastly over-weight condition. The battle still rages, but I have lost two stone and I do feel a lot better. The trouble with dieting and exercise, as you all know, is that it gives you an enormous appetite...

It takes our whole lives. We try and we fail and we try again and we fail again, but this is the temple of the Holy Spirit, so let's not give up.

Help us to do it for you.

FILLED WITH THE SPIRIT AND THE SKILL

Exodus 35:30–35 (NIV)

Then Moses said to the Israelites, 'See, the Lord has chosen Bezalel son of Uri, the son of Hur, of the tribe of Judah, and he has filled him with the Spirit of God, with skill, ability and knowledge in all kinds of crafts—to make artistic designs for work in gold, silver and bronze, to cut and set stones, to work in wood and to engage in all kinds of artistic craftsmanship. And he has given both him and Oholiab son of Ahisamach, of the tribe of Dan, the ability to teach others. He has filled them with skill to do all kinds of work as craftsmen, designers, embroiderers in blue, purple and scarlet yarn and fine linen, and weavers—all of them master craftsmen and designers.

I find it deeply satisfying—indeed, quite wonderful—that these radiantly enthusiastic verses identify such a specific link between being filled with the Spirit of God and being filled with the craftsmanship and artistic ability needed to construct and decorate the tabernacle that Moses had been commanded to build. Not only were Bezalel and Oholiab highly capable artists themselves, but they were also gifted by God with the ability to teach others to acquire those same skills.

Why am I so uplifted by this passage? Well, even as I write, a list forms in my mind of all the Christian artists I have known who at various points in their lives have felt marginalized or actively disapproved of by sections of the Church. Such disapproval is frequently fuelled by fear, the fear that art is a maverick pursuit, one that will help to undermine the foundations of 'church' as it is understood, or reflect critically on negative aspects of Christianity. One friend of mine laid down his art materials for 20 years because of attitudes prevailing at the time of his conversion. He is so much more complete as a Christian and a human being since taking them up again.

So, all you tentative Christian artists—out with your brushes and your pens and your tools and your needles and your music and whatever else you need to do your thing. God has filled you with his Spirit and with the skills to celebrate that fact. Hallelujah!

Father, don't let me waste my gifts.

In the resurrection everyone will receive that
bodily stature which he had in his prime,
even though he has died an old man.

ST AUGUSTINE

POWER TO PERSEVERE

THE MIRACLE OF RESURRECTION

Have you heard of Bert Hinkler?

I was about to say, 'No, neither had I until last year'—but I expect someone is replying, 'Yes, actually, I have.' There are always a few clever Dicks around to put us all straight, aren't there? You know the sort of people I mean. They're the ones who go along to watch TV quiz shows being made, and shout out the right answer when the contestants are stumped and the question master says, 'Let's ask our audience.' They're the ones who have been aware for years that a pregnant goldfish is called a 'twit'. They're the ones who came out of their mother's womb, not clearing their lungs with a good old vulgar cry, but reeling off the entire list of the kings and queens of England, the ones who are programmed within their genes to know that a 'pucket' is a congress of caterpillars. They're the ones who, if ever they entered for the *Mastermind* contest on television, would choose General Knowledge as their specialist subject.

Anyway, leaving them aside, for all those who are honest enough to admit that they do not have an encyclopedic knowledge of Bert Hinkler, I would like to tell you how Bridget and I came to hear about him, and about the unusual act of resurrection that has been organized in his honour.

In the summer of 1996 we took three of our children on a speaking tour that involved three weeks in Australia, a week in New Zealand and a week in America. In the course of the Australian part of the tour, we made a return visit to the state of Queensland, a vast tract of country that we have come to love very much, not just because it is a beautiful and fascinating part of the world, but also because we have many good friends there (and I can nearly do the accent). One evening we were booked to speak in Bundaberg, a small coastal town where we had stayed during a previous trip. The only thing we really knew about Bundaberg was the fact that a very good ginger beer was manufactured there, one which is sold in its stubby brown glass bottles all over Australia—we've consumed many a gallon of ice-cold ginger beer during long, hot car-trips in Oz.

This particular evening was a specially significant one for Bridget and me. August the first was our 26th wedding anniversary, and the children had stayed behind for the night with a friend in the Sunshine Coast apartment that was to be our base while we were in Queensland.

A large sign over the entrance to the motel we had been booked into informed us and the rest of the world that it was called simply 'The Bert Hinkler Motor Inn'. Even as we registered and found our way to the room where we were to stay the night, I found myself idly wondering if Bert Hinkler was the owner of a whole chain of motels, or whether he was some famous ex-resident of Bundaberg whose name was likely to appear on garages and restaurants and memorial halls all over town, rather as King Arthur's does in Tintagel.

Our room was well-equipped and comfortable, except for one item, a double water-bed, something neither of us had ever experienced before. I lay down tentatively on one side, only to find that the tide immediately came in, as it were, on the other, causing it to expand and rise bulbously. I nervously anticipated, rightly as it turned out, that trying to relax on the stomach of a giant suffering from gastro-enteritis would be easier than sleeping on this thing. Bridget took one look at my overweight form encased in its deep rubber trough, and said dispassionately, 'We might as well cancel our trip to Harvey Bay to see the whales.'

Very amusing. Deciding to change the subject, I spoke from my watery grave.

'Who do you think Bert Hinkler is?'

'No idea. Who do you think he is?'

'No idea—that's why I asked you.'

Conversation always sparkles like that in the Plass household. That's the way it is with writers.

Our performance went well that evening. It was one of those very local events where everyone knows everyone else, and they've all set out from home with the firm intention of having a really good evening whatever happens. It was fun and friendly and we felt good. As our host drove us home we asked him who Bert Hinkler was.

'I'll show you tomorrow,' he said.

After a passionless night spent on our water-bed (a stand-up comic would undoubtedly have felt constrained to say that we were drifting apart) we checked out and set off with our host to a different part of town, where we found an extensive, beautifully maintained area of ornate gardens devoted exclusively to the memory of this same Bert Hinkler. Right in the centre of this area stood a house, and, so strange did this building appear to my eyes, that I stood quite still for a moment, trying to make sense of what I was seeing. For this unpretentious little villa, set in the middle of a small Queensland town halfway up the east coast of Australia, and 15,000 miles away from the islands of Great Britain was, without any doubt at all, a typically English house, dating perhaps from the mid-1920s. There it was—standing there—an English house.

'Come in and have a look round,' said our host.

Inside, we found that the furnishings and decoration were of exactly the same era, and that the house itself was a sort of museum—more than that, it was a shrine—to the memory of Bert Hinkler, one-time resident of the town of Bundaberg and a pioneer of international air travel.

We found out lots of facts about him.

Born in Bundaberg in 1892, by the age of 19 Bert Hinkler had already constructed and flown his own glider. He ate, slept, breathed and dreamed flying. Arriving in England just as war broke out he offered himself to the Royal Naval Air Service and was accepted as a volunteer. After 122 flights over France, including 36 night bombing raids he was awarded the DSM and demobilized in 1919, having graduated as a pilot.

Hinkler then concentrated on record-breaking flights, including, in 1928, a new record for the trip from England to Australia, when he took fifteen and a half days to fly from Croydon to Darwin. The previous record had been 29 days. Other exploits, adventures and records followed until, in 1933, in the course of a further flight to Australia, Hinkler's plane crashed in the Italian Alps and he was killed on impact. The Italian nation showed great sympathy, organizing and paying for a funeral with full military honours in Florence on Monday, 1 May 1933.

During his lifetime *The Times* newspaper had spoken of Hinkler's exceptional skill, daring judgment, and genius amounting almost to a sixth sense for the discovery of navigational facts, adding that his triumphs were ones of which the 'British race' must justly be proud.

And I had never heard of him.

We moved slowly from room to room in the little house, studying the faded old photographs of Bert greeting the press, Bert standing beside one of his planes waving goodbye before yet another record-challenging trip, and Bert being presented with an award by some long-dead dignitary. There were items of clothing and other bits and pieces that had actually belonged to Bert, together with framed documents of various kinds, all relating to his achievements and successes. There was no doubt at all that, in his time, Bert Hinkler had been a real celebrity, not just in Australia, but also in Great Britain (we discovered that he had been a long-time resident of Southampton), and in other parts of the world as well.

Pausing to look out across the gardens from one of the upstairs windows, I felt a sudden wave of sadness and a momentary shiver of something akin to fear. The inside of that house was so intimate and Bert Hinkler-ish. He and it had been so important once. Could it be possible that he simply didn't exist any more, and that hardly anybody really cared whether he ever had done or not? His name had meant nothing to me before arriving at the motel last night. I had vaguely assumed that he must be some kind of motel boss. I had been wrong, but what difference did it really make? All that fame and press coverage and excitement and sheer intensity of life had been more or less forgotten in England, where he had obviously been extremely well known at one time. I wondered how many Australians remained familiar with his name and exploits.

It suddenly occurred to me that I had still not solved the mystery of the house.

'Why,' I asked the lady who sat by the front door taking money, 'have you built a copy of an English house in an Australian town?'

'We haven't,' she replied.

'You haven't?'

'No, this isn't a copy of an English house, sir. This is an English house.'

'But how——?'

'This is the actual house that Bert Hinkler owned when he was living in England. The whole building was taken to pieces brick by brick, everything was numbered and recorded and packed up, and then it was all transported over to Australia and put together again exactly as it was in Southampton. Amazing, isn't it?'

I nodded. 'Yes, it is, quite amazing.'

I wandered outside after that and stood for a moment leaning on a fence in the bright Queensland sunshine, just staring at Bert Hinkler's Southampton house and indulging in a little fantasy. Imagine, I thought, if Bert were to be given a little holiday from wherever he was now—heaven, hopefully—and allowed to pay a brief visit to his old home town of Bundaberg. He finds himself walking along the street, taking in all the old familiar sights and sounds that he once knew so well, when suddenly he comes to a dead stop.

'Cripes!' he exclaims, being an Australian, 'that looks just like my old house in England! What the heck is something like that doing here in Bundaberg?'

Slowly approaching the building he studies it in detail, becoming more and more puzzled as it dawns on him that this is not only like his old house. This is his old house. How could his Southampton residence possibly have got to Bundaberg, for goodness' sake? How could it? Some angel due for a rocket, no doubt, when the boss finds that the reality-reconstruction plans have been studied a little too carelessly.

I think that once he had learned what actually happened Bert would be really pleased, don't you? What an honour for him that the citizens of Bundaberg thought it worthwhile to take his house like some giant building kit, and carry it right across to the other side of the world, so that it could be rebuilt in the town that is proud to claim him as a son.

Of course, they were not able actually to resurrect Bert Hinkler, although I think that they would have done if they could. They had a jolly good try, didn't they? The following notes are about resurrection, which, for each of us, will be much more total and spectacular than Bert's. We shall be alive again, complete down to the last detail with the personalities that are unique to us, fully aware and able to recognize and communicate with each other. We shall not be in Bundaberg, beautiful though that town is, but in an even better place, where God himself will welcome us proudly as returned sons and daughters, and we shall take our rightful place as citizens of heaven.

I do hope Bert will be there.

Prayer
Father, we sometimes get a bit worried about the reality of resurrection and eternal life. Help us to hold as tightly to the words of Jesus as if we were clinging to his cloak in a crowd. Thank you for his costly and ultimate gift to us of life in heaven with you.

A CHANGE OF LANDSCAPE

John 20:1–4 (RSV)

Now on the first day of the week Mary Magdalene came to the tomb early, while it was still dark, and saw that the stone had been taken away from the tomb. So she ran, and went to Simon Peter and the other disciple, the one whom Jesus loved, and said to them, 'They have taken the Lord out of the tomb, and we do not know where they have laid him.' Peter then came out with the other disciple, and they went toward the tomb. They both ran, but the other disciple outran Peter and reached the tomb first.

A friend of mine had a very frightening experience when he was a teenager. Walking home in the dark after a late party, he suddenly became aware that the landscape near his parents' house was 'all wrong'. A field that had been empty twelve hours earlier was now occupied by something that, on that cloudy starless night, appeared to be a castle-like building. Simon stood stock-still for a moment as his mind attempted in vain to accommodate this logical impossibility. Then, seized by scalp-prickling horror, he sprinted away to the safety of home, only to learn from his amused parents that the 'castle' was actually a huge marquee, erected for some event on the following day.

Mary's experience was probably worse. The stone was gone, the soldiers were gone and the body was gone. It was all wrong, and it must have shaken her up. Mysterious empty tombs on dark nights are the stuff that Hammer films are made of. No wonder she ran to where Peter and John were, gasping out as she arrived the quite reasonable hypothesis that someone had moved the body. What an impact her news made on the disciples!

Bleary-eyed and unwashed, the Steve Ovett and Sebastian Coe of the New Testament hitched their skirts up and gave it everything they'd got. On the final bend John overtook Peter and was first to arrive at the tomb, where, ironically after all that explosive effort, he stopped abruptly and was unable to bring himself actually to enter it. What a tumult of emotions, questions and speculations must have filled the mind and heart of the disciple whom Jesus loved.

Is there anybody or anything in the world or the universe that would make me run like that?

MOMENTS OF TRUTH

John 20:5–10 (RSV)

Stooping to look in, he saw the linen cloths lying there, but he did not go in. Then Simon Peter came, following him, and went into the tomb; he saw the linen cloths lying, and the napkin, which had been on his head, not lying with the linen cloths but rolled up in a place by itself. Then the other disciple, who reached the tomb first, also went in, and he saw and believed; for as yet they did not know the scripture, that he must rise from the dead.

One of the most significant moments in my life occurred on the top of a double-decker bus when I was about ten years old. That morning I had read the words 'Everyone is I' in some obscure book, and I was frowningly anxious to work out what it meant. As the bus arrived in Tunbridge Wells and stopped at a zebra crossing, I looked down and, seeing an elderly lady making her laborious way from one side of the road to the other, the truth suddenly hit me. That lady was as important to herself as I was to myself. I was not the star player in the universe, and the rest of the world's population were not bit-players in my life. That recognition changed my perception fundamentally.

A much more famous moment of recognition happened in Israel when Malcolm Muggeridge, feeling cynical and sickened by commercialism and tourist exploitation of the (alleged) scene of Jesus' birth, gradually became aware of the way in which the faces of visiting pilgrims were quite transfigured by the idea that they were in the place where the great life began. Muggeridge saw a vital truth on that day and was deeply affected on a personal level.

Such moments of recognition impart knowledge that cannot be taught in normal ways and they change lives.

Here, in the empty tomb, Peter and John gaze with growing awareness at the way in which the grave clothes are lying in an undisturbed position, as though the body had melted quietly away. In John's mind at least the awe-inspiring truth chimed like heavenly bells. It wasn't all over. The story was not finished. Somewhere, somehow—Jesus was alive!

Have we told others about the significant moments of recognition in our lives? Perhaps we think they weren't spiritual enough.

BLIND GRIEF

John 20:11–14 (RSV)

But Mary stood weeping outside the tomb, and as she wept she stooped to look into the tomb; and she saw two angels in white, sitting where the body of Jesus had lain, one at the head and one at the feet. They said to her, 'Woman, why are you weeping?' She said to them, 'Because they have taken away my Lord, and I do not know where they have laid him.' Saying this, she turned round and saw Jesus standing, but she did not know that it was Jesus.

Mary must have been pretty tough to withstand the traumas of this extraordinary day. When she got to the tomb, she experienced two encounters that my son would (with typical irreverence) describe as gobsmackers. The first was with the two angels.

When we read that Mary, still weeping, leaned down and saw two angels sitting in the tomb, then had a little chat with them, we tend to forget the drama and tension of the situation. This is partly due to the brevity with which the event is recorded, and partly to the dismal presentation of the scriptures that we have allowed and endured for generations. Public readings of the Bible have been conducted in tones of such sepulchral monotony for so long now that there is a corporate perception of biblical characters as two-dimensional, unemotional, cardboard cut-out figures who trot out their appointed lines in semi-anaesthetized voices. This distraught lady must have come very near to braining herself on the roof of the tomb when she saw these two strange figures who'd posted themselves at either end of the place where Jesus' body had lain. Did she know they were angels? I don't know, but such odd behaviour from human beings would have been no less alarming.

Perhaps the strength of grief overpowered fear, though. As soon as it became clear that these two beings knew nothing about the where-abouts of the body, Mary turned away to search elsewhere. How ironic that the angels asked their 'silly' question about why was she weeping because they could see Jesus standing behind her! Her sight was blurred by tears when she turned. She didn't recognize him.

Do we grieve his absence even as he stands before us?

GETTING EXCITED

John 20:15–17 (RSV)

Jesus said to her, 'Woman, why are you weeping? Whom do you seek?' Supposing him to be the gardener, she said to him, 'Sir, if you have carried him away, tell me where you have laid him, and I will take him away.' Jesus said to her, 'Mary.' She turned and said to him in Hebrew, 'Rab-bo'ni!' (which means Teacher). Jesus said to her, 'Do not hold me, for I have not yet ascended to the Father, but go to my brethren and say to them, I am ascending to my Father and your Father, to my God and your God.'

I have seen films, pictures and mimes of this wonderful encounter, the second and most staggering of Mary's 'gobsmackers'. In most of these presentations Jesus is standing like some product of the taxidermist's art, stiffly gesturing away a remarkably restrained Mary who has attempted to touch him in an elegant, saint-like manner. If it really happened like that, let's all give up and go and become frog-worshippers. G.K. Chesterton made the point that believers and non-believers alike have great problems about genuinely accepting the fact that 'he became man'. The divine ordinariness of Jesus should be one of our greatest comforts. Instead, it's a serious stumbling block to many, perhaps because it brings the reality of God so close that we are forced to respond from the heart, rather than from bits of our minds.

Do you really believe that Jesus was not smiling broadly when he asked Mary why she was crying and who she was looking for? Do you really think that Mary didn't throw herself at her beloved friend and master after he said her name in a way that was specially his? And do you not think he would have chucklingly retreated with both arms extended as he warned her that she must not touch him because he had not yet ascended to his Father ('not cooked yet' as a small friend put it)?

How we need some of this Mary-style excitement in the modern Church, the kind of excitement that follows real meetings with this real Jesus who is more down-to-earth than many of his followers.

Can you see her running and leaping, her eyes now wet with tears of joy, on her way to tell the disciples?

We want to be excited, Lord.

WHO NEEDS WHO?

John 20:19–23 (RSV)

On the evening of that day, the first day of the week, the doors being shut where the disciples were, for fear of the Jews, Jesus came and stood among them and said to them, 'Peace be with you.' When he had said this, he showed them his hands and his side. Then the disciples were glad when they saw the Lord. Jesus said to them again, 'Peace be with you. As the Father has sent me, even so I send you.' And when he had said this, he breathed on them, and said to them, 'Receive the Holy Spirit. If you forgive the sins of any, they are forgiven, if you retain the sins of any, they are retained.'

Neither John's perception of the truth nor Mary's account of that first sparkling meeting seems to have inspired any courage in the disciples. Here they are on the evening of that same Sunday, securely locked in for fear of the Jewish authorities tracking them down, probably discussing the day's events over and over again, but unable to do anything without the direct leadership and guidance of Jesus.

A lot of prayer groups, churches and fellowships are in the same position. I've belonged to some of them. I've led one or two of them. Personally, I think it's far better to wait for Jesus to come, than to fabricate or role-play religious activity that is not authorized or commissioned. It's interesting to note that Jesus sends the disciples as he has been sent by the Father. In other words, he is asking for the kind of love and obedience that characterized his own ministry—a tall order for most of us without the comfort and assistance of the Holy Spirit. William Barclay points out how, from this speech, we learn that Jesus needs the Church, and the Church needs Jesus. Our failing groups might do well to abandon religion and invite Jesus to stand in their midst.

Once again the drama of the moment is rather inadequately expressed by the writer's assertion that 'the disciples were glad when they saw the Lord'. I'm quite sure that their responses varied from stunned silence to wild, celebrated joy. These people were not stained-glass window types. Jesus was alive—anything was possible.

Do we believe that Jesus needs us? Do we need him?

STAYING HONEST

John 20:24–25 (RSV)

Now Thomas, one of the twelve, called the Twin, was not with them when Jesus came. So the other disciples told him, 'We have seen the Lord.' But he said to them, 'Unless I see in his hands the print of the nails, and place my finger in the mark of the nails, and place my hand in his side, I will not believe.'

I like the sound of Thomas. He may have been a bit of an Eeyore ('Let us also go, that we may die with him'), but he was honest and straightforward, and more than ready to commit himself when the evidence was clear. We could do with a few more like him in the church today.

A friend of mine had to attend a foundation course run by a fellowship in the Midlands (attendance was compulsory for all prospective church members). The leader read out 1 John 3:6, and said it meant that anyone who became a Christian would stop sinning. My friend (a Christian for many years) interjected. 'You're not saying, are you, that Christians never sin? Because they do, don't they?'

Reproof, Christian forgiveness, humble disagreement and heavily veiled human annoyance met in the crinkly smile of the leader. 'If that's what the scripture says,' he replied, 'then that must be the truth, mustn't it?' 'Well, I sin,' said my friend, 'don't you? And anyway, it says later on in the same letter that if we do sin—' 'I think we'd better agree to differ, friend,' interrupted the leader. 'We'll talk about it afterwards, OK?'

They did—and what horrified my friend was that it wasn't just a matter of mistaken teaching.

'Between you and me,' said the leader, 'of course Christians sin, but I didn't want to mislead all those new Christians on the course.'

Maybe Thomas was at fault for going off to be solitary with his grief (I would have missed Jesus' first appearance as well), but he stuck to his guns when faced with the emotional intensity of the others' experience. He wasn't going to say anything he didn't actually believe, however much he wanted it to be true. I like him.

Father, help us to be honest and loving like Thomas, and help those of us who get a bit solitary, to be part of the Church, for your sake. We don't want to miss anything good!

A MESSAGE FROM THE PAST

John 20:26–31 (RSV)

Eight days later, his disciples were again in the house, and Thomas was with them. The doors were shut, but Jesus came and stood among them, and said, 'Peace be with you.' Then he said to Thomas, 'Put your finger here, and see my hands, and put out your hand, and place it in my side: do not be faithless, but believing.' Thomas answered him, 'My Lord and my God!' Jesus said to him, 'Have you believed because you have seen me? Blessed are those who have not seen and yet believe.' Now Jesus did many other signs in the presence of the disciples, which are not written in this book; but these are written that you may believe that Jesus is the Christ, the Son of God, and that believing you may have life in his name.

Eight days after his first appearances Jesus stood among his disciples again, a real, touchable man. But the Bible doesn't say that Thomas did touch him, and I doubt if he bothered. That man standing in front of him, the man who had been at the front of his mind for the last eight days, as the other disciples endlessly discussed recent events, was Jesus. He was alive.

'My Lord and my God!' Thomas was as direct and uncompromising in his newfound belief as he had been in his doubt. As I said, Thomas (and all the others present behind those locked doors) were lucky. They met the risen Jesus and knew that death was somehow defeated. But now Jesus speaks a message down through the passage of 2,000 years to those of us who were not able to be there at the time.

'Blessed are those who have not seen and yet believe.' That's us, folks! We can meet the risen Jesus in the Bible, in personal or corporate prayer, and in the lives of others, but (except for a minuscule minority) we cannot meet him face to face as the disciples did. Jesus says we are blessed if we believe in him without that benefit. Let's face it, however good we may be at debating, it is only our personal experience of the risen Jesus that will convince others of the truth.

Sceptic: Why did God create evil, then?
Disciple: I don't know, but Jesus came back to life...

WORKING AND WAITING

John 21:1–3 (RSV)

After this Jesus revealed himself again to the disciples by the Sea of Tiberias; and he revealed himself in this way. Simon Peter, Thomas called the Twin, Nathanael of Cana in Galilee, the sons of Zebedee, and two others of his disciples were together. Simon Peter said to them, 'I am going fishing.' They said to him, 'We will go with you.' They went out and got into the boat, but that night they caught nothing.

'Blow this for a game of soldiers—I'm going fishing!' This may not be an exact rendering of the Greek text, but I suspect it sums up Peter's feelings and attitudes. How long was a volatile character like him going to put up with hiding behind locked doors and waiting for something to happen? Jesus had said he was sending the disciples out to forgive and retain sins, empowered by the Holy Spirit, but somehow the 'Go!' had not yet been said. Perhaps, also, Peter was secretly troubled by his triple denial. Did it disqualify him? Was he forgiven? Would it ever be brought up? Peter was neither the first nor the last man to seek refuge from his anxieties in a day's fishing. They spent the whole night in the boat, but caught nothing. I bet they enjoyed it, though. A spot of hard physical effort can be an excellent antidote to the poison of emotional or spiritual turmoil. (This applies particularly to overweight, sedentary writers whose only exercise is eating.)

Whatever else was happening in the hearts of these disciples as they toiled with their nets, they must have been filled with a constant, buzzing excitement, an excitement that sprung from the knowledge that Jesus could turn up at any moment, in any place. Perhaps he would come walking across the surface of the water just as he had done before. Perhaps this time, Peter would keep his footing, join his master and do a little dance of joy with him across the Sea of Tiberius.

The Christian life at its best is like that, isn't it? Jesus can enter any situation, transforming it, and you and me. As the dawn breaks, that is what is about to happen to Peter.

Am I watching for him? Do I expect him?

UNCONDITIONAL LOVE

John 21:4–8 (RSV)

Just as day was breaking, Jesus stood on the beach; yet the disciples did not know that it was Jesus. Jesus said to them, 'Children, have you any fish?' They answered him, 'No.' He said to them, 'Cast the net on the right side of the boat, and you will find some.' So they cast it, and now they were not able to haul it in, for the quantity of fish. That disciple whom Jesus loved said to Peter, 'It is the Lord!' When Simon Peter heard that it was the Lord, he put on his clothes, for he was stripped for work, and sprang into the sea. But the other disciples came in the boat, dragging the net full of fish, for they were not far from the land, but about a hundred yards off.

If you want to know what the Christian faith is really about, this incident will provide as good an answer as any. It is about the kind of spontaneous, non-religious, extravagant love and affection that has motivated true followers of Jesus for generations.

At first, in the half-light of dawn, the disciples failed to recognize Jesus. As far as they were concerned, he was a stranger who shouted advice from the shore (quite a common occurrence apparently), and very good advice it turned out to be.

Then, as the sky lightened and visibility improved, John happened to look towards the shore as he paused from his efforts for a moment, and something about the silhouette and stance of the solitary figure on the beach seemed terribly familiar.

'It's the Lord!' he whispered to Peter. Seconds later he must have been rocking in the slipstream of his large piscatorial colleague, who had stayed for only as long as it took to throw some clothes on before leaping into the water and splashing his way towards Jesus. Thoroughly confused at that point about the meaning of Jesus' past ministry, uncertain about the present, totally ignorant of what the future might hold, and with the knotty tissue of those three denials still unresolved, Peter just wanted to be with the person he loved. God grant us that same unconditional desire to be with Jesus.

Father, help us to recognize Jesus when he helps us with ordinary things. We want to love him as much as Peter did.

GOD IN HIS OWN WORLD

John 23:9–14 (RSV)

When they got out on land, they saw a charcoal fire there, with fish lying on it, and bread. Jesus said to them, 'Bring some of the fish that you have just caught.' So Simon Peter went aboard and hauled the net ashore, full of large fish, a hundred and fifty-three of them; and although there were so many, the net was not torn. Jesus said to them, 'Come and have breakfast.' Now none of the disciples dared asked him, 'Who are you?' They knew it was the Lord. Jesus came and took the bread and gave it to them, and so with the fish. This was now the third time that Jesus was revealed to the disciples after he was raised from the dead.

I have already mentioned, in connection with Mary's first sight of her risen Master, the divine ordinariness of Jesus. Here, in this little scene on the beach, the same quality is even more dramatically evident. How wonderful that God doesn't approach such moments in his own history as though he was an epic film producer. No stirring music, no cast of thousands, no apocalyptic visions in the sky. The risen Jesus—God himself, the glory of the universe—was cooking breakfast for his friends. Real and solid, he nudged the fire into more effective life and moved his head to avoid getting smoke in his eyes. Ordinary. Peaceful.

Like waking up after a nightmare, a real encounter with God nearly always feels like a blessedly reassuring return to the familiar and warm sensation of true reality. That's why it's so important to make it clear to non-believers that they are not being asked to give their hearts to some alien, faraway, irrelevant concept. They might be more willing to give their hearts to a God who knows how to get an open fire going without matches or paraffin. This is the world he made. He and it are parts of the same reality.

Do you feel ignorant sometimes when you read the Bible? I often do. That's why I had to find out what other writers thought about the significance of the 153 fish that were caught by the disciples, and I was amazed at the number of complex explanations that have been suggested over the years. Do you think they just enjoyed counting their big catch, do you? Is that a possible explanation? No—too ordinary, eh?

What is 'real life'?

IT HAS TO BE SAID

John 21:15–19 (RSV)

When they had finished breakfast, Jesus said to Simon Peter, 'Simon, son of John, do you love me more than these?' He said to him, 'Yes, Lord, you know that I love you.' He said to him, 'Feed my lambs.' A second time he said to him. 'Simon, son of John, do you love me?' He said to him, 'Yes, Lord, you know that I love you.' He said to him. 'Tend my sheep.' He said to him the third time, 'Simon, son of John, do you love me?' Peter was grieved because he said to him the third time, 'Do you love me?' And he said to him, 'Lord, you know everything; you know that I love you.' Jesus said to him, 'Feed my sheep. Truly, truly, I say to you, when you were young, you girded yourself and walked where you would; but when you are old, you will stretch out your hands, and another will gird you and carry you where you do not wish to go.' (This he said to show by what death he was to glorify God). And after this he said to him. 'Follow me.'

A young friend phoned me to describe a visit she had made to her grandmother in Germany. The old lady is matriarchal, stubborn and full of strong opinions—a force to be reckoned with. My friend, Greta, is a considerable force in her own right, but on this particular occasion she wasn't feeling very sure about anything. Since her baby son had died she had been struggling back to some level of hopefulness. Grandmother had clearly decided that the process would be accelerated by a detailed analysis of Greta's faults, weaknesses and recent failures, and that she would be the one to do it. Greta listened to this barrage of criticism until she just couldn't take any more. 'Even if that's all true, Gran,' she said, 'why don't you say nice things as well? Why don't you tell me you love me? That's what I need to hear.' 'Tell you I love you?' said her grandmother. 'I don't need to tell you that, it goes without saying.' But it didn't. Love needs to be spoken and heard. Peter needed to express his love for Jesus. His words sealed the total commitment that was being asked of him if he was to follow his master to the death.

God needs to be told that he's loved.

Revelation explains all mysteries
except her own.

WILLIAM COWPER, 'THE TASK'

PICTURES IN THE SKY

REVELATION 19—22

There are just as many fads and fashions and waves and trends in the Christian world as there are in any other. The book of Revelation is a good example. Certainly, in the evangelical world, there was a time when we tended to regard it as being too abstruse and intellectually demanding to be of much use to us wide-eyed believers. You couldn't sing it or clap in time to it, so how could it have any real value? The pendulum swung, of course, as it always does. Suddenly, the book of Revelation was vitally important, crucial even, to our ongoing spiritual development and growth. Was our particular church in danger of losing its lampstand, and what could we do to avert the threat? The vivid, epic imagery, the dark warnings, the mysteriously specific number of the beast (whoever or whatever he was), the lake of fire, the book of life, the extravagant promises, the lowering threats, all of these elements conspired to present a hugely impressive but profoundly puzzling picture of God's plans for heaven, earth, humankind and the devil.

Fortunately, in recent years we have received excellent teaching on the subject of this fascinating book. Rightly understood, it is a clear call from God to keep going through the difficult and dark times. There may be problems now, but when this life is over we are going to live with God in his glorious new world. The central message of the book seems to be that Jesus really is the Lord of heaven and earth. Evil will be defeated in the end, and the climax of history will be the union of Christ with his bride, the Church.

These readings from chapters 19—22 are about the victory of Christ, the new Jerusalem, and the simple but monumental fact that Jesus is coming!

MY DOG WOULD UNDERSTAND

Revelation 19:1–5 (NIV)

After this I heard what sounded like the roar of a great multitude in heaven shouting: 'Hallelujah! Salvation and glory and power belong to our God, for true and just are his judgments. He has condemned the great prostitute who corrupted the earth by her adulteries. He has avenged on her the blood of his servants.' And again they shouted: 'Hallelujah! The smoke from her goes up for ever and ever.' The twenty-four elders and the four living creatures fell down and worshipped God, who was seated on the throne. And they cried: 'Amen, Hallelujah!' Then a voice came from the throne, saying: 'Praise our God, all you his servants, you who fear him, both small and great!'

It will be electrifying one day to see clearly the conflicts of good and evil as they are played out on the canvas of ultimate reality. Just now I am simply glad that God seems to be the winner. One day I shall understand how dramatic the process of that victory has been.

My dog would understand what I'm talking about here if she were a human being. Yesterday, the noise of the garden strimmer must have spooked Lucy, our slightly nervy two-year-old border collie. Bridget and I suddenly realized that she had disappeared, something she had never done before. We panicked. Had she been stolen? Had a car hit her? Had she run off and got lost? After driving around for half an hour, we met a lady who told us that a dog answering to Lucy's description had been found running up and down one of the nearby roads and taken to a boarding kennels a couple of miles away. We arrived to find Lucy safe and sound and none the worse for her adventure. From her point of view she had simply got lost, found herself in a strange place and then, miraculously, we turned up to collect her. She knew nothing of the anguish and the driving round in circles that had preceded our arrival. She will never know.

We, on the other hand, have a glimpse in these words of all that has been going on without our knowing and will fully understand, one day, the vastness and complexity of God's triumph over evil on our behalf and will be amazed.

Lord, thank you for all that you have done behind the scenes to make sure we can come home.

THE FOOD WILL BE FANTASTIC!

Revelation 19:6–9 (NIV)

Then I heard what sounded like a great multitude, like the roar of rushing waters and like loud peals of thunder, shouting: 'Hallelujah! For our Lord God Almighty reigns. Let us rejoice and be glad and give him glory! For the wedding of the Lamb has come, and his bride has made herself ready. Fine linen, bright and clean, was given her to wear.' (Fine linen stands for the righteous acts of the saints.) Then the angel said to me, 'Write: "Blessed are those who are invited to the wedding supper of the Lamb."' And he added, 'These are the true words of God.'

It seems inevitable that anything involving Jesus will end up with a meal of some sort. In this case, it is the wedding supper that will be held when Jesus and his followers are finally united by an indissoluble bond that, in its closeness and commitment, is akin to marriage. Those of you who are immediately put off by the very idea of a wedding supper need not worry. Mind you, I do understand how you feel. I have some very negative memories of wedding receptions. There was the wedding of a close friend where I was the best man, but nobody had allocated a seat to me. Then there was my cousin's marriage, the whole of which was overshadowed and infected with gloom by the presence of Great-Aunt Mab, who disapproved of alcohol in particular and just about everything else in general. At yet another of these joyous occasions a different aunt, clearly coming from the opposite end of the spectrum to Mab, drank far too much gin and became extremely tired and emotional. She took the opportunity to loudly express her long-held views on most other members of the family, many of whom felt obliged to reply in detail.

Depressing memories, but the wonderful thing about this happy-ever-after reunion with Jesus is that none of these dark and dismal things will happen. All of us, including Great-Aunt Mab and I, will, by the grace of God, be clothed in virtue. Only the brightest and whitest of linen will be allowed. We shall be filled with joy and immense relief and the food will be fantastic.

Lord, it will be so good to be really clean in spirit. We look forward to that great celebration.

THREE NAMES

Revelation 19:11–16 (NIV)

I saw heaven standing open and there before me was a white horse, whose rider is called Faithful and True. With justice he judges and makes war. His eyes are like blazing fire, and on his head are many crowns. He has a name written on him that no one knows but he himself. He is dressed in a robe dipped in blood, and his name is the Word of God. The armies of heaven were following him, riding on white horses and dressed in fine linen, white and clean. Out of his mouth comes a sharp sword with which to strike down the nations. 'He will rule them with an iron sceptre.' He treads the winepress of the fury of the wrath of God Almighty. On his robe and on his thigh he has this name written: KING OF KINGS AND LORD OF LORDS.

Not much of the 'gentle Jesus meek and mild' about this image, is there? The Son of God is riding into battle with his troops, a vision of brilliant whiteness, the symbol of purity and righteousness and the reason none will stand before such a force.

Intriguingly, the Lord is given three names. One is the Word of God. Jesus will be revealed as the fulfilment of all the scriptures have taught about his nature and destiny. This is the son in whom the Father was well pleased now grown to full spiritual stature and ready to cleanse creation of all that offends.

He is also King of kings and Lord of lords—the ultimate authority over all powers, whether temporal or spiritual. What a tragic shock for those who have mocked and derided the figure of Christ when he returns with such awesome authority and power.

Most intriguingly, we are told that he has a name known only to himself. There is a suggestion elsewhere in Revelation that each of God's people will one day be given a new and very special name, known only to them and to the creator. I look forward to hearing what mine is, but will I be able to keep it to myself?

It is impossible to know if these dramatic pictures are fact or helpful fantasy, but it occurs to me that I might actually qualify to ride into battle with him. Want to come?

DOLPHINS AND MARTYRS

Revelation 20:4–6 (NIV)

I saw thrones on which were seated those who had been given authority to judge. And I saw the souls of those who had been beheaded because of their testimony for Jesus and because of the word of God. They had not worshipped the beast or his image and had not received his mark on their foreheads or their hands. They came to life and reigned with Christ for a thousand years. (The rest of the dead did not come to life until the thousand years were ended.) This is the first resurrection. Blessed and holy are those who have part in the first resurrection. The second death has no power over them, but they will be priests of God and of Christ and will reign with him for a thousand years.

This passage makes me think about two things—dolphins and martyrs.

The dolphin bit is connected with a television programme I watched the other night. I have nothing against dolphins—on the contrary, I really like them—but the man doing most of the talking on this programme had a rather eerily dolphin-like expression. By that I mean that, when he smiled, the corners of his mouth seemed to go an awfully long way round towards the back of his head and I have never seen so many small but regimented teeth lining one set of human jaws before. He was speaking with eloquent intensity about prophecy and end-times, including the details contained in this passage. As he talked, his eyes began to gleam and more and more of his teeth became visible. The feverish excitement in this man made me feel quite uncomfortable, so I switched him off. We really mustn't get hung up on the details.

As for the martyrs, well, they are mentioned here, aren't they? How wonderful it will be for these quiet heroes who held on to their faith up to and past the point of death when they find that the one they stood up for values their courage and loves them so highly. I don't suppose they had the faintest idea about the technical aspects of eschatology, but then, that never was their priority, was it?

Lord, I would like a martyr's reward, but without being martyred. Help me to keep my eyes fixed on you to the exclusion of all else.

ENDLESS TORMENT?

Revelation 20:7–10 (NIV)

When the thousand years are over, Satan will be released from his prison and will go out to deceive the nations in the four corners of the earth—Gog and Magog—to gather them for battle. In number they are like the sand on the seashore. They marched across the breadth of the earth and surrounded the camp of God's people, the city he loves. But the fire came down from heaven and devoured them. And the devil, who deceived them, was thrown into the lake of burning sulphur, where the beast and the false prophet had been thrown. They will be tormented day and night for ever and ever.

Like something out of *Lord of the Rings*, isn't it? A final battle in which the devil and his followers will be destroyed by fire from heaven and thrown into the burning lake. An end to turmoil and tears and failure and the gulf between God and human beings that has caused so much pain for him and for us. We followers of Jesus shall be fine, but in the lake of burning sulphur will be a boiling stew of evil. The beast, the false prophet, the devil and those who were deceived into following him will suffer torment for eternity.

This is the kind of thing that can turn a lot of people, Christians and non-Christians, away from faith. How could a God who is the essence of love allow anyone to suffer torment for eternity, let alone those who have been unfortunate enough to be deceived into joining the wrong side? The idea of anyone or anything screaming with pain for ever offends some of us both in the heart and the head.

I suspect that we need to take ourselves sternly in hand over this. Jesus died an agonizing death so that we can go home to the Father. We cannot possibly comprehend the depth and extent of the suffering involved in that sacrifice. It happened because we would be lost if it didn't. That act of love invites our trust, even when we are faced with questions that are tough and unanswerable in this world. Ask the questions by all means (I always do), but bear in mind that one day they will be fully answered.

Lord, do we hurt you with our doubts?

THE BOOK OF LIFE

Revelation 20:11–15 (NIV)

Then I saw a great white throne and him who was seated on it. Earth and sky fled from his presence, and there was no place for them. And I saw the dead, great and small, standing before the throne, and books were opened. Another book was opened which is the book of life. The dead were judged according to what they had done as recorded in the books. The sea gave up the dead that were in it, and death and Hades gave up the dead that were in them, and each person was judged according to what he had done. Then death and Hades were thrown into the lake of fire. The lake of fire is the second death. If anyone's name was not found written in the book of life, he was thrown into the lake of fire.

This jolly little scenario encapsulates a central problem that we Christians face when communicating with the rest of the world.

Yes, God is loving and forgiving and unwilling that any should be lost. I believe that with all my heart. Yes, there will be surprises in heaven and none of us is allowed to make any judgments about the ultimate destination of a specific person. I believe that, too. Yes, of course it is perfectly proper to speculate on the compassion of God towards those who have never been given the chance to accept or reject Jesus. I do it myself all the time. Yes, I will happily concede that the lurid image of hell given here by John is probably a picture of separation from God's presence. That is fine. All these things are fine. However, when we have made all these points, added multiple provisos, admitted our own uncertainties and acknowledged the great mystery that surrounds all things, we shall still be faced with one unavoidable fact. It is that the New Testament teaches that, literally or metaphorically, there is a book of life that supersedes and overrules the records of human deeds. It lists those who belong to Jesus and they are the ones who will be saved, whatever that turns out to mean.

Whether they consider it true or false, the world simply does not want to hear this and who can blame them? Our task is not an easy one.

Wake us up to reality, Lord.

THE BIG PICTURE

Revelation 21:1-4 (NIV)

Then I saw a new heaven and a new earth, for the first heaven and the first earth had passed away, and there was no longer any sea. I saw the Holy City, the new Jerusalem, coming down out of heaven from God, prepared as a bride beautifully dressed for her husband. And I heard a loud voice from the throne saying, 'Now the dwelling of God is with men, and he will live with them. They will be his people, and God himself will be with them and be their God. He will wipe every tear from their eyes. There will be no more death or mourning or crying or pain, for the old order of things has passed away.'

As I read these words I find my brain searching for and juggling with words like 'crux', 'climax' and 'pinnacle'. For God, the one we are allowed to know as our Father, this is the fulfilment of a dream. This is the triumphant realization of a divine longing that has been beating like a grieving heart at the centre of the universe ever since Adam and Eve allowed Satan to tempt them into tearing the peace of Eden apart. It really does not matter whether we believe in the historical accuracy of the creation story or not. Suffice it to say that something went terribly, fundamentally wrong. As a result we were deprived of close contact with God and he has been obliged to come among us in the form of a voice in a burning bush or a pillar of light or the inner part of some sacred tent or in dreams and visions or in the form of a man called Jesus. Spectacular, fulfilling and wonderful though some of those contacts have been and still are, none will compare with the glowing perfection of this moment when the history of the Spirit completes a full circle and God is able to live among his people once more in the way that he had always intended.

Whatever you do, don't be distracted by the details. Look at the big picture. God and his children will be back together again. He will wipe the tears from our eyes and, I suspect, we might even wipe one or two from his.

Just think—what a day that will be!

THE SECOND DEATH

Revelation 21:5–8 (NIV)

He who was seated on the throne said, 'I am making everything new!' Then he said, 'Write this down, for these words are trustworthy and true.' He said to me: 'It is done. I am the Alpha and the Omega, the Beginning and the End. To him who is thirsty I will give to drink without cost from the spring of the water of life. He who overcomes will inherit all this, and I will be his God and he will be my son. But the cowardly, the unbelieving, the vile, the murderers, the sexually immoral, those who practise magic arts, the idolaters and all liars—their place will be in the fiery lake of burning sulphur. This is the second death.'

The trips that Bridget and I have made to Third World countries in recent years have affected us on many levels. Witnessing grinding poverty on the dusty streets of isolated Zambian communities, for instance, has forced us to face the fact that we are rich beyond the dreams of many we met during our travels. We are also increasingly conscious of the need to add our voices to the demand that governments apply themselves rigorously to the need for debt reduction or cancellation in countries where, in some cases, the interest on their loans exceeds the total income of the nation.

For me, though, the major impact is a spiritual one. Time after time we heard the same words from people on the edge of starvation or dying of AIDS or finding it impossible to earn enough money to support large, hungry families: 'When we get to heaven all things will be well. We shall be with Jesus.'

Of course this spiritual optimism must never dull the edge of our resolve to offer material support to those who are starving and sick but, in countries like England, we seem to have moved too far in the opposite direction: 'Why hasn't God answered my prayer about the mortgage?', 'If God loves my children more than I do, why doesn't he provide the things they need?'

Read this passage. There is going to be a second death. Followers of Jesus will not die this second death. That is the real cause for rejoicing and the joy of it will eclipse anything you can imagine in this world.

Fix our priorities, Lord.

WHAT ABOUT THE DAPPLED THINGS?

Revelation 22:1–5 (NIV)

Then the angel showed me the river of the water of life, as clear as crystal, flowing from the throne of God and of the Lamb down the middle of the great street of the city. On each side of the river stood the tree of life, bearing twelve crops of fruit, yielding its fruit every month. And the leaves of the tree are for the healing of the nations. No longer will there be any curse. The throne of God and of the Lamb will be in the city, and his servants will serve him. They will see his face, and his name will be on their foreheads. There will be no more night. They will not need the light of a lamp or the light of the sun, for the Lord God will give them light. And they will reign for ever and ever.

In one of the most evocative lines of poetry ever written, Gerard Manley Hopkins gave glory to God for 'dappled things'. I often recall his words, especially during spring and summer. The rich complexity of light and shade is unspeakably delicious. Early summer sun turns the silver birch in our garden into a whispering, shimmering lightshow of sparkle and shadow each time a sea breeze arrives from the other side of the Pevensey levels.

Autumn is my favourite season. I love the stage-set vividness with which everyday items are picked out and illuminated against the lowering sky as brilliant sunsets blaze and die. I love lamps and open fires, flames that flicker in the half-light.

I love the light and shadow of life itself. Relief and sudden joy after disappointment. Success after and at the centre of failure. Healing after suffering. The extraordinary mix of elation, despair and blessed ordinariness that makes up our lives with family and friends.

In this passage, we learn that there will be no more night. No need for sun or lamps. Contrasts will be impossible because God will give us light and that light will never fade. Rightly or wrongly, the prospect depresses me a little.

Lord Jesus, this is probably only a picture anyway and I know that the reality of being with you will be greater than anything we have known here. It's just that I feel sad at the idea of losing dappled things. Forgive me.

By the same author

REPORTAGE

America 1968: The Fire this Time
Ulster 1969: The Struggle for Civil Rights in Northern Ireland
The Battle for the Falklands (with Simon Jenkins)

BIOGRAPHY

Montrose: The King's Champion
Yoni: Hero of Entebbe

AUTOBIOGRAPHY

Going to the Wars
Editor
Did You Really Shoot the Television?

MILITARY HISTORY

Bomber Command
The Battle of Britain (with Len Deighton)
Das Reich
Overlord
Victory in Europe
The Korean War
Warriors: Extraordinary Tales from the Battlefield
Armageddon: The Battle for Germany 1944–45
Nemesis: The Battle for Japan 1944–45

COUNTRYSIDE WRITING

Outside Days
Scattered Shots
Country Fair

ANTHOLOGY (EDITED)

The Oxford Book of Military Anecdotes

'A nuanced, fully rounded portrait of a man who blundered as often as he succeeded, who could be appallingly cruel as well as inspiring, but who dragged his country through the war through sheer force of personality'

ANDREW HOLGATE, *Sunday Times*, Books of the Year

'A vivid, moving, warts-and-all picture of a leader who was determined to be a hero'

DAVID CANNADINE, *TLS*, Books of the Year

'Max Hastings tells us that he has 100 books on Churchill on his shelves, yet he has managed to write another genuinely surprising one. Drawing on his vast knowledge as a military historian, he comes at it from new angles and with new opinions. Hastings gives full credit to his overall greatness of leadership'

PETER LEWIS, *Daily Mail*, Books of the Year

MAX HASTINGS

Finest Years

Churchill as Warlord 1940–45

Harper
Press

In memory of Roy Jenkins,
and our Indian summer friendship

Harper*Press*
An imprint of HarperCollins*Publishers*
77–85 Fulham Palace Road
Hammersmith
London W6 8JB

Visit our authors' blog at www.fifthestate.co.uk
Love this book? www.bookarmy.com

This Harper*Press* paperback edition published 2010
1

First published in Great Britain by Harper*Press* in 2009

Copyright © Max Hastings 2009

Max Hastings asserts the moral right to be identified as the author of this work

A catalogue record for this book is available from the British Library

ISBN 978-0-00-726368-4

Set in Minion by
Palimpsest Book Production Limited, Falkirk, Stirlingshire

Printed and bound in Great Britain by Clays Ltd, St Ives plc

Mixed Sources
Product group from well-managed
forests and other controlled sources
www.fsc.org Cert no. SW-COC-001806
© 1996 Forest Stewardship Council

FSC

FSC is a non-profit international organisation established to promote the responsible
management of the world's forests. Products carrying the FSC label are independently
certified to assure consumers that they come from forests that are managed to meet the
social, economic and ecological needs of present and future generations.

Find out more about HarperCollins and the environment at
www.harpercollins.co.uk/green

CONTENTS

LIST OF ILLUSTRATIONS   ix

LIST OF MAPS   xii

INTRODUCTION   xv

1	The Battle of France	1
2	The Two Dunkirks	36
3	Invasion Fever	60
4	The Battle of Britain	79
5	Greek Fire	111
	1 Seeking Action	111
	2 The War Machine	139
6	Comrades	150
7	The Battle of America	171
	1 Strictly Cash	171
	2 Walking Out	190
8	A Glimpse of Arcadia	214
9	'The Valley of Humiliation'	234
10	Soldiers, Bosses and 'Slackers'	259
	1 An Army at Bay	259
	2 Home Front	272
11	'Second Front Now!'	283
12	Camels and the Bear	315
13	The Turn of Fortune	334
14	Out of the Desert	368
15	Sunk in the Aegean	401

16	Tehran	422
17	Setting Europe Ablaze	451
18	Overlord	476
19	Bargaining with an Empty Wallet	493
20	Athens: 'Wounded in the House of Our Friends'	523
21	Yalta	546
22	The Final Act	557

ACKNOWLEDGEMENTS	599
NOTES AND SOURCES	601
SELECT BIBLIOGRAPHY	636
INDEX	644

ILLUSTRATIONS

Churchill in Whitehall with Halifax in March 1938. *(Getty Images)*

Churchill outside Downing Street in May 1940. *(Getty Images)*

German columns advancing through France in May 1940. *(Imperial War Museum RML193)*

Churchill in Paris on 31 May 1940 with Dill, Attlee and Reynaud. *(Getty Images)*

British troops awaiting evacuation from Dunkirk. *(Imperial War Museum NYP68075)*

Dead British soldier at Dunkirk. *(ECPAD, France)*

Churchill inspecting a roadblock. *(Imperial War Museum H2653)*

The Mid-Devon Hunt patrol Dartmoor.

French warships blaze at Mers-el-Kebir under British bombardment, 3 July 1940. *(© Musée National de Marine)*

The Battle of Britain: Hurricane pilots scramble. *(Time & Life Pictures/Getty Images)*

The filter room at RAF Fighter Command, Bentley Priory. *(MoD Air Historical Branch)*

A Luftwaffe Heinkel over the London docks in September 1940. *(Imperial War Museum C5422)*

The blitz: a street scene repeated a thousand times across the cities of Britain. *(Popperfoto/Getty Images)*

Churchill portrayed by Cecil Beaton in the Cabinet Room at 10 Downing Street on 20 November 1940. *(Courtesy of the Cecil Beaton Studio Archive at Sotheby's)*

Blazing shore facilities on Crete in May 1941. *(Imperial War Museum E3104E)*

A Russian soldier surrenders to the Wehrmacht during the first year of Operation *Barbarossa*. *(Bundesarchiv, Bild 101I-136-0877-08/Bruno Plenik)*

Harry Hopkins and Churchill outside Downing Street on 10 January 1941. *(Getty Images)*

Roosevelt and Churchill at Placentia Bay on 10 August 1941. (*Imperial War Museum H12739*)

British troops advance through a minefield in North Africa. (*Imperial War Museum E18542*)

Some of the tens of thousands of Italian prisoners who fell into British hands during Wavell's Operation *Compass*. (*Imperial War Museum E1591*)

George King. (*Courtesy of Judith Avery*)

Vere Hodgson.

Sir John Kennedy. (*National Portrait Gallery, London*)

Sir Alexander Cadogan. (*Press Association Images*)

Harold Nicolson. (*Getty Images*)

Charles Wilson, Lord Moran. (*National Portrait Gallery, London*)

Hugh Dalton. (*National Portrait Gallery, London*)

Leo Amery. (*Getty Images*)

Cuthbert Headlam. (*Press Association Images*)

Oliver Harvey. (*Press Association Images*)

Lt.Gen. Sir Henry Pownall. (*Imperial War Museum FE556*)

Churchill working on his train. (*Imperial War Museum H10874*)

Churchill viewing new aircraft with Lindemann, Portal and Pound. (*Imperial War Museum H10306*)

Jock Colville's September 1941 farewell to Downing Street. (*Harriet Bowes-Lyon*)

Churchill at the controls of the Boeing Clipper which brought him home from Washington in January 1942. (*Imperial War Museum H16645*)

One of the many Second Front rallies held in Britain in 1942–43. (*Imperial War Museum D4593*)

The Cairo conference, August 1942. (*AP/Press Association Images*)

Harriman and Churchill with Molotov on their arrival in Moscow. (*Imperial War Museum MoI FLM115*)

Dieppe after the disastrous August 1942 raid. (*Imperial War Museum HU1904*)

Soviet troops advance towards Stalingrad. (*The Archive of the Panoramic Museum of the Battle of Stalingrad*)

The British advance at El Alamein, November 1942. (*Imperial War Museum E18807*)

American war leaders at Casablanca, January 1943. (© *Bettmann/Corbis*)

Aneurin Bevan. (*Getty Images*)

Stafford Cripps. (*Getty Images*)

Clement Attlee. (*Getty Images*)

Ernest Bevin. *(Getty Images)*

Lord Beaverbrook. *(Getty Images)*

Churchill with General Anderson at the Roman amphitheatre at Carthage, May 1943. *(Imperial War Museum NA3253)*

US troops advance through Italy. *(NARA)*

Beaufighters attack German shipping off Kos on 3 October 1943. *(Hansjürgen Weissenborn/Anthony Rogers Collection)*

German troops land on Kos. *(Imperial War Museum HU67424)*

Algiers, June 1943. *(Imperial War Museum NA3286)*

Churchill with Clementine in the saloon of his special train in Canada in August 1943. *(Imperial War Museum H32954)*

The 'Big Three' at Tehran on 30 November 1943. *(Imperial War Museum E26640)*

The Anzio landing, January 1944. *(Time & Life Pictures/Getty Images)*

Instructing French *maquisards* on the use of the sten sub-machine gun. *(Getty Images)*

An SOE mission in occupied Yugoslavia. *(Imperial War Museum HU67565)*

American troops approaching the Normandy beaches, 6 June 1944. *(Imperial War Museum EA25641)*

Operation *Overlord*, 6 June 1944. *(Imperial War Museum EA29655)*

Churchill with Alexander in Italy, 26 August 1944. *(Imperial War Museum NA18041)*

Churchill with De Gaulle in Paris on Armistice Day, 11 November 1944. *(Imperial War Museum BU1294)*

Churchill meeting the warring Greek factions in Athens on 26 December 1944. *(Imperial War Museum NAM163)*

King, Brooke, Ismay and Marshall at Yalta in February 1945. *(Liddell Hart Centre for Military Archives)*

Victorious Russian soldiers in Sofia, the Bulgarian capital. *(Courtesy of the Central Museum of the Armed Forces/Nik Cornish)*

Churchill overlooks the Rhine with Brooke and Montgomery in March 1945. *(Liddell Hart Centre for Military Archives)*

On the balcony of Buckingham Palace with the royal family on VE-Day. *(Imperial War Museum MH21835)*

Churchill broadcasts from Downing Street. *(Imperial War Museum H41846)*

Churchill with Truman and Stalin at Potsdam on 17 July 1945. *(Getty Images)*

MAPS

May 1940 deployments   6

The German advance   23

The Dunkirk perimeter   29

Operation *Sealion*   94

Operation *Compass*   122

The North African campaign   340

Operation *Torch*   342

The Italian campaign   384

The Dodecanese   407

Overlord and *Anvil*   496

It may well be that the most glorious chapters of our history have yet to be written. Indeed, the very problems and dangers that encompass us and our country ought to make English men and women of this generation glad to be here at such a time. We ought to rejoice at the responsibilities with which destiny has honoured us, and be proud that we are guardians of our country in an age when her life is at stake.

WSC, April 1933

History with its flickering lamp stumbles along the trail of the past, trying to reconstruct its scenes, to revive its echoes, and kindle with pale gleams the passion of former days.

WSC, November 1940

INTRODUCTION

Winston Churchill was the greatest Englishman and one of the greatest human beings of the twentieth century, indeed of all time. Yet beyond that bald assertion there are infinite nuances in considering his conduct of Britain's war between 1940 and 1945, which is the theme of this book. It originated nine years ago, when Roy Jenkins was writing his biography of Churchill. Roy flattered me by inviting my comments on the typescript, chapter by chapter. Some of my suggestions he accepted, many he sensibly ignored. When we reached the Second World War, his patience expired. Exasperated by the profusion of my strictures, he said: 'You're trying to get me to do something which you should write yourself, if you want to!' By that time, his health was failing. He was impatient to finish his own book, which achieved triumphant success.

In the years that followed I thought much about Churchill and the war, mindful of some Boswellian lines about Samuel Johnson: 'He had once conceived the thought of writing The Life Of Oliver Cromwell . . . He at length laid aside his scheme, on discovering that all that can be told of him is already in print; and that it is impracticable to procure any authentick information in addition to what the world is already possessed of.' Among the vast Churchillian bibliography, I was especially apprehensive about venturing anywhere near the tracks of David Reynolds's extraordinarily original and penetrating *In Command of History* (2004). The author dissected successive drafts of Churchill's war memoirs, exposing contrasts between judgements on people and events which the old statesman initially proposed to make, and those which he finally deemed it prudent to publish. Andrew Roberts has painted a striking portrait of wartime Anglo–American relations, and especially of the great summit meetings, in *Masters and Commanders* (2008). We have been told more about Winston Churchill than any other human being. Tens of thousands of people of many nations have recorded even the most trifling encounters, noting every word they heard him utter. The most vivid wartime memory of one soldier of Britain's Eighth Army derived from a day in 1942 when he found the prime minister his neighbour in a North African desert latrine. Churchill's speeches and writings fill many volumes.

Yet much remains opaque, because he wished it thus. Always mindful of his role as a stellar performer upon the stage of history, he became supremely so after 10 May 1940. He kept no diary because, he observed, to do so would be to expose his follies and inconsistencies to posterity. Within months of his ascent to the premiership, however, he told his staff that he had already schemed the chapters of the book which he would write as soon as the war was over. The outcome was a ruthlessly partial six-volume work which is poor history, if sometimes peerless prose. We shall never know with complete confidence what he thought about many personalities – for instance Roosevelt, Eisenhower, Alanbrooke, King George VI, his cabinet colleagues – because he took good care not to tell us.

Churchill's wartime relationship with the British people was much more complex than is often acknowledged. Few denied his claims upon the premiership. But between the end of the Battle of Britain in 1940 and the Second Battle of El Alamein in November 1942, not only many ordinary citizens, but also some of his closest colleagues, wanted operational control of the war machine to be removed from his hands, and some other figure appointed to his role as Minister of Defence. It is hard to overstate the embarrassment and even shame of British people as they perceived the Russians playing a heroic part in the struggle against Nazism, while their own army seemed incapable of winning a battle. To understand Britain's wartime experience, it appears essential to recognise, as some narratives do not, the sense of humiliation which afflicted Britain amid the failures of its soldiers, contrasted – albeit often on the basis of wildly false information – with the achievement of Stalin's.

Churchill was dismayed by the performance of the British Army, even after victories began to come at the end of 1942. Himself a hero, he expected others likewise to show themselves heroes. In 1940, the people of Britain, together with their navy and air force, wonderfully fulfilled his hopes. Thereafter, however, much of the story of Britain's part in the war seems to me that of the prime minister seeking more from his own nation and its warriors than they could deliver. The failure of the army to match the prime minister's aspirations is among the central themes of this book.

Much discussion of Britain's military effort in World War II focuses upon Churchill's relationship with his generals. In my view, this preoccupation is overdone. The difficulties of fighting the Germans and Japanese went much deeper than could be solved by changes of commander. The British were beaten again and again between 1940 and 1942, and continued to suffer battlefield difficulties thereafter, in consequence of failures of tactics, weapons, equipment and culture even more significant than lack of mass or inspired leadership. The gulf between Churchillian aspiration and reality extended to the peoples of occupied Europe, hence his faith in 'setting Europe ablaze' through the agency of Special Operations Executive, which had malign consequences that he failed to anticipate. SOE armed many occupied peoples to fight more energetically against each other in 1944–45 than they had done earlier against the Germans.

It is a common mistake, to suppose that those who bestrode the stage during momentous times were giants, set apart from the personalities of our own humdrum society. I have argued in earlier books that we should instead see 1939–45 as a period when men and women not much different from ourselves strove to grapple with stresses and responsibilities which stretched their powers to the limit. Churchill was one of a tiny number of actors who proved worthy of the role in which destiny cast him. Those who worked for the prime minister, indeed the British people at war, served as a supporting cast, seeking honourably but sometimes inadequately to play their own parts in the wake of a titan.

Sir Edward Bridges, then Cabinet Secretary, wrote of Churchill between 1940 and 1942: 'Everything depended upon him and him alone. Only he had the power to make the nation believe that it could win.' This remains the view of most of the world, almost seventy years later. Yet there is also no shortage of iconoclasts. In a recent biography Cambridge lecturer Nigel Knight writes contemptuously of Churchill: 'He was not mad or simple; his misguided decisions were a product of his personality – a mixture of arrogance, emotion, self-indulgence, stubbornness and a blind faith in his own ability.' Another modern biographer, Chris Wrigley, suggests that Sir Edward Bridges' tribute to Churchill 'may over-state his indispensability'.

Such strictures seem otiose to those of us convinced that, in his absence, Britain would have made terms with Hitler after Dunkirk. Thereafter, beyond his domestic achievement as war leader, he performed a diplomatic role of which only he was capable: as suitor of the United States on behalf of the British nation. To fulfil this, he was obliged to overcome intense prejudices on both sides of the Atlantic. So extravagant was Churchill's – and Roosevelt's – wartime rhetoric about the Anglo–American alliance, that even today the extent of mutual suspicion and indeed dislike between the two peoples is often under-estimated. The British ruling class, in particular, condescended amazingly towards Americans.

In 1940–41, Winston Churchill perceived with a clarity which eluded some of his fellow countrymen that only American belliger-ence might open a path to victory. Pearl Harbor, and not the prime minister's powers of seduction, eventually brought Roosevelt's nation into the war. But no other statesman could have conducted British policy towards the United States with such consummate skill, nor have achieved such personal influence upon the American people. This persisted until 1944, when his standing in the US declined precipi-tously, to revive only when the onset of the Cold War caused many Americans to hail Churchill as a prophet. His greatness, which had come to seem too large for his own impoverished country, then became perceived as a shared Anglo-American treasure.

From June 1941 onwards, Churchill saw much more clearly than most British soldiers and politicians that Russia must be embraced as an ally. But it seems important to strip away legends about aid to the Soviet Union, and to acknowledge how small this was in the decisive 1941–42 period. Stalin's nation saved itself with little help from the Western Allies. Only from 1943 onwards did supplies to Russia gain critical mass, and Anglo-American ground operations absorb a significant part of the Wehrmacht's attention. The huge popularity of the Soviet Union in wartime Britain was a source of dismay, indeed exasperation, to the small number of people at the top who knew the truth about the barbarity of Stalin's regime, its hostility to the West, and its imperialistic designs on Eastern Europe.

The divide between the sentiments of the public and those of the prime minister towards the Soviet Union became a chasm in May 1945. One of Churchill's most astonishing acts, in the last weeks of his premiership, was to order the Joint Planning Staff to produce a draft for Operation *Unthinkable*. The resulting document considered the practicability of launching an Anglo-American offensive against the USSR, with forty-seven divisions reinforced by the remains of Hitler's Wehrmacht, to restore the freedom of Poland. Though Churchill recognised this as a remote contingency, it is remarkable that he caused the chiefs of staff to address it at all.

I am surprised how few historians seem to notice that many things which the British and Americans believed they were concealing from the Soviets – for instance, Bletchley Park's penetration of Axis ciphers and Anglo–American arguments about launching a Second Front – were well known to Stalin, through the good offices of communist sympathisers and traitors in Whitehall and Washington. The Soviets knew much more about their allies' secret policy-making than did the British and Americans about that of the Russians.

It is fascinating to study public mood swings through wartime British, American and Russian newspapers, and the diaries of ordinary citizens. These often give a very different picture from that of historians, with their privileged knowledge of how the story ended. As for sentiment at the top, some men who were indifferent politicians or commanders contributed much more as contemporary chroniclers. The diaries of such figures as Hugh Dalton, Leo Amery and Lt.Gen. Henry Pownall make them more valuable to us as eye-witnesses and eavesdroppers than they seemed to their contemporaries as players in the drama.

Maj.Gen. John Kennedy, for much of the war the British Army's Director of Military Operations, kept a diary which arguably ranks second only to that of Gen. Sir Alan Brooke for its insights into the British military high command. On 26 January 1941, in the darkest days of the conflict, Kennedy expressed a fear that selective use of accounts of the meetings of Britain's leaders might mislead posterity:

It would be easy by a cunning or biased selection of evidence to give the impression for instance that the P.M.'s strategic policy was nearly always at fault, & that it was only by terrific efforts that he is kept on the right lines – and it would be easy to do likewise with all the chiefs of staff. The historian who has to deal with the voluminous records of this war will have a frightful task. I suppose no war has been so well documented. Yet the records do not often reveal individual views. It is essentially a government of committees . . . Winston is of course the dominating personality & he has in his entourage and among his immediate advisers no really strong personality. Yet Winston's views do not often prevail if they are contrary to the general trend of opinion among the service staffs. Minutes flutter continually from Winston's typewriter on every conceivable subject. His strategic imagination is inexhaustible and many of his ideas are wild and unsound and impracticable . . . but in the end they are killed if they are not acceptable.

These observations, made in the heat of events, deserve respect from every historian of the period. Another banal and yet critical point is that circumstances and attitudes shifted. The prime minister often changed his mind, and deserves more credit than he sometimes receives for his willingness to do so. Meanwhile, others vacillated in their views of him. Some who revered Churchill in the first months of his premiership later became bitterly sceptical, and vice versa. After Dunkirk, Britain's middle classes were considerably more staunch than some members of its traditional ruling caste, partly because they knew less about the full horror of the country's predicament. History perceives as pivotal Britain's survival through 1940, so that the weariness and cynicism that pervaded the country by 1942, amid continuing defeats, are often underrated. Industrial unrest, manifested in strikes especially in the coalfields, and in the aircraft and ship-building industries, revealed fissures in the fabric of national unity which are surprisingly seldom acknowledged.

This book does not seek to retell the full story of Churchill at war, but rather to present a portrait of his leadership from the day on which he became prime minister, 10 May 1940, set in the context of Britain's national experience. It is weighted towards the first half of the conflict, partly because Churchill's contribution was then much greater than it became later, and partly because I have sought to emphasise issues and events about which there seem new things to be said. There is relatively little in this book about the strategic air offensive. I addressed this earlier in *Bomber Command* and *Armageddon*. I have here confined myself to discussion of the prime minister's personal role in key bombing decisions. I have not described land and naval campaigns in detail, but instead considered the institutional cultures which influenced the performance of the British Army, Royal Navy and RAF, and the three services' relationships with the prime minister.

To maintain coherence, it is necessary to address some themes and episodes which are familiar, though specific aspects deserve reconsideration. There was, for instance, what I have called the second Dunkirk, no less miraculous than the first. Churchill's biggest misjudgement of 1940 was his decision to send more troops to France in June after the rescue of the BEF from the beaches. Only the stubborn insistence of their commander, Lt.Gen. Sir Alan Brooke, made it possible to overcome the rash impulses of the prime minister and evacuate almost 200,000 men who would otherwise have been lost.

The narrative examines some subordinate issues and events in which the prime minister's role was crucial, such as the strategic contribution of SOE – as distinct from romantic tales of its agents' derring-do – the Dodecanese campaign and Churchill's Athens adventure in December 1944. I have attempted little original research in his own papers. Instead, I have explored the impression he made upon others – generals, soldiers, citizens, Americans and Russians. Moscow's closure of key archives to foreign researchers has curtailed the wonderful bonanza of the post-Cold War period. But much important material was published in Russian documentary collections.

It seems mistaken to stint on quotation from Alan Brooke, John Colville and Charles Wilson (Lord Moran), merely because their records have been long in the public domain. Recent research on Moran's manuscript suggests that, rather than being a true contemporary record, much of it was written up afterwards. Yet most of his anecdotes and observations appear credible. The diaries of Churchill's military chief, junior private secretary and doctor provide, for all their various limitations, the most intimate testimony we shall ever have about Churchill's wartime existence.

He himself, of course, bestrides the tale in all his joyous splendour. Even at the blackest periods, when his spirits sagged, flashes of exuberance broke through, which cheered his colleagues and contemporaries, but caused some people to recoil from him. They were dismayed, even disgusted, that he so conspicuously thrilled to his own part in the greatest conflict in human history. 'Why do we regard history as of the past and forget we are making it?' he exulted to Australian prime minister Robert Menzies in 1941. It was this glee which caused such a man as the aesthete and diarist James Lees-Milne to write fastidiously after it was all over: 'Churchill so evidently enjoyed the war that I could never like him. I merely acknowledge him, like Genghis Khan, to have been great.'

Lees-Milne and like-minded critics missed an important aspect of Churchill's attitude to conflict in general, and to the Second World

War in particular. He thrilled to the cannon's roar, and rejoiced in its proximity to himself. Yet never for a moment did he lose his sense of dismay about the death and destruction that war visited upon the innocent. 'Ah, horrible war, amazing medley of the glorious and the squalid, the pitiful and the sublime,' he wrote as a correspondent in South Africa in January 1900. 'If modern men of light and leading saw your face closer simple folk would see it hardly ever.' Hitler was indifferent to the sufferings his policies imposed upon mankind. Churchill never flinched from the necessity to pay in blood for the defeat of Nazi tyranny. But his sole purpose was to enable the guns to be silenced, the peoples of the world restored to their peaceful lives.

Appetite for the fray was among Churchill's most convincing credentials for national leadership in May 1940. Neville Chamberlain had many weaknesses as prime minister, but foremost among them was a revulsion from the conflict to which his country was committed, shared by many members of his government. One of them, Rob Bernays, said: 'I wish I were twenty. I cannot bear this responsibility.' A nation which found itself committed to a life-and-death struggle against one of the most ruthless tyrannies in history was surely wise to entrust its leadership to a man eager to embrace the role, rather than one who shrank from it. This book discusses Churchill's follies and misjudgements, which were many and various. But these are as pimples upon the mountain of his achievement. It is sometimes said that the British and American peoples are still today, in the twenty-first century, indecently obsessed with the Second World War. The reason is not far to seek. We know that here was something which our parents and grandparents did well, in a noble cause that will forever be identified with the person of Winston Churchill, warlord extraordinary.

Max Hastings
Chilton Foliat, Berkshire
May 2009

ONE

The Battle of France

For seven months after the Second World War began in September 1939, many British people deluded themselves that it might gutter out before there was a bloodbath in the West. On 5 April 1940, while the armed but passive confrontation which had persisted since the fall of Poland still prevailed on the Franco–German border, prime minister Neville Chamberlain told a Conservative Party meeting: 'Hitler has missed the bus.' Less than five weeks later, however, on 7 May, he addressed the House of Commons to explain the disastrous outcome of Britain's campaign to frustrate the German occupation of Norway. Beginning with a tribute to British troops who had 'carried out their task with magnificent gallantry', in halting tones he continued:

> I hope that we shall not exaggerate the extent or the importance of the check we have received. The withdrawal from southern Norway is not comparable to the withdrawal from Gallipoli . . . There were no large forces involved. Not much more than a single division . . . Still, I am quite aware . . . that some discouragement has been caused to our friends, and that our enemies are crowing . . . I want to ask hon. Members not to form any hasty opinions on the result of the Norwegian campaign so far as it has gone . . . A minister who shows any sign of confidence is always called complacent. If he fails to do so, he is labelled defeatist. For my part I try to steer a middle course – [Interruption] – neither raising undue expectations [Hon. Members: 'Hitler missed the bus'] which are unlikely to be fulfilled, nor making

1

people's flesh creep by painting pictures of unmitigated gloom. A great many times some hon. Members have repeated the phrase 'Hitler missed the bus' – [Hon. Members: 'You said it'] . . . While I retain my complete confidence on our ultimate victory, I do not think that the people of this country yet realise the extent or the imminence of the threat which is impending against us [An Hon. Member: 'We said that five years ago'].

When the debate ended the following night, thirty-three Tories voted against their own party on the Adjournment Motion, and a further sixty abstained. Though Chamberlain retained a parliamentary majority, it was plain that his Conservative government had lost the nation's confidence. This was not merely the consequence of the Norway campaign, but because through eight fumbling months it had exposed its lack of stomach for war. An all-party coalition was indispensable. Labour would not serve under Chamberlain. Winston Churchill became Britain's prime minister following a meeting between himself, Chamberlain, Foreign Secretary Lord Halifax and Tory chief whip David Margesson on the afternoon of 9 May 1940, at which Halifax declared his own unsuitability for the post, as a member of the House of Lords who would be obliged to delegate direction of the war to Churchill in the Commons. In truth, some expedient could have been adopted to allow the Foreign Secretary to return to the Commons. But Halifax possessed sufficient self-knowledge to recognise that no more than Neville Chamberlain did he possess the stuff of a war leader.

While much of the ruling class disliked and mistrusted the new premier, he was the overwhelming choice of the British people. With remarkably sure instinct, they perceived that if they must wage war, the leadership of a warrior was needed. David Reynolds has observed that when the Gallipoli campaign failed in 1915, many people wished to blame Churchill – then, as in 1940, First Lord of the Admiralty – while after Norway nobody did. 'It was a marvel,' Churchill wrote in an unpublished draft of his war memoirs, 'I really do not know how – I survived and maintained my position in public esteem while all the blame was thrown on poor Mr Chamberlain.' He may also have perceived his own good fortune that he had not achieved the highest office in earlier years, or even in the earlier months of the war. Had he done so, it is likely that by May 1940 his country would have tired of the excesses which he would surely have committed, while being no more capable than Chamberlain of stemming the tide of fate on the Continent. Back in 1935, Stanley Baldwin explained to a friend his unwillingness to appoint Churchill to his own cabinet: 'If there is going to be a war – and who can say there is not – we must keep him fresh to be our war Prime Minister.' Baldwin's tone was jocular and patronising, yet there proved to be something in what he said.

In May 1940 only generals and admirals knew the extent of Churchill's responsibility for Britain's ill-starred Scandinavian deployments. Nonetheless the familiar view, that he was sole architect of disaster, seems overstated. Had British troops been better trained, motivated and led, they would have made a better showing against Hitler's forces, which repeatedly worsted them in Norway while often inferior in numbers. The British Army's failure reflected decades of neglect, together with institutional weaknesses that would influence the fortunes of British arms through the years which followed. These were symbolically attested by a colonel who noticed among officers' baggage being landed at Namsos on the central Norwegian coast 'several fishing rods and many sporting guns'. No German officer would have gone to war with such frivolous accoutrements.

Now Halifax wrote disdainfully to a friend: 'I don't think WSC will be a very good PM though . . . the country will think he gives them a fillip.' The Foreign Secretary told his junior minister R.A. Butler, when they discussed his own refusal to offer himself for the premiership: 'It's all a great pity. You know my reasons, it's no use discussing that – but the gangsters will shortly be in complete control.' Humbler folk disagreed. Lancashire housewife Nella Last wrote in her diary on 11 May: 'If I had to spend my whole life with a man, I'd choose Mr Chamberlain, but I think I would sooner have Mr Churchill if there was a storm and I was shipwrecked. He has a funny face, like a bulldog living in our street who has done more to drive out unwanted dogs and cats . . . than all the complaints of householders.' London correspondent Mollie Panter-Downes told *New Yorker* readers: 'Events are moving so fast that England acquired a new Premier almost absent-mindedly . . . It's paradoxical but true that the British, for all their suspicious dislike of brilliance, are beginning to think they'd be safer with a bit of dynamite around.' National Labour MP Harold Nicolson, a poor politician but a fine journalist and diarist, wrote in the *Spectator* of Churchill's 'Elizabethan zest for life . . . His wit . . . rises high in the air like some strong fountain, flashing in every sunbeam, and renewing itself with ever-increasing jets and gusts of image and association.'

Though Churchill's appointment was made by the King on the advice of Chamberlain, rather than following any elective process, popular acclaim bore him to the premiership – and to the role as Minister of Defence which he also appropriated. Tory MP Leo Amery was among those sceptical that Churchill could play so many parts: 'How Winston thinks that he can be Prime Minister, co-ordinator of defence and leader of the House all at once, is puzzling, and confirms my belief that he really means the present arrangement to be temporary. Certainly no one can coordinate defence properly who is not prepared to be active head of the three Chiefs of Staff and in fact directly responsible for plans.' Critics were still expressing dismay about Churchill's joint role as national leader and defence minister three years later. Yet this was prompted not by mere personal conceit, but by dismay at the shocking lack of coordination between the services which characterised the Norway campaign. And posterity perceives, as did he himself at the time, that beyond his own eagerness to run Britain's war machine, there was no other political or military figure to whom delegation of such power would have been appropriate.

In one of the most famous and moving passages of his memoirs, Churchill declared himself on 10 May 'conscious of a profound sense of relief. At last I had the authority to give directions over the whole scene. I felt as if I were walking with destiny, and that all my past

4

life had been but a preparation for this hour and this trial.' He thrilled to his own ascent to Britain's leadership. Perhaps he allowed himself a twitch of satisfaction that he could at last with impunity smoke cigars through cabinet meetings, a habit that had annoyed his predecessor. If, however, he cherished a belief that it would be in his gift to shape strategy, events immediately disabused him.

At dawn on 10 May, a few hours before Churchill was summoned to Buckingham Palace, Hitler's armies stormed across the frontiers of neutral Holland, Belgium and Luxembourg. Captain David Strangeways, serving with the British Expeditionary Force near Lille just inside the French border, bridled at the impertinence of an orderly room clerk who rushed into the quarters where he lay abed shouting: 'David, sir, David!' Then the officer realised that the clerk was passing the order for Operation *David*, the BEF's advance from the fortified line which it had held since the previous autumn, deep into Belgium to meet the advancing Germans. Though the Belgians had declared themselves neutrals since 1936, Allied war planning felt obliged to anticipate an imperative requirement to offer them aid if Germany violated their territory.

David perfectly fulfilled Hitler's predictions and wishes. On 10 May the British, together with the French First and Seventh Armies, hastened to abandon laboriously prepared defensive positions. They mounted their trucks and armoured vehicles, then set off in long columns eastward towards the proffered 'matador's cloak', in Liddell Hart's phrase, which the Germans flourished before them in Belgium. Further south in the Ardennes forest, Panzer columns thrashed forward to launch one of the war's great surprises, a thrust at the centre of the Allied line, left inexcusably weak by the deployments of the Allied supreme commander, France's General Maurice Gamelin. Guderian's and Reinhardt's tanks, racing for the Meuse, easily brushed aside French cavalry posturing in their path. Luftwaffe paratroops and glider-borne forces burst upon the Dutch and Belgian frontier fortresses. Stukas and Messerschmitts poured bombs and machine-gun fire upon bewildered formations of four armies.

DENMARK

NORTH
SEA

GREAT
BRITAIN

NETHERLANDS

German
reserves
42 divisions

Belgian Army
18 divisions + res

Reserves
2 divisions

The Hague

Amsterdam

Utrecht

Dutch Army
8 divisions + res

Army Group B
(Bock)
29.5 divisions, inc 3 armoured

French Seventh Army
(Giraud)
7 divisions, inc
1 light mechanised
and 2 motorised

Rotterdam

Breda

Maas

GERMANY

Supreme Commander,
Armed Forces – Hitler

Supreme Commander,
OKH (Army High Command)
C and C, Brauchitsch

Dover

Ostend

Dunkirk

Reserves
4 divisions

Schelde

Albert Canal

Louvain

Brussels

Wavre

BELGIUM

Meuse

Namur

Liège

Aachen

Army Group A
(Rundstedt)
45.5 divisions,
inc 7 armoured
and 3 motorised

Abbeville

BEF
(Gort)
9 divisions

Somme

Sedan

Ardennes

Luxembourg

West Wall
(Siegfried Line)

French 1st Army Group
(Billotte)
22 divisions, inc 2 light mechanised

Longuyon

Brit

French 2nd Army Group
(Prételat)
35 divisions + 1 British

Seine

Paris

FRANCE

Haguenau

Meuse

Army Group C
(Leeb)
19 divisions

French 3rd Army Group
(Besson)
14 divisions

Maginot Line

Basle

SWITZERLAND

Bern

0   100 miles

0   200 km

May 1940 deployments

No more than his nation did the prime minister grasp the speed of approaching catastrophe. The Allied leaders supposed themselves at the beginning of a long campaign. The war was already eight months old, but thus far neither side had displayed impatience for a decisive confrontation. The German descent on Scandinavia was a sideshow. Hitler's assault on France promised the French and British armies the opportunity, so they supposed, to confront his legions on level terms. The paper strengths of the two sides in the west were similar – about 140 divisions apiece, of which just ten were British. Allied commanders and governments believed that weeks, if not months, would elapse before the critical clash came. Churchill retired to bed on the night of 10 May knowing that the Allies' strategic predicament was grave, but bursting with thoughts and plans, and believing that he had time to implement them.

Events which tower in the perception of posterity must at the time compete for attention with trifles. The BBC radio announcer who told the nation of the German invasion of Belgium and Holland followed this by reporting: 'British troops have landed in Iceland,' as if the second news item atoned for the first. *The Times* of 11 May 1940 reported the issue of an arrest warrant at Brighton bankruptcy court for a playwright named Walter Hackett, said to have fled to America. An army court martial was described, at which a colonel was charged with 'undue familiarity' with a sergeant in his searchlight unit. What would soldiers think, demanded the prosecutor, on hearing a commanding officer address a sergeant as 'Eric'? Advertisements for Player's cigarettes exhorted smokers: 'When cheerfulness is in danger of disturbance, light a Player . . . with a few puffs put trouble in its proper place.' The Irish Tourist Association promised: 'Ireland will welcome you.' On the front page, a blue Persian cat was offered for sale at £2.10s: 'house-trained: grandsire Ch. Laughton Laurel; age 7 weeks – Bachelor, Grove Place, Aldenham'. Among Business Offers, a 'Gentleman with extensive experience wishes join established business, Town or Country, capital available.' A golf report on the sports page was headed: 'What the public want.' There was a poem by Walter de la Mare:

'O lovely England, whose ancient peace/War's woful dangers strain and fret.'

The German blitzkrieg was reported under a double-column headline: 'Hitler strikes at the Low Countries'. Commentaries variously asserted: 'Belgians confident of victory; ten times as strong as in 1914'; 'The side of Holland's economic life of greatest interest to Hitler is doubtless her agricultural and allied activities'; 'The Military Outlook: No Surprise This Time'. *The Times*'s editorial column declared: 'It may be taken as certain that every detail has been prepared for an instant strategic reply . . . The Grand Alliance of our time for the destruction of the forces of treachery and oppression is being steadily marshalled.'

A single column at the right of the main news, on page six, proclaimed: 'New prime minister. Mr Churchill accepts'. The newspaper's correspondence was dominated by discussion of Parliament's Norway debate three days earlier, which had precipitated the fall of Chamberlain. Mr Geoffrey Vickers urged that Lord Halifax was by far the best-qualified minister to lead a national government, assisted by a Labour leader of the Commons. Mr Quintin Hogg, Tory MP for Oxford, noted that many of those who had voted against the government were serving officers. Mr Henry Morris-Jones, Liberal MP for Denbigh, deplored the vote that had taken place, observing complacently that he himself had abstained. The news from France was mocked by a beautiful spring day, with bluebells and primroses everywhere in flower.

'Chips' Channon, millionaire Tory MP, diarist and consummate ass, wrote on 10 May: 'Perhaps the darkest day in English history . . . We were all sad, angry and felt cheated and out-witted.' His distress was inspired by the fall of Chamberlain, not the blitzkrieg in France. Churchill himself knew better than any man how grudgingly he had been offered the premiership, and how tenuous was his grasp on power. Much of the Conservative Party hated him, not least because he had twice in his life 'ratted' – changed sides in the House of Commons. He was remembered as architect of the disastrous 1915 Gallipoli campaign, 1919 sponsor of war against the Bolsheviks in

Russia, 1933–34 opponent of Indian self-government, 1936 supporter of King Edward VIII in the Abdication crisis, savage backbench critic of both Baldwin and Chamberlain, Tory prime ministers through his own 'wilderness years'.

In May 1940, while few influential figures questioned Churchill's brilliance or oratorical genius, they perceived his career as wreathed in misjudgements. Robert Rhodes-James subtitled his 1970 biography of Churchill before he ascended to the premiership *A Study in Failure*. As early as 1914, the historian A.G. Gardiner wrote an extraordinarily shrewd and admiring assessment of Churchill, which concluded equivocally: ' "Keep your eye on Churchill" should be the watchword of these days. Remember, he is a soldier first, last and always. He will write his name big on our future. Let us take care he does not write it in blood.'

Now, amidst the crisis precipitated by Hitler's blitzkrieg, Churchill's contemporaries could not forget that he had been wrong about much even in the recent past, and even in the military sphere in which he professed expertise. During the approach to war, he described the presence of aircraft over the battlefield as a mere 'additional complication'. He claimed that modern anti-tank weapons neutered the powers of 'the poor tank', and that 'the submarine will be mastered . . . There will be losses, but nothing to affect the scale of events.' On Christmas Day 1939 he wrote to Sir Dudley Pound, the First Sea Lord: 'I feel we may compare the position now very favourably with that of 1914.' He had doubted that the Germans would invade Scandinavia. When they did so, Churchill told the Commons on 11 April: 'In my view, which is shared by my skilled advisers, Herr Hitler has committed a grave strategic error in spreading the war so far to the north . . . We shall take all we want of this Norwegian coast now, with an enormous increase in the facility and the efficiency of our blockade.' Even if some of Churchill's false prophecies and mistaken expressions of confidence were unknown to the public, they were common currency among ministers and commanders.

His claim upon his country's leadership rested not upon his contribution to the war since September 1939, which was equivocal,

but upon his personal character and his record as a foe of appease-
ment. He was a warrior to the roots of his soul, who found his being
upon battlefields. He was one of the few British prime ministers to
have killed men with his own hand – at Omdurman in 1898. Now
he wielded a sword symbolically, if no longer physically, amid a
British body politic dominated by men of paper, creatures of com-
mittees and conference rooms. 'It may well be,' he enthused six years
before the war, 'that the most glorious chapters of our history have
yet to be written. Indeed, the very problems and dangers that encompass us and our country ought to make English men and women of
this generation glad to be here at such a time. We ought to rejoice
at the responsibilities with which destiny has honoured us, and be
proud that we are guardians of our country in an age when her life
is at stake.' Leo Amery had written in March 1940: 'I am beginning
to come round to the idea that Winston with all his failings is the
one man with real war drive and love of battle.' So he was, of course.
But widespread fears persisted, that this erratic genius might lead
Britain in a rush towards military disaster.

Few of the ministers whom he invited to join his all-party coalition were equal to the magnitude of their tasks. If this is true of
all governments at all times, it was notably unfortunate now. Twenty-
one out of thirty-six senior office-holders were, like Halifax, David
Margesson, Kingsley Wood and Chamberlain himself, veterans of the
previous discredited administration. 'Winston has not been nearly
bold enough with his changes and is much too afraid of the
[Conservative] Party,' wrote Amery, who had led the Commons
charge against Chamberlain.

Of the Labour recruits – notably Clement Attlee, A.V. Alexander,
Hugh Dalton, Arthur Greenwood and Ernest Bevin – only Bevin was
a personality of the first rank, though Attlee as deputy prime minister
would provide a solid bulwark. Sir Archibald Sinclair, the Liberal
leader who had served as an officer under Churchill in France in
1916 and now became Secretary for Air, was described by those
contemptuous of his subservience to the new prime minister as 'head
of school's fag'. Churchill's personal supporters who received office

or promotion, led by Anthony Eden, Lord Beaverbrook, Brendan Bracken and Amery, were balefully regarded not only by Chamberlain loyalists, but also by many sensible and informed people who were willing to support the new prime minister, but remained sceptical of his associates.

Much of the political class thought Churchill's administration would be short-lived. 'So at last that man has gained his ambition,' an elderly Tory MP, Cuthbert Headlam, noted sourly. 'I never thought he would. Well – let us hope that he makes good. I have never believed in him. I only hope that my judgement . . . will be proved wrong.' The well-known military writer Captain Basil Liddell Hart wrote gloomily on 11 May: 'The new War Cabinet appears to be a group devoted to "victory" without regard to its practical possibility.' Lord Hankey, veteran Whitehall *éminence grise* and a member of the new government, thought it 'perfectly futile for war' and Churchill himself a 'rogue elephant'.

Even as Hitler's Panzer columns drove for Sedan and pushed onward through Holland and Belgium, Churchill was filling lesser government posts, interviewing new ministers, meeting officials. On the evening of 10 May Sir Edward Bridges, the shy, austere Cabinet Secretary, called at Admiralty House, where Churchill still occupied the desk from which he had presided as First Lord. Bridges decided that it would be unbecoming for an official who until that afternoon had been serving a deposed prime minister, too obsequiously to welcome the new one. He merely said cautiously: 'May I wish you every possible good fortune?' Churchill grunted, gazed intently at Bridges for a moment, then said: 'Hum. "Every good fortune!" I like that! These other people have all been congratulating me. Every good fortune!'

At Churchill's first meeting with the chiefs of staff as prime minister on 11 May, he made two interventions, both trifling: he asked whether the police should be armed when sent to arrest enemy aliens, and he pondered the likelihood of Sweden joining the war on the Allied side. Even this most bellicose of men did not immediately attempt to tinker with the movements of Britain's army on the Continent. When Eden, the new Secretary for War, called on the prime minister that day, he noted in his diary that Churchill 'seemed well satisfied with the way events were shaping'. If these words reflected a failure to perceive the prime minister's inner doubts, it is certainly true that he did not perceive the imminence of disaster.

Churchill cherished a faith in the greatness of France, the might of her armed forces, most touching in a statesman of a nation tradition-ally wary of its Gallic neighbour. 'In Winston's eyes,' wrote his doctor later, 'France is civilisation.' Even after witnessing the German conquest of Poland and Scandinavia, Churchill understood little about the disparity between the relative fighting powers of Hitler's Wehrmacht and Luftwaffe, and those of the French and British armies and air forces. He, like almost all his advisers, deemed it unthinkable that the Germans could achieve a breakthrough against France's Maginot Line and the combined mass of French, British, Dutch and Belgian forces.

In the days that followed his ascent to Downing Street on 10 May, Churchill set about galvanising the British machinery of war and government for a long haul. As war leader, he expected to preside over Britain's part in a massive and protracted clash on the Continent. His foremost hope was that this would entail no such slaughter as that which characterised the 1914–18 conflict. If he cherished no expectation of swift victory, he harboured no fear of decisive defeat. On 13 May, headlines in *The Times* asserted confidently: 'BRITISH FORCES MOVING ACROSS BELGIUM – SUCCESSFUL ENCOUNTERS WITH ENEMY – RAF STRIKES AGAIN'.

Addressing the Commons that day, the prime minister apologised for his brevity: 'I hope that . . . my friends . . . will make allowance, all allowance, for any lack of ceremony with which it has been neces-sary to act . . . We have before us an ordeal of the most grievous kind. We have before us many, many long months of struggle and of suffering . . . But I take up my task with buoyancy and hope. I feel sure that our cause will not be suffered to fail among men. At this time I feel entitled to claim the aid of all, and I say: "Come then, let us go forward together with our united strength."'

Churchill's war speeches are usually quoted in isolation. This obscures the bathos of remarks by backbench MPs which followed those of the prime minister. On 13 May, Major Sir Philip Colfox, West Dorset, said that although the country must now pursue national unity, he himself much regretted that Neville Chamberlain had been removed from the premiership. Sir Irving Albery, Gravesend, recalled the new prime minister's assertion: 'My policy is a policy of war.' Albery said he thought it right to praise his predecessor's commitment to the cause of peace. Colonel John Gretton, Burton, injected a rare note of realism by urging the House not to waste words, when 'the enemy is almost battering at our gates'. The bleakest indication of the Conservative Party's temper came from the fact that while Neville Chamberlain was cheered as he entered the chamber that day, Churchill's appearance was greeted with resentful Tory silence.

This, his first important statement, received more applause from abroad than it did from some MPs. The *Philadelphia Inquirer* editorialised: 'He proved in this one short speech that he was not afraid to face the truth and tell it. He proved himself an honest man as well as a man of action. Britain has reason to be enheartened by his brevity, his bluntness and his courage.' *Time* magazine wrote: 'That smart, tough, dumpy little man, Prime Minister Winston Churchill, knows how to face facts . . . Great Britain's tireless old firebrand has changed the character of Allied warmongering.'

That day, 13 May, the threat of German air attack on Britain caused Churchill to make his first significant military decision: he rejected a proposal for further fighter squadrons to be sent to France to reinforce the ten already committed. But while the news from the Continent was obviously bleak, he asserted that he was 'by no means sure that the great battle was developing'. He still cherished hopes of turning the tide in Norway, signalling to Admiral Lord Cork and Orrery on 14 May: 'I hope you will get Narvik cleaned up as soon as possible, and then work southward with increasing force.'

Yet the Germans were already bridging the Meuse at Sedan and Dinant, south of Brussels, for their armoured columns emerging from the Ardennes forests. A huge gap was opening between the

French Ninth Army, which was collapsing, and the Second on its left. Though the BEF in Belgium was still not seriously engaged, its C-in-C Lord Gort appealed for air reinforcements. Gort commanded limited confidence. Like all British generals, he lacked training and instincts for the handling of large forces. One of the army's cleverest staff officers, Colonel Ian Jacob of the war cabinet secretariat, wrote: 'We have for twenty years thought little about how to win big campaigns on land; we have been immersed in our day-to-day imperial police activities.'

This deficiency, of plausible 'big battlefield' commanders, would dog British arms throughout the war. Gort was a famously brave officer who had won a VC in World War I, and still carried himself with a boyish enthusiasm. Maj.Gen. John Kennedy, soon to become Director of Military Operations at the War Office, described the BEF's C-in-C as 'a fine fighting soldier' – a useful testimonial for a platoon commander. In blunter words, the general lacked brains, as do most men possessed of the suicidal courage necessary to win a Victoria Cross or Medal of Honor. A shrewd American categorised both Gort and the Chief of the Imperial General Staff, Sir Edmund Ironside, as 'purely physical soldiers who had no business in such high places'. Yet Sir Alan Brooke or Sir Bernard Montgomery would have been no more capable of averting disaster in 1940, with the small forces available to the BEF. Unlike most of Continental Europe, Britain had no peacetime conscription for military service until 1939, and thus no large potential reserves for mobilisation. The army Gort commanded was, in spirit, the imperial constabulary of inter-war years, starved of resources for a generation.

On 14 May, for the first time Churchill glimpsed the immensity of the Allies' peril. Paul Reynaud, France's prime minister, telephoned from Paris, reporting the German breakthrough and asking for the immediate dispatch of a further ten RAF fighter squadrons. The chiefs of staff committee and the war cabinet, which met successively at 6 and 7 o'clock, agreed that Britain's home defences should not be thus weakened. At seven next morning, the 15th, Reynaud telephoned personally to Churchill. The Frenchman spoke emotionally, asserting in English: 'The battle is lost.' Churchill urged him to steady himself, pointing out that only a small part of the French army was engaged, while the German spearheads were now far extended and thus should be vulnerable to flank attack.

When Churchill reported the conversation to his political and military chiefs, the question of further air support was raised once more. Churchill was briefly minded to accede to Reynaud's pleas. But Chamberlain sided with Air Chief Marshal Sir Hugh Dowding, C-in-C of Fighter Command, who passionately demurred. No further fighters were committed. That day Jock Colville, the prime minister's twenty-five-year-old junior private secretary and an aspiring Pepys, noted in his diary the understated concerns of Maj.Gen. Hastings 'Pug' Ismay, chief of staff to Churchill in his capacity as Minister of Defence. Ismay was 'not too happy about the military situation. He says the French are not fighting properly: they are, he points out, a volatile race and it may take them some time to get into a warlike mood.'

Sluggish perception lagged dreadful reality. Churchill cabled to US president Franklin Roosevelt: 'I think myself that the battle on land has only just begun, and I should like to see the masses engage. Up to the present, Hitler is working with specialized units in tanks and air.' He appealed for American aid, and for the first time begged the loan of fifty old destroyers. Washington had already vetoed a request that a British aircraft-carrier should dock at an American port to embark uncrated, battle-ready fighters. This would breach the US Neutrality Act, said the president. So too, he decided, would the dispatch of destroyers.

In France on the 15th, the RAF's inadequate Battle and Blenheim bombers suffered devastating losses attempting to break the Germans' Meuse pontoon bridges. A watching Panzer officer wrote: 'The summer landscape with the quietly flowing river, the light green of the meadows bordered by the darker summits of the more distant heights, spanned by a brilliantly blue sky, is filled with the racket of war . . . Again and again an enemy aircraft crashes out of the sky, dragging a long black plume of smoke behind it . . . Occasionally from the falling machines one or two white parachutes release themselves and float slowly to earth.' The RAF's sacrifice was anyway too late. Much of the German armour was already across the Meuse, and racing westward.

On the morning of the 16th it was learned in London that the Germans had breached the Maginot Line. The war cabinet agreed to deploy four further fighter squadrons to operate over the battle-field. At 3 o'clock that afternoon the prime minister flew to Paris, accompanied by Ismay and Gen. Sir John Dill, Ironside's Vice-CIGS. Landing at Le Bourget, for the first time they perceived the desper-ation of their ally. France's generals and politicians were waiting upon defeat. As the leaders of the two nations conferred at the Quai d'Orsay, officials burned files in the garden. When Churchill asked about French reserves for a counter-attack, he was told that these were already committed piecemeal. Reynaud's colleagues did not conceal their bitterness at Britain's refusal to dispatch further fighters. At every turn of the debate, French shoulders shrugged. From the British embassy that evening, Churchill cabled the war cabinet urging the dispatch of six more squadrons. 'I . . . emphasise the mortal gravity of the hour,' he wrote. The chief of air staff, Sir Cyril Newall, proposed a compromise: six further squadrons should operate over France from their British airfields. At 2 a.m., Churchill drove to Reynaud's flat to communicate the news. The prime minister thereafter returned to the embassy, slept soundly despite occasional distant gunfire, then flew home via Hendon, where he landed before 9 a.m. on the 17th.

He wore a mask of good cheer, but was no longer in doubt about the catastrophe threatening the Allies. He understood that it had become essential for the BEF to withdraw from its outflanked pos-itions in Belgium. Back in Downing Street, after reporting to the war cabinet he set about filling further minor posts in his government, telephoning briskly to prospective appointees, twelve that day in all. Harold Nicolson recorded a typical conversation:

'Harold, I think it would be wise if you joined the Government and helped Duff [Cooper] at the Ministry of Information.'

16

'There is nothing I should like better.'

'Well, fall in tomorrow. The list will be out tonight. That all right?'

'Very much all right.'

'OK.'

Sir Edward Bridges and other Whitehall officials were impressed by Churchill's 'superb confidence', the 'unhurried calm with which he set about forming his government'. At the outset, this reflected failure to perceive the immediacy of disaster. Within days, however, there was instead a majestic determination that his own conduct should be seen to match the magnitude of the challenge he and his nation faced. From the moment Churchill gained the premiership, he displayed a self-discipline which had been conspicuously absent from most of his career. In small things as in great, he won the hearts of those who became his intimates at Downing Street. 'What a beauti-ful handwriting,' he told Jock Colville when the private secretary showed him a dictated telegram. 'But, my dear boy, when I say stop you must write stop and not just put a blob.' Embracing his staff as an extension of his family, it never occurred to him to warn them against repeating his confidences. He took it for granted that they would not do so – and was rewarded accordingly.

Churchill lunched on 17 May at the Japanese embassy. Even in such circumstances, diplomatic imperatives pressed. Japan's expansion-ism was manifest. Everything possible must be done to promote its quiescence. That afternoon he dispatched into exile former Foreign Secretary Sir Samuel Hoare, most detested of the old appeasers, to become ambassador to Spain. He also established economic com-mittees to address trade, food and transport. A series of telegrams arrived from France, reporting further German advances. Churchill asked Chamberlain, as Lord President, to assess the implications of the fall of Paris – and of the BEF's possible withdrawal from the Continent through the Channel ports. His day, which had begun in Paris, ended with dinner at Admiralty House in the company of Lord Beaverbrook and Brendan Bracken.

Posterity owes little to Churchill's wayward son Randolph, but a debt is due for his account of a visit to Admiralty House on the morning of 18 May:

> I went up to my father's bedroom. He was standing in front of his basin and shaving with his old-fashioned Valet razor . . .
>
> 'Sit down, dear boy, and read the papers while I finish shaving.' I did as told. After two or three minutes of hacking away, he half turned and said: 'I think I see my way through.' He resumed his shaving. I was astounded, and said: 'Do you mean that we can avoid defeat?' (which seemed credible) 'or beat the bastards?' (which seemed incredible).
>
> He flung his Valet razor into the basin, swung around and said: – 'Of course I mean we can beat them.'
>
> Me: 'Well, I'm all for it, but I don't see how you can do it.'
>
> By this time he had dried and sponged his face and turning round to me, said with great intensity: 'I shall drag the United States in.'

Here was a characteristic Churchillian flash of revelation. The prospect of American belligerence was remote. For years, Neville Chamberlain had repeatedly and indeed rudely cold-shouldered advances from Franklin Roosevelt. Yet already the new prime minister recognised that US aid alone might make Allied victory possible. Eden wrote that day: 'News no worse this morning, but seems to me too early to call it better. PM and CIGS gave, however, optimistic survey to Cabinet.' Whatever Churchill told his colleagues, he was now obliged to recognise the probability – though, unlike France's generals, he refused to bow to its inevitability – of German victory on the Continent. Reports from the battlefield grew steadily graver. Churchill urged the chiefs of staff to consider bringing large reinforcements from India and Palestine, and holding back some tank units then in transit from Britain to the BEF. The threat of a sudden German descent on England, spearheaded by paratroops, seized his imagination, unrealistic though it was.

A Home Intelligence report suggested to the government that national morale was badly shaken: 'It must be remembered that the defence of the Low Countries had been continually built up in the press . . . Not one person in a thousand could visualise the Germans breaking through into France . . . A relieved acceptance of Mr Churchill as prime minister allowed people to believe that a change of leadership would, in itself, solve the consequences of Mr Chamberlain. Reports sent in yesterday and this morning show that disquiet and personal fear have returned.'

That evening of 18 May, the war cabinet agreed that Churchill should broadcast to the nation, making plain the gravity of the emergency. Ministers were told that Mussolini had rejected Britain's proposal for an Italian declaration of neutrality. This prompted navy minister A.V. Alexander to urge the immediate occupation of Crete, as a base for operations against Italy in the Mediterranean. Churchill dismissed the idea out of hand, saying that Britain was much too committed elsewhere to embark upon gratuitous adventures.

On the morning of Sunday, 19 May, it was learned that the BEF had evacuated Arras, increasing the peril of its isolation from the main French forces. Emerging together from a meeting, Ironside said to Eden: 'This is the end of the British Empire.' The Secretary for War noted: 'Militarily, I did not see how he could be gainsaid.' Yet it was hard for colleagues to succumb to despair when their leader marvellously sustained his wit. That same bleak Sunday, the prime minister said to Eden: 'About time number 17 turned up, isn't it?' The two of them, at Cannes casino's roulette wheel in 1938, had backed the number and won twice.

At noon, Churchill was driven across Kent to Chartwell, his beloved old home, shuttered for the duration. He sought an interlude of tranquillity in which to prepare his broadcast to the nation. But he had been feeding his goldfish for only a few minutes when he was interrupted by a telephone call. Gort, in France, was seeking sanction to fall back on the sea at Dunkirk if his predicament worsened. The C-in-C was told instead to seek to re-establish contact with the French army on his right, with German spearheads in between. The French, in their turn, would be urged to counter-attack towards him. The Belgians were pleading for the BEF to hold a more northerly line beside their own troops. The war cabinet determined, however, that the vital priority was to re-establish a common front with the main French armies. The Belgians must be left to their fate, while British forces redeployed south-westwards towards Arras and Amiens.

Broadcasting to the British people that night, Churchill asserted a confidence which he did not feel, that the line in France would be stabilised, but also warned of the peril the nation faced. 'This is one of the most awe-striking periods in the long history of France and Britain. It is also beyond doubt the most sublime. Centuries ago words were written to be a call and a spur to the faithful servants of Truth and Justice: "Arm yourselves, and be ye men of valour . . . for it is better for us to perish in battle than to look upon the outrage of our nation and our altar. As the will of God is in Heaven, even so let it be."'

This was the first of his great clarion calls to the nation. It is impossible to overstate its impact upon the British people, and indeed upon the listening world. He asserted his resolve, and his listeners responded. That night he dispatched a minute to Ismay, reasserting his refusal to send further RAF squadrons to France. Every fighter would be needed 'if it becomes necessary to evacuate the BEF'. It was obvious that this decision would be received badly by the French, and not all his subordinates supported it. His personal scientific and economic adviser, Frederick Lindemann – 'the Prof' – penned a note of protest.

Britain's forces could exert only a marginal influence on the outcome of the battle for France. Even if every aircraft the RAF possessed had been dispatched to the Continent, such a commitment would not have averted Allied defeat. It would merely have sacrificed the squadrons that later won the Battle of Britain. In May 1940, however, such things were much less plain. As France tottered on the brink of collapse, with five million terrified fugitives clogging roads in a fevered exodus southwards, the bitterness of her politicians and generals mounted against an ally that matched extravagant rhetoric with refusal to provide the only important aid in its gift. France's leaders certainly responded feebly to Hitler's blitzkrieg. But their rancour towards Britain merits understanding. Churchill's perception of British self-interest has been vindicated by history, but scarcely deserved the gratitude of Frenchmen.

He sent an unashamedly desperate message to Roosevelt, regretting America's refusal to lend destroyers. More, he warned that while his own government would never surrender, a successor administration might parley with Germany, using the Royal Navy as its 'sole remaining bargaining counter . . . If this country was left by the United States to its fate, no one would have the right to blame those men responsible if they made the best terms they could for the surviving inhabitants. Excuse me, Mr President, putting this nightmare bluntly.' In Hitler's hands, Britain's fleet would pose a grave threat to the United States.

If this was a brutal prospect to lay before Roosevelt, it was by no means a bluff. At that moment Churchill could not know that Parliament and the British people would stick with him to the end. Chamberlain remained leader of the Conservative Party. Even before the crisis in France, a significant part of Britain's ruling class was susceptible to a compromise peace. Following military catastrophe, it was entirely plausible that Churchill's government would fall, just as Chamberlain's had done, to be replaced by an administration which sought terms from Hitler. Only in the months which followed would the world, and Churchill himself, gradually come to perceive that the people of Britain were willing to risk everything under his leadership.

On the 20th he told the chiefs of staff that the time had come to consider whether residual Norwegian operations around Narvik should be sustained, when troops and ships were urgently needed elsewhere. On the Continent, the Germans were driving south and west so fast that it seemed doubtful whether the BEF could regain touch with the main French armies. Gort was still striving to pull back forces from the Scheldt. That night, German units passed Amiens on the hot, dusty road to Abbeville, cutting off the BEF from its supply bases. Still Churchill declined to despair. He told the war cabinet late on the morning of the 21st that 'the situation was more favourable than certain of the more obvious symptoms would indicate'. In the north, the British still had local superiority of numbers. Fears focused on the perceived pusillanimity of the French, both politicians and soldiers. That day, a British armoured thrust south from Arras failed to break through. The BEF was isolated, along with elements of the French First Army. Calais and Boulogne remained in British hands, but inaccessible by land.

The House of Commons on 20 May, with the kind of inspired madness that contributed to the legend of 1940, debated a Colonial Welfare Bill. Many people in Britain lacked understanding of the full horror of the Allies' predicament. Newspaper readers continued to receive encouraging tidings. The *Evening News* headlined on 17 May: 'BRITISH TROOPS SUCCESS'. On the 19th, the *Sunday Dispatch* headline read 'ATTACKS LESS POWERFUL'. Even two days later, the *Evening News* front page proclaimed 'ENEMY ATTACKS BEATEN OFF'. An editorial in the *New Statesman* urged that 'the government should at once grapple with the minor, but important problem of Anglo–Mexican relations'.

Gort's chief of staff, Lt.Gen. Henry Pownall, complained bitterly on 20 May about the absence of clear instructions from London: 'Nobody minds going down fighting, but the long and many days of indigence and recently the entire lack of higher direction . . . have been terribly wearing on the nerves of all of us.' But when orders did come from the prime minister three days later – for a counter-attack south-eastwards by the entire BEF – Pownall was even angrier: 'Can nobody prevent him trying to conduct operations himself as a super Commander-in-Chief? How does he think we are to collect eight divisions and attack as he suggests? Have we no front to hold? He can have no conception of our situation and condition . . . The man's mad.'

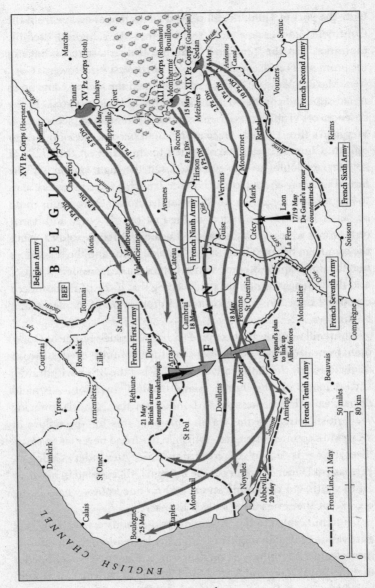

The German advance

Only the port of Dunkirk still offered an avenue of escape from the Continent, and escape now seemed the BEF's highest credible aspiration. On the 22nd and 23rd, the British awaited tidings of the promised French counter-offensive north-eastward, towards Gort. Gen. Maxime Weygand, who had supplanted the sacked Gamelin as Allied supreme commander, declared this to be in progress. In the absence of visible movement Churchill remained sceptical. If Weygand's thrust failed, evacuation would become the only British option. Churchill reported as much to the King on the night of 23 May, as Boulogne was evacuated. On the night of the 24th he fumed to Ismay about Gort's failure to launch a force towards Calais to link up with its garrison, and demanded how men and guns could be better used. He concluded, in the first overtly bitter and histri-onic words which he had deployed against Britain's soldiers since the campaign began: 'Of course, if one side fights and the other does not, the war is apt to become somewhat unequal.' Ironside, the CIGS, told the Defence Committee that evening that if the BEF was indeed evacuated by sea from France, a large proportion of its men might be lost.

Churchill was now preoccupied with three issues: rescue of Gort's men from Dunkirk; deployment of further units of the British Army to renew the battle in France following the BEF's withdrawal; and defence of the home island against invasion. Reynaud dispatched a bitter message to London on the 24th, denouncing the British retreat to the sea and blaming this for the failure of Weygand's counter-offensive – which in truth had never taken place. 'Everything is complete confusion,' Sir Alexander Cadogan, Permanent Under-Secretary at the Foreign Office, noted in his diary on the 25th, 'no communications and no one knows what's going on, except that everything's black as black.'

Churchill cabled to the Dominion prime ministers, warning that an invasion of Britain might be imminent. He rejoiced that reinforce-ments from the Empire were on their way, and asserted his confidence that the Royal Navy and RAF should be able to frustrate an assault, following which 'our land defence will deal with any sea-borne survivors after some rough work'. He rejected the notion of a public appeal to the United States. He feared, surely correctly, that such a message would have scant appeal to a nation already disposed to dismiss aid to Britain as wasted motion. In this, as in his judgement of shifting American moods through the months that followed, he displayed much wisdom. A Gallup poll showed Americans still overwhelmingly opposed, by thirteen to one, to participation in the European conflict.

On 25 May, Churchill dispatched a personal message to Brigadier Claude Nicholson, commanding the British force in Calais, ordering that his men must fight to the end. The Belgians were collapsing. Gort cancelled his last planned counter-attack southward, instead sending north the two divisions earmarked for it, to plug the gap between British and Belgian forces. That evening, at a meeting of the Defence Committee, Churchill accepted the conclusion which Gort, now out of contact with London, had already reached and begun to act upon. The BEF must withdraw to the coast for evacuation. The commander-in-chief's order, issued in advance of consent from Britain, represented his most notable contribution to the campaign, and by no means a negligible one. The prime minister ordered that six skeleton divisions in Britain should be urgently prepared for active service, though scant means existed to accomplish this. Artillery, anti-tank weapons, transport, even small arms were lacking. He acknowledged that France's leaders, resigned to defeat, would probably depose Reynaud and make terms with Hitler. Henceforward, the future of the French fleet was much in his mind. In German hands, these warships might drastically improve the odds favouring a successful invasion of Britain. That night, Ironside resigned as CIGS, to become commander-in-chief home forces. The general had never commanded Churchill's confidence, while Sir John Dill, Ironside's vice-chief, did. Next day Dill, fifty-nine years old, clever and sensitive though seldom in good health, became head of the British Army.

At 9 o'clock on the morning of the 26th, Churchill told the war cabinet there was a good chance of 'getting off a considerable proportion of the British Expeditionary Force'. Paul Reynaud arrived in London. He warned the prime minister over lunch that if Germany occupied a large part of France, the nation's old hero Marshal Philippe Pétain would probably call for an armistice. Reynaud dismissed British fears that the Germans were bent on an immediate invasion of their island. Hitler would strike for Paris, he said, and of course he was right. Churchill told Reynaud that Britain would fight on, whatever transpired. Following a break while he met the war cabinet, the two leaders resumed their talks. Churchill pressed for Weygand to issue an order for the BEF to fall back on the coast. This was designed to frustrate charges of British betrayal. Reynaud duly requested such a message, to endorse the reality of what was already taking place.

At a four-hour war cabinet meeting that afternoon, following Reynaud's departure, the merits of seeking a settlement with Hitler were discussed. Churchill hoped that France might receive terms that precluded her occupation by the Germans. Halifax, the Foreign Secretary, expressed his desire to seek Italian mediation with Hitler, to secure terms for Britain. He had held preliminary talks with Mussolini's ambassador in London about such a course. Churchill was sceptical, saying this presupposed that a deal might be made merely by returning Germany's old colonies, and making concessions in the Mediterranean. 'No such option was open to us,' said the prime minister.

Six Alexander Cadogan, who joined the meeting after half an hour, found Churchill 'too rambling and romantic and sentimental and temperamental'. This was harsh. The prime minister bore vast burdens. It behoved him to be circumspect in all dealings with the old appeasers among his colleagues. There were those in Whitehall who, rather than being stirred by Churchill's appeals to recognise a great historic moment, curled their lips. Chamberlain's private secretary, Arthur Rucker, responded contemptuously to the ringing phrases in one of the prime minister's missives: 'He is still thinking of his books.' Eric Seal, the only one of Churchill's private secretaries who established no close rapport with him,* muttered about 'blasted rhetoric'.

---

* Seal departed from Downing Street in 1941.

A substantial part of the British ruling class, MPs and peers alike, had since September 1939 lacked faith in the possibility of military victory. Although Churchill was himself an aristocrat, he was widely mistrusted by his own kind. Since the 1917 Russian Revolution, many British grandees, including such dukes as Westminster, Wellington and Buccleuch, and such lesser peers as Lord Phillimore, had shown themselves much more hostile to Soviet communism than to European fascism. Their patriotism was never in doubt. However, their enthusiasm for a fight to the finish with Hitler, which they feared would end in rubble and ruin, was less assured. Lord Hankey observed acidly before making a speech to the House of Lords early in May that he 'would be addressing most of the members of the Fifth Column'.

Lord Tavistock, soon to become Duke of Bedford, a pacifist and plausible quisling, wrote to former prime minister David Lloyd George that Hitler's strength was 'so great . . . it is madness to suppose we can beat him by war on the continent'. On 15 May, Tavistock urged Lloyd George that peace should be made 'now rather than later . . . If the Germans received fair peace terms a dozen Hitlers could never start another war on an inadequate . . . pretext.' Likewise, some financial magnates in the City of London were sceptical of any possibility of British victory, and thus of Churchill. Harold Nicolson wrote: 'It is not the descendants of the old governing classes who display the greatest enthusiasm for their leader . . . Mr Chamberlain is the idol of the business men . . . They do not have the same personal feelings for Mr Churchill . . . There are awful moments when they feel that Mr Churchill does not find them interesting.'

There were also defeatists lower down the social scale. Muriel Green, who worked at her family's garage in Norfolk, recorded a conversation at a local tennis match with a grocer's roundsman and a schoolmaster on 23 May. 'I think they're going to beat us, don't you?' said the roundsman. 'Yes,' said the schoolmaster. He added that as the Nazis were very keen on sport, he expected 'we'd still be able to play tennis if they did win'. Muriel Green wrote: 'J said Mr M. was saying we should paint a swastika under the door knocker ready. We all agreed we shouldn't know what to do if they invade.

After that we played tennis, very hard exciting play for 2 hrs, and forgot all about the war.'

In those last days of May, the prime minister must have seen a real possibility, even a likelihood, that if he himself appeared irrationally intransigent, the old Conservative grandees would reassert themselves. Amid the collapse of all the hopes on which Britain's military struggle against Hitler were founded, it was not fanciful to suppose that a peace party might gain control in Britain. Some historians have made much of the fact that at this war cabinet meeting Churchill failed to dismiss out of hand an approach to Mussolini. He did not flatly contradict Halifax when the Foreign Secretary said that if the Duce offered terms for a general settlement 'which did not postulate the destruction of our independence . . . we should be foolish if we did not accept them'. Churchill conceded that 'if we could get out of this jam by giving up Malta and Gibraltar and some African colonies, he would jump at it'. At the following day's war cabinet he indicated that if Hitler was prepared to offer peace in exchange for the restoration of his old colonies and the overlordship of central Europe, a negotiation could be possible.

It seems essential to consider Churchill's words in context. First, they were made in the midst of long, weary discussions, during which he was taking elaborate pains to appear reasonable. Halifax spoke with the voice of logic. Amid shattering military defeat, even Churchill dared not offer his colleagues a vision of British victory. In those Dunkirk days, the Director of Military Intelligence told a BBC correspondent: 'We're finished. We've lost the army and we shall never have the strength to build another.' Churchil did not challenge the view of those who assumed that the war would end, sooner or later, with a negotiated settlement rather than with a British army marching into Berlin. He pitched his case low because there was no alternative. A display of exaggerated confidence would have invited ridicule. He relied solely upon the argument that there was no more to lose by fighting on, than by throwing in the hand.

How would his colleagues, or even posterity, have assessed his judgement had he sought at those meetings to offer the prospect of

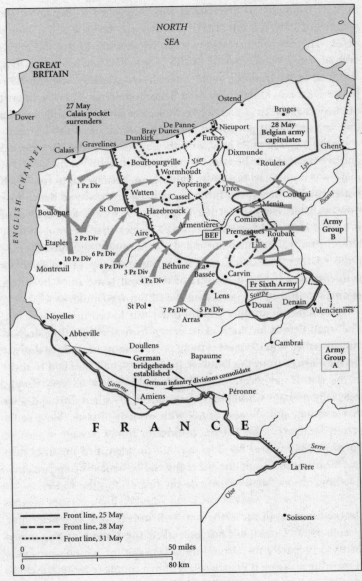

The Dunkirk perimeter

military triumph? To understand what happened in Britain in the summer of 1940, it is essential to acknowledge the logic of impending defeat. This was what created tensions between the hearts and minds even of staunch and patriotic British people. The best aspiration they, and their prime minister, could entertain was a manly determination to survive today, and to pray for a better tomorrow. The war cabinet discussions between 26 and 28 May took place while it was still doubtful that any significant portion of the BEF could be saved from France.

At the meeting of 26 May, with the support of Attlee, Greenwood and eventually Chamberlain, Churchill summed up for the view that there was nothing to be lost by fighting on, because no terms which Hitler might offer in the future were likely to be worse than those now available. Having discussed the case for a parley, he dismissed it, even if Halifax refused to do so. At 7 o'clock that evening, an hour after the war cabinet meeting ended, the Admiralty signalled the Flag Officer Dover, Vice-Admiral Bertram Ramsay: 'Operation *Dynamo* is to commence.' The destroyers of the Royal Navy, aided by a fleet of small craft, began to evacuate the BEF from Dunkirk.

That night yet another painful order was forced upon Churchill. The small British force at Calais, drawn from the Rifle Brigade, had only nuisance value. But everything possible must be done to distract German forces from the Dunkirk perimeter. The Rifles had to resist to the last. Ismay wrote: 'The decision affected us all very deeply, especially perhaps Churchill. He was unusually silent during dinner that evening, and ate and drank with evident distaste.' He asked a private secretary, John Martin, to find for him a passage in George Borrow's 1843 prayer for England. Martin identified the lines next day: 'Fear not the result, for either thy end be a majestic and an enviable one, or God shall perpetuate thy reign upon the waters.'

On the morning of the 27th, even as British troops were beginning to embark at Dunkirk, Churchill asked the leaders of the armed forces to prepare a memorandum setting out the nation's prospects of resisting invasion if France fell. Within a couple of hours the chiefs of staff submitted an eleven-paragraph response that identified the key issues with notable insight. As long as the RAF was 'in being', they wrote, its aircraft together with the warships of the Royal Navy should be able to prevent an invasion. If air superiority was lost, however, the navy could not indefinitely hold the Channel. Should the Germans secure a beachhead in south-east England, British home forces would be incapable of evicting them. The chiefs pinpointed the air battle, Britain's ability to defend its key installations, and especially aircraft factories, as the decisive factors in determining the future course of the war. They concluded with heartening words: 'The real test is whether the morale of our fighting personnel and civil population will counter-balance the numerical and material advantages which Germany enjoys. We believe it will.'

The war cabinet debated at length, and finally accepted, the chiefs' report. It was agreed that further efforts should be made to induce the Americans to provide substantial aid. An important message arrived from Lord Lothian, British ambassador in Washington, suggesting that Britain should invite the US to lease basing facilities in Trinidad, Newfoundland and Bermuda. Churchill opposed any such unilateral offer. America had 'given us practically no help in the war', he said. 'Now that they saw how great was the danger, their attitude was that they wanted to keep everything that would help us for their own defence.' This would remain the case until the end of the battle for France. There was no doubt of Roosevelt's desire to help, but he was constrained by the terms of the Neutrality Act imposed by Congress. On 17 May Gen. George Marshall, chief of the army, expounded to US Treasury Secretary Henry Morgenthau his objections to shipping American arms to the Allies: 'It is a drop in the bucket on the other side and it is a very vital necessity on this side and that is that. Tragic as it is, that is it.' Between 23 May and 3 June US Secretary of War Harry Woodring, an ardent isolationist, deliberately delayed shipment to Britain of war material condemned as surplus. He insisted that there must be prior public advertisement before such equipment was sold to the Allies. On 5 June, the Senate foreign relations committee rejected an administration proposal to sell ships and planes to Britain. The US War Department declined to supply bombs to fit dive-bombers which the French had already bought and paid for.

In the last days of May, a deal for Britain to purchase twenty US patrol torpedo boats was scuttled when news of it leaked to isolationist Senator David Walsh of Massachusetts. As chairman of the Senate's Navy Affairs Committee, Walsh referred the plan to the attorney-general – who declared it illegal. In mid-June, the US chiefs of staff recommended that no further war material should be sent to Britain, and that no private contractor should be allowed to accept an order which might compromise the needs of the US armed forces. None of this directly influenced the campaign in France. But it spoke volumes, all unwelcome in London and Paris, about the prevailing American mood towards Europe's war.

It was a small consolation that other powerful voices across the Atlantic were urging Britain's cause. The *New York Times* attacked Colonel Charles Lindbergh, America's arch-isolationist flying hero, and asserted the mutuality of Anglo-American interests. Lindbergh, said the *Times*, was 'an ignorant young man if he trusts his own premise that it makes no difference to us whether we are deprived of the historic defense of British sea power in the Atlantic Ocean'. The Republican *New York Herald Tribune* astonished many Americans by declaring boldly: 'The least costly solution in both life and welfare would be to declare war on Germany at once.' Yet even if President Roosevelt had wished to heed the urgings of such interventionists and offer assistance to the Allies, he had before him the example of Woodrow Wilson, in whose administration he served. Wilson was renounced by his own legislature in 1919 for making commitments abroad – in the Versailles Treaty – which outreached the will of the American people. Roosevelt had no intention of emulating him.

Chamberlain reported on 27 May that he had spoken the previous evening to Stanley Bruce, Australian high commissioner in London, who argued that Britain's position would be bleak if France surrendered. Bruce, a shrewd and respected spokesman for his dominion, urged seeking American or Italian mediation with Hitler. Australia's prime minister, Robert Menzies, was fortunately made of sterner stuff. From Canberra, Menzies merely enquired what assistance his country's troops could provide. By autumn, three Australian divisions were deployed in the Middle East. Churchill told Chamberlain to make plain to Bruce that France's surrender would not influence Britain's determination to fight on. He urged ministers – and emphasised the message in writing a few days later – to present bold faces to the world. Likewise, a little later he instructed Britain's missions abroad to entertain lavishly, prompting embassy parties in Madrid and Berne. In Churchill's house, even amid disaster there was no place for glum countenances.

At a further war cabinet that afternoon, Halifax found himself unsupported when he returned to his theme of the previous day, seeking agreement that Britain should solicit Mussolini's help in exploring terms from Hitler. Churchill said that at that moment, British prestige in Europe was very low. It could be revived only by defiance. 'If, after two or three months, we could show that we were still unbeaten, we should be no worse off than we should be if we were now to abandon the struggle. Let us therefore avoid being dragged down the slippery slope with France.' If terms were offered, he would be prepared to consider them. But if the British were invited to send a delegate to Paris to join with the French in suing for peace with Germany, the answer must be 'no'. The war cabinet agreed.

Halifax wrote in his diary: 'I thought Winston talked the most frightful rot. I said exactly what I thought of [the Foreign Secretary's opponents in the war cabinet], adding that if that was really their view, our ways must part.' In the garden afterwards, when he repeated his threat of resignation, Churchill soothed him with soft words. Halifax concluded in his diary record: 'It does drive one to despair when he works himself up into a passion of emotion when he ought to make his brain think and reason.' He and Chamberlain recoiled from Churchill's 'theatricality', as Cadogan described it. Cold men both, they failed to perceive in such circumstances the necessity for at least a semblance of boldness. But Chamberlain's eventual support for Churchill's stance was critically important in deflecting the Foreign Secretary's proposals.

Whichever narratives of these exchanges are consulted, the facts seem plain. Halifax believed that Britain should explore terms. Churchill must have been deeply alarmed by the prospect of the Foreign Secretary, the man whom only three weeks earlier most of the Conservative Party wanted as prime minister, quitting his government. It was vital, at this moment of supreme crisis, that Britain should present a united face to the world. Churchill could never thereafter have had private confidence in Halifax. He continued to endure him as a colleague, however, because he needed to sustain the support of the Tories. It was a measure of Churchill's apprehension about the resolve of Britain's ruling class that it would be another seven months before he felt strong enough to consign 'the Holy Fox' to exile.

The legend of Britain in the summer of 1940 as a nation united in defiance of Hitler is rooted in reality. It is not diminished by asserting that if another man had been prime minister, the political faction resigned to seeking a negotiated peace would probably have prevailed. What Churchill grasped, and Halifax and others did not, was that the mere gesture of exploring peace terms must impact disastrously upon Britain's position. Even if Hitler's response proved unacceptable to a British government, the clear, simple Churchillian posture, of rejecting any parley with the forces of evil, would be irretrievably compromised.

It is impossible to declare with confidence at what moment during the summer of 1940 Churchill's grip upon power, as well as his hold upon the loyalties of the British people, became secure. What is plain is that in the last days of May he did not perceive himself proof against domestic foes. He survived in office not because he overcame the private doubts of ministerial and military sceptics, which he did not, but by the face of courage and defiance that he presented to the nation. He appealed over the heads of those who knew too much, to those who were willing to sustain a visceral stubbornness. 'His world is built upon the primacy of public over private relationships,' wrote the philosopher Isaiah Berlin in a fine essay on Churchill, 'upon the supreme value of action, of the battle between simple good and simple evil, between life and death; but above all battle. He has always fought.' The simplicity of Churchill's commitment, matched by the grandeur of the language in which he expressed this, seized popular imagination. In the press, in the pubs and everywhere that Churchill himself appeared on his travels across the country, the British people passionately applauded his defiance. Conservative seekers after truce were left beached and isolated; sullenly resentful, but impotent.

Evelyn Waugh's fictional Halberdier officer, the fastidious Guy Crouchback, was among many members of the British upper classes who were slow to abandon their disdain for the prime minister, displaying an attitude common among real-life counterparts such as Waugh himself:

> Some of Mr Churchill's broadcasts had been played on the mess wireless-set. Guy had found them painfully boastful and they had, most of them, been immediately followed by the news of some disaster ... Guy knew of Mr Churchill only as a professional politician, a master of sham-Augustan prose, an advocate of the Popular Front in Europe, an associate of the press-lords and Lloyd George. He was asked: 'Uncle, what sort of fellow is this Winston Churchill?' 'Like Hore-Belisha [sacked Secretary for War, widely considered a char-latan], except that for some reason his hats are thought to be funny' ... Here Major Erskine leant across the table. 'Churchill is about the only man who may save us from losing this war,' he said. It was the first time that Guy had heard a Halberdier suggest that any result, other than complete victory, was possible.

Some years before the war, the diplomat Lord D'Abernon observed with patrician complacency that 'An Englishman's mind works best when it is almost too late.' In May 1940, he might have perceived Churchill as an exemplar of his words.

TWO

The Two Dunkirks

On 28 May, Churchill learned that the Belgians had surrendered at dawn. He repressed until much later his private bitterness, unjustified though this was when Belgium had no rational prospect of sustaining the fight. He merely observed that it was not for him to pass judgement upon King Leopold's decision. Overnight a few thousand British troops had been retrieved from Dunkirk, but Gort was pessimistic about the fate of more than 200,000 who remained, in the face of overwhelming German air power. 'And so here we are back on the shores of France on which we landed with such high hearts over eight months ago,' Pownall, Gort's chief of staff, wrote that day. 'I think we were a gallant band who little deserve this ignominious end to our efforts . . . If our skill be not so great, our courage and endurance are certainly greater than that of the Germans.' The stab of self-knowledge reflected in Pownall's phrase about the inferior professionalism of the British Army lingered in the hearts of its intelligent soldiers until 1945.

That afternoon at a war cabinet meeting in Churchill's room at the Commons, the prime minister again – and for the last time – rejected Halifax's urgings that the government could obtain better peace terms before France surrendered and British aircraft factories were destroyed. Chamberlain, as ever a waverer, now supported the Foreign Secretary in urging that Britain should consider 'decent terms if such were offered to us'. Churchill said that the odds were a thousand to one against any such Hitlerian generosity, and warned that 'nations which went down fighting rose again, but those which surrendered tamely were finished'. Attlee and Greenwood, the Labour members, endorsed Churchill's view. This was the last stand of the old appeasers. Privately, they adhered to the view, shared by former prime minister Lloyd George, that sooner or later negotiation with Germany would be essential. As late as 17 June, the Swedish ambassador reported Halifax and his junior minister R.A. Butler declaring that no 'diehards' would be allowed to stand in the way of peace 'on reasonable conditions'. Andrew Roberts has convincingly argued that Halifax was not directly complicit in remarks made during a chance conversation between Butler and the envoy. But it remains extraordinary that some historians have sought to qualify verdicts on the Foreign Secretary's behaviour through the summer of 1940. It was not dishonourable – the lofty eminence could never have been that. But it was craven.

Immediately following the 28 May meeting, some twenty-five other ministers – all those who were not members of the war cabinet – filed into the room to be briefed by the prime minister. He described the situation at Dunkirk, anticipated the French collapse, and expressed his conviction that Britain must fight on. 'He was quite magnificent,' wrote Hugh Dalton, Minister of Economic Warfare, 'the man, and the only man we have, for this hour . . . He was determined to prepare public opinion for bad tidings . . . Attempts to invade us would no doubt be made.' Churchill told ministers that he had considered the case for negotiating with 'that man' – and rejected it. Britain's position, with its fleet and air force, remained strong. He concluded with a magnificent peroration: 'I am convinced that every man of you would rise up and tear me down from my place if I were for one moment to contemplate parley or surrender. If this long island story of ours is to end at last, let it end only when each one of us lies choking in his own blood upon the ground.'

He was greeted with acclamation extraordinary at any assembly of ministers. No word of dissent was uttered. The meeting represented an absolute personal triumph. He reported its outcome to the war cabinet. That night, the British government informed Reynaud in Paris of its refusal of Italian mediation for peace terms.

FINEST YEARS

A further suggestion by Halifax of a direct call upon the United States was dismissed. A bold stand against Germany, Churchill reiterated, would carry vastly more weight than 'a grovelling appeal' at such a moment. At the following day's war cabinet, new instructions to Gort were discussed. Halifax favoured giving the C-in-C discretion to capitulate. Churchill would hear of no such thing. Gort was told to fight on at least until further evacuation from Dunkirk became impossible. Mindful of Allied reproaches, he told the War Office that French troops in the perimeter must be allowed access to British ships. He informed Reynaud of his determination to create a new British Expeditionary Force, based on the Atlantic port of Saint-Nazaire, to fight alongside the French army in the west.

All through those days, the evacuation from the port and beaches continued, much hampered by lack of small craft to ferry troops out to the larger ships, a deficiency which the Admiralty strove to make good by a public appeal for suitable vessels. History has invested the saga of Dunkirk with a dignity less conspicuous to those present. John Horsfall, a company commander of the Royal Irish Fusiliers, told a young fellow officer: 'I hope you realise your distinction. You are now taking part in the greatest military shambles ever achieved by the British Army.' Many rank-and-file soldiers returned from France nursing a lasting resentment towards the military hierarchy that had exposed them to such a predicament. Horsfall noticed that in the last phase of the march to the beaches, his men fell unnaturally silent: 'There was a limit to what any of us could absorb, with those red fireballs flaming skywards every few minutes, and I suppose we just reached the point where there was little left to say.' They were joined by a horse artillery major, superb in Savile Row riding breeches and scarlet and gold forage cap, who said: 'I'm a double blue at this, old boy – I was at Mons [in 1914].' A young Grenadier Guards officer, Edward Ford, passed the long hours of waiting for a ship reading a copy of Chapman's Homer which he found in the sands. For the rest of his days, Ford was nagged by unsatisfied curiosity about who had abandoned his Chapman amid the detritus of the beaches.

Though the Royal Navy's achievement at Dunkirk embraced its

highest traditions, many men noted only the chaos. 'It does seem to me incredible that the organisation of the beach work should have been so bad,' wrote Lt. Robert Hichens of the minesweeper *Niger*, though he admired the absence of panic among embarking soldiers.

> We were told that there would be lots of boats and that the embarkation of the troops would all be organised . . . That was what all the little shore boats were being brought over from England for . . . One can only come to the conclusion that the civilians and small boats packed up and went home with a few chaps instead of staying there to ferry to the big ships which was their proper job. As for the shore organisation, it simply did not exist . . . It makes one a bit sick when one hears the organisers of the beach show being cracked up to the skies on the wireless and having DSOs showered upon them, because a more disgraceful muddle and lack of organisation I have never seen . . . If a few officers had been put ashore with a couple of hundred sailors . . . the beach evacuation would have been a different thing . . . When the boats were finally hoisted I found that I was very tired and very hoarse as well as soaking wet. So I had a drink and then changed. I had an artillery officer in my cabin who was very interesting. They all seem to have been very impressed by the dive bombers and the vast number of them, and by the general efficiency of the German forces. The soldiers are not very encouraging, but they were very tired which always makes one pessimistic, and they had been out of touch for a long time. This officer did not even know that Churchill had replaced Chamberlain as Premier.

Pownall arrived in London from France to describe to the defence committee on 30 May Gort's plans for holding the Dunkirk perimeter. 'No one in the room,' wrote Ian Jacob of the war cabinet secretariat, 'imagined that they could be successful if the German armoured divisions supported by the Luftwaffe pressed their attack.' It was, of course, a decisive mercy that no such attack was 'pressed'. In the course of the Second World War, victorious German armies displayed a far more consistent commitment to completing the destruction of their enemies when opportunity offered than did the Allies in similarly advantageous circumstances. Dunkirk was an exception. Most of the BEF escaped not as a consequence of Hitler's forbearance, but through a miscellany of fortuities and misjudgements. Success beyond German imagination created huge problems of its own. Commanders' attention was fixed upon completing the defeat of Weygand's forces, of which large elements remained intact. The broken country around Dunkirk was well suited to defence. The French First Army, south of the port, engaged important German forces through the critical period for the BEF's escape, a stand which received less credit from the British than it deserved.

On 24 May von Rundstedt, commanding Army Group A, ordered his Panzers, badly in need of a logistical pause, not to cross the Aa canal and entangle themselves with British 'remnants', as Gort's army was now perceived. Hitler supported his decision. He was amenable to Goering's eagerness to show that his aircraft could complete the destruction of the BEF. Yet, in the words of the most authoritative German history, 'The Luftwaffe, badly weakened by earlier operations, was unable to meet the demands made on it.' In the course of May, Goering's force lost 1,044 aircraft, a quarter of them fighters. Thanks to the efforts of the RAF's Fighter Command over Dunkirk, the German Fourth Army's war diary recorded on the 25th: 'The enemy has had air superiority. This is something new for us in this campaign.' On 3 June the German air effort was diverted from Dunkirk, to increase pressure on the French by bombing targets around Paris.

Almost the entire RAF Air Striking Force was reduced to charred wreckage, strewn the length of northern France. It scarcely seemed to the Germans to matter if a few thousand British troops escaped in salt-stained battledress, when they left behind every tool of a modern army – tanks, guns, trucks, machine-guns and equipment. Hitler's failure to complete the demolition of the BEF represented a historic blunder, but an unsurprising one amid the magnitude of German triumphs and dilemmas in the last days of May 1940. The Allies, with much greater superiority, indulged far more culpable strategic omissions when they returned to the Continent for the campaigns of 1943–45.

Ian Jacob was among those impressed by the calm with which Churchill received Pownall's Dunkirk situation report of 30 May. Thereafter, the war cabinet addressed another budget of French requests: for troops to support them on the Somme front; more aircraft; concessions to Italy; a joint appeal to Washington. Churchill interpreted these demands as establishing a context for French surrender, once Britain had refused them. The decision was taken to withdraw residual British forces from north Norway. The prime minister determined to fly again to Paris to press France to stay in the war, and to make plain that Britain would dissociate itself from any parley with Germany mediated by the Italians. Next morning, as Churchill's Flamingo took off from Northolt, he knew that 133,878 British and 11,666 Allied troops had been evacuated from Dunkirk.

The prime minister's old friend Sir Edward Spears, viewed by his fellow generals as a mountebank, was once more serving as a British liaison officer with the French, a role he had filled in World War I. Spears, waiting at Villacoubray airfield to meet the party, was impressed by the prime minister's imposture of gaiety. Churchill poked the British officer playfully in the stomach with his stick, and as ever appeared stimulated by finding himself upon the scene of great events. He beamed upon the pilots of the escorting Hurricanes which had landed behind him, was driven into Paris for lunch at the British embassy, then went to see Reynaud at the Ministry of War.

Amid the gloom that beset all France's leaders, gathered with her prime minister, Pétain and Admiral Jean François Darlan showed themselves foremost in despair. As Ismay described it: 'A dejected-looking old man in plain clothes shuffled towards me, stretched out his hand and said: "Pétain." It was hard to believe that this was the great Marshal of France.' The rationalists, as they saw themselves, listened unmoved to Churchill's outpouring of rhetoric. He spoke of the two British divisions already in north-western France, which he hoped could be further reinforced to assist in the defence of Paris.

He described in dramatic terms the events at Dunkirk. He declared in his extraordinary franglais, reinforced by gestures, that French and British soldiers would leave arm in arm – '*partage – bras dessus, bras dessous*'. On cabinet orders, Gort was to quit Dunkirk that night. If, as expected, Italy entered the war, British bomber squadrons would at once strike at her industries. Churchill beamed once more. If only France could hold out through the summer, he said, all manner of possibilities would open. In a final surge of emotion, he declared his conviction that American help would come. Thus this thirteenth meeting of the Allied Supreme War Council concluded its agenda.

Reynaud and two other ministers were guests for dinner that night at the palatial British embassy in the rue Saint-Honoré. Churchill waxed lyrical about the possibility of launching striking forces against German tank columns. He left Paris next morning knowing he had done all that force of personality could achieve to breathe inspiration into the hearts of the men charged with saving France. Yet few believed a word of it. The Allies' military predicament was irretrievably dire. It was impossible to conceive any plausible scenario in which Hitler's armies might be thrown back, given the collapse of French national will.

Paul Reynaud was among a handful of Frenchmen who, momentarily at least, remained susceptible to Churchill's verbiage. To logical minds, there was an absurdity about almost everything the Englishman said to ministers and commanders in Paris. Britain's prime minister paraded before his ally his own extravagant sense of honour. He promised military gestures which might further weaken his own country, but could not conceivably save France. He made wildly fanciful pledges of further military aid, though its impact must be insignificant. Britain's two divisions in the north-west were irrelevant to the outcome of the battle, and were desperately needed to defend the home island. But Churchill told the war cabinet in London on 1 June that more troops must be dispatched across the Channel, with a suitable air component. Even as the miracle of Dunkirk unfolded, he continued to waver about dispatching further fighters to the Continent. He trumpeted the success of the RAF in preventing the Luftwaffe from frustrating the evacuation, which he declared a splendid omen for the future.

Chamberlain and Halifax urged against sending more men to France, but Churchill dissented. He felt obliged to respond to fresh appeals from Reynaud. He envisaged a British enclave in Brittany, a base from which the French might be inspired and supported to maintain 'a gigantic guerrilla . . . The B.E.F. in France must immediately be reconstituted, otherwise the French will not continue in the war.' Amid the dire shortage of troops, he committed to France 1st Canadian Division, which had arrived in Britain virtually untrained and unequipped. The prime minister told one of the British generals who would be responsible for sustaining the defence of north-west France that 'he could count on no artillery'. An impromptu new 'division' was created around Rouen from lines of communications personnel equipped with a few Bren and anti-tank guns which they had never fired, and a single battery of field artillery that lacked dial sights for its guns. Until Lt.Gen. Alan Brooke, recently landed from Dunkirk, returned to France on 12 June, British forces there remained under French command, with no national C-in-C on the spot.

By insisting upon resumption of an utterly doomed campaign, Churchill made his worst mistake of 1940. It is unsurprising that his critics in the inner circle of power were dismayed. The strength of Churchill's emotions was wonderful to behold. But when sentiment drove him to make deployments with no possibility of success, he appalled his generals, as well as the old Chamberlainite umbrella-men. Almost every senior civilian and uniformed figure in Whitehall recognised that the Battle of France was lost. Further British commitments threatened to negate the extraordinary deliverance of Dunkirk. The Air Staff closed ranks with Halifax, Chamberlain and others to resist Churchill's demands that more fighters should be sent to France, in addition to the three British squadrons still operating there. On the air issue, Churchill himself havered, then reluctantly gave way. This was the first of many occasions on which he mercifully subordinated his instincts to the advice of service chiefs and colleagues. Chamberlain and Halifax were not wrong about everything. The moral grandeur in Churchill's gestures towards his ally in the first days of June was entirely subsumed by the magnitude of France's tragedy and Britain's peril.

The Dunkirk evacuation approached a conclusion on 4 June, by which time 224,328 British troops had been evacuated, along with 111,172 Allied troops, most of whom subsequently elected to be repatriated to France rather than fight on as exiles. For thirty-five minutes that afternoon, Churchill described the operation to the Commons, concluding with some of his greatest phrases: 'We shall fight on the beaches, we shall fight on the landing grounds, we shall fight in the fields and in the streets, we shall fight in the hills, we shall never surrender.'

That evening he found time to dispatch brief notes, thanking the King for withdrawing his objections to Brendan Bracken's membership of the Privy Council on the grounds of character; and to former prime minister Stanley Baldwin, expressing appreciation for a letter offering good wishes. Churchill apologised for having taken a fortnight to respond. 'We are going through v[er]y hard times & I expect worse to come,' he wrote; 'but I feel quite sure better days will come; though whether we shall live to see them is more doubtful. I do not feel the burden weigh too heavily, but I cannot say that I have enjoyed being Prime Minister v[er]y much so far.'

The German drive on Paris began on 5 June. Anglo–French exchanges in the days that followed were dominated by increasingly passionate appeals from Reynaud for fighters. Five RAF squadrons were still based in France, while four more were operating from British bases. The war cabinet and chiefs of staff were united in their determination to weaken Britain's home defence no further. On 9 June, Churchill cabled to South African premier Jan Smuts, who had urged the dispatch of more aircraft, saying: 'I see only one sure way through now, to wit, that Hitler should attack this country, and in so doing break his air weapon. If this happens he will be left to face the winter with Europe writhing under his heel, and probably with the United States against him after the Presidential election is over.' The Royal Navy was preoccupied with fears about the future of the French fleet. Admiral Sir Dudley Pound, the First Sea Lord, declared that only its sinking could ensure that it would not be used by the Germans.

Yet perversely, and indeed indefensibly, Churchill continued to dispatch troops to France. The draft operation order for 1st Canadian Division, drawn up as it embarked on 11 June, said: 'The political object of the re-constituted BEF is to give moral support to the French Government by showing the determination of the British Empire to assist her ally with all available forces . . . It is the intention . . . to concentrate . . . in the area North and South of Rennes . . . A division may have to hold 50 miles of front.' At a meeting of ministers in London that day, Dill was informed that a study was being undertaken for the maintenance of a bridgehead in Brittany, 'the Breton redoubt'. As late as 13 June, Royal Engineers were preparing reception points and transit camps on the Brittany coast, to receive further reinforcements from Britain.

Churchill recognised the overwhelming likelihood of French surrender, yet still cherished hopes of maintaining a foothold across the Channel. It seemed to him preferable to face the difficulties of clinging on in France, rather than those of mounting from Britain a return to a German-defended coast. He sought to sustain French faith in the alliance by the deployment of a mere three British divisions. He seemed unmoved by Mussolini's long-expected declaration of war on 10 June, merely remarking to Jock Colville: 'People who go to Italy to look at ruins won't have to go as far as Naples and Pompeii again.' The private secretary noted his master's bitter mood that day. On the afternoon of 11 June, Churchill flew with Eden, Dill, Ismay and Spears to the new French army headquarters at Briare on the Loire, seventy miles from Paris, to meet the French government once again. The colonel who met their plane, wrote Spears, might have been greeting poor relations at a funeral. At their destination, the Château du Muguet, there was no sense of welcome. At that evening's meeting of the Supreme War Council, after the

French had unfolded a chronicle of doom, Churchill summoned all his powers. He spoke with passion and eloquence about the forces which Britain could deploy in France in 1941 – twenty, even twenty-five divisions. Weygand said dismissively that the outcome of the war would be determined in hours, not days or weeks. Dill, pathetically, invited the supreme commander to use the makeshift British forces now in France wherever and however he saw fit.

The French, with the Germans at the gates of Paris, could scarcely be blamed for thinking themselves mocked. Eden wrote: 'Reynaud was inscrutable and Weygand polite, concealing with difficulty his scepticism. Marshal Pétain was overtly incredulous. Though he said nothing, his attitude was obviously "*C'est de la blague*" – "It's a joke."' The harshest confrontation came when Weygand asserted that the decisive point had been reached, that the British should commit every fighter they had to the battle. Churchill replied: 'This is not the decisive point. This is not the decisive moment. The decisive moment will come when Hitler hurls his Luftwaffe against Britain. If we can keep command of the air over our own island – that is all I ask – we will win it all back for you.' Britain would fight on 'for ever and ever and ever'.

Reynaud seemed moved. The newly appointed army minister, Brigadier-General Charles de Gaulle, was much more impressed by the prime minister's representation of himself as an Englishman than as an ally: 'Mr Churchill appeared imperturbable, full of buoyancy. Yet he seemed to be confining himself to a cordial reserve towards the French at bay, being already seized – not, perhaps, without an obscure satisfaction – with the terrible and magnificent prospect of an England left alone in her island, with himself to lead her struggle towards salvation.' The other Frenchmen present made nothing of the prime minister's words. Though courtesies were sustained through a difficult dinner that night, Reynaud told Britain's leader over brandy that Pétain considered it essential to seek an armistice.

To his staff, Churchill fumed at the influence upon Reynaud of his mistress, the comtesse de Portes, an impassioned advocate of surrender: 'That woman . . . will undo everything during the night that I do during the day. But of course she can furnish him with facilities that I cannot afford him. I can reason with him, but I cannot sleep with him.' For all the hopes which Churchill reposed in Reynaud, even at his best the French prime minister never shared the Englishman's zest for war à l'outrance. The American Under-Secretary of State, Sumner Welles, reported a conversation with France's leader earlier that summer: 'M. Reynaud felt that while Mr C[hurchill] was a brilliant and most entertaining man with a great capacity for organization, his kind has lost elasticity. He felt that Mr C could conceive of no possibility other than war to the finish – whether that resulted in utter chaos and destruction or not. That, he felt sure, was not true statesmanship.' This seems a convincing representation of Reynaud's view in June 1940. Like a significant number of British politicians in respect of their own society, the French prime minister perceived, as Churchill did not, a limit to the injury acceptable to the fabric and people of France in the cause of sustaining the struggle against Nazism.

Next morning, 12 June, Churchill told Spears to stay with the French, and to do everything possible to sustain them: 'We will carry those who will let themselves be carried.' Yet Britain had no power to 'carry' France. Pétain absented himself from the ensuing meeting of the Supreme War Council. His own decision was reached. Churchill raged at news that a planned RAF bombing mission to Italy the previous night had been frustrated by farm carts pushed across the runway by French airmen. Reynaud said that any further such missions must be launched from England. At Briare airfield, Ismay observed encouragingly that with no more allies to worry about, 'We'll win the Battle of Britain.' Churchill stared hard at him and said: 'You and I will be dead in three months' time.' There is no reason to doubt this exchange. Churchill claimed later that he had always believed Britain would come through. He certainly had a mystical faith in destiny, however vague his attachment to a deity. But it is plain that in the summer of 1940 he suffered cruel moments of rationality, when defeat seemed far more plausible than victory, when the huge effort of will necessary to sustain the fight was almost too much for him.

Six months later, Eden confessed to the prime minister that during the summer he and Pound, the First Sea Lord, had privately acknowledged despair to each other. Churchill said: 'Normally I wake up buoyant to face the new day. Then, I awoke with dread in my heart.' In the fevered atmosphere of the time, some MPs panicked. Harold Macmillan was among the prime movers in the so-called 'under-secretaries' revolt' by Tories demanding that the old 'men of Munich' should be summarily expelled from the government. 'All this,' in Leo Amery's words, 'on the assumption that France is going out altogether and that we shall be defeated.' The young turks were squashed.

When so many others were dying, Churchill could scarcely take for granted his own survival. A German bomb, a paratroop landing in Whitehall, an accident by land, sea or air such as befell many other prominent wartime figures, could extinguish him at any time. His courage, and that of those who followed and served him, lay in defying probability, sweeping aside all thought of the most plausible outcome of the struggle, and addressing each day's battles with a spirit undaunted by the misfortunes of the last. That Wednesday morning of 12 June, his Flamingo hedgehopped home over the lovely countryside of Brittany. Near the smoking docks of Le Havre, the pilot dived suddenly to avoid the attentions of two German planes which were strafing fishing boats. The Flamingo escaped unseen, landing safely at Hendon, but this was one of Churchill's closest calls. Later in the afternoon he told the war cabinet that it was obvious French resistance was approaching an end. He spoke admiringly of De Gaulle, whose resolution had made a strong impression on him.

Churchill had been back in London less than thirty-six hours when Reynaud telephoned, soon after midnight, demanding a new and urgent meeting at Tours, to which he had now retreated. The prime minister left next morning, accompanied by Halifax and Beaverbrook, driving through the incongruous London summer shopping crowds. He was greeted at Hendon with news that bad weather required a take-off postponement. 'To hell with that,' he growled. 'I'm going, whatever happens. This is too serious a situation to bother about the weather!' They landed at Tours amid a thunderstorm, on an airfield which had been heavily bombed the previous night, and solicited transport from a jaded rabble of French airmen. Churchill, Beaverbrook and Halifax crowded with difficulty into a small car which took them to the local prefecture, where they wandered unrecognised through the corridors. At last a staff officer escorted them to a nearby restaurant for cold chicken and cheese. This was black comedy. It is not difficult to imagine Halifax's disdain for the ordeal to which Churchill had exposed him.

Back at the prefecture, the British waited impatiently for Reynaud. It was essential that they take off again in daylight, because the bomb-cratered and unlit runway was unfit for night operations. At last the French prime minister arrived, with Spears. He told the English party that while Weygand was ready to surrender, it was still possible that he could persuade his colleagues to fight on – if he received a firm assurance that the Americans would fight. Otherwise, would Britain concede that it was now impossible for France to continue the war? Churchill responded with expressions of sympathy for France's agony. He concluded simply, however, that Britain would sustain its resistance: no terms, no surrender. Reynaud said that the prime minister had not answered his question. Churchill said he could not accede to a French capitulation. He urged that Reynaud's government should make a direct appeal to President Roosevelt before taking any other action. Some of the British party were dismayed that nothing was said about continuing the fight from France's North African empire. They were fearful that Reynaud's nation would not only cease to be their ally, but might join Germany as their foe. They were acutely aware that, even though the French leader still had some heart, his generals, excepting only De Gaulle, had none.

In the courtyard below, a throng of French politicians and officials, emotional and despairing, milled around Churchill as he left. Hands were wrung, tears shed. The prime minister murmured to De Gaulle: 'L'homme du destin.' He ignored an impassioned intervention by the comtesse de Portes, who pushed forward crying out that her country was bleeding to death, and that she must be heard. French officials told the assembled politicians that Churchill at this last meeting of the Supreme War Council had shown full understanding of France's position, and was resigned to her capitulation. Reynaud did not invite Churchill to meet his ministers, as they themselves wished. They felt snubbed in consequence, though the omission changed nothing.

Churchill landed back at Hendon after a two-and-a-half-hour flight. At Downing Street he learned that President Roosevelt had responded to an earlier French appeal with private promises of more material aid, and declared himself impressed that Reynaud was committed to fight on. Churchill told the war cabinet that such a message came as close to an American declaration of war as was possible without Congress. This was, of course, wildly wishful thinking. Roosevelt, on Secretary of State Cordell Hull's advice, rejected Churchill's plea that he should allow his cable to be published.

On 12 June, the 51st Highland Division at Saint-Valery was forced to join a local capitulation by troops of the French Tenth Army, to which the British formation was attached. Had an order been given a few days earlier, it is plausible that the troops could have been evacuated to Britain through Le Havre. Instead, they became a sacrifice to Churchill's commitment to be seen to sustain the campaign. That same day, Gen. Sir Alan Brooke arrived with orders to lead British forces to the aid of the French. Reinforcements were still landing at the Brittany ports on the 13th.

When Ismay suggested that British units moving to France should hasten slowly, Churchill said: 'Certainly not. It would look very bad in history if we were to do any such thing.' This was of a piece with his response to chancellor Kingsley Wood's suggestion a few weeks later, that since Britain was financially supporting the Dutch administration in exile, in return the government should demand an increased stake in the Royal Dutch Shell oil company. 'Churchill, who objected to taking advantage of another country's misfortunes, said that he never again wished to hear such a suggestion.' At every turn, he perceived his own words and actions through the prism of posterity. He was determined that historians should say: 'He nothing common did or mean upon that memorable scene.' Indeed, in those days Marvell's lines on King Charles I's execution were much in his mind. He recited them repeatedly to his staff, and then to the House of Commons. Seldom has a great actor on the stage of human affairs been so mindful of the verdict of future ages, even as he played out his own part and delivered his lines.

On 14 June, the Germans entered Paris unopposed. Yet illusions persisted in London that a British foothold on the Continent might even now be maintained. Jock Colville wrote from Downing Street that day: 'If the French will go on fighting, we must now fall back on the Atlantic, creating new lines of Torres Vedras behind which British divisions and American supplies can be concentrated. Paris is not France, and . . . there is no reason to suppose the Germans will be able to subdue the whole country.' Colville himself was a very junior civil servant, but his fantasies were fed by more important people. That evening, Churchill spoke by telephone to Brooke in France. The prime minister deplored the fact that the remaining British formations were in retreat. He wanted to make the French feel that they were being supported. Brooke, with an Ulster bluntness of which Churchill would gain much more experience in the course of the war, retorted that 'it was impossible to make a corpse feel'. After what seemed to the soldier an interminable and absurd wrangle, Churchill said: 'All right, I agree with you.'

In that conversation, Brooke saved almost 200,000 men from death or captivity. By sheer force of personality, not much in evidence among British generals, he persuaded Churchill to allow his forces to be removed from French command and evacuated. On the 15th, orders were rushed to Canadians en route by rail from the Normandy coast to what passed for the battlefront. Locomotives were shunted from the front to the rear of their trains, which then set off once more for the ports. At Brest, embarking troops were ordered to destroy all vehicles and equipment. However, some determined and imaginative officers laboured defiantly and successfully to evacuate precious artillery. For the French, Weygand was further embittered by tidings of another British withdrawal. It seems astonishing that his compatriots did nothing to impede the operation, and even something to assist it.

Much has been written about Churchill's prudence in declining to reinforce defeat by dispatching further fighter squadrons to France in 1940. The contrary misjudgement is often passed over. Alan Brooke understood the prime minister's motive – to demonstrate to the French that the British Army was still committed to the fight. But he rightly deplored its futility. If Dunkirk represented a miracle, it was scarcely a lesser one that two weeks later it proved possible to evacuate almost all of Brooke's force to Britain through the north-western French ports. There were, in effect, two Dunkirks, though the latter is much less noticed by history. Churchill was able to escape the potentially brutal consequences of his last rash gesture to Reynaud, because of Brooke's resolution and the Germans' preoccupation with completing the destruction of the French army. Had not providence been merciful, all Brooke's men might have been lost, a shattering blow to the British Army's prospects of reconstitution.

On 15 June, at Churchill's behest Dill telephoned Brooke on a weak, crackling line, and told him to delay evacuation of 52nd Division from Cherbourg. In London there were renewed hopes of clinging to a foothold in France, though these had no visible foundation in reality. The French anyway discounted all such British aspirations. Brooke was exasperated. He told the CIGS: 'It is a desperate job being faced with over 150,000 men and a mass of material, ammunition, petrol, supplies etc, to try to evacuate or dispose of, and nothing to cover this operation except the crumbling French army . . . We are wasting shipping and precious hours.' Next day, London grudgingly agreed that the 52nd Division could continue returning to Britain. Yet administrative confusion persisted. Some troops were embarked at Le Havre for Portsmouth, only to be offloaded at Cherbourg and entrained for Rennes. A ship arrived at Brest on the morning of the 18th, bearing artillery and ammunition from England. At a dozen north-west French ports, tens of thousands of British troops milled in chaos, many of them lacking orders and officers.

German preoccupation with the French army alone made it possible to get the men and a few heavy weapons away, amid chaos and mismanagement. There were skirmishes between British and enemy forces, but no fatal clash. Between 14 and 25 June, from Brest and Saint-Nazaire, Cherbourg and lesser western French ports, 144,171 British troops were successfully rescued and brought home, along with 24,352 Poles and 42,000 other Allied soldiers. There were losses, notably the sinking of the liner *Lancastria* at a cost of at least 3,000 lives;* but these were negligible in proportion to the forces at risk – two-thirds of the numbers brought back from Dunkirk.

It is hard to overstate the chaos of British command arrangements in France during the last three weeks of the campaign, even in areas where formations were not much threatened by the Germans. Two trainloads of invaluable and undamaged British tanks were gratuitously abandoned in Normandy. 'Much equipment had been unnecessarily destroyed,' in the angry words of Maj.Gen. Andrew McNaughton, commanding 1st Canadian Division. Though the war had been in progress for almost nine months, Lt.Gen. Sir Henry Karslake, commanding at Le Mans until Brooke's arrival, wrote in a report: 'The lack of previous training for our formations showed itself in many ways.' Men of the 52nd Division arrived in France in June with equipment issued two days earlier, never having fired their anti-tank guns or indeed seen a tank. Karslake was appalled by the perceived indiscipline of some regular units, even before they were engaged: 'Their behaviour was terrible!' Far more vehicles, stores and equipment could have been evacuated, but for administrative disorder prevailing at the ports, where some ships from England were still being unloaded while, at nearby quays, units embarked for home. The commitment to north-west France represented a serious

---

* Estimates that as many as 8,000 people perished on the *Lancastria* are rendered implausible by the overall casualty figures for the campaign in France, which show a total British loss of life of only 11,000.

misjudgement by Churchill, which won no gratitude from the French, and could have cost the Allies as many soldiers as the later disasters in Greece, Crete, Singapore and Tobruk put together.

While the horror of Britain's predicament was now apparent to all those in high places and to many in low, Churchill was visibly exalted by it. At Chequers on the warm summer night of 15 June, Jock Colville described how tidings of gloom were constantly telephoned through, while sentries with steel helmets and fixed bayonets encircled the house. The prime minister, however, displayed the highest spirits, 'repeating poetry, dilating on the drama of the present situation . . . offering everybody cigars, and spasmodically murmuring: "Bang, bang, bang, goes the farmer's gun, run rabbit, run rabbit, run, run, run."' In the early hours of morning, when US ambassador Joseph Kennedy telephoned, the prime minister unleashed upon him a torrent of rhetoric about America's opportunity to save civilisation. Then he held forth to his staff about Britain's growing fighter strength, 'told one or two dirty stories', and departed for bed at 1.30, saying, 'Goodnight, my children.' At least some part of this must have been masquerade. But it was a masquerade of awesome nobility. Churchill's private secretary Eric Seal thought him much changed since 10 May, more sober, 'less violent, less wild, less impetuous'. If this was overstated, there had certainly been an extraordinary accession of self-control.

On 16 June the war cabinet dispatched a message to Reynaud, now in Bordeaux, offering to release France from its obligation as an ally to forswear negotiations with Germany, on the sole condition that the French fleet should be sailed to British harbours. De Gaulle, arriving in London, was invited to lunch with Churchill and Eden at the Carlton Club. He told the prime minister that only the most dramatic British initiative might stave off French surrender. He urged formalising a proposal for political union between France and Britain over which the cabinet had been dallying for days. Amid crisis, these desperate men briefly embraced this fanciful idea. An appropriate message, setting forth the offer in momentous terms, was dispatched to Reynaud. Churchill prepared to set forth once more for France, this time by sea, to discuss a draft 'Proclamation of Union'. He was already aboard a train at Waterloo with Clement Attlee, Archibald Sinclair and the chiefs of staff, bound for embarkation on a destroyer, when word was brought that Reynaud could not receive them. With a heavy heart, the prime minister returned to Downing Street. It was for the best. The proposal for union was wholly unrealistic, and could have changed nothing. France's battle was over. Reynaud's government performed one last service to its ally: that day in Washington, all the French nation's American arms contracts were formally transferred to Britain.

During the night, it was learned at Downing Street that Reynaud had resigned as prime minister and been replaced by Marshal Pétain, who was seeking an armistice. Pétain's prestige among the French people rested first upon his defence of Verdun in 1916, and second upon an ill-founded belief that he possessed a humanity unique among generals, manifested in his merciful handling of the French army during its 1917 mutinies. In June 1940 there is little doubt that Pétain's commitment to peace at any price reflected the wishes of most French people. Reynaud, however, probably committed a historic blunder by agreeing to forsake his office. Had he and his ministerial colleagues chosen instead to accept exile, as did the Norwegian, Belgian and Dutch governments, he could have prevented his nation's surrender of democratic legitimacy, and established French resistance to tyranny on strong foundations in London. As it was, he allowed himself to be overborne by the military defeatists, led by Pétain and Weygand, and denied himself a famous political martyrdom.

A British sergeant named George Starr, who escaped from the Continent through Dunkirk, belatedly reached home in Yorkshire on 18 June. He found his father listening to the radio announcement of France's surrender. The Starr family had for many years run a travelling circus on the Continent. George's father switched off the set, shook his head and said: 'The French will never forgive us for this.' His son could not understand what he meant. Later in the war, however, George Starr spent three years as a British agent with the French Resistance. He enjoyed ample opportunity to explore the sense of betrayal harboured by many French people towards Britain, which never entirely faded.

De Gaulle, Reynaud's army minister, almost alone among prominent Frenchmen chose to pitch camp in London, and secured the evacuation of his wife. The war cabinet opposed his request that he should be permitted to broadcast to his people on the BBC. Churchill however, urged on by Spears, insisted that the renegade – for so De Gaulle was perceived by many of his own people – should be given access to a microphone. The general's legal adviser, Professor Cassin, enquired of his new chief what was the status of his embryo movement in Britain. De Gaulle answered magnificently: 'We are France! . . . The defeated are those who accept defeat.' The general had an answer, too, to the problem of establishing his own stature: 'Churchill will launch me like a new brand of soap.' The British government indeed hired an advertising agency, Richmond Temple, to promote Free France. De Gaulle would need all the help he could get. Few Frenchmen, even those evacuated to Britain from the battlefield, were willing to fight on if their government quit. De Gaulle asked the captain of the French destroyer *Milan*, which carried him across the Channel, if he would serve under British colours. The naval officer answered that he would not. Most of his compatriots proved like-minded. 'Mr Churchill finds that there are not enough French and German bodies to satisfy him,' declared a sulphurous front-page editorial in the Paris paper *Le Matin*, in one of its first issues after the surrender. 'We ask if the British prime minister has lost his head. If so, what a pity that our ministers did not perceive it sooner.' The paper went on to denounce De Gaulle, and to accuse the British of fomenting revolt in France's overseas empire.

In 1941 and 1942, the prime minister would be obliged to preside over many British defeats, and indeed humiliations. Yet no trauma was as profound, no shock as far-reaching, as that which befell him in his first weeks of office, when the German army destroyed France as a military power, and swept the British from the Continent. Henceforward, the character of the war thus became fundamentally different from that of 1914–18. All assumptions were set at naught upon which Allied war policy, and Churchill's personal defiance of Hitler, had been founded. Whatever Britain's continuing capabilities at sea and in the air, since September 1939 it had been taken for granted that the British Army would confront the Nazi legions alongside the French, in the frankly subordinate role demanded by its inferiority of numbers – just ten divisions to ninety-four French on the western front. The British Army could never alone aspire to dispute a battlefield with the Wehrmacht, and this knowledge dominated British strategy.

It was hard for many people, even the highest in the land, to absorb the scale of the disaster which had befallen Allied arms, and which now threatened to overwhelm Britain. Alan Brooke was struck by a Churchillian observation about human nature. The prime minister said that the receptive capacity of a man's mind was like a three-inch pipe running under a culvert. 'When a flood comes the water flows over the culvert whilst the pipe goes on handling its 3 inches. Similarly the human brain will register emotions up to its "3 inch limit" and subsequent additional emotions flow past unregistered.' So it now seemed to Brooke himself, and to a host of others. They perceived that a catastrophe was unfolding, but their hearts could not keep pace with the signals from their brains about its significance. Harold Nicolson wrote in his diary on 15 June: 'My reason tells me that it will now be almost impossible to beat the Germans, and that the probability is that France will surrender and that we shall be bombed and invaded . . . Yet these probabilities do not fill me with despair. I seem to be impervious both to pleasure and pain. For the moment we are all anaesthetised.'

Another eye-witness, writer Peter Fleming, then serving as an army staff officer, identified the same emotional confusion: 'This period was one of carefree improvisation as far as most civilians were concerned. It was as though the whole country had been invited to a fancy-dress ball and everybody was asking everybody else "What are you going as?" A latent incredulity, and the fact that almost everybody had more than enough to do already, combined to give problems connected with invasion the status of engrossing digressions from the main business of life . . . The British, when their ally was pole-axed on their doorstep, became both gayer and more serene than they had been at any time since the overture to Munich struck up in 1937.'

British casualties in France were large in relation to the size of the BEF, but trifling by comparison with those of the French, and with the infinitely more intense struggles that would take place later in the war. The army lost just 11,000 killed and missing, against at least 50,000 French military dead. In addition, 14,070 British wounded were evacuated, and 41,030 BEF prisoners fell into German hands. The loss of tanks, artillery and weapons of all kinds was, of course, calamitous. It is a familiar and ill-founded cliché that the 1940 British Expeditionary Force was ill-equipped. In reality it was much better supplied with vehicles than the Germans, and had good tanks if these had been imaginatively employed. When Hitler's Field Marshal Fedor von Bock saw the wreckage at Dunkirk, he wrote in astonishment: 'Here lies the material of a whole army, so incredibly well-equipped that we poor devils can only look on with envy and amazement.' The BEF was driven from Dunkirk after relatively light fighting and very heavy retreating, because it lacked mass to change the outcome of the campaign once the French front was broken, and was outfought by German formations with better leadership, motivation and air support. The British Army was now, for all practical purposes, disarmed. Almost a thousand RAF aircraft were gone, half of these fighters.

But Britain had human material to forge a new army – though not one that alone could ever be large enough to face the Germans in a Continental war – if only time was granted before it must fight again. An American correspondent reported home that Londoners received news of the French surrender in grim silence rather than with jokes or protestations of defiance. The Battle of France was over, Churchill told the British people on the following night. The Battle of Britain was about to begin. The position of Churchill's nation on 17 June was scarcely enviable. But it was vastly better than had seemed possible a month earlier, when the BEF faced annihilation.

THREE

Invasion Fever

In the months after September 1939, Britain found itself in the bleak – indeed, in some eyes absurd – position of having declared war on Germany, while lacking means to undertake any substantial military initiative, least of all to save Poland. The passivity of the 'Phoney War' ate deeply into the morale of the British people. By contrast, the events of May and June 1940 at least had the merit, brilliantly exploited by Churchill, that they thrust before the nation a clear and readily comprehended purpose: to defend itself against assault by an overwhelmingly powerful foe. The Royal Irish Fusiliers, back from Dunkirk, staged a mess party to celebrate news that the French had surrendered. 'Thank heavens they have,' said an officer gaily. 'Now at last we can get on with the war.' A middle-aged court shorthand writer named George King, living in Surrey, wrote in a diary letter intended for his gunner son, left behind in France and on his way to captivity in Germany: 'Winston Churchill has told us just exactly where we stand. We are on our own, and have got to see this thing through; and we can do it, properly led. Goodness knows what the swines will try, but somehow we've got to stick it.'

Naval officer Robert Hichens wrote on 17 June: 'Now we know that we have got to look to ourselves only, I have an idea that England will respond wonderfully to this setback. She is always greatest in taking reverses.' After Churchill addressed the Commons on the 18th, a Labour backbencher, Dr Hastings Lees-Smith of Keighley, stood up: 'My hon. friends on these benches have asked me on their behalf to say one or two sentences. They wish to say to the PM that in their experience among the broad masses of the people of this country never in their lives has the country been more united than it is today in its support of the PM's assertion that we shall carry on right to the end. One sentence can summarise what we feel. Whatever the country is asked for in the months and, if necessary, in the years to come, the PM may be confident that the people will rise to their responsibilities.'

Yet, if the grit displayed by King, Hichens and Lees-Smith was real enough, it would be mistaken to suppose that it was universal. Not all sceptics about Britain's chances of survival were elderly politicians or businessmen. An RAF Hurricane pilot, Paul Mayhew, wrote in a family newsletter: 'Now I suppose it's our turn and though my morale is now pretty good . . . I can't believe that there's much hope for us, at any rate in Europe. Against a ferocious and relentless attack, the Channel's not much of an obstacle and with the army presumably un-equipped, I don't give much for our chances. Personally I have only two hopes; first that Churchill is more reliable than Reynaud and that we will go on fighting if England is conquered, and secondly that Russia, in spite of our blunders, will now be sufficiently scared to stage a distraction in the East. In America I have little faith; I suppose in God's own time God's own country will fight. But at present their army is smaller than the Swiss, their Air Force is puny and rather "playboy", and I doubt whether we need their Navy.' A week later, Mayhew apologised to his family for being 'ludicrously defeatist'. But here was a young airman voicing fears widely shared among his elders.

The summer and autumn of 1940 were poor seasons for truth-telling in Britain. That is to say, it was hard for even good, brave and honourable men to know whether they better served their country by voicing their private thoughts, allowing their brains to function, or by keeping silent. Logic decreed that Britain had not the smallest chance of winning the war in the absence of American participation, which remained implausible. Churchill knew this as well as anyone. Yet he and his supporters believed that the cause of freedom, the defiance of tyranny, made it essential that the British people should fight on regardless, sweeping aside all calculations of relative strengths and strategic disabilities. Posterity has heaped admiration upon the grandeur of this commitment. Yet at the time it demanded from intelligent men and women a suspension of reason which some rejected. For instance, Captain Ralph Edwards, Director of Naval Operations at the Admiralty, was an almost unwavering sceptic. On 17 June he noted in his diary: '[Captain] Bill Tennant came in to say that he'd told Sir Walter Monckton of all our misgivings about the higher direction of the war.' And again on the 23rd: 'Our cabinet with that idiot Winston in charge changes its mind every 24 hours ... I'm rapidly coming to the conclusion that we're so inept we don't deserve to win & indeed are almost certain to be defeated. We never do anything right.' Through the lonely eighteen months ahead, Churchill was galled that such scourges as Aneurin Bevan MP taxed him in the Commons with unwelcome facts of which he was thoroughly aware, painful realities such as he confronted every hour. From the outset, while he always insisted that victory would come, his personal prestige rested upon the honesty with which he acknowledged to the British people the gravity of the ordeal they faced.

Churchill told MPs on 4 June: 'Our thankfulness at the escape of our Army and so many men, whose loved ones have passed through an agonising week, must not blind us to the fact that what has happened in France and Belgium is a colossal military disaster. I have myself full confidence that if all do their duty, if nothing is neglected, and if the best arrangements are made, as they are being made, we shall prove ourselves once again able to defend our island home, to ride out the storm of war, and to outlive the menace of tyranny, if necessary for years, if necessary alone. That is the resolve of His Majesty's Government.' After the prime minister sat down, as always exchanges between MPs degenerated into commonplaces. Dr Lees-Smith delivered words of appreciation. Glaswegian maverick Jimmy Maxton, an Independent Labour MP, raised a point of order, which led to cross words and pettiness. Captain Bellenger of Bassetlaw rebuked Mr Thorne of Plaistow, whom Bellenger believed had impugned his courage: 'You have no right to make remarks of that kind.'

Clausewitz wrote in 1811: 'A government must never assume that its country's fate, its whole existence, hangs on the outcome of a single battle, no matter how decisive.' Churchill's conduct after the fall of France exasperated some sceptics who perceived themselves as clear thinkers, but conformed perfectly to the Prussian's dictum. His supreme achievement in 1940 was to mobilise Britain's warriors, to shame into silence its doubters, to stir the passions of the nation, so that for a season the British people faced the world united and exalted. The 'Dunkirk spirit' was not spontaneous. It was created by the rhetoric and bearing of one man, displaying powers that will define political leadership for the rest of time. Under a different prime minister, the British people in their shock and bewilderment could as readily have been led in another direction. Nor was the mood long-lived. It persisted only until winter, when it was replaced by a more dogged, doubtful and less exuberant national spirit. But that first period was decisive: 'If we can get through the next three months, we can get through the next three years,' Churchill told the Commons on 20 June.

Kingsley Martin argued in that week's *New Statesman* that Churchill's 18 June 'finest hour' broadcast to the nation was too simplistic: 'He misunderstood [the British people's] feelings when he talked of this as the finest moment of their history. Our feelings are more complex than that. To talk to common people in or out of uniform is to discover that determination to defend this island is coupled with a deep and almost universal bitterness that we have been reduced to such a pass.' Yet the prime minister judged the predominant mood much more shrewdly than the veteran socialist. In 1938 the British had not been what Churchill wanted them to be. In 1941 and thereafter they would often disappoint his hopes. But in 1940, to an extraordinary degree he was able to shape and elevate the nation to fulfil his aspirations.

Mollie Panter-Downes wrote in the *New Yorker* of 29 June:

It would be difficult for an impartial observer to decide today whether the British are the bravest or merely the most stupid people in the world. The way they are acting in the present situation could be used to support either claim. The individual Englishman seems to be singularly unimpressed by the fact that there is now nothing between him and the undivided attention of a war machine such as the world has never seen before. Possibly it's lack of imagination; possibly again it's the same species of dogged resolution which occasionally produces an epic like Dunkirk. Millions of British families, sitting at their well-stocked breakfast tables eating excellent British eggs and bacon, can still talk calmly of the horrors across the Channel, perhaps without fully comprehending even now that anything like that could ever happen in England's green and pleasant land.

Many Americans, by contrast, thought it unlikely that Britain would survive. In New York, 'one thing that strikes me is the amount of defeatist talk', wrote US General Raymond Lee, 'the almost pathological assumption that it is all over bar the shouting . . . that it is too late for the United States to do anything'. Key Pittman, chairman of the Senate Foreign Relations Committee, called on Churchill to send the British fleet to the New World: 'It is no secret that Great Britain is totally unprepared for defense and that nothing the US has to give can do more than delay the result . . . It is to be hoped that this plan will not to be too delayed by futile encouragement to fight on. It is conclusively evident that Congress will not authorize intervention in the European war.' *Time* magazine reported on 1 July: 'So scared was many a US citizen last week that he wanted to shut off aid to Britain for fear that the US would weaken its own defenses, wanted to have the US wash its hands of help for Britain, for fear of getting involved on the losing side.'

A *Fortune* opinion survey showed that even before France collapsed, most Americans believed that Germany would win the war. Only 30.3 per cent saw any hope for the Allies. A correspondent named Herbert Jones wrote a letter to the *Philadelphia Inquirer* which reflected widespread sentiment: 'The great majority of Americans are not pacifists or isolationists, but, after the experience of the last war and Versailles, have no desire to pull Britain's chestnuts out of the fire for her, under the slogan of "Save the World for Democracy". They rightly feel that that little is to be gained by pouring out our money and the lives of our young men for the cause of either the oppressor of the Jews and Czechs or the oppressor of the Irish and of India . . .' Richard E. Taylor of Apponaugh, Rhode Island, wrote to a friend in England urging him to draw the attention of the authorities to the danger that the Germans might tunnel under the Channel.

Yet some Americans did not despair. An 'aid to Britain' committee gathered three million signatures on petitions to the White House. The organisation spawned a Historians' Committee under Charles Seymour of Yale; a Scientists' Committee under Nobel Prize-winner Harold Urey; a Theatre Committee under playwright and Roosevelt speechwriter Robert Sherwood. Americans were invited to set aside their caricature view of Britain as a nation of stuffed-shirt sleepy-heads, and to perceive instead battling champions of freedom. Novelist Somerset Maugham, arriving in New York, predicted a vastly different post-war Britain, and hinted at the beginnings of one more sympathetic to an American social vision: 'I have a feeling . . . that in the England of the future evening dress will be less important than it has been in the past.' America was still far, far from belligerence, but forces favouring intervention were stirring.

In 1941 Churchill devoted immense energy to wooing the US. But in 1940, once his June appeals to Roosevelt had failed, for several weeks he did not write to the president at all, and dismissed suggestions for a British propaganda offensive. 'Propaganda is all very well,' he said, 'but it is events that make the world. If we smash the Huns here, we shall need no propaganda in the United States . . . Now we must live. Next year we shall be winning. The year after that we shall triumph. But if we can hold the Germans in this coming month of July . . . our position will be quite different from today.'

But how to 'hold them'? the anglophile General Raymond Lee, military attaché at the London embassy, wrote: 'One queer thing about the present situation is that it is one which has never been studied at the Staff College. For years [British officers] had studied our [American Civil War] Valley campaign, operations in India,

Afghanistan, Egypt and Europe, had done landings on a hostile shore, but it had never occurred to them that some day they might have to defend the non-combatants of a country at war.' An MP recounted Churchill saying at this time: 'I don't know what we'll fight them with – we shall have to slosh them on the head with bottles – empty ones, of course.' This joke was almost certainly apocryphal, but as the prime minister himself observed of the manner in which spurious Churchilliana accrued, he became 'a magnet for iron filings'.

On 8 June, Britain's Home Forces boasted an inventory of just fifty-four two-pounder anti-tank guns, 420 field guns with 200 rounds of ammunition apiece, 613 medium and heavy guns with 150 rounds for each; 105 medium and heavy tanks and 395 light tanks. There were only 2,300 Bren light machine-guns and 70,000 rifles. Visiting beach defences at St Margaret's Bay in Kent on 26 June, Churchill was told by the local brigadier that he had three anti-tank guns, with six rounds of ammunition apiece. Not one shot must be wasted on practice, said the prime minister. He dismissed a suggestion that London might, like Paris, be declared an open city. The British capital's dense streets, he said, offered peerless opportunities for local defence. So dire was the shortage of small arms that when a consignment of World War I-vintage rifles arrived from the US on 10 July, Churchill decreed that they must be distributed within forty-eight hours. He rejected a proposal that Britain should try to deter Spain from entering the war by promising talks about the disputed sovereignty of Gibraltar as soon as peace returned. The Spanish, he said, would know full well that if Britain won, there would be no deal.

His wit never faltered. When he heard that six people had suffered heart failure following an air-raid warning, he observed that he himself was more likely to die of overeating. Yet he did not want to perish quite yet, 'when so many interesting things were happening'. Told that the Luftwaffe had bombed ironworks owned by the family of Stanley Baldwin, arch-appeasing thirties prime minister, he muttered, 'Very ungrateful of them.' When his wife Clementine described how she had marched disgusted out of a service at St Martin-in-the-Fields after hearing its preacher deliver a pacifist sermon, Churchill said: 'You ought to have cried "Shame," desecrating the House of God with lies.' He then turned to Jock Colville: 'Tell the Minister of Information with a view to having the man pilloried.' General Sir Bernard Paget exclaimed to Colville: 'What a wonderful tonic he is!'

Between June and September 1940, and to a lessening degree for eighteen months thereafter, the minds of the British government and people were fixed upon the threat that Hitler would dispatch an army to invade their island. It is a perennially fascinating question, how far such a peril was ever realistic – or was perceived as such by Winston Churchill. The collapse of France and expulsion of the British Army from the Continent represented the destruction of the strategic foundations upon which British policy was founded. Yet if the German victory in France had been less swift, if the Allies had become engaged in more protracted fighting, the cost in British and French blood would have been vastly greater, while it is hard to imagine any different outcome. John Kennedy was among senior British soldiers who perceived this: 'We should have had an enormous army in France if we had been allowed to go on long enough, and it would have lost its equip[men]t all the same.' Sir Hugh Dowding, C-in-C of Fighter Command, claimed that on news of the French surrender 'I went on my knees and thanked God,' because no further British fighters need be vainly destroyed on the Continent. Only German perceptions of the BEF's marginal role permitted so many of Britain's soldiers to escape from the battlefield by sea not once, but twice, in June 1940. No staff college war game would have allowed so indulgent an outcome. Though it was hard to see matters in such terms at the time, if French defeat had been inevitable, Britain escaped from its consequences astonishingly lightly.

The British in June 1940 believed that they were threatened by imminent invasion followed by likely annihilation. Unsurprisingly, they thought themselves the focus of Hitler's ambitions. Few comprehended his obsession with the East. They could not know that Germany was neither militarily prepared nor psychologically committed to launch a massive amphibious operation across the Channel. The Wehrmacht needed months to digest the conquest of France and the Low Countries. The Nazis' perception of Britain and its ruling class was distorted by pre-war acquaintance with so many aristocratic appeasers. Now, they confidently awaited the displacement of Churchill's government by one which acknowledged realities. 'Are the English giving in? No sure signs visible yet,' Goebbels wrote in his diary on 26 June. 'Churchill still talks big. But then he is not England.' Some historians have expressed surprise that Hitler prevaricated about invasion. Yet his equivocation was matched by the Allies later in the war. For all the aggressive rhetoric of Churchill and Roosevelt, the British for years nursed hopes that Germany would collapse without an Allied landing in France. The Americans were much relieved that Japan surrendered without being invaded. No belligerent nation risks a massive amphibious operation on a hostile shore until other options have been exhausted. Germany in 1940 proved no exception.

Churchill's people might have slept a little easier through that summer had they perceived that they were more happily placed to withstand the siege and bombardment of their island than any other conceivable strategic scenario. Their army had been delivered from the need to face the Wehrmacht on the battlefield, and indeed would not conduct major operations on the Continent for more than three years. The Royal Navy, despite its Norwegian and Dunkirk losses, remained an immensely powerful force. A German fleet of towed barges moving across the Channel at a speed of only three or four knots must remain within range of warship guns for many hours. On 1 July, the German navy possessed only one heavy and two light cruisers, together with four destroyers and some E-boats, available for duty as escorts. The Royal Air Force was better organised and equipped to defend Britain against bomber attack than for any other operation of war. If a German army secured a beachhead, Churchill's land forces were unfit to expel it. But in the summer of 1940 England's moat, those twenty-one miles of choppy sea between rival chalk cliffs, represented a formidable, probably decisive obstacle to Hitler's landlubbing army.

Among the government's first concerns was that of ensuring that the Vichy French fleet did not become available to Hitler. During days of cabinet argument on this issue, Churchill at one moment raised the possibility that the Americans might be persuaded to purchase the warships. In the event, however, a more direct and brutal option was adopted. Horace Walpole wrote two centuries earlier: 'No great country was ever saved by good men, because good men will not go to the lengths that may be necessary.' At Mers-el-Kebir, Oran, on 3 July, French commanders rejected an ultimatum from Admiral Sir James Somerville, commanding the Royal Navy's Force H offshore, either to scuttle their fleet or sail to join the British. The subsequent bombardment of France's warships was one of the most ruthless acts by a democracy in the annals of war. It resulted from a decision such as only Churchill would plausibly have taken. Yet it commands the respect of posterity, as it did of Franklin Roosevelt, as an earnest of Britain's iron determination to sustain the struggle. Churchill told the House of Commons next day: 'We had hoped until the afternoon that our terms would be accepted without bloodshed.' As to passing judgement on the action, he left this 'with confidence to Parliament. I leave it also to the nation, and I leave it to the United States. I leave it to the world and to history.'

As MPs cheered and waved their order papers in a curiously taste-less display of enthusiasm for an action which, however necessary, had cost 1,250 French lives, Churchill resumed his seat with tears pouring down his face. He, the francophile, knew the bitter fruits that had been plucked at Oran. He confided later: 'It was a terrible decision, like taking the life of one's own child to save the State.' He feared that the immediate consequence would be to drive Vichy to join Germany in arms against Britain. But, at a moment when the Joint Intelligence Committee was warning that invasion seemed imminent, he absolutely declined to acquiesce in the risk that French capital ships might screen a German armada.

Pétain's regime did not declare war, though French bitterness about Oran persisted for years to come. The bombardment was less decisive in its strategic achievement than Churchill claimed, because one French battle-cruiser escaped, and a powerful fleet still lay at Toulon under Vichy orders. But actions sometimes have consequences which remain unperceived for long afterwards. This was the case with the attack on Mers-el-Kebir, followed by the failure two months later of a Free French attempt to take over Dakar, the capital of France's African colony Senegal. When General Francisco Franco, Spain's dictator, submitted to Hitler his shopping list for joining the Axis, it was headed by a demand that Hitler should transfer to Spain French colonies in Africa. Yet Vichy France's rejection of both British diplomatic advances and military threats, together with the refusal of most of France's African colonies to 'rally' to De Gaulle, persuaded Hitler to hope that Pétain's nation would soon become his fighting ally. He therefore refused to satisfy Franco at French expense. The attack on Oran, a painful necessity, and Dakar, an apparent fiasco, contributed significantly to keeping Spain out of the war.

One part of the British Commonwealth offered no succour to the 'mother country': the Irish Free State, bitterly hostile to Britain since it gained independence in 1922, sustained nominal allegiance by a constitutional quirk under the terms of the island's partition treaty. Churchill had heaped scorn upon Neville Chamberlain's 1938 surrender of Britain's Irish 'Treaty Ports' to the Dublin government. As First Lord of the Admiralty in 1939 he contemplated military action against Eire, as the southern Irish dominion was known. Amid the desperate circumstances of June 1940, however, he responded cautiously to a suggestion by Chamberlain – of all people – that Ireland should be obliged by force to yield up its harbours, which might play a critical role in keeping open Britain's Atlantic lifeline. Churchill was moved to oppose this by fear of a hostile reaction in the United States. Instead, the British government urged Lord Craigavon, prime minister of the Protestant north, which remained part of the United Kingdom, to seek a meeting with Irish prime minister Éamon de Valera to discuss the defence of their common island. Craigavon, like most of his fellow Ulstermen, loathed the Catholic southerners. He dismissed this notion out of hand.

Yet in late June, London presented a remarkable and radical secret proposal to Dublin: Britain would make a principled commitment to a post-war united Ireland in return for immediate access to Irish ports and bases. Britain's ambassador in Dublin reported De Valera's stony response. The *Taoiseach* would commit himself only to the neutrality of a united Ireland though he said unconvincingly that he 'might' enter the war after the British government made a public declaration of commitment to union.

The British government nonetheless urged Dublin to conduct talks with the Belfast regime about a prospective union endorsed by Britain, in return for Eire's belligerence. Chamberlain told the cabinet: 'I do not believe that the Ulster government would refuse to play their part to bring about so favourable a development.' De Valera again declined to accept deferred payment. MacDonald cabled London, urging Churchill to offer personal assurances. The prime minister wrote in the margin of this message: 'But all contingent upon Ulster agreeing & S. Ireland coming into the war.'

On 26 June Chamberlain belatedly reported these exchanges to Craigavon, saying: 'You will observe that the document takes the form of an enquiry only, because we have not felt it right to approach you officially with a request for your assent unless we had first a binding assurance from Eire that they would, if the assent were given, come into the war . . . If therefore they refuse the plan you are in no way committed, and if they accept you are still free to make your own comments or objections as may think fit.' The Ulsterman cabled back: 'Am profoundly shocked and disgusted by your letter making suggestions so far-reaching behind my back and without any pre-consultation with me. To such treachery to loyal Ulster I will never be a party.' Chamberlain, in turn, responded equally angrily to what he perceived as Craigavon's insufferable parochialism. He concluded: 'Please remember the serious nature of the situation which requires that every effort be made to meet it.'

The war cabinet, evidently unimpressed by Craigavon's anger, now strengthened its proposal to Dublin: 'This declaration would take the form of a solemn undertaking that the Union is to become at an early date an accomplished fact from which there shall be no turning back.' When Craigavon was informed, he responded: 'Your telegram only confirms my confidential information and conviction De Valera is under German dictation and far past reasoning with. He may purposely protract negotiations till enemy has landed. Strongly advocate immediate naval occupation of harbours and military advance south.'

Craigavon asserted in a personal letter to Churchill that Ulster would only participate in an All-Ireland Defence Force 'if British martial law is imposed throughout the island'. The two men met in London on 7 July. There is no record of their conversation. It is reasonable to assume that it was frosty, but by then Churchill could assuage the Ulsterman's fears. Two days earlier, De Valera had finally rejected the British plan. He, like many Irishmen, was convinced that Britain was doomed to lose the war. He doubted Churchill's real willingness to coerce Craigavon. If he ever seriously contemplated accepting London's terms, he also probably feared that once committed to belligerence, Ireland would become a British puppet.

Churchill makes no mention of the Irish negotiation in his war memoirs. Since the British offer to Dublin was sensational, this suggests that recollection of it brought no pleasure to the prime minister. Given De Valera's implacable hostility, the Irish snub was inevitable. But it represented a massive miscalculation by the Irish leader. Ernest Bevin wrote in confidence to an academic friend who was urging a deal on a united Ireland: 'There are difficulties which appear at the moment almost insurmountable. You see, De Valera's policy is, even if we get a united Ireland, he would still remain neutral. On that, he is immovable. Were it not for this attitude, I believe a solution would be easy . . . You may rest assured that we are watching every possible chance.' If Ireland had entered the war on the Allied side at any time, even after the US became a belligerent in December 1941 and Allied victory was assured, American cash would have flooded into the country, perhaps advancing Ireland's economic take-off by two generations.

The exchanges of July were not quite the end of the story. In December 1940, Churchill suggested in a letter to President Roosevelt that 'If the Government of Eire would show its solidarity with the democracies of the English-speaking world . . . a Council Of Defence of all Ireland could be set up out of which the unity of the island would probably in some form or other emerge after the war.' Here was a suggestion much less explicit than that of the summer, obviously modified by the diminution of British peril. It is impossible to know whether, if De Valera had acceded to the British proposal of June 1940, Churchill would indeed have obliged the recalcitrant Ulster Protestants to accept union with the south. Given his high-handed treatment of other dominions and colonies in the course of the war – not least the surrender of British overseas bases to the United States – it seems by no means impossible. So dire was Britain's predicament, of such vital significance in the U-boat war were Irish ports and airfields, that it seemed worth almost any price to secure them.

Churchill threw himself into the struggle to prepare his island to resist invasion. He decreed that if the Germans landed, all measures including poison gas were to be employed against them. On 6 July he inspected an exercise in Kent. 'Winston was in great form,' Ironside wrote in his diary, 'and gave us lunch at Chartwell in his cottage. Very wet but nobody minded at all.' A consignment of 250,000 rifles and 300 old 75mm field guns arrived from America – poor weapons, but desperately welcome. Ironside expected the German invasion on 9 July, and was surprised when it did not come. On 10 July, instead, the Luftwaffe launched its first big raid on Britain, by seventy aircraft against south Wales dockyards. Churchill knew this was the foretaste of a heavy and protracted air assault. Two days later he visited RAF Hurricane squadrons at Kenley, to the south of London. Straining to harness every aid to public morale, he demanded that military bands should play in the streets. He urged attention to gas masks, because he feared that Hitler would unleash chemical weapons. He resisted the evacuation of children from cities, and deplored the shipment of the offspring of the rich to sanctuary in the US. He argued vigorously against over-stringent rationing, and deplored pessimism wherever it was encountered. Dill, less than two months head of the army, was already provoking his mistrust: the CIGS 'strikes me as tired, disheartened and over-impressed with the might of Germany', wrote the prime minister to Eden. In Churchill's eyes, all through the long months which followed, defeatism was the only crime beyond forgiveness.

On 19 July, Ironside was dismissed as C-in-C Home Forces, and replaced by Sir Alan Brooke. Ironside wanted to meet an invasion with a thin crust of coastal defences, and to rely chiefly upon creating strong lines inland. Brooke, by contrast, proposed swift counter-attacks with mobile forces. Brooke and Churchill were surely correct in anticipating that if the Germans secured a lodgement and airfields in south-east England, the battle for Britain would be irretrievably lost. Inland defences were worthless, save for sustaining a sense of purpose among those responsible for building them.

Peter Fleming argued in his later history of the period that although the British went through the motions of anticipating invasion, they did not in their hearts believe in such an eventuality, because they had no historical experience of it: 'They paid lip-service to reality. They took the precautions which the Government advised, made the sacri-fices which it required of them and worked like men possessed . . . But . . . they found it impossible, however steadfastly they gazed into the future, to fix in a satisfactory focus the terrible contingencies which invasion was expected to bring forth.' Fleming added a percep-tive observation: 'The menace of invasion was at once a tonic and a drug . . . The extreme and disheartening bleakness of their long-term prospects was obscured by the melodramatic nature of the predica-ment in which . . . the fortunes of war had placed them.'

Churchill understood the need to mobilise the British people to action for its own sake, rather than allowing them time to brood, to contemplate dark realities. He himself thought furiously about the middle distance. 'When I look around to see how we can win the war,' he wrote to Beaverbrook on 10 July, 'I see only one sure path. We have no continental army which can defeat the German military power. The blockade is broken and Hitler has Asia and probably

Africa to draw upon. Should he be repulsed here or not try invasion, he will recoil eastward and we have nothing to stop him. But there is one thing that will bring him back and bring him down, and that is an absolutely devastating, exterminating attack by very heavy bombers from this country upon the Nazi homeland.' Likewise at Chequers on 14 July: 'Hitler must invade or fail. If he fails he is bound to go east, and fail he will.' Churchill had no evidential basis in intelligence for his assertion that the Germans might lunge towards Russia. At this time only a remarkable instinct guided him, shared by few others save Britain's notoriously erratic ambassador in Moscow, the Independent Labour MP Sir Stafford Cripps. Not until March 1941, three months before the event, did British intelligence decide that a German invasion of the Soviet Union was likely.

As for aircraft production, while fighters were the immediate need, the prime minister urged the creation of the largest possible bomber force. This, a desperate policy born out of desperate circumstances, absolute lack of any plausible alternative, would achieve destructive maturity only years later, when victory was assured by other means. Churchill appointed Admiral Sir Roger Keyes, the brainless old hero of the 1918 Zeebrugge raid, to become Director of Combined Operations, with a brief to prepare to launch raids on the Continent of Europe. He wanted no pinprick fiascos, he said, but instead attacks by five to ten thousand men. He ordered the establishment of Special Operations Executive, SOE, under the direction of Hugh Dalton as Minister of Economic Warfare, with a mandate to 'Set Europe ablaze.' He endorsed De Gaulle as the voice and leader of Free France. Brooke, at Gosport with Churchill on 17 July, found him 'in wonderful spirits and full of offensive plans for next summer'. Most of the commitments made in those days remained ineffectually implemented for years to come. Yet they represented earnests for the future that inspired Churchill's colleagues; which was, of course, exactly as he intended.

And above all in those days, there were his words. 'Faith is given to us to help and comfort us when we stand in awe before the unfurling scroll of human destiny,' he told the British people in a broadcast on

14 July, Bastille Day, in which he recalled attending a magnificent military parade in Paris just a year before. 'And I proclaim my faith that some of us will live to see a Fourteenth of July when a liberated France will once again rejoice in her greatness and her glory.' He continued:

> Here in this strong City of Refuge which enshrines the title-deeds of human progress and is of deep consequence to Christian civilization; here, girt about by the seas and oceans where the Navy reigns; shielded from above by the prowess and devotion of our airmen – we await undismayed the impending assault. Perhaps it will come tonight. Perhaps it will come next week. Perhaps it will never come. We must show ourselves equally capable of meeting a sudden violent shock or – what is perhaps a harder test – a prolonged vigil. But be the ordeal sharp or long, or both, we shall seek no terms, we shall tolerate no parley; we may show mercy – we shall ask for none.

One of the prime minister's listeners wrote: 'Radio sets were not then very powerful, and there was always static. Families had to sit near the set, with someone always fiddling with the knobs. It was like sitting round a hearth, with someone poking the fire; and to that hearth came the crackling voice of Winston Churchill.' Vere Hodgson, a thirty-nine-year-old London woman, wrote: 'Gradually we came under the spell of that wonderful voice and inspiration. His stature grew larger and larger, until it filled our sky.' Vita Sackville-West wrote to her husband Harold Nicolson, saying that one of Churchill's speeches 'sent shivers (not of fear) down my spine. I think that one of the reasons why one is stirred by his Elizabethan phrases is that one feels the whole massive backing of power and resolve behind them, like a great fortress: they are never words for words' sake.' Mollie Panter-Downes told readers of the *New Yorker*: 'Mr Churchill is the only man in England today who consistently interprets the quiet but completely resolute national mood.'

Isaiah Berlin wrote: 'Like a great actor – perhaps the last of his kind – upon the stage of history, he speaks his memorable lines with a large, unhurried, and stately utterance in a blaze of light, as is appropriate to a man who knows that his work and his person will remain the objects of scrutiny and judgement to many generations.' Tory MP Cuthbert Headlam wrote on 16 July: 'It is certainly his hour – and the confidence in him is growing on all sides.' Churchill's sublime achievement was to rouse the most ordinary people to extraordinary perceptions of their own destiny. Eleanor Silsby, an elderly psychology lecturer living in south London, wrote to a friend in America on 23 July 1940: 'I won't go on about the war. But I just want to say that we are proud to have the honour of fighting alone for the things that matter much more than life and death. It makes me hold my chin high to think, not just of being English, but of having been chosen to come at this hour for this express purpose of saving the world . . . I should never have thought that I could approve of war . . . There is surprisingly little anger or hate in this business – it is just a job that has to be done . . . This is Armageddon.' Churchill was much moved by receiving through the post a box of cigars from a working girl who said that she had saved her wages to buy them for him. One morning at Downing Street, John Martin found himself greeting a woman who had called to offer a £60,000 pearl necklace to the service of the state. Told of this, Churchill quoted Macaulay:

> Romans in Rome's quarrel,
> Spared neither land nor gold

Much of the German press editorialised about Churchill's 14 July speech, describing him as 'Supreme Warlord of the Plutocracy'. The *Deutsche Allgemeine Zeitung* was among the titles which suggested that his foolish determination to fight to the last would bring down upon London the same fate as had befallen other conquered cities: 'The unscrupulous rulers of Warsaw did not perceive the consequences of obstinacy until their capital lay in ruins and ashes. Likewise, Rotterdam paid the price for its failure to reach a rational

decision, such as saved other Dutch cities and – at the eleventh hour
– Paris.' German forces, Hitler's people were told, felt well rested after
the French campaign, and now stood poised to launch an assault on
Britain whenever the Führer gave the order. Meanwhile, the
Luftwaffe's air attacks on Churchill's country, which had hitherto
been on a small scale, would escalate dramatically. A quick victory
over Britain was to be confidently anticipated. German radio's
English-language propaganda broadcasts conveyed the same message,
of imminent doom.

On 19 July Hitler addressed the Reichstag and the world, publicly
offering Britain a choice between peace and 'unending suffering and
misery'. Churchill responded: 'I don't propose to say anything in
reply to Herr Hitler's speech, not being on speaking terms with him.'
He urged Lord Lothian, Britain's ambassador in Washington, to press
the Americans to fulfil Britain's earlier request for the 'loan' of old
destroyers. On 1 August he delivered a magisterial rebuke to the
Foreign Office for the elaborate phrasing of its proposed response
to a message from the King of Sweden, who was offering to mediate
between Britain and Germany. 'The draft errs,' he wrote, 'in trying
to be too clever, and to enter into refinements of policy unsuited to
the tragic simplicity and grandeur of the times and the issues at
stake.' That day, Hitler issued his Directive No. 17, unleashing the
Luftwaffe's massive air campaign against Britain.

FOUR

The Battle of Britain

Thus began the events that will define for eternity the image of Britain in the summer of 1940. Massed formations of German bombers with their accompanying fighter escorts droned across blue skies towards Kent and Sussex, to be met by intercepting Hurricanes and Spitfires, tracing white condensation trails through the thin air. The most aesthetically beautiful aircraft the world has ever seen, their grace enhanced in the eyes of posterity by their role as the saviours of freedom, pierced the bomber formations, diving, twisting, banking, hammering fire. Onlookers craned their heads upwards, mesmerised by the spectacle. Shop-workers and housewives, bank clerks and schoolchildren, heard the clatter of machine-guns; found aircraft fragments and empty cartridge cases tinkling onto their streets and littering suburban gardens; sometimes even met fallen aircrew of both sides, stumbling to their front doors.

Stricken planes spewing smoke plunged to the ground in cascades of churned-up earth if their occupants were fortunate enough to crash-land, or exploded into fiery fragments. This was a contest like no other in human experience, witnessed by millions of people continuing humdrum daily lives, bemused by the fact that kettles boiled in kitchens, flowers bloomed in garden borders, newspapers were delivered and honey was served for tea a few thousand feet beneath one of the decisive battlefields of history. Pilots who faced oblivion all day sang in their 'locals' that night, if they lived. Their schoolboy slang – 'wizard prang' and 'gone for a Burton' – passed into the language, fulfilling the observation of a French writer quoted by Dr Johnson: '*Il y a beaucoup de puerilities dans la guerre.*'

Once bombs began to fall on Britain's cities in August, blast caused a layer of dust to settle upon every surface, casting over the urban fabric of the country a drab greyness which persisted throughout the blitz. Yet islands of seasonal beauty survived. John Colville was struck by the tortoiseshell butterflies fluttering gaily over the lawn behind Downing Street: 'I shall always associate that garden in summer, the corner of the Treasury outlined against a china-blue sky, with 1940.' Churchill, intensely vulnerable to sentiment, witnessed many scenes which caused him to succumb. While driving to Chequers one day, he glimpsed a line of people. Motioning the driver to stop, he asked his detective to enquire what they were queuing for. Told that they hoped to buy birdseed, Churchill's private secretary John Martin noted: 'Winston wept.'

10 July was later officially designated as the first day of the Battle of Britain, though to the aircrew of both sides it seemed little different from those which preceded and followed it. The next month was characterised by skirmishes over the Channel and south coast, in which the Luftwaffe never lost more than sixteen aircraft in a day's combat – on 25 July – and Fighter Command no more than fifteen. Churchill insisted that coastal convoys should continue to sail the Narrows, partly to assert British rights of navigation, partly to provoke the Luftwaffe into action on what were deemed favourable terms for the RAF. On 11 August, attrition sharply increased: thirty British aircraft were shot down for thirty-five German. In the month thereafter, Goering launched his major assault on Fighter Command, its airfields, control centres and radar stations. Between 12 and 23 August, the RAF lost 133 fighters in action, a further forty-four to mishaps, while the Luftwaffe lost 299 aircraft to all causes.

By early autumn, British casualties and damage to installations had reached critical proportions. Among Dowding's squadron commanders, eleven out of forty-six were killed or wounded in July and August, along with thirty-nine of ninety-seven flight commanders. One Fighter Command pilot, twenty-one-year-old George Barclay of 249 squadron, a Norfolk parson's son, wrote after the bitter battles of 7 September: 'The odds today have been unbelievable (and we are all really very shaken!) . . . There are bombs and things falling around tonight and a terrific gun barrage. Has a blitz begun? The wing-commander's coolness is amazing and he does a lot to keep up our morale – very necessary tonight.' As in every battle, not all participants showed the stuff of heroes. After repeated German bombings of the RAF's forward airfield at Manston, ground crews huddled in its air-raid shelters and rejected pleas to emerge and service Hurricanes. The work was done by off-duty Blenheim night-fighter crews.

The prime minister intently followed the progress of each day's clashes. The Secret Intelligence Service warned that a German landing in Britain was imminent. Yet it was not easy to maintain the British people at the highest pitch of expectancy. On 3 August, Churchill felt obliged to issue a statement: 'The Prime Minister wishes it to be known that the possibility of German attempts at invasion has by no means passed away.' He carried this spirit into his own household. Downing Street and the underground Cabinet War Rooms were protected by Royal Marine pensioners, Chequers by a Guards company. The prime minister took personal charge of several practice alerts against the possibility of German paratroop landings in St James's Park. 'This sounds very peculiar today, but was taken quite seriously by us all in the summer of 1940,' a war cabinet secretariat officer recalled.

Churchill practised with a revolver and with his own Mannlicher rifle on a range at Chequers, entirely in earnest and not without pleasurable anticipation. It was odd that the Germans, having used special forces effectively in the May blitzkrieg on the Continent, never thereafter showed much interest in their possibilities. A direct assault on Churchill in 1940, most plausibly by a paratroop landing at Chequers, could have paid handsome dividends. Britain was fortunate that such piratical ventures loomed far less prominently in Hitler's mind, and in Wehrmacht doctrine, than in Churchill's imagination. In the summer of 1940 the Germans had yet to understand how pivotal to Britain's war effort was the person of the prime minister.

The supply of aircraft to Fighter Command was a critical factor.

While propaganda lauded the achievements of the Ministry of Aircraft Production, in Whitehall its conduct by Lord Beaverbrook provoked bitter criticism. For some weeks he ran the department from his private residence, Stornoway House in Cleveland Row, behind the Ritz Hotel. It is easy to perceive why many people, Clementine Churchill prominent among them, deplored the press baron, then sixty-one. He was a former appeaser, who had secretly subsidised the pre-war political career of Sir Samuel Hoare, most egregious of Chamberlain's ministers. In January 1940 Beaverbrook addressed the Duke of Windsor, the former King Edward VIII, about a possible peace offer to Germany. On 6 May he asserted in his own *Daily Express* that London would not be bombed, and that the Germans would not attack the Maginot Line. Deputy Führer Rudolf Hess later told Beaverbrook: 'Hitler likes you very much.' The historian G.M. Young suggested that Beaverbrook looked like a doctor struck off for performing an illegal operation. It was once said of his newspapers that they never espoused a cause which was both honourable and successful. The King opposed his inclusion in the cabinet, but among all men Churchill chose this old colleague from the 1917–18 Lloyd George government as his luncheon companion on 10 May 1940.

Beaverbrook cast a spell over Churchill which remained unbroken by his old friend's petulance, disloyalty and outrageous mischief-making. The Canadian-born magnate's command of wealth, such as the prime minister had always craved, impressed him. Churchill recognised in 'dear Max' a fellow original, full of impish fun, which was scantily available in Downing Street that summer. It is often remarked that Churchill had acolytes, but few intimates. More than any other person save his wife, Beaverbrook eased the loneliness of the prime minister's predicament and responsibilities. Churchill's belief in his old comrade's fitness for government was excessive. But who among Beaverbrook's cabinet colleagues was more blessed with dynamism and decision, such as seemed vital to meet the challenges of 1940?

As a minister, Beaverbrook trampled on air marshals, browbeat industrial chiefs, spurned consultation and cast aside procedure in pursuit of the simple objective of boosting fighter output. He ruled by row. Jock Colville once suggested that Beaverbrook took up more of Churchill's time than Hitler. The prime minister himself remarked a resemblance between Beaverbrook and the film star Edward G. Robinson, most notable for his portrayals of gangsters. It is hard to dispute that Beaverbrook was a monster. The Royal Air Force detested him. Much of his success in increasing aircraft output was achieved in consequence of decisions and commitments made before he took office. Yet for a brief season he deserved gratitude for injecting into the key element of British weapons production an urgency which matched the needs of the hour. He was supported by three great civil servants – Eaton Griffiths, Edmund Compton and Archibald Rowlands – together with Sir Charles Craven, former managing director of Vickers Armstrong, and Patrick Hennessy, forty-one-year-old boss of Ford at Dagenham. His other key prop, and sometimes adversary, was Air Marshal Sir Wilfred Freeman, who loathed Beaverbrook as a man, but grudgingly conceded his usefulness that summer.

Daily pressures upon the prime minister were unrelenting. The war cabinet met 108 times in the ninety-two days between 10 May and 31 July. His black dispatch box contained a pile of papers which seemed never to diminish, 'a farrago of operational, civil, political and scientific matters'. Overriding War Office objections, he promoted Maj. Millis Jefferis, a clever soldier engaged in weapons experimental work, and ordered that he should report directly to Lindemann at the Cabinet Office. He insisted that the maverick armoured enthusiast Maj.Gen. Percy Hobart should be given suitable employment, over-ruling Dill's objections with the assertion that he should remember that not only good boys help to win wars: 'It is the sneaks and stinkers as well.' He harassed the service chiefs in support of one of 'the Prof's' most foolish personal initiatives, aerial rocket deployments against enemy aircraft. Sir Hugh Dowding of Fighter Command wanted his pilots to kill German aircrew who took to their para-chutes. Churchill, recoiling from what he perceived as dishonourable conduct, would have none of this. Travelling with Roger Keyes at the end of July, he told the admiral that he had 'many detractors' as chief of combined operations. Keyes responded tartly: 'So had you, but you are now there in spite of it.' Churchill said: 'There are no competitors for my job now – I didn't get it until they had got into a mess.'

Beyond pressing the urgency of fighter production, Churchill made few tactical interventions in the Battle of Britain, but one of the most justly celebrated took place in the Downing Street cabinet room on 21 June. There was fierce controversy between Lindemann and Sir Henry Tizard, chairman of the Aeronautical Research Committee, about a suggestion from air intelligence that the Luftwaffe intended to use electronic beams to guide its night raiders to British targets. Tizard dismissed the feasibility of such a technique. Churchill summoned him, together with Lindemann and senior airmen, to a meeting attended by twenty-eight-year-old scientific intelligence officer R.V. Jones. It soon became obvious that Jones alone understood the issue. Though awed by finding himself in such company, he said to the prime minister: 'Would it help, sir, if I told you the story right from the start?' Churchill was initially taken aback, then said: 'Well, yes, it would!' Jones spent twenty minutes explaining how his own researches, aided by 'Ultra' German signals decrypted by the codebreakers at Bletchley Park – still fragmentary at this stage of the war – had led him to an understanding of the Luftwaffe's navigational aids. Churchill, characteristically, found himself paraphrasing in his mind lines from the parodic nineteenth-century folklore collection *The Ingoldsby Legends*: 'But now one Mr Jones/Comes forth and depones/That fifteen years since, he had heard certain groans.'

When Jones finished, Tizard expressed renewed scepticism. Churchill overruled him, and ordered that the young scientist should be given facilities to explore the German beams. Initially much dismayed by Jones's revelations, he thrilled when the young 'boffin' told him that, once wavelengths were identified, the transmissions could be jammed. Jones himself, of course, was enchanted by the prime minister's receptiveness: 'Here was strength, resolution, humour, readiness to listen, to ask the searching question and, when convinced, to act.' The beams were indeed jammed. Jones became